MULTIMEDIA MODELING

Modeling Multimedia Information and Systems

MULTIMEDIA MODELING

Modeling Multimedia Information and Systems

Ottawa, Canada October 4 – 6, 1999

Editor

Ahmed Karmouch

School of Information Technology and Engineering

University of Ottawa, Canada

Organizers

Multimedia and Mobile Agent Research Laboratory
School of Information Technology & Engineering
University of Ottawa
&
Network Computing
Institute for Information Technology
National Research Council of Canada

Sponsors

Mitel Corporation
Nortel Networks
Communications and Information Technology Ontario
The Ottawa Center for Research & Innovation

In cooperation with Computer Graphics Society

World Scientific

Singapore • New Jersey • London • Hong Kong

Published by

World Scientific Publishing Co. Pte. Ltd.

P O Box 128, Farrer Road, Singapore 912805

USA office: Suite 1B, 1060 Main Street, River Edge, NJ 07661

UK office: 57 Shelton Street, Covent Garden, London WC2H 9HE

British Library Cataloguing-in-Publication Data
A catalogue record for this book is available from the British Library.

MULTIMEDIA MODELING: MODELING MULTIMEDIA INFORMATION AND SYSTEMS

ISBN 981-02-4146-1

Printed in Singapore.

MMM99

PREFACE

Multimedia systems result from the merging of the computing, communications and broadcasting industries. This merging is made possible today due to the technical advances in high-speed broadband networks, computer desktop workstations and information storage and compression techniques.

Currently, text and image are the predominant forms of information exchanged over Internet. However, there are clear signs that the situation is rapidly changing with the recent emergence of multimedia applications in the area of education, business, e-commerce and entertainment. Resulting, therefore, in increased consumption of network bandwidth and in the creation of very large volume of information that needs to be processed and stored. This trend has put strong requirements and pressure on the multimedia modeling research community to develop new semantic models that will further facilitate the creation, representation, manipulation, and animation of multimedia content with a better level of (semantic) granularity than what is possible to achieve with today's multimedia systems.

Multimedia Modeling can be seen as the next important step in multimedia information research. It will help to better understand, organize and extract knowledge from still images, video streams and audio segments that are viewed by today's technology as binary large objects. It is our belief that the next three years will still see the research and development on various aspects of multimedia modeling growing in a staggering fashion.

This volume contains a collection of articles that were selected for presentation at the International Conference on Multimedia Modeling held in Ottawa, Canada, on October 4-6, 1999. The articles are grouped into seven chapters corresponding to the conference sessions: authoring and presentation of multimedia information, interactive multimedia, model based graphics, video, vision and virtual reality, information modeling, storage and integration, topological and geometric modeling, indexing & retrieval of multimedia information, and distributed multimedia systems and applications.

The success of MMM'99 would not be possible without many people providing the motivations and efforts. Therefore, I would like to express my appreciation and thanks to the authors for their contributions in preparing and revising the papers, as well as the technical program committee and the reviewers who have helped put together an excellent technical program for the conference. Special thanks are due to Hamid Harroud who kindly contributed his time and put a great effort in helping with the conference organization. Thanks to Roger Impey, Tet yeap, Kathy Mahoney, Dianne Dinsdale, Alex Pugh, and Marilyn Cheek for their assistance with the conference organization. Finally I would like to acknowledge to our sponsors and co-organizers for their support and for making this conference possible

A. Karmouch

MMM99

TABLE OF CONTENTS

CHAPTER 1 AUTHORING AND PRESENTATION OF MULTIMEDIA INFORMATION

CHAPTER 2 INTERACTIVE MULTIMEDIA

CHAPTER 3 MODEL BASED GRAPHICS, VIDEO, VISION AND VIRTUAL REALITY

CHAPTER 4 INFORMATION MODELING, STORAGE AND INTEGRATION

CHAPTER 5 TOPOLOGICAL AND GEOMETRIC MODELING

Chapter 1

Authoring and Presentation of Multimedia Information

MMM99

THE USE OF SMIL: MULTIMEDIA RESEARCH CURRENTLY APPLIED ON A GLOBAL SCALE

LLOYD RUTLEDGE, LYNDA HARDMAN AND JACCO VAN OSSENBRUGGEN
CWI (Centrum voor Wiskunde en Informatica), P.O. Box 94079, NL-1090 GB Amsterdam, The Netherlands
E-Mail: {Lloyd.Rutledge, Lynda.Hardman, Jacco.van.Ossenbruggen}@cwi.nl

This paper describes the current use of the multimedia standard SMIL. SMIL features that relate to active areas of multimedia research are discussed. SMIL current implementation in existing browsers is described. Examples from the Web of SMIL applications representing different types of multimedia are presented. These discussions together provide an overview of how SMIL currently addresses the needs of multimedia distributed on the Web.

1. Introduction

SMIL (Synchronized Multimedia Integration Language, pronounced "SMIL") is the W3C format for multimedia on the Web [9]. Its HTML-like syntax encodes the screen layout, interaction, adaptivity and timing of multimedia presentations. With its W3C status and several free browsers currently available, SMIL is gaining a substantial presence on the Web. Various concepts from multimedia research have a presence in the SMIL format. This gives SMIL the potential to apply multimedia research on a global scale — putting multimedia into common use, just as HTML put hypertext into common use.

This paper discusses SMIL as a result of multimedia research. First, SMIL is discussed in terms of ongoing multimedia research, showing the relationship between this research and its existing, and potential, impact on large-scale multimedia use. Then, existing software for processing SMIL is described, specifying what SMIL is capable of today. Finally, some current applications of SMIL on the Web are presented, showing the manner with which SMIL is — and can be — used.

2. Multimedia Research Applied to SMIL

SMIL, as a format for multimedia, also serves as a model for multimedia. Its constructs define a distinct set of multimedia concepts. The structure within which these constructs fit in is one model for how these concepts can be composed into multimedia presentations. These concepts and this model are related with concepts and models that come from multimedia research. This shows the impact research has had on the SMIL standard, and it demonstrates the potential impact ongoing research can still have on SMIL and Web-based multimedia. Some research has started as a result of the SMIL standard, such as the adaptation of existing models and systems to incorporate SMIL, and the comparison of the format with other models to suggest extensions to it. This section presents some examples of multimedia research that relates to the SMIL format and its implementation.

2.1 Top-level Document Structuring

SMIL is an XML-defined format. Its XML structure is time-based — the primary semantic impact of the syntactic composition and progression the XML code is on the timing of the document. This contrasts with typical XML documents and HTML documents. Their structure is textflow-based, with its primary semantic impact being on how far along the wrapped-around single flow of text a part of the document appears. In other words, a component's position in SMIL structure says *when* it appears, and a component's position in HTML and typical XML structure says *where* it appears. This distinction and its ramifications have been investigated in recent research [7]. These ramifications include how temporal information can be applied to mainly textual documents, and how text-flow information can be applied to mainly temporal documents. An example of where these issues applies with HTML+Time, which uses SMIL-based temporal constructs in HTML documents. With HTML+Time, the XML structure can be either textflow-based or time-based or a mixture of both.

2.2 User Adaptation

There is much research on adapting presentations to individual users. SMIL has constructs that provide some user-centered adaptation. Research with the CMIFed system has investigated means of encoding user-centered adaptation in SMIL and also in non-standardized extensions to SMIL [3].

The primary SMIL constructs for user-centered adaptation are the `switch` element and the test attributes. These specify that one or zero selections are to be made among a collections of alternatives for inclusion at individual locations in the temporal hierarchy of a SMIL document. These alternatives can be, for example, equivalent media objects in different formats. They can also be different subtrees of SMIL temporal composition and media objects.

CMIFed's approach is to put adaptation not in the temporal/media structure but on the devices for presented individual media objects. The CMIFed construct for such media devices is the *channel*. The CMIFed channel corresponds to the SMIL `region` element, except that the region applies only to visual media, while the channel can apply to any medium.

Channel-based adaptation consists of having channels be turned on or off. For example, in CMIFed, subtitling for the hearing impaired would consist of audio media objects throughout the temporal/media hierarchy that output to one subtitle channel. This subtitle channel would be turned on for the hearing impaired and turned off for other users. To encode this in SMIL, each piece of subtitling in the hierarchy would have to be have test attributes assigned to it an be put in a `switch` element. With channels, neither additional attributes nor the additional layers of the temporal/media hierarchy are needed. Since SMIL subtitles would be assigned a region, which is the equivalent of a channel, assigning subtitles in CMIFed a channel involves the use of no addition constructs over SMIL.

The use of channels also facilitates the enabling of different combinations of adaptation. For example, a presentation can adapt by providing subtitles and also by being in different languages. Both the main spoken soundtrack and the subtitles can be in these different languages. Adaptation can consist of providing just sound, just subtitles, sound and subtitles in the same language, or sound and subtitles in the different languages. With SMIL, each different combination would need to be explicitly accounted for in the temporal/media hierarchy, its `switch` elements, and the test attributes. With the use of CMIFed channels, the temporal/media hierarchy is simpler because it encodes little of the adaptive information. The hierarchy is structured as if both soundtracks and subtitles in all languages are played simultaneously. In CMIFed, the selection is made with the channels, not with the media objects and temporal hierarchy. The different combinations are specified by the turning on and off of different channels, where there is one channel for each language in sound and subtitles.

2.3 Authoring Multimedia

Much research has taken place regarding the authoring of multimedia [14,18,24]. Some of this has been applied to authoring SMIL [4,12,15]. The primary authoring issue that applies to SMIL is the author's specification of temporal constraints. The research authoring system CMIFed [18], which was later developed into the commercial authoring system GR*i*NS [4], used a timing model that is similar to that used in SMIL. When CMIFed was extended to output SMIL as well as its own format, not many changes were required.

Other systems have used a different model for temporal constraints than that which SMIL uses and have thus needed to perform a transformation between the models to output SMIL code. Mikado [12], for example, primarily generates multimedia presentations in the format Madeus [13], whose model is based on sets of temporal constraints, not parallel and sequential composites. Mikado has a component named SMILY [15] that generates a subset of SMIL. SMILY has an algorithm for translating the temporal constraints inherent in Mikado and Madeus into SMIL temporal composites along with SMIL delay and event synchronization attributes. This algorithm describes the relationship between the two timing models.

2.4 Dynamic Quality-of-Service

Recent research with the REMDOR architecture has explored means of extending SMIL to support more dynamic graceful degradation of quality-of-service [26].

These extensions would provide the author more power to specify what media to start downloading and when to adapt the presentation to varying bandwidth and processing constraints. REMDOR is an architecture using a transport level partial-order/partial-reliability model for selecting media components for multimedia integration. This model has been compared with the SMIL timing model to investigate how dynamic QoS control could be incorporated into SMIL processing and the SMIL syntax.

This research is producing suggestions for the extension of the SMIL standard to handle more dynamic control of graceful degradation. The `strong` and `weak` values of their proposed `start` attribute state for a SMIL `par` (parallel) element whether the elements the `par` states should be played in parallel must all start at the same time, thus waiting for all the elements' media objects to be loaded before any start playing, or if each element can start playing as soon at it's media objects are downloaded. The proposed `reliability` attribute states whether a media object in a presentation is essential or expendable. From this attribute, when it is time to play a media object that has not yet been downloaded, the browser can determine whether to wait for the download and then play the object before continuing, or to continue the presentation without playing the object. The proposal also includes adding new event types to SMIL synchronization, such as when a media object has been downloaded.

2.5 The Automatic Generation of SMIL

Research with the Berlage architecture has investigated the potential automatic generation of SMIL encoded multimedia presentations [22]. The presentations are generated from media archives and metadata describing that media. Berlage is structured in terms of the Standard Reference Model for Intelligent Multimedia Presentation Systems (SRM-IMMPSs), an established model for generating multimedia in general [2]. The SRM-IMMPSs accounts for having different multimedia output formats generated by the same system. This way, the same code that generates SMIL could also be used to generate other formats as well. Such a multi-format system would need a base multimedia presentation model from which presentations in the particular formats would be generated. A transform would have to occur from this model to an output format such as SMIL.

3. SMIL Implementations

The extent to which an idea can be exercised is the extent to which tools exist for applying it. Breaking down the idea into intellectually manageable components, developing models from these for expressing the idea in its various forms and then designing architectures for processing the idea are crucial first steps. Toward the end of the research life cycle comes the making of running tools. The nature of these tools can have a large impact on how the community in general applies an idea on a larger scale. While an idea or model may be influenced strongly by the research community, industry has naturally a stronger impact on final implementations and thus to how an idea or model is realized. The impact a particular implementor has on the general, long-term execution of an idea can be influenced by that implementor's other work, or by the nature of an existing implementation that was adapted for incorporating the new idea. This section describes the existing tools for processing SMIL, and how these tools shape, and have the potential to shape, the use of SMIL.

3.1 G2

RealPlayer G2 is a SMIL player made by RealNetworks [17]. RealPlayer G2 is free-of-charge and has a commercially available version called RealPlayer Plus G2. G2 is a player for the media formats developed by RealNetworks, such as RealAudio and RealVideo. These formats include much timing information, and G2 can play multiple formats simultaneously, making G2 effectively a player for synchronized multimedia. One G2 focus is the ability to play a lot of media efficiently without noticeable delays in presentation. Another focus has been to function with RealNetworks streaming servers.

With the release of SMIL last year, G2 was extended to play SMIL presentations as well as Real media files. With tens of millions of G2 players having been downloaded since, there is an enormous amount of SMIL browsers hooked up with the Web. While not having implemented all of the SMIL constructs, the SMIL-related features of G2 are regularly enhanced and extended. G2 has recently been made to play many more media formats and to function as a plug-in within HTML players. The impact RealNetworks and G2 are having on SMIL is in terms of well-processed timing and of the integration and large-scale distribution of high-volume media in multimedia presentations.

The community authors that write for the G2 player sometimes produce SMIL code that relies on external media file for specifying timing rather than putting the synchronization data in the SMIL file itself. Before SMIL was developed, G2 was a player primarily for specialized mono-media formats. The formats that RealNetworks developed and that G2 played were typically mono-medium with timing information for that medium embedded in the format. The arrival and implementation of SMIL has enabled G2 presentations to have a more intricate spatial layout by encoding it in SMIL. However, authors that have been familiar primarily with the G2 player often create SMIL presentations with much of the timing information not in SMIL but in the integrated media objects encoded with RealNetworks media formats, even though G2 properly plays the equivalent SMIL code. This results in SMIL presentations with timing information spread between multiple files in multiple formats, rather than in one, integrating file. It also results in presentations that are difficult to adapt for players other than G2.

3.2 GRiNS

GR*i*NS (GRaphical *i*Nterface to SMIL) is an authoring and player system developed by CWI and Oratrix Development [16]. The GR*i*NS player is available free-of-charge and has had several thousand downloads. Compared to other players, GR*i*NS has a focus on the SMIL standard itself. It has implemented almost all of the SMIL constructs, more than the other players. But it does not have some of the browser environment integration features of other players, such as the ability to operate as a plug-in.

The GR*i*NS player was made as a companion to the GR*i*NS authoring environment (see Figure 2). This provides a tool for large-scale authoring of SMIL presentations. Graphical interfaces are provided for direct manipulation of SMIL temporal compositional, fine-tuned synchronization, spatial layout and hyperlinking.

GR*i*NS was originally the research multimedia authoring system CMIFed [18]. Multimedia presentations created with CMIFed were stored in the format CMIF. When SMIL was developed, CMIFed was adapted to output SMIL as well as CMIF. CMIF encodes some behavior that SMIL does not encode. Such behavior can be edited with GR*i*NS. When it is, this behavior is encoded in SMIL as an extension of SMIL. The SMIL specifications specifies some techniques and constructs for output such extensions. GR*i*NS uses these constructs and techniques in its SMIL output of non-SMIL behavior. Still, even with the proper use of extension constructs, GR*i*NS may make presentations that do not play well on other browsers.

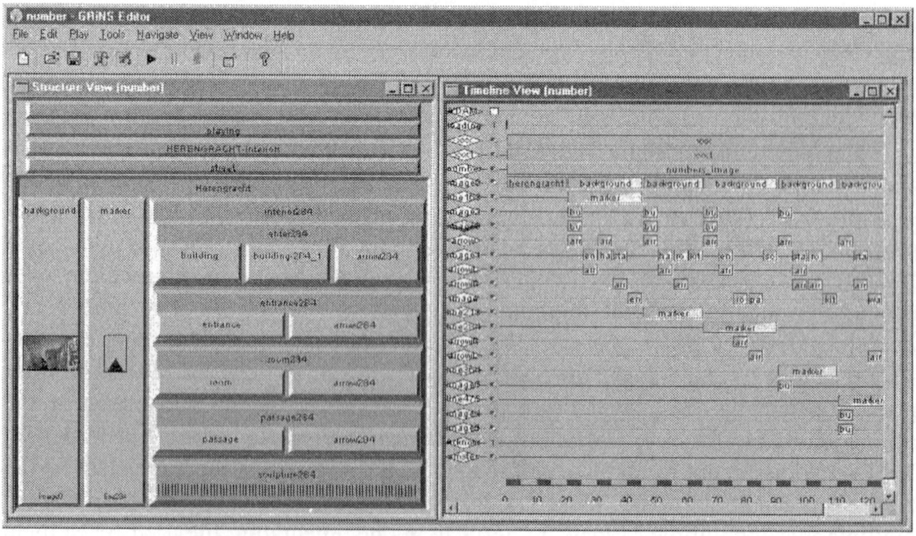

Figure 1. Screen Display from the GR*i*NS Authoring System

3.3 SOJA

The Helio organization has developed a SMIL browser called SOJA [8]. It is available free-of-charge and has had several thousand downloads. As a Java-based player, it integrates well within HTML presentations on HTML browsers. A typical presentation of a SMIL document on SOJA involves downloading not just the SMIL and media files but also the SOJA applet itself. The applet itself takes up relatively small system space. In relation to the other players, SOJA's focus is on having SMIL integrate well with the general Web browsing environment in terms of user interface, data transfer and software processing. Since SOJA was created only for SMIL presentations, and since work on it began only after SMIL became a standard, its use is less likely to develop SMIL dialects than the other players.

4. Some SMIL Applications

Once tools are made for expressing and processing an research result, a community can use them on a large enough scale to develop conventions for their use and for the application of the research result. These conventions consist of established patterns of how features in a tool, or constructs in a format, are applied. Conventions then effectively become tools and languages themselves.

This section presents some examples of the application of SMIL. These examples of the early use of SMIL provide insight into how the standard can be used, and into what conventions for its use may form. The multimedia applications discussed in this section fall in three different areas: infotainment, accessibility, and conceptual multimedia art. These analyses not only describe how multimedia research is applied to SMIL as it exists today, but also how in can continue to contribute the development of future versions of SMIL and further integration of it with other Web standards [20].

4.1 Infotainment Multimedia

Perhaps the most typical type of multimedia presentations is "infotainment", in which the presented information is made more entertaining and engaging through increased use of audio and video media and more interaction with the user. One example of infotainment multimedia is *Fiets* (Dutch for "bicycle", pronounced "feets"), a collection of SMIL presentations about Amsterdam [11,23] (see Figure 2). Fiets consists of 9 different presentations on Amsterdam. Each conveys either the spatial, temporal, or relational information inherent to Amsterdam itself by using either the spatial, temporal or navigational aspects of the multimedia presentation [23]. Experience with Fiets as infotainment provides insight into how SMIL encodes a primary genre of multimedia, while focusing on the three main constructs of multimedia: screen display, timeline and navigational links. This section presents

Fiets' encoding in SMIL of these three areas and how the coding for each could be facilitated with improvements to SMIL itself or its use with other Web formats. Some of these changes have been proposed in earlier work [20], but not in the context of Fiets.

One measurement of SMIL is its ability to provide the basic components for multimedia upon which the bulk of typical multimedia presentations can be made. For Fiets, SMIL did provide the basic components needed for defining the spatial layout, timeline and hyperlinking desired. However, the means needed to encode some behaviors with SMIL was sometimes bulky and inefficient.

The SMIL `region` element and its attributes for two-dimensional placement and sizing provide the basics for screen placement of visual media objects. While this was able to represent all the placement in Fiets, the coding would have been more efficient if a mechanism for centering visual media in their assigned regions was available to SMIL processing. Without it, any centering would have to be explicitly calculated for each media object of different size. Grouping regions within other regions and relative positioning of regions would also facilitate positioning calculation by the author and make the code more efficient. The means of implementing these improvements could be put in a future SMIL version.

SMIL's hierarchical temporal composition and pair-wise synchronization successfully encoded all the timing desired in Fiets. However, the requirement in SMIL that synchronization be only between siblings in the temporal hierarchy

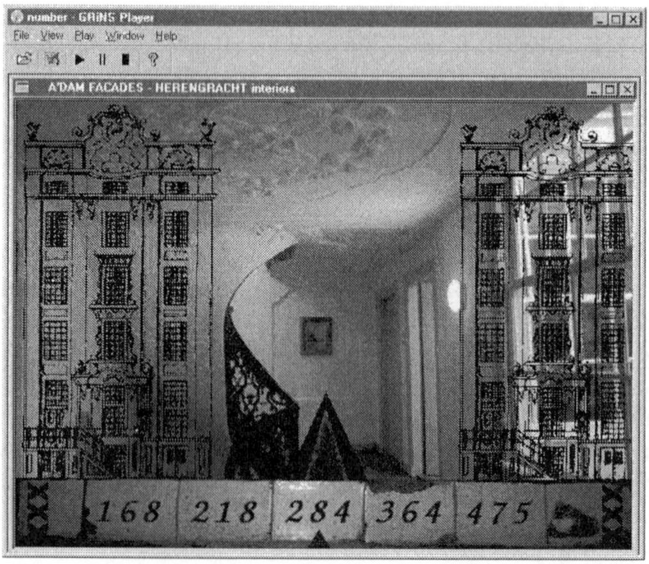

Figure 2. Screen Display from *Fiets*

necessitated either cumbersome rearranging of the hierarchy or chaining multiple synchronizations together. Allowing broader synchronization in SMIL would remove the need for these inefficiencies.

Finally, the SMIL-encoded linking in Fiets would have required less repeated code if a constructs such as the *choice node*, discussed in earlier work [6,20], were introduced into SMIL. This would enable behavior similar to that provided by frames in HTML: having part of the presentation stay the same while the rest changes. This is only possible in SMIL by repeating the code for the static part of the presentation.

4.2 Accessible Multimedia

While infotainment multimedia makes the presentation of information more engaging, accessible multimedia serves to adapt the presentation of information for users who may otherwise not be able to perceive it. Sight- and hearing-impaired may need additional visual or audio descriptions of information they cannot perceive. Media also needs to be adapted for users under special circumstances, such as driving a car, or users with certain systems, such as portable, hand-held devices.

The "Physics Interactive Video Tutor" (PIVOT) is a Web-based multimedia physics curriculum (see Figure 3). It is being developed by The CPB/WGBH

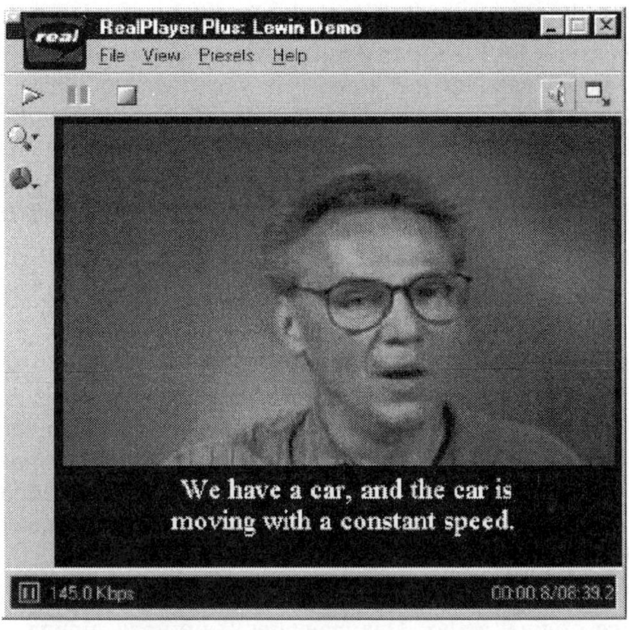

Figure 3. Screen Display from *PIVOT*

National Center for Accessible Media (NCAM) [5] and the Center for Advanced Educational Services at the Massachusetts Institute of Technology (MIT). PIVOT is built around MIT Professor Walter Lewin's class on Classical Newtonian Mechanics.

A primary goal of PIVOT is to have it be accessible to students who are deaf or blind. The source presentations, without any accessibility features used typically have one audio and one video, where the video shifts from face-and-gesticulating-hand shots of the professor to diagrams being drawn by the professor. There are three basic accessibility components for PIVOT that can be added to these source presentations: closed captions, tucked audio descriptions, and pausing audio descriptions. For each of these three, the use of SMIL for them, and possibilities of SMIL extensions for them, are discussed below.

4.2.1 Closed Captions

If closed captions are to be used, then pieces of text must be shown in a portion of the display, and their display must be timed with the audio. In PIVOT, closed captioning is represented with a SMIL `switch` element containing a `text` element with the captioned text. The `text` element would have its `system-captions` attribute set to `"on"`. This would cause a browser to recognize that `text` element as appropriate to select for playing, as a child of the `switch` element, only if captions are desired for the presentation. The `text` element would assign a screen display region on which to display the captions. All of this behavior can be encoded in SMIL.

Desired behavior for PIVOT that cannot be encoded in SMIL is the altering of the layout if closed captions are used. This would enable screen display to be rearranged to make room for the captions in a graceful way. A possible extension to SMIL that would enable this behavior would be to allow `layout` elements to have test attributes like `system-captions` so that alternative layouts could be specified and at runtime selected based on the browser's setting for the use of captions.

4.2.2 Tucked Audio Descriptions

Some presentations require audio descriptions, which describe visual events in the video. For example, when a video shows a ball bouncing as part of a physics experiment, visually impaired users will not perceive it. An audio description such as "the ball bounces on the table" would provide these users with information essential to the presentation that they would otherwise miss. Such audio descriptions would be in addition to the original audio of the presentation, which both sighted and visually impaired users would hear.

One technique for putting audio descriptions in a presentation is to "tuck" them into gaps in the original audio. This maintains the original timing of the original audio and video. This is important if the presentation is a scheduled broadcast to be adapted on an individual basis to each member of the audience watching it simultaneously.

The SMIL encoding for this is similar to the encoding for closed captions. A `switch` element contains a single `audio` element contain a clip of audio description. If this audio clip is considered appropriate for playing, then it is played —otherwise, it is not. SMIL-defined synchronization between the audio clips and the original audio and video put the descriptive audio in the natural gaps in the original audio track. A useful addition to SMIL for specifically defining this behavior would be a `system-audio-desc` test attribute, which works for audio descriptions in the same manner that the `system-captions` attribute works for captions.

4.2.3 Pausing Audio Descriptions

Instead of tucking, audio descriptions can be played during pauses imposed on the original audio and video. The advantage of pausing the original video and audio is that more elaborate and informative audio descriptions can be used. SMIL can define this behavior by cutting the audio and video into clips that begin and end with the pausing points. The clips would be played sequentially if there is no audio description. The video clip would have its `fill` attribute set to `"freeze"`, and the audio descriptions would push the timing of the `video` elements to be longer than the clips themselves. This causes the pausing behavior when the audio descriptions are played and thus changes the timeline.

Currently, no SMIL browser performs this behavior without error or without visible distortion in the video progress with audio description turned off. Improving the performance of this behavior is necessary to make pausing audio descriptions effective. A possible extension to SMIL that may encode this behavior better is a "pause" command that can work at multiple places on a single clip of video. This might enable browsers to more seamlessly play the video when audio descriptions are not used.

4.3 Conceptual Multimedia Art

Infotainment and accessible multimedia each typically uses the same basic model and behavior for most of their presentations. On the other hand, artists that use multimedia to express certain concepts often make presentations that have models of interaction and display that vary widely. Since it is impossible to make a model that applies to all possible conceptual multimedia art, artists usually must struggle to find a mapping between their concept and the multimedia presentation models that exist, often with the need to make compromises on the original vision.

One example of conceptual multimedia is *GoTo0*, an interactive story by Maja Kuzmanovic [10] (see Figure 4). It's SMIL-encoding is a multimedia storyboard for a planned virtual reality presentation. In the final virtual reality, the user's interface with the story will be more physically immersive. The multimedia version emulates the virtual reality with a point-and-click interface with which the user navigates through the story. The challenge with writing the SMIL version what choosing what media objects (sound, images and video), screen display layouts, timing relationships and navigational interface will best convey the final virtual reality.

Another example of conceptual multimedia comes from the artwork *Off the Wall*[1], by Margret Wibmer and Günther Zechberger. *Off the Wall* involves multiple photographs from different perspectives of one object: a person entirely encased in an outfit made of loose-fitting yellow industrial material [22] (see Figure 5). A CD-ROM is being made for *Off the Wall* containing different QuickTime VRs of this object. With the object being represented in QuickTime VR, the user can spin the object around in all different orientations, and zoom in and out: like a 3-D digital image. As a companion to the project and its QuickTime VR CD-ROM, a SMIL presentation is being made for installation on the Web for emulating the behavior of the QuickTime VR [22].

Figure 4. Screen Display from *GoTo0*, by Maja Kuzmanovic

---

[1] An exhibition of this work premiered in July 1999 at the Museum Ferdinandeum in Innsbruck, Austria.

4.3.1 Encoding the Manipulating of a Object

An important aspect of the concept being conveyed in *Off the Wall* is that of an object being manipulated by the user. The QuickTime VR provides the user with the interface to move the object around in a virtual space. The primary design for representing this type of interaction in SMIL is to replace the QuickTime VR objects with "linear" videos and integrate them in SMIL. Each video would represent the object being moved in one particular way.

For example, there could be a separate video for the object being rotated along each of the three axes of rotation. For each rotation, there could be a separate video for each different distance the view could be from the object as it rotates. There could also be video clips of the object being moved toward/away from the user, with each clip having a particular orientation of the object along the three axes. Different videos could display varying speeds of each movement. Of course, there are infinite possibilities for such movement, and each video can only capture one. For an effective presentation with these videos, they should represent a broad sample of the types of motion that the artist desires to convey.

Links can be established for specific points in the movement that trigger other video clips moving the object from that position and orientation to another. The video clips loaded as a result of these triggers can be portions of video files. In SMIL, these would be defined with begin clip attributes. The reason for using clips is to have the object in the same position and orientation for starting the next movement as it was when ending the previous.

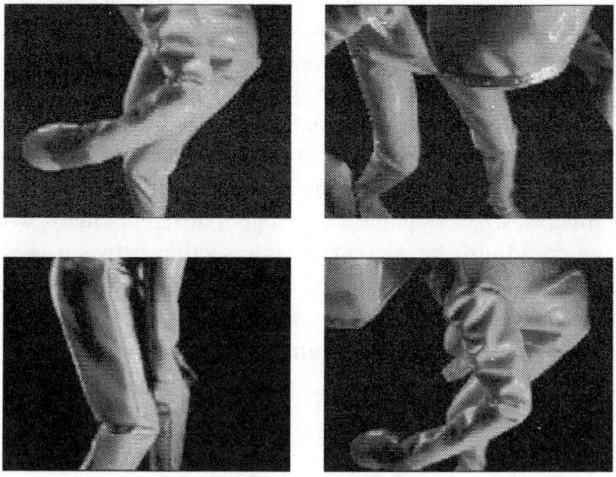

Figure 5. Screen Displays from *Off the Wall*, by Margret Wibmer and Günther Zechberger

With QuickTime VR, you have virtually infinite possibilities for interaction with the grabbing of the object to rotate it and the motion of the mouse to move it in and away. With the multimedia presentation described here, all movement is along the linear paths of rotation and motion established by the videos. Also, the number of potential interactions is finitely set with the discrete number of hotspots for the links.

4.3.2 Encoding a Dynamic Object

This SMIL-based approach can be used to convey the object changing form. Described above is a collection of videos conveying the motion of one static object. An equivalent (in terms of motion along the axes) collection can be made for the object in a different shape. Transition videos showing the object change from one shape another can also be used. The transition videos could also convey movement during the transformation. SMIL links can trigger shape changes in the same manner as they convey movement of the object.

This requires having anchors within individual media objects that effect the entire integrated presentation. Because QuickTime VR is multi-dimensional, it is harder to have portions of its display trigger events. With SMIL and the "linear" video approached described, it is easier to encode that there is a perceived change of the object during a period of time.

4.3.3 Reducing Storage Space And Bandwidth

A concern that arises is the space required. More videos mean more freedom of control. Increasing the amount of video also greatly increases the space required. QuickTime VR has an implicit compression over this multi-video model in that one collection of 3D pixels can be used for all movement at all speeds of a static object. With multiple videos, there is much repeated visual information stored.

A further compromise to save space would be to use all images and no videos. Each video would be replaced with a sequence of images, set up as a sequence in SMIL code. The exact same user interaction model would apply, with the same buttons and the same number of state changes. There would be much reuse of images. For example, conveying the same movement at different speeds could use the exact same images, whereas in the video model different videos would have to be used. One image could also be a common intersection between movements along different axes. The disadvantage would be the visual chunkiness of the progression. This could be lessened with more images shown at shorter durations, with a cost in space and possibly also in processing-incurred delays.

5. Summary

This paper presented SMIL as applied multimedia research. Examples of established and ongoing research were presented, along with their existing and potential impact on SMIL. Existing software was described, showing the tools that are available for demonstrating research concepts with SMIL. Examples of SMIL applications were given, illustrating some potential conventions for use of the standard, and illustrating how the standard can be used to demonstrate multimedia research ideas. Issues that arose include the need to transform some multimedia models into SMIL.

6. Acknowledgments

The Fiets artwork and graphic design was made by Maja Kuzmanovic. Many images used in Fiets come from the Amsterdam Heritage Website [1]. The creation of Fiets was funded by the European Union ESPRIT Chameleon project. Funding for the PIVOT project comes from Mitsubishi Electric America Foundation (MEAF).

7. References

[1] City of Amsterdam Municipal Department for Preservation and Restoration of Historic Buildings and Sites. *Amsterdam Heritage*, http://www.amsterdam.nl/bmz/adam/adam_e.html.

[2] Bordegoni, M., Faconti, G., Feiner S., Maybury, M.T., Rist, T., Ruggieri, S., Trahanias, P. and Wilson, M. Standard Reference Model for Intelligent Multimedia Presentation Systems." *Computer Standards and Interfaces*, **18**(6,7) (December 1997), pp. 477-496.

[3] Bulterman, D.C.A. User-Centered Abstractions for Adaptive Hypermedia Presentations, *Proceedings of ACM Multimedia 98* (Bristol, England, September, 1998) pp. 247-256.

[4] Bulterman, D.C.A, Hardman, L., Jansen, J. Mullender, K.S. and Rutledge, L. GRiNS: A GRaphical INterface for Creating and Playing SMIL Documents, *Proceedings of the Seventh International World Wide Web Conference (WWW7)* (Melbourne, Australia, April 1998).

[5] Freed, G. *NCAM Web Access Project*, http://www.wgbh.org/wgbh/pages/ncam/webaccess/aboutproject.html.

[6] Hardman, L., Bulterman, D.C.A. and van Rossum, G. The Amsterdam Hypermedia Model: Adding Time and Context to the Dexter Model. *Communications of the ACM*, **37**, 2 (ACM, 1994) pp. 50-62.

[7] Hardman, L., van Ossenbruggen, J., Rutledge, L. and Bulterman, D.C.A. Do You Have the Time? Composition and Linking in Time-based Hypermedia, *Proceedings of ACM Hypertext 99* (Darmstadt, Germany, February, 1999) pp. 189-196.

[8] Helio, *SOJA "Cherbourg 2"*, http://www.helio.org/products/smil/.

[9] Hoschka, P. (ed.). *Synchronized Multimedia Integration Language*, World Wide Web Consortium Recommendation (June 1998) http://www.w3.org/TR/REC-smil.

[10] Kuzmanovic, M., *GoToO*, http://www.cwi.nl/SMIL/GoTo0/.

[11] Kuzmanovic, M., and Rutledge, L. *Fiets: A Tour of Historic Amsterdam Buildings*, http://www.cwi.nl/SMIL/fiets.html.

[12] Jourdan, M., Layaïda, N. and. Roisin, C., A survey on authoring techniques for temporal scenarios of multimedia documents, *Handbook of Internet and Multimedia Systems and Applications, part 1: Tools and Standards* (CRC Press, April 1998).

[13] Jourdan, M., Layaïda, N., Roisin, C., Sabry-Ismail, L. and Tardif, L., "Madeus, an Authoring Environment for Interactive Multimedia Documents", *Proceedings of ACM Multimedia 98* (Bristol, England, September, 1998) pp. 267-272.

[14] Jourdan, M., Tardif, L. and Villard, L., Multiviews Interfaces for Multimedia Authoring, *Proceedings of Multimedia Modeling 98 (MMM98)* (Lausanne, Switzerland, October 1998) pp. 72-79.

[15] Jourdan, M., Tardif, L. and Villard, L., SMILY, a Smil Authoring environment, Technical Demonstration, *Proceedings of ACM Multimedia 99* (Orlando, Florida, USA, November 1999).

[16] Oratrix Development BV. *GRiNS*, http://www.oratrix.com/GRiNS/.

[17] RealNetworks, Inc. *RealPlayer G2*, http://www.real.com/products/player/.

[18] van Rossum, G., Jansen, J., Mullender, M.S., and Bulterman, D.C.A. CMIFed: a presentation environment for portable hypermedia documents, *Proceedings of ACM Multimedia 93* (Anaheim, California, USA, August 1993) pp. 183-188.

[19] Rutledge, L. Hardman, L. and van Ossenbruggen, J. Evaluating SMIL: Three User Case Studies, *Proceedings of ACM Multimedia 99* (Orlando, Florida, USA, November 1999).

[20] Rutledge, L., van Ossenbruggen, J., Hardman, L. and Bulterman D.C.A. Anticipating SMIL 2.0: The Developing Cooperative Infrastructure for Multimedia on the Web, in *Proc. The Eighth International World Wide Web Conference (WWW8)* (Toronto, Canada, May 1999).

[21] Rutledge, L. Hardman, L. and van Ossenbruggen, J. Evaluating SMIL: Three User Case Studies, Poster Paper, *Proceedings of ACM Multimedia 99* (Orlando, Florida, USA, November 1999)

[22] Rutledge, L., Hardman, L., van Ossenbruggen, J. and Bulterman, D.C.A. Implementing Adaptability in the Standard Reference Model for Intelligent Multimedia Presentation Systems, *Proceedings of Multimedia Modeling 98 (MMM98)* (Lausanne, Switzerland, October, 1998) pp. 12-20.

[23] Rutledge, L. Hardman, L., van Ossenbruggen, J. and Bulterman, D.C.A. Structural Distinctions Between Hypermedia Storage and Presentation, *Proceedings of ACM Multimedia 98* (Bristol, England, September 1998), pp. 145-150.

[24] Saade, D.C.M., Soeares, L.F.G, Costa, F.R. and Souza Filho G.L., Graphical Structured-Editing of Multimedia Documents with Temporal and Spatial Constraint, *Proceedings of Multimedia Modeling 97 (MMM97)* (Singapore, October 1997) pp. 279-295.

[25] Schmitz, P., Yu, J. and Santangeli, P. *Timed Interactive Multimedia Extensions for HTML (HTML+TIME): Extending SMIL into the Web Browser*, Note submitted to the Wide Web Consortium. September 1998. http://www.w3.org/TR/NOTE-HTMLplusTIME/. (note for discussion)

[26] Urbano, M. J., Mendes, A.J., Monteiro, E.H. and Amer, P.D. Specification of Order and Reliability in SMIL Documents, *Proceedings of the IEEE Workshop on Internet Applications (WIAPP'99)* (San Jose, California, USA, July 1999).

[27] Wibmer, M. and Zechberger, G. *Off the Wall*, http://www.off-the-wall.at/.

IMPROVING SMIL DOCUMENTS WITH NCM FACILITIES

L.M. RODRIGUES, R.F. RODRIGUES, D.C. MUCHALUAT-SAADE, L.F.G. SOARES
{leandro, rogerio, debora}@telemidia.puc-rio.br; lfgs@inf.puc-rio.br

Laboratório TeleMídia, Depto. de Informática, PUC-Rio
R. Marquês de São Vicente, 225 – 22453-900 – Rio de Janeiro, Brasil

The use of the World-Wide Web to distribute multimedia documents with temporal and spatial relations is a research topic that has recently gained a lot of attention. Following the same proposal of simplicity found in HTML, the WWW consortium has published the SMIL recommendation for declarative authoring of multimedia documents. However, the SMIL simplicity leads to some limitations in the authoring process. In order to overcome these limitations, this work presents in details the integration of the SMIL language with NCM (Nested Context Model), an event-driven and object-oriented hypermedia model. The integration allows one to refine and manipulate SMIL documents in a Web-integrated hypermedia system with version control and high-level authoring tools.

1 Introduction

The use of the World-Wide Web (WWW) to distribute multimedia documents with temporal and spatial relations, besides the usual hypermedia navigation relations, is a research topic that has recently gained a lot of attention. As HTML, the main language used to create Web documents, does not support the definition of such synchronization relations, other proposals have been arisen to achieve this goal.

One of these proposals is a declarative language called SMIL (Synchronized Multimedia Integration Language) [11], adopted as a recommendation by the WWW Consortium. SMIL allows defining multimedia presentations on the Web in a simple way. However, as it happens with HTML, SMIL simplicity leads to some limitations in the authoring process.

The conceptual model of the HyperProp hypermedia system, *Nested Context Model* – NCM [8], is an object-oriented and event-driven model that allows logically structuring a document using compositions. Relationships among components are modeled by compositions and links. Compositions define structural relationships among nodes, while links define synchronous and asynchronous relationships among them.

Aiming to overcome HTML limitations, HyperProp has been integrated with the WWW, offering its features to manipulate Web documents [7]. Following a similar goal, this work presents the integration of SMIL with NCM.

The paper is organized as follows. Section 2 briefly describes the SMIL language. Section 3 presents some SMIL limitations and how they can be overcome by its integration with NCM. Section 4 presents some NCM relevant concepts for the paper scope. Section 5 describes the mapping between the two models. Section 6 comments related work and Section 7 is reserved to final remarks.

2 SMIL

The SMIL language offers a declarative form to specify the presentation of multimedia documents. A document is divided in two sections: head and body. The *head* contains general information about the document and the specification of the presentation spatial layout. The *body* contains the definition of objects and their temporal relations, as well as the specification of anchors and navigation links.

The spatial layout contains the definition of presentation window regions where objects will be shown. There is a special region that represents the whole window where the SMIL document will be presented. All other regions are defined in relation to this region.

SMIL basic objects, called *media objects*, can be of several types, such as text, image, video and audio. The object does not have the content of the associated data, but a description that includes a reference (URI) to the content itself. Media objects can also have *clip-begin* and *clip-end* attributes, which limit the object content to be presented.

SMIL uses the concept of composition to structure the document presentation. A composition can contain media objects and other compositions, establishing the way its components will be presented. There are two composition types, parallel (*par*) and sequential (*seq*). In a *parallel* composition, components are simultaneously presented, while in a *sequential* composition they are presented in sequence. The document body implicitly defines a sequential composition.

Every media object or composition has a duration that establishes how long its presentation will last. Continuous media objects, such as audio and video, have an implicit duration derived from its content, while discrete media objects, such as text and image, have a null implicit duration. The implicit duration of a composition corresponds to the result of the duration of its components. Besides the implicit duration, every element can have its duration explicitly defined by the author, through an optional attribute called *duration* (*dur*). The explicit duration of an element can be *indefinite*, indicating that the end of its presentation will coincide with the end of the presentation of the composition that contains it.

SMIL elements have two other optional temporal attributes, called *begin* and *end.* If an element with a defined begin/end attribute is contained in a parallel composition or if it is the first component of a sequential composition, it starts/finishes its presentation after the specified time interval since the beginning of the composition. If the element is a component, other than the first, of a sequential composition, the attribute value specifies a time interval to start/finish its presentation, in relation to the end of the previous component. In both parallel and sequential compositions, begin and end attributes can also be specified in relation to the beginning or end of any other element contained in the composition.

Additionally, parallel compositions have an attribute called *endsync*. It specifies the end of the composition in relation to the end of one of its components, which can be the first one to finish, the last one to finish or any specific component.

The same element can be presented several times in sequence. The number of presentations is specified in the *repeat* attribute, whose value can be an integer or *indefinite*. In the latter case, the element presentation will be repeated until the end of the composition that contains it.

SMIL also allows the specification of temporal and spatial sub-regions (anchors) in media objects and the definition of hyperlinks between them. Links can be defined not only between sub-regions of an object, but also among elements (whole media objects or compositions), or associations of these possibilities. Links can also be defined from an element or sub-region to a whole document or a specific element in another document. A SMIL link has an attribute called *show*, which defines the behavior of the link source object when a link is fired. The attribute value can be: *replace*, which specifies that the presentation of the source object will be replaced by the presentation of the target object; *new*, which specifies that the presentation of the target object will happen in another context, without affecting the source object; and *pause*, which specifies that the presentation of the source object will be suspended and resumed after the end of the presentation of the target object, which is done in another context.

Finally, SMIL provides means to define alternatives for a document presentation, depending on factors related to the system or to the user (e.g. language, bandwidth, etc.). In order to define multiple behavior options for a presentation, the language provides the *switch* element. This element allows the author to specify a group of alternative elements, from which at most one will be chosen, according to one or more tests that are made during runtime. These alternative elements are declared in order, and the first one that satisfies its tests is chosen to be presented.

3 Benefits of the integration of the SMIL language with NCM

As previously commented, SMIL simplicity leads to some limitations in the authoring process. Among these limitations, we can mention:

- SMIL offers two types of compound elements to define temporal relations, which are parallel and sequential compositions. The logical structure of a document is necessarily the presentation structure built by a hierarchy of nested compositions. Using this temporal model, changes in a document specification may result in a completely new structure for the document.
- SMIL does not provide data reuse or presentation structure reuse. Structures can only be reused by making copies, which makes maintenance tasks difficult. The language only provides reuse of media object content, identified by a URI, and reuse of presentation layouts inside the same document.

- Asynchronous relations in a SMIL document are always *1:1* links triggered by user selection, while all synchronous relations are specified by parallel and sequential compositions and element attributes (begin, end, dur, repeat, etc.). Thus, more complex relations among objects cannot be defined (e.g. "if the presentation of object *A* is in paused state when the presentation of anchor α of object *B* finishes, then restart the presentation of object *A* and increase the presentation rate of object *B* by 5%").
- There is no support for specifying behavior changes that may happen during an object presentation (e.g. "increase the audio volume to *X db*, *t* seconds after the beginning of its presentation").
- SMIL does not offer much flexibility for specifying presentation and preparation duration of objects, for example, allowing the definition of intervals for this duration. This flexibility would allow a presentation control system to adjust time in order to improve the presentation quality and reduce the chance of having temporal inconsistencies [1,4].

The integration of the SMIL language with NCM aims to overcome these limitations. Among the integration benefits, we can highlight:

- Using compositions not only for structuring a document presentation, but also for other logical structuring of its components, for example, context, derivation and task relations [9].
- The possibility of defining temporal synchronization among components using also links, allowing users to change a presentation specification without modifying the document global structure.
- The possibility of reusing data and presentation structure. In NCM, as compositions can be contained in different compositions, it is possible to reuse parts of a document structure (objects and relations) in the same document or in other documents, besides its data items.
- Support for the definition of *m:n* relationships among components of a SMIL document using NCM links, combining user interaction, presentation events and also the manipulation of node attributes.
- The possibility of specifying behavior changes that may happen during an object presentation.
- More flexibility in the specification of temporal behavior of objects, allowing possible adjustments during its presentation, for example, due to network delays.
- Support for version control and cooperative work.
- Using the HyperProp authoring tool, which offers a graphical interface to create and edit structured documents.
- Using the HyperProp formatter (analogous to a SMIL player) to present SMIL documents. The current version of the HyperProp formatter does not

implement, but foresees, support for adjustments during runtime in order to guarantee a better presentation quality according to a user platform.

4 Nested Context Model

NCM is based on the usual concepts of nodes and links. In NCM, a *node* has as main attributes its content, an anchor ordered list and a descriptor. The *content* identifies a set of *information units*. An *anchor* identifies a marked subset of the content. The exact notion of information unit is part of the definition of node class. For example, an information unit of a video node could be a frame, while an information unit of a text node could be a character or a word. Every NCM node has an anchor called λ *anchor*, which identifies the whole content of the node. The *descriptor* contains information determining how the node should be presented in time and space.

NCM distinguishes two basic classes of nodes, called content node and composite node. Intuitively, a *content node* contains data whose internal structure is application dependent, modeling traditional hypermedia nodes. Content nodes may be specialized in other classes (text, graphic, audio, video, etc.) as required by applications. For example, a specialization of the text node class, called HTML node, was defined in [7] to integrate HTML pages with NCM documents. The logical structuring of a document is made by introducing the composition concept. In NCM, the content of a *composite node* is a list of links and nodes, which may be content or composite nodes, recursively. An important restriction is made: a node cannot be recursively contained in itself.

As a node can be contained in different compositions and composite nodes can be nested to any depth, it is necessary to introduce the concept of perspective. Intuitively, the *perspective* of a node identifies through which sequence of nested composite nodes a given node instance is being observed.

The basic synchronization unit in NCM is an event. As stated in [5], an *event* is an occurrence in time that can be instantaneous or can occur over some time period. NCM defines three types of events: *presentation event*, which is defined by the presentation of an anchor of a node in a given perspective; *selection event*, which is defined by the selection of an anchor of a node in a given perspective; and *attribution event*, which is defined by a change in the value of an attribute of a node in a given perspective.

In NCM, an event can be in one of the following states: *sleeping, preparing, prepared, occurring*, *paused* and *aborted*. Every event has an associated attribute, called *occurrences*, which counts how many times it transits from *occurring* to *prepared* state during a document presentation. Presentation events also have an attribute named *repeat*, which indicates how many times the event should sequentially be presented. As in SMIL, this attribute can contain a finite value or the *indefinite* value. Moreover, presentation events contain five other attributes:

minimum duration, optimum duration, maximum duration, expected duration and elastic cost. The *minimum* and *maximum duration* together define the valid interval for the event presentation duration, while the *optimum duration* specifies the duration that leads to the best quality of presentation. *Elastic cost* is a function that determines the cost if the best quality of presentation is not chosen. The *expected duration* is initialized with the optimum duration. Based on synchronization procedures like the ones described in [1,4], a formatter can change the expected duration to achieve a better presentation quality for the document as a whole, optimizing the global cost. The NCM event state machine is presented in Figure 1.

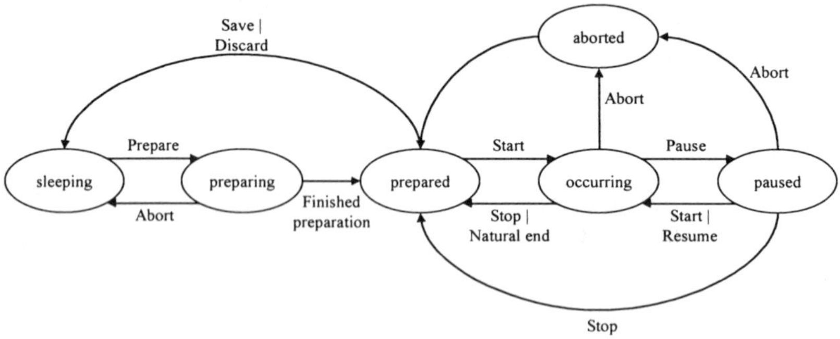

Figure 1 – NCM event state machine

A presentation event can change from *occurring* to *prepared* in two situations: as a consequence of the natural end of the presentation duration, or due to an action that stops the event. As in SMIL, an event duration can be intrinsic or specified by the author. Furthermore, the transition from *aborted* to *prepared* always occurs automatically. The actions that generate state transitions will be explained later in this section.

A *link* represents *m:n* relationships among objects. It is composed by *m* source end points, *n* target end points and a meeting point. *End points* define events, while the *meeting point* contains the description of the relationship among them. Since a node may pertain to more than one composite node, the source and target end points of a link are identified by tuples of the form $<(N_k,...,N_l)$, α, *type*$>$, such that: $(N_k,...,N_l)$ is the nested node sequence to reach N_l, in relation to the composition that contains the link; α is the identification of an anchor or an attribute of N_l; and *type* specifies the event associated to α (presentation, selection or attribution). N_l is called an *anchor node* of the link.

The meeting point contains a condition and an action. Conditions are related to source end points, while actions are operations that should be applied to target end points. When a condition is satisfied, its associated action is fired.

Meeting point *condition* evaluates boolean values and can be binary simple or compound. Every *binary simple condition* is expressed by two unary conditions: a *previous condition*, to be satisfied immediately before the condition evaluation instant, and a *current condition*, to be satisfied at the condition evaluation instant. A binary simple condition is satisfied when both unary conditions are satisfied. A unary condition is a comparison concerning event states, event attributes or node attributes. It can also receive the *true* value, if it is not relevant in the binary simple condition evaluation. Comparison operators used in the evaluation of unary conditions are: =, ≠, <, ≤, > and ≥. A *compound condition* consists of a logical expression involving other conditions, simple or compound, and based on the operators ∧ (and), ∨ (or), ¬ (not) and ⊕ (delay). The logical operators ∧, ∨ and ¬ have the usual meanings of the propositional logic. An expression ($C \oplus d$) is satisfied at a time t if condition C was satisfied at time $[t - d]$, where $d \in \Re$. When d is non-negative, the meeting point defines a traditional causal relationship. When d is negative, satisfied conditions imply actions that should be fired in the past. In these cases, the meeting point semantically specifies constraint relations among events. Like the event duration, d is specified with minimum, optimum, expected and maximum values and an elastic cost.

Meeting point *actions* can also be simple or compound. A *simple action* is executed over an event contained in the destination end point set. Simple actions applied on end points that define presentation events are described in Table 1. The model also defines simple actions over attribution events, but they are not relevant in this paper.

A compound action is defined by an expression based on the operators | (parallel) and → (sequential), specifying the execution order of each action of the expression. Moreover, every simple or compound action has an optional attribute called *wait*. This attribute determines the time that must be waited before executing the action. Like the event duration and the condition delay operator, the *wait* attribute is specified as a tuple <minimum, optimum, maximum, expected, elastic cost>.

A hypermedia document model should permit the definition of the expected behavior of each node when it is presented, specifying its presentation layout and how the presentation should be modified in time. NCM defines this information separately from the associated node, which allows a better reuse of objects. For example, using distinct layouts, one can define different presentations for the same media object. A string can be presented as text, or it can be synthesized as audio, depending on the layout specification. Note that as different layouts can lead to different event duration intervals, different qualities of presentation and different platform requirements, the definition of all these issues should also be part of the layout and not part of the media object (node).

In NCM, spatial and temporal specification of a node and behavior changes during its presentation are defined in the descriptor object. The presentation of a node to the final user (document reader) is done by the association of this node with a descriptor. The model also allows a descriptor to be specified by the reader during the presentation. If it does not happen, the system will use a descriptor previously defined by the author. In this case, the descriptor can be specified in the link (action parameter), in the composition that contains the node or as an attribute of the node.

Action	Description
Prepare(E, d)	If event *E* is in the sleeping state, it goes to the preparing state; otherwise, there is no transition. The action can optionally specify a descriptor to be associated to the anchor node of the target end point that defines *E*. At the end of the procedure, the repeat attribute of *E* is initialized with the value specified in the associated descriptor. If there is no specified value, the attribute is set to one (default value).
Start(E, d, n)	If event *E* is in the sleeping, preparing, prepared or paused state, it goes to the occurring state through the state machine (see Figure 1), starting its presentation from the beginning. Otherwise, nothing happens. As in the prepare action, the start action can optionally specify a descriptor to be associated to the anchor node of the target end point that defines *E*. This action also has another optional parameter *n* to initialize the *repeat* attribute of *E*. If this parameter is not specified, the *repeat* attribute is initialized with the value declared in the associated descriptor.
Stop(E)	If event *E* is in the occurring or suspended state, it goes to the prepared state; otherwise, there is no transition. This action increases by one unit the *occurrences* attribute of *E* and decreases by one unit the *repeat* attribute of *E*. If the value of *repeat* is still greater than zero after being decreased, a new presentation of *E* is automatically started.
Pause(E)	If event *E* is in the occurring state, it goes to the paused state, otherwise, nothing happens.
Resume(E)	If event *E* is in the paused state, it goes back to the occurring state, otherwise, nothing happens. The presentation of *E* is resumed from the last information unit presented before the event has been paused.
Abort(E)	If event *E* is in the occurring or paused state, it goes to the aborted state and immediately after it goes to the prepared state. The *occurrences* attribute of *E* is not increased and the *repeat* attribute is set to zero. If *E* is in the preparing state it goes to the sleeping state. If *E* is in any other state, nothing happens.

Table 1 – NCM simple actions applied on presentation events

This is the respective priority order used to choose the descriptor. If there is no descriptor specified, a default descriptor of the node class is used.

A *descriptor* has as main attributes the node exhibition/edition method and a collection of event descriptions. NCM allows descriptor attributes to be extended with other attributes depending on the node class.

The *node exhibition/edition method* can identify any program or can be a method implemented in the descriptor itself. Each *event description* consists in a tuple $<\alpha$, *type*, *dur*, *rep*, *oper*$>$. The first parameter (α) identifies an anchor of the node to which the descriptor will be associated. *Type* specifies the event type associated to the anchor (presentation, selection or attribution). *Dur* is a tuple $<d_{min}, d_{opt}, d_{max}, f_c>$, which defines values to initialize, respectively, the minimum duration, optimum duration, maximum duration and elastic cost attributes of the event. *Rep* specifies the number of repeated exhibitions for the event. This parameter initializes the *repeat* attribute value of the event, if it is not initialized by a link action. *Dur* and *Rep* are only used for presentation events. *Oper* specifies an ordered sequence of operations, which are executed whenever the event state changes. Each operation is composed by a condition and an action, which are similar to link meeting point conditions and actions. The only difference is that their entry scope are limited to events and attributes of the node associated to the descriptor, or to attributes defined in the descriptor itself.

5 Conversion of SMIL documents into NCM documents

5.1 Media objects and anchors

SMIL media objects are converted into content nodes and descriptors in NCM. A content node is created from the *type* and *src* attributes declared in the media object. Its class corresponds to the media object type (text, image, etc.), and the value of its *content* attribute is assigned with the reference (URI) stored in the *src* attribute of the media object. Two or more distinct media objects with the same values for their *type* and *src* correspond to the same NCM content node, inserted in different perspectives and with distinct descriptors. The information stored in descriptors is discussed in Section 5.2.

For each media object anchor, an equivalent NCM anchor is created and inserted in the anchor list of the node. If the media object has *clip-begin* and *clip-end* attributes, an additional anchor is created and inserted in the anchor list of the node, defining this sub-region of the node content. In this case, all synchronization relationships associated to this node will make reference to this anchor, instead of the λ anchor of the node (see Section 4). In this paper, we will not consider media objects with clip attributes, without generality loss.

5.2 Spatial layout, object duration and repetitions

Given the region attribute of a media object, the information about spatial localization is extracted from the SMIL document layout and stored in the descriptor. In order to store the object duration, an entry is created in the event description list associated to the λ anchor of the node (see Section 4). The event type is defined as presentation. The minimum, optimal and maximum duration are all set to the same value (the object duration), and the cost function is set to a null value, since SMIL does not provide flexibility in the duration declaration, as mentioned in Section 3. The *rep* parameter is set to the value of the *repeat* attribute specified in the media object, if it is specified.

Descriptors are also created for composite nodes. NCM compositions will represent SMIL parallel and sequential compositions, as will be seen in Sections 5.3 and 5.4. In this case, descriptors will be important to store the duration, the number of repetitions and additional node attributes.

5.3 *Parallel Compositions*

A SMIL parallel composition is represented in NCM as a composite node containing other content or composite nodes corresponding to the components of the SMIL composition. The NCM composition also has links to express synchronization among its components. The generic structure of an NCM composite node that represents a SMIL parallel composition is presented in Figure 2, while its links are described in Table 2.

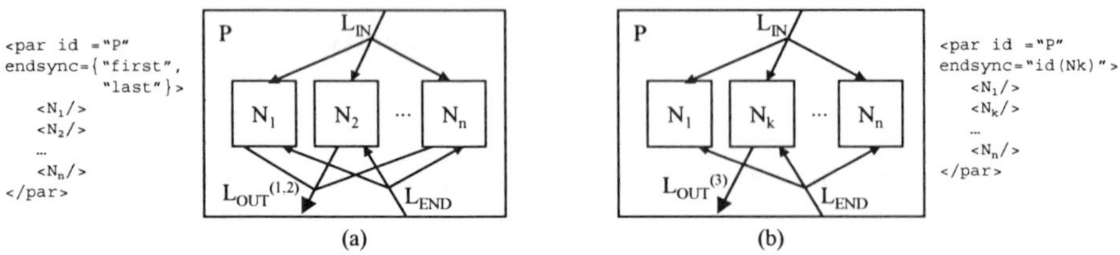

Figure 2 – Representation of SMIL parallel compositions in NCM. (a) Compositions ending by the first or the last component. (b) Compositions ending by a specific component.

Link L_{IN} is responsible for the beginning of the parallel presentation of the nodes contained in composition *P* as soon as the presentation of *P* starts.

Links $L_{OUT}^{(1,2,3)}$ are responsible for the end of the presentation of *P*. The component of *P* responsible for the end of its presentation depends on the *endsync* attribute of the SMIL parallel composition. If the composition is finished by the last component (link $L_{OUT}^{(1)}$), each time the presentation of a node contained in *P* finishes, the link meeting point verifies if all nodes have already finished their presentations (including possible repetitions). If the composition is finished by the first component (link $L_{OUT}^{(2)}$), the first component that finishes its presentation fires the link. Finally, if *P* is finished by a specific component (link $L_{OUT}^{(3)}$), the link only tests the component presentation event.

When *P* leaves the *occurring* state, it must abort the presentation of each node it contains, if it is still occurring. This action is performed by link L_{END}, which is fired when the presentation event state of node *P* changes from *occurring* to *prepared*, or from *occurring* to *aborted*. The former transition occurs as a consequence of the *stop* action of a link (e.g., $L_{OUT}^{(1,2,3)}$) or the expiration of the duration specified in node *P* descriptor, if an explicit duration is defined for this node. The latter transition occurs as a consequence of the *abort* action over the presentation event of *P*, caused by a link contained in another composition in which *P* is contained.

The beginning of a component may be defined explicitly in relation to the parallel composition. Supposing that a component N_k of the parallel composition *P* presented in Figure 2 has an explicit begin of *t* units of time in relation to the parallel composition itself, a new link $L_{IN,k}$ is created in order to warrant the specified delay to start N_k presentation. This link has a source end point defined in *P* and a target end point defined in N_k. Besides, link L_{IN} is modified so that it does not

Link	Source Events	Target Events	Meeting Point
L_{IN}	**E_P**: <(P), λ, *pres*>	**E_1**: <(N_1), λ, *pres*> **E_2**: <(N_2), λ, *pres*> … **E_n**: <(N_n), λ, *pres*>	***Condition***: <st(E_P)=prepared, st(E_P)=occurring> ***Action***: start(E_1) $\mid$ start(E_2) $\mid$ … $\mid$ start(E_n)
$L_{OUT}^{(1)}$	**E_1**: <(N_1), λ, *pres*> **E_2**: <(N_2), λ, *pres*> … **E_n**: <(N_n), λ, *pres*>	**E_P**: <(P), λ, *pres*>	***Condition***: (<st(E_1)=occurring, st(E_1)=prepared> ∨ <st(E_2)=occurring, st(E_2)=prepared> ∨ … ∨ <st(E_n)=occurring, st(E_n)=prepared>) ∧ (<true, rep(E_1)=0> ∧ <true, rep(E_2)=0> ∧ … ∧ <true, rep(E_n)=0>) ***Action***: stop(E_P)
$L_{OUT}^{(2)}$	**E_1**: <(N_1), λ, *pres*> **E_2**: <(N_2), λ, *pres*> … **E_n**: <(N_n), λ, *pres*>	**E_P**: <(P), λ, *pres*>	***Condition***: (<st(E_1)=occurring, st(E_1)=prepared> ∧ <true, rep(E_1)=0>) ∨ (<st(E_2)=occurring, st(E_2)=prepared> ∧ <true, rep(E_2)=0>) ∨ … ∨ (<st(E_n)=occurring, st(E_n)=prepared> ∧ <true, rep(E_n)=0>) ***Action***: stop(E_P)
$L_{OUT}^{(3)}$	**E_k**: <(N_k), λ, *pres*>	**E_P**: <(P), λ, *pres*>	***Condition***: <st(E_k)=occurring, st(E_k)=prepared> ∧ <true, rep(E_k)=0> ***Action***: stop(E_P)
L_{END}	**E_P**: <(P), λ, *pres*>	**E_1**: <(N_1), λ, *pres*> **E_2**: <(N_2), λ, *pres*> … **E_n**: <(N_n), λ, *pres*>	***Condition***: <st(E_P)=occurring, st(E_P)=prepared> ∨ <st(E_P)=occurring, st(E_P)=aborted> ***Action***: abort(E_1) $\mid$ abort(E_2) $\mid$ … $\mid$ abort(E_n)

pres = presentation
$L_{OUT}^{(1)}$ - compositions finished by the last component (endsync = "last" – default)
$L_{OUT}^{(2)}$ - compositions finished by the first component (endsync = "first")
$L_{OUT}^{(3)}$ - compositions finished by a specific component N_k (endsync = "id(N_k)")

Table 2 – Specification of links in parallel compositions. In meeting point conditions, we adopted the following representation conventions: st(*E*) evaluates the state of event *E*, and rep(*E*) evaluates the *repeat* attribute of event *E*.

start N_k presentation, but just prepares it. The reason to prepare N_k presentation is due to the need to initiate the *repeat* event attribute, in order to avoid firing link $L_{OUT}^{(1)}$ before N_k presentation. Table 3 presents the descriptions of the modified link (L_{IN}) and the new link ($L_{IN,k}$).

Link $L_{IN,k}$ has a condition that verifies if the presentation event of composition *P* remains in the *occurring* state after the specified delay. The state can have changed for three reasons: i) the end of the composition was determined by a node, other than the last, that has finished its presentation before the specified delay; ii) composition *P* has finished its presentation as a consequence of the definition of an explicit duration for the composition; iii) an *abort/stop* action has been performed over the presentation event of *P*.

The explicit begin of a component can also be given in relation to another node of the composition. In this case, the new link created will have this node as its source end point. Table 3 describes the new link ($L_{m,k}$) created to express the explicit begin of a node N_k in relation to another node N_m of the same composition.

Link	Source Events	Target Events	Meeting Point
L_{IN}	**E_P**: <(P), λ, *pres*>	**E_1**: <(N_1), λ, *pres*> … **E_k**: <(N_k), λ, *pres*> … **E_n**: <(N_n), λ, *pres*>	***Condition***: <st(E_P)=prepared, st(E_P)=occurring> ***Action***: start(E_1) | start (E_2) | … | prepare(E_k) | … | start(E_n)
$L_{IN,k}$	**E_P**: <(P), λ, *pres*>	**E_k**: <(N_k), λ, *pres*>	***Condition***: (<st(E_P)=prepared, st(E_P)=occurring> ⊕ t) ∧ <true, st(E_P)=occurring> ***Action***: start(E_k)
$L_{m,k}$	**E_m**: <(N_m), λ, *pres*> **E_P**: <(P), λ, *pres*>	**E_k**: <(N_k), λ, *pres*>	***Condition***: (<st(E_m)=prepared, st(E_m)=occurring> ⊕ t) ∧ <true, st(E_P)=occurring> ***Action***: start(E_k)

Table 3 – Specification of links for explicit begin in parallel compositions

5.4 Sequential Compositions

Like a parallel composition, a SMIL sequential composition is represented in NCM as a composite node containing other content or composite nodes associated with the components of the SMIL composition, and links to express synchronization among its components. The SMIL document body is represented in the same way. The generic structure of an NCM composite node that represents a SMIL sequential composition is presented in Figure 3, while its links are described in Table 4.

```
<seq id ="S">
   <N1/>
   <N2/>
   ...
   <Nn/>
</seq>
```

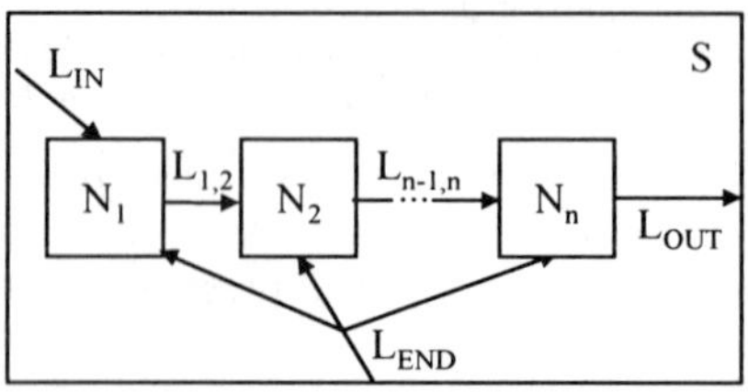

Figure 3 – Representation of SMIL sequential compositions in NCM

Link L_{IN} starts the presentation of the node corresponding to the first component of the SMIL sequential composition, as soon as the presentation of composition *S* starts. The beginning of the presentation of each subsequent node is caused by the end of the presentation of the previous node (considering possible repetitions). These relations are established by links $L_{i-1,i}$, with i ∈ [2,n]. Finally, link L_{OUT} finishes the presentation of *S* after the last node presentation.

When the presentation event of composition *S* leaves the *occurring* state, the presentation of all its component nodes must be aborted. These actions are performed by link L_{END}, and typically occur when the presentation event of *S* is aborted, or when it finishes as a consequence of the definition of an explicit duration.

Link	Source Events	Target Events	Meeting Point
L_{IN}	E_S: <(S), λ, *pres*>	E_1: <(N_1), λ, *pres*>	***Condition***: <st(E_S)=prepared, st(E_S)=occurring> ***Action***: start(E_1)
$L_{i-1,i}$ (i∈[2,n])	E_{i-1}: <(N_{i-1}), λ, *pres*>	E_i: <(N_i), λ, *pres*>	***Condition***: <st(E_{i-1})=occurring, st(E_{i-1})=prepared> ∧ <true, rep(E_{i-1})=0> ***Action***: start(E_i)
L_{OUT}	E_n: <(N_n), λ, *pres*>	E_S: <(S), λ, *pres*>	***Condition***: <st(E_n)=occurring, st(E_n)=prepared> ∧ <true, rep(E_n)=0> ***Action***: stop(E_S)
L_{END}	E_S: <(S), λ, *pres*>	E_1: <(N_1), λ, *pres*> E_2: <(N_2), λ, *pres*> ... E_n: <(N_n), λ, *pres*>	***Condition***: <st(E_S)=occurring, st(E_S)=prepared> ∨ <st(E_S)=occurring, st(E_S)=aborted> ***Action***: abort(E_1) | abort(E_2) | ... | abort(E_n)

Table 4 – Specification of links in sequential compositions

The beginning of a component presentation may be defined explicitly in relation to the end of the previous component, specifying a delay. When the explicit specification is made in the first component, link L_{IN} is slightly modified. If the specification is made in component *k*, link $L_{k-1,k}$ is modified. Table 5 presents the description of the modified links for the specified cases.

5.5 Navigation links

SMIL allows the definition of traditional hypermedia links activated by user interaction. These links are always *1:1*, that is, with a source anchor and a target anchor. The anchors are defined in the link itself.

SMIL links are converted into NCM links. If the *show* attribute of the SMIL link is *replace*, the NCM link action stops the source document presentation before starting the target object presentation. If it is *pause*, the action pauses the source object presentation, which is resumed by another link after the end of the target

Link	Source Events	Target Events	Meeting Point
L_{IN}	E_S: <(S), λ, *pres*>	E_1: <(N_1), λ, *pres*>	***Condition***: (<st(E_S)=prepared, st(E_S)=occurring> $\oplus$ t) $\wedge$ <true, st(E_S)=occurring> ***Action***: start(E_1)
$L_{k-1,k}$	E_{k-1}: <(N_{k-1}), λ, *pres*> E_S: <(S), λ, *pres*>	E_k: <(N_k), λ, *pres*>	***Condition***: ((<st(E_{k-1})=occurring, st(E_{k-1})=prepared> $\wedge$ <true, rep(E_{k-1})=0>) $\oplus$ t) $\wedge$ <true, st(E_S)=occurring> ***Action***: start(E_k)

Table 5 – Specification of links for explicit begin in sequential compositions

object presentation. If it is *new*, the action simply starts the target object presentation, without affecting the source document presentation.

For example, consider a SMIL link from an element of the document "origin.smil" to an element of the document "destination.smil", with the *show* attribute equal to *replace*. Let S_1 and S_2 be the NCM compositions that represent the body of these documents, respectively, and let N_1 and N_2 be the NCM nodes corresponding to the source and the target SMIL elements, respectively. Link L, created in NCM to represent this SMIL link, is specified in Table 6. Its source end point corresponds to the selection event of N_1, and its target end points correspond to the presentation events of S_1 and N_2. The link action stops the presentation of S_1, and then starts the presentation of N_2. The node lists (S_1,..., N_1) and (S_2,..., N_2) specify the perspectives of N_1 and N_2 in the context given by the conversion of the documents "origin.smil" and "destination.smil", respectively. The link is inserted into a third composition that also contains nodes S_1 and S_2.

Link	Source Events	Target Events	Meeting Point
L	E_S: <(S_1,..., N_1), λ, *sel*>	E_1: <(S_1), λ, *pres*> E_2: <(S_2,..., N_2), λ, *pres*>	***Condition***: <st(E_S)=prepared, st(E_S)=occurring> ***Action***: stop(E_1) $\rightarrow$ start (E_2)

sel = selection

Table 6 – Specification of a traditional hypermedia navigation link

5.6 Alternative presentations

As previously mentioned, SMIL provides the *switch* element, which allows the definition of alternatives for media object and composition presentation, according to system characteristics or user preferences.

NCM does not directly offer this kind of feature. Instead, it proposes that users create structures and virtual links with queries that define the presentation behavior according to the context. However, virtual entities and query languages are not implemented in the system yet, and are left for future work. Nevertheless, it is possible to simulate the specification of alternative presentations through composite nodes, links and operation lists in event descriptions.

In order to convert a *switch* element to an NCM object, a composite node is created containing nodes that correspond to the components of the *switch* element. Associated with this composite node, there is a descriptor with an attribute *attr*, over which the test must be done. Figure 4 describes the generic structure of a composition that represents alternative components. Table 7 presents the description of the links shown in the figure. The attribute *attr* is declared in attribution event A_S.

```
<switch id ="S">
   <N1 attr=val1/>
   <N2 attr=val2/>
   ...
   <Nn attr=valn/>
</switch>
```

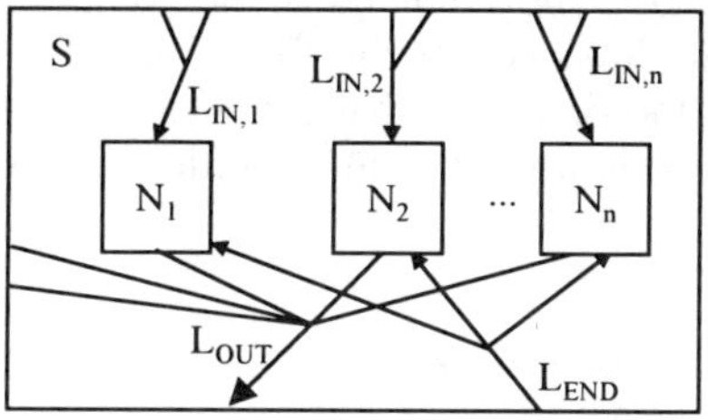

Figure 4 – Generic structure of a switch element as an NCM composition

Link	Source Events	Target Events	Meeting Point
$L_{IN,i}$ ($i \in [1,n]$)	E_S: <(S), λ, *pres*> A_S: <(S), *attr*, *attrib*>	E_i: <(N_i), λ, *pres*>	***Condition***: <st(E_S)=prepared, st(E_S)=occurring> ∧ <true, at(A_S)=val_i> ***Action***: start(E_i)
L_{OUT}	E_1: <(N_1), λ, *pres*> E_2: <(N_2), λ, *pres*> ... E_n: <(N_n), λ, *pres*> E_S: <(S), λ, *pres*> A_S: <(S), *attr*, *attrib*>	E_S: <(S), λ, *pres*>	***Condition***: (<st(E_1)=occurring, st(E_1)=prepared> ∧ <true, rep(E_1)=0>) ∨ (<st(E_2)=occurring, st(E_2)=prepared> ∧ <true, rep(E_2)=0>) ∨ ... ∨ (<st(E_n)=occurring, st(E_n)=prepared> ∧ <true, rep(E_n)=0>) ∨ (<st(E_S)=prepared, st(E_S)=occurring> ∧ (¬<true, at(A_S)=val_1> ∧ ¬<true, at(A_S)=val_2> ∧ ... ∧ ¬<true, at(A_S)=val_n>)) ***Action***: stop(E_S)
L_{END}	E_S: <(S), λ, *pres*>	E_1: <(N_1), λ, *pres*> E_2: <(N_2), λ, *pres*> ... E_n: <(N_n), λ, *pres*>	***Condition***: <st(E_S)=occurring, st(E_S)=aborted> ∨ <st(E_S)=occurring, st(E_S)=prepared> ***Action***: abort(E_1) | abort(E_2) |...| abort(E_n)

attrib = attribution

Table 7 – Specification of links in switch compositions

Links $L_{IN,i}$, with $i \in [1,n]$, start the presentation of the node N_i whose value val_i is equal to the value of the *attr* attribute of the composition descriptor. Link L_{OUT}

stops the presentation of S when the presentation of the chosen node is finished, or if no component satisfies the condition. Link L_{END} warrants that the end of the composition presentation aborts the chosen node presentation.

It is worth to note that some attributes defined in SMIL cannot be tested in the proposed solution. For example, this is the case of tests related to the available network bandwidth. For this kind of attribute, the node being tested must be chosen not only when its attribute value is equal to the value defined by the system, but also when it is smaller than this value. Moreover, in this case, more than one link $L_{IN,i}$ could be satisfied. Simply changing the comparison operator in the meeting point conditions of the links solves the first point. The second point is overcome by the computation of the first node that satisfies its tests, following the declaration order. This computation is done in the operation list specified in the presentation event description.

5.7 Example of conversion

This section presents an example of conversion of a SMIL document into an NCM document. The SMIL document is presented in Figure 5. The document body is composed of a sequential element with two parallel elements, each one with two media object elements. The first parallel element is finished by the last component, and the second one is finished by a specific component (the video element).

```
<smil>
  <head>
    <meta name="title" content="matise"/>
    <layout>
      <root-layout id="matise" background-color="#fcedc4" width="721" height="587"/>
      <region id="m_title" left="4%" top="4%" width="47%" height="22%"/>
      <region id="V-Main" left="52%" top="5%" width="45%" height="42%"/>
      <region id="music"/>
    </layout>
  </head>
  <body>
      <seq id="News-at">
        <par>
          <text id="Leader-Title" region="m_title" src="leader_title.html"/>
          <audio id="Leader-Music" region="music" src="logo1.aiff"/>
        </par>
        <par endsync="id(DCAB-Video)">
          <text id="DCAB-Intro" region="m_title" src="intro.html" dur="8s"/>
          <video id="DCAB-Video" region="V-Main" src="zoomin.mpv"/>
        </par>
      </seq>
  </body>
</smil>
```

Figure 5 – Example of a SMIL document

The NCM document generated by the conversion is shown in Figure 6. The body element has been converted into a composite node ("example.smil"), containing another composite node that corresponds to the sequential element

("News-at"). Both nodes "example.smil" and "News-at" contain links to represent the sequential behavior, as described in Section 5.4. The parallel elements have been converted into composite nodes ("$par1" and "$par2") containing terminal nodes that correspond to the media object elements, and links to represent the parallel behavior, as described in Section 5.3.

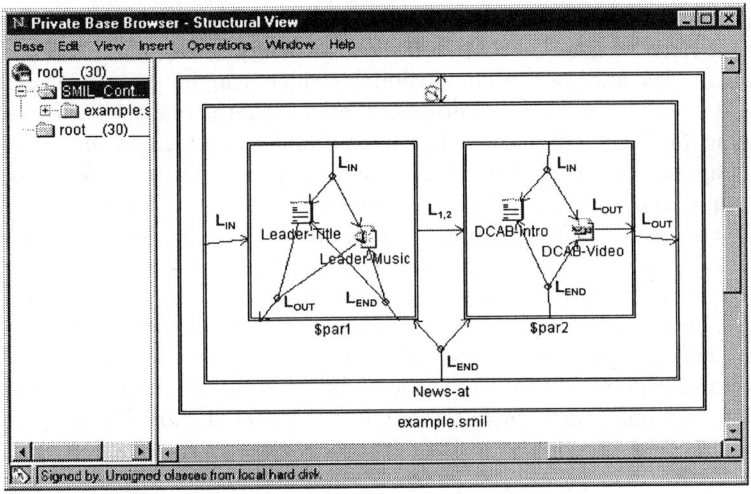

Figure 6 – The generated NCM document

5.8 *Implementation*

The screen presented in Figure 6 is the client browser of the HyperProp system. This browser provides a graphical structural view of NCM documents, allowing both authoring and navigation operations. The conversion of SMIL documents into NCM documents is called by a menu item. The translator automatically imports a set of SMIL documents and adds them to a special composite node, called "SMIL Context", which also contains NCM links corresponding to external links between the SMIL documents.

The process of conversion is divided in two parts. The first one is a parser that reads the SMIL document, verifies its syntactic correctness and builds a data structure that represents the SMIL elements in an object-oriented basis. The second one translates this data structure to the NCM data structure, which represents NCM documents. The reason for dividing the conversion in these two parts is that the SMIL document is read only once, and the translation is started only after verifying that the document is correctly specified.

6 Related Work

There are some proposals to allow the presentation of multimedia documents on the Web. One of them is HTML+TIME (*Timed Interactive Multimedia Extensions for HTML*) [12]. This proposal aims to incorporate synchronization facilities, creating temporal extensions to HTML, and not using a new substitute language. As a result, any HTML element could be presented at a specific moment with a given duration. Besides the new attributes, HTML+TIME also incorporates some SMIL elements, such as *par*, *seq* and *switch* compositions, which can be used to specify more complex relations. However, the proposed model inherits many HTML limitations, such as the fact that links are unidirectional and embedded in the node content (HTML pages). This limitation hinders, among other things, node content reuse without inheriting relations, link creation in pages where users do not have permission to write, and knowing which links make reference to a given page.

Another proposal following the SMIL approach of defining a declarative language to specify multimedia presentations on the Web is presented in [6]. This proposal is based on three concepts: *hypertime links* for temporal compositions, *time bases* for close lip-sync synchronization between media objects, and *dynamic layout* for positioning and movement. Hypertime links are similar to traditional hyperlinks, containing only one source anchor and only one target anchor. The difference from hyperlinks is that, similarly to NCM presentation events, source anchors on hypertime links do not need user interaction to be activated. The time base concept defines how an object should adjust its presentation rate. One time base can be shared by several objects, establishing a master-slave way to specify fine synchronization among them. Therefore, similarly to NCM, the model presents the elastic time concept, that is, an object duration can be calculated depending on the environment and the author specification. The layout contains spatial information to present the objects. In order to make no distinction between temporal and spatial synchronization, layouts are also considered objects. The authors also defined an execution architecture and implemented a prototype using Java and Dynamic HTML. This prototype allows presenting documents defined in the proposed extended language using commercial browsers. This proposal, like SMIL and NCM, separates link from data content. However, the proposed model does not present any composition concept, making difficult or even impossible a structured authoring process. Defining relationships among more than two objects is not allowed either. Behavior changes in the presentation of objects are previewed as future work.

Madeus [3], an authoring and presentation system for multimedia documents based on a constraint model, developed a work similar to the one presented in this paper, permitting importing SMIL documents into its environment [2]. Madeus conceptual model also offers compositions for logical structuring of documents, and temporal and spatial relationships among components. However, it also has some limitations, as it does not offer *m:n* relations and does not allow the specification of behavior changes during an object presentation. The work presented in [2] is concentrated on the SMIL temporal model, and does not consider all SMIL elements. For example, SMIL *switch* compositions are not mentioned.

7 Final Remarks

This paper presented how to overcome the limitations of the SMIL language through its integration with the NCM event-driven model. The exercise of representing SMIL documents has led to refinements in some aspects of NCM, as the definition of the *repeat* attribute of events and how its value is set. It was shown that all SMIL functionality could be represented in NCM. However, the way parallel and sequential compositions were modeled caused a little difference in relation to the SMIL recommendation. According to this recommendation, when a link is fired by a user selection, the destination document is presented from the target element until the end of the document. In the conversion to NCM, when a hyperlink has as target end point the presentation of a node *N* contained in a parallel or switch composition, only this node will be presented. When *N* is contained in a sequential composition, only the nodes in the composition (node *N* and subsequent nodes) will be presented. NCM could be easily extended to embed SMIL behavior. However, we think that we should try a general solution, since this SMIL behavior is not always desirable.

NCM is the conceptual data model of the HyperProp system. HyperProp is implemented in Java and is integrated with the Web. This integration, presented in details in [7], has allowed providing support for structured authoring of documents, version control and definition of relationships for temporal and spatial synchronization. The integration also provided a graphical structural view of Web sites using fisheye techniques. As a result of the work presented in this paper, a SMIL-NCM translator was added to the system, to automatically import SMIL documents to NCM. It is now possible to incorporate the facilities offered by NCM and implemented in HyperProp to SMIL documents.

In spite of NCM complex syntax for the definition of links, we are working on the HyperProp system in order to offer a high-level graphical interface for document edition. The aim of the system is to provide an interface with templates of the main types of links, for authors that are not familiar with the model. For advanced authors, the system provides methods to directly edit the meeting point of links, allowing the specification of more complex relations.

As a future work, it is intended to define NCM extensions to allow a direct specification of the main facilities of the SMIL language. An example of extension is the definition of NCM *parallel* and *sequential composition* classes, which would have the same semantics of the homonym SMIL classes. This extension would allow generating SMIL documents from NCM documents, with the restriction that only a subset of the NCM documents would be appropriate to be converted, due to SMIL limitations. Another future work is the definition of an XML DTD to support a declarative specification of documents that complies with these extensions of

NCM. The aim is that this new language incorporates facilities that overcome SMIL limitations, while keeping its present simplicity for the definition of presentations.

References

1. Buchanan, M.C.; Zellweger, P.T. "Automatically Generating Consistent Schedules for Multimedia Documents", *Multimedia Systems*, Springer-Verlag, April 1993.
2. Collomb, P. "De Smil à Madeus: deux langages de synchronisation de documents multimédia", *Rapport de Maîtrise Informatique de l'Université Joseph Fourier (Grenoble 1)*, September 1998.
3. Jourdan, M.; Layaïda, N.; Roisin, C.; Sabry-Ismail, L.; Tardif, L. "Madeus, an Authoring Environment for Interactive Multimedia Documents", *Proceedings of the ACM Multimedia Conference 98*, pp. 267-272, ACM, Bristol, September 1998.
4. Kim, M.Y.; Song J. "Multimedia Documents with Elastic Time", *Proceedings of the ACM Multimedia Conference 95*, San Francisco, November 1995.
5. Pérez-Luque, M.J.; Little, T.D.C. "A Temporal Reference Framework for Multimedia Synchronization". *IEEE Journal on Selected Areas in Communications (Special Issue: Synchronization Issues in Multimedia Communication)*, Vol. 14, No. 1, January 1996. pp. 36-51.
6. Rousseau, F.; Duda, A. "Synchronized Multimedia for the WWW". *Proceedings of the Seventh International World-Wide Web Conference*, Brisbane, April 1998.
7. Rodrigues, R.F.; Muchaluat-Saade, D.C.; Soares, L.F.G. "Composite Nodes, Contextual Links and Graphical Structural Views on the WWW". *Special Issue on World Wide Web of the Journal of the Brazilian Computer Society (JBCS)*, Vol. 5, No. 2, November 1998. pp. 31-44.
8. Soares, L.F.G.; Casanova, M.A.; Rodriguez, N.L.R. "Nested Composite Nodes and Version Control in an Open Hypermedia System". *International Journal on Information Systems (Special Issue on Multimedia Information Systems)*, Vol. 20, No. 6. Elsevier Science Ltd, 1995. pp. 501-519.
9. Soares, L.F.G.; Muchaluat-Saade, D.C.; Rodrigues, R.F. "Authoring and Formatting of Hypermedia Documents", *Workshop on Multimedia Authoring Systems in the IEEE International Conference on Multimedia Computing and Systems*, Austin, June 1998.
10. Soares, L.F.G.; Souza, G.L.; Rodrigues, R.F.; Muchaluat-Saade D.C. "Versioning Support in the HyperProp System". *Multimedia Tools and Applications - An international Journal*, Kluwer Academic Publishers, Vol. 8, No. 3, May 1999.
11. "Synchronized Multimedia Integration Language (SMIL) 1.0 Specification". *W3C Recommendation.* Available in http://www.w3.org/TR/REC-smil,June 1998.
12. "Timed Interactive Multimedia Extensions for HTML (HTML+TIME)". *W3C Note*. Available in http://www.w3.org/TR/NOTE-HTMLplusTIME, September 1998.

MULTIDIMENSIONAL SHAPE MODELING IN MULTIMEDIA APPLICATIONS

VALERY ADZHIEV[*], ANATOLI OSSIPOV[#] AND ALEXANDER PASKO[*]

(*) *Shape Modeling Laboratory, University of Aizu, Aizu-Wakamatsu, Fukushima Prefecture, 965-8580 Japan*
E-mail: v.adzhiev@computer.org, pasko@u-aizu.ac.jp

(#) *Department of Computer Science, Moscow Engineering Physics Institute Kashirskoe sh. 31, Moscow 115409 Russia*
E-mail: tolos@glasnet.ru

An approach is proposed to represent functionally defined multidimensional shapes as multimedia objects. A multimedia object can be described using 2D/3D world coordinates, visual, audio, haptic and other "multimedia coordinates". We introduce a space mapping between geometric coordinates and multimedia coordinates. The approach is supported by the interactive modeling system which integrates high-level language HyperFun and its interpreter, tools for defining mappings to multimedia coordinates, visualization software for polygonization, ray-tracing and animation. Examples are provided for modeling multidimensional shapes, mapping them onto multimedia space, and subsequent visualization.

1 Introduction

Multidimensional point sets (shapes) appear in different areas such as:

- *Mathematics*, where the notion of n-dimensional space is well-developed with specific abstract techniques of operating with it.
- *Physics* and other natural sciences explore mathematical models expressed with functions of several variables. Scientific visualization provides some tools for visual analysis of such functions.
- *Data mining* deals with large sets of experimental data and provides retrieval and subsequent interpretation of specified data.
- *Aesthetic and industrial design* of objects described with multiple parameters, constraints and optimization criteria.

Multimedia applications combine hypertext, sound, images, video, animation, 2D/3D geometric models. In this sense, a multimedia object can be treated as a multidimensional object with Cartesian, visual, audio, haptic and other "multimedia coordinates". These two worlds (multidimensional shapes and multimedia objects) coexist without much interaction. The known areas bridging this gap are computer animation and multidimensional visualization. Time-dependent 3D shapes can be treated in animation as 4D objects. Multidimensional visualization represents multidimensional points, surfaces, and voxel data as image sets.

In this paper, we propose an approach to more close integration of multidimensional spaces of shape modeling and multimedia. In shape modeling, objects are defined with continuous functions of several geometric coordinate variables (so-called *function representation*) [23]. Each geometric coordinate variable takes values within a given interval. On the other hand, "multimedia coordinates" also have their own variation intervals. For example, a time interval means life time of the multimedia object, color varies inside color space (RGB cube). The essence of the proposed approach is introducing a space mapping between geometric coordinates and multimedia coordinates. Such mapping establishes correspondence between the multidimensional shape and the multimedia object. This allows for

- Interpretation of the multidimensional shape involving more human senses;
- Uniform treatment of all kinds of multimedia coordinates (Cartesian coordinates of "real life" 2D and 3D geometry, time, color, sound, etc.). It becomes possible to set correspondence between the entire multimedia object and a single functional dependence;
- New visual representations of multidimensional shapes such as animated spreadsheets of images or 3D objects;
- Non-traditional behavior descriptions for animation;
- Emerging of new multimedia applications such as synthesis of music, color and dynamic 3D shapes based on strict mathematical definitions.

The approach is supported by a suite of tools oriented towards an end user. We have been developing a hybrid (multi-representational) modeling system with the function representation (F-rep) in its core. High-level language HyperFun is the user's instrument for describing a multidimensional model. An interactive modeling environment provides the user diverse possibilities to built his/her model in step-by-step manner. Finally, the user defines a mapping of the model to a multimedia object that can currently include time-dependent colored spreadsheets of 3D shapes and raytraced images.

The paper is structured as follows. A brief survey of related works is given in Section 2. In Section 3, we discuss problems of using existing modeling and animation systems from the perspectives of the declared approach. Inclusion of the function representation in a hybrid modeling system is advocated in Section 4. Mappings of multidimensional shapes to multimedia objects are discussed in Section 5. The proposed modeling language and interactive system implementation are described in Sections 6 and 7. Examples of modeling multidimensional shapes and mapping them onto multimedia objects are given in Section 8. Section 9 concludes the paper.

2 Related works

In this section, we discuss works related to multidimensional visualization and multimedia modeling. In visualization, one can obtain an image of multidimensional data by mapping initial numerical data onto the multidimensional geometric object (point set in n-dimensional geometric space). Then, problems of mapping of this object onto the 2D plane and definition of optical properties of the received 2D object have to be solved. Methods exist for the visualization of multidimensional objects of various types. Traditionally, visualization methods for multidimensional points, straight segments and surfaces of various dimensions are discussed.

In the case of points and segments, it is possible to directly project objects onto some 2D plane [21]. A similar method can be applied to visualize a 2D surface defined in n-dimensional space using its "wireframe" representation by a set of curves [2]. Several methods of visualization of multidimensional points use mnemonic graphic images ("icons", "glyphs"). The "glyph" has a set of parameters corresponding to coordinates of the multidimensional point [29]. Interactive mapping of multidimensional discrete points onto space-time was presented in [6].

The function representation of multidimensional shapes is based on explicit real functions of several variables $x_{n+1} = F(x_1,x_2,...,x_n)$ [23]. The geometric model of such a function is a hypersurface or a n-dimensional surface in n+1-dimensional space. Hypersurfaces for n=3 can be visualized using either isosurfaces or semi-transparent density clouds. There are several methods for isosurface polygonal approximation and graphic representation [4]. Ray tracing can be applied for rendering semi-transparent clouds with hue and opacity used for the function value representation [28]. There are several methods for fast interactive visualization of a hypersurface in 4D space: tiny cubes and vanishing cube, hypersurface projection graph [20]. It was proposed to polygonize quadric and cubic hypersurfaces for $n \geq 2$ with further displaying their projections in 3D space [1]. "Worlds within worlds" metaphor allows to visualize hypersurfaces for n>3 by specifying assignment of variables to nested coordinate systems [9].

Most universal approaches for cases n>3 were proposed in the descriptive geometry [10], in the method of parallel coordinates [12] and in the hierarchical axis method [18]. These approaches are based on searching for 2D and 3D models of a hypersurface. The descriptive geometry provides mapping onto 3D space for simplest hypersurfaces (planes, quadratic surfaces) defined in spaces with $2 < n < 7$. The methods described in [12,18] practically have no upper limit of space dimension but are restricted in the visual sense by 2D models of hypersurfaces.

As the above overview shows, methods of visualization exist for many types of multidimensional objects. However, most of methods have the upper limit of the space dimension. Therefore, the problem often appears to visualize the object of the same type defined in the space with dimension higher than the limit of the method at least by one. The general approach to this problem was formulated as icon based reference model in [3]. It was extended to the case of continuous functions of several variables in [22]. In particular, we proposed to use an animated graphic spreadsheet with polygonized or ray-traced isosurfaces as elementary images. A matrix of orthogonal two-dimensional slices is used in HyperSlice system [30] to visualize a scalar function of many variables. Spreadsheets of images are also applied in large data sets visualization [7] and in operations on images [14].

Multimedia objects are essentially multidimensional, where time, color, sound, and other characteristics can be considered as coordinates. This consideration provided the basis to introduction of multidimensional language for multimedia [5] using spatial/temporal compositions of generalized icons. Existing temporal models for multimedia are based on points and intervals in a time space [13], which provides an additional coordinate to a model. Considering time-dependent 3D shapes as four-dimensional objects is common in computer animation.

3 Problems with current tools

Modern modeling, rendering and animation systems (such as 3D Studio Max 2 [16], Maya [17] or POV-Ray [8]) provide variety of tools to model 3D shapes, generate still images and animation sequences [27]. However, there are problems of applying existing tools from the perspectives of our approach. These problems are caused by the underlying shape models and traditional computer animation technologies.

From the shape modeling point of view, existing systems provide the following basic tool-set. Objects can be modeled with polygonal meshes, NURBS surfaces (de-facto standard), and skeleton based implicit surfaces (so-called metaballs). The following operations are supported: linear transformations, set (Boolean) operations, extrusion, lofting, twisting, tapering, bending and free-form deformations. Animation sequences can be defined using key-frame technique, forward and inverse kinematics.

Let us outline some common drawbacks of the surface based systems from multidimensional modeling point of view.

3.1 Objects

- Fixed set of initial objects (primitives) with no tools for its extension by the user.
- Objects are thought as one-, two- or three-dimensional point sets. It is not possible to directly model higher dimensional objects.
- Limited object parametrization, for example, parameters' dependencies are not supported.

- Although "implicit surfaces" (blobby, metaballs, soft objects) proved to be a powerful tool, support of them is quite limited (see Operations below).

3.2 Operations

- Fixed set of operations with no tools for its extension by the user.
- Blending or generating rounds and fillets is not usually provided for all set (Boolean) operations (intersection, union, difference) yielding sharp edges.
- Set-theoretic operations are provided for the restricted types of objects, for example, polygonal meshes or NURBS surfaces. Implicit surfaces need to be polygonized first with the loss of their attractive features.
- Deformations can result in self-intersections of polygonal meshes. Even if the original surface is smooth, sharp edges and undesirable spikes can appear.
- Reconstruction of 3D shape from 2D cross-sections is still questionable when so-called branching appears. If there are different number of contours with different topology in two adjacent cross-sections, no automatic method exists for the polygonal surface reconstruction [19].
- Conditional and looped operations are not supported. These operations make it easier for the end user to introduce new types of objects (e.g., metaballs like).

3.3 Animation

- Time dependence is usually introduced after the shape is defined. Direct modeling of a 4D object with time as one coordinate is not supported.
- Metamorphosis or transformation of one shape into another is poorly supported. The main problem here is the necessity to manually establish one-to-one correspondence between vertices of two shapes. Moreover, robust methods of metamorphosis between surface models of different genus are not known [15] (e.g., transformation of a sphere in a two-holed torus or to a sphere with several handles).
- Time dependence of shape parameters is not fully supported (e.g., tabular, graphical, analytical, and procedural definitions are needed).
- Mapping of higher-dimensional objects on space-time is not supported.

It is well known that no single shape representation can handle all the problems encountered in geometric modeling. The idea of hybrid (or multi-representational) systems brings a possible solution. For example, the combination of the boundary representation (B-rep) and Constructive Solid Geometry (CSG) makes solid modeling systems more universal and robust [24]. On the other hand, CSG is unable to solve most of the problems mentioned above. In the next section, we consider the function representation (F-rep) [23] as a possible candidate for the inclusion in a hybrid system.

4 F-rep modeling in a hybrid system

Here, we discuss solutions available with F-rep to the problems listed in Section 3. In general, F-rep defines a geometric object by a single continuous real function of several variables $F(X) \geq 0$, where X is a vector of point coordinates in n-dimensional Euclidean space. A set of operations closed on the representation is provided. It means that the result of any operation is expressed by a function and can be an argument of another operation. No special restrictions are imposed on the function definition. In principle, it can be a "black box" with coordinates as input and a function value as output. Let us discuss the advantages of F-rep from the multimedia applications' point of view.

4.1 Objects

- The set of primitives is not fixed and can be extended by the end user by providing a defining function in various forms (analytical, procedural, tabular, etc.).
- Objects modeled in different representational schemes can be converted to F-rep: implicit surfaces, CSG, sweeping, voxel data, and closed parametric surfaces. This provides a reach variety of shapes.
- Objects can be modeled directly in multidimensional space and treated uniformly in spite of the dimension.
- Parametrization of objects is provided by the parametrization of defining functions.

4.2 Operations

- The set of operations is not fixed and can be extended by the end user.
- Set-theoretic operations, blending, offsetting and other operations [23] are closed on F-rep.
- There are special operations for modeling in multidimensional space: Cartesian product (increasing object's dimension) and projection (decreasing object's dimension).
- Non-linear deformations of different types are generalized by so-called extended space mappings [25].
- Reconstruction of 3D shapes from branching contours is solved automatically [26].

4.3 Animation

- Time dependent shape can be modeled directly as a 4D object with the following generation of time cross-sections (or 3D frames).
- Metamorphosis is performed automatically and handles objects of different topology (e.g., genus change and generation of disjoint components).

Taking into account the discussed advantages, we consider F-rep as a promising representation for a hybrid multidimensional shape modeling system. In Section 6 we discuss a high-level language as an F-rep model specification tool and its interpreter.

5 Mapping to multimedia coordinates

In this section, we discuss a space mapping of abstract geometric coordinates onto multimedia coordinates. Such mapping establishes correspondence between the multidimensional shape and the multimedia object. Informally, the multimedia object is an element of the multimedia space, which is characterized by multimedia coordinates. In general, multimedia coordinate variables are heterogeneous non-elementary structures. To operate with multimedia coordinates, one can introduce a system of normalized numerical coordinates (unit cube) and its one-to-one correspondence to the multimedia space. By defining a real normalized value, one can select the corresponding value of the multimedia coordinate.

The following types of multimedia coordinates with their variation intervals can be introduced:

- *World* coordinates of 2D and 3D "real life" geometry. They can be Cartesian, cylindrical and other coordinates. The selection of these types and their variation intervals defines the "elementary" image or 2D/3D shape within the bounding box in the selected geometric space. An "elementary" shape (i.e., curve, surface, isosurface) is a projection of a cross-section of the initial multidimensional shape.
- *Dynamic* coordinates represent continuous values that can be linearly or non-linearly mapped onto physical time. The interval of such coordinate means life time of the multimedia object. One can define an animation sequence by selecting a set of discrete points along any dynamic coordinate. Each frame of animation corresponds to a cross-section of the multidimensional shape.
- *Spreadsheet* coordinates take discrete values in the given bounding box. This type allows for spreadsheet-like spatial organization of elementary images or shapes in the regularly or irregularly placed 1D, 2D or 3D nodes.
- *Photometric* coordinates include color, transparency, texture and other parameters of visual appearance of the multimedia object. These multiple coordinates can be introduced differently depending on the application. For example, color can be assigned to the shape, background or light source in the scene.
- *Transformation* coordinates define transformations (rotation, scaling, filtering, etc.) of the elementary image or shape. In particular, it allows for the implementation of "glyph" visualization discussed in Section 2.
- *Audio/Video* coordinates have complex structure and are dynamic by their nature. One needs to synchronize them with other dynamic variables when defining the mapping.

The above list is not complete. Depending on applications and available devices, one can extend it by other types such as force feedback (for haptic interfaces).

Each geometric coordinate variable takes values within a given interval. On the other hand, multimedia coordinates also have their own variation intervals. To define the mapping, one has to establish correspondence between these intervals. Generally, more than one multimedia coordinate can correspond to one geometric coordinate. For instance, one can map a certain geometric coordinate simultaneously onto a dynamic coordinate and a color coordinate. It results in associating the geometric coordinate with "dynamic color" allowing to produce differently colored frames of animation sequence.

It is possible to assign constant value to a geometric coordinate variable; it defines a cross-section of the multidimensional shape and decreases its dimension by one. The function value of the shape definition $xn+1 = F(x1, x2, \ldots, xn)$ provides additional geometric coordinate xn+1 of the multidimensional space resulting in the so-called extended space [25]. Mapping the functional coordinate onto multimedia coordinates provides several types of elementary images and shapes (e.g., contour map, nested isosurfaces, color height map). In the combination with mappings of other coordinates, this allows for the construction of unconventional objects such as animated spreadsheet of colored contour maps.

6 HyperFun language and interpreter

To make it possible effective and convenient exploiting of F-rep paradigm, flexible high-level tools are necessary. F-rep can be considered as a suitable base for a high-level language that lets the user specify his/her model. Such model's symbolic representation can also be used as a high-level geometric exchange protocol independent of specific modeling systems. There are different categories of users having different levels of expertise and working in a variety of application fields. A high-level language should enable us to create a kernel geometric modeling system with limited (or even empty) set of built-in functionally-based objects, transformations and relations. Such system can serve as a universal base for building modeling systems with specifics depending on a particular application domain or even designed for a particular user.

6.1 Language overview

HyperFun is a modeling language designed to be a high-level tool suitable for specifying functionally based models. There was an intention to keep the language as simple as possible to provide its easy mastering. While being minimalist it should not limit the user in creating quite complex geometric models. It supports all main notions of F-rep, in particular "geometric object" and "geometric operation".

The program in HyperFun can contain a specification of several geometric objects. Each object is defined by a function parametrized using input arrays of point coordinates and free numerical parameters. A number of coordinate variables can be more than three to provide multidimensional objects description. The function can be quite complex: it is represented with help of assignment statements (using auxiliary local variables and arrays, if necessary); conditional selection ('if-then-else') and iterative ('while-loop') statements can be used too. The functional expressions are built using conventional arithmetic and relational operators. It is possible to use standard mathematical functions ('exp', 'log', 'sqrt', 'sin', etc.). Such fundamental operations as set-theoretic ones are supported by a special built-in operators with reserved symbols ("|" - union, "&" - intersection, "\" - subtraction, "~" - negation, "@" - Cartesian product).

The principled feature of the language is a possibility of using a special 'F-rep library' that contains functions representing geometric primitives and transformations. The library is extendible, and its composition can be varied depending on a particular domain. The library version in general use contains the most common primitives ('Sphere', 'Torus', 'Ellipsoid', 'Cylinder', 'Blobby object', 'Metaball object', etc.) and transformations ('Blending union/intersection', 'Rotation', 'Scaling', 'Twisting', etc). The functional expressions can also include references to previously defined geometric objects. The user can create his/her own library of objects to be reused. Examples of HyperFun programs can be found in Section 8.

On-line manual on HyperFun language containing a description of the current version of 'F-rep library' as well as numerous examples of programs in HyperFun can be found at the devoted Web-site [11].

6.2 Interpreter of the language

HyperFun interpreter is implemented as a suite of functions in ANSI C. Actually, these functions are considered as API that can be used as self-contained procedures in different applications. The interpreter provides parsing with syntax and semantic analysis for a program in HyperFun containing symbolic function definitions. Let us describe two most important functions that correspondingly build an internal interpretable representation and perform function evaluation in the given point for the given actual parameters.

Function 'Parse' performs syntax analysis in the accordance with language grammar and semantic rules. For each object described in the program, the function generates its internal representation. Another output result is the list of messages about errors together with their locations and specifics, if they are present in the program. As to the form of the object's internal representation, it is supposed to be optimal for the subsequent function evaluation (we need to evaluate the function in given points of modeling space, and the number of them can be very large). Accordingly, the internal representation can be considered as a tree structure ready to effective evaluation of all formula expressions defining the complete function.

Function 'Calc' performs the function evaluation for the given object in the given point and for the actual external parameters. The object's internal representation serves as an input parameter for the function that returns a value of the evaluated function in the given point; if a certain error appears, the function generates a correspondent message about the error and its location.

In the whole, the interpreter provides an effective procedure for building internal representation and for the function evaluation. It should be emphasized that module 'Parse' works just once for the program; the internal representation it creates can be treated as Java-like "byte-code" (note that it is platform-independent) and can in principle serve as a protocol for data exchange between system components.

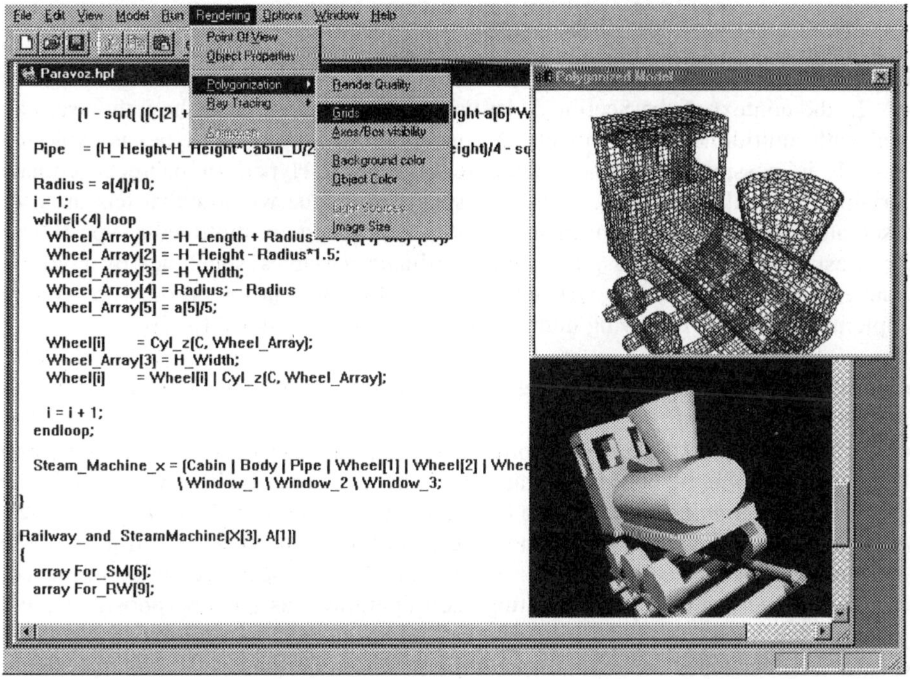

Figure 1. Screenshot of Hyperfun for Windows interactive system.

7 Interactive system "HyperFun for Windows"

HyperFun for Windows is an interactive system that is being implemented on Windows NT platform. The system provides the user a means allowing to

a) Specify a functionally-based model in HyperFun language using built-in editor and interpreter;
b) Use standard 'F-rep library' of geometric objects and transformations as well as the user's own library of geometric objects written in HyperFun;
c) Define mappings of geometric space to multimedia space by assigning "multimedia types" to geometric coordinates;

d) Compose scenes consisting of a few objects, each defined in its own modeling space;
e) Generate images of polygonized or ray-traced elementary shapes, animation sequences, 1D and 2D spreadsheets in accordance with assigned multimedia types.

Fig. 1 demonstrates a screenshot of the system in the process of modeling.

In the context of the Section 5, let us describe in more detail how the user can deal with multidimensional models. A conception of multimedia types is exploited here. It is possible to define geometric objects in HyperFun using coordinate variables x[1], x[2], ..., x[n]. There is a special dialogue window that lets the user associate each geometric coordinate variable with a certain multimedia type. These types establish conventions governing coordinate variables' semantics by giving a concrete interpretation of x[i] on the fly. In the current prototype system implementation, the following multimedia types can be assigned to x[i]:

- "**x**", "**y**" and "**z**" types correspond to *world* coordinates in the Cartesian coordinate system;
- "**t**" corresponds to *dynamic* coordinates. This type can be assigned to one, two or three geometric coordinate variables. The user can actually give a path in the space of variables with "t" type by filling out a table with their discrete values. Each row of the table corresponds to certain time value. Then, the frames of the animation sequence in the form of the model's cross-sections can be produced. This is the basis for implementing such operations as metamorphosis of quite complex form;
- "**u**" and "**v**" types correspond to 2D *spreadsheet* coordinates. By assigning only one of these types, the user can construct a horizontal or vertical 1D spreadsheet.
- "**c**" corresponds to a *photometric* coordinate, namely the color. Color is interpreted differently depending on the selected type of the elementary image or shape. For example, if the elementary shape is a 3D surface, color is assigned to a light source of the scene. In fact, color is a vector of three real values (R,G,B) defining red, green and blue components of RGB color model. Therefore, the mapping should be provided from a geometric coordinate onto all (R,G,B) components.

To define a cross-section of the multidimensional model the user can assign a constant numerical value to the corresponding x[i]. By assigning one or several constant values to the function x[n+1], the user can select a contour map or a set of isosurfaces as an elementary shape.

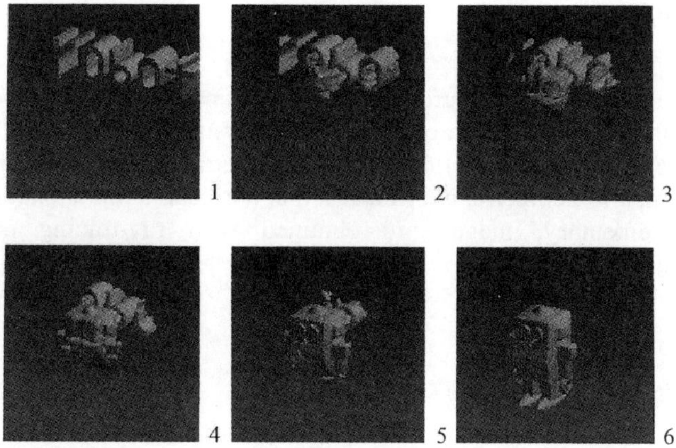

Figure 2. Metamorphosis as a four-dimensional object: six frames of animation.

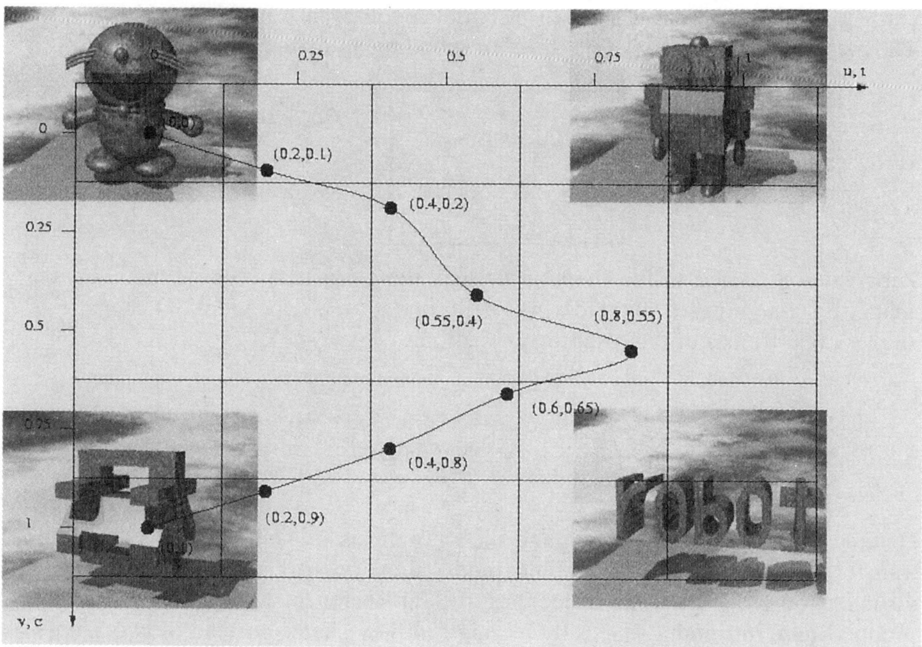

Figure 3. Bi-directional metamorphosis: spreadsheet and animation path design

8 Examples

Several examples of using the introduced concepts and implemented tools are given in this section. The models are created and visualized using "HyperFun for Windows" interactive system. After getting the model in HyperFun, the multimedia types are assigned to geometric coordinates, and corresponding animation frames or spreadsheet elementary images are obtained with ray-tracing or isosurface polygonization.

8.1 Metamorphosis as a 4D object

Metamorphosis (shape transformation) between two 3D shapes is modeled as a 4D object (Fig. 2). The initial 3D shapes are modeled with set-theoretic operations on quadratic primitives. Metamorphosis defines intermediate shapes according to the value of the fourth coordinate. It provides smooth transformation ("tooth paste extrusion" like) between shapes of different topology placed in different locations. The mapping allowing to define the corresponding animation is as follows:

```
x[1] → x
x[2] → y
x[3] → z
x[4] → t
```

Zero value assigned to the function defines the isosurface type of the elementary shape. By assigning "**t**" type to x[4], we define a time-dependent 3D shape. Fig. 2 shows a few frames of the resulting animation.

8.2 Bi-directional metamorphosis as a 5D object

Here, we present a bi-directional metamorphosis, which is not a traditional transformation in computer graphics and animation. Implemented modeling and visualization tools allow us to increase the dimension of the previous example to produce quite intriguing shapes by mixing four key-shapes instead of two shapes as in 8.1. The selected key-shapes (see Fig. 3) are, to some extent, "cultural key signs" in Japan:

1) A cat (upper left in Fig. 3) resembles the cult character of kids' animation. Its complete model in HyperFun can be found at [11];

2) "NiHon" (lower left) is a 3D puzzle representing word "Japan". First, two 3D Chinese characters "*Ni*" and "*Hon*" are constructed independently as unions of blocks. Note that the defining function for each 3D character is obtained by the system with R-functions [23] and therefore is continuous in entire 3D space. Then, the solids are oriented along Z and X axes respectively and combined as $NiHon = Ni \cap Hon$, where $\cap$ represents intersection operation. The idea of this puzzle construction is that the resulting 3D solid looks like a single initial 2D character "*Ni*" or "*Hon*" when projected along Z and X axes respectively onto a plane.
3) A robot (upper right) and
4) A 3D word "robot" (lower right) are the same used in 8.1 and Fig. 2.

```
Meta5D(x[5],a[1])
{
array xx[3];
xx[1]  = x[1]; xx[2]  = x[2]; xx[3]  = x[3];

-- (0,0): Cat
     Cat = Cat3D(xx);

-- (0,1): NiHon
     NiHon = NiHon3D(xx);

-- (1,0): Robot
     Robot = Robot3D(xx);

-- (1,1): Rob_word
     Rob_word = Rob_word3D(xx);

-- Bi-directional metamorphosis
Meta5D = (Cat*(1.-x[4])+Robot*x[4])*(1.-x[5])
         + (NiHon*(1.-x[4])+Rob_word*x[4])*x[5];
}
```

Figure 4. HyperFun model of the bi-directional metamorphosis.

The HyperFun model of the bi-directional metamorphosis is shown in Fig. 4. Note that each initial 3D shape is defined by its own real function in the HyperFun object <name>3D. Algebraically, the model of the metamorphosis is the bilinear interpolation between four real-valued functions by coordinates x[4] and x[5]. Geometrically, it is a 5D object defined by the real function as $f(x_1, x_2, x_3, x_4, x_5) \geq 0$.

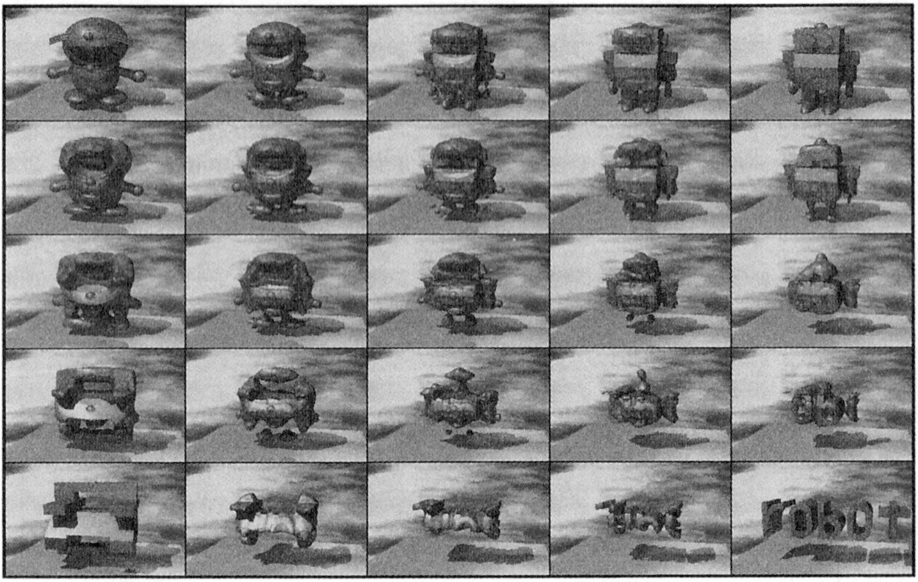

Figure 5. Spreadsheet of bi-directional metamorphosis between four shapes

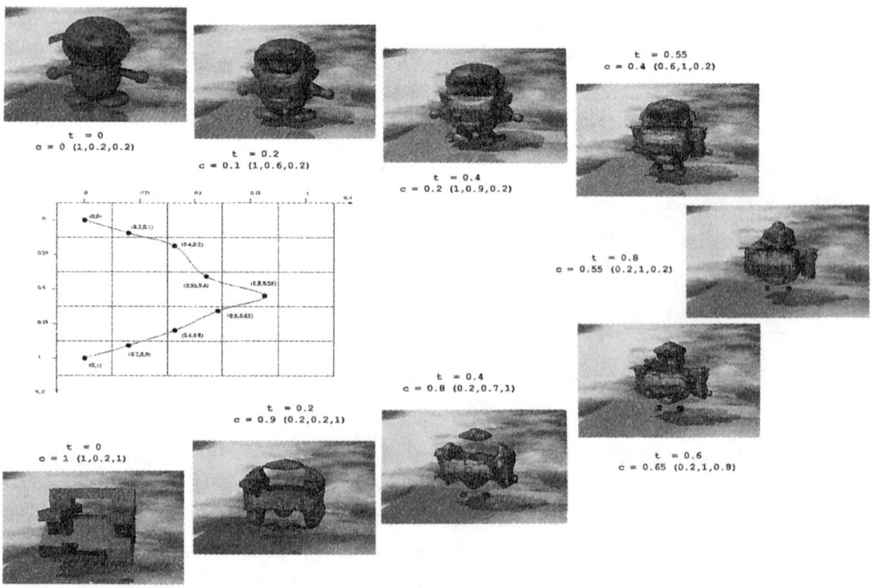

Figure 6. Frames of animation along the path defined in time-color space. A frame caption includes values for time and color coordinates with (R,G, B) values.

A 2D spreadsheet is the most adequate visual representation of this 5D object. The following mapping defines such spreadsheet:

```
x[1] → x
x[2] → y
x[3] → z
x[4] → u
x[5] → v
```

Fig. 3 shows the four key-shapes in the corners of the 5×5 spreadsheet pattern with **u** and **v** coordinates varying at [0,1] interval with 0.25 step. Fig. 5 shows the actual spreadsheet of elementary images, each placed in a cell with discrete (u,v) coordinates. For example, (0.5,0.5) cell contains the image of the equal-weighted mixture of all four shapes. Note that any direction (horizontal, vertical or diagonal) in the spreadsheet corresponds to one-directional metamorphosis between the end-point shapes of the interval. It would be quite difficult to understand the entire model behavior through observing one-directional transformations without the spreadsheet viewing.

On the other hand, the spreadsheet can be considered as a set of frames of animation with two dynamic variables. It can serve as a reference for constructing an animation sequence containing particularly interesting shape transformations. Let us create such animation with the following mapping:

```
x[1] → x
x[2] → y
x[3] → z
x[4] → t
x[5] → c
```

This assigns the *dynamic* type to x[4] interpreted as time and the *color* type to x[5]. The specific animation corresponds to a curve in the time-color space. The spreadsheet helps to introduce such curve (see Fig. 3) and to select the points on the curve for the animation frames. The interval [0,1] of the type "**c**" variable corresponds to the color spectrum ranging from red to purple. The frames of the obtained animation are shown in Fig. 6. We would like to emphasize that, in contrast with traditional computer animation, time, color and world coordinates likewise influence the shape transformation. Regarding the color, it can be interpreted as the influence of the light source color on the shape of the illuminated object.

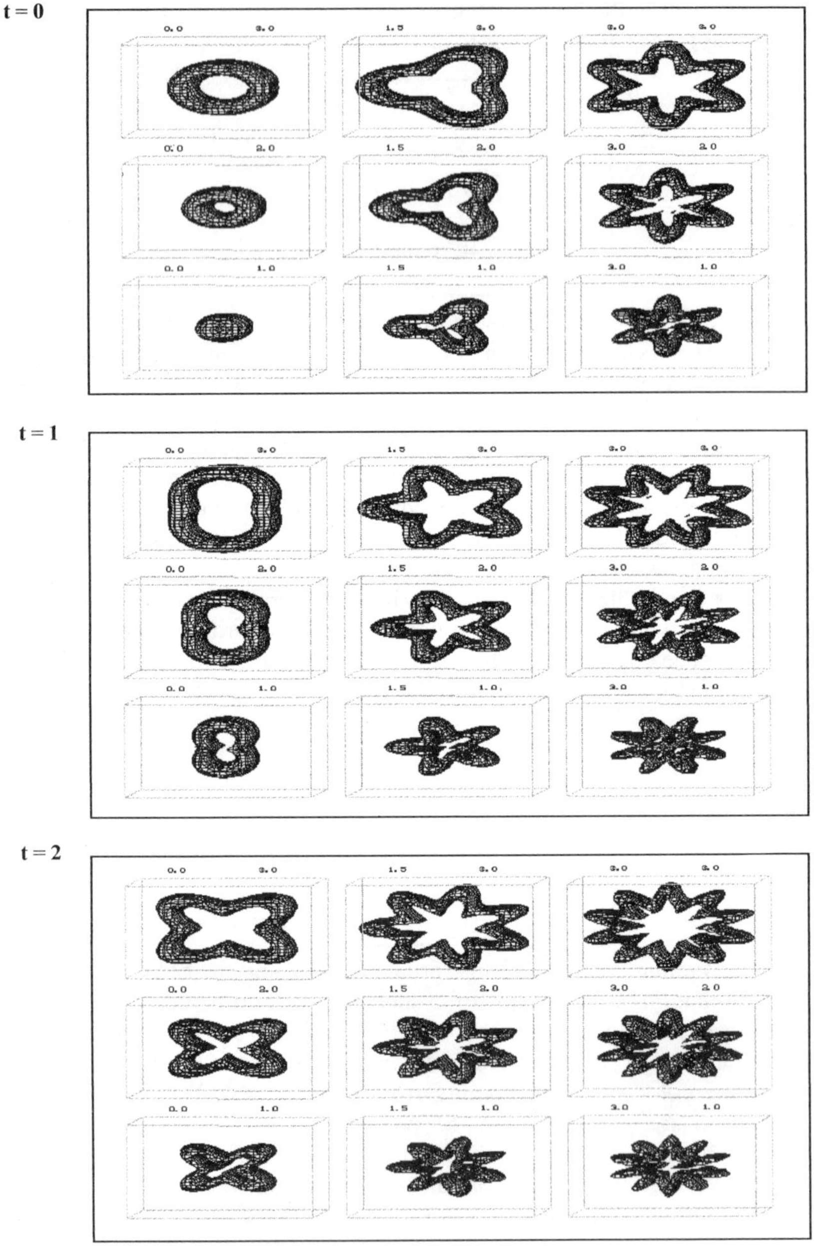

Figure 7. Animated spreadsheet of a function of six variables: three frames of animation for t = 0, 1, 2.

8.3 Visualization of functions of several variables

The previous examples illustrated generation and animation of interesting "real life" shapes that in particular appear in the field of multimedia entertainment (and edutainment!). On the other hand, abstract multidimensional models are conventional in mathematics, natural sciences and data mining. Here, we illustrate application of our approach to scientific visualization. As an example, the concept of the animated spreadsheet of elementary shapes (see Fig. 7) is used to construct a visual representation of a function of six variables $x_7 = f(x_1, x_2, x_3, x_4, x_5, x_6)$. This function was introduced to illustrate unstable states in plasma physics. The HyperFun code for the function is given in Fig. 8.

```
Star6(x[6],a[2]){

-- Amplitude a[1] and
-- "cord" radius a[2] to be input interactively
array xc[3];
xc[1] = x[1]; xc[2] = x[2]; xc[3] = x[3];

-- Mapping from Cartesian to cylindrical coordinates
-- x1 - angle Phi, x2 - radius Ro, x3 - Z
tmp = hfTCartCyl(xc);
x1 = xc[1]; x2 = xc[2]; x3 = xc[3];

-- Radius oscillation
s = sin((x[5]+x[4])*x1);
xs2 = x2 - a[1]*s^2;

-- Cartesian product: disk in (Ro,Z) and Phi segment
xs2 = xs2 - x[6];
disk = a[2]^2-xs2^2-x3^2;
pi = 3.1418;
segment = x1 & (2*pi-x1);
Star6 = disk @ segment;
}
```

Figure 8. HyperFun code of the function of six variables.

The following types are assigned to the geometric coordinates:

```
x[1] → x
x[2] → y
x[3] → z
x[4] → t
x[5] → u
x[6] → v
```

Assigning zero value to the function defines an isosurface as an elementary shape in the cells of the spreadsheet. The elementary shape illustrates function dependence on three variables x[1], x[2], and x[3]. Changes of isosurfaces along rows and columns of the spreadsheet illustrate function dependence on x[5] and x[6]. Changes of the entire spreadsheet in time show how the function depends on x[4]. The image in Fig. 7 helps to grasp the entire function behavior in the 6D space of its arguments. In accordance with our approach, a function of more variables can be visualized by assigning color and other types to additional geometric coordinates.

9 Conclusions

In this paper, we proposed an approach to represent functionally defined multidimensional shapes as multimedia objects. A multimedia object can be treated as a multidimensional object with 2D/3D world, visual, audio, haptic and other "multimedia coordinates". We introduced a space mapping between geometric coordinates and multimedia coordinates. It makes possible to involve more human senses to percept multidimensional shapes, to set correspondence between the entire multimedia object and a single functional dependence, and to introduce new visual representations of multidimensional shapes.

The approach is supported by the interactive modeling system which integrates high-level language HyperFun and its interpreter, tools for defining mappings to multimedia types, visualization software for polygonization, ray-tracing and animation. We have provided examples of modeling multidimensional shapes, mapping them onto multimedia space, and subsequent visualization. Further development supposes implementation of texture, video and audio types, as well as GUI for multidimensional interactive modeling.

Acknowledgements

We would like to thank Eric Fausett for his work on rendering. The three-dimensional shapes were modeled by students Kensuke Masuda, Yukio Hashimoto, Kou Setoguchi, Masayuki Tetsuka, and Tetsurou Tobe.

References

1. Bajaj C.L., Rational hypersurface display, *Computer Graphics* **24** (1990) pp. 117-127.
2. Banchoff T., Computer animation and the geometry of surfaces in 3- and 4-space, *International Congress of Mathematics*, Helsinki (1978) pp. 1005-1013.
3. Bergeron R.D., Grinstein G.G., A reference model for the visualization of multidimensional data, *EUROGRAPHICS'89* (1989) pp. 393-399.
4. Bloomenthal J. et al., *Introduction to Implicit Surfaces*, Morgan Kaufman, (1997).
5. Chang S.-K., Extending visual languages for multimedia, *IEEE Multimedia* **3** (1996) pp.18-26.
6. Chi E. et al., Flexible information visualization of multivariate data from biological sequence similarity searches, *Visualization'96*, IEEE Computer Society (1996) pp. 133-140.
7. Chi E. et al., Principles for information visualization spreadsheets, *IEEE Computer Graphics and Applications* **18** (1998) pp. 30-38.
8. Enzmann A., Kretzchmar L., Young C., *Ray Tracing Worlds with POV-Ray*, Waite Group Press (1994).
9. Feiner S., Visualizing n-dimensional virtual worlds with n-Vision, *Computer Graphics* **24** (1990) pp. 37-38.
10. Filippov P.V., *Descriptive Geometry of Multidimensional Space and its Applications*, Leningrad State University, Leningrad, USSR (1979).
11. *HyperFun: Language for F-rep Geometric Modeling*, http://www.u-aizu.ac.jp/labs/sw-sm/FrepWWW/HF_descr.html
12. Inselberg A., Multi-dimensional graphics: algorithms and applications, *EUROGRAPHICS'86*, North-Holland (1986) pp. 7-18.
13. Keramane C., Duda A., Interval Expressions - a functional model for interactive dynamic multimedia presentations, *International Conference on Multimedia Computing and Systems*, IEEE Computer Society (1996) pp. 283-286.
14. Levoy M., Spreadsheet for images, *Computer Graphics* **28** (1994) pp. 139-146.

15. Lazarus F., Verroust A., Three-dimensional metamorphosis: a survey, *The Visual Computer* **14** (1998) pp. 373-389.
16. Maestri G. et al., *Inside 3D Studio MAX 2*, New Riders, (1998).
17. *Using Maya: Modeling*, Alias|Wavefront Inc., Canada (1998).
18. Mihalisin T., Timlin J., Schwegler J., Visualizing multivariate functions, data and distributions, *IEEE Computer Graphics and Applications* **11** (1991) pp. 28-35.
19. Meyers D., Skinner S., Sloan K., Surfaces from contours, *ACM Transactions on Graphics* **11** (1992) pp. 228-258.
20. Nielson G.M. et al., Visualizing and modeling scattering multivariate data, *IEEE Computer Graphics and Applications* **11** (1991) pp. 47-55.
21. Noll A., A computer technique for displaying n-dimensional hyperobjects, *Communications of ACM* **10** (1967) pp. 469-473.
22. Pasko A., Adzhiev V., Prostakov I., Multivariate functions visualization: the inductive approach, *Proceedings of 3rd Eurographics Workshop on Scientific Visualization*, Viareggio, Italy (1992) pp. 303-316.
23. Pasko A., Adzhiev V., Sourin A., Savchenko V., Function representation in geometric modeling: concepts, implementation and applications, *The Visual Computer* **11** (1995) pp. 429-446.
24. Requicha A. A. G., Representations of rigid solids: theory, methods and systems, *Computing Surveys* **12** (1980) pp. 437-464.
25. Savchenko V., Pasko A., Transformation of functionally defined shapes by extended space mappings, *The Visual Computer* **14** (1998) pp. 257-270.
26. Savchenko V.V., Pasko A.A., Okunev O.G., Kunii T.L., Function representation of solids reconstructed from scattered surface points and contours, *Computer Graphics Forum* 14 (1995) pp. 181-188.
27. Thalmann N., Thalmann D., *Interactive Computer Animation*, Prentice Hall, (1996).
28. Upson C., Keeler M., V-buffer: visible volume rendering, *Computer Graphics* **22** (1988) pp. 59-64.
29. Wong P., Bergeron R., Multivariate visualization using metric scaling, *Visualization '97*, IEEE Computer Society (1997) pp. 111-118.
30. van Wijk J., van Liere R., HyperSlice - Visualization of scalar functions of many variables, *Visualization'93*, IEEE Computer Society (1993) pp.119-125.

EDITING AND PROCESSING OF MULTIVIEW DOCUMENTS IN CROSS-MEDIA PUBLISHING

THOMAS CORTE, JENS DEPONTE, HEINRICH MÜLLER

University of Dortmund
Department of Computer Science VII
Otto-Hahn-Str. 16, D-44221 Dortmund, Germany

email: {corte|deponte|mueller}@ls7.cs.uni-dortmund.de

Publishing for different media is burdened by the desire to take optimum advantage of the capabilities of each medium and the often redundant work implicated by this. In most cases the result of the work is a collection of documents in different formats that contain basically the same information. Cross-media publishing tries to ease this burden by converting the same document base into formats for different media. But because of different media characteristics simple conversion is often not enough to get optimal results. In this paper we approach these problems with a concept called MultiView Documents. This concept covers the whole document cycle from the creation and modification of documents to their output using different media. While the document structure has been defined and a tool for processing such documents is completed, work on an appropiate editor is still in progress.

1 Introduction

Publishing today often means to produce documents with essentially the same information for different media. With traditional publishing technologies this results in a lot of divergent, often redundant processes. Cross-media publishing is a strategy for making this job easier by providing a set of technologies and a publishing workflow which opens the user a way to serve different media with only one source. The key for reaching this goal lies in powerful tools for the creation and processing of suitable documents.

Cross-media publishing seems to be an adequate answer to a number of common publishing problems. A first example is the publishing of scientific papers. First the author has to create a print version of the information he likes to make public. If accepted, he has to prepare slides for the presentation at the conference itself and often there is an electronic version of the proceedings or an online version in the WWW. Another field of application for cross-media publishing is multimedia enhanced education. Here the same information can be used for the lectures itself, a printed version for the students preparation and maybe an online or cd-rom version as a self guided course. Additionally these documents could be published in variations e.g. with more or less basics for beginners and advanced readers. Also the software industry can profit from the advantages of cross-media publishing when they sell products which run on different operating systems. In this case there is the problem of creating input files for the different help systems of the supported operating systems. Besides that, printed documentation with special sections for each operating system has to be published.

In all examples there is a common problem of supporting several media with mostly the same content. This problem could be solved by developing output filters for the different file formats. While this approach covers a large range of problems, it fails when it comes to use special features of the target media. The author can only use a common subset of features from all of the media used. For example a HTML document can contain animations, which illustrate some processes. This feature is very useful for the author, because this way it is easier for the reader to see how things work. Books do not have animations. So the author has to extract some pictures from the animation and write some illustrating text to pass the same information via print media. In other words: he has to use different views on the same information for different media.

The examples show that it is often useful to have different views on the same information without having to keep several documents up to date. Although there are clear advantages of this approach there is a lack of tools that support this kind of publishing. In the next section we propose concepts for implementing and using document views. Section 3 describes an SGML-application that implements those concepts. The following section gives an outlook on the projected editor. In Section 5 we introduce an already developed tool that supports authors by extracting document views from the root document and formatting the output. The last Section summarizes first experiences with the existing parts of the system.

2 Cross-Media Publishing with Document Views

Publishing documents for different media suffers from the problem that it is extremely difficult to support all features the media provide. This often leads to relative simple cross-media publishing systems that support only basic features common to all output media, which results in documents or presentations that are not as sophisticated as they could be. Examples are Microsoft Word or the wordprocessor in Stardivisions StarOffice package. They promise to make it easy to publish documents for print and online (HTML) media, but the results are often not satisfying. On the other hand, the preparation of distinct special versions for different media that use all the features is too error prone and costs too much time and money.

Therefore the main goal is a document processing system that keeps the document together, while there must still be a possibility to include special parts which are only used for the medium they are meant for. One of the main problems of such a system is to support the user in managing these special parts and keeping track of the desired information flow.

With our approach to this problem we open a way for the author to use special features of the target media without having to produce an extra document for each additional medium. This goal is reached by keeping the common document parts together and split up the textflow only where it is needed. I.e. where traditional publishing methods do not provide sufficient mechanisms to use special features of the different output media. The main concept behind this approach is to group those special parts into viewgroups. This allows to detect which parts represent the same information for different views. Since there can be some document views that share the same information representation there are three different types of viewgroups (see Fig. 1).

A *complete viewgroup* (Fig. 1a) contains a content variant for each document view. This is needed if all views need different representations for the information contained in this viewgroup. Each representation or content variant can hold a list of one or more document views.

If there are views that can use the same representation the author can use a *complete viewgroup with wildcards* (Fig. 1b). In this type of viewgroups the author specifies some content variants for the viewgroups that need distinct representations and a common variant for the remaining viewgroups. This reduces redundancy within the group.

The third type of viewgroups allows the specification of incomplete content variants (Fig. 1c). This is useful if certain information shall appear only in some document views. In this case the author may specify content variants only for those views and skip this information for the remaining views.

Distinction of views can be useful in all levels of document hierarchies starting from chapters, sections to sentences or even words. Although it is possible to put completely different information into a single viewgroup, the variants in a viewgroup should always contain only different representations of the same information. This helps to keep track of the textflow for authors and publishing tools that are able to process viewgroups.

3 The MultiDoc DTD

MultiDoc is our implementation of the above described concept of multiple document views with viewgroups. It acts as a reference implementation for

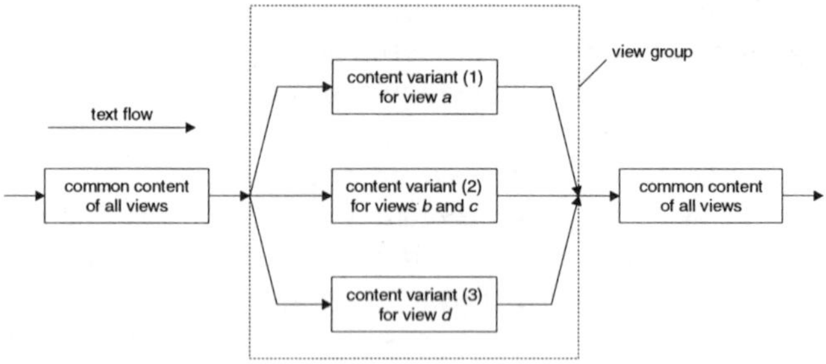

(a) complete viewgroup

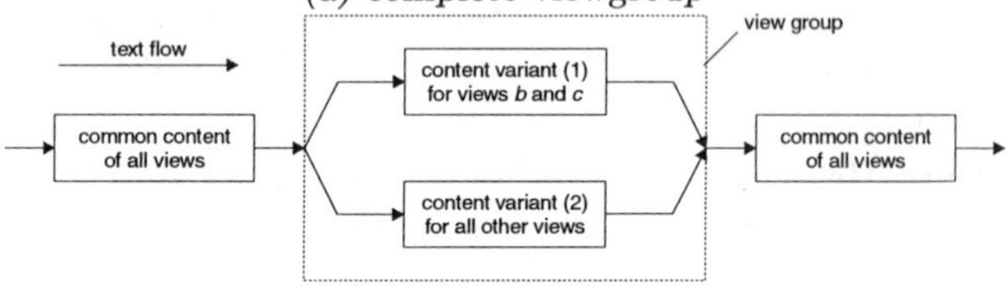

(b) complete viewgroup with wildcards

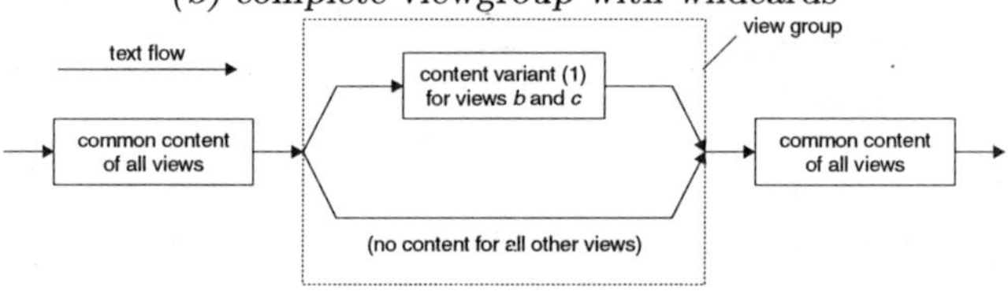

(c) incomplete viewgroup

Figure 1. Types of viewgroups

the use of viewgroups especially in scientific publications, but the universality of the concept helpes to implement it for all kinds of cross-media publishing. MultiDoc uses the SGML technology, because it provides an ideal base to add the viewgroup concept.

SGML stands for *Standard Generalized Markup Language* and is an ISO standard for the definition of markup languages for electronic documents. Markup languages use tags to define the structure of documents. This can be used to split up a document into chapters, section, paragraphs and so on. But also more sophisticated concepts like viewgroups can be implemented using SGML. The main advantage of this concept is that authors can concentrate on the subject of their document instead of being occupied by formatting it. The formatting is done later by a tool, which evaluates the structure information and generates the appropiate output. The specification of the visual presentation of a document is completely separated from its content. Another vital term in the world of SGML is DTD which stands for *Document Type Definition*. It holds a formal specification of the markup language and therefore defines which tags can or must be used for structuring documents of this type. Tags are mostly defined as strings like <TAGNAME> and have an associated end-tag </TAGNAME>. Tags can be expanded by attributes which consist of a name value pair, e.g. <SECTION STATUS="DRAFT">.

The probably most known application of SGML is the HTML-DTD [8,13] which is used for describing the content of web pages. A more thorough overview of SGML can be found in [16,17].

3.1 Essential DTD Elements

As a starting point for the developement of the MultiDoc DTD the *DocBook DTD* was taken. It is now maintained by the DocBook Technical Committee of OASIS, the *Organisation for the Advancement of Structured Information Standards* [14]. Although DocBook was primarily developed for technical documentation, the main structural components can be used for many other types of documents. For the support of tables the *SGML Open CALS table model*, a de facto standard for the representation of tabular data with SGML elements (see [15]), is used. But MultiDoc is not just a subset of DocBook. Its main extensions are the implementation of support for document views with viewgroups and add-ons in the field of multimedia features. Besides, many DocBook tag classes were replaced by fewer, more general markup concepts.

The DTD elements are divided into *block oriented* and *inline* elements. *Block oriented* or *object level elements* are used to give the documents a vertical structure like chapters, sections, lists or tables. *Inline* or *text level elements* are used to mark footnotes, hyperlinks and so on. This division corresponds to the *block level elements* and *text level elements* in the HTML-specification [8].

The root element for all MultiDoc documents is `publication` which contains the following elements:

1. the optional `header` element contains information about the publication like `title`, `subtitle`, `author/authorgroup`, `date` and an `abstract`. More information can be given by using a `meta` tag, whose semantics must be specified by its `class` attribute.

2. definition of document views with the `viewdef` tag. For each document view a `viewdef` definition is needed, which specifies details about the view by using `viewproperty` tags. E.g. a document view for a book with the default format "TEX" could be declared with:

```
<viewdef id="book">
  <viewproperty name="defaultfmt" value="tex">
</viewdef>
```

3. definitions of pool elements which may contain text passages that are either used at multiple locations in the document or have been gathered in an earlier preparation for the document. pool elements are identified by unique ID's which are used to reference them within the document.

4. a sequence of books or articles which make up the actual document. These tags where taken from the DocBook DTD, because they are well known for authors of print media, but this does not imply a preference of the MultiDoc DTD for print media.

A book conforming to the MultiDoc DTD may consist of a header (see above), a dedication, a sequence of table of contents (toc), list of figures (lof) or tables (lot), a preface, a bibliograhy or a glossary. The actual body of the book is a combination of parts, chapters or articles, which can be followed by an undefined number of appendices (appendix) or indices (index).

In parts, chapters or articles the author can use elements like sections, paragraphs, tables, lists, floats or quotes (blockquote). In addition to these elements, which can be used to define the main structure of the document, there are more elements the author can use to express his thoughts. Examples for such tags are hypertext elements like links, anchors and URL's (ulink). They are completed by elements for multimedia data like graphics or objects specified by the more generic multimedia tag. These objects are normally stored in extra files, because an inclusion of binary data into the textoriented document specification would make it extremly difficult to handle. Nevertheless textoriented graphics data can be included into the document. For example, mathematical formulars could be included in LaTeX [11] notation, which could be directly used if the output format is LaTeX or has to be rendered into another graphics format which can be processed with any other document output format. Both the graphic tag and the multimedia tag contain an attribute format which gives the SGML processor the information it needs to convert the data format into something the output processor is capable of.

For the localization of string literals like headings for a table of contents or a list of figures, the author can specify a lang attribute in any tag. The value is inherited by all included tags. E.g. the tag <publication lang="EN"> specifies english as the language for this publication unless not stated otherwise. The lang attribute takes two-character country codes as defined in [9].

The last part of this section is dedicated to the document view/viewgroup concept of the MultiDoc DTD. The view definitions as mentioned above provide all information the SGML processor needs to distinguish between different views onto the same document. The differentiation of views inside the document itself can be done on different levels:

1. on the level of `chapters` or `sections` the author can use `viewgrps` to indicate that he wants to specify different `variants` of the same information for different views. Each `variant` holds a list of views in its `targetviews` attribute to announce for which document views it has to be used.

2. on the level of paragraphs and alike there is a similar kind of viewgroups. The `sviewgrp` contains `svariants` which have the same semantics as `viewgrp` and `variant`. These tags were included to preserve the possibility of a strict automatic check of the documents structure.

3. the third form of viewgroups works the level of paragraphs or even words. The combination of the tags `viewswitch` and `viewcase` can be used analog to the above. For this kind of viewgroups there is a short form for the case that a piece of information shall be included in only one view or in all except one. The tags are called `viewincl` and `viewexcl`, respectively.

For the realisation of viewgroups with wildcards as in Figure 1b the author can use a wildcard variant by defining a view with the `viewproperty name` set to the value `"iswildcard"`. Using the ID of this view in a viewgroup tells the processor to include this variant into every view not explicitly specified in this viewgroup.

3.2 Some MultiDoc Examples

The first example shows a simple header with document title, authors and an abstract. It corresponds to the header of this paper.

```
<header>
  <title>Editing and Processing of MultiView Documents in
    Cross-Media Publishing</title>
  <authorgroup>
    <author><name>Thomas Corte</name></author>
    <author><name>Jens Deponte</name></author>
    <author><name>Heinrich M&uuml;ller</name>
      <addresspart>Dep. of Computer Science VII (Computer Graphics)
      </addresspart>
      <addresspart>University of Dortmund, D-44221 Dortmund
```

```
      </addresspart>
      <addresspart>http://ls7-www.cs.uni-dortmund.de/</addresspart>
    </author>
  </authorgroup>
  <abstract>Publishing for different media ... </abstract>
</header>
```

The following viewgroup examples use the same view definitions (for ”book”, ”www” and ”cdrom”):

```
<viewdef id="book"><viewproperty name="defaultfmt" value="ps">
</viewdef>
<viewdef id="www"><viewproperty name="defaultfmt" value="html">
</viewdef>
<viewdef id="cdrom"><viewproperty name="defaultfmt" value="html">
</viewdef>
<viewdef id="else"><viewproperty name="iswildcard">
</viewdef>
```

While the first view definition has a default output format PS, the others use HTML. The fourth view definition is a wildcard view, which is used in viewgroups with wildcards.

The first viewgroup example shows a simple viewgroup:

```
<section><title>A viewgroup example</title>
  <para>The following text contains variants for different media:</para>
  <sviewgrp>
  <svariant targetviews="book"><para>Books are great!</para></svariant>
  <svariant targetviews="www"><para>HTML is great!</para></svariant>
  </sviewgrp>
</section>
```

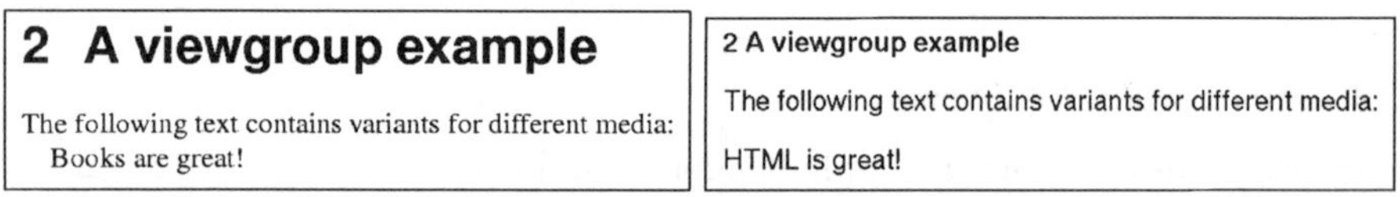

Figure 2. Example output of a simple viewgroup (left: view ”book”, right: view ”www”)

The resulting output is shown in Figure 2 for the book view (a) and the WWW (b). In fact it is an *incomplete viewgroup*, because there is no variant for the view ”cdrom”. The same output results from this code fragment:

```
<para>The same output results from:</para>
<para><viewswitch>
  <viewcase targetviews="book">Books are</viewcase>
  <viewcase targetviews="www">HTML is</viewcase>
```

```
  </viewswitch> great!
</para>
```

An other form of viewgroup is the *complete viewgroup with wildcards.* It is used to specify a variant for any not explicitly mentioned view in a group and can be used as the following fragment shows:

```
<section>
  <title>A complete viewgroup with wildcards</title>
  <para>The following text contains variants for different media:</para>
  <sviewgrp>
    <svariant targetviews="book"><para>Books are great!</para>
    </svariant>
    <svariant targetviews="else"><para>Digital media are great!</para>
    </svariant>
  </sviewgrp>
</section>
```

In the described context this viewgrp defines the text "Books are great!" for the view "book" and "Digital media are great!" for every other document view (here: "www" and "cdrom").

4 Editing MultiDoc Documents

There are already a number of software tools that are specially designed for editing SGML documents. A very basic one is the GNU Emacs [7] with an additional SGML-Package. It supports the user by validating the document structure (i.e. test if it complies to a given DTD) and giving him hints which tag can be used at an arbitrary point in the document. Since the tags are represented as normal text and the document is shown with nearly no formatting, Emacs shows a very technical representation of SGML documents. A more sophisticated editing system can be found in the ArborText ADEPT Series editor [1]. It has a powerful mechanism for producing special editors that comply to a given DTD and a description of the semantics of its tags. The advantage of this is the performance of a specially tailored system that can be created for any DTD the user likes to work with.

Another class of editors that support SGML are DTP programs (e.g. the Adobe FrameMaker+SGML [2]) with additional features to produce SGML documents. While such tools were mainly developed as pure WYSIWYG editors, extra functionality had to be integrated to manage and verify structural information in an SGML conform style.

With both kinds of text processors it is possible to create valid MultiDoc documents. But these tools cannot assist the author in managing document views, because they do not know about the semantics of the corresponding tags. Also the further processing of MultiDoc documents can be a problem, especially the extraction of single document views.

As a conclusion from this, a special MultiDoc editor is desirable that supports the author in all aspects of document views. The key features of such an editor would be the ability to handle the MultiView concept, reaching from the basics of SGML support to (semi-)automatic actions in all views triggered by changes in a single view that are made by the author. While working on the MultiDoc system we identified two main problems that are related to editing MultiDoc documents. The first one pertains the handling of document views in the editor, the second one is how the onscreen rendering of documents is influenced by the contained tags.

4.1 Handling Document Views

The representation of MultiDoc documents in the editor should contain a window that shows structural information about the document and, for the ease of use, a somehow "WYSIWYG-like" content-oriented rendering of the document. While the structural information can be used to navigate through the different views contained in the document, the "WYSIWYG-like" representation gives the author an idea of how the selected document view would look like.

The structural information can be shown in a tree-like form as it is often used to display e.g. the contents of file systems. Besides the conventional options to expand and show single branches of the tree, there should be the possibility to manipulate the tree representation on a higher level. This could be switches to toggle the display of certain tags, e.g. to show only the main structure of the document as sections and similar. Regarding the document views it should be possible to show the structural information for all views or only the selected one (maybe with a mark that there are alternative views for a particular part). It should also be possible to maintain the document structure within this representation, i.e. adding viewgroup-related tags and more content-related tags as sections, tables and so on. With all these actions a correct document structure must be preserved, so the user must get information about valid and invalid actions he can perform at a certain point.

The content oriented representation should give the author all information he needs to imagine the form and substance of the selected document view. Since it can be useful to compare different views, the editor should be able to display different views side by side. The number of simultaneous viewable document views should only be limited by the size of the computer screen.

The arrangement of the common and separate parts of the different document views can be done in various ways. One possibility is to render each document view on its own. This gives the best approximation for the output for each view, but would make it difficult to trace which part belongs to which viewgroup. A simple technique to make this easier would be a colored rendering of the parts in viewgroups, with a unique color for each viewgroup. Another possibility is to horizontally align the corresponding viewgroup parts, which makes it much easier to see which parts belong together, but might result in more or less large holes in the representation of single views. To support the recognition of shared and separate parts, an additional coloring scheme can be implemented.

Both possibilities are supposed to work fine with text, tables and pictures. A problem arises with the use of media like video or even worse, media that do not have a visual representation (e.g. audio streams). For both classes of media the author should use special editors, but it should be possible to play them on request via internal or external media players.

Another form of support for editing MultiDoc documents could be a mechanism to change (automatically or semi-automatically) the other alternatives in a viewgroup when one view is altered. This could be useful if e.g. two views contain the same information in different representations, like numbers in a simple table and a pie chart. The problem with this case is to describe the representations of the information in different groups. Since a formal description of the needed data conversions would be too complicated to use, we thought about including program calls to let the conversion be done by other tools as it is realised with the graphics conversion mentioned in section 5.1.

4.2 Rendering SGML documents for editing

Rendering SGML documents is a non trivial problem, because neither the DTD nor the document itself contains any information about it. Since users often like a more sophisticated onscreen representation than simple, monospaced text, the developer of an SGML editor has to think about connecting SGML tags with an individual rendering of its content. Hard coding the rendering directives would restrict the editor to a single DTD and therefore drops out. A first idea for a more general approach is to use DSSSL stylesheets as described in section 5.1, but the DSSSL standard would imply too complex computations to meet the realtime needs of an editor. Another solution could be the use of Cascading Style Sheets (CSS) [4], but developing a rendering engine for the complete CSS specification is also a quite pretentious task. A third idea is to provide a set of commonly used rendering patterns and let the user do the assignment of tags to them for each DTD in an interactive process.

The main advantage of the third approach is that the user does not have to learn and use a difficult description mechanism like CSS or DSSSL. On the other hand there is the disadvantage of being much less flexible and general.

5 Processing of MultiDoc Documents

The first step from the MultiDoc Document to any output format is to extract the desired document view. The output format can be classified into two classes: SGML and non SGML applications. While the SGML applications only need a transformation from the filtered MultiDoc instance into an instance of another SGML DTD, other output formats need specifications regarding the style in which the information shall be represented. These specifications are needed, because SGML DTDs normally describe only the *syntax* of a document type but not its *semantics*. I.e. the SGML document contains only information concerning the structure and not the meaning of tags or how the information should be rendered.

All of the steps mentioned above can be described in the *Document Style and Semantics Specification Language (DSSSL)*[6]. It is, as expressed in its name, a set of formalisms to describe the semantics of DTD elements and the style in which they have to be rendered in the resulting documents. It is as well as SGML standardized by the ISO. It mainly defines the syntax, semantics and process model for two languages:

1. the *Transformation Language* is used to define rules for the transformation of a document from one DTD to another. Source and target DTD can be the same, which is useful for restructuring documents.

2. the *Style Language* is used to describe the formatting of documents.

A DSSSL specification consists of a *Transformation Specification* and a *Style Specification* (short form: *Stylesheet*). They are used in the main two steps of the DSSSL process model. The *Transformation Process* maps the SGML source document into an SGML result document. This result document is formatted in the *Formatting Process* using a Style Specification.

5.1 The MultiDoc Processor

Since the MultiDoc DTD is useless without an appropriate document processor, we developed a tool which hides the complexity of all these transformations and other process steps. It provides a simple frontend for the analysis of

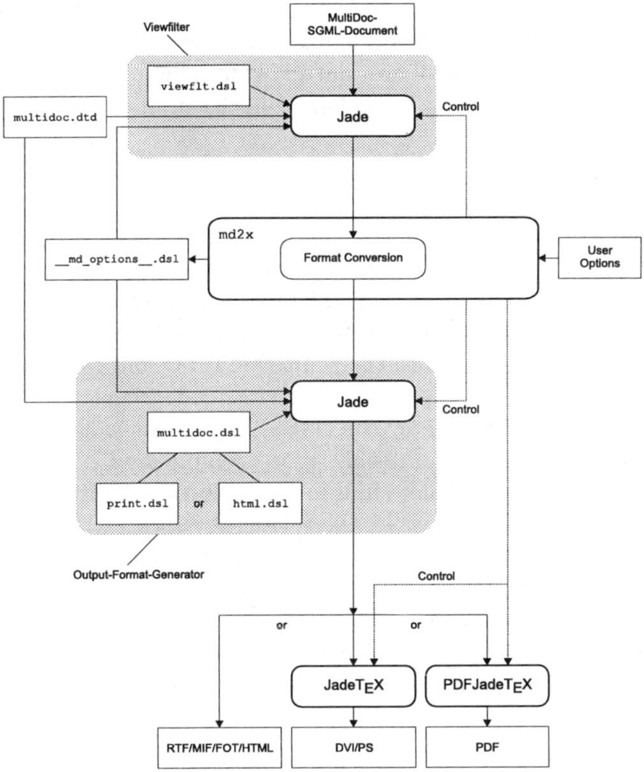

Figure 3. Process model of the MultiDoc processor

MultiDoc documents, the extraction of document views, automatic graphics conversions where needed and the formatting of the output. When the MultiDoc editor will be implemented, this processor will be used by it, hiding the command line syntax of its calls. But also then it still will be useable as a standalone tool, enabling the user to do document processing as batch jobs.

The MultiDoc processor *md2x* is based on James Clarks Jade [3], a partial, free DSSSL implementation. Although Jade does not implement the complete DSSSL standard and the included backends for the generation of formatted output do have some problems, this approach seemed to be the best one. An alternative could have been a completely new developed program with some special purpose output filters. As a consequence of this approach the work could be utilized only with this software. On the other hand, the DSSSL specification from this project can be used with every DSSSL processor available on any operating system, with any output filter available for that system.

Figure 3 shows the control and data flow for the processing of documents in the MultiDoc processor. It is explained in detail in the following sections.

Extracting Document Views

The first step from the multiview to an output document is the extraction of the selected document view. This process step is done by the view filter which is shown in the top part of Figure 3. The main tasks of the view filter are the processing of viewgroups and to resolve internal references. The result is a document that is still conform to the MultiDoc DTD, but lacks any viewgroup related elements.

The transformations done by the DSSSL stylesheet *viewflt.dsl* simply pass through most of the tags. Somewhat more complicated is the processing of viewgroup elements. In complete and incomplete viewgroups all variants that do not contain the active view in their `targetviews` attribute are ignored. A special treatment of viewgroups with wildcards checks if the active view is referenced in the wildcard variant. Furthermore the tags `viewexcl` and `viewincl` have to be processed appropriately.

After the first Jade run the MultiDoc processor does all needed graphics conversions, by calling one or more of the NetPBM [20] utilities.

Formatting the Output

In this state of development there are two main DSSSL stylesheets that cover different print media (*print.dsl*) and HTML (*html.dsl*) as an example for online media. Figure 4 shows an overview of the hierarchy of the MultiDoc stylesheets.

The modules in the left column of Figure 4 implement the Style Specification for print media. The right column contains the Style Specification for HTML. In the middle column there are modules that implement general useful functions. That reaches from list operators and comparison of strings over the definition of global parameters to the localization of automatically generated literals. The structuring of the Stylesheets is inspired by the DocBook-Stylesheets by N. Walsh [19], from which the grey parts are taken.

The functionality of the stylesheets in combination with the formatting backends provided by Jade offer the author a variety of common output formats for the MultiDoc system and the modular structure of it makes it easy to include more. At the moment the supported output formats are HTML, RTF

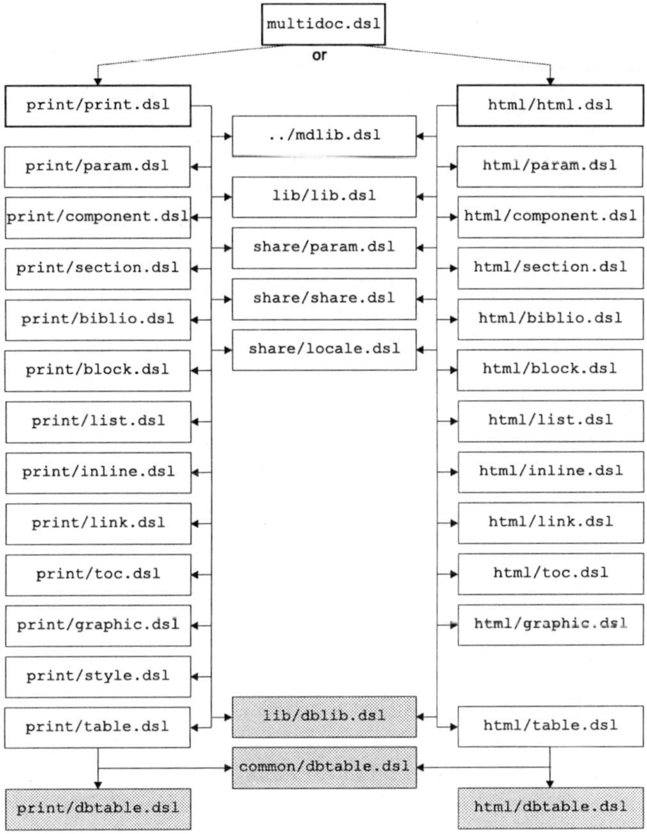

Figure 4. Hierarchy of the MultiDoc DSSSL stylesheets

(*Rich Text Format*, used in many Windows Textprocessors), MIF (*Maker Interchange Format* of the Adobe FrameMaker), DVI (meta output of TEX [10]), PS (*PostScript* page description language from Adobe), PDF (*Portable Document Format* also from Adobe) and FOT, an XML [12] representation of the *Flow Object Tree. Flow Object Trees* are representations of SGML documents, which are often used during the processing of those documents.

While the first three formats are direct outputs of the Jade processing controlled by the MultiDoc system, the other formats need further steps of processing, which are completely integrated into the MultiDoc processor and do not need user interaction.

6 Conclusion

First experiences with the system show that the concept of document views is a flexible instrument to group and select data for different purposes. People who are used to write HTML or LaTeX documents get along fine with the ideas and notation of MultiDoc documents. But the projected editor has to be implemented before the system is usable for a broader range of users.

Although there are some commonly used output formats, more formats especially in the field of multimedia systems should be implemented.

Further research has to be done to develop a method for integrating the concept of document views into other DTDs. For the implementation of an editor there are problems regarding the consistency of multiview documents (e.g. links to anchors in viewgroups) to be solved. A formal modell for document views should be helpful for both tasks.

With the advance of XML a port to XML and XSL (*Extensible Stylesheet Language*) gains importance. With an XML/XSL capable browser it would then be possible to view MultiView documents directly without the need for converters.

References

1. ArborText Inc.: *ADEPT Series*, `http://www.arbortext.com/Products/ADEPT_Series/adept_series.html`
2. Adobe Systems Inc.: *Adobe FrameMaker+SGML*, `http://www.adobe.com/prodindex/framemaker/prodinfosgml.html`
3. Clark, J.: *Jade – James' DSSSL Engine*, `http://www.jclark.com/jade/`, 1998
4. World Wide Web Consortium (W3C): *Cascading Style Sheets (CSS)*, `http://www.w3.org/Style/`
5. *ISO/IEC 10179:1996 – Document Style Semantics and Specification Language (DSSSL)*, the official ISO-Document, `ftp://ftp.ornl.gov/pub/sgml/WG8/DSSSL/`
6. Germán, D. M.: *An Introduction to DSSSL*, `http://csg.uwaterloo.ca/~dmg/dsssl/tutorial/tutorial.html`, 1997
7. Free Software Foundation: *GNU Emacs*, `http://www.gnu.org/software/emacs/emacs.html`
8. World Wide Web Consortium (W3C): *Hypertext Markup Language (HTML)*, `http://www.w3.org/TR/REC-html40/`
9. *ISO 639:1988 – Codes for the representation of names of languages*, 1988
10. Knuth, Donald E.: *The Texbook : A Complete Guide to Computer Type-*

setting With Tex, Addison Wesley, 1984.

11. Lamport, Leslie and Bibby, Duane: *LaTeX: A Documentation Preparation System User's Guide and Reference Manual*, Addison Wesley, 1994.
12. W3C Recommendation: *Extensible Markup Language (XML) 1.0*, `http://www.w3.org/TR/1998/REC-xml-19980210`, 1998
13. Musciano, C./Kennedy, B.: *HTML: The Definitive Guide*, 2nd Edition, O'Reilly & Associates, 1997
14. Organization for the Advancement of Structured Information Standards (OASIS): *The DocBook DTD*, `http://www.oasis-open.org/docbook/`, 1998
15. Severson, E./Bingham, H.: *Table Interoperability: Issues for the CALS Table Model*, OASIS Technical Research Paper 9501, `http://www.oasis-open.org/html/a501.htm`, 1995
16. *ISO 8879: Information processing – Text and office systems – Standard Generalized Markup Language (SGML)*, Genf, 1986
17. Travis, B./Waldt, D.: *The SGML implementation guide: a blueprint for SGML integration*, Springer-Verlag Berlin, Heidelberg, New York, 1995
18. Wall, L./Christiansen, T./Schwartz, R. L.: *Programming Perl*, O'Reilly & Associates, 2nd Edition, 1996
19. Walsh, N.: *The Modular DocBook Stylesheets*, `http://nwalsh.com/docbook/dsssl/index.html`
20. NetPBM: Various tools for the conversion of bitmap graphics, `ftp://ftp.informatik.uni-oldenburg.de/pub/grafik/netpbm/`

TOWARDS A CATEGORIZATION OF HYPERMEDIA DATA MODELS

CARLOS MIGUEL TOBAR

Institute of Informatics, Pontifical Catholic University of Campinas,.
Rod. D. Pedro I, Km 136, CP 317, Campinas, SP, CEP 13020-904, Brazil
E-mail: tobar@zeus.puccamp.br

IVAN LUIZ MARQUES RICARTE

School of Electrical and Computer Engineering, State University of Campinas
Cidade Universitária "Zeferino Vaz", CP 6101, Campinas, SP, CEP 13081-970, Brazil
E-mail: ricarte@dca.fee.unicamp.br

Several hypermedia data models have been proposed in order to face hypermedia as a paradigm to develop information-oriented systems. However, hypermedia modeling introduces very specific requirements not found within conventional database modeling due to several issues must be considered during a design effort, such as modeling of data navigation, data perception, and human-machine interaction. Most of present data models oriented to hypermedia present differences on abstraction level, modeling issues, and considered data aspects. An *Abstract Categorization Map* is proposed as a graphical tool through which it is possible to assess and compare existing specification mechanisms of data models oriented to hypermedia. The map allows an analysis of existing models as an exercise to relate them and therefore derive strengths, weaknesses, overlaps, or omissions. It also allows observing existing gaps between the modeling of data considering different levels of abstraction†.

1 Introduction

The term hypertext, originally defined as "non sequential writing" [1], has been continuously evolving. Presently, it covers much more than its creators could imagine. Hypertext introduces a new organizational perspective to data modeling, allowing a customization for the order into which data perception can be performed.

Multimedia corresponds to the use of different media types to register information in the same application. Through multimedia it is possible to create very complex information objects that present basic components interrelated differently and which can be used to explore the different perception abilities of humans.

Hypermedia extends the combination of hypertext characteristics with those of multimedia allowing the composition of an associative structure equivalent to a semantic network where nodes can be expanded into a variety of forms, visual,

† The work reported in this paper has been funded by Grant No. 97/12807-1 from the State of São Paulo Foundation for Research Support (FAPESP), Brazil.

audible, and, why not, sensorial. Hypermedia modeling introduces very specific requirements not found within other types of conventional modeling.

Considering hypermedia as a paradigm to develop information-oriented systems, there is a need for hypermedia data models. However, hypermedia modeling requirements are different from those of conventional data base modeling or structured document modeling, mainly when aspects such as navigation through data, human-machine interaction, data perception, and synchronization of components with temporal continuity are considered.

Some existing models oriented to database or document design were adapted to incorporate hypermedia, such as Hypermedia/Time-based Document Structuring Language (HyTime) [2] ascribed to Standard Generalized Markup Language (SGML) [3]. There is a great diversity of data models proposed to cover few specific issues related to multimedia and hypertext, such as modeling of time based media [4], navigation [5], data perception and exchange [6], and browsing semantics [7]. There are reference models, such as the Dexter reference model [8], and extensions, such as the Amsterdam Hypermedia Model [9]. There are also model-based approaches to hypermedia design, such as Relationship Management Methodology (RMM) [10] and Object-Oriented Hypermedia Design Methodology (OOHDM) [11].

An *Abstract Categorization Map* is presented as a graphical tool through which it is possible to assess and compare existing specification mechanisms of data models oriented to hypermedia regarding three different points of view: abstraction level of the modeling; manipulation services that are considered; and aspects for data specification. The map allows an analysis of existing models as an exercise to relate them and therefore derive strengths, weaknesses, overlaps, or omissions. It also allows observing existing gaps between the modeling of data considering different levels of abstraction.

2 Categorizing Hypermedia Data Models

Data models currently in use to model data with hypermedia characteristics present limited coverage related to the broad intrinsic requirements of hypermedia modeling. But it is possible to find several mechanisms among those models for the specification of several characteristics of hypermedia data. These mechanisms can present coverage overlapping for the characteristics that can be modeled through them. There are also several similar mechanisms among them, which allow the same kind of specification, configuring specification alternatives.

Integration efforts exist combining several available data models, but unfortunately those do not present a complete coverage of known characteristics that could be present in hypermedia applications. The analysis of this scenario rises the following open questions:

1. Given a data model, how is it possible to know and visualize the existence of overlapping or complementary coverage of hypermedia characteristics with another data model?
2. How is it possible to compare data models considering characteristics of their specification mechanisms?
3. How wide should be the coverage of a hypermedia system in order to support a complete set of data manipulation activities?

In the following section, an answer is proposed to these questions in the form of a graphical map, named *Abstract Categorization Map*, through which it is possible to categorize data models according to three points of view:

- abstract level emphasis that they support to represent data;
- services for data manipulation that are considered in order to dispose specification mechanisms; and
- specification dimensions defined for data modeling; *e.g.*, the structural and the behavioral dimensions.

Data models usually fit at one level of abstraction, but nothing prevents that they comprehend more than one level or restrict themselves to part of one level. Data models are usually oriented to few manipulation services, such as perception and navigation, but ideally should consider each of the supported services in isolation to allow separation of concerns. Data models by convention are regarded to structural concerns but should comprehend a broader set of specification dimensions.

Abstraction levels are explored in the R-Model of the Trellis System [7] and also in the Premo proposal for standardization [12]. While the R-Model presents five abstraction levels – abstract component, abstract hypertext, concrete context, concrete hypertext, and visible hypertext – it does not consider information elements at a higher abstraction level, closer to the modeling domain of interest.

The Premo standard also presents five levels – construction, virtual, vision, logic, and realization. Premo also does not consider information elements and is mainly concerned with implementation elements to support presentation and interaction of graphical interfaces.

A very important reference to abstraction levels is the ANSI/SPARC architecture [13] developed to allow categorization of database schemas, something very close to what is proposed here for data models.

Manipulation services are explored by Steinmetz [14] when he compares the SGML standard to ODA [15] and to MHEG. One architecture is defined with three operation models: representation, presentation, and manipulation. Considering hypermedia, at least navigation and interaction should also be considered, but they are not. In the Abstract Categorization Map several other services are considered, as it is presented in the next section.

Specification aspects are explored in the most known and used data models. While in record-oriented models the structural aspect is strongly explored, little is done with the restriction-related, the content-related, and the behavioral aspects, mainly when considering information elements at high levels of abstraction. Semantic data models, extensions to the record-oriented approach, consider meaning for the structural elements. Object-oriented models are more complete, strongly directed to consider the structural and behavioral aspects in an integrated form. When restriction-related issues are considered, they are oriented to computational matters. Usually content-related issues are considered isolated and cannot be forgotten since they are essential to multimedia modeling.

3 An Abstract Categorization Map

Although three viewpoints are used in the definition of the proposed Abstract Categorization Map, the abstraction level view is followed in order to simplify its presentation.

The Abstract Categorization Map (Figure 1) presents three main abstraction levels: external, intermediate, and physical. The intermediate level is further divided into abstract and concrete sublevels.

On the top of the map are considered data models at the external level that closer to how individuals perceive the domain of interest. They are used to identify information elements, their characteristics, and relationships, without any concern with user profiles or activity types that users perform to manipulate data. On the bottom of the map are considered data models at the physical level; they provide mechanisms that allow and offer different facilities to the specification of computational elements that, when constructed, will be actually responsible by the manipulation of data. These mechanisms establish how users are going to perform different activities to manipulate data through a computer.

Models located at the intermediate levels of the map introduce abstract mechanisms that are related to the computational world and facilitate application development. Ideally, a data model at the intermediate level should allow the adaptation between information elements and computational elements.

The information-element adaptation could be done preferentially through mappings that begin at the external level, somewhat abstractly, and gradually are transformed into implementation specifications, *i.e.*, into concrete elements at the physical level.

In practice, intermediate data models are the most common, offering abstractions to computational elements without considering information elements that exist in the domain of interest.

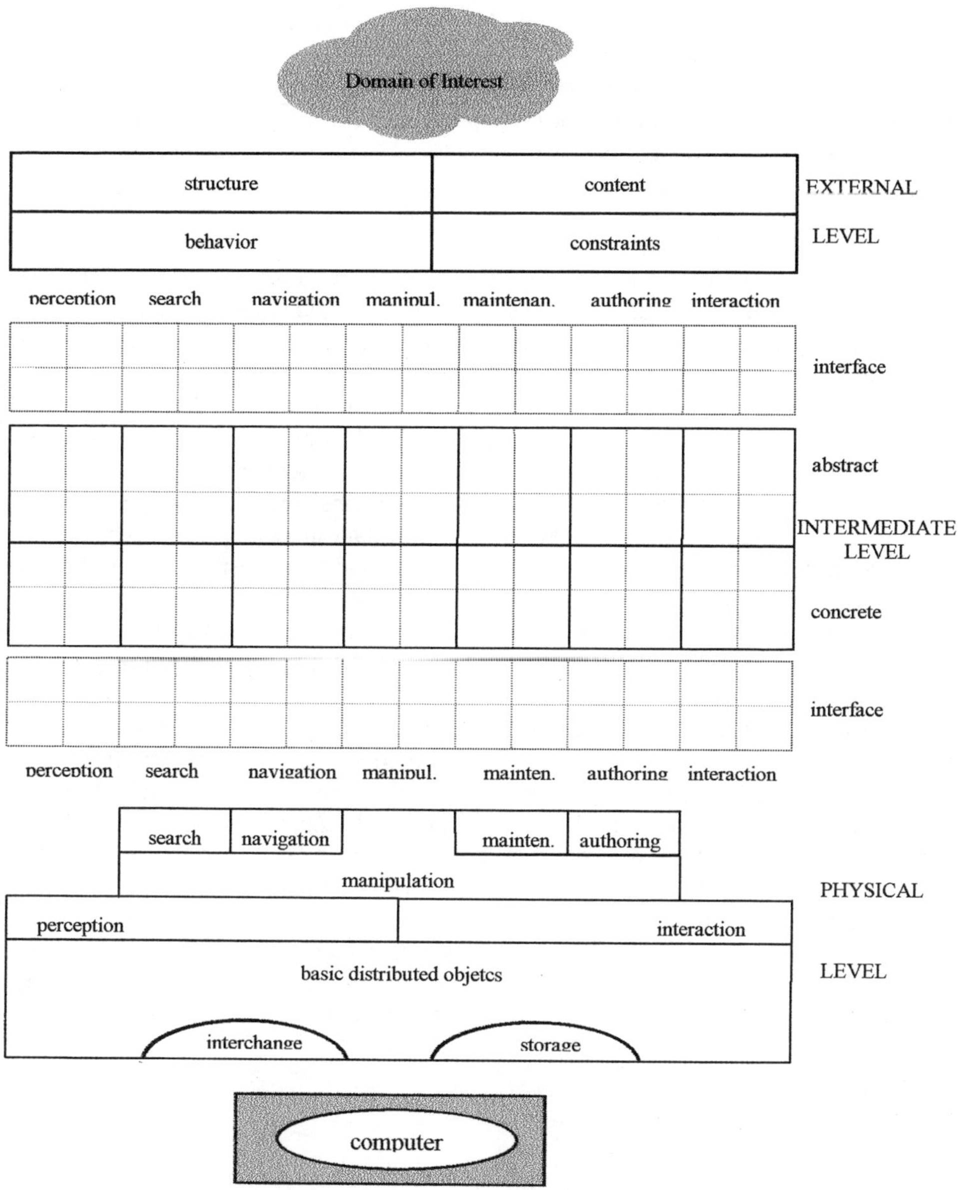

Figure 1. Abstract Categorization Map.

The easiness of a mapping between data models that belong to different abstraction levels depends on the available mechanisms supported by the higher-level data level data model. If some of these mechanisms offer some adaptation type for the elements specified through them to elements that can be obtained through the lower-level data model, they are named *mapping facilitators*. For instance, a relationship identified through a conceptual model can be used to identify and specify links in a navigational model.

3.1 The External Level

Data models at the external level should allow representation of information elements, which are perceived as interesting in the world under investigation. This representation should be as close as possible to the real target world regarding aspects that are considered relevant to the application designer. There should be no concerns with computational matters, such as navigational links or anchors because they do not exist in the actual world. Computational elements will be specified afterwards from the already defined information elements.

Four specification aspects or dimensions are considered in the external level, in order to categorize existent mechanisms of a data model. Each mechanism is analyzed in order to identify what kind of specification aspect is considered: structural, content-oriented, behavioral, or restriction-oriented. These four specification aspects constitute a proposal for infologic data specifications named *T-vision* [16], which establishes for each aspect three specification components: description, meaning, and perception delimiters.

The specification component named perception delimiter allows delimitation of description parts in order to define data-component chunks for afterwards perception. Usually, data components equivalent to perception delimiters are associated to content and are defined together with computational elements, *e.g.*, the classical definition of hypertext links. However, it is worth to note that perception delimiters are not restricted to content but can also be specified considering the other three specification aspects, allowing the delimitation of behavioral descriptions, *e.g.*, a method; structural descriptions; and constraints descriptions, *e.g.*, a set of rule-firing conditions. Perception delimiters applied to content can be easily mapped to anchors of data models oriented to navigation such as the Dexter reference model [8].

3.2 The Physical Level

The physical level represents something like a computational platform where a support is provided to users perform different types of activities based on data manipulation. During data modeling, several user profiles should be considered together with their possible activity necessities and presently this is partially accomplished through the use of different data models.

The activities that users can perform are better supported if divided into services that are traditionally considered in the computational arena. In addition, separation of services allows different degrees of data independence, *e.g.*, the separation of concerns between navigation and interface allows the construction of different interfaces for the same navigation modeling [11].

Usually, data models at the physical level are oriented to at most two services, thus an integration of data models should be provided in order to obtain a broad, complete, and consistent coverage of services.

Present hypermedia data models, with abstraction levels higher than physical, consider at most three different services: *navigation*, *presentation*, and *interaction*. In the physical level, these three services are also considered, but "perception" is used instead of "presentation" because several media explore cognitive sensations other than visual and audible. Other services considered are *search*, *manipulation*, *maintenance*, and *authoring*.

At the base of the physical level in Figure 1 the existence of several basic distributed services is considered, amongst which two are closely related to hypermedia – *interchange* and *storage*, that are basic rendering services. In principle, the facilities of these services are activated transparently to the user by other physical level services providing higher physical abstractions. This does not prevent the existence of specific data models for interchange and storage, establishing how data should be represented in order to be better operated upon.

It is interesting to note that some services give support to other services, such as the manipulation, perception, and interaction services. Every support service comprehends a support-interface between itself and each of the supported services. These support-interfaces correspond, in abstract terms, to the real role of the "anchoring" and "presentation specifications" interfaces in the Dexter reference model. In the graphical representation of the Abstract Categorization Map, those interfaces are not represented for sake of visibility.

Data can be retrieved in traditional database systems through identifiers, attributes, and keywords. The same facilities are expected for hypermedia data, although they present high generation and maintenance costs, besides not being easily available to some types of descriptions, such as with continuous media.

A search-service support to hypermedia modeling should provide specification mechanisms that allow the definition of elements through which the user should be able to search and query data, based on the different data aspects. An infrastructure with dictionaries, thesaurus, taxonomies, templates, onthologies, and subjectivity levels is the objective of the search-oriented modeling service.

Manipulation mechanisms aim the calling and articulation control of other services in order to establish computational requirements, such as non-volatile storage, real-time, transactions, and exception handling treatment. Manipulation modeling regards to the basic operations for data manipulation from repositories, through networks, until availability to other services. The user through the manipulation service might define rules and restrictions directly or indirectly.

Maintenance issues comprehend configuration, failures, security, performance, and service billing [17]. Considering data modeling, manipulation mechanisms should support the specification of policies related to behavioral control and monitoring of the other services, which require planning, monitoring, and modification of computational resources.

Authoring covers all steps necessary to define hypermedia data, amongst which are capturing or content generation, composition, and final art. Hypermedia information definition is the objective of the authoring service. Software engineering issues beyond hypermedia data specific issues are covered by the authoring service. For instance, policies for configuration management, reuse management, and facilities to maintain different representations for the same information are examples of authoring issues.

3.3 The Intermediate Level

Data models at the intermediate level support mechanisms that allow information element adaptation into computational elements, or, at least, they introduce computational-oriented mechanisms that are not related to the domain of interest.

Intermediate data models present mechanisms that allow the specification of computational elements in very high levels of abstraction, such as an *index* or a *tour* mechanism considering the navigation service. Elements modeled through intermediate mechanisms with high levels of abstraction, in order to be implemented, must be specified through mechanisms of other data models with lower levels of abstraction belonging to the intermediate or physical level. If they belong to the intermediate level, other lower level adaptations must be provided until a modeling is obtained at the physical level in order to permit the realization of the original modeling. Sometimes, these adaptations produce computational elements that do not preserve the characteristics of the respective information element or to the respective higher level element. Other times, the computational elements do not correspond to any information element.

The intermediate level is divided into two sublevels to allow the localization of data models regarding the abstract influence of the other two levels. If the influence is due to the external level and its four specification aspects of information, the data model belongs to the abstract sublevel. If, otherwise, the influence is due the physical level and its computational services, then it belongs to the concrete sublevel.

For instance, considering the modeling of nested contexts or of m-slices through the orientation of, respectively, OOHDM [11] and RMM [18], an external physical influence takes place from the content dimension in order to obtain computational elements with very high level of abstraction oriented to the navigation service. Afterwards these high-level elements are adapted through lower-level mechanisms, such as the ones that constitute the HTML model [19].

A modeling that is oriented entirely to a specific service relates to the abstract sublevel, if an infologic modeling previously specified influences it. The moment when abstract data models are used is the very first moment to consider computational issues, although at high levels of abstraction.

A concrete modeling represents computational elements that were identified through abstract mechanisms and to which are aggregated detailed characteristics determined by the influence of the other services, not previously considered.

For instance, consider elements related to the navigation service. Each identified navigation mechanism can have aggregated a set of characteristics influenced by the other services, such as:

- The perception service, if destination anchors should be treated like transclusions, substitutions, or new visual elements.
- The interaction service, if the navigation activation is to be triggered by the user or automatically by the system.
- The manipulation service, if the specification of the navigation mechanism is internal or external to the description; and if the destination anchors belong to a group of related anchors and should be manipulated together.
- The search service, if the destination anchors should be located through some kind of query.

3.4 A Complete Vision of the Map

In addition to the three basic levels of the Abstract Categorization Map, there are additionally two interfaces located between the external and intermediate levels, and between the intermediate and physical levels.

The seven services that appear at the upper side of the physical level are projected from the bottom of the map towards the external level, through the intermediate level and interfaces. Each resulting column represents the influence of the respective service at each abstraction sublevels and interfaces. However, the interchange and storage services, that appear at the bottom side of the physical level, are not projected towards the external level because they do not need elements with high level of abstraction in order to be activated. Furthermore, of the known data models oriented to these two services, none covers other service, *i.e.*, they are concerned only with codification matters.

The four specification aspects of the external level are also projected towards the physical level through the intermediate level and interfaces, producing quadrants in each abstraction sublevel of each service-column. Each quadrant represents the influence of the respective aspect at the abstraction level of the considered service.

The motivation for the Abstract Categorization Map is to graphically indicate the existence of mechanisms through which it is possible to specify elements with a specific abstraction level, and related to one of the computational services and one of the information aspects. The quadrants in the intermediate sublevels establish an influence crossing between the physical level services and the four external level aspects.

Considering each quadrant of the external and intermediate levels, it could be pointed out the existence of mechanisms that facilitate data specification mappings to elements that can be obtained through a data model with adjacent lower level of abstraction. If such mechanisms exist, they play the role of *mapping facilitators* between models of distinct abstraction levels, and their existence is represented in the correspondent quadrant of the respective interface, *i.e.*, the interface between the two considered levels.

A mapping facilitator is an existent mechanism of a high-level data model, regarding abstraction, whose resulting modeled elements could be mapped directly into elements produced by some other mechanism in a lower-level data model. That would be the case of an infologic data model supporting perception delimiters for content, such as attributes of a semantic data model, which could be mapped into anchors of a data model oriented to navigation which could, in turn, be used in the navigational design step in RMM. Another example that can be also observed in RMM is the mapping facilitator of relationships. Relationships that are defined during the E-R design step of RMM are mapped afterwards into links of the application diagram or of m-slices [18].

The interface between the external and intermediate levels allows the presentation of existent mechanisms of the external data model under consideration that facilitates mappings to any data model of the intermediate level. The interface division is a mirror of the division that exist in each intermediate level, allowing the indication of characteristics (abstraction, service, and aspect) for the target mechanism in the intermediate data model. The second interface plays the same role, except that it applies to the intermediate and physical levels.

Although there is the consideration of data models at each of the intermediate sublevels, there is no interface between them since there is not a real mapping between data models of the two sublevels. What happens is the production of details, not element transformation or new element introduction.

4 Using the Abstract Categorization Map

The Abstract Categorization Map is a tool that allows graphical visualization to represent the existence and sophistication of specification mechanisms according to their adequate abstraction level, computational service and specification aspect. As an example, the categorization of RMM is commented here.

RMM corresponds to one of few methodologies for model-based approaches to hypermedia design that covers most of the different abstraction levels of the map, allowing a step-by-step design development through these levels. This set of models addresses the design and construction of hypermedia applications. It is based on data models that support data representation schemes but provide few procedures for the representation usage in a design process. One of its basics is the Entity-Relationship model.

RMM focuses on applications that present regular structure, *i.e.*, whose domain of interest offers the possibility to model entity-classes, relationships between classes, and multiple instances in each class.

RMM provides specification primitives to structure information divided into three points of view: E-R domain, slice domain, and access. In the slice domain, the *slice* primitive allows modeling of how the information should be presented. Access primitives model navigation through data.

RMM consists of the following eight steps, some of which can be conducted in parallel:

a) Entity-Relationship design, when the information domain of interest is modeled through entities and their relationships.
b) Application diagram design, when presentation units and links among them are defined.
c) M-Slice design, when information units are sub-divided for presentation.
d) Navigational design, when it is modeled how users will access information.
e) User-Interface design, when it is modeled how data will be presented.
f) Protocol Conversion design, when it is established how abstract constructs are to be transformed into physical-level constructs.
g) Run-time Behavior, when decisions about how link transversal, history, backtracking, and navigational mechanisms are to be implemented, and how to populate the application with data.
h) Construction and testing.

Although first presented as a linear methodology, RMM was conceived to be flexible by supporting rapid feedback loops.

The existence of mechanisms is represented by the occupation of the quadrant that corresponds to their characteristics. All parts of the map can be used to point out mechanism existence, including the three abstraction levels, the four specification aspects of the external level, and the nine computational services of the physical level (considering also interchange and storage). For RMM the considered services are mainly navigation together with perception and authoring, as can be visualized in Figure 2.

Indication of existence of mechanisms in a quadrant is performed through a graphical occupation of the quadrant which means that the data model under consideration support one or more mechanisms with the abstraction level, computational service, and specification aspect defining the quadrant. Comments justifying a given categorization should be written.

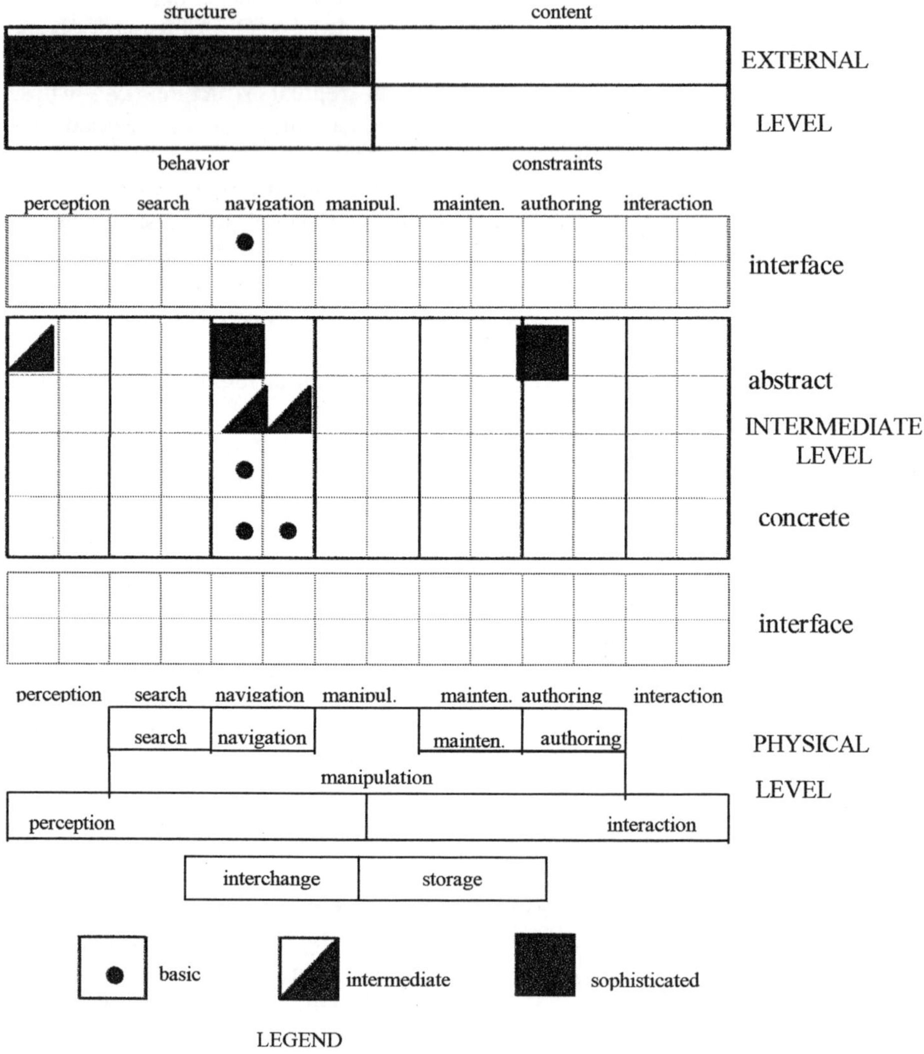

Figure 2. Abstract categorization map for RMM.

In order to indicate the sophistication of a mechanism that is represented in the map, a simple scale with three values – basic, intermediate, sophisticated – is proposed. Different patterns used to occupy a quadrant represent the sophistication degrees.

In RMM, an infologic structural modeling is created in the first step using the E-R data model followed by an application diagram through which a global vision of the final application is defined, that is composed by presentation units.

Each presentation unit is decomposed into m-slices (with E-R attributes and nested m-slices) which can be seen as navigation nodes. The most basic m-slices constitute WWW pages equivalents or part of them.

Usually m-slices belong to one of the E-R entities but can be composed by attributes of other entities, even those that are not directly related to the owner entity. An m-slice describes which data is to be presented but does not describe how it is presented.

Very powerful mechanisms that define indexes, groups, and guided tours are available during m-slice design. It is also possible to associate conditions to the related entities in order to establish which instances are involved in the presentation.

The two interfaces that are present in the Abstract Categorization Map between the basic abstraction levels can also have existence and sophistication indications for mapping facilitators. Only the sophistication degree of a mapping facilitator must be considered in a categorization when it comes to the interface. It could happen to have different sophistication indications in two correspondent quadrants. The first at one of the interfaces and the second at the correspondent upper abstraction level, because the mechanisms considered in one quadrant are different from those considered in the other – only mapping facilitators are represented in the interface. In RMM, the domain analysis using the E-R data model helps to identify important relationships through which navigation can be supported. It is considered natural that the infologic relationships establish navigational paths.

During the protocol conversion step is necessary to map or convert the already obtained modeling into available tools that can be categorized at the concrete intermediate level or at the physical level. This step is not easily performed because of the lack of mapping facilitators to these lower abstraction levels.

A designed application through RMM can be realized with any data base tool oriented to the WWW. Depending on the information volatility, applications can be constructed using HTML (statically) or SQL query (dynamically).

4.1 Orientations for a Categorization

A categorization requires a set of guidelines in order to orient the use of the Abstract Categorization Map. These guidelines should reflect the categorization objective and their definition is a responsibility to be accomplished before the categorization could be initialized.

Some objectives that can be considered are:

- identification of coverage overlapping between data models, aiming the analysis of potential integration;
- comparison of data models;
- specification of a new authoring methodology; or
- adherence assessment of data models to specific available tools.

Considering the first objective, several categorizations were produced [16]. In order to perform these categorizations, the following orientations were established:

1. Any mechanism that is oriented to one of the computational services, mainly to those strongly related to hypermedia, *i.e.*, navigation, perception, and interaction, cannot be considered at the external level.
2. The existence of a mechanism is pointed out at least as basic, no matter how simple it is.
3. The reference for a mechanism to be considered intermediate sophisticated, related to the navigational service, is the Dexter reference model. Related to the perception service, the reference is the HyTime standard. For the interaction service, ADVcharts [20] were adopted. For the remaining services there is no referential other than the decision of the analyst responsible by the assessment.
4. The determination of the abstraction level for a given mechanism should follow the motivations that are presented below together with the definition of the Abstract Categorization Map.
5. If several different mechanisms exist and relate to the same quadrant in the Abstract Categorization Map, the indication of the most sophisticated prevails.
6. A given mechanism of a given data model can only be considered a mapping facilitator if, through it, it is possible to specify elements which are going to be used as a specification basis for other elements with lower abstraction level, which can be specified through another data model.

It is also recommended that each graphical categorization be produced together with the following textual information:

a) A presentation of the data model.
b) Observations and justifications for the map coverage, regarding abstraction levels, computational services, and specification aspects.
c) Observations and justification about how each of the basic abstractions levels is explored.
d) Observations and justifications for mapping facilitators.
e) Relevant features of the data model.
f) Other observations.

4.2 Map User Profiles

The Abstract Categorization Map is directed to designers that work with hypermedia, mainly those involved with:

- Application development and whose interest is to choose a set of data models that can be used to support their work.
- Hypermedia systems and who are interested in determine how broad a system is regarding the map coverage.
- Hypermedia systems and whose interest is to define mapping facilitators and mapping rules, mainly when involving data models at the physical level.
- New data models which are the result of an integration effort, involving existing or new data models.
- Development methodologies to information systems and whose interest is with coverage and transition strategies between abstraction levels, computational services, and specification aspects.

5 Conclusions

The *Abstract Categorization Map* has two main objectives. First, it allows comparisons and assessment of each mechanism for multimedia and hypermedia modeling that composes data models, according to an abstraction level, a computational service, and a specification aspect. Second, it constitutes a reference framework for the definition of new data models or for the integration of existent data models in order to support multimedia and hypermedia information applications. The map can also be used for the analysis of conventional data models.

When a specific data model is categorized, representations for all of its specification mechanisms should be located in the Abstract Categorization Map according to the abstraction level, the service to which it is oriented, and the specification aspect that is considered. In addition if any of the mechanisms plays a role of mapping facilitator, its existence should be displayed in the respective quadrant of the applicable interface.

Through the analysis of several data models using the Abstract Categorization Map, it was observed that the abstraction emphasis is directed to the concrete intermediate level, *i.e.*, it is operationally oriented, presenting more concern with computational elements than with information elements.

The Abstract Categorization Map allows figuring out how broad should be a support environment for multimedia and hypermedia. Actually it is possible to find good, if not excellent, data models supporting several aspects and services that are considered in the external and intermediate levels. It is also possible to find good authoring methodologies that focus some of the computational services. However, they usually do not offer a complete vertical coverage with support to different abstraction levels. The reasons for this situation should be investigated and some questions are proposed in order to orient further efforts:

1. Is it possible to integrate some of the good models in order to obtain either a complete vertical coverage for any of the services or a horizontal coverage for one of the abstraction levels?
2. Is there any model oriented to some of the quadrants, mainly to those located through the intersections of the search, manipulation, and maintenance services, in addition to those of the behavioral and restriction-oriented specification aspects?
3. How broad are the available tools in terms of map coverage?
4. How much effort should be located on creating more abstract data models for multimedia and hypermedia?
5. What mechanisms of existent data models can be considered mapping facilitators?

The Abstract Categorization Map can be improved through the introduction of a graphical representation for the existence of elements, regarding one computational service, which give support to other services.

Orientations and criteria for the use of the Abstract Categorization Map vary according to the defined objectives of the categorization and are not fixed. One important open issue to consider is the definition of metrics to measure the sophistication scale for the different representation and manipulation mechanisms. The subjective scale presented here can be adequate for one to compare different models. However, in order to enable the use of the map as a tool to exchange information, the sophistication scale can be refined to consider deeper details of data models.

References

1. T. H. Nelson, "Getting it out of our System Information Retrieval: A Critical Review", G. Schechter, ed., Thompson Books, (1967).
2. International Standard Organization, "The Hypermedia Timed-Based Structuring Language, HyTime", ISO/IEC 10744, (1992).
3. International Standard Organization, "Standard Generalized Markup Language (SGML)", ISO/IEC IS8879 (1986).
4. A. Karmouch and J. Emery, "A Playback Schedule Model for Multimedia Documents", IEEE Multimedia, 3(1), Spring, (1996), pp.50-61.
5. W. Hall and H. Davis, "Hypermedia link services and their application to Multimedia information management", Information and Software Technology, 36(4), (1994), pp.197-202.

6. International Standard Organization, "Coding of Multimedia and Hypermedia Information, MHEG part I – object representation and base notation (ASN.1)", ISO/IEC CD13522-1, (1995).
7. R. Furuta and P. Stotts, "The Trellis Hypertext Reference Model", in Proceed. of the Hypertext Standardization Workshop by NIST, (1990).
8. F. Halasz and M. Schwartz, "The Dexter Hypertext Reference Model", CACM, 37(2), (Feb. 1994), pp.30-39.
9. L. Hardman, D. Bulterman and G. van Rossun, "The Amsterdam Hypermedia Model – Adding Time and Context to the Dexter Model", CACM, 37(2), (Feb. 1994), pp.50-62.
10. T. Isakowitz, E. A. Stohr and P. Balasubramanian, "RMM: A Methodology for Structured Hypermedia Design", CACM, 38(8), (Aug. 1995), pp.34-44.
11. D. Schwabe, G. Rossi and S. Barbosa, "Abstraction, composition and lay-out definition mechanisms in OOHDM", in ACM Workshop of Effective Abstractions in Multimedia (1995).
12. I. Herman, G. J. Reynolds and J. van Loo, "Premo: An Emerging Standard for Multimedia Presentation, Part II: Specification and Applications", IEEE Multimedia, 3(4), (Winter, 1996), pp.72-75.
13. D. C. Tsichritzis and A. Klug, "The ANSI/X33/SPARC DBMS Framework: Report of the Study Group on Data Base Management Systems", Information Systems, 3 (1978).
14. R. Steinmetz and K. Nahrstedt, "Multimedia: Computing, Communication and Applications" (Prentice Hall, 1995).
15. W. Appelt and N. Tetteh-Lartey, "The Formal Specification of the ISO Open Document Architecture (ODA) Standard", The Computer Journal, 36(3), (1993), pp.267-279.
16. C. M. Tobar, "Categorization of Hypermedia Data Models Through a Multidimensional View", Ph.D. Thesis, State University of Campinas, Brazil (1998); In Portuguese.
17. B. Kinane, "Distributing Public Network Management Systems Using CORBA", in IFIP International Conference on Open Distributed Processing, (Feb. 1995), pp.117-130.
18. T. Isakowitz, A. Kamis and M. Koufaris, "Extending the Capabilities of RMM: Russian Dolls and Hypertext", in Proceed. of the 13th Annual Hawaii International Conference on System Science (1996).
19. World Wide Web Consortium, W3C, "HyperText Markup Language (HTML)", reachable at http://www.w3.org/MarkUp/ .
20. L. M. F. Carneiro, M. H. Coffin, D.D. Cowan and C. J. P. Lucena, "ADVCharts, a Visual Formalism for Highly Interactive Systems", in M. D. Harrison and C. Johnson (eds.), Software Engineering in Human-Computer Interaction, Cambridge University (1994).

CHAPTER 2

INTERACTIVE MULTIMEDIA

MMM99

ELECTRONIC COMMERCE OF MULTIMEDIA SERVICES

Jaime DELGADO, Isabel GALLEGO, José POLO
Telematic Applications Group, Departament d'Arquitectura de Computadors
Universitat Politècnica de Catalunya
Campus Nord, Mòdul D6, Jordi Girona 1-3, E-08034 Barcelona, Spain
E-mail: delgado, isabel, jpolo@ac.upc.es

This paper presents the issues related to the implementation of electronic commerce of services, in contrast to the more usual electronic commerce of products, focussing on the use of multimedia facilities. After presenting some introductory ideas on electronic commerce, the paper provides a classification of electronic commerce activities in order to put in context different kinds of electronic commerce applications. Then, the specificity of electronic commerce of multimedia services is considered, proposing some solutions based on the use of brokerage systems. Models to clarify the role broker agents should take, is also provided. Finally, the paper presents a concrete implementation of an application for electronic commerce of services in the consultancy sector, that of the TRADE project. The developed system is classified according to the initially described activities, and the main issues and results of the project are introduced.[1]

1 Introduction

Electronic commerce (see [3], as an example, for some generic work), as the electronic counterpart of traditional commerce, generally involves many buyers and sellers. A buyer is a subject (individual or organisation) interested in obtaining goods or services from a seller. A seller is a subject (individual or organisation) that owns certain goods or can provide certain services and who is interested in providing them (sell) to a potential buyer. This situation is illustrated in Figure 1.

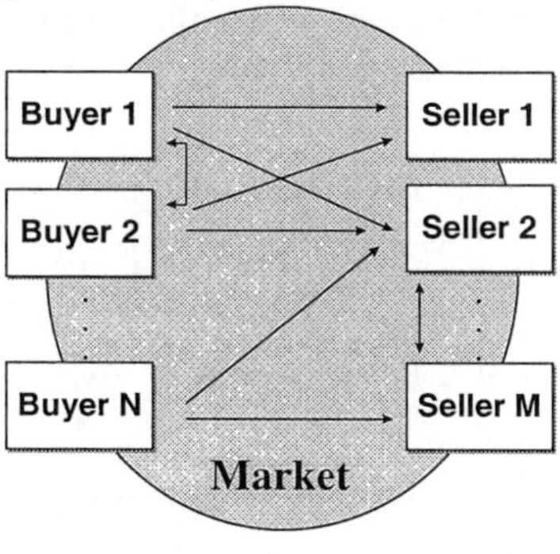

Figure 1. General scenario for commerce

[1] This work has been partly supported by the European Commission (TRADE, ACTS project 328) and the Spanish government (TEL98-0699-C02-01).

In commerce, there are interrelations between buyers and sellers, between buyers and buyers (e.g. associations) and between sellers (e.g. shop grouping). Nevertheless, the normal situation can be represented by a one-to-one situation between a buyer and a seller.

This is illustrated in Figure 2 where a buyer requests goods or services from a seller, who in turn provides responses to the buyer (in the form of products or services). Negotiation can be also considered within the request-response paradigm.

Figure 2. The request response paradigm

In the case of electronic commerce, part of these requests and responses are carried out by electronic means which may include, or not, payment and delivery. It is not necessary for all the interactions to take place electronically. For example, in traditional commerce, we use electronic payment by credit cards and we still call it traditional commerce. We understand that electronic commerce takes place if the decision to buy and the purchase take place electronically (see Figure 3). Electronic delivery is only possible in those cases where the result of the request is electronic in nature (e.g. multimedia products or services).

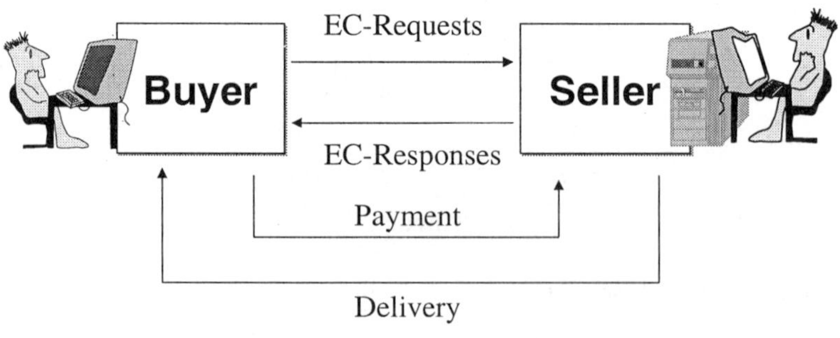

Figure 3. Electronic Commerce general situation

2 Classification of electronic commerce activities

This section attempts to provide a classification of electronic commerce activities. The characteristics of the different activities are used to establish this classification.

Several characteristics (in bold) can be identified in electronic commerce activities depending on several aspects. Each of these characteristics can assume different values (in italics), which are listed after the characteristic.

The characteristics and their values are summarised in Table 1.

Table 1. Characteristics of electronic commerce activities (1 of 3)

Characteristic	Values	Description
Result	*Tangible*	The result of the activity is a product, something tangible. Examples: a digital picture or just a pizza.
	Intangible	The result is something intangible (normally a service), such as financial investments, entertainment services (chat, etc.), consultancy, tax payments.
Electronic	*Electronic result*	The result of the commerce is electronic goods that can be transferred over the network. Examples: digitised images, translation of electronic documents, etc. In case of service provision, the service is provided through the network (e.g., by the interchange of documents).
	Non-electronic result	The result of the activity is not electronic or cannot be transferred over the network. Examples: buying CDs, pizza service, etc. In case of service provision, no network interchange is done after the purchase (e.g., an hotel room rental).
Existence	*Pre-defined*	The results of the activity are known since the beginning. The buyer buys a specific product (like an existing picture) or a well-known predefined service (automatic format conversion).
	Customised	The result of the activity will be a customised product or service. This not only implies ordering, but also negotiation of the parameters of the service.

Table 1. Characteristics of electronic commerce activities (2 of 3)

Characteristic	Values	Description
Availability	*Immediate*	The results are sent electronically or physically just after the activity. Examples: buying electronic pictures, shopping malls, etc.
	Delayed	The results need some time to be delivered because a predefined action needs to be taken. Examples: printing of brochures, translation of a document, etc
	Negotiated	The results need to be negotiated after the request and before the delivery, because they need to be produced or customised according to the instructions of the buyer. Example: design of a customised publicity brochure.
	Ordered	The request has been made, but the results have not yet been used. In the meantime there may be modifications of the result (e.g. cancellation) depending on certain conditions. Examples: hotel bookings, reservation of flight tickets, etc.
Contract	*No contract*	There is no explicit contract, but there are probably some specific rules or an implicit contract. For example, in a supermarket there is an implicit contract that specifies that you pay for the goods before you take them home, some rules for exchange, etc. The electronic purchase of "small" (in a monetary sense) things can be also done without an explicit contract.
	Previous	The buyer has previously established a framework contract. For example, manufacturers have long-term contracts with their suppliers.
	Contract per activity	The activity requires the existence of a specific contract and there is no previous contract. Ex.: buying a house.

Table 1. Characteristics of electronic commerce activities (3 of 3)

Characteristic	Values	Description
Payment	*Electronic payment*	Payment is done through the network. Example: Credit card payment using the SET protocol.
	Non electronic payment	Payment is done outside the network used by the customer. Example: Cash payment.
Buyer	*Re-seller* (Intermediary)	The buyer will sell the results, as they are, to other users. Brokerage systems are included here.
	Transformer	The buyer will use the results to produce other results.
	End-user	The buyer uses the results directly.

Of course, it is difficult to select an appropriate set of characteristics, but those mentioned above allow a distinction to be made between most situations (at least, those discussed in this paper).

3 Multimedia services

When the objects of commerce are electronic, the use of electronic commerce provides the best advantages in the sense of speed in accessing the services and, more importantly, the delivery of the results. The commerce of multimedia information is one of the areas best suited to electronic commerce, since the goods being sold can be also transferred over the network. Some discussions on applications of this kind can be found in [1], [4], [6] and [7].

The electronic commerce can be also of services, rather that of products. To provide those services, an ordered sequence of electronic interchange of documents may be needed, being the service provision an added value to that multimedia information interchange, not only the set of documents alone. In this case, we are dealing with electronic commerce of multimedia services. Then, these multimedia services take maximum benefit of electronic commerce.

It is also possible another kind of electronic commerce of services where either no interchange is needed or the objects to interchange are not electronic ones.

3.1 Characteristics of electronic commerce activities with multimedia services

Following the previous considerations, this situation corresponds to all those activities where the characteristic "**result**" takes the value of *´Intangible´* and the characteristic "**electronic**" takes the value of *´Electronic result´*.

On the other hand, in this context, a buyer can request a customised service. This situation requires negotiation of service parameters.

Then, the characteristics of the activities in the case of multimedia services are:

Characteristic	Values
Result	*Intangible*
Electronic	*Electronic result*
Availability	*Negotiated*
Existence	*Customised*
Payment	*ANY*
Contract	*ANY*
Buyer	*ANY*

The following sections concentrate on those aspects of electronic commerce activities where the result is electronic and the existence is customised. The electronic activities handled are those that involve intermediaries (brokers), where the buyer is a re-seller.

3.2 Electronic contract management

Full electronic commerce activities, especially in the case of customised services, require electronic contracts to be established between buyer and seller. There are two main problems in electronic contract management, the first is the technical development of the systems to establish and manage flexible contracts. The second problem is the legal recognition of this type of contract.

This paper does not elaborate on this point but considers it important enough to be mentioned.

3.3 Solutions based on Electronic Brokerage of multimedia services

Brokerage is an activity that is widely extended in traditional commerce and it has, of course, a counterpart in electronic commerce. Electronic brokerage is becoming a core activity in electronic commerce systems because of the rapidly increasing number of sellers. Brokers help buyers by simplifying selection and access to sellers. This is illustrated in Figure 4. For electronic commerce activities in the area of brokerage, the "**buyer**" characteristic for the broker agent takes the value *´re-seller´*.

To take benefit of the features provided by broker–based electronic commerce systems, it is necessary to develop models to help in their implementation.

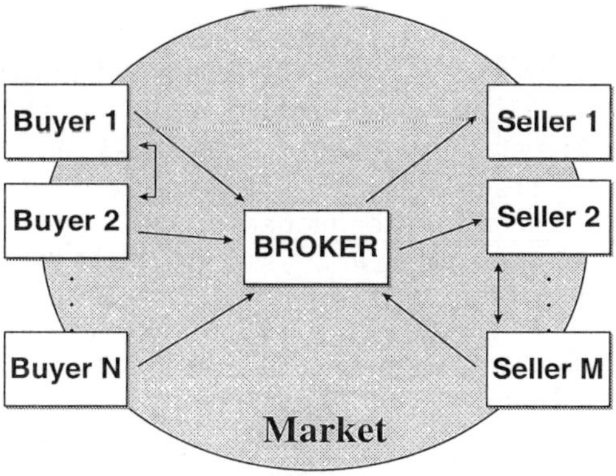

Figure 4. The role of a broker agent in Electronic Commerce

In the following, two of these models (functional and operational) are presented. This paper is more focussed in the operational model. More details can be found in [5]. The models are general and apply to both electronic commerce of products and electronic commerce of services, either on physical goods or on multimedia objects.

3.3.1 Functional model

A functional model for an electronic brokerage system may have the following levels, illustrated in Figure 5:

- **Buyer level:** these are the users of the service.
- **Broker level:** in this level, one electronic broker or several electronic brokers provide the service requested by the customer, using the services offered by the suppliers.
- **Seller level:** sellers offer their services to one or more brokers.
- **Complementary Services level:** electronic brokerage requires additional non-specific services, such as electronic security and payment.
- **Distribution level**: the result of the service must be distributed from the buyers to the sellers: this distribution may be electronic (in the case of electronic information) or physical, in the general case.

At the *buyer* level, the end users can interact with the electronic brokerage system in two different ways:

- **Direct access:** if the user previously knows the service to be ordered (or the products to be bought), access can be made directly without any browsing or searching.

- **Navigation access**: if the user does not have previous knowledge of the service to be ordered. This mechanism allows browsing and searching broker information.

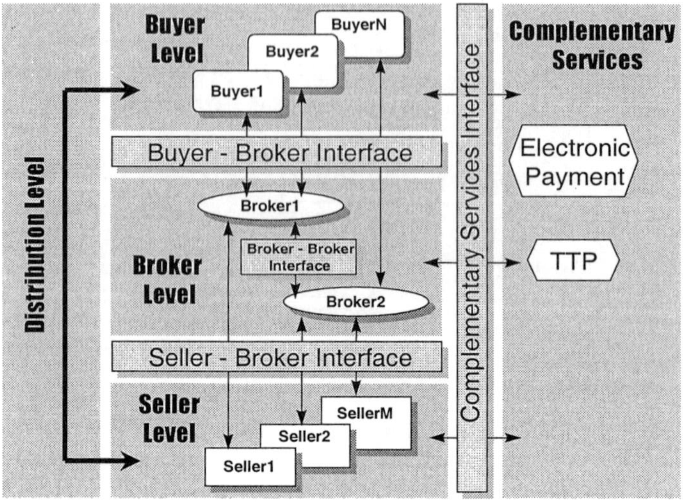

Figure 5. Functional Model for electronic brokerage

At the *seller* level, there is an additional function to allow the broker (or brokers) access to the local information (detailed information and final products):

- **Seller Database:** allows a broker (or brokers) to access information stored in the seller system.

The *broker* level is the most complex system, and provides, in addition, the following functions:

- **General & Management Database:** This module manages the Database of the broker which contains management information (e.g. accounting information), user information (e.g. user profiles) and service information.
- **Searching:** This module provides specific search functions to assist system users. The search function may include some intelligent behavior such as multi-lingual searching.

3.3.2 Operational model

The operations related to an electronic brokerage system can be categorised into two types:

- **Service-oriented**: those that occur while providing the services to buyers;
- **System-oriented**: those that provide the users with some added-value system operations.

We can identify the phases that generally occur when a buyer requests a service from a seller through an electronic brokerage system.

In the case of the **service-oriented** phases, we can identify the following sub-phases:

Phase	Description
Service Identification	The user makes a selection in order to identify those services that fulfil his interest.
Service Request	The user must perform formal ordering for purchasing the service. In this case both parts, the seller and the buyer, assume responsibility to fulfil the conditions and statements of an established contract.
Agreement	The conditions for provision of the service (service parameters, delivery specifications, etc.) are to be agreed at this point.
Post-agreement	It is necessary to specify a procedure (after the agreement) that allows follow-up of the service until final delivery.

In the case of the **system-oriented** phases, the following sub-phases can be identified:

Phase	Description
Maintenance	Allows users to access some maintenance services such as automatic software upgrading from the broker.
Service-Update	The sellers should also be able to update the information that the broker holds on them.
Contract re-negotiation	Allows buyers and sellers that may have some contractual relationship with the broker, to modify the previously established contract.

4 Case study: TRADE

The ideas presented in this paper have been put into practice in a specific case: the TRADE (TriAls in the Domain of Electronic commerce) project [12] [8], that started in March 1998 and will finish in February 2000.

TRADE (a European Commission co-funded project in the ACTS programme [2]) has implemented a distributed system for the lawyer and administrative consultant professionals to offer legal and administrative services by electronic means. Customers can contract these kinds of services. Then, this is a clear example of electronic commerce of multimedia services.

4.1 Main features

The main component of the system is a Server Machine that acts as a simple broker between suppliers and customers. The TRADE server machine has the basic functionality of a broker, as to select a supplier or to store temporarily the information interchange among customer and suppliers. The real commerce takes place between the customers and the server and between the server and the suppliers. Although there is no direct electronic communication between customers and suppliers, as in a normal broker situation, customers and suppliers interact between them without the broker avoiding the disclosure of their identities. Furthermore, the TRADE server could be even exploited by one provider itself.
More information on the TRADE applications presented here can be found in [11] and [9].

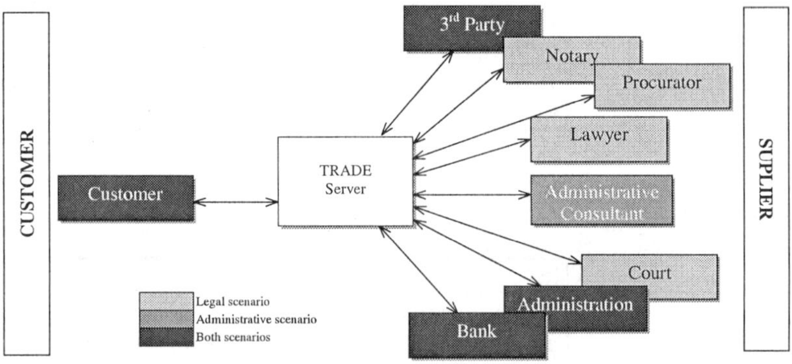

Figure 6. Architectural Model of the Legal and Administrative Scenarios.

As already said, lawyer and administrative consultants offer their services through the TRADE server in two different scenarios. They have similarities and differences as can be seen in Table 2 and Table 3.

Following the client-server paradigm in both scenarios, the TRADE server corresponds to the server and all other constituents to the clients, see Figure 6. The TRADE server centralises all interchanges done by the clients, also named actors. These can be: customers, lawyers, administrative consultants, notaries, procurators, courts, administrations, 3rd parties, etc. The activity in these scenarios is basically a document and information interchange in a specific order between the actors. In the legal scenario, the lawyer is the actor that controls the correct operation of the interchanges (legal cases) between him and the other actors. In the administrative scenario, the actor who controls the interchanges (administrative cases) is the administrative consultant.

The server contains all information about documents and information to interchange, the actors that have to take part, and the interchange order (workflow rules). It allows lawyers or administrative consultants to carry out all case steps.

Table 2. TRADE Legal Scenario

	Values	Comments
Result	*Intangible*	A legal service could be considered as an added value to a sequence of steps that could lead to an interchange of electronic documents.
Electronic	*Electronic result*	An aim of the TRADE project is, if possible, that the documents produced as a result are electronic.
Availability	*Negotiated*	Each legal service needs a special negotiation. Furthermore, the evolution of a legal case uses to be different in every case.
Existence	*Customised*	Each legal professional decides the steps to follow in the legal service provision depending on the case.
Payment	*Electronic*	Electronic payment is an objective of the TRADE project.
Contract	*Contract per activity*	It is necessary to consider each legal case with their specificity.
Buyer	*Re-seller*	Applies to the TRADE server.
	End-user	Applies to the Consumer.

Table 3. TRADE Administrative Scenario (1 of 2)

	Values	Comments
Result	*Intangible*	An administrative service could be considered as an added value to a sequence of steps that could lead to an interchange of electronic documents.
Electronic	*Non electronic result*	When the service consists of an only step (like in a VAT three-monthly return handling) then no electronic interchange is needed as a result.
	Electronic result	An aim of the TRADE project is, if possible, that the documents produced as a result are electronic. This is the case of services that need more than one step, like a National Insurance medical fitness or sick leave.
Availability	*Delayed*	The results needs some time to be delivered.
Existence	*Pre-defined*	This is a characteristic of an administrative service.

Table 3. TRADE Administrative Scenario (2 of 2)

	Values	Comments
Payment	*Electronic*	Electronic payment is an objective of the TRADE project.
Contract	*Previous*	Each administrative case has a specific treatment and normally always the same.
Buyer	*Re-seller*	Applies to the TRADE server.
	End-user	Applies to the Consumer.

4.2 Operation

The TRADE server and actor's components can be seen in Figure 7. The actors only need a web browser. On the other hand, the TRADE server structure is more complex. It is composed of the following components:

- Relational database: SQL Server. It is the database containing all information about documents, information, actors, cases steps, etc.
- HTTP Server. To serve the HTML pages to the actor.
- Electronic Commerce Software (such as Microsoft Site Server Commerce Edition). To save temporally information when the HTML pages are processed.
- ASP pages: HTML + Script code (such as Microsoft Visual Basic Script Edition). Using the information from the database to generate the HTML page.
- CGI application: ANSI C. To file transfer.

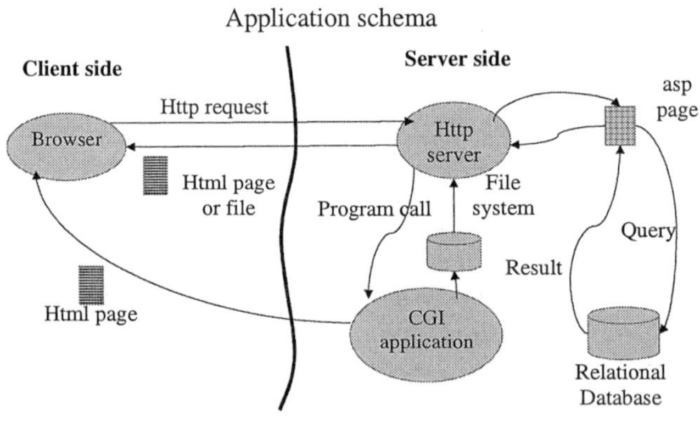

Figure 7. Structure of the client or actor and the TRADE server.

The sequence of actions between the TRADE server and an actor could be summarised in the following steps [10]:

1. The actor connects to the server using a standard web browser (no extra software is needed in his site).
2. He requests a web page.

3. The TRADE server, using the ASP (Active Server Pages) pages and the information in the database, generates an HTML page.
4. This page is sent to the actor's browser.
   Steps 2 to 4 are repeated until the actor disconnects from the server.

5 Conclusions

The paper has presented a top-down approach to electronic commerce activities, focussing on electronic brokerage of customised multimedia services. The classification of electronic commerce activities is intended to put into context the area of interest of the paper.

The electronic commerce of multimedia services has some specific aspects that make it more complex than other kinds of commerce. This paper has presented a brief discussion of that point.

Electronic brokerage provides a new paradigm in electronic commerce, where customers do not deal directly with the producer of the goods or the provider of the services. The main aspects of electronic brokerage have been also addressed in the paper as a solution to develop systems for electronic commerce of multimedia services.

Finally, a presentation of a specific implementation, within the TRADE European project, of a system that covers most of these aspects has been given.

References

1. ACEBRÓN, J.J. and DELGADO J. "Electronic brokers as intermediaries for electronic publishing", ICCC/IFIP 2nd Conference on Electronic Publishing, 20-22 April 1998, Budapest (Hungary). ICCC Press, ISBN 1-891365-02-9.
2. ACTS Web Page, http://www.infowin.org/acts/.
3. CEN/ISSS: CEN / Information Society Standardisation System, http://www.cenorm.be/isss/.
4. DELGADO J., GALLEGO I. and ACEBRÓN J.J. "Electronic Commerce of Multimedia Products", 7th IFIP/ICCC Conference on Information Networks and Data Communications (INDC'98), 1998 Aveiro (Portugal). ICCC Press, ISBN 1-891365-03-7.
5. GALLEGO I., DELGADO J. and ACEBRÓN J.J. "Distributed Models for Brokerage on Electronic Commerce", International IFIP Working Conference Trends in Electronic Commerce (TREC'98), 3-5 June 1998, Hamburg (Germany). Springer, ISBN 3-540-64564-0.
6. MARTÍ R. and DELGADO J. "Use of WWW technology for Client/Server Brokerage Applications in MULTIMEDIATOR", Intelligence in Services and Networks (IS&N'97), May 1997. Springer, ISBN 3-540-63135-6.
7. MULTIMEDIATOR Web Page, http://www.ac.upc.es/multimediator/.

8. TRADE Document AC328/COS/R&D/DS/P/018/a1 "TRADE Trials Application Scenarios", July 1998.
9. TRADE Document AC328/UPC/DAC/PI/I/029/a1 "Electronic Commerce Pilots Operations - 1st TRADE Trial", July 1999.
10. TRADE Document AC328/UPC/DAC/PI/I/031/a1 "Electronic Commerce Applications Development - 2nd TRADE Trial", July 1999.
11. TRADE Legal and Administrative applications Web Page, http://trade.ac.upc.es/.
12. TRADE Web Page, http://trade.cosi.it/.

FORMAL DESIGN OF INTERACTIVE MULTIMEDIA DOCUMENTS AND AUTOMATIC GENERATION OF JAVA APPLICATIONS

R. WILLRICH[1], P. de SAQUI-SANNES[2,3], P. SÉNAC[2,3] AND M. DIAZ[3]

[1]INE/CTC/UFSC, Caixa Postal 476, 88040-900 Florianópolis SC, Brazil
[2]ENSICA, 1 place Emile Blouin, 31056 Toulouse Cedex 05, France
[3]LAAS-CNRS, 7 avenue du Colonel Roche, 31077 Toulouse Cédex 04, France
Email: willrich@inf.ufsc.br, {pdss, senac}@ensica.fr, diaz@laas.fr

Java has increasingly been used for multimedia applications deployment over the Internet. The paper advocates that complex applications to be coded in Java should be first modeled using Hierarchical Timed Stream Petri Nets (HTSPN) and checked against design errors before actual implementation. How Java applications can be automatically generated from HTSPN models is discussed in depth in the paper. A development environment has been prototyped. Java practitioners find it a convenient, high level interface for the production of structured, hierarchical and temporally coherent documents in multimedia applications running on top of the Java Virtual Machine.

1 Introduction

Use of formal modeling techniques has increasingly been recommended in the literature to support authoring of multimedia and hypermedia documents [2, 3, 4, 5]. Following [6], the paper introduces Java Interpreted Hierarchical Time Stream Petri Nets to support the automatic generation of Java applications from hypermedia document modeled in I-HTSPN. The latter can be checked against synchronization problems and temporal inconsistencies using validation techniques described in [7]. Starting from a validated I-HTSPN model, new results in the paper make it possible to derive a portable application that can run on top of any workstation or PC supporting a Java Virtual Machine (JVM). Java has been selected for its well-known advantages: portability, support of advanced multimedia applications via the Java Media Framework API (JMF), multitasking and advanced networking capabilities.

The paper is organized as follows. Section 2 gives the intuition behind the Java I-HTSPN model and outlines principles of Java application generation. A formal introduction to I-HTSPNs follows in Section 3. How Java applications are derived from Java I-HTSPN models is detailed in Section 4. Other components of the Java I-HTSPN toolkit are described in Section 5. A distance-learning application serves as example in Section 6. Conclusions on the proposed methodology are finally given in Section 7.

2 Methodology

2.1 Related Work

Users of multimedia authoring tools include artists, designers, journalists, and other people scarcely attracted by mathematical models. Among formal models so far applied to hypermedia document design, Petri nets graphically feature parallel/serial composition and thus implement a digital studio paradigm. Little [5] demonstrated that switching from a timeline description to a Petri net model is straightforward (figure 1). Each multimedia unit processing depicted in the timeline is modeled by a place in the net. Synchronization points become transitions in the net. Petri nets supersede timelines by the possibility to endow places and/or transitions with attributes. For example, Little's OCPNs give a finite and fixed duration to places. Sénac [6] identified OCPN's shortfalls in the context of networked - and therefore asynchronous - multimedia applications. He proposed to replace fixed duration on places by temporal intervals on arcs.

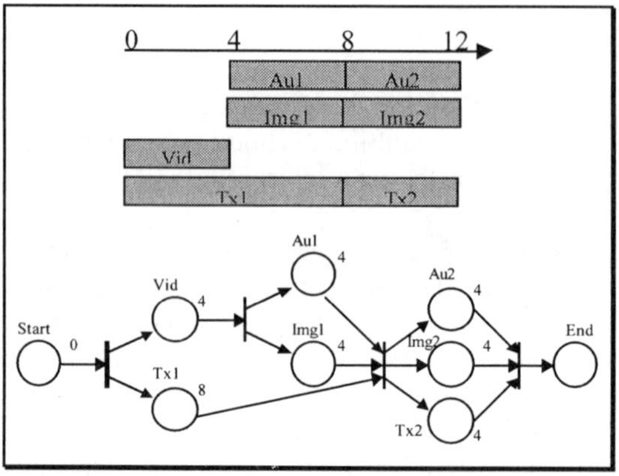

Figure 1. A timeline diagram and its OCPN counterpart

2.1.1 The TSPN Model [1]

The Timed Stream Petri Net model (TSPN) associates a Temporal Validity Interval (TVI) with each arc outgoing from a place. TVI = [x, n, y] where n denotes the nominal duration of the processing modeled by the arc's output place, whereas x and y denote the earliest and latest firing time, respectively. Jitter and other usual defects in multimedia flow synchronization are thus taken into account (figure 2).

TSPNs rely on Petri nets, a modeling technique that gives ability to describe serial and parallel flows. In such a model, a transition acts as synchronization point for its incoming flows (arcs). TSPNs offer nine synchronization strategies, including the possibility to dynamically privilege the earliest or latest stream, respectively.

Synchronization can also be driven by a "master" flow whose characteristics are statically predefined in the model.

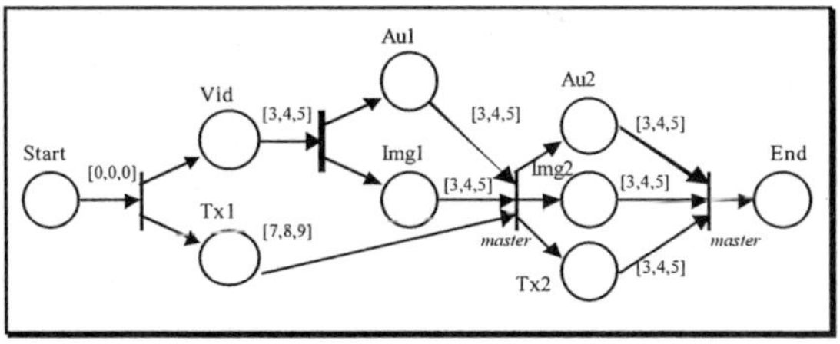

Figure 2. A simple Time Stream Petri Net

The TSPN in figure 2 depicts a multimedia scenario that starts with a video (Vid) and text information (Tx1). When Vid finishes, both an audio (Au1) and a still picture (Img2) start. When master flow Au1 finished, Img1 and Tx1 presentation are stopped. An audio (Au2), a still picture (Img2) and a text information (Tx2) start immediately. When master flow Au2 finishes, the multimedia scenario finishes too.

2.1.2 HTSPN Model [6]

Like OCPNs and timelines, TSPNs are limited to basic multimedia synchronization scenarios. Enhanced TSPNs, called HTSPNs (Hierarchical Time Stream Petri Nets) [6] extends TSPNs with structuring facilities. HTSPNs also give the possibility to model user interaction by means of timed links (figure 3). HTSPNs borrow three basic concepts from the Dexter reference model [3]: atomic, composite and links components (section 3.1.1). Atomic, composite and links places are represented by normal, dotted and boldfaced circles, respectively.

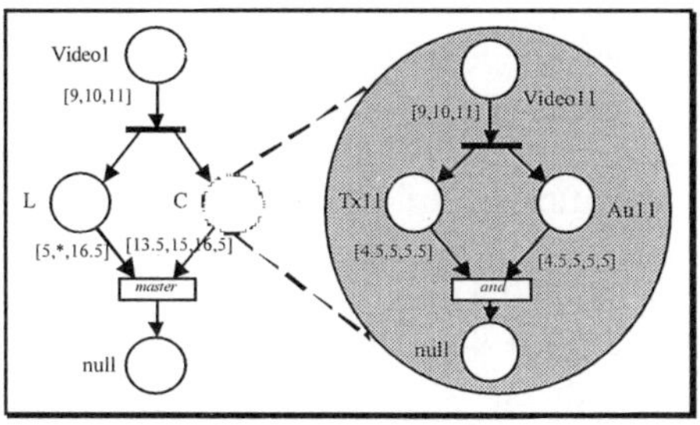

Figure 3. A HTSPN sample

Let us comment the HTSPN in figure 3. A composite place C has been refined into a TSPN sub-net. The latter is temporally equivalent to the interval of the arc outgoing from C. A timed link starts from place L. The arc outgoing from link place L is constrained by a TVI, making thus a timed link. In figure 3, a token cannot exit place L before five units of time even though the user activated the corresponding link. At the latest, the transition must be fired 16.5 units of time after it was enabled. The nominal duration cannot be known in advance; as a matter of fact, nobody can predict when the user will activate the link; consequently, the nominal duration is denoted by a star (*).

2.1.3 The Java Interpreted HTSPN Model

The expression power of the HTSPN model is limited to temporal and logical synchronization in multimedia and hypermedia documents. In other words, HTSPN give ability to specify the conceptual structure of documents. Willrich's extension in [10] gives ability to write a more complete and realistic model. The so-called "Interpreted HTSPN model" or I-HTSPN for short gives a particular semantics to places and transitions in the net. Places in a HTSPN are given a semantic to support the specification of the conceptual structure, content and presentation structures of multimedia and hypermedia documents. Names given to the structures vary with authors. The following definitions apply in the paper:

- The **conceptual structure** specifies the semantic organization, *i.e.* components along with the logical and temporal relationships between components.
- The **presentation structure** describes how and where the components will be presented.
- The **content structure** describes information within components.

Verification techniques [6] developed for HTSPNs remain applicable to I-HTSPNs.

This paper presents a new interpretation of the I-HTSPN model: Java I-HTSPN. The latter specifically addresses the conceptual structure, content and presentation structures relevant for Java multimedia applications.

2.2 Life-cycle

The Java I-HTSPN model supports a four steps methodology for hypermedia documents formal design and subsequent generation of Java applications:

1. Document specification in Java I-HTSPN, a formal model that allows complete and unambiguous specification of interactive multimedia documents, including the description of conceptual, presentation and content structures.
2. Analysis of the Java I-HTSPN specification: the purpose is to check multimedia scenarios against incorrect logical behaviors, temporal inconsistencies and resource allocation conflicts.
3. Final test of the multimedia document through an interpretation (presentation) of the analyzed Java I-HTSPN specification. The author can see the multimedia document. Would the behavior or the layout of the presentation differs from that expected, then go back to step a.
4. Automatic production of the Java multimedia application implementing the specified multimedia document.

3 The Java I-HTSPN Model

This section extends HTSPNs to cover the specification and analysis of interactive multimedia documents as well as the generation of Java multimedia applications. This extension is not a complete reformulation of the I-HTSPN model presented in Section 2. Changes are limited to presentation and content structure attributes that make it now possible to model data access information and presentation characteristics within the Java context.

3.1 Content Structure Modeling

In I-HTSPN, multimedia data used by a multimedia document are specified by a list of *Data* objects. Each *Data* class make it possible to specify one medium type. Java I-HTSPNs support four presentation media: still picture, audio, video, text and animation (a sequence of still pictures presented at fixed intervals). The list is limited to presentation media currently treated by the graphical library of the Java Toolkit (AWT) and by the Java Media Framework (JMF) API. Multimedia data can be specified by the following *Data* classes: *StillPicture*, *Audio*, *Video*, *Text* and *Animation*.

All *Data* classes contain the URL (*Uniform Resources Locator*) attribute. The latter specifies access information for multimedia data used by a multimedia document. Different media types specified by different object classes allows to verify which URL really specifies the media data type modeled (identified by the file extension). In addition to the URL attribute, the *Animation* class specifies the original speed and duration of the animation.

An example of still picture specification follows:

StillPicture Photo1 {
URL http://www.inf.ufsc.br/~willrich/Photo1.gif; }

3.2 Presentation Structure Modeling

A multimedia document is made up of several presentations specified by a set of *Presentation* objects. The Java I-HTSPN model, the following *Presentation* classes are defined:

- The *PSStillPicture* class contains presentation characteristics for one still picture. A *PSStillPicture* object specifies a *StillPicture* object, its presentation size and position, and an alternative presentation. The latter specifies the maximal preparation duration of the still picture as well as an alternative presentation specified by another *Presentation* object. The alternative presentation will replace the initially scheduled presentation in case of either access problems or preparation time overflow.

- The *PSVideo* class allows the specification of the characteristics of one audio presentation. A *PSVideo* object specifies an *Video* object (which describes the video to be presented), the termination type and an alternative presentation. The termination attribute specifies the action to be executed during the wait for a synchronization point. It specifies a choice between three actions: (i) to freeze the last position, (ii) interrupt the presentation, and (iii) present an alternative presentation. Similar mechanisms are proposed by [8] and [4].
- The *PSAudio* class allows the specification of the characteristics of one audio presentation. A *PSAudio* object specifies an *Audio* object (which describes the audio to be presented), the termination type and an alternative presentation.
- The *PSText* class allows the specification of the characteristics of one text presentation. A *Text* object specifies a *Text* object (which describes the text to be presented), the presentation style (*area* or *field*), the font (*dialog*, *helvetica*, *timesRoman*, *courier* and *symbol*), the font style (*bold*, *italic*, *and plain*), the character size, and an alternative presentation.
- The *PSAnimation* class allows the specification of the characteristics of one animation presentation. A *PSAnimation* specifies an *Animation* object (which describes the animation to be presented), its presentation size, position, speed, start and end point, the termination type and an alternative presentation.
- The *PSLink* class allows specifying the characteristics of one button in a multimedia document. A *PSLink* objet specifies the presentation position of the button, its background and foreground colors, and the text font.

For instance, a presentation of the still picture specified by the *Photo1* object can be specified by bellow *PSStillPicture* object:

```
PSStillPicture PresPhoto1 {
        Data                      Photo1
        Presentation-position     [ 100 420 ] }
```

3.3 Conceptual Structure Modeling

In a Java I-HTSPN model, a HTSPN specifies the semantic organization, *i.e.* components and their logical and temporal relationships. The model also includes additional information, such as the document's title and author as well as the size of the main window characteristics (size, background and foreground colors).

3.4 Java I-HTSPN and the Hypermedia Document Modeling

The model Java I-HTSPN does not apply to any type of multimedia or hypermedia documents. The latter should be codified using Java. Therefore, several mechanisms reached in classical, non Java, multimedia or hypermedia documents cannot be expressed by Java I-HTSPN model. Examples include both intra-media synchronization and inter-media synchronization between internal point of components, such as temporal relation between video frames and audio samples.

4 Automatic Production of Java Multimedia Applications

The Java I-HTSPN model supports automatic generation of Java multimedia applications using a standard Java code. Java multimedia applications derived from previously validated documents are composed by two classes: (i) *Document class* contains the document specification in Java I-HTSPN and serves as starting point of the Java application (ii) *Interpretation* classes permit interpretation of any document specified in Java I-HTSPN.

4.1 Document class

The *Document class* is automatically generated from the Java I-HTSPN specification. It contains the internal representation of the Java I-HTSPN specification as attribute. This internal representation is an object of the *DocumentSpecification* class. The latter implements a data structure used to store the Java I-HTSPN specification.

Based on the *documentSpecification* attribute, *Document* class specifies the following operations:

- Creation of the main window where the document is to be presented. The *Description* object (Section 4.3) defines the size, title, foreground and background colors of the application. The menu in the main window allows the user to start or interrupt the presentation and to quit the application.
- Instantiation of one *Interpreter* objet (presented in the sequel).

4.2 Interpretation classes

Interpretation classes are responsible for the presentation of any document specified by a Java I-HTSPN net. Among these classes, the *Interpreter* class is responsible for the creation and control of an *Interpretation Structure.* This structure is generated from the Java I-HSTPN specification. It is composed by a set of active and communicating objects, implemented by threads and monitors. These active objects implement the capabilities modeled by the places, arcs and transitions of a Java I-HTSPN specification. The *Interpreter* creates and connects active objets in order to create an Interpretation Structure corresponding to the Java I-HTSPN specification.

The creation process of the Interpretation Structure is recursive. A *Sub-net* module represents the Interpretation Structure of a generic sub-net S (including the root or one of sub-nets of S). This module is an abstract representation of active objects (instances of the Interpretation classes) responsible for the interpretation of the sub-net S.

The Sub-net module is the elementary block of creation of the Interpretation Structure of the Java I-HTSPN specification. Figure 4 presents the Sub-net module in an AS/RT based notation. The circles represent functional process, the oriented arcs in plain traces represent data flows and dot traces represent control flows.

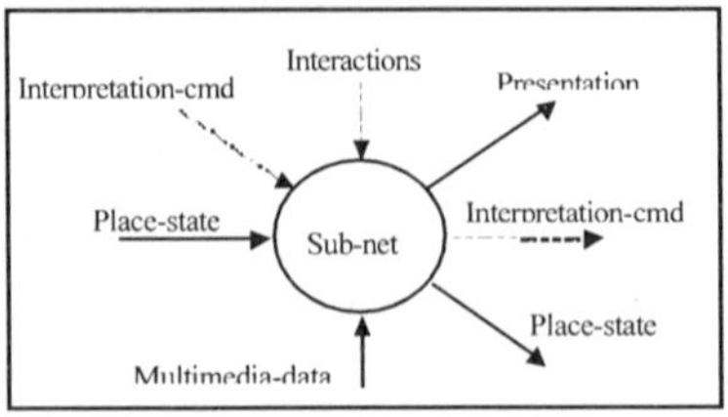

Figure 4 Elementary block for the construction of the Interpretation Structure

A Sub-net module receives interpretation commands (*interpretation-cmd*) from both its parent sub-net and the user (*interactions*). If the sub-net is the specification root, then it receives interpretation commands from the user via the main menu. Input data of a Sub-net module include the state information of its children sub-nets (*state-place*) and multimedia data. Its output data are the composite place status representing the sub-net (*state-place*). These data are sent at state change. The Sub-net module sends interpretation commands to its children sub-nets (*interpretation-cmd*).

Figure 5 exemplifies a structure necessary to the interpretation of a Java I-HTSPN specification. The root contains one composite place "A" and its associated sub-net contains another composite place "B". This Interpretation Structure contains 3 connected Sub-net modules. This structure implements all the capabilities specified by the Java I-HTSPN net.

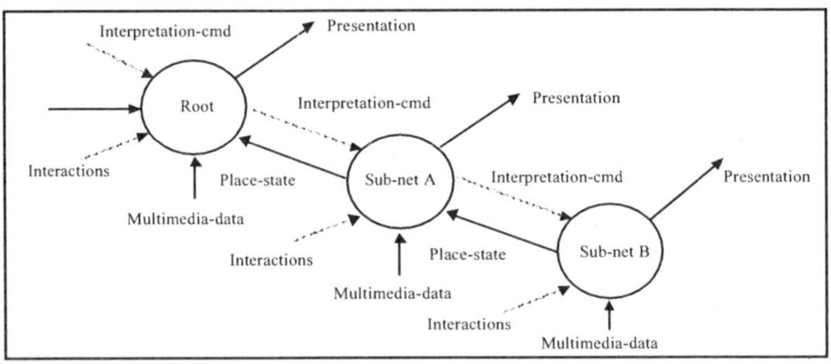

Figure 5. An example of Interpretation Structure

A Sub-net module S manages presentation of components modeled by composite, link and atomic places of sub-net S. It also control temporal validity of associated activities. The scheduler of sub-net S is realized by one instance of the *Scheduler* module. The presentations modeled by the places of S are supported by instances of the following modules: *Text-Presentation*, *Image-Presentation*, *Audio-*

Presentation, *Video-Presentation*, *Button-Presentation*, and *Animation-Presentation*.

- Each presentation of a text modeled by an atomic place is implemented by an instance of the *Text-Presentation* module.
- Each presentation of an image modeled by an atomic place is implemented by an instance of the *Image-Presentation* module.
- Each presentation of an audio modeled by an atomic place is implemented by an instance of the *Audio-Presentation* module.
- Each presentation of a video modeled by an atomic place is implemented by an instance of the *Video-Presentation* module.
- Each presentation of animations modeled by an atomic place is implemented by an instance of the *Animation-Presentation* module.
- Each presentation of buttons modeled by a link place is implemented by an instance of the *Button-Presentation* module.
- Each presentation of a multimedia scenario modeled by a composite is implemented by an instance of the Sub-net module place (the root of a Java I-HTSPN specification is always associated with an abstract composite place).

During the Interpretation Structure creation associated with a sub-net S, the *Interpreter* performs the connection of the *Scheduler* object (which implements the composite object associated with sub-net S) with the active objects that implement the places of sub-net S (possibly including another *Scheduler* objects). From these connections, the *Scheduler* can react to changing states and send Start/Stop presentation commands to the objects associated with the places of the represented sub-net. For instance, Figure 6 presents the refinement of a Sub-net module necessary to interpret a sub-net specifying a multimedia scenario with one text, one image, one audio, one button and one animation.

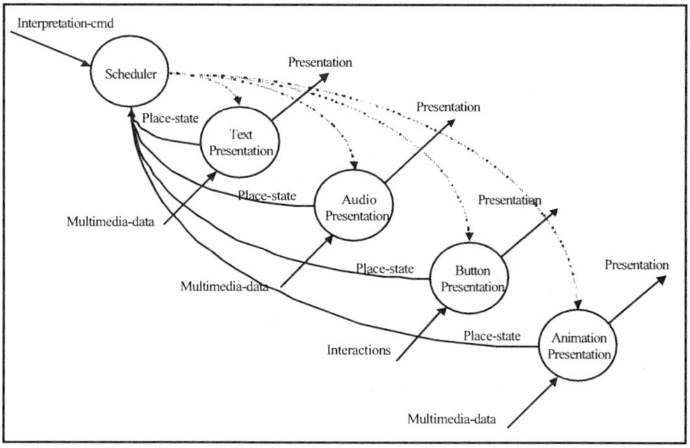

Figure 6. Example of Interpretation Structure

4.2.1 Scheduler Module

The *Scheduler* module is responsible for the scheduling of the presentations modeled by the places of a sub-net S. It is made up of two active objects:

- *TVI-Control* performs validity temporal control on S. This object behaves as an alarm signaling to the *PetriNet-Engine,* associated with the mother sub-net of S, the instants at which the minimal and maximal duration of S alive.
- *PetriNet-Engine* guarantees sub-net S evolves. From the net's current state, *PetriNet-Engine* identifies firable transitions and fires them. Firing transition leads to interrupt the transition's input presentation, the starting of output presentations, and to prevent the Petri net marking from changing. Search for firable transitions starts after a new (stable) state is entered. When an output place of the sub-net becomes marked, the *PetriNet-Engine* object sends the state information of composite place to its mother sub-net.

4.2.2 Presentation Modules

The *Text-Presentation*, *Image-Presentation*, *Video-Presentation*, *Audio-Presentation* and *Animation-Presentation* modules control component presentation (modeled by atomic places in S). They are composed of the following active objects:

- *Presentation* controls the presentation modeled by an atomic place type. There is one *Presentation* class dedicated to the presentation of one type of medium (text, still picture, video, audio and animation).
- *TVI-Control* performs the temporal validity control of the presentation. This object behaves as an alarm. It denotes the *PetriNet-Engine* associated with sub-net S. it also indicates the occurrence of the minimal and maximal duration of the treatment modeled by the atomic place.
- *Alternative-Presentation* replaces the principal presentation in case the latter cannot be totally prepared in a determined time interval.

4.2.3 Button-Presentation Module

The *Button-Presentation* module is responsible for the presentation of a button modeled by a link place type. It is made up of the following active objects:

- *Button* controls the button presentation and handles interaction events of the button represented by the place.
- *TVI-Control* performs the temporal validity control of the presentation.

5 Current State of the Java I-HTSPN Toolkit

A Java I-HTSPN toolkit based on the Java I-HTSPN model is being developed in order to assist the design of Java multimedia applications.

5.1. The Java I-HTSPN Editor

The Java I-HTSPN editor guides the author through a graphical construction of the multimedia document. The Java I-HTSPN editor makes it easy to specify the *Data* and *Presentation* objects as well as the logical and temporal composition of the multimedia document.

We specify *Data* objects within a *Data Specification Window*, a scrolling list of *Data* objects managed by user-commands to add, set-up and remove *Data* objects. For example, the Data Specification window in Figure 7 illustrates how we specify an audio information accessed by URL http://www.inf.ufsc.br/~willrich/audio1.au.

The presentation and conceptual structures of a multimedia document are specified using the HTSPN graphical editor. To build a net, the author can create places, transitions and arcs of the net. He/she also uses dialog window to set up attributes associated with these elements. In particular, the Place Editor Window can be used to specify a *Presentation* object associated with an atomic or link place of the Java I-HTSPN specification. Figure 7 shows how multimedia document presentation and conceptual structures are specified. This figure illustrates the presentation characteristics that apply when *Audio1Data,* specified by *audio1* place, is presented.

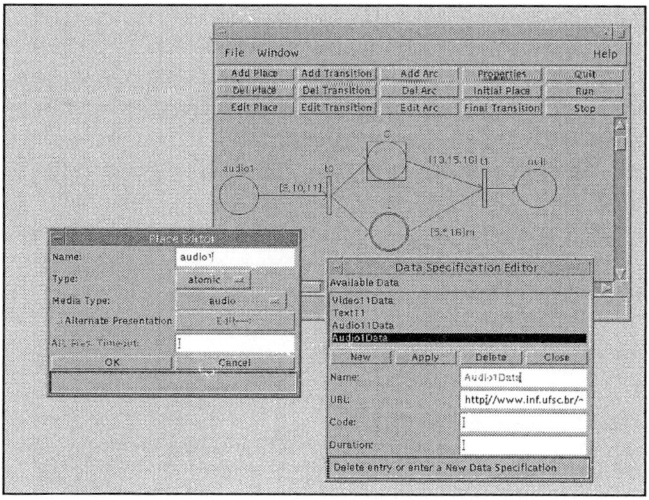

Figure 7. The Java I-HTSPN Editor

5.2 Java I-HTSPN Player

The Java I-HTSPN Player allows the interpretation (presentation) of the Java I-HTSPN specification. This module is implemented as a Java application that uses the Java Abstract Window Toolkit (AWT) and the Java Media Framework API to play the multimedia document. Using the Java I-HTSPN player, the author can really verify "how the document behaves" during its presentation.

The interpretation commands are provided to the author via a main menu. The latter includes the following interpretation commands: read a Java I-HTSPN specification file (generated by the Java I-HTSPN Editor), start the interpretation (presentation) of the loaded specification, and interrupt the interpretation of the document.

The Java I-HTSPN Player is made up of interpretation classes presented in Section 4.2. These classes generate an interpretation structure associated with the Java I-HTSPN specification. The user commands the interpretation structure via the main menu offered by the Interpreter module.

6 Example

VACBI (Video and Audio Computer Based Instruction) [9] is the Computer Aided Learning system developed by Airbus Training for pilot and maintenance staff training. This case study illustrates the use of the design approach based on the Java I-HTSPN model, and highlights its advantages.

The teaching material of VACBI is organized in chapters and modules. The case study in this section relies on the module of the Landing Gear chapter in the flight part. This module has been chosen for both its size and complexity. Figure 8 presents the user interface of the prototype implemented using the Java I-HTSPN toolkit. One can identify the following components:

- wheel and doors graphic representations (to graphically animate this procedure);
- textual instructions to guide students and assist them in case of wrong manipulations;
- sound information, usually repeating text instructions;
- video, such as the landing gear extension still picture sequence;
- a button set to control the procedure executions.

6.1.1 Conceptual Structure Specification

The conceptual structure of the landing gear extension module is specified by a HTSPN made up of 5 sub-nets, 69 places and 61 transitions. This paper presents only one sub-net in Figure 9. For simplicity, we select [∞,., ∞] as default value for all the TVI appearing in the net. This figure depicts the root of the HTSPN specification of the landing gear extension module. Firstly, a set of still ($Pict_i$), texts (Tx_i) and an audio information (Au_1) are presented in parallel with two buttons (*Start* and *End*). The student has the possibility to either start the study (*Start*) or to stop it (*End*). *Start* is a timed link; its temporal validity interval [0,*,20] specifies that this link is automatically triggered if the student does nothing during 20 seconds after its entrance in this module. If the *Start* link is activated, the procedure teaching of the landing gear extension is started (it is specified by composite place *Procedure*). This procedure is presented in parallel with buttons *Restart* and *End*. Thus, during the landing gear extension, the student can restart the study (*Restart* link) or end the presentation (*End* link).

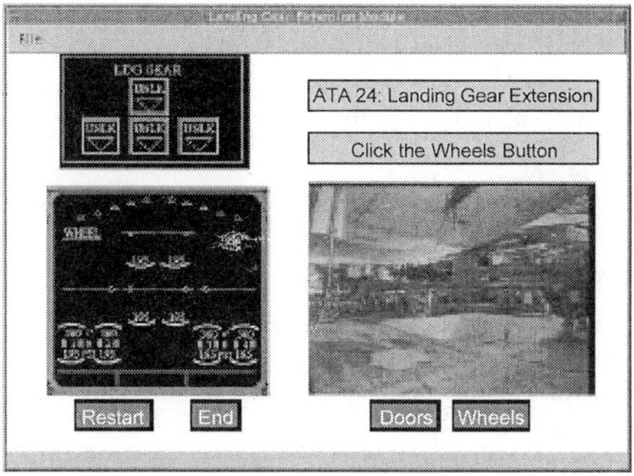

Figure 8. VACBI user interface

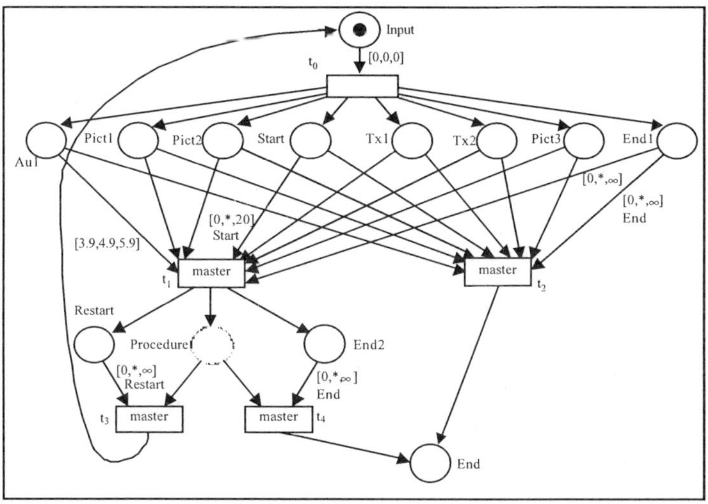

Figure 9. The root of the Java I-HTSPN specification

The HTSPN specification describes the components of the landing gear extension module and the logical and temporal behavior of this module. Multimedia data as well as the module's layout are specified in Java I-HTSPN. Multimedia data are modeled by a set of *Data* objects and presentation characteristics are modeled by a set of *Presentation* objects.

6.1.2 Content Structure Specification

The landing gear extension module has 34 *Data* objects that describe all the used multimedia data: 2 video files, 10 audio files, 9 text files and 13 still pictures. For instance, object *PhotoA340* bellow specifies a still picture that relates to component *Pict1* specified by place Pict1 (Figure 9).

```
StillPicture PhotoA340 {
        URL http://www.inf.ufsc.br/~willrich/htspn/Spec/IMG/A340.gif }
```

6.1.3 Presentation Structure Specification

Besides data, the author also specifies presentation characteristics for each component in the module landing gear extension. Therefore, an object of a *Presentation* class must be associated with each atomic and link type place of the HTSPN specification. This object describes presentation characteristics (including the data information specification) of the presentation modeled by the associated place. For instance, object *Pict1* bellow (*PSStillPicture* class) is associated with place *Pict1* (Figure 9) to specify data and presentation characteristics.

```
PSStillPicture Pict1 {
        Data                     PhotoA340
        Presentation-position    [ 340 175 ] }
```

7 Conclusions

The paper proposed a methodology for the specification and validation of hypermedia documents modeled using a timed extension of Petri nets, a formal technique endowed with both a graphical syntax and formal semantics. Timed Stream Petri Nets, as introduced in [1], have been enhanced with structuring capabilities and ability to take user interactions into account. The new model has been named HTSPN (Hierarchical Time Stream Petri Nets) [6]. It gives ability to check a document against synchronization and timing errors.

An interpreted version of HTSPN, named I-HTSPN, has been proposed in [10]. I-HTSPNs add semantic information to places and transitions in the net. They make it possible to specify presentation details, such as window size and access procedure to the content and presentation characteristics of document components.

The paper proposed and discussed Java Interpreted-HTSPN (Java I-HTSPN), a novel extension designed with automatic generation of Java applications in mind. Main results include a hypermedia document authoring and Java application prototyping methodology, and a toolkit developed in Java. Any operating system or machine on top of which a Java interpreter can run, becomes able to interpret the authoring tool as well as the Java applications derived from the formal model. A HTSPN editor has been prototyped and automatic generation of Java code works too. Validation algorithms are currently under optimization and will be introduced in the tool's new release under development at UFSC, Santa Catarina, Brazil.

First experiences with postgraduate students indicate the latter appreciate to model multimedia scenarios and by extension, hypermedia documents, prior to coding in Java. To our knowledge, temporal interval composition strategies have no counterpart in graphic models accessible on the variety of platforms allowed by the Java language. Further practice is needed to compare automatically generated code with hand-coded one.

References

1. M. Diaz, P. Sénac. Time Streams Petri Nets, a Model for Multimedia Streams Synchronization. In proc. Of the First International Conference on Multimedia Modeling - Vol. 1, Singapore, World Scientific, Tat-Seng Chua & T. L. Kunii (Eds.), pp. 257-273, November 1993.
2. J.P. Coutiat, R.C. de Oliveira. Proving Temporal Consistency in a New Multimedia Synchronization Model. ACM Multimedia'96, Boston, USA, Nov. 1996.
3. F. Halasz, M. Schwartz. The Dexter Hypertext Reference Model. Communication of the ACM 37(2):29-39, February 1994.
4. S.E. Hudson, C.H. Hsi. A Framework for Low Level Analysis and Synthesis to Support High Level Authoring of Multimedia Documents. Graphics Visualization and Usability Center Technical Report GVU-93-14. Georgia Institute of Technology, 1993.
5. T.C.D. Little, A. Ghafoor. Synchronization and Storage Models for Multimedia Objects. IEEE Journal on Selected Areas in Communication 8(3):413-427, April 1990.
6. P. Sénac, M. Diaz, A Léger, P. de Saqui-Sannes. Modeling Logical and Temporal Synchronization in Hypermedia Systems. IEEE Journal on Selected Areas in Communication 14(1):84-103, 1996.
7. P. Sénac. Contribution à la modélisation des systèmes multimédias et hypermédias. Ph.D. dissertation, Université Paul Sabatier, Toulouse, June 1996.
8. R. Steinmetz. Synchronization Properties in Multimedia Systems. IEEE Journal on Selected Areas in Communication, 8(3):401-412, 1990.
9. VACBI Utilization Guide. Aeroformation - Airbus Industrie/Flight Safety.
10. R. Willrich, P. Sénac, M. Diaz, P. de Saqui-Sannes. A Formal Framework for the Specification, Analysis and Generation of Standardised Hypermedia Documents. Third IEEE International Conference on Multimedia Computing and Systems (ICMCS'96), pp. 399-406, Hiroshima, Japan, 1996.

METADATA MANAGEMENT FOR MULTIMEDIA INTERACTIVE TELELEARNING SYSTEM

LEI YUAN, AHMED KARMOUCH
Multimedia & Mobile Agent Research Laboratory
School of Information and Technology Engineering (SITE), University of Ottawa
161 Louis-Pasteur, Ottawa, ON, Canada, K1N 6N5
Tel: 1+(613)5625800 x 6203 Fax: 1+(613)562-5175
Email: lyuan@scs.carleton.ca, karmouch@site.uottawa.ca

This paper describes the system design and the components of a web-based multimedia interactive telelearning system (MITS) with emphasis on metadata management mechanism. Metadata model is defined and exploited in designing the overall architecture to support courseware creating, management, delivery, and learner performance evaluation. Metadata was generated, stored, and utilized to facilitate the search and on-demand presentation of learning objects. Learner preference, performance and progress information is maintained by profile database to make courseware presentation adaptable and more interactive. The system provides a multimedia interactive learning environment with easy-to-search and highly reusable learning objects.

1 Introduction

1.1 TeleLearning: History and Background

The terms "Distance Education" and "TeleLearning" have been used interchangeably by various researchers based on their knowledge and backgrounds. "It puts emphasis on the separation of the learner and the educator in space and/or time, where the volitional control of the learning process is driven by the student rather than the distant teacher" [1].

Distance education came into being in the late 1950's and early 1960's, when broadcasting TV/Radio classes were transmitted to audiences in Europe. This form of educational classes did not provide any sort of interaction or bi-directional communications between students and teacher, which are supported in the traditional classrooms and play very important role. In the late 1970's, newly designed and produced TV series introduced students to new subject matter that was not being taught, so they were considered to be an important complement to the classroom curriculum [1]. Meanwhile, the distance learning trend had been affected by communication technologies, such as Email, to provide some sort of interaction between teacher and students.

From the early 1990's, the extensive research in multimedia information processing and enhanced achievements within networking technologies produced a new era of multimedia information applications, which ambitiously aimed to deliver complex multimedia information to distributed users over networks. One of the areas that exploited the high technology growth is distance education. Thus, the education process is shifting from traditional learning style that is based on lecture-and-book model towards non-traditional learning styles where courses are provided through TV classes, CD-ROM and distributed computer systems. The non-traditional learning styles might lead to a totally different way for learners to acquire knowledge in the near future [2].

Currently, distance education is gaining high interest especially in regions where students are geographically scattered and/or involved by a number of factors that could affect their learning demands. Specifically, it is necessary to address the needs of small rural school districts or under-served urban school districts. Also, some university students may need courses to meet graduation requirements that their own schools are unable to offer, or there is time conflict, so distance education will be beneficial for them.

This paper is organized as follows: the current section provides an overview of the distance education models, distant education participants and their roles. Section 2 gives an introduction to metadata and addresses the importance of metadata management. Section 3, presents our system architecture. In section 4, we describe the metadata model, courseware structure and other data services. Section 5 discusses the system's middle tier applications where metadata is mostly utilized. Finally in section 6, we draw our conclusions and discuss future work.

1.2 Distance Education Models

The traditional "lecture-and-book" education model is still the foundation of education. Broadcasting model and CD-ROM Courseware Model are widely spread but are gradually being replaced by Distributed Computer Based Model.

With the emerging infrastructure and enhanced multimedia information processing technologies, innovative TeleLearning Systems can be designed and implemented to deliver courseware content locally or remotely to distant learners. Courseware is an educational software entity that contains different knowledge components, yet it resembles the objectives of a traditional course. TeleLearning Systems have offered several features to build a seamless education environment. First, these systems aim at making the education process more accessible and reachable by large groups of Learners. Second, because of the achievement within multimedia computing and networking infrastructure, computer–based learning becomes more powerful by integrating multiple media of information into the system and providing more effective and expressive ways to represent knowledge. Third, Telelearning Systems try to present knowledge structure in a form closer to the reality, by using sophisticated multimedia presentation environments. In addition, students are offered a real-time, interactive and reusable information interchange through different platforms. For instance, a student can be easily connected to a teacher or an on-line facilitator to obtain help on a specific topic using e-mail, chat, telephone connections and video conferencing. Furthermore, these systems also provide the ability to come in contact with other students from different social, cultural, economic and experiential backgrounds to discuss topics of similar interests. In other words, sophisticated Telelearning systems involve interactivity between teachers and students, between students and the learning environment, and among students themselves, thus resembling active learning in the classroom [1][5].

Nevertheless, TeleLearning systems are being restricted by networking capabilities and information CODEC methods [3]. Meanwhile, the World Wide Web (WWW), in particular, opens wide the door for offering courses to distant learners. What makes the WWW attractive to an educational institute, is a large communication network to exchange information in two ways; namely, on-line browsing and the courseware package distribution [6].

Currently, several practical and experimental forms of Telelearning systems are being developed and placed on the WWW. For example, IMS Project in the US [4], United Kingdom's Open University, Vancouver's Open Learning Agency, K-12 programs, Project BIO [7], Norway's NKS Distance Education System, etc [1], as well as our TeleLearning System "**MITS**".

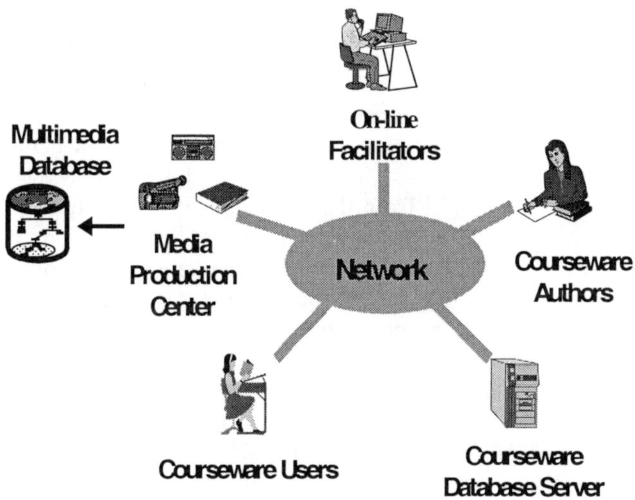

Figure 1: MITS' major components

1.3 Distance Education Participants

As shown in Fig. 1, a lot of participants are involved in distance education environment. Each participant has specific roles to play in order to integrate the distance education environment.

1.3.1 Distance Education Designers

Distance education designers have to consider a variety of issues that could affect the distance education process. The most important issues that need to be considered are: the learner's characteristics and needs, the influence of media upon the education process, strategies to increase interactivity as well as active learning, accessibility, and the new roles of teacher, on-line facilitator and student. Although, technology is an integral part of distance education, any successful distance education system must focus on the instructional needs of the students, rather than on the technology itself [1]. It is also essential to consider students' interests and experiences, educational levels, instructional problems and familiarity with TeleLearning methods and courseware delivery. Thus, designers must build distance education systems that should stand on solid ground. Intelligently designed TeleLearning system can make a significant and positive difference in the way students are learning.

1.3.2 Teacher

In a conventional education environment, teachers interact directly with their students. It is face-to-face or one-on-one communication. Teachers prepare their supported materials, lecture notes, assignments and tests. However, the distant teacher's role has been changed from the controller of a classroom to a consultant who could help students. In distance education, teachers have to be allowed to choose, willing to make choices and qualified to implement their choices effectively [1]. In other words, flexibility should be granted to teachers to develop their personal teaching approach utilizing a variety of options offered by technology [8]. In addition, distant teachers are not in direct classroom contact with their students. Communication is provided through videoconferencing, chat or e-mail and is mediated by a host of team partners, which may include editors, designers, producers, technicians, media specialists, site facilitators and service providers [1]. Therefore, it is essential to prepare a well-set plan and coordinate staff's activities to construct a courseware as well as provide enhanced interaction mechanisms in order to deliver courseware content to distant learners.

1.3.3 On-line Facilitator

The on-line facilitator is an extension of the site teacher, though he/she need not be a teacher [1]. The on-line facilitator monitors and tutors students via e-mail, chat, telephone or video conferencing facilities, as well as provides help when students encounter problems during the learning process.

1.3.4 Courseware Author

Courseware author is responsible for constructing a courseware. It is possible that there is not just one author but many authors for the courseware, including multiple secondary-authors. Courseware authoring is based on a courseware data model, which is generated according to multimedia document model [9][10] and teaching architecture [5]. The proposed courseware data model will be addressed in section 3.

1.3.5 Distant Learners

Distant learners are students who access courseware content and being able to work on their own. They are the center of the learning process. Moreover, they have additional duties to do, e.g. they must learn how to discriminate between "junk" information and "quality" information, to distinguish facts from persuasion, and to understand how the technology itself shapes the information it carries [1]. In other words, distant learners must analyze the information that they are reading, listening and viewing, and then contribute their analysis to distant teachers and/or on-line facilitators. Such analysis and hard work provide more opportunities for students to understand the courseware content and improve learning effects.

2 Metadata of Distance Learning Resources

2.1 Introduction to Metadata

As our needs for learning expand dramatically, the number of distance learning resources continues to grow exponentially over the Internet. Suppose someone wants to take an online course about Java programming, and he/she needs the course to be multimedia-enabled and interactive. To find such a resource, naturally the first thing to do is a search of the World Wide Web with keywords like "multimedia, interactive, Java, course". It won't be a surprise that such a search indicate over 4 million pages that are related. Then the next step is to try these links one after another. Normally such a "try and error" experience is very inefficient and frustrating, and very often it doesn't bring learner the resources with the properties they have in mind. Educators are also especially frustrated by the infinite amount of resources on the Web. The potential of the Web for providing rich materials and experiences is often abandoned as teachers and learners find themselves relying solely on strategies of hits and misses. The result is an over-reliance on serendipity, coupled with persistent filtering [11].

The World Wide Web requires a common methodology and language for describing online learning resources that will facilitate purposeful and effective searching. Just like the multiple categories of the card catalogue system of libraries (e.g. subject, author, title) provide effective means to search for books, online materials also need a descriptive catalogue system: the metadata.

Metadata is "data about data". It's descriptive information about an object. The learning resources are the data; the descriptive information about these resources is the metadata. As mentioned above, the lack of metadata about these resources has produced a critical and fundamental constraint on our ability to discover, manage and use these objects [12]. To address this problem, Metadata allows the user to locate, evaluate, access, and manage available online learning resources. Examples of metadata for learning materials are the title, the author, the targeted learning level, and the educational objectives of the material.

Metadata is distinct from, but intimately related to, its contents. The author of the learning materials might change the title without changing the content. This may alter the user's initial perception of the material, but the data itself remains unchanged. Conversely, the author may change the content, which increases the appropriate learning level of the material. The metadata must then be changed appropriately. Overall, metadata serves as a complement to its contents and reflects the content's attributes to interested users [11].

2.2 *Metadata of Digital Media*

Development of TeleLearning systems also faces the serious problem of how to handle large amounts of digital media. Therefore, there is a need to explicitly capture content information as well as application-specific semantics by means of a variety of metadata, e.g., multimedia indexes, attribute-based annotations, and intentional descriptions, to allow appropriate access to, selection of, and processing of digital media.

One of the key problems to be solved is the development of metadata, that is, the generation, structuring, representation, management, and proper utilization of data or information about data.

Metadata plays a more important role in managing multimedia learning objects than does the management of traditional well-structured data or information retrieval techniques applied to text-only data. Furthermore, different query paradigm, inadequate processing techniques and lack of efficiency in content-based search against multimedia data all make metadata very important in managing multimedia information.

Various multimedia learning objects involve large raw data volume, which has negative consequences on effective management and retrieval of the digital media. Content-based search and retrieval techniques of raw data are very limited in capability, furthermore, it's inefficient to execute queries on large data sets. However, indirect retrieval and processing that utilizes metadata of these digital media seems to be a promising approach to enhance querying and processing as metadata will be much less in volume than the digital media themselves.

Metadata derived or extracted from digital media have the additional advantages of being more amenable to traditional data retrieval and manipulation techniques than the raw digital media. Therefore metadata can be easily applied or analyzed using text processing or information retrieval techniques and database management systems. For fuller exploitation of data and to provide information system interoperability, it is necessary to support correlation of data. It is often more convenient and useful to identify and specify correlation at the metadata level rather than between raw data items.

2.3 XML: Data interchange format

XML can be thought of as a self-explaining data format that is entirely in text, therefore it becomes an ideal mechanism for information exchange between clients and servers. This notion of XML as a common language of the Web opens the door to new opportunities in terms of clients and servers [15].

Internet and Intranet applications open up some possibilities for which XML is an ideal choice. Although there are more efficient data representations, XML text permits very loose coupling between clients and servers. It will become possible for future clients to discover a desired exchange format from a server previously unknown to it and conduct a transaction.

In general, a client-server XML application needs to answer some specific challenges:

- Formatting a message for the server
- Transferring XML between the client and server
- Parsing client message on the server and performing a task
- Dynamically generating an XML document for return to the client

Typically, (client-server) Web applications consist of a browser and a user interacting with it on the client side, and some process on the server generating HTML. The data exchange is synchronous. There is no motivation to use XML in a system like this because the user can view the result of the server process and HTML can serve this purpose very well. But if there is an automated process like a software agent instead of a human being on the client side, the situation changes. In such cases, data has to be separated from a user-friendly presentation. Compared with some other proprietary data interchange format like EDI (Electronic Data Interchange) [13], XML is easier to write, and more important, it can be transmitted over HTTP.

Much has been made of automated agents roving the Internet, performing tasks on behalf of users. XML is an excellent format for agent interactions. It is a simple format, easily implemented on any computing platform. Because XML is tagged, agents expecting only well-formed XML can be extremely fault-tolerant, ignoring tags they do not understand.

2.4 *Metadata in Multimedia Format*

Can metadata itself be multimedia? In most metadata standard, metadata is limited to "tags and labels", which means it is textual and monomedia in nature. However, in many situations metadata, as it is traditionally defined, is not sufficient for managing digital media and multimedia data. For instance, to describe the color of a piece of image as "blend of red, blue, orange" can not give the feeling of "sunrise", while a small icon is more expressive in describing the image.

The incorporation of non-textual information as metadata is also possible. For example thumbnail stills from video could be stored alongside textual elements as descriptors in a searchable index [16]. Presentation of search results could include these thumbnails and also other information such as color histograms. In the JPEG community it has been recognized that the small icon of a large image could be treated as a description criterion [14].

It has also been suggested that database queries aimed at retrieval of sound or images could be made using sound or pictures. For instance with the Query-by-Example paradigm a user searching for a piece of music could give their input by humming the tune, or by making a sketch using a graphics editor when searching for a picture. A great deal of work has already been done on pattern matching on non-text information, which could provide the basis for non-text-based searching. With current technology it is already possible to search video data streams for some specific factors which may align with motion detection or person detection, for example by a change in the color balance parameters of encoded data blocks [16].

Although it is difficult to apply such techniques in an open environment, our definition of metadata should not exclude such possibilities and we conclude therefore that the definition of metadata should not be restricted to either textual or monomedia information.

An alternative of applying multimedia metadata to Query-by-Example paradigm is to only use it to facilitate browsing and navigation of multimedia content. A user may search for a picture by keywords and browse returned thumbnails to judge if it suits the needs. This alternative doesn't involve a lot of complex algorithms and can provide a lot more descriptive information about the image, although it is still limited in capability. However, this method is employed in the metadata management of the MITS system.

3 System Architecture

As is illustrated in the Figure 2, MITS employs a three-tier client/server system architecture, which consists of User Service tier, Business Logic tier (the middle tier), and Data Service tier. Client user interacts with the system using Web Browser through the Internet or Intranet; Data Service tier hosts Courseware Database, Media Content Database, Profile Database and optional Email Server. The middle tier and Data Service tier will be addressed in the next two sections.

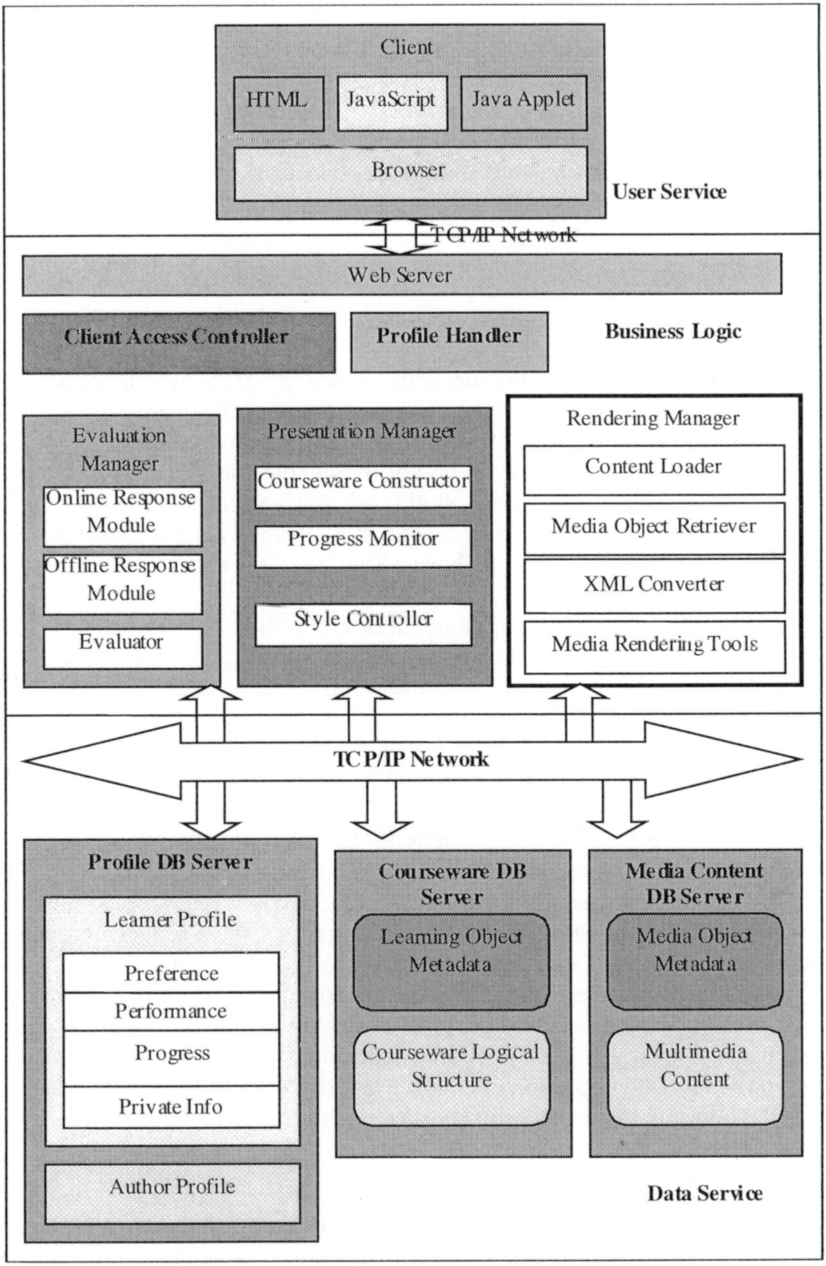

Figure 2: Three-tier System Architecture of MITS

4 The Data Service of MITS

4.1 The Metadata Model of MITS

The metadata model of MITS is based on three concepts:

- Roles of Actors
- Metadata structures
- Actions

4.1.1 Actors in MITS

There are three major actors in the metadata system of MITS, which are defined in terms of different roles involved in the process of learning. They are:

Learners: The Learner entity is an abstraction of a human student. The Learner may represent a single student, a group of students learning individually or collaboratively. They will vary in age, skill level, and learning style.

Authors: authors may create courseware all by themselves from scratch, or take advantage of some existing learning objects. They decide what to teach and the style of teaching.

Service providers: may be an individual or group; may or may not be affiliated with a specific professional organization or institution; may provide content and/or services; contents provided may be original works or may be aggregated works of others (e.g. publisher role).

The same entity in real life can play different roles at the same time, e.g., someone who is an author may also act as a learner and vice versa; similarly, a service provider may also engage in activities associated with the role of an author.

All actors expect the whole system to be easy to use, interoperable, and customizable, but their concerns of the Metadata Management system vary. Authors want to be able to find materials easily, handle copyright restrictions, have more powerful tools for responding to learner requests, and have a greater quality of excellent content and systems from which to create a customized environment. Learners want to find the exact courseware suit their needs, have more authentic learning experiences and personal control over their learning process with multiple paths for gaining the skills and experience they seek. Service providers want to provide richer opportunities for learners, lower deployment costs, and leverage the time and money already invested in various technologies [16].

4.1.2 Actions for metadata

Three major actors all make different use of metadata in the system [16].

Author: Create, capture, prepare, edit (combine, assemble, update, reuse, disassemble, discard), store persistently.

Service Provider: The service provider offers services of information and metadata. Maintain, store, backup, integrate, preserve, archive, discard, validate, quality control, deliver, guard, advertise, sell, etc.

Learner: Learners make use of information resource and metadata during learning process. Their action includes search, locate, selection, achieve right to access, access (read/reuse/forward...), feedback to author/service provider.

4.1.3 Metadata Structures

Metadata structures can be arbitrarily simple or complex and metadata information can be classified according to different criteria. MITS adopted the classification proposal from the IEEE Learning Object Metadata Working Group [12]. This classification identifies nine classes of metadata. We added a tenth only for digital media objects: multimedia metadata.

General: Basic reference to the resource. This class includes an identifier and titles for the resource.

Characteristics: Groups non-contextualized features of the resource, i.e. characteristics that are independent of its educational use, like language (of the user interface or content), descriptions in several languages, the subject presented, etc.

Life Cycle: Characteristics related to the different phases of the resource. This class includes versioning information, lists the authors and the publisher, and may includc information about when the resource ceases to be accessible.

Meta-metadata: Characteristics of the description rather than the resource, such as who created the metadata, under whose authority, using what kind of structure, who the metadata was validated by, etc.

Technical: Technical features of the resource. This class includes data elements on format, size, location, hardware and software requirements, etc.

Use dependent: Features that need to be interpreted according to the use of the resource. An example of such a class groups data elements that are specific to resources being used in an educational context, in which case it includes prerequisites, objectives, target audience, difficulty, pedagogical duration, etc.

Rights Management: Includes data elements on how the resource can be procured, whether or not support is available, pricing, etc.

Relation: Characteristics of the resource in relationship to other resources, such like other versions of a resource, resources referred to, etc.

Annotation: These are comments on the use of the resource.

Multimedia metadata: metatdata in multimedia format. This class applies for digital media objects only.

The data fields for each class are illustrated in table 1.

Metadata Class	Data Fields
General	Identifier, Title, Catalog Entry
Characteristics	Language, Description, Discipline
Life Cycle	Version, Create, Publish
Meta-metadata	Create, Scheme, Validate
Technical	Format, Size, Location Specific, OS Requirement, Installation Remarks, Duration
Educational Use dependent	Role, Description, Prerequisite, Educational objective, Level, Difficulty, Duration
Rights Management	Role, Description, Contact, Support, Conditions
Relation	Kind, Resource
Annotation	Person, Date, Description
Multimedia metadata	Binary data (mainly images)

Table 1: Data Fields for each class of Metadata

4.1.4 Metadata Generation

Metadata values of MITS are created in one of four ways:

1. Automatically generated by the DBMS or authoring tool.
2. Read in from an authoring profile.
3. Selected from a list by the author.
4. Entered directly by the author.

After being generated, metadata of learning objects is maintained by Courseware Database Server. System utilization of metadata will be addressed in Section 5.

4.2 Courseware Database

The design of an appropriate data model for a multimedia information system will ensure smooth navigation and fast access between real-world application entities and multimedia information objects.

In MITS, we have adopted the metadata model mentioned in Section 4 and object-oriented paradigm to design our Courseware Data Model (CDM). The Courseware Data Model describes and represents courseware content by specifying the logical structure and presentation information, in order to facilitate courseware authoring and ensure its delivery to distributed educational groups. In other words,

CDM aims to simplify the creation of courses and facilitate their manipulation into database systems. In addition, the Courseware Data Model incorporates a courseware with teaching architecture, and guides students through the learning process by specifying the presentation information of the courseware content.

The Courseware Data Object Model (CDOM) is the logical structure of courseware. It describes how a courseware is organized into major components and sub-components, as regards Courses and Modules, respectively. As illustrated in Figure 4, three levels of data components are maintained: base components, learning units, and pure container. All data components have the nine classes of metadata but each of them has a different collection of metadata field extensions in addition to the core set.

Since the CDOM is designed based on object-oriented paradigm, it satisfies different object-oriented features. For instance, it supports the "*reuse*" of logical structures and media objects. The courseware logical structure can be reused to create a new courseware by using the same learning object in constructing different courses.

Base Components are a group of granular learning objects. Each of them can reference one or more media objects stored in Multimedia Content Database. In another words, they contain learning specific metadata of media objects, which differentiate them from ordinary multimedia objects. Base Components are highly reusable: each of them can be referenced by one or more Learning Units at the same time. Authors can create new Learning Units with existing Base Components directly, or after some modification to suit different real-life semantics. MITS Base components include:

- Audio clip
- Video clip
- Image
- Graph
- Text block
- Animation
- Question/Answer block
- Downloadable Files

What deserves more description is Question/Answer block. In early approach of MITS this type is not included. This type of data object provides a template so authors can create some questions with answers for each learning module to enhance the interactivity. Currently only multiple-choice questions are available.

Learning Unit is a kind of container type. Each Learning Unit references one or more Base Components, and some spatial, temporal or behavioral relationships are defined. Learning Units can be very well mapped into real-life entities. This group includes:

- Notes: Mainly composed of static media like text blocks, images and graphs. No interaction provided. Notes are easy to author but notes-only courses won't bring learners with impressive learning experience because of the lack of interaction and it's linear nature.

- Online Instruction: Well-designed animation with necessary audio and video support. The authoring of Online Instruction involves more work than other objects in this group. Authors tend to make a great deal of reuse of this type of object.
- Presentation: Composed of audio clips, video clips, text block and images. Spatial and temporal relationships must be specified for final layout. Presentation can be specified in SMIL format. User interaction includes VCR-like control: play, fast forward, rewind, and stop.
- Assignment: consists of static media like text block and image.
- Exam: a group of Question/Answer blocks related to the corresponding learning module. Authors can reuse existing Q/A blocks to construct new exams, or create new Q/A blocks themselves.

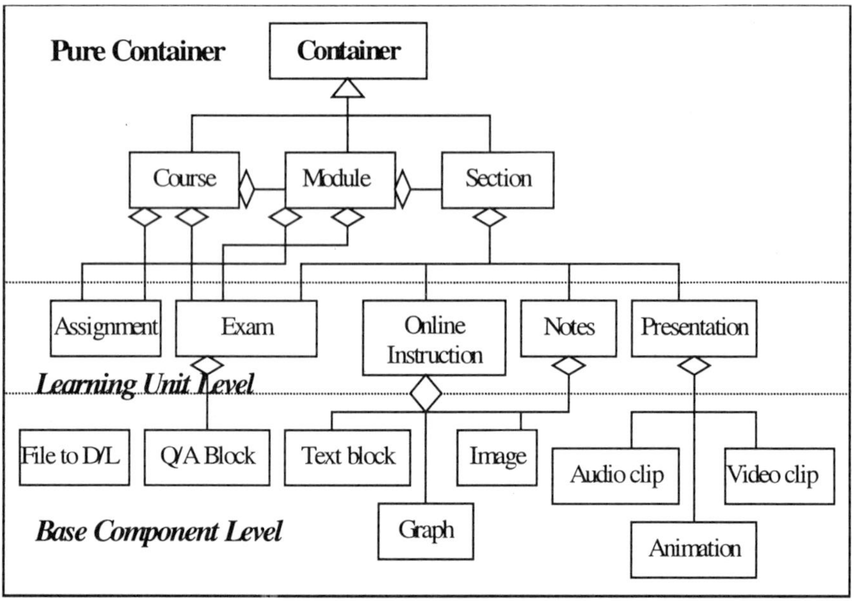

Figure 3. Courseware Data Object Model

The highest level is Pure Container. This group includes Course, Module, and Section. Courses are organized into multiple Modules, which are in turn composed of Sections, although sometimes a Module has no Section. This level of objects is more context-related. Generally speaking, Pure Containers are not as reusable as

Learning Units and Base Components. Authors often design and create Pure Containers based on a large quantity of Base Components and Learning Units.

4.3 Multimedia Content Storage

The design of such information systems starts with a media content production phase where new contents are created from scratch, or by importing and editing existing ones, and stored on servers to allow their sharing and reuse by a maximum of users. In our system, we distinguish archiving servers (for media contents long-term storage) from media contents' servers (for contents' real-time delivery to users). We also distinguish between the courseware DB server, which provides database management systems services to the TeleLearning applications, from the application server which implements more specific and end user-oriented functionality.

The consideration of synchroneous media contents (video, audio and animation) and their interactive presentation in real-time put new requirements on content storage and delivery servers' capacity and performances. Media content servers store the subset of contents which are frequently or recently accessed. They must be equipped with storage devices of very fast access time and must have a very high throughput capacity. Contents which are not frequently accessed or not accessed recently are stored on the archive servers which must present a very high capacity storage devices but not necessarily of rapid access time.

Media content servers maintain Databases of archives' media content indexing information (contents' semantic and external descriptions). Media contents referenced by courseware documents and requested by a user, at presentation time, are searched locally and if they are not found, they are loaded from the archiving servers. Media content servers deliver a content to the user through the distribution network, using the RTP protocol [3] and control its presentation by adapting their throughput according to media type and the user's interactions (fast forward, pause, etc.).

5 Middle Tier Components

5.1 Client Access Controller

Client Access Controller is responsible for user authenticity check and user session management. It checks the user login request against Profile. Once the login request is validated, a separate session is created for each authenticated user.

5.2 *Profile Handler*

Profile handler is a data access component works like a bridge between other middle tier components to Profile Database. Other components can not access Profile Database directly, instead, all requests are handled by Profile Handler.

5.3 *Evaluation Manager*

The existence of Evaluation Module makes the TeleLearning system different from other online multimedia entertainment. It is the major component that constructs the feed back loop in learning process. The Evaluation process uses the metadata of Learning Content to provide context to the Learner's response to determine the appropriate Evaluation. For example, a Learner is expected to select an answer from a multiple choice question and the correct answer is "B", but the Evaluation process has no context that "B" is the correct answer -- the metadata of Learning Content provides the context ("question #1234, the correct answer is B") to correlate the correct response (e.g., the selection of "B"). The Evaluation Module receives the Learner's response to the questions provided with courseware, then query the courseware database for metadata of the Exam and Q/A blocks in order to assess learner performance. Performance information is then sent to the Presentation Manager. At the same time, the Evaluation stores Performance information in the Profile Database.

5.4 *Presentation Manager*

Presentation Manager is the kernel of the middle tier applications. Its functionality includes:

- Negotiates the Learning Style with the Learner.
- Determine the appropriate Learning Content.
- Generate treatment to learner performance.
- Utilize Performance Information from Evaluation Module and Profile Database to make courseware adaptable to learner requirement.
- Determine appropriate content (e.g., current lesson, and schedule of lessons) by integrating Preference information, the Learner's Performance information (past history, future objectives), and the availability of learning materials (searched and retrieved via Index).

Presentation Manager consists of Progress Monitor, Style Controller and Courseware Constructor. Progress Monitor simply records the Learner's learning progress information and stores it to Profile Database. Style Controller is responsible for preference negotiating with learners. When learner logs on the system for the first time, it accepts learner selection for preference information and stores into Profile Database. Later in learning process, it will first query the metadata of learning objects to determine if these preferences can be satisfied. If not, it will start the negotiating process again until conflict is eliminated; otherwise it will let Courseware Constructor to decide learning contents.

Courseware Constructor determines the Learning Content and format for courseware presentation. It requests and receives Performance and Progress information from the Profile Database. Typically, historical information is retrieved, but current information may be available as well from Evaluation Manager. Combining these with preference information and context information from Style Controller, Courseware Constructor determines the appropriate learning content to present. Constructed learning content structure is sent to Rendering Manager to be delivered to learner in multimedia format.

5.5 Rendering Manager

Courseware Rendering Manager is responsible for rendering course contents in the format of an HTML page. Courseware Rendering Manager is composed of three modules: Content Loader, XML Converter, and Media Object Rendering Tools.

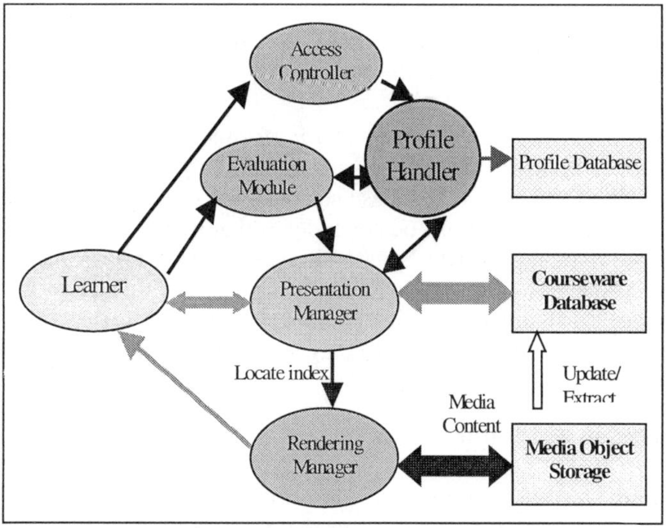

Figure 4: System Data Flow

Rendering Manager is composed of three modules: Content Loader, XML Converter, and Media Object Rendering Tools.

Content Loader queries media content archive database and gets the media objects. Texts are retrieved to construct the XML Data Island. For other media types like images and videoclips, locator index get from their metadata are applied instead of the media itself. These textual data are organized into XML format and will be sent to XML Converter. Other media are not retrieved, instead, a request to

Multimedia Content Server is embeded in the <OBJECT> or <EMBED> tags of HTML page dynamically generated.

Courseware Loader accepts "play back" requests from Courseware Explorer, gets the locator of media objects and the presentation template of courses from Courseware Database, then asks Media Object Retriever to retrieve necessary static media contents (texts, images, etc.) from the media contents database. XML Converter detects the capability of client Web browser and converts XML data into HTML, or sends XML Island in HTML directly. References to continuous media objects are included in generated pages inside <EMBED> or <OBJECT> tag and will be retrieved and streamed directly from the media contents server to the learner's terminal upon the learner's request, at presentation time.

Media Object Rendering Tools are a group of Java applets to help render media objects such as streamed audio, video and SMIL documents.

As illustrated in Figure 4, generally, a full cycle for learning content online presentation is described below.

Step #1: Learner logs on to system.

Step #2: The Presentation Manager negotiates the Learning Style with the Learner.

Step #3: The Presentation Manager receives Preference, Progress and Performance information from the Profile Database to support the decision-making process.

Step #4: Based on the Progress and Performance information, the Presentation Manager sends Query to the Courseware Database to search for appropriate learning materials. The Courseware Database searches learning object metadata and returns Content Indexes, i.e., a list of Locator Indexes that match the search query.

Step #5: The appropriate Locator Indexes (e.g., a lesson plan) are sent to the Rendering Manager to delivery to Learner.

Step #6: Evaluation Manager receives learner response, queries Courseware Database and notices Presentation Manager of Learner Performance. Go to Step #4.

6 Conclusion and Future Work

In summary, distance education is a highway to 21st century learning styles, which might be entirely different from those of today. The Multimedia Interactive Telelearning System that is presented in this paper, aims to build a seamless education environment that supports the delivery of electronic courses to distributed users over the network. The system also aims to combine the learning theory and the emerging technology for facilitating the education process of scattered students. Thus, the increased popularity of the Internet and its usage as a communication technology has offered a suitable opportunity to develop such a TeleLearning system in order to help students to access courses from any access point at any time.

However, As the number of learning resources over the Internet continues to grow exponentially and especially as our needs for learning expand equally dramatically, the lack of this information or metadata about these objects has produced a critical and fundamental constraint on our ability to discover, manage and use these objects. To address this problem, TeleLearning systems must provide effective metadata management mechanism to enable efficiency searching, evaluating, and utilization of Learning resources. Metadata management played a key role in the design and implementation of MITS. MITS adopted and extended the metadata standard proposed by IEEE LTSC Learning Object Metadata working group and focused on the generation and utilization of metadata in middle tier applications. In order to provide an optimum learning experience, learner profile information is also collected and utilized by the system to dynamically generate adaptable courseware.

In the future, the metadata management of MITS will be refined to satisfy more user requirement, which includes:

- To enable the development of learning objects in units that can be combined and decomposed in meaningful ways.
- To enable computer agents to automatically and dynamically compose personalized lessons for an individual learner.
- To complement the direct work on standards that are focused on enabling multiple Learning Objects to work together within open distributed learning environment.

Based on the client-server architecture, another major area of research is to investigate the adoption of **mobile-agent** architecture in designing and developing an enhanced version of the system, in order to serve a large number of distributed users.

REFERENCES

1. L. Sherry, "Issues in Distance Learning", *International Journal of Distance Education*, Volume 1, Number 4, September 1996, pp. 337-365.
2. R. Wang, and A. Karmouch, "A Broadband Multimedia Telelearning System", Proceedings of 5th Int. IEEE Symposium on HPDCMCE, August 1996, Syracuse, USA.
3. R. Wang, "A Broadband Multimedia Telelearning System ", Master Thesis, June 1996, Ottawa, Canada
4. "IMS Project", http://www.imsproject.com
5. R. C. Schank, "Active Learning through Multimedia", IEEE Multimedia, Volume 1, Number 1, Spring 1994, pp. 69-78.
6. C. Vieville, "Organising Distance Learning Process thanks to Asynchronous Structured Conversations", *Proceedings of WebNet'97,* November 1997, Toronto, Canada.
7. T. Ingebritsen, G. Brown, and J. Pleasants, "Teaching Biology on the Internet", Proceedings of WebNet'97, November 1997, Toronto, Canada.

8. Office of Technology Assessment, "Power on New Tools for teaching and Learning", US. Congress Library, OTA-SET-379, Washington DC, USA.
9. J. Emery, and A. Karmouch, "A Playback Schedule Model for Multimedia Documents", *IEEE Multimedia*, Volume 3, Number 1, Spring 1996, pp50-61.
10. N. Hirzalla, O. Megzari, and A. Karmouch, "An Object-Oriented Data Model and A Query Language for Multimedia Database", *IEEE ICECS*, December 1995, Amman, Jordan.
11. "Introduction to metadata", http://www.imsproject.org/metadata/Mdintro.html
12. IEEE LTSC Draft Document, "Learning Object Metadata, v2.5", 14-December-1998.
13. "XML and EDI", http://www.xmledi.com
14. Val Jones, "Draft Deliverable 1: Model for Metadata for Multimedia Information", CEN/ISSS - MMI Workshop, Sep. 1998, Buffalo, USA.

SQL EXTENSION FOR SUPPORTING MULTIMEDIA DATA

JUNGHWA LEE, YOOHYUN PARK, KYONGSOK KIM
Department of Computer Science, Pusan National University
Pusan, 609-735, South Korea.
{jhlee, yhpark, gimgs}@asadal.cs.pusan.ac.kr

As the importance and utilization of multimedia data increase, we need to study representing and processing multimedia data within databases. Especially, to process multimedia data within databases, we need to precisely model multimedia data, to define data types and operations, and to make up query language supporting them. However, since most previous studies are dependent on specific media or defined multimedia data without using formal modeling techniques, it is hard to reuse or extend the results of these studies. Therefore, in this paper, we modeled multimedia data using OMT so that we can support multimedia within databases. We also propose an extended SQL, MMSQL (MultiMedia SQL), which can efficiently query stored multimedia data.

1 Introduction

As the user's need of multimedia data increases, the study on how to process the multimedia data in the computer is in progress vigorously. Since 1990s the development of internet and WWW (World Wide Web) has caused the common users to use multimedia data widely. So its importance has increased daily.

The traditional data processing methods have many difficulties in processing multimedia data that are characteristics of conceptually complex structure and large capacity. Because managing multimedia data in databases is indispensable to process large amounts of data effectively, DBMS must present the supports for multimedia data, such as storage structure for large volumes, multimedia data types and operations, and queries. Recently many studies have been under way to solve these requirements and most DBMS developed these days support multimedia data. But except some of commercial systems, most systems only support the storage structures that store multimedia data into the existing database systems. There are a few studies on how to express and query the multimedia data. Especially multimedia data require new data type such as text, image, audio, and video. And each of data have temporal and spatial relationship each other. So in order to express multimedia data very well above all, data modeling which reflect the characteristics of multimedia data is indispensable[1,2,3,4]. But most of the previous studies are dependent on specific application or defined multimedia data without using formal modeling techniques, it is hard to reuse or extend the results of these studies[5,6,7].

Because proper organization and structuring of multimedia information through data modeling help us better understand it, we must do data modeling before implementing application system. The key challenge in data modeling is to find a logical representation for the entities of interest. Among many methodologies proposed for multimedia information modeling, the object-oriented approach has seen more attention, mostly due to the fact that it can hide the internal representation and implementation details and emphasize the interrelationships between entities. It also supports reuse or extension[8].

So this paper has studied the method that will be used in more applications by using the proven data modeling techniques in classifying and defining the multimedia data.

Also we extend SQL, standard query language used widely, so that multimedia data defined in this paper can be processed efficiently. The extended SQL provides how to define the multimedia data types and represent temporal and spatial relationships, which exist within multimedia object or between multimedia objects.

The constitution of this paper is as following. Section 2 inspects the previous studies relating with data modeling and extension of query language for multimedia data. Section 3 describes our data modeling for giving effective support to multimedia data within database. Section 4 explain about SQL extension and section 5 says conclusion and future works.

2 Related Research

To manage multimedia data in database, it is necessary to define data types which is logical structure for data in database, to define operations for new data types, and to make natural expression of the temporal and spatial relationship existing in separate object internally and externally. So more systematic modeling is needed. In this section, we inspect the previous studies of the multimedia data modeling and models to express temporal and spatial characteristics within multimedia object or between multimedia objects.

If the users can store multimedia data into databases and query them, query languages are extended to support the data types and operations specified during data modeling stages. In this section, we also inspect the previous studies related to extension of query language.

2.1 Studies on Data Modeling

Generally data modeling is to classify the stored data into the set of logical structures, and to define operations of manipulating them. If it can be called data object modeling, multimedia data needs other additions, that is, data relationship modeling to express temporal and spatial relationships as well as data object modeling.

2.1.1 Data Object Modeling

The studies on definition of multimedia data's logical structure classes are constituted as part of the ones that give shape to multimedia application system[8,9]. These studies are focused on multimedia objects that are the target of application system and on definition of their attributes. So they cannot make good reflection on the characteristics of media data or not be reused in other application system because they only define the objects and attributes without object modeling stages for definition of media data. Also these studies cannot analyze the semantically common attributes originated from organic combination between media data. So, they can cause the problems such as redundant expression of attributes.

The modeling studies on definition of multimedia data object can be seen in [10, 11]. These studies classify the text, image, audio, and video, according to the temporal and spatial characteristics and define the attributes of individual media object and operations. The object's attributes defined in these studies express the physical features of objects, but they are in lack of definition of attributes for using in other applications.

2.1.2 Data Relationship Modeling

Mostly general modeling techniques deal with whole system aspects, but synchronization, which is important portion in multimedia application system, needs to be modeled more precisely. Synchronization can be precisely modeled with Time-line model, TPN, OCPN, and etc.

All events are expressed on absolute time line in Time-line model. Synchronization information between data can be expressed properly on screen by start and end time points [12].

Fig. 1 describes the example of synchronization expressed by using Time-line model.

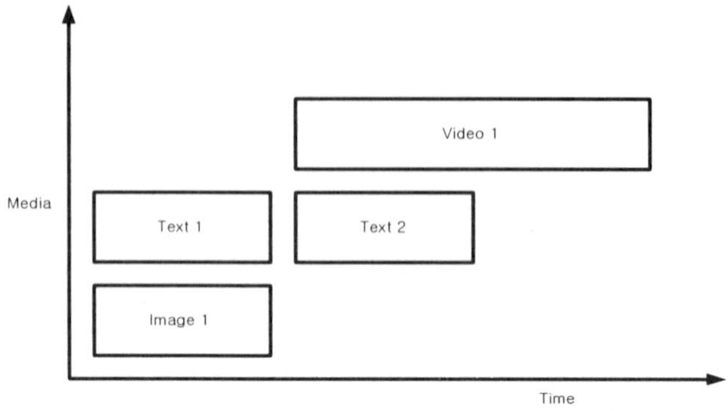

Figure 1. Example of Time-line Model

TPN extends petrinet to express temporal relationships between media data[13]. In TPN model, each synchronization information is expressed according to 13 temporal relationships defined by Allen. TPN model can express synchronization information more effectively than Time-line. But, it provides no way to express spatial information between media data and can express only binary temporal relationships.

Fig. 2 describes the example of synchronization which is expressed by using TPN model when video data are simultaneously played with text and audio data. Only when all of three events are finished, the next stage can be played the same as in petrinet[14].

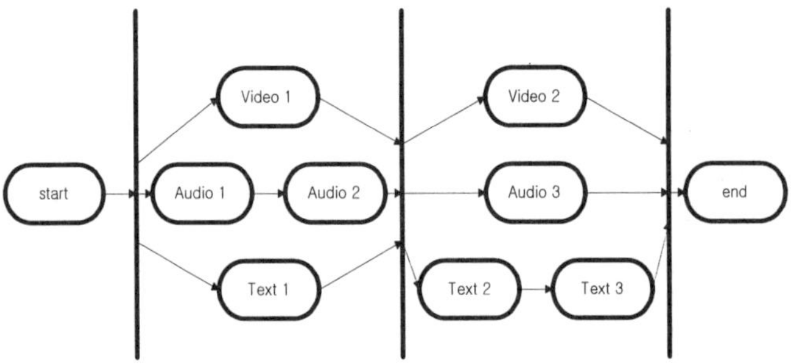

Figure 2. Example of TPN model

When multimedia data are used in application systems, they are more used as combined by temporal and spatial relationships between media data than used as individual. So it is necessary to study the models that define the structure of temporal and spatial relationships and express them conceptually.

OCPN (Object Component Petri Net) model is the method that expresses 13 temporal relationships defined by Allen by extending petrinet. OCPN can express temporal information between media data in multi-dimensional relation and spatial information between media data[15]. Fig. 3 express temporal and spatial information between media data using OCPN model.

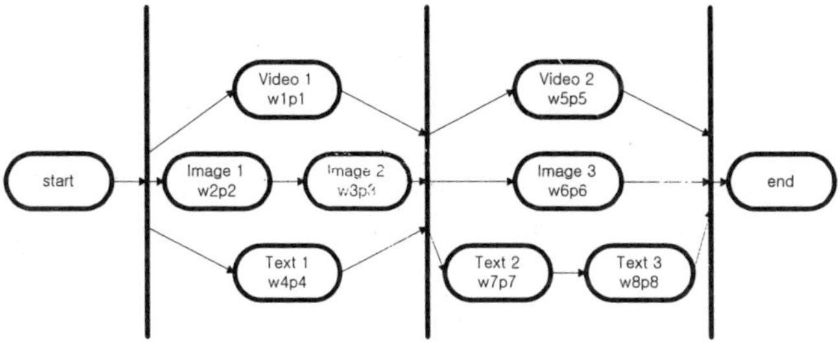

Figure 3. Example of OCPN model

[11] specified temporal and spatial relationships between multimedia data based on object oriented model. And it also defined temporal and spatial operations to express those relationships between objects.

2.2 *Studies on query language for multimedia data*

With the above studies, query language for multimedia data must provide the methodology to specify temporal and spatial relationship between multimedia data. The development of query language is under way as form of extending SQL, which is used as standard query language in database, with adding temporal and spatial keyword or developing query language which has new structure.

As one of studies extending SQL for multimedia data, ISO(International Organization for Standardization) is developing SQL3, object-oriented database standard query language.

Trigger, recursive query expressions, boolean type, enumeration type, cursor, and stored procedure are added or expanded in SQL3. Also abstract data type, inheritance, parameterized type, type generator, and function and procedure described by SQL will be supported. But SQL3 only describes storage representation of multimedia data and there are few studies on how to express associated relationships between multimedia data.

OVID is the study on query language and user interface, which are used in object-oriented video database system[6]. VideoSQL is the video query language used in OVID. It gives the user the ability to specify video objects where and when to be shown by extending SELECT clause of SQL. But it does not contain expressions for specifying temporal relationships between video objects. Also it is dependent on video data because it is developed as the query language of only OVID. So it has demerit that cannot be used for querying other multimedia data.

The studies on query language that has new language structure are [16, 17]. But the user will have difficulty in constructing queries using these query languages because they have different structures from SQL, standard query language.

Multimedia query language must enable the users to specify not only queries retrieving attributes of multimedia data being stored in database but also queries including temporal and spatial relationships within media data and between the multimedia data to be presented. So multimedia data modeling, which defines the attributes and the kinds of media and prescribes temporal and spatial relationships between media data, must precede the design of multimedia query language.

It is impossible to obtain the abilities of specifying temporal and spatial relationships as well as the perfect definition of media's attributes without the multimedia data modeling. In this paper, we model multimedia data and propose MMSQL, query language for multimedia data. MMSQL is defined to satisfy requirements of multimedia query language based on our modeling results.

2.3 OMT (Object Modeling Techniques)

When modeling multimedia data, the characteristics of them that have complicate relationships and complex structures make it more appropriate to model them using object-oriented data model[5,18,19,20]. Multimedia data that are modeled by object-oriented methodology, which guarantee reusability and extensibility, can be used in much more multimedia applications. The representative technique of object-oriented data modeling is OMT suggested by Rumbaugh[21].

Object modeling in OMT describes the kinds of objects, relationships between objects, attributes of objects, and operations of objects. It also makes visual expression using object diagram which includes object classes and etc. Object modeling provides essential framework needed for dynamic modeling or functional modeling. An object class defines the operation for the object itself and the attribute values that individual object instance preserves. Its higher class defines common attributes and operations that object classes have.

It is needed for the users to specify the attributes and the operations of objects, and relationships between objects in query language. We will analyze the expected queries, make up data dictionary including discrimination of objects and definition of terms, refine each stage repeatedly and defines perfect object according to object modeling. OMT have already been used for geographical information systems to store great capacity data objects[22].

3 Multimedia Data Modeling

As it was mentioned before, the complexity and relevance of multimedia make OMT modeling more desirable to define certain data. The objects which are well-defined by OMT can be used for various application because they can be transplanted and reusable. Therefore, in this paper, we use the most widely used one among OMT modeling methods to model multimedia data.

In this section, the process of modeling multimedia data through OMT will be shown. Object modeling represent data into a static structure by discerning object, and defining the attributes of an object and the relationship between objects through data dictionary. In this step, defined object and its attributes come to be defined into a new data type in database. Fig. 4 show the steps modeling object.

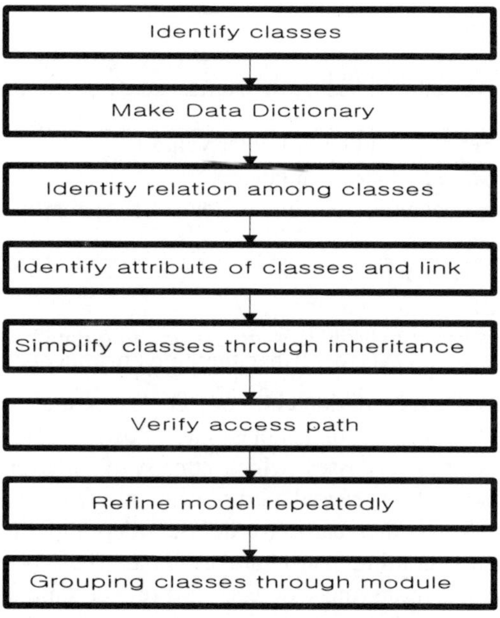

Figure 4. The Steps of Object Modeling

Identifying different categories of user queries about multimedia data is very important because user's demands are expressed by queries. Expected queries about multimedia data which are processed in database, are divided as follows.

Table 1. The Division of Queries about Multimedia Data

Types of queries	Examples of queries
Query about attribute	Retrieve this image's resolution
Query about content	Retrieve clips with a sunset scene
Query about structure	Retrieve video's title having this frame

After classifying queries, we can define attributes of multimedia objects for satisfying user's demands in those queries. For example, we must contain attributes, which are file format, and size, etc. of an image, in Image class for querying about its physical attributes. By previous step, we define representative classes for multimedia objects and construct the data dictionary as shown in Table 2.

Table 2. Class definition in the data dictionary

Class	Description
Text	Stream of characters
Image	Set of pixel that has color value
Graphic	Stored as script language. It becomes to image data if rendering by application programs.
Audio	Sound data
Video	Stream of images. It can synchronize with text or audio data

Multimedia data can be divided into object classes such as text, image, graphic, video and audio, etc. and each object class has its own proper attributes. Video and audio classes are complex classes, which consist of video and audio clip classes, respectively. Because clip is a small part of original video or audio object, but has a logical distinction from other parts, we define video and audio clip classes. And video and audio are continuous stream of data. Therefore they have a strong relation to time in presenting these objects. To reflect temporal properties of video and audio objects, we define new Temporal Media class from generalizing video and audio classes. That class has attributes and methods related to temporal properties of video and audio.

Multimedia data have common attributes such as the title, the author, and creation date of them. So we define Media class, which has those attributes, as a root of all other classes using class generalization.

Following Fig. 5 shows the inheritance relationships of each media class which is made as a result of object modeling

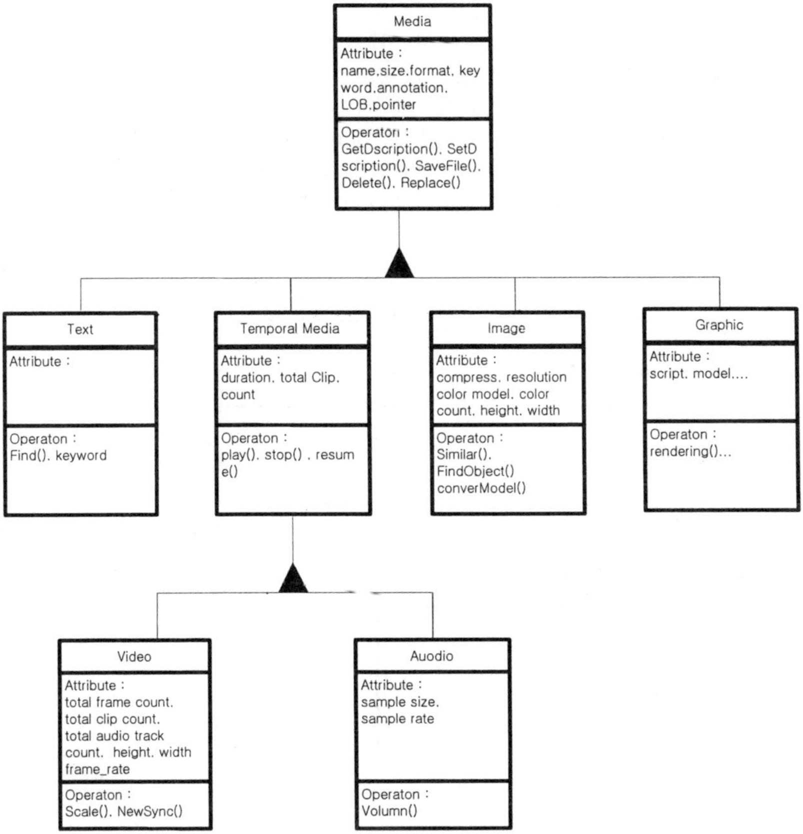

Figure 5. Inheritance Relationship among Media Class

In finger 5, we define temporal media class to express temporal information in continuous media such as video, audio. It has duration, total clip count as temporal attributes, and has play(), stop(), resume() as temporal method.

Specially, video class has information than any other classes. In Video class, meta information such as a title, author, or production date must expressed. In addition, video also provides other information, such as the counts of audio tracks, the happening of the activities, events, and the shapes of object. The nature of video information is different from textual data since video has both temporal and spatial dimensions.

Fig. 6 is the object diagram which defines relations between image and graphic class, necessary attributes and operations. Image class represents the instance of object class which is extracted to save information for content-based search. Object class has information about object appearing in image such as domain, name, texture, color and out line pointer set. Out line pointer is stored as pointers set object's shape or vectors represent them. If it stored as pointers set, we calculate the object's region, location and length of object's out line. The location is used to topology among objects. Recently researches about retrieve objects from image have progressed and if object retrieved from image, object's information can be stored into that class. Graphic class saves only the script data save script data, the set of vector representing object, which can be changed into image data through rendering operation.

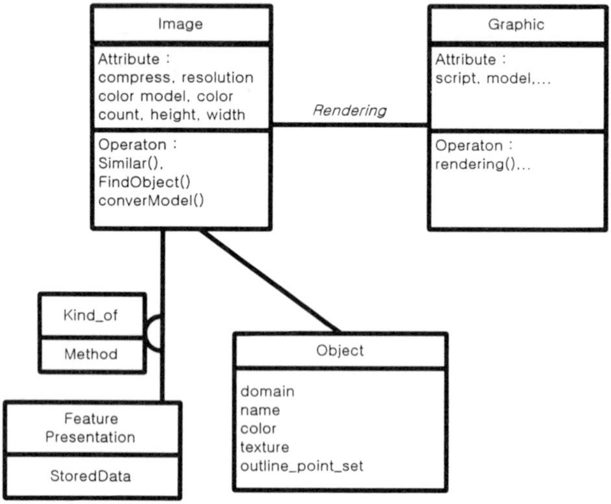

Figure 6. Image Class

The proper attributes of image class include compress method, resolution, height, width, color model, color count, scale which can control resolution and so on. A number of currently studied image search methods such as similarity search operation, do not take a real-time, but take a real-time processing by saving metadata which can be representative of image data. For example, metadata such as histogram (color distribution) of total image, signature can be maintained. Therefore, this paper defines feature_presentation class which is for saving object information which is represented in image.

As Fig. 7 shows, video sets clip, the set of frames within the same scene, as a basic unit for motivation, and uses activity and event to show the contents of a clip.

A video clip can include various activities, and each of these activities consists of the set of various events. For example, activity of driving consists of events of putting on the accelerator, changing gears, and applying the break and so on.

In most case, video is synchronized with media such as text and audio. Text is used to describe caption for video data, the title of video, actors and actress listed at the beginning and all cast listed at end of a film, and so on. At this moment, text should be able to describe the location of showing on the video screen (left, right, top, bottom), the effect (raising, blink, fade out, fade in) etc. Audio represents itself as speech, sound effect, background music, etc. The synchronization of these is realized by describing video's frame number that start (sFrame) with audio or text and finish (eFrame).

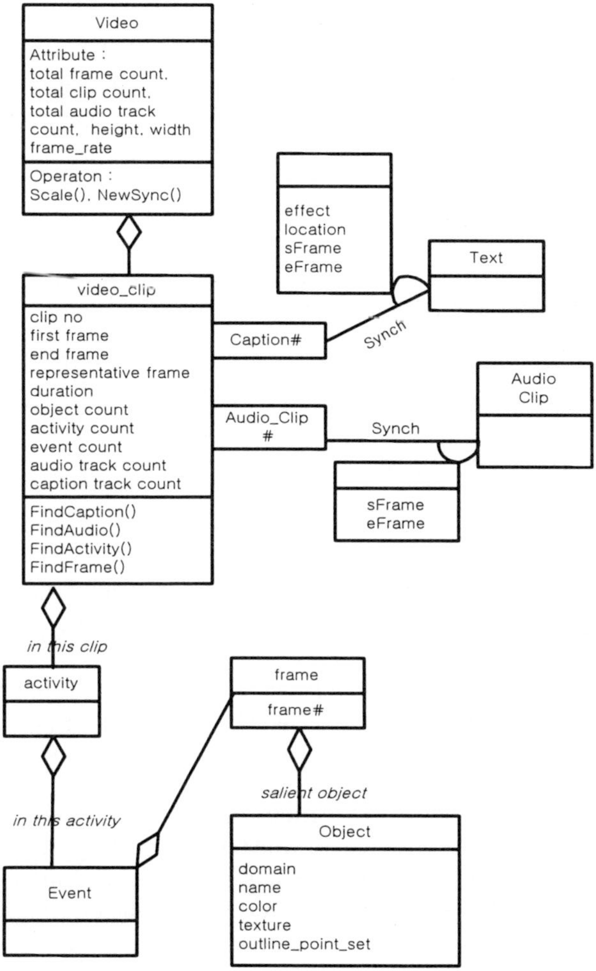

Figure 7. Synchronization among Video, Audio, Clip and Caption

4 SQL Extension for Supporting Multimedia Data

4.1 The Support of Temporal and Spatial Operator for multimedia data

The internal constituents of each media object have temporal and spatial relationship with one another, and users should be able to query this. To do this, it is necessary to define operators which are used to query the temporal and spatial relationship of the object. Following is about temporal and spatial operator for multimedia data.

Temporal relations among objects can be expressed 13 cases by Allen's model. Temporal relations among objects, as in Fig. 8, define reserved words which represent the characteristics of temporal relations and realize them as operator to be used in query words.

```
<tp_exp> ::= <tp_obj> <tp_cond> <tp_obj>

<tp_cond> ::=  EQUAL|BEFORE|AFTER|MEET|METBY|OVERLAP
               |OVERLAPEDBY|DURING|INCLUDE|START
               |STARTEDBY|FINISH|FINISHEDBY

<tp_obj> ::= <query>|<clip>|FRAME|CAPTION

<clip> ::= VIDEO_CLIP|AUDIO_CLIP
```

Figure 8. The syntax of the temporal condition within the media

Allen's temporal relations consists of equal, before, meet, overlap, during, start and finish relations, and in reverse of them, after, metby, overlapedby, include, startedby and finishedby relations.

These temporal relations can be used among the frame in the step of object modeling, caption, video_clip and audio_clip. The end and the beginning of audio_clip can be expressed as "AUDIO_CLIP AFTER VIDEO_CLIP" according to the grammar of Fig. 8.

Media like video or image can consist of various objects which have spatial relations such as topology and direction. The query which is suggested by this paper defines operator to be able to express the spatial relation of objects, and to be used in extracted query by a user. Fig. 9 shows the grammar of extended query which supports spatial relation of objects.

```
<sp_expr> ::= <sp_obj> <sp_cond> <sp_obj>
<sp_cond> ::= <topological_cond>
| <directional_cond>
<topological_cond> ::= TOUCH|CONTAINS
            |OVERLAP|DISJOINT|EQUAL
<directional_cond> ::= LEFT|RIGHT|ABOVE|BELOW
            |LEFT_ABOVE|LEFT_BELOW
            |RIGHT_ABOVE|RIGHT_BELOW
 <sp_obj> ::= <query> | OBJECT
```

Figure 9. The syntax of the spatial condition within the media

As well-known, spatial operator can be divided into topological information and directional information. Topology among objects can be expressed into touch, contain, overlap, disjoint and equal relations. Also, direction among objects can be expressed into left, right, above, below, left_above, left_below, right_above and right_below relations.

4.2 The Disposition of Media According to the Result of Query

When different media are extracted by query, users want to see them as forms they need. Generally user wants to specify temporal and spatial relationship also. So, in this paper we suggest the method which uses SQL into which a new clause PRESENT is added like Fig. 10.

```
SELECT ...
  FROM ...
  [WHERE ...]
  [PRESENT present_spec {,present_spec}]
```

Figure 10. The form of SELECT sentence with PRESENT

As Fig. 11 shows, in PRESENT clause, spatial condition of each media is represented by WIN_POS() function. Spatial condition-defined media is shown according to temporal relations. The start time of play is expressed by TIME_POINT() function, continuous media such as video and audio by PLAY() function, and discontinuous media such as image and text by DISPLAY() function. Timestamp in PLAY() and DISPLAY() represents only the delayed time from the start time of play or the time which is shown after the delayed time. Mode in PLAY() function decides the play speed of continuous media. A minus in play speed means backward play and a plus means forward play.

```
<present_spec> ::= <spatial_layout>|<synchronize>
<spatial_layout> ::= WIN_POS (ID,POINT,POINT)
| WIN_POS (ID,<alignment>)
<alignment> ::= CENTER | RIGHTALIGN |LEFTALIGN
<synchronize> ::= <event> <play_operator> <event>
<event> ::= <view_event>[TIME_POINT(<time>)]
|<play_event>|<reduce_event>
<view_event> ::= DISPLAY(ID,<timestamp>[,<timestamp>])
<play_event> ::= PLAY(ID,<timestamp>
            [,<timestamp>[,<mode>]])
<reduce_event> ::= REDUCE(ID,INTEGER[,INTEGER])
<timestamp> ::= INTEGER[<temporal_granularity>]
<mode> ::= FLOAT|NORMAL
<play_operator> ::= START_WITH|END_WITH
<temporal_granularity> ::= YEAR|MONTH|DAY|HOUR
                  |MINUTE|SECOND|MS
<time> ::= <year>/<month>/<day>/<hour>:<min>:<sec>
```

Figure 11. The syntax of expressing disposition as a result of query

As it mentioned before, synchronization among media is realized into 13 temporal relations which, like table 2, can be expressed through the relationship between timestamp of operator (START_WITH) and that of operator (END_WIDTH). For example, in "PLAY(IDa, Sa, Ea...), START_WITH PLAY(IDb, Sb, Eb...)", if relation between timestamp of IDa and that of IDb is Sa<Sb<Eb<Ea, it means OVERLAP relationship, and if it is Ea<Sb, it means BEFORE relationship.

Table 3. The 13 cases of temporal relation using timestamp

Relation	Constraints	Operator
EQUAL	Sa = Sb AND Ea,= Eb	START_WITH
BEFORE	Ea < Sb	START_WITH
AFTER	Sa > Eb	END_WITH
MEET	Ea = Sb	START_WITH
METBY	Eb = Sa	END_WITH
OVERLAP	Sa < Sb < Ea < Eb	START_WITH
OVERLAPEDBY	Sb < Sa < Eb < Ea	END_WITH
DURING	Sa < Sb AND Eb < Ea	START_WITH
INCLUDE	Sb < Sa AND Ea < Eb	END_WITH
START	Sa = Sb	START_WITH
STARTEDBY	Sb = Sa	END_WITH
FINISH	Ea = Eb	END_WITH
FINISHEDBY	Eb = Ea	START_WITH

The following shows the example of multimedia query using MMSQL

```
Select img.lob, t.lob
From image img, text t, img.object o1, img.object o2
Where o1.domain = "man" and o2.domain = "gun"
    And o1 touch o2
    And img.title = "Shiri" and t.title = "Shiri"
Present win_pos(img.lob, (200, 200), (500, 450))
     and win_pos(t.lob, (450, 100), (750, 350))
     and display(t.lob,10,20) start_with display(img.lob,10);
```

Above example shows text and image data that pose in spatial and temporal constraint. Spatial relationship between text and image is shown at “touch” reserved word and temporal relationship is shown at “start_with”. The location of presented media is shown in win_pos() function and the start time is shown in display().

5 Implementation

A prototype system is implemented to illustrate the capabilities of MMSQL. This prototype system is implemented using the JAVA language and Object Store storage system. The system architecture is briefly introduced in the following.

5.1 System architecture

In Fig. 12, the architecture of our prototype system is shown. It can be divided into four components: User interface, MMSQL query processor, Presentation controller and Object Store storage system. Users can input query through Query input window in MMSQL user interface. And then user query is sent to server part by query sending module. It is parsed and executed by query parser and executor in MMSQL query processor. Finally, the presentation control information that is made by presentation controller and query results are sent to Client and shown by Result viewer in MMSQL user interface.

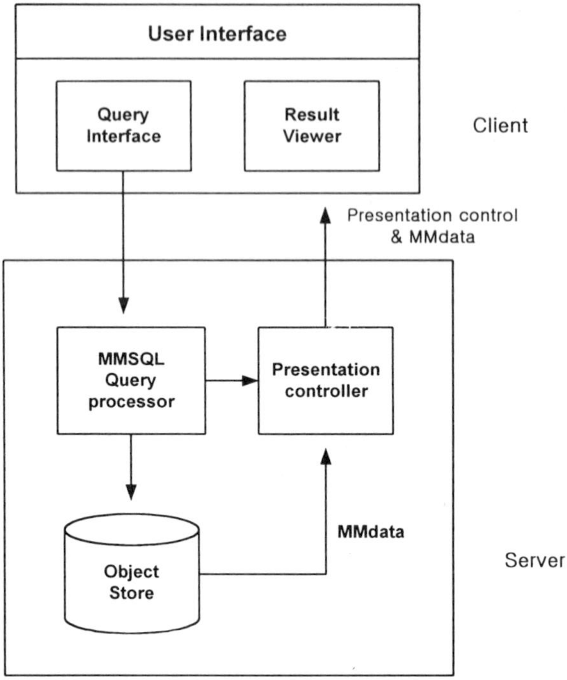

Figure 12 Architecture of the MMSQL prototype system

5.2 Example of executing MMSQL

Example of query input window is shown in Fig. 13.

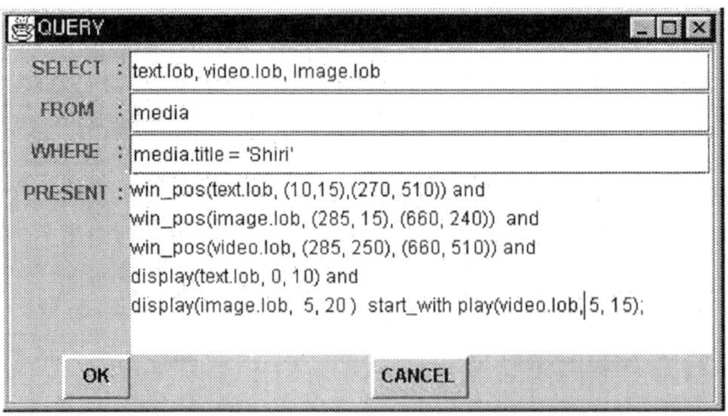

Figure 13. Example of Query input window

This query retrieves that video, image and text that their title is SHIRI . Query results also are shown in Fig. 14.

Figure 14. Example of Query result

6 Conclusion and Future work

This paper used object-oriented technique for multimedia modeling to process multimedia data in database. Data object was defined using OMT, one of object-oriented modeling technique.

Multimedia data was classified into five categories - video, audio, image, graphic and text and audio and video which have temporal characteristic was defined the lower class of time media. These classes have own attribute and succeed to the registration data of media class as higher class.

Multimedia classes that we defined are divided two categories, non-temporal media and temporal media. Temporal media such as audio and video consists of clips aggregation and temporal synchronization information with other media was stored.

Image and video have spatial status or direction information between automatically extracted objects. And extracted objects have storage for content-based retrieval. In this paper, we expand SQL that is the standard query language to query multimedia data efficiently. The expanded query language (MMSQL) can retrieve multimedia data using spatial and temporal relationship, synchronization and interaction with user. It also can express various query results using PRESENT clause. In that clause, query results are expressed size of windows, locations and synchronization information. By using MMSQL, users can various queries about multimedia and make spatial and temporal schedule for query results.

We outlined the implementation of our prototype design based on result of modeling for MMSQL. But we can execute the simple and restrictive query in this prototype system.

We will continue to improve our system and revise the proposed model in this paper.

7 Acknowledgements

This paper was supported by the Research Institute of Computer, Information and Communication grant, Pusan National University, in 1998.

References

1. G. Blakowski, et. al., "A Media Synchronization Survey : Reference Model, Specification, and Case Studies," IEEE Journal on Selected Areas in Communications, Vol. 14, No. 1, Jan. 1996.
2. K. Fujikawa, S. shimojo, et. al., "Multimedia Presentation System Harmony with Temporal and Active Media". proc. of the Summer 1991 USENIX Conf. JUNE, 1991.
3. T.D.C. Little, A. Ghafoor, "Multimedia Object Models for Synchronization and Databases". Proc. of 6th Data Engineering, 1990.
4. Y. Masunaga, "An Object-Oriented Approach to Multimedia Database organization and Management". Proc. Int. Sympo. on Database Systems for Advanced Applications(DASFAA), 1989.
5. S.Adali, K.S.Candan, V.S.Subrahmanian. "Advanced video information system: Data Structures and query processing". ACM Multimedia Journal, 1995.
6. Oomoto, E. and Tanaka, K., "OVID: Design and Implementation of a video-object database system", IEEE Trans. on Knowledge and Data Engineering, Vol.5, No.4, Aug 1993, p.629-643.
7. Jia-Ling Koh, A.L.P. Chen, "A Query Language and Interface for Integrated media and Alphanumeric Database System".1996.
8. Arun Hampapur, "Design Video Data Management Systems.", PhD thesis, The University of Michigan, 1995.
9. J.A Rody, A. Karmouch, "A Remote Presentation Agent for Multimedia Databases", Proc. of the International Conference on Multimedia Computing and Systems, May 1995.
10. M. Vazirgiannis, M. Hatzopoulos, "Intergrated Multimedia Object and Application Modeling based on events and scenarios", Proc. of 1st International Workshop for MMDBMSs, August 1995.

11. M. Vazirgiannis, "Multimedia Database object and application modeling", Multimedia Database System, Kluwer Acamedic Pub. 1996.
12. A. Gibbs, "Composite Multimedia and Active Object", Proc. OOPSLA "91, 1991.
13. T.D.C.Little and A. Ghafoor, "Synchronization and Storage Models for Multimedia Objects", IEEE Journal on Selected Areas in Communications, Vol. 8, No. 3, May, 1990.
14. J. L. Peterson, "Petri Net Theory and the Modeling of Systems", Prentice Hall inc., Englewood Cliffs, NJ., 1990.
15. M. Iino, Y. F. Day, and A. Ghafoor, "An Object-Oriented Model for Spatio-Temporal Synchronization of Multimedia Information". In Proc. IEEE Intl. Conference on Multimedia computing and Systems, pp.110-119, Boston, Ma, May 1994.
16. Nael B. Hirzalla, Ahmed Karmouch, "A Multimedia Query Specification Language", Multimedia Database System, Kluwer Acamedic Pub. 1996.
17. A. F. Cardenas, I. T. Ieong, R. K. Taira, R. Barker, and C. M. Breant, "The knowledge-based object-oriented PICQUERY+ language", IEEE Transactions on Knowledge and Data Engineering, August 1993.
18. I.Hiroshi, S.Fumio, "The model, language, and implementation of an object-oreinted multimedia knowledge base management system", ACM Transaction on Database Systems, Vol.18, No.1, pp.1-50, March, 1993.
19. G.Booch, Object-Oriented VS. Structured Design, IEEE Trans. Software Engineering, Vol SE-12, No.2, pp.211-221.
20. Chulwoong Yang, Woosuk Yang, Yoonjoon Lee, Myoungho Kim, "Multimedia Database Technology", Korea Information Science Society Riview, 1997. 9.
21. Rumbaugh, James, M.Blaha, W.Premerlani, F,Eddy, W.Lorensen, "Object-Oriented Modeling and Design", Prentice Hall, 1991.
22. Anak Agung, "Object Modeling in an Object-Relational Database for large scale mapping", 1994.

CHAPTER 3

MODEL BASED GRAPHICS, VIDEO, VISION AND VIRTUAL REALITY

MMM99

CMC'S 3D VIRTUAL REALITY THEATRE VR TOURS OF TWO TOMBS DURING THE MYSTERIES OF EGYPT EXHIBITION

GEORGE MACDONALD AND FRANK CORCORAN

Canadian Museum of Civilization, 100 Laurier, Hull, Québec, Canada, J8X 4H2

JOHN TAYLOR, PIERRE BOULANGER AND MARC RIOUX

National Research Council of Canada, Ottawa, Ontario, Canada, K1A 0R6

E-mail: john.taylor@iit.nrc.ca

In May 1998, the exhibition, Mysteries of Egypt opened at the Canadian Museum of Civilization in conjunction with the world première of the IMAX movie Mysteries of Egypt. As a new feature, the Museum constructed a Virtual Reality 3D Theatre for the presentation of VR Tours of the Tombs of Nefertari and Tutankhamun. This paper presents an overview of the VR Theatre experience including a summary of the challenges experienced in integrating several hardware and software systems. The latter will be useful to museums and cultural institutions planning similar installations in the future.

1 Introduction

The Canadian Museum of Civilization (CMC) is among the forefront of international museums using new technology to enhance the display of its collections within the Museum as well as in making electronic images and information accessible in keeping with its "Museum Without Walls" mandate. CMC has also collaborated extensively with the National Research Council of Canada (NRC) on the development of new 3D imaging and display technology for museum applications.

In conjunction with the world première of the IMAX movie *Mysteries of Egypt*, in May 1998, CMC opened the related exhibition, Mysteries of Egypt. The exhibition is thematically related to the movie and it borrows heavily from the imagery and even uses some of the objects seen in the film. CMC did not have the timeframe or the budget to produce an exhibition on ancient Egypt, which featured high-quality and rare artworks. Instead, the exhibition relied heavily on contextualization. This meant the use of models, artist's renderings, replicas, photographic blowups and virtual reality technology as well as some original artifacts. With an attendance of nearly 700,000, it was the most popular exhibition presented by the Museum and the second all-time highest attendance generator for a temporary exhibition in Canada. A key point this demonstrated is that the concept of contextualization in museum exhibitions is a valid and acceptable supplementary approach.

For the virtual reality display, CMC collaborated with NRC and several industrial partners, on the construction of a Virtual Reality 3D Theatre for the presentation of *VR Tours of the Tombs of Nefertari and Tutankhamun*. In a 3D virtual reality presentation, a graphic computer recreates viewpoints of a scene in real time as the viewer "moves through" the scene from an accurate digital model of the site. In addition to providing "virtual" access to sites, VR systems also offer the potential of "digital reconstruction" of sites as well as "digital repatriation" of models of artifacts, back into the virtual copy of their original site. As such, VR technology offers some new and potentially promising museum exhibition applications.

This paper presents an overview of the VR Theatre experience during the Mysteries of Egypt exhibition. It includes information on the preparation of the VR Tours, a description of the theatre including hardware and software systems, as well as the visitors' response. It also includes a summary of the challenges experienced in integrating several hardware and software systems into a new VR theatre environment as well as areas which need to be addressed in making improvements to future VR Tour presentations. The latter will be useful to museums and cultural institutions planning similar installations in the future.

2 Production of the VR Tours of the Tombs of Nefertari and Tutankhamun

Many important international heritage sites have become endangered as a result of heavy public visitation – some have been closed. In producing the VR Tour, CMC's objective was to demonstrate the use of the technology to provide "virtual visits" to sites that have become endangered. Queen Nefertari's Tomb was temporarily closed in 1997 for conservation treatment due to damages caused, in part, by humidity resulting from public visitation. While Tutankhamun's Tomb is partially open to the public, the burial chamber, which is the only painted room in the Tomb, is closed to the public.

The tour of Nefertari's tomb was prepared by Infobyte s.p.a. of Italy (http://www.infobyte.it) with the assistance of the Getty Conservation Institute (GCI). It was previously featured during the 1997 exhibition *Nefertari: Light of Egypt* organized by the GCI and Fondazione Memmo. The tour, complete with audio track, includes a display of the tomb before and after conservation treatment.

CMC collaborated with NRC and two Canadian companies, IVS Canada Inc. and Le Groupe Parallèle, on the production of the Tutankhamun Tour. It featured a virtual visit into the burial chamber. Visitors to the actual tomb can enter only the first undecorated antechamber; a railing prevents entry into the burial chamber. The 3D model of the tomb (Figure 1a) was provided by the Theban Mapping Project (http://www.kv5.com). It was prepared from survey data using a CAD program. Texture maps of the paintings in the burial chamber were mapped on the 3D model (Figure 1b) using detailed color slides provided by the GCI (http://www.getty.edu/gci). Permission to use the slides was also granted by the Supreme Council of Antiquities in Egypt.

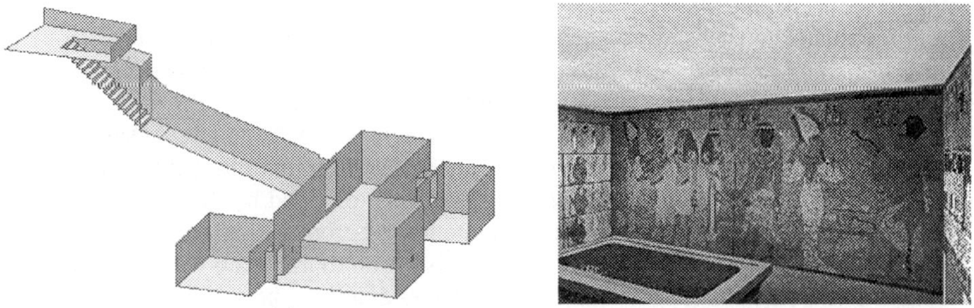

(a) (b)

Figure 1. The 3D model of Tutankhamun's tomb (a) was prepared using ArchiCAD from survey data, by the Theban Mapping Project. Texture maps of the paintings in the burial chamber obtained from detailed color slides taken during a conservation survey in 1992 by the Getty Conservation Institute were mapped on the 3D model. Figure 1b illustrates the view of the tomb model looking into the burial chamber from the antechamber. The digital model of Tutankhamun's funeral mask is just visible in the sarcophagus. In the actual tomb, a railing at this point prevents visitors from entering the burial chamber.

To illustrate the concept of "digital repatriation", a 3D model of a replica of Tutankhamun's funeral mask was integrated into the 3D model of the tomb. For this, the replica was scanned at CMC (Figure 2a) using the Hymarc COLORSCAN system [1]. The mask model was placed inside the sarcophagus where it was found (Figure 1b). The model is introduced into the display at the conclusion of the Tour to demonstrate how models of objects, which are originally associated with a site, can be reintegrated in a digital reconstruction (Figure 2b).

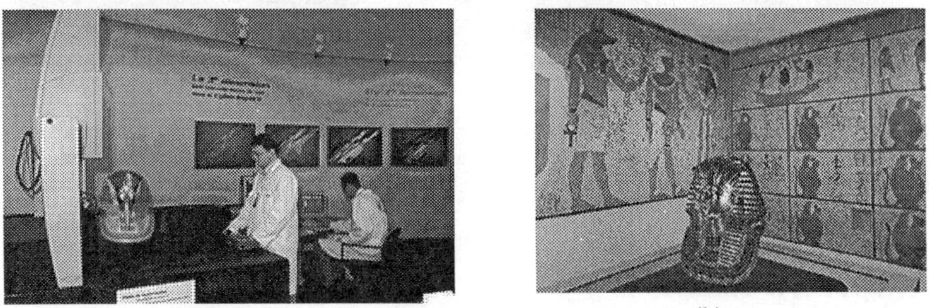

(a) (b)

Figure 2. The Hymarc COLORSCAN 3D digitizing system at the Canadian Museum of Civilization was used to scan a replica of Tutankhamun's funeral mask. The 3D digital model of the mask was then "digitally repatriated" into the model of the tomb.

It is interesting to note that the Tutankhamun Tour is a combination of virtual reality (tomb modeled from photographs and survey data in a CAD program) and virtualized reality (mask model based on a 3D image digitized directly from the actual object) [2].
The original storyboard scripted the VR Tour to last approximately 12 minutes. It was designed to be presented either interactively by a host from the computer console at the rear of the theatre or non-interactively in a linear fly through mode. The presentation commenced with a short introduction which included a selection of graphic stills of world heritage sites and an explanation that many have become endangered as a result of heavy visitation. This was followed by the Tour of Nefertari's tomb, which featured the complete tomb before and after conservation treatment. It also explained how VR enables visitation to the tomb without further damage. The Tour concluded with a visit to Tutankhamun's burial chamber. It took visitors down the limestone stairs, through the antechamber and stopped at the door to the burial chamber. The narration explained that, although visitors to the tomb today are not allowed beyond this point, the VR tour allows them to enter and examine the burial chamber and paintings in detail. It also includes an interactive display of a replica of the funeral mask originally found in the tomb.

(a) (b)

Figure 3. In the interactive mode, the tour guide can use the mouse to take the visitors through any part of the 3D model of Nefertari's tomb (a) and visit it as if they were there. They can also follow Howard Carter's footsteps down the stairs of Tutankhamun's Tomb model (b) and enter the burial chamber.

3 CMC 3D VR Theatre

The VR theatre was included in the main hall of the Mysteries of Egypt exhibition. It was located near the exit area, adjacent to a full size recreation of Tutankhamun's Tomb. The theatre occupies a floor area of approximately 26' x 15' (8 m x 5 m) and is designed to seat 20-25 visitors (Figure 4).

To cut sound transmission from the theatre to the exhibition hall, a double-layer of gyproc was used for the walls, the floor was carpeted and absorbent fabric was used for the seating. The walls were painted black to minimize reflections. Toadstool type seating was used for the first three rows, which could easily be moved for wheelchair access. One problem, which became apparent, was that too much space was left at the back of the theatre for the host-operator or tour guide. This space could have been used for seating an additional 7-8 people.

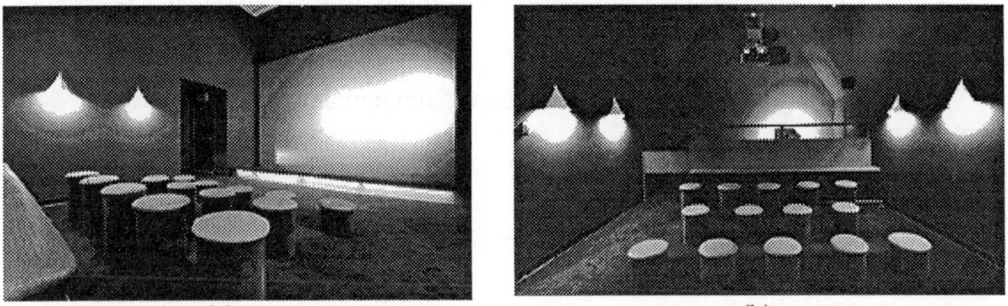

(a) (b)

Figure 4. The CMC 3D VR Theatre. Figure 4a is a side view from the rear. Three rows of stools and a rear bench provided seating for 20 – 25 visitors. The 10' x 15' screen covered the front wall. Visitors were provided with a pair of passive stereo viewing glasses on entry. Figure 4b is a rear view from the front. The host or tour guide, operated the presentation in either an interactive or linear "fly through" mode from the computer console at the rear of the theatre. The overhead projection system visible at the top of the rear wall.

The tour was projected in stereo on a flat 10' x 15' (3 m x 4.6 m) aluminized screen using an Electrohome Marquee 9501LC overhead projection system driven with a Silicon Graphics Onyx 2 Reality computer. On entry, visitors are provided with a pair of passive polarizing glasses. The Tour is presented by a guide from the computer console at the rear of the theatre in either a linear "fly through" mode or interactively.

4 Visitor and Media Response

The response to the VR Tours from the media as well as from exhibition visitors was quite positive, despite the technical problems experienced, as discussed in the next section.

In a review of the exhibition in the Ottawa Citizen, Paul Gessell [3] wrote, "*The virtual reality tours are thrilling, but all too brief. One wants to linger longer at the fabulous wall paintings, but the camera seems to be on an urgent mission, carrying us at times at breakneck speed through subterranean corridors. You will leave these tours wishing for more, or at least a desire to return for a rerun*". In a Globe and Mail review, Graham Fraser [4] wrote, "*The major innovation in the show is the 3D virtual-reality tour of the tombs*".

In the month before the exhibition closed, CMC carried out a number of visitor surveys of the VR Theatre users with the following results:

- 88% of the respondents felt that their expectations were met.
- 86% of the respondents got the message "Virtual Reality offers a way of seeing world heritage sites without causing further deterioration of these places."
- 64% had never seen a Virtual Reality program before.
- A significant number of people were confused between this technology and Imax film technology.

The following are some direct quotations from people interviewed post-screening...

- “We can visit these sites without causing further damage.”
- “We can appreciate these sites with the help of technology.”
- “We can see old and rare materials.”
- “This can replace a real visit.”
- “It's better to use 3D than to damage anything.”
- “We don't have to go there (Egypt) to see stuff like this”.
- “Ça a permit de s'approcher de plus près des tombes.”
- “C'est une technologie de remplacement.”
- “Ça permet de préserver les articles sans les toucher, préserver ce que les touristes peuvent détruirent.”
  “Ça permet la préservation des lieux.”

5 3D VR Theatre Challenges

In preparing the VR Tours as well as running them during the exhibition, we experienced a variety of challenges – several unanticipated. In the process, we learned a great deal about the “reality of virtual reality” for museum applications. As we believe our experiences will be useful to museums and cultural institutions planning similar installations in the future, the following are notes on these aspects. Although VR presentations do offer some new and exciting applications to museums, clearly a number of substantial issues need to be addressed if the technology is to be used successfully on a broad scale for similar museum applications.

5.1 Equipment Costs

Apart from the VR theatre construction costs, the costs to purchase the computer and display hardware required for an interactive 3D presentation are substantial. In this project, we went to considerable effort to test various computer and display systems, which would yield a satisfactory performance at the lowest cost. Although higher performance systems were available, which would have offered improved display results, the costs of these systems can best be described as a well beyond the budget available. While this will change, the reality at present is that for museums with tight budgets, there is not an off-the-shelf system at a reasonable cost.

5.2 VR Production Companies

The number of companies with experience in developing programs (software) for museum 3D VR presentations is extremely small. Consequently, museums wishing to set up a 3D VR theatre may have problems in getting a range of programming from quality suppliers. Instead, it is likely that they will need to collaborate with several small start up companies to develop and produce the programs locally. If so, it is important that museums carefully evaluate the technical competence as well as the financial stability of these companies to ensure that they can not only deliver the program on time but also continue to support it technically throughout the run of the show. The current shortage of experienced VR production companies also suggests that museums will likely encounter problems in getting other theatres to share software and to do co-production.

5.3 System Crashes and Software Bugs

During the first three months of the exhibition, the VR Tour presentation was literally plagued with a large number of unusual technical problems. These ranged from software incompatibility problems, bugs, projection system failures, UPS crashes and computer hardware problems including a computer fire. One of the authors (Corcoran) described it from his non-technical perspective as a "warring within the bosom of the computer". These problems led to many crashes during the early stages – often in the middle of a show. Understandably, this led to considerable frustration for the Museum staff as well as to disappointment to visitors – some who came specifically to see the show only to find the theatre closed.

In preparing a VR show such at this, it is necessary to integrate several sophisticated hardware systems and software programs from several manufacturers. This inevitably leads to some hardware and software problems and to component failures. In this project, the extent to which this occurred, particularly software incompatibility problems and bugs, was unanticipated and clearly underestimated. Accordingly, for museums planning similar projects, we strongly recommend an extended period of testing of the integrated hardware and software systems prior to the opening of the exhibition. A technically qualified – on-site – system administrator who can quickly identify the source of a problem and arrange the appropriate repair and/or patch is also a necessity.

5.4 Interactive vs. Linear Presentation

One of the attractive features of VR technology is interactivity. As discussed above, to demonstrate this, the Tours were designed to be presented either interactively by a host from the computer console at the rear of the theatre or non-interactively in a linear fly through mode. After the show opened, however, it was found that one joystick among 20 members of an audience does not make for a smooth or practical interactive presentation. Moreover, a quick move of the mouse by the operator can make the images appear fuzzy or out of focus or introduce artifacts such as strobing. This is not only unsettling for the audience, in instances it can also cause nausea. As a result, the Tours were presented in the linear or fly through mode through much of the exhibition. The interactive feature was used primarily for special demonstrations.

5.5 Resolution and Brightness Issues

Visitors to museum exhibitions and movies to day are accustomed to bright and sharp (high-resolution) images. Generally speaking, audiences are quite unforgiving if a presentation is either dark or "out of focus". Both of these aspects became important issues.

The Nefertari Tour, when projected on the 10' x 15' (3 m x 4.6 m) screen in the theatre, was less sharp than movie visitors are used to. This led to frequent comment from visitors as well as the press that the Nefertari Tour was "out of focus". While we were aware of this aspect when we planned the exhibit, we were not aware of the extent that it would be a concern to the public. Consequently, resolution issues should be carefully considered in planning future VR presentations in theatres such at this. (Although Infobyte has prepared a higher resolution version of the Nefertari Tour, it was not available until just before the Exhibition closed.)

We also received comments that some of the images, particularly in the Tutankhamun Tour, were too dark. Our assessment was that this problem was related to where the visitors sat or stood in the theatre. While the theatre was designed to seat 21 visitors, frequently up to 33 crowded into the theatre by standing around the periphery. For those seated, brightness did not appear to be an issue. However, the images appeared darker – accompanied by an image-ghosting problem – to those standing around the periphery.

Similar to the resolution issue, the brightness of the presentation – as well as the uniformity of it in the theatre – should be considered for future presentations. Brighter and higher resolution projection systems as well as a theatre design, which limits the seating to the best viewing angles, are needed. One approach to this is the use of a rear projection system, which is capable of producing a constant illumination.

5.6 When You Advertise 3D VR, People Want To See 3D

A major criticism of both Nefertari and Tutankhamun Tours was the apparent lack of 3D impact on the audience. This reaction was also unanticipated. In retrospect however, most of the images in each presentation are fundamentally flat 2D images of wall paintings in the tombs. The 3D visual impact is primarily apparent when the scene pans across the rooms in Nefertari's Tomb or into Tutankhamun's burial chamber. Part of the problem here also rests with the modeling techniques used to prepare the presentations. Rather than being prepared from an actual 3D range scan of the Tombs, the models were prepared using CAD programs from survey data. This did not capture the irregular shape details of the surfaces of each tomb and results in a flat presentation of the walls (Figure 5). As discussed in the Conclusions, in planning future presentations, more 3D visual details will have a greater visitor impact.

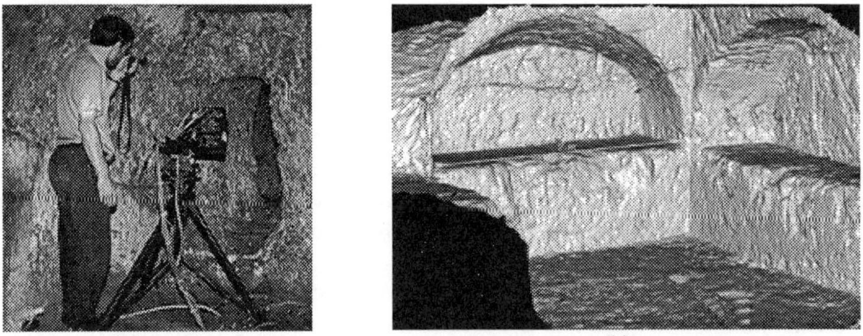

(a) (b)

Figure 5. A major criticism the 3D VR tours was the apparent lack of 3D impact on the audience. In the future, 3D imaging systems will be used to record archaeological sites directly. This will enable the creation of accurate digital models of sites, such as St James' Tomb in Israel, shown in (b) above, recorded using a laser scanner system (a) developed by NRC. The combination of color and the 3D surface shape details will add considerable 3D impact as well as reality to future productions.

5.7 Other Issues

Due to the fact that this is a leading edge technology, many of the "usual issues" one faces in publishing or filmmaking have not been resolved. For example, in negotiating the rights to use an image as a texture map to make a 3D model, people are not familiar with the technology and have no idea what kind of pricing structure is appropriate. Others are also somewhat concerned about how the images may be manipulated or altered either intentionally or unintentionally. As a result, copyright and other intellectual property issues of this nature remain to be discussed and resolved.

Another issue which became clear in this project is that there is a steep learning curve for both the museum professionals (on VR technology and its limitations) and the scientific and technical VR people (on museum programming requirements). For example in the Tutankhamun Tour, in order to demonstrate the concept of "digital repatriation", it was decided to include a 3D model of a replica of the funeral mask which was originally found in the Tomb. To the technical people, this meant simply inserting the 3D model in the center of the burial chamber space and rotating it 360º. In itself, this is a significant technical achievement which "demonstrates the concept". For the museum people, however, it did not present the mask in its proper context. Instead of a simple insertion and rotation, the museum staff requested that it be placed in the sarcophagus and raised up at the end of the show. This required an additional amount of non-trivial modeling. Consequently, in planning future programs, it is most important that the museum staff have a good grasp of the limitations of VR technology and that the technical VR staff clearly understand the museum programming requirements.

6 Conclusions

When *Mysteries of Egypt* closed, the Museum made the decision to keep the theatre and to prepare a new program to accompany the next exhibition, *Iqqaipaa: Celebrating Inuit Art. 1948 - 1970*. This decision was prompted in part by visitor surveys that indicated that they wanted to see 3D programs.

Rather than featuring tours of the sites such as the tombs, the current show features images of three-dimensional Inuit art objects, which literally jump out of the screen and into the middle of the theatre. Prior to opening the show, CMC tested segments of the new program with both staff and public and the overwhelming majority indicated they wanted to see strong "in your face" 3D elements. While people today see new special effects in music videos, commercials and at the theatre, they seldom see 3D. This is the unique feature of the 3D VR technology and is emphasized in the current programming. As a result, visitor response to the programming has been quite positive.

CMC is also in the process of planning a new VR theatre program for a forthcoming exhibition on India. For this show, they plan to integrate some of the built environment features presented in the Tutankhamun and Nefertari programs with the better use of artifacts and their manipulation extant in the current program. The Museum would also like to explore means of enriching the program offering without adding or adding significantly to the existing hardware.

As a result of this experience, we have learned a great deal about 3D VR theatre museum applications. While the visitors' response was positive, there are many challenges to be resolved before 3D VR technology can move into the mainstream of museum applications. At the present, it is safe to say that CMC remains committed to using the 3D VR technology as a display enrichment device as long as it is practical and cost-effective to do so. Paramount in this decision, however, is the need for the establishment of 3D VR production companies to provide programming content for museums. Included is the requirement for the companies to apply 3D imaging technology for the direct recording of accurate digital models of sites and objects. In doing so, it will enable them to display much more accurate virtualized reality presentations, with more 3D visual details. This will have a greater visitor impact.

7 Acknowledgements

The authors wish to acknowledge the Getty Conservation Institute, the Theban Mapping Project, the Supreme Council of Antiquities and Hymarc Ltd. for their support for this project. The contributions of Jean-Claude Gavrel, Gina Ierullo and Gregor Shapiro formerly of IVS Canada were greatly appreciated. Finally, the authors from NRC wish to thank George MacDonald for his longstanding support and encouragement for the development of 3D imaging and display technology.

This paper was originally published in ICHIM99 (International Cultural Heritage Informatics Meeting), September 22-26, Washington, D.C., by Archives & Museum Informatics.

References

1. Livingstone, F., Evans, K., Taylor, J., Rioux, M., and Arsenault-Desfossés, H., "The 3rd Dimension: A New Way of Seeing in Cyberspace", Electronic Imaging and the Visual Arts, EVA'97 Paris, Musée du Louvre, Conference Proceedings, 2 Septembre 1997, 10.1 - 10.13.
2. Boulanger, P., Taylor, J., El-Hakim, S. and Rioux, M., "How to Virtualize Reality: An Application to the Re-creation of World Heritage Sites", VSMM98, International Society on Virtual Systems and Multimedia, Vol. I of II, 18-20 November 1998, Gifu, Japan, 39 - 45.
3. Gessell, P., "Story gets in the way of beautiful sights of Egypt", Ottawa Citizen, 2 June 1998.
4. Fraser, G., Museum opens 'Everyman show' on old Egypt", The Globe and Mail, 9 May 1998.

STRATIFICATION APPROACH TO MODELING VIDEO

Tat-Seng Chua, Liping Chen and Mohan Kankanhalli
School of Computing
National University of Singapore,Singapore 119260
{chuats, chenlp, mohan}@comp.nus.edu.sg

Last few years have seen an explosion of audiovisual information from many sources around the world. There is an urgent need to develop advanced modeling tool to manage the vast quantity of video information effectively. In this research, we investigate the use of stratification approach to represent the contextual information of video contents as multi-layered strata. Each stratum models the multiple occurrences of a simple concept in the video stream. Strata may overlap and thus the meaning of video at any instance is simply the integration of meanings of all strata present. By using the strata as the base, we can develop advanced functionalities to support flexible retrieval and content-based browsing of video. A prototype has been developed to support the whole process of video management from indexing, retrieval to browsing. The prototype is tested in the domain of News video and the results have been found to be highly satisfactory.

1. Introduction

The wide spread acceptance of MPEG video standards [MPEG 93] has accelerated the use of digital video in our daily life. The use of digital video permits seamless integration of broadcast, telecommunication and computer in a single framework. Such integration facilitates the development of advanced innovative applications that will have profound effects in our everyday life. One such application is the personalized news broadcast that enables the users to view their preferred news summaries, and able to browse quickly to regions of news of their interests.

To support the above application, the video data must be properly modeled and indexed. As video is a complex temporal medium that captures both the sights and sounds of the real world, the modeling of semantic contents of video is a complex task. There are generally two approaches to modeling video data. They are the segmentation approach [Rubin & Davenport 89], and the stratification approach [Aquierre-Smith & Pincever 91]. In the segmentation approach, the video is divided into atomic units called shots. Each shot consists of a visually continuous sequence of frames. The content of each shot is then described individually. To provide the necessary context information, a concept structure is normally superimposed on top of the set of shots. The two-layered structure is used to support effective modeling and retrieval of video sequences based on users' queries [Chua & Ruan 95]; cinematic rules are used to sequence the retrieved video shots into a coherent sequence for presentation.

The stratification approach, on the other hand, focuses on segmenting the contextual information into chunks, rather than dividing physically contiguous frames into shots as is traditionally done. Each chunk is known as a *stratum*, which describes the occurrences of a simple concept like the appearance of a specific person. Strata may overlap and thus the meaning of the video at any instance can be flexibly modeled as the union of all strata present. A *stratosphere* [Aquierre-Smith & Pincever 91] has been prototyped to demonstrate the idea of stratification. More recently, the AVIS system (The Advanced Video Information System) [Adali et al 96] developed a formal model similar to the stratification model, but focused more on the efficient organization and data structure of video data. They modeled video sequences as simple entities and developed a linear algorithm to support efficient query processing.

Browsing is another significant task that merits quality computer-based support. The major technological precedent for video browsing is the VCR, with its support for sequential fast-forwarding and reverse play. Browsing a video this way is a matter of skipping frames at an even rate regardless of its content. Therefore there is always the danger that some skipped frames may contain information of greatest interest. One approach to overcome this problem is to employ the segmentation model of detecting cuts, dividing the video into shots, and selecting key frames to represent each shot. The list of key frames is then used as summary of video contents to support effective browsing [Ueda et al 91; Taniguchi et al 95]. [Zhang et al 95] proposed a hierarchical organization of key frames to facilitate browsing. [Hisashi et al 96] presented a method to reduce the browsing space by eliminating repetitive key frames using a combination of chromatic histograms and differences in local average luminance values. A better approach to overcome the browsing problem is to support browsing of video based on contents.

Research on video retrieval in the past has focused on either low level or high level features. The low level techniques have relied on features like color, texture, shape and free text. The resulting system is fully automated but the retrieval effectiveness is limited. The high level techniques model video contents with elaborate concept structure with entities and relations [Prié. et al 98]. They are effective for providing high level queries in a limited domain. However, the setting up of the concept structure is a tedious manual process. Stratification represents a middle ground that models video contents as overlapping strata of concepts. By judiciously choosing the right level of concepts, the extraction of most strata can be automated. It offers high modeling power to permit most complex retrieval and browsing operations to be supported.

This paper describes the design, implementation and testing of the prototype for news video retrieval. The main contributions of this paper include: a) the extension of stratification approach to model audio and structured data, and high level concepts such as categories and events; b) the use of stratification as the basis to support fast content-based browsing; c) the development of an actual prototype which models video contents to demonstrate complex retrieval and browsing operations.

The rest of this paper is organized as follows. Section 2 describes the stratification model. Sections 3 and 4 discuss the design and implementation of the system respectively. The evaluation of the system is presented in Section 5. Finally, section 6 contains the conclusion and discussion of limitations and future work.

2. The Stratification Model

Stratification is a context-based approach to modeling video content as strata. Strata may overlap and thus any frame can have a variable number of strata associated with it. Stratification is therefore a way to model video content as rich multi-layered descriptions that can be parsed by a wide range of applications.

A comparison between the traditional segmentation model and the stratification model is given below.

- In the segmentation model, the basic atomic unit and therefore the granularity of video data is a shot. It is not possible for users to access video contents within the shot boundaries. For stratification, the granularity of information is a frame. It thus permits users the greatest flexibility to access and present video contents.
- The segmentation model imposes authors' intentionality early during the shot creation stage. Thus once the video is segmented, it is difficult to support other users who may need to use the same material for a different purpose. The stratification model views video contents as layers of overlapping strata. Thus users may combine strata to flexibly retrieve video, or easily build additional strata to cater to their specific needs.

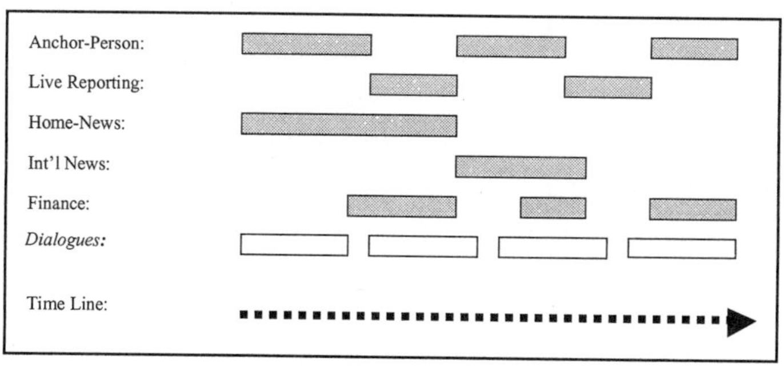

Figure 1: Stratification modeling of a news video

Figure 1 shows an example of the stratification modeling of news video, in which the content is modeled as multiple occurrences of strata. In order to enhance the modeling power of the stratification model, we have extended the model to cover not just single concepts, but also audio dialogue, structured data and high level concepts such as categories and events. Thus, under the extended model, a stratum can be an object such as a person, a category such as the sports news, or audio dialogue. It may occur over many, possibly overlapping time periods.

The strata act as meta-information that provides concise interpretation of video's semantics in terms of multiple layers of concepts. By applying simple union and/or intersection operations, many interesting higher level concepts can be derived from the basic strata. Also, it is possible to use the strata information to support many interesting video manipulation functions such as the content-based fast-forwarding, retrieval, and video summarization. In this paper, we will only present two major applications: video retrieval and fast-forwarding. The research on the other aspects of video management is still going on.

3. System Design

In this section, we describe the design of the Stratification Video Modeling System (SVMS). SVMS is a general-purpose video management system, which supports the whole process of video indexing, retrieval to browsing. We will discuss the details of video representation, query processing and retrieval, and video browsing below.

3.1 Video Representation

3.1a Strata and Frame Sequence

Video can be organized as a set of frames. By following the symbols employed in [Adali et al 96], a frame sequence is defined as a pair [i,j] where $1 \leq i \leq j \leq n$. [i,j) represents the set of all frames between i (inclusive) and j (non-inclusive). Thus each strata is mapped to a set of frame sequences to indicate its multiple occurrences in the video. One property that we would like the frame sequence to have is so-called "solid". A set $\underline{X}$ of frame sequences $\{[i_1,j_1) \ldots [i_r,j_r)\}$ is said to be solid if $[i_1, j_1) \subset [i_2, j_2) \subset \ldots \subset [i_r, j_r)$. Here $\subset$ is a partial ordering on the set of all frame sequences as follows: $[i_1, j_1) \subset [i_2, j_2)$ if $i_1 < j_1 < i_2 < j_2$. Intuitively, $[i_1, j_1) \subset [i_2, j_2)$ means that the sequence of frames denoted by $[i_1, j_1)$ precedes the sequence of frames denoted by $[i_2,j_2)$.

We can now briefly define the stratum. As described previously, there are three types of stratum: the first is based on dialogue and the other two are on entity and structured data.

Thc dialogue stratum D_s of a video stream s is defined as:

$$D_s :== \{(d_{s1},f_1), (d_{s2},f_2), .. (d_{sN},f_N)\}$$

where d_{sk} denotes the paragraph k of audio dialog of video stream s; and f_k denotes the frame sequence that contains dialogue d_{sk}.

The entity stratum E_i is defined as:

$$E_i :== \{e_i, \underline{X}\}$$

where e_i denotes the entity i; $\underline{X}$ is the list of solid frame sequences that e_i appears. The strata for structured data are defined in the same way as the entity strata.

We now describe each type of stratum in detail.

3.1b The Dialogue Stratum: Paragraphs in a Video Database

Audio dialogue provides rich information about the video and is modeled at the paragraph level. To extract text from audio dialogue, the audio track must be analyzed using speech recognition [Rudnicky et al 94]. There are a lot of commercial and prototype speech recognition systems that could achieve a reasonably high degree of accuracy. Thus in most general applications, the identification of most essential words in a dialogue is not a big problem. We will rely on a commercial IBM product[ViaVoice 98] to automatically identify the majority of sentences on the news video's audio track.

Currently the paragraphs are transcribed manually. Each paragraph is associated with a frame sequence to indicate the start and end frames where the dialogue takes place. An example of a dialogue stratum is shown in Figure 1. From a query, partial match free text retrieval technique [Salton & McGill 83] can be used to identify relevant paragraphs which in turn maps into a list of relevant frame sequences.

3.1c The Entity Stratum

Entities are items that are of interest to the users. How to select an appropriate set of entities to suit an application is an open question that has no uniform answer. Although stratification is rich in data representation, the indexing of entity strata manually is a very tedious task. This is because the same video needs to be parsed multiple times in order to index a good collection of entities. Thus in SVMS, only primitive concepts and well-defined categories are chosen as strata. We are using pseudo-object models together with relevance feedback [Chua & Chu 98] and other learning method to identify and track objects automatically. We are also employing face location [Sung. et al 1998] and tracking methods to identify important faces. We aim to automate as much as possible the process of extracting strata data.

The consideration of what can be automated affects our decisions of what entities should be modeled in SVMS. The various types of entities are discussed below.

- ***Object***: The video objects may be people in the news video such as the Prime Minister of Singapore, Bill Clinton, or anchor person etc. They may also be buildings/places, landmarks, animals or items which are of general interest to the users. Although automatic detection of objects is not possible in the current image processing research, with pre-knowledge of the objects involved, locating and tracking of objects in a video sequence using video analysis techniques is possible using the techniques as described in the preceding paragraph.
- ***Category:*** The semantic structure of news video is quite unique and well structured. Its contents can generally be classified into the categories of: home news, international news, finance, weather, sports and commercial breaks. Among these, the home and international news are rather high-level and require sophisticated analysis for their identification. As it is not possible to automatically identify these high-level categories directly, low level categories such as the shots of anchor person, live reporting, sports, or even reports on money/stock market and weather etc can be used instead. These low-level categories, together with their visual features, audio dialogues, and knowledge of the structure of news video, may be used as the basis to identify high-level categories. This is an area of current research.

- ***Location and Event:*** Location specifies the place where the event took place; and the event entity captures notable occurrences of news items. We are now researching into techniques to identify stories and events using a combination of audio and visual cues together with time based specification of the characteristics of events or stories. These will contribute towards automatic detection of events.

- ***Structured Data:*** In addition to the above, structured data such as the dates, times, and source of video streams etc must be encoded. Such information can be used to support queries based on dates and times such as the “financial news in the last two days”.

Since each entity may occur multiple times within one video stream, each entity is associated with a solid set of frame sequences. When queried about the entities, it is usual to retrieve the whole set of frame sequences that the entities appear. Thus the entity data is organized in an inverted structure with entity names as the inverted index for retrieval. Hence with keys such as Bill Clinton (Object), Indonesia

(Location), or Home News (Category), we are able to retrieve the whole set of frame sequences that these entities appear. Figure 2 shows the data structure for organizing the entity strata.

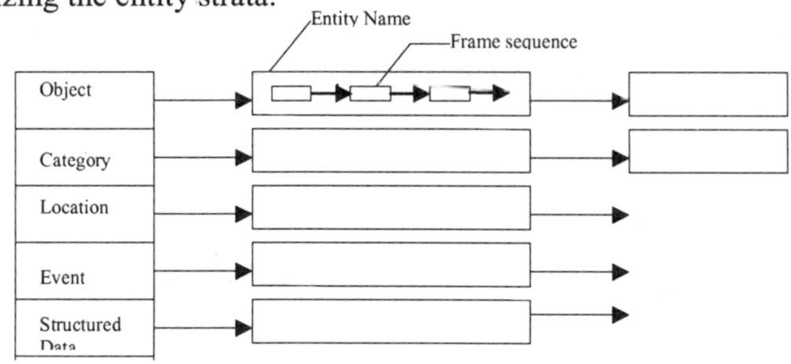

Figure 2: Inverted file structure for entity strata

3.2 Query Processing and Retrieval

The semantic of video is modeled as strata of dialogues and entities. We employ logical exact match operations to combine entities to support complex queries; whereas we use free-text partial match technique to locate relevant paragraphs. The combination of both Boolean exact match and IR best match techniques provides a powerful mechanism for querying the database.

3.2a Free Text Retrieval of Paragraphs

SVMS uses Vector Space Model [Salton & McGill 83] to support paragraph level free text retrieval. Vector Space model maps each paragraph to a vector space of non-trivial terms of dimension N, where N is number of stems extracted from the paragraphs. The stem terms in each paragraph is indexed using the standard tf*idf term weighting formula. The similarity between the query and a paragraph is simply the distance between them in the vector space. This is computed using the well-known cosine similarity formula as follows

$$Sim(D_i,Q) = \frac{\sum_{k=1}^{t}(d_{ik} \times q_k)}{\sqrt{\sum_{k=1}^{t}(d_{ik})^2 \times \sum_{k=1}^{t}(q_k)^2}}$$

where $Sim(D_i,Q)$ gives the similarity between query **Q** and paragraph $\mathbf{D_i}$. In general, the retrieval returns a list of up to n paragraphs whose similarity values are above a threshold.

3.2b Logical Operations on Entity Strata

The exact match technique is used to retrieve entity level strata such as the object, category, location and event. Since the result of the logical AND or OR operation on two solid frame sequences is also a solid frame sequence, the logical operations can be used to construct complex queries based on simple entities.

Figure 3 shows the logical operations on two solid sets of frame sequences. In the *AND* (or *OR*) operation, those frame sequences that *are common to (*or *appear in*) both sets are returned. The exact match is also used to filter video streams based on structured information such as dates, times, broadcast companies or programs etc.

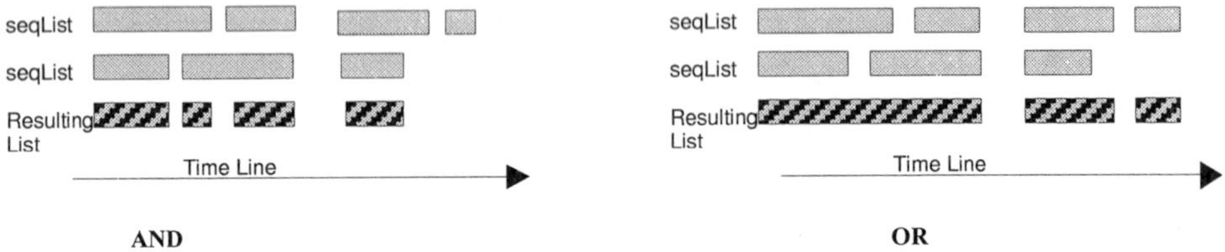

Figure 3: Logical operations on two frame sequences

3.2c Presentation of Query Results

The result of the query is a list of frame sequences. Since the frame sequence can begin or end at any position along the time line of video, a presentation formed by simply concatenating all the frame sequences returned may not be effective. To smoothen out the abrupt effects of simple concatenation, we first extend the frame sequence to match the beginning and end of an audio sentence. We then modify the start frame number by searching for the MPEG GOP (group of picture) where the start frame belongs and starting from the beginning of GOP. Similarly, for each end frame, we search for the GOP that it belongs to and use the ending of GOP as the end frame of our frame sequence. Thus we extend the original frame sequence a bit longer in order to give a smoother presentation with better visual and audio continuity.

The presentation of query result is a major topic of research. In order to have a really meaningful presentation of the query result, other factors such as the semantic and cinematic continuity [Balasz 52] of presentation needs to be considered. This is beyond the scope of this paper.

3.3 Video Browsing

The task of browsing is intimately related to query processing. Furthermore, browsing may serve not only as an aid to the formulation of queries but also as a means for examining the results. Thus an effective browsing tool should base on some level of analysis of the video contents.

As video is modeled as multiple occurrences of simple entities in the stratification model, the meaning of video at any instance is simply the union of strata occurring at that time. This brought us to the idea that fast-forwarding, or more accurately, fast-skipping, can be supported directly using the strata information. For instance, suppose that the user is interested in Bill Clinton, he may choose the entity "Clinton" as the context for browsing. So each time the user clicks the fast-forward button, the video will skip to the next occurrence of Bill Clinton. In this way, the user is able to browse through all the news related to Bill Clinton within a short duration without missing any interesting information. This will be a major improvement over the even-rated fast skipping method used in traditional fast-forwarding.

4. System Implementation

The Stratification Video Modeling System (SVMS) is implemented on the Sun workstation running Solaris 2.0. Figure 4 shows the overall system structure of SVMS. It consists of three modules: *Video Logger*, *Video Query Processor* and *Video Browser*. The *Video Logger* is designed to facilitate the manual indexing of video data. It has a VCR like interface which provides standard functionalities such as play, pause, stop, etc. Two additional buttons are provided to mark the start and end of frame sequences and add in the strata information accordingly. It also provides a stratagraph that gives users an overall view of all the strata information indexed.

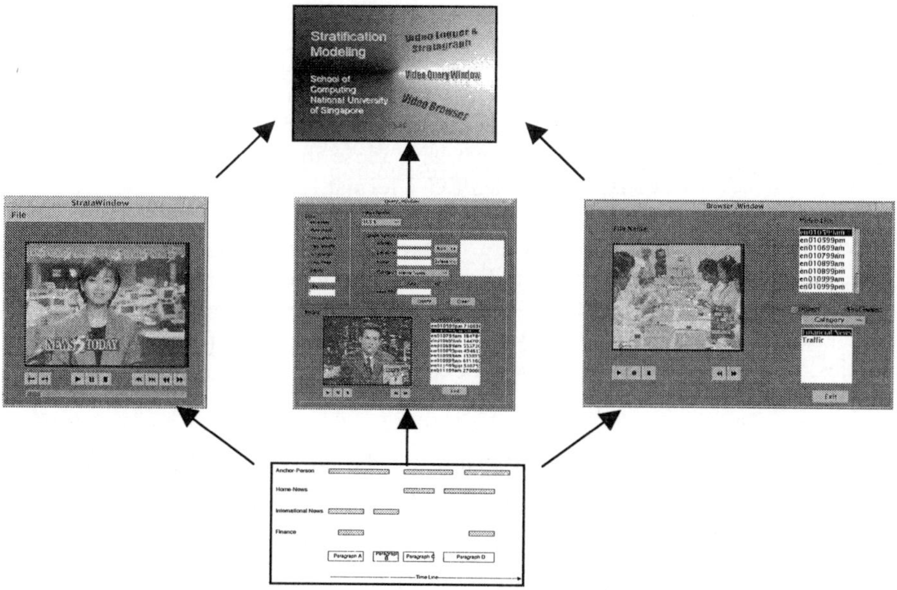

Figure 4: Overall system structure of SVMS

The user interacts with the *Video Query Processor* to perform queries and view the results. The upper part of the screen is the query composer, which supports three types of queries. It supports the free-text queries to locate relevant paragraphs using the IR partial match technique. It permits the users to compose complex entity-level queries by using the AND/OR operator to combine entity specifications. It also supports the use of structured data such as the dates and times to filter video streams. The common interface permits these three types of query specifications to be combined to support complex query like "international news (category) about Bill Clinton (object) in the last two dates (structured data in dates) about 'US-China relations' (free-text description)". The results of the query are presented at the lower part of the screen. A picture in picture display is designed to let the user view the current frame sequence, while previewing the content of the next sequence in the smaller picture display. With the preview sub-window, the user can make the choice of whether to watch or skip the next sequence.

The *Video Browser* facilitates content-based browsing of video. The user can choose any interesting object (indexed in strata) as the context to browse through the entire video database. Whenever the fast-forward button is pressed, the next occurrence of the object is displayed.

5. Evaluation

The system is evaluated using the domain of news video. We utilized one-week of English news from TCS (Television Corporation of Singapore) channel 5 from Jan 5 to Jan 11,1999. For each day, we used both the morning (10 minutes) and evening news (30 minutes). Thus altogether we have close to 280 minutes of news video data. All the news video is stored in MPEG-1 format.

Three types of strata information are indexed: entities, paragraphs and structured data. Four types of entities are identified: object, category, event and location. Only entities involving simple and well-defined concepts are chosen. For this prototype, all entities are extracted manually. However, with the use of simple concepts as entities, it is possible to automate the extraction most strata information. It is the subject of our current research.

Seven types of categories are used. They are the home news, international news, finance, sports, weather, traffic and commercial break. More than 10 objects are identified and each contributes about 5-10 strata to the total database. Each paragraph corresponds to a piece of news. All key words for each paragraph are recorded manually. Altogether, 135 paragraphs are identified.

The following retrieval examples are used to demonstrate the three types of queries supported by SVMS:

- Free-text query: Figure 5 shows the results of issuing the free-text query "currency crisis". The retrieval is based only on the paragraphs indexed. All frame sequences are correctly retrieved except sequence (e).

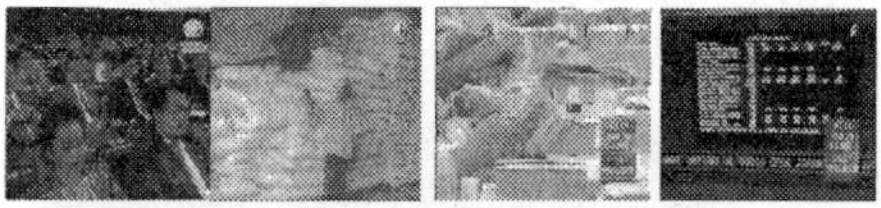

a) Indonesia currency crisis (05/01/99 am)

b) Indonesia currency crisis (05/01/99 pm)

c) S.K. currency crisis (05/01/99 pm)

d) Asia currency crisis (08/01/99 pm)

e) UK cow disease crisis (10/01/99 pm)

Figure 5: Retrieval results of free-text query "Currency Crisis"

- Query combining both free-text and logical Boolean operation on entity strata: Figure 6 shows the result of the combined query "currency crisis in Indonesia", which combines free-text ('currency crisis') and location entity (Indonesia). All sequences are correctly retrieved.

a) 05/01/99 am

b) 05/01/99 pm

c) 08/01/99 pm

Figure 6: Retrieval result of the query "Currency Crisis in Indonesia"

- Query with additional time constraint: Suppose we specify that we only want news on "currency crisis in Indonesia" from 1st-7thJanuary 1999, then only frame sequences (a) and (b) of Figure 6 will be shown; frame sequence (c) will be excluded.

Figure 7 shows the typical frame sequences encountered by performing the object-based browsing on news of 5th January 1999. Figure 7(a) shows the sequences generated by using the object "Bill Clinton" as the browsing context. The context for browsing for sequences shown in Figure 7(b) is the category "Home News".

a) Bill Clinton

b) Home News

Figure 7: Results of object-based browsing on News on 5th January, 1999

6. Conclusion and Future Work

The aim of this project is to develop a prototype news video modeling system that models the video data using the stratification approach. By using the strata information indexed, we are able to explore advanced video manipulation functionalities such as retrieval and content-based fast-forwarding. The prototype is developed using the news video supplied by the Television Corporation of Singapore. The results of initial testing indicate that these advanced functions can be adequately supported using the stratification approach.

Current research is carried out in the following direction in an attempt to automate the indexing of strata as much as possible.

a) Better techniques for segmenting video sequence into shots and audio stream into sentences. For video sequence, we are developing a new multi-resolution technique[Lin. et al 1999] that could detect a wide range of cut, dissolve and wipe. The shots and sentences provide a basis for identifying stratum boundaries.

b) Techniques for identifying and tracking pseudo objects [Chua & Chu 98] and faces [Sung. et. al 1998] by extending current research in the lab.

c) Techniques to identify stories and events in video sequence. A story is defined as a coherent semantic sequence of news/narratives such as a news item on "Election in Indonesia". A story normally consists of multiple shots with little visual coherence and sentences. An event involves a specified sequence of action that constitute notable occurrences. Examples include riots, war, signing ceremony etc. The stories and events are high level strata.

d) The presentation of retrieval result using both cinematic and semantic rules to ensure visual and audio continuity.

References:

Adali S, Candan KS, Chen SS, Erol K, Subrahmanian VS (1996). "The Advanced Video Information System: data structures and query processing", ACM Multimedia Systems, 4, 172-186.

Aguierre Smith TG and Pincever NC (1991). "Parsing Movies in Context", USENIX-summer'91, 157-168.

Balazs B (1952). "Theory of the Film". London, Dennis Dobson Ltd.

Chua TS & Chu CX (1998). "Color-based Pseudo Object Model for Image Retrieval with Relevance Feedback". Proceedings of 1st International Conference on advanced Multimedia Content Processing, Nov, Osaka, Japan, 148-162.

Chua TS & Ruan LQ (1995). "A Video Retrieval and Sequencing System". ACM Trans of Information Systems, 13(4): 373-407, Oct.

Hisashi A, Shigeyoshi S & Osamu H (1996). "A Shot Classification Method of Selecting Effective Key-frames for Video Browsing". ACM Multimedia '96, ACM Press, 1-10

Y. Lin, T. S. Chua, M. S. Kankanhalli, (1999). "Temporal Multiresolution Analysis for Video Segmentation". Technical Report, School of Computing, NUS, 1999

MPEG (1993). "Information Technology – Coding of moving pictures and associated audio for digital storage media at up to about 1.5 Mbit/s", Moving Picture Expert Group Committee, ISO/IEC 11172-1,2,3,4.

Yannick Prié, Alain Mille, and Jean-Marie Pinon (1998). "AI-STRATA: A User-centered Model for Content-based Description and Retrieval of Audiovisual Sequences". Proceedings of 1st International Conference on advanced Multimedia Content Processing, Nov, Osaka, Japan, 333-348

Rubin B & Davenport G (1989). "Structured Content Modeling For Cinematic Information", SIGCHI Bulletin, 21(2), 78-79.

Rudnicky AI, Lee KP & Hauptmann AG (1994). "Survey of current speech technology". Communications of the ACM, 37(3): 52-57.

Salton G & McGill M (1983). "Introduction to Modern Information Retrieval", McGraw-Hill, New York.

Sung, Kah Kay and Poggio, Tomaso (1998). "Example-based Learning for View based Human Face Detection". IEEE Transactions on Pattern Analysis and Machine Intelligence, vol. 20, no. 1, 39-51.

Taniguchi Y, Akutsu A, Tonomura Y & Hamada H (1995). "An Intuitive and Efficient Access Interface to Real-time Incoming Video Based On Automatic Indexing", ACM Multimedia 95, ACM Press

Ueda H, Miyatake T & Yoshizawa S (1991). "Impact: An Interactive Natural-Motion-Picture Dedicated Multimedia Authoring System", Proc. ACM Multimedia 91, ACM Press, 343-350

ViaVoice (1998). IBM's speech recognition technology. http://www.software.ibm.com/speech/

Zhang HJ, Smoliar SW & Wu JH (1995). "Content-Based Video Browsing Tools". Proc. SPIE Multimedia Computing and Networking, 2417: 389-398.

EVENT-DRIVEN VIDEO ABSTRACTION AND VISUALIZATION

JEHO NAM AND AHEMD H. TEWFIK

Department of Electrical and Computer Engineering
University of Minnesota at Twin Cities
Minneapolis, MN 55455, USA
E-mail: {jnam, tewfik}@ece.umn.edu

We propose a novel video abstraction technique that produces a dynamic (video) summarization of the original video sequence. Our technique compactly summarizes a video data by preserving its original temporal characteristics (visual activity) and semantically essential information. It relies on an adaptive nonlinear sampling. The local sampling rate is directly proportional to the amount of *visual activity* in localized sub-shot units of the video. The resulting video abstract is highly compact.

To get very short, yet semantically meaningful summaries, we propose an *event-oriented* abstraction scheme, in which two semantic events; *emotional* dialogue and *violent* featured action, are characterized and abstracted into the video summary before all other events. If the length of the summary permits, other non key events are then added.

1 Introduction

Remarkable advance, in both speed and capacity of communication, storage media and computer technologies, has spurred the proliferation of various types of digitized information. Especially, ever-increasing large collection of video data demands efficient database management solutions. A series of content-based video analysis techniques has been one of the most noteworthy topics for past few years [1]-[3]. Particularly, compactly summarized video representation is fundamental for content-based indexing, browsing and retrievals in video database.

Most video representation and summarization approaches that have appeared in the literature rely on *static* arrangements of key frames. Specifically, a set of key frames is selected from each video shot and spatially arranged in a variety of pictorial summary forms [2]-[6]. Such compact representations of video provide viewers with a global picture of the entire video content on a single screen. However, a common drawback of static video summaries are that they do not preserve the time-evolving dynamic nature of video content. Furthermore, these static representations are not natural to non-experts and can be hard to grasp on a single screen, particularly when the underlying video is complex.

Alternatively, video content can be summarized using a *dynamic* time varying presentation. In this case, sample frames extracted at regular time intervals (uniform sampling), or selected key frames from component shots are assembled in a time ordered sequence [9,10]. A slideshow display allows a viewer to display and navigate the sequence while preserving essential dynamic nature of the underlying video. Dynamic representations can speed up the browsing of large video databases through its fast sequential playback. The drawback of the slideshow display studied in [9] is that it simply presents a sequence of *static* key frames at a certain fixed rate without considering any time relationship between successive key frames. A video player in [10] requires a user's control of the summarization level for changing the number of selected key frames. More sophisticated techniques in [11,12] summarize a video data by selecting and re-organizing only *semantic* contents.

In this paper, we present a novel compact and dynamic video summarization and visualization scheme. Our approach relies on an adaptive and dynamic sampling of the underlying video sequence. We begin by describing our temporal video segmentation technique to extract meaningful sub-shot units of the video sequence. Next, we calculate motion activity in each of these units and propose a simple motion index quantization approach followed by explaining how to derive time-varying video sampling rates from the quantized motion index. Sub-shot units characterized by a high quantized motion intensity index are sampled at a higher rate than those characterized by a low index.

To get very short, yet semantically meaningful summaries, we propose an *event-oriented* abstraction scheme (e.g., for feature films). Two semantically meaningful events; *emotional dialogue* and *violent featured action*, are characterized and included in the video summary. As a result, conceptually meaningful video contents are compactly summarized and, through fast sequential playback, presented to a viewer for effective browsing and searching of video data.

2 Temporal Video Segmentation

In our dynamic video summarization scheme, we begin with decomposing a continuous video sequence into temporally isolated short visual segments (basic video unit). Note that those segment units are bounded at *subshot* level beyond the traditional shot boundaries [2,3,7]. The use of such temporally finer units is more suitable to create a conceptually well-organized video summary.

2.1 Semantically Meaningful Video Unit

Generally, since a "shot" is considered as an elemental video unit which is expected to capture individual content of meaningful information, many algorithms have been developing to accurately identify the actual shot boundaries [1,2,7].

However, there exist many video shots containing more than a single *semantic* content. This fact entails the additional key frame selection algorithms for more detailed video representation [8]. Here, we note that some false detection (considered as no actual shot boundaries) often correspond to the important clues for key frame selections (especially, involved with dynamic shots of significant object/camera motions). In addition, some sudden and/or significant changes in global/local illumination are indicative of semantically meaningful events, e.g., camera flashlight for appearing of important person [7] and gunshot/explosion of violent features [22].

Therefore, for more detailed content-based representation, we need to initially segment a video sequence into ''subshot'' unit levels, i.e., *inter-shot* boundaries, which are supplement the actual shot boundary units with more conceptually refined granulites.

2.2 *Coarse Identification of Candidate Segmentation Boundaries*

Here, we present a novel approach that decomposes a continuous video sequence directly into at *sub-shot* units. The first step in our method identifies a set of potential segment boundaries from temporally sub-sampled video data, and then we analyze the localized imagery information to verify the candidate boundaries. The basic idea of this coarse-to-fine approach is similar to a multi-pass method proposed by Zhang *et al.*[2]. Advantages in this strategy are that it speeds up the overall processing with reduced number of video frames, and also effectively detects the gradual transitions (fade in/out, dissolve and wipe). However, potential drawbacks of this approach are the possibility of too many spurious candidate boundaries caused by increased inter-frame differences due to the temporal sub-sampling and difficulty in the final verification stage. In particular, poor verification of candidate boundaries results in severe degradation in final performance of boundary detection.

In our approach for coarse boundaries identification, we begin with a temporally sub-sampled video sequence. For example, we typically sub-sample the video data by a factor of 2^2 or 2^3 in time domain. Then, we perform a 2-D wavelet decomposition on each frame, $f(m,n)$, of the temporally sub-sampled sequence to extract four sequences of the spatially filtered and reduced wavelet coefficient subimages,

$$\{S_{2^{-J}} f, D_{2^{-J}}^{LH} f, D_{2^{-J}}^{HL} f, D_{2^{-J}}^{HH} f\},$$

as its multiresolution representation form with a scale factor $J=4$. The subimage $S_{2\text{-}J} f$ is a coarse version of original image and subimages $\{D_{2\text{-}J}{}^{LH}f,\ D_{2\text{-}J}{}^{LH}f,\ D_{2\text{-}J}{}^{LH}f\}$ contain detail information for different orientation and resolutions [15].

On these subimages, we now perform the coarse identification to get candidate boundaries. Particularly, we take a 1-D wavelet filtering on each subimage sequence along a time axis to detect *temporal edges* (segment boundaries) using our previous method in [16], and then combine the results of four subimage sequences by a correlation using direct multiplication in time domain. This can be written as

$$S(i) = \prod_{k=1}^{4} E_k(i),$$

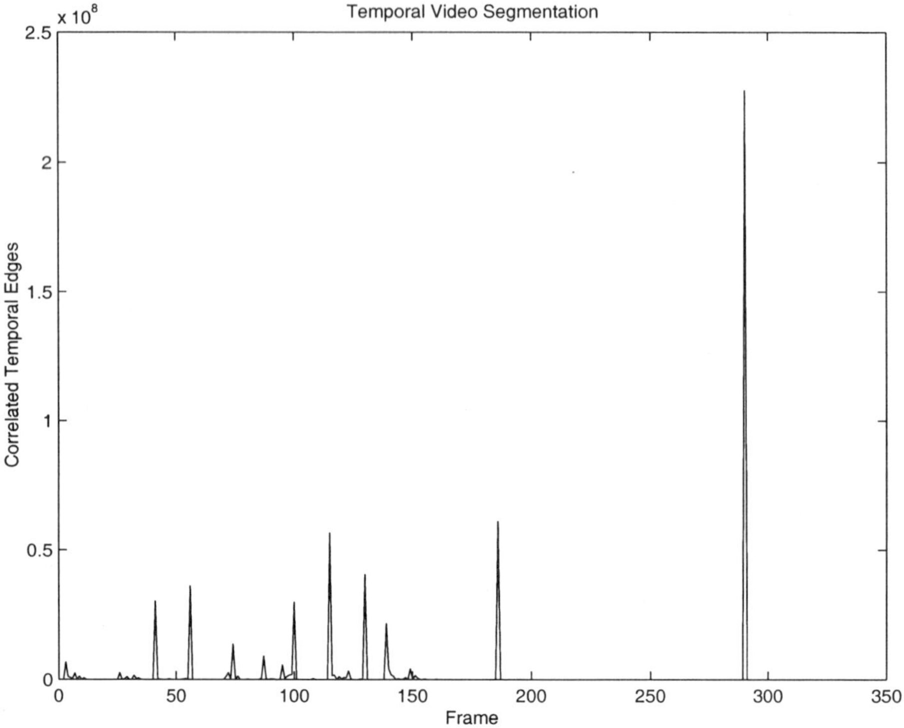

Figure 1. Coarse identification of candidate boundaries in sub-sampled sequence by a factor of 4

where each E_k, for $k=1,..,4$, is the detected temporal edge signal on four spatial wavelet coefficient sequences respectively. Note that combination of wavelet filtering's inherent noise-removing properties for edge detection [16] and their temporally correlated results of four subimage sequences, can clearly identify the sharp edges (segment boundaries) by effectively suppressing the increased inter-frame differences due to the initial temporal sub-sampling as well as other object/camera motions. Figure 1 shows the effectiveness of our proposed technique.

Given the correlated (temporal) edge signal $S(i)$, a set of candidate boundaries is determined by thresholding. Unlike the global threshold [1], we make use of the local threshold to define a candidate boundary if it satisfies the following condition;

$$S(i) > \frac{T_L}{m}\sum_{j=i-m}^{i-1} S(j) \qquad \text{and} \qquad S(i) > \frac{T_L}{m}\sum_{j=i+1}^{i+m} S(j).$$

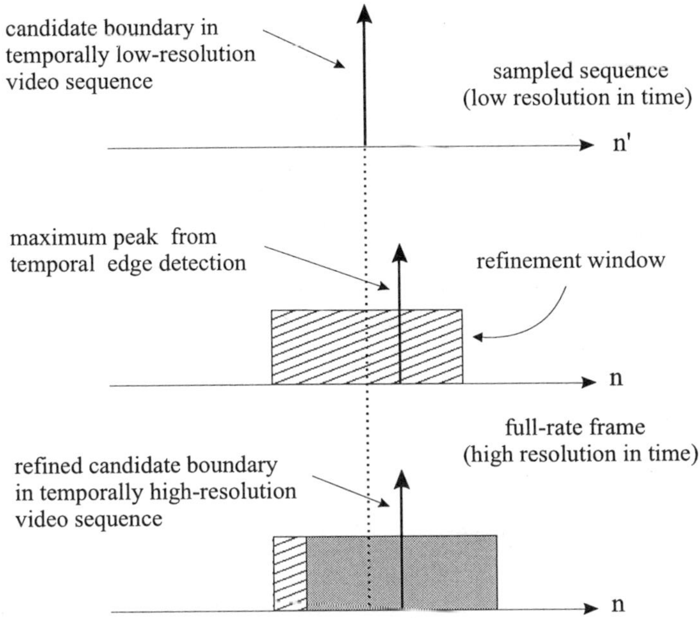

Figure 2. Progressive refinement of boundaries

This local thresholding condition identifies the peaks whose local activity is T_L times higher than average values of neighbors within a window of size $2m+1$.

2.3 Progressive Refinement and Verification

Recall that since our coarse segmentation initially analyzes a temporally sub-sampled sequence, we need to identify the exact locations at full-rate frames (original temporal resolution) from the candidate boundary set. By focusing on temporally localized neighbor regions of each candidate boundary, *coarse-to-fine* refinement is applied on this step. When the temporal video sub-sampling factor is 2^M, the full-rate frame number n of the boundary is simply computed by

$$n = 2^M (n' - 1) + 1,$$

from the frame number n' at sub-sampled sequence. Based on this approximate boundary location, the exact boundary position is identified by performing temporal edge detection again within only a window (at original full-rate frames) centered on each candidate boundary. Note that, unlike previous coarse segmentation, the temporal edge detection is performed on $S_{2^{-J}}f$ (J=3, i.e., spatially higher resolution) subimage sequence alone at this refinement stage. Finally, the candidate boundary at full-rate frames is simply obtained by picking a maximum peak within the window. Figure 2 illustrates the overall coarse-to-fine refinement procedure within a certain sized window.

Note again that the potential problem of our procedure is that there may exist false detections in the candidate boundary set because of the increased inter-frame differences due to the initial temporal sub-sampling and object/camera motions. Thus, it demands verification procedure of each candidate detection. A simple possible way is to investigate the localized imagery data statistics (e.g., mean images or histograms) with simple Euclidean metric and a thresholding. However, it is hardly reliable to obtain such a threshold value that equally handles with a variety of input video signals of gradual transitions and other special effects. Besides, we need to carefully treat this verification procedure because it may seriously degrades the overall detection performance by rejecting the real detection if we have wrong decision here.

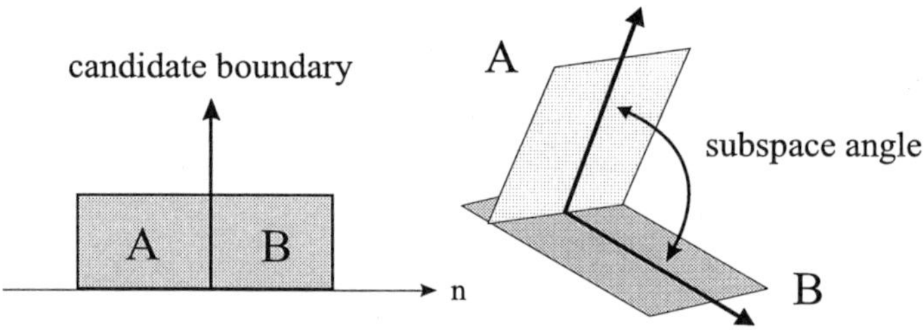

Figure 3. Boundary verification using a subspace angle

To attack this challenging problem, we propose a novel method to verify each candidate detection. In our approach, we measure the visual similarity by computing a *principal angle* between data subspaces of two imagery information; backward (region *A*) and forward (region *B*) within a time-localized window centered on each candidate boundary to be verified (see Figure 3). First, two imagery feature data sets, X_A and X_B, are formed by

$$X_A = [x_{n-w}, x_{n-w-1}, \ldots, x_{n-w}] \qquad \textit{and} \qquad X_B = [x_{n+1}, x_{n+2}, \ldots, x_{n+w}],$$

where x_i is a "zig-zag" scanned *K*-dim vector of each subimage frame S_2^{-3} f within the analysis window of size *2w+1*. Note that a parameter *w* depends on the original temporal resolution of video sequence, e.g., sampling rates of *30 fps* or *15 fps* etc., but should be less than the minimum shot length of *1~10* seconds [13]. Then, we perform the principal component analysis (PCA) on X_A and X_B to obtain two orthonormal matrices,

$$Q_A = [e_A^1, e_A^2, ..., e_A^k] \quad and \quad Q_B = [e_B^1, e_B^2, ..., e_B^k],$$

whose column vectors, e^i_A's and e^i_B's, are the partial set of k eigenvectors ($k < K$) of each X_A and X_B through PCA; i.e., they are associated eigenvectors corresponding to the first k largest eigenvalues of correlation matrix of X_i [21]. Therefore, Q_A and Q_B compactly represent each imagery signal space in region A and B respectively.

Now, we compute the *principal angles*, θ_i, ..., θ_k, between two imagery data spaces A and B using the singular value decomposition (SVD) of $Q^T_A Q_B$;

$$Q_A^T Q_B = U \Sigma V^T, \qquad \Sigma = diag\ (\sigma_1, \sigma_2, ..., \sigma_k),$$

From these singular values σ_m's (m = *1, 2, ..., k*), the principal angles θ_m's are defined by

$$\cos(\theta_m) = \sigma_m, \qquad \text{where} \quad \theta_m \in [0, \frac{\pi}{2}].$$

Here, we take only the largest (first) singular value σ_1 and use its corresponding principal angle value θ_1 to compare the visual similarity between two imagery data spaces of region A and B. Finally, we determine any candidate boundary as a real boundary detection if its principal angle θ_1 exceeds a given threshold T.

Since we exploit two time-localized image clusters of successive video frames before and after a candidate boundary, our verification technique effectively detect boundaries of gradual transitions as well as abrupt transitions. Note again that we consider any boundaries whose imagery information is visually dissimilar as the *semantic unit* boundary. These cases usually involve with significant object/camera motions.

3 Dynamic Video Sequence Summarization

As we described in introduction, our method summarizes a video by dynamically changing the rate (i.e., temporal resolution) at which the underlying video is sampled. That rate is determined by the local motion activity in sub-shots of the video. Therefore, our sequential video summarization technique begins with a temporal segmentation step. We decompose the continuous video sequence into "sub-shot" level units, i.e., *intra-shot* boundaries by modifying a method in [16]. We have elected to use "sub-shots" rather than shots, because they provide a more meaningful and detailed representation of the visual content of the video than a shot for our purposes. Note that besides the approach of [16], several other techniques could be used as well to extract the sub-shots.

3.1 Motion Intensity Index

3.1.1 Motion Intensity Index

Once sub-shots have been extracted, our procedure calculates the amount of *visual activity* within each sub-shot unit. To efficiently measure this motion activity, we extract the *motion sequence* from a video using the approach of [20]. Specifically, the motion sequence produced by the temporally high-passed filtering function of 1-D wavelet transform captures only the spatial variations within a sub-shot unit. Then, we compute the *motion intensity index* from each sliding windowed video frames of motion sequence as follows;

$$\text{motion intensity index} = \frac{1}{L}\sum_{i=b+1}^{e}\sum_{m,n}\left|m_i^k(m,n)\right| ,$$

where $m_i^k\,(m,n)$ is the ith frame of motion sequence within the kth sub-shot unit, and L is the length of the analysis window beginning at b^{th} frame and ending at e^{th} frame; i.e., $L = e\text{-}b\text{+}1$ and L is smaller than a length of the shortest sub-shot in video sequence. Therefore, the resulting motion intensity index curve indicates the temporal variations of visual activity in the original video sequence.

Other well-known techniques can be adapted for this task as well.

3.1.2 Temporally Localized Sampling Structure

In order to obtain a localized sampling rate, we partition the time axis into discrete regions of different sampling rates. The motion intensity index curve signal is quantized and converted into different sampling rate levels with a predefined quantization table (see Figure 4). Next, we sample the full-rate sequence in each interval of time at the corresponding appropriate sampling rate that we determined in the previous step. As a result, we use a higher temporal resolution to represent areas characterized by high visual activity and a lower time resolution for static contents. Therefore, the underlying video data is compactly summarized into a moving image sequence that effectively preserves its dynamic nature.

3.1.3 Video Abstract Rendition

Note that if we simply playback the summary sequence produced by our technique at a certain fixed rate, static segments would be rendered at a faster speed than dynamic segments because they are represented by relatively fewer frames. This, of course, distorts the temporal nature of the underlying video. Temporal structure, i.e., variations in shot duration, is an important factor for establishing "visual rhythm" in moving image sequences [13]. Hence, accurate recovery of the time-relationship between clusters of sub-sampled frames is necessary to fully represent the information in the underlying video.

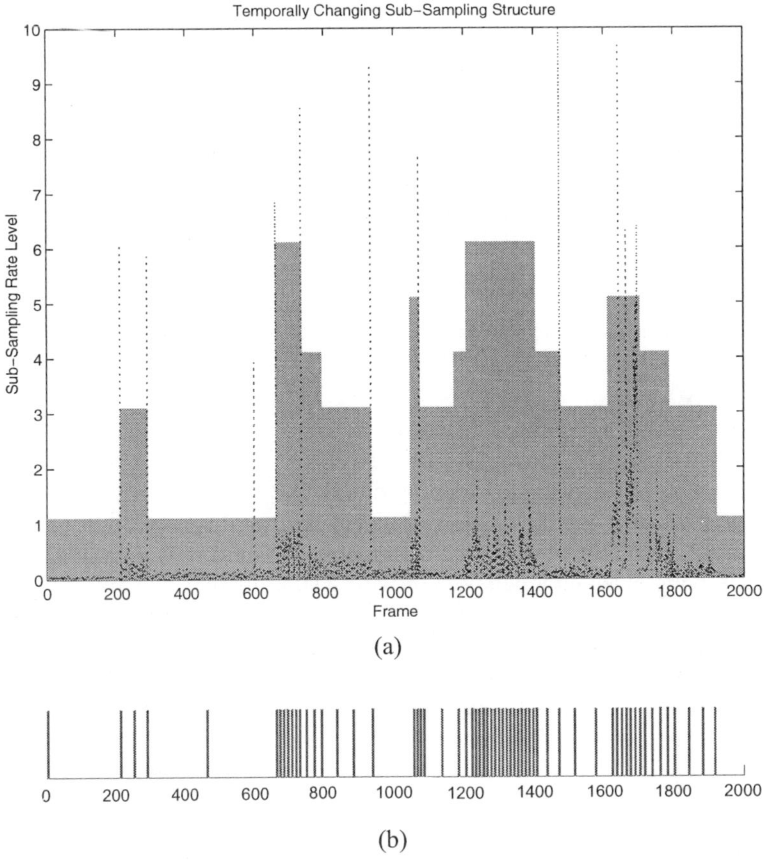

Figure 4. Temporal sub-sampling structure: (a) quantized motion intensity levels mapping to different sub-sampling rates (b) sub-sampled video frames

To quickly and faithfully render the true temporal nature of video, we use a simple piece-wise constant frame interpolation scheme. Given a summary sequence (i.e., dynamically sub-sampled frames) and corresponding information about the local sampling rates, we produce intermediate frames between successive retained frames by simply copying the preceding frame sample as many times as desired (see Figure 5). The target interpolating frame rate is determined by the highest sub-sampling rate used in dynamic regions corresponding to the highest motion intensity index.

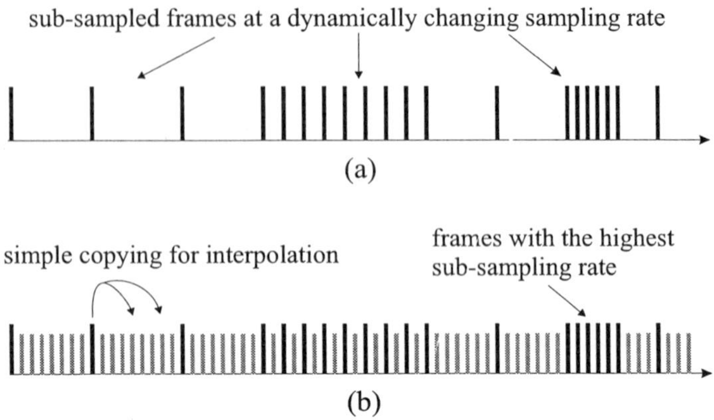

Figure 5. Recovering time-relationship for linear playback: (a) dynamically summarized sequence (b) interpolated sequence

That highest frame sampling rate therefore now becomes the globally uniform frame rendition rate f_S in playback mode. Note that this rate f_S is much lower than the frame rate f_N of the original video by design since our goal is to summarize the video in a short time interval. Note also that the resulting rendition of the video abstract is *very* different from that corresponding to a uniformly subsampled version of the underlying video although both provide a constant playback rate.

Viewers who want to quickly preview only the spatial contents of video data without consideration of any temporal structure (specially, suitable to fast browsing of long video sequences) can turn off the interpolation mode and play the video summary at a constant rate without computing any intermediate frame.

4 Event-Driven Abstraction

Highly compact summarization of a very long video sequence (e.g., feature films) requires that we abstract only conceptually meaningful contents rather than handle the entire material in the video data. In our video summarization scheme, we focus on two representative high-level semantic contents; *emotional dialogues* and *violent featured actions*. Both semantic contents often capture vital messages in the underlying story and many exciting specific events in general movie genres. Note that we characterize these contents at conceptually more specific levels than in previous similar works [6,12]. Note also that we apply our adaptive nonlinear sampling scheme on these events. Therefore, we can achieve a very high compaction rate in the final video summary form.

4.1 Emotional Dialogues Detection

4.1.1 Actual Conversations of Main Characters

We begin with an algorithm proposed by Yeung *et al.* [6]. The basic idea is to detect the time-constrained clusters of shots, specially which consist of alternately recurring two visual contents. In [6] theses visual contents are depicted with a label sequence as follows;

$$\ldots,\ \underbrace{A,\ B,\ A},\ W,\ X,\ Y,\ Z,\ \overbrace{A,\ B,\ A,\ B,\ A,\ B},\ C,\ D,\ E,\ldots,$$

where each alphabet is a label representing each shot and two subsequences (*A, B, A, …,*) are detected subsequence of dialogue-like visual content.

Here, with visually located above dialogues, we make sure if they are actual conversation events by investigating their accompanied audio information. Specifically, we sift only dialogues with speeches by speech/music signal discrimination techniques [17,18]. To discriminate speech signals from music and other sounds, we use a simple classification method using a zero-crossing rate (ZCR) [17].

We now present a novel method to derive information of main characters attending in dialogue scenes. Given these actual conversations, we first classify speakers based on the conversation speeches using a method in our previous work [19]. Then, derived speaker IDs are assigned to the associated dialogue label sequences as following;

$$\{A_1, B_2, A_1, B_2\}, \{C_1, D_3, C_1, D_3\}, \{E_1, F_3, E_1, F_3\}, \ldots,$$

where X_i is a visual shot of a speaker *i*. Although each dialogue shot most likely captures only one speaker's speech, some shots may contain more than two speakers' speeches [19], i.e., asynchronized speech and visual boundaries between different speaker identities (Figure 6). In those cases, we need a sub-division of shot label to represent each speaker's identity (e.g., $A_{1,2} \rightarrow A_1A_2$: a visual shot *A* containing the conversation speech between speaker 1 and 2). Finally, information of main characters is derived by listing the speaker IDs in descending order with the number of appearing in the dialogue label sequences. One or two highest ranked (i.e., the most frequently appearing) speakers are considered as main character(s). For example, main characters in above dialogue labels are order of speaker *1, 3, 2*.

Recall that our goal in this paper aims at the highly compact summarization of a long video. In general, there exist many conversation scenes in a film, especially in drama, romance and comedy genres. Among many dialogues, now we can select only main characters' dialogues for summarization. Furthermore, we focus on more specific events, emotional conversations of main characters, as described in next section.

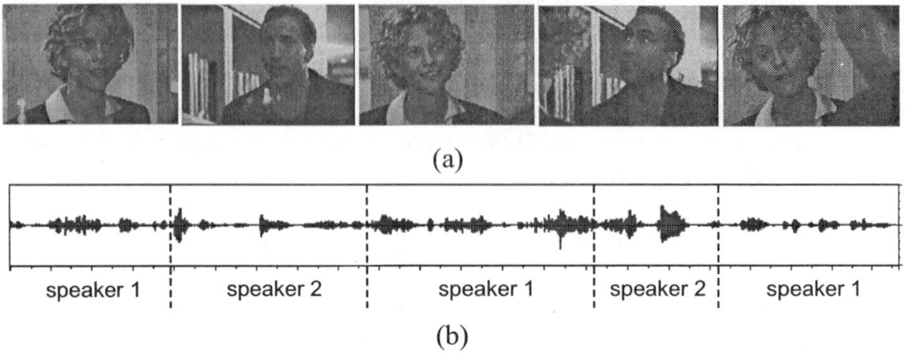

Figure 6. Dialogue: (a) visual content (b) speeches

4.1.2 Vocal Emotion Change

Generally, a film (very long video data) enacts a variety of *emotional* signatures through its whole story [14]. Those emotional dialogue contents often attract viewers' attention and present important messages (especially, of main characters) effecting upon the flow of story. Hence, it is reasonable and effective approach for video abstraction to enclose such conceptually meaningful contents into a summary. Particularly, in this paper we focus on *main characters' conversations containing certain emotions* by discerning from many other ordinary dialogues.

In efforts to detect the emotional dialogues, we analyze speech signal which is a rich source of information containing vocal emotion status as well as speaker identity. Relevant literatures [24,25] on human vocal emotion report that human voices change with emotions and those affective voices are reflected by certain audible signatures (e.g., pitch, speed and loudness etc.) of speech signals.

Particularly, in [25] the five primary emotions (anger, fear, sadness, happiness and disgust) with more subtle secondary emotions, are categorized. Although preliminary studies showed promising results in this literature, these affective recognition still remain as a challenging research issue.

Since our goal is to select certain conceptually meaningful semantic contents for video summarization, we simplify vocal emotional states into only two manifestly distinguishable categories; i.e., *emotional* and *no emotion (neutral)* states. The categorization of emotions in detail is not our main concern here.

Note that we discriminate the conversation speeches of individual speaker (i.e., speaker dependent and text independent continuous speech). Specifically, given each speaker's dialogue speech, we compute two acoustic features; average pitch frequency and temporal variations of speech signal intensity levels. The pitch frequency is estimated by 12-order linear prediction coding (LPC) parameters [25]. For second feature, we compute a variance of signal power levels (dB) within successive 20 msec windowed voice signal segments. Note that, since these two acoustic features effectively indicate the pitch average and temporal intensity structure respectively, we mainly detect the strongly distinguishable emotions; e.g., anger and happiness. These two primary vocal emotions commonly have much higher average pitch value and higher intensity levels than neutral (no emotion) speeches [24].

Our preliminary experimental results are presented in Figure 7. Both male and female speaker cases show that the emotional (O) and neutral (X) speeches are clearly separated in 2-dim feature space. Finally, we perform *K*-mean clustering (*K*=2) on each speaker's feature space, and the emotional speech is defined as any speech belong to a cluster whose mean has both higher feature values than the other cluster's mean.

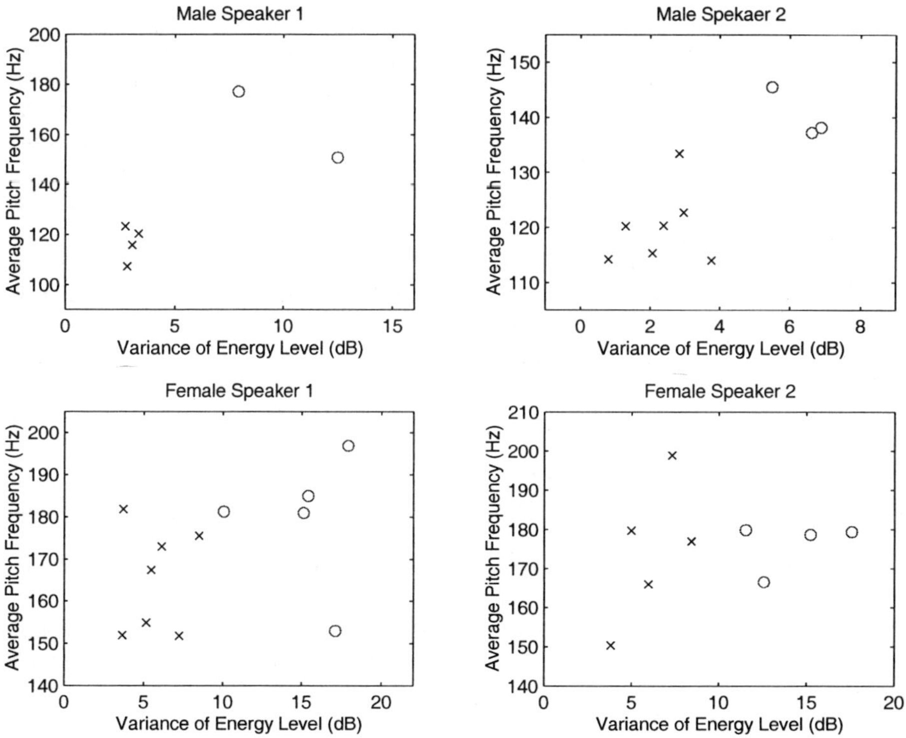

Figure 7. Vocal emotion change: (a) male speakers (b) female speakers; emotional (O) and neutral speeches (X)

4.2 Action Contents with Violent Features

As another conceptually meaningful story content, we also focus on *action event*. These action scenes are often found in general TV drama and films, especially in action, war and adventure genres. Note that, unlike previous works [6,12], we characterize more specific and distinct *violent featured* action events. Particularly, we apply our novel techniques used in [22] for an event-oriented video abstraction. With the emotional dialogue contents in previous section, the detected action events are included into a video summary form.

4.2.1 Visual Signatures

Most action scenes involve rapid and significant movements of persons and objects (e.g., fighting or chasing scenes). To characterize those action contents, we begin with locating a set of time-constrained successive video shots, in which little or no visually similar contents recurring [6]. In addition, we identify successive shots containing dynamic contents of high variations in spatial (object/scene motions) and temporal (shot duration) domains. Specifically, we measure such spatio-temporally dynamic visual activities using a technique in [22]. It is basically similar to the method for computing the motion intensity used in previous section 3. As a result, the shorter length and more spatial motion each shot has, the higher value its motion density metric indicates (refer to [22] for details).

In addition, we investigate more visual features to identify more distinct violent action events. Gunfire and explosion are the most obvious and typical violent events. Those events have very unique audio-visual signatures. To characterize those visual features, we focus on *flame* which can be instantaneously generated by gunfire and explosion (Figure 8). Similar to the effect of a camera flashlight, such a sudden short-time intra-frame variation of global/local intensity leads to a potential false-detection of shot boundaries. These false-detections can be easily be recognized by identifying two sharp peaks close to each other at the temporal video segmentation step [7,22]. Compared with gunfire cases, the flame from explosion mostly show over longer time duration and cover wider areas on the screen. The flames due to explosions have dominant yellow, orange and/or red color histogram components. Hence, we use a predefined color table (palette) containing a certain range of color values matched to flame colors and identify the explosion events.

Some extremely violent actions (e.g., beating, stabbing, gunshot and explosion) result in *bleeding*. Hence, as another violence-related visual feature, we identify bloody color pixels in video frames by simple pixel-matching with the predefined color table (Figure 9). Note that we focus on the temporal location of video frames, which show a noticeable increase in the number of bloody pixels, rather than on the number of such pixels because blood-like colors may appear in non-violent scenes.

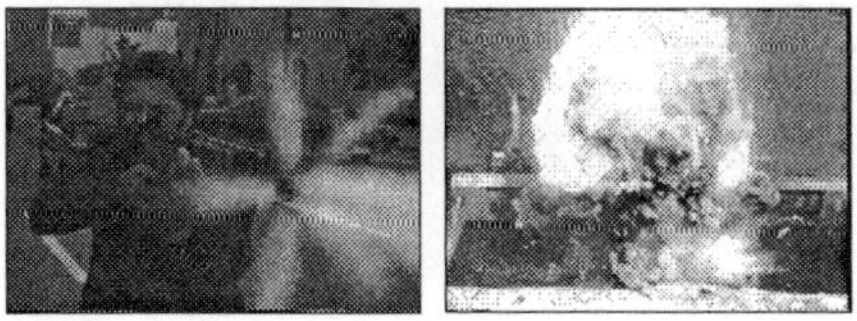

(a) (b)

Figure 8. Flame (a) gunfire (b) explosion

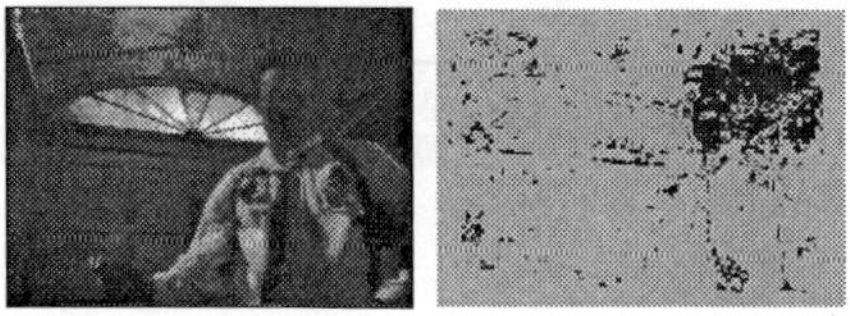

(a) (b)

Figure 9. (a) original frame (b) detected bloody pixels

4.2.2 Audio Signatures

In general, violent scenes are inherently accompanied by unique non-speech audio (e.g., beating, gunshot, explosion, crashing of objects, etc.). With all our visual signatures before, the associated audio information provides a supplement to the identification of violent events. A characterizing feature of violent scenes is the background soundtrack with the unique "sound texture". Particularly, given the audio track for specific successive shots, we discriminate its class (i.e., violent or non-violent soundtrack) based on a Gaussian modeling used in [22]. Once Gaussian model's mean and covariance of the training audio data are obtained, the likelihood ratio between the input audio track and the two sound classes, is computed to determine which class (violent or non-violent) the associated sound belong to.

Additionally, we focus on unique sound effects of beating, gunshot, explosion, crashing of objects and etc. These actions usually happen in a very short time duration (i.e., time-localized events) and cause a *sudden burst of sound*, which is *temporally synchronized* with visual signatures such as flame, bleeding and visually dynamic activities. Here, we detect the abrupt change in energy level of the audio signal as another feature associated with violence. To effectively measure this temporal signature, we use the *energy entropy* criterion I, defined as follows;

$$I = -\sum_{i=1}^{J} \sigma_i^2 \log_2 \sigma_i^2,$$

where J is the total number of segments in a audio analysis frame (each frame is divided into smaller J segments) and σ^2_i is the normalized energy of the ith short segment in a frame (In our experiments, we use K=15 and J=64 with about 46 msec frame of 22 kHz sampled audio signals). Like probabilistic entropy, the value of the energy entropy measure falls down in frames with sudden energy transitions while the energy entropy is largest in a frame with nearly constant energy (Figure 10). Therefore, we can identify the time-localized violent events based on these burst sounds. Note again that we combine these audio cues with synchronized visual cues (e.g., flames and/or bleeding) for more reliable performance [22].

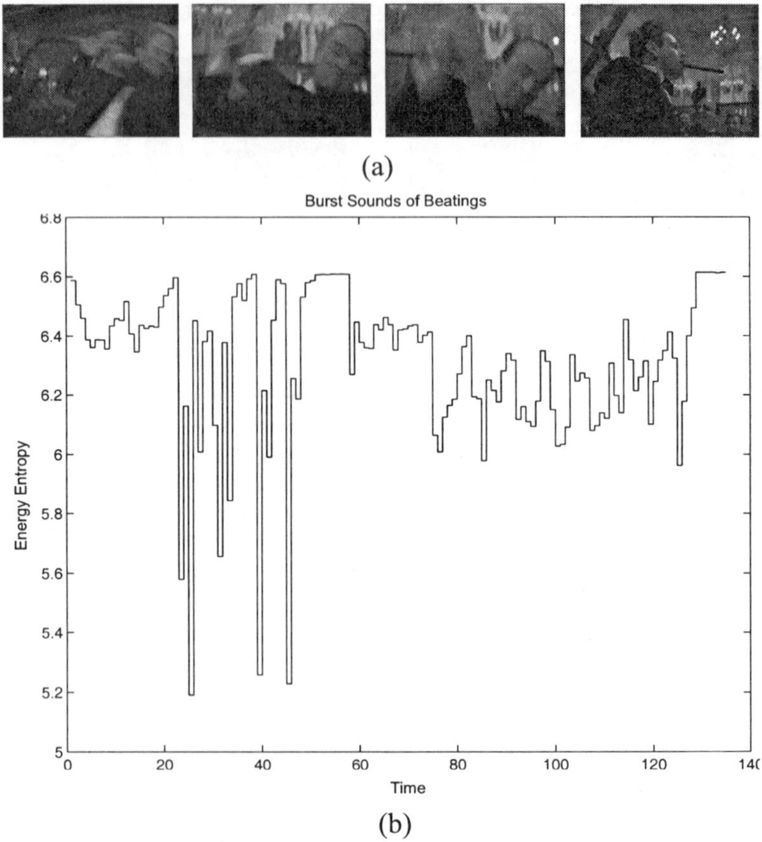

Figure 10. (a) violent beating scene in "The Untouchables" (b) energy entropy of sudden burst sounds

4.3 Summarization of a Long Video

Given the entire sequence of a long video, it demands the elaborate selection of certain temporal events only, to achieve a high compaction rate while preserving essential messages of the underlying story contents of its original video, e.g., short trailer of a movie [12]. Characterization of such meaningful events play an important role to create conceptually well-abstracted summary.

Given a user-defined target length of a short video summary clip (in maximum time length), we first select particular events of interest from a source data (an original long video such as a feature film). Specifically, *emotional dialogues* and *violent actions* are selected with priority over any other portions of video. Then, the remaining parts in the video summary clip are completed by uniformly selecting shot blocks from the original source video. A shot block consists of successive shots. Recall that these shot blocks are also abstracted by the dynamic nonlinear frame sampling method unlike previous related works [9]-[12]. This procedure aims to capture the temporally balanced additional information while preserving the conceptually important events conveying the essential messages of the original source video data.

5 Experimental Results

Let us now present some preliminary experimental results illustrating our video abstracting technique. Figure 11 shows the recovery of the time-relationship for sequential playback of a summarized sequence. A total of 82 frames (marked with O) were retained from 1200 frames. The interpolated rendered sequence consists of 188 frames (82 sub-sampled frames plus 106 interpolations) and is marked with X. Note that it appears much more linear. Therefore, sequential playback of this interpolated sequence preserves the temporal structure of the original video and is visually pleasant.

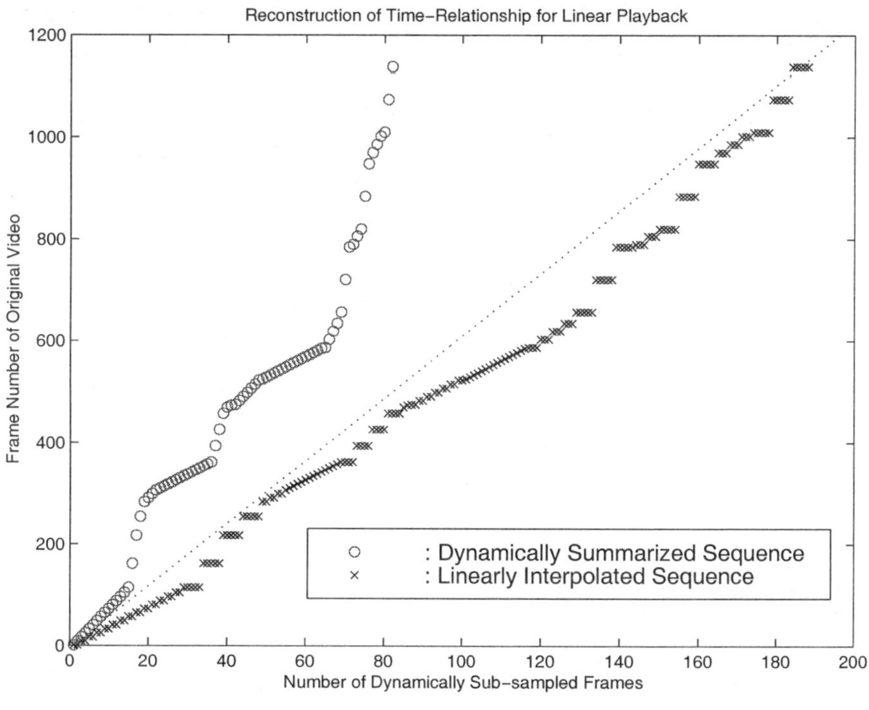

Figure 11. Video abstract rendition: reconstruction of time-relationship for linear playback

Figure 12 shows the summarization of 1200 video frames sampled at 15 frame/sec from the last scene in "FARGO". The motion intensity index levels corresponding to each sub-shot are quantized to different sub-sampling rates with a given sampling rate table. Two different cases are shown in (c) and (d). In each case dynamic and static contents are summarized with different temporal resolutions (i.e., sub-sampling with sequentially changing sampling rate) depending on the amount of local visual activity.

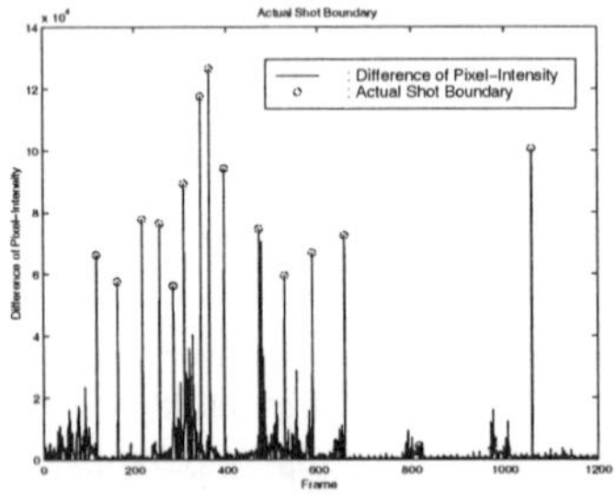

(a)

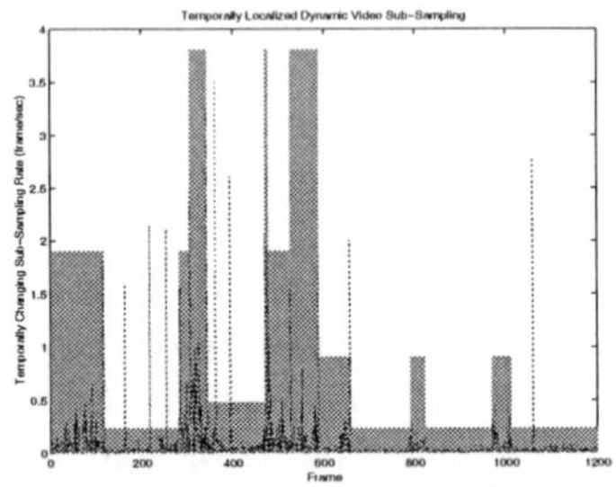

(b)

Sampling Rate (fps)	Sampling Factor
15.00	$2^0=1$
7.50	$2^1=2$
3.75	$2^2=4$
1.88	$2^3=8$
0.94	$2^4=16$
0.48	$2^5=32$
0.23	$2^6=64$

(c)

(d)

Figure 12. Dynamic video summarization (a) actual shot boundaries (b) temporally localized sub-sampling rates (c) successive video shots with different summarizing resolution (d) a video shot consisting of two subshots with different summarizing resolution

Figure 13 shows a violent action event with its relevant experimental results. This scene has a gunfire event causing the sudden bleeding and its sound effect. The results of combining visual features (bleeding, significant activities in shot 3 and 4) and audio feature (bursting sound effects due to gunfires in shot 2 and 7) are presented.

6 Conclusion

In this paper, we have described the technique of dynamically visualized video summarization. Through sequentially changing sub-sampling rate, our proposed

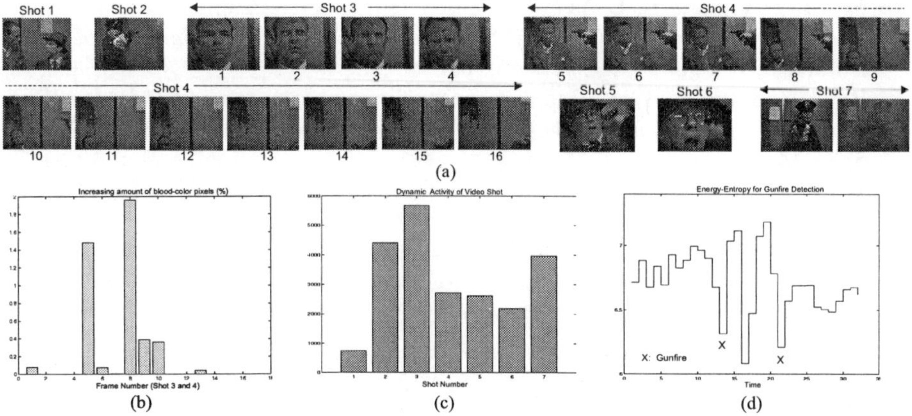

Figure 13. Violent featured action event: (a) gunfire scene (b) blood detection (c) dynamic activity (d) energy-entropy of burst sounds

scheme adapts temporal resolution to its time-localized visual activities (i.e., static and dynamic contents) to preserve temporal nature of its original video. Also, two conceptually meaningful story events (emotional dialogues of main characters and violent featured actions are characterized and selected for highly compact summarization of a long video data.

Although we here mainly focus on abstracting visual stream of video data, its accompanying audio contents, i.e., speech, music and special effect sounds, also need to be carefully abstracted. We are currently investigating the characterization and summarization of audio information, to create a compact audio-visual abstraction of video data. Such a perceptually united summary would convey the essential information of source video in more effective and efficient manner.

References

1. S. W. Smoliar and H. Zhang, "Content-based video indexing and retrieval," *IEEE Multimedia*, vol. **1(2)** (1994) pp. 62-72.
2. B. Furht, S. W. Smoliar, and H. Zhang, *Video and Image Processing in Multimedia Systems*, Kluwer Academic Publishers (1995).
3. Y. Tonomura, A. Akutsu, Y. Taniguchi, and G. Suzuki, "Structured video computing," *IEEE Multimedia*, **1(3)** (1994) pp. 34-43.
4. M. Mills, J. Cohen, and Y. Y. Wong, "A magnifier tool for video data," *Proc. of ACM Computer Human Interface* (1992) pp. 93-98.
5. M. M. Yeung and B. L. Yeo, "Time-constrained clustering for segmentation of video into story units," *ICPR*, vol. **C** (1996) pp. 375-380.

6. M. M. Yeung and B. L. Yeo, "Video content characterization and compaction for digital library," *Proc. of SPIE: Storage and Retrieval for Image and Video Database*, vol. **3022** (1997) pp. 45-58.
7. B. L. Yeo and B. Liu, "Rapid scene analysis on compressed videos," *IEEE Trans. on Circuits and Systems For Video Technology*, vol. **5**, no. **6** (1995) pp. 533-544.
8. W. Wolf, "Key frame selection by motion analysis," *Proc. of IEEE ICASSP*, vol. **2** (1996) pp. 1228-1231.
9. W. Ding, G. Marchionini, and T. Tse, "Previewing video data: browsing key frames at high rates using a video slide show interface," *International Symposium on Research, Development & Practice in Digital Libraries* (1997).
10. D. DeMenthon, V. Kobla, and D. Doermann, "Video summarization by curve simplification," *Proc. of ACM Multimedia* (1998) pp. 211-218.
11. M. A. Smith and T. Kanade, "Video skimming and characterization through the combination of image and language understanding techniques," *Proc. of IEEE CVPR* (1997) pp. 775-781.
12. R. Lienhart, S. Pfeiffer, and W. Effelsberg, "Video abstracting," *Communications of The ACM* (1997) pp. 55-62.
13. B. F. Kawin, *How movies work*, University of California Press, Ltd., London, England (1992).
14. D. Bordwell and K. Thompson, *Film art: an introduction*, McGraw-Hill, 1997.
15. S. Mallat, "A Theory for Multiresolution Signal Decomposition: The Wavelet Representation," *IEEE Trans. Pattern Analysis and Machine Intelligence*, vol. **2**, no. **7** (1989) pp. 674-693.
16. J. Nam and A. H. Tewfik, "Combined audio and visual streams analysis for video sequence Segmentation," *Proc. of IEEE ICASSP*, vol. **4** (1997) pp. 2665-2668.
17. J. Saunders, "Real-Time discrimination of broadcast speech/music," *Proc. of IEEE ICASSP*, vol. **2** (1996) pp. 993-996.
18. E. Scheirer and M. Slaney, "Construction and evaluation of a robust multifeature speech/music discriminator," *Proc. of IEEE ICASSP*, vol. **2** (1997) pp. 1331-1334.
19. J. Nam, A. E. Cetin, and A. H. Tewfik, "Speaker identification and video analysis for hierarchical video shot classification," *Proc. of IEEE ICIP*, vol. **2** (1997) pp. 550-553.
20. J. Nam and A. H. Tewfik, "Progressive resolution motion indexing of video object," *Proc. of IEEE ICASSP*, vol. **4** (1998) pp. 3701-3704.
21. G. H. Golub and C. F. Van Loan, *Matrix Computations*, The Johns Hopkins University Press (1996).
22. J. Nam, M. Alghoniemy, and A. H. Tewfik, "Audio-visual content-based violent scene characterization," *Proc. of IEEE ICIP*, vol. **1** (1998) pp. 353-357.
23. H. Levin and W. Lord, "Speech pitch frequency as an emotional state indicator," *IEEE Trans. Systems, Man and Cybernetics* (1975) pp. 259-273.

24. I. R. Murray and J. L. Arnott, "Toward the simulation of emotion in synthetic speech: a review of the literature on human vocal emotion," *Journal of Acoustical Society of America*, **93:2** (1993).
25. L. R. Rabiner and B. H. Juang, *Fundamentals of speech recognition*, Englewood Cliffs, New Jersey: Prentice-Hall (1993).

MULTIMODAL ANIMATION SYSTEM BASED ON THE MPEG-4 STANDARD

SUMEDHA KSHIRSAGAR, MARC ESCHER, GAEL SANNIER,
NADIA MAGNENAT-THALMANN

MIRALab, CUI, University of Geneva, 24 rue du Général Dufour, 1211 Genéve 4, Switzerland

Tel:+41.22.705.7763 Fax:+41.22.705.7780

Web: http://www.miralab.unige.ch

E-mail:[sumedha, escher, sannier, thalmann]@cui.unige.ch

In this paper we describe experiments of real-time facial animation for generation of various virtual actors using high level-actions, compatible with *MPEG-4* standard specifications. An *MPEG-4* compatible synthetic face and body are integrated into an interactive real-time application allowing the user-friendly control of virtual humans' facial animation and its speech in real-time. This application provides tools for an interactive creation of virtual stories or storyboard. The faces are animated using high-level actions that allow the user to forget the technical side of the animation, and focus only on the more abstract and intuitive part of the facial animation. They represent a top layer constructed over the *MPEG-4* Facial Animation Parameters (FAP).

1 Introduction

The ISO/IEC JTC1/SC29/WG11 (Moving Pictures Expert Group - MPEG) has formulated a new *MPEG-4* standard [1,2,3]. *MPEG-4* sets its objectives beyond "plain" compression. Instead of regarding video as a sequence of frames with fixed shape and size and with attached audio information, the video scene is regarded as a set of dynamic objects. The objects are spatially and temporally independent and therefore can be stored, transferred and manipulated independently. The composition of the final scene is done at the decoder, potentially allowing great manipulation freedom to the consumer of the data.

Video and audio acquired by recording from the real world is called natural. In addition to the natural objects, synthetic, computer generated graphics and sounds are being produced and used in ever increasing quantities. *MPEG-4* aims to enable the integration of synthetic objects within the scene. It will provide support for 3D graphics, synthetic sound, Text to Speech, as well as synthetic faces and bodies. This paper will describe the use of facial and body definitions and animations parameters, as defined in *MPEG-4* in an interactive real-time animation system.

1.1 *Face definition and animation in* MPEG-4

The Face and Body animation Ad Hoc Group (FBA) deals with the coding of human faces and bodies, i.e. efficient representation of their shape and movement. This is important for a number of applications ranging from communication, entertainment to ergonomics and medicine. The group has defined in detail the parameters for both definition and animation of human faces and bodies. These are being updated within the current *MPEG-4* Committee Draft. Definition parameters allow detailed definition of body and face shape, size and texture. Animation parameters allow the definition of facial expressions and body postures. The parameters are designed to cover all naturally possible expressions and postures, as well as exaggerated expressions and motions to some extent (e.g. for cartoon characters). The animation parameters are precisely defined in order to allow accurate implementation of any facial/body model. In the following paper we will mostly discuss about face animation. To define a face, two types of parameters are defined; both based on a set of feature points located at morphological places on the face (Figure 1). The two following sections will briefly describe the Face Animation Parameters (*FAP*) and the Face Definition Parameters (*FDP*). These play a key role in facial animation systems based on the MPEG-4 standard.

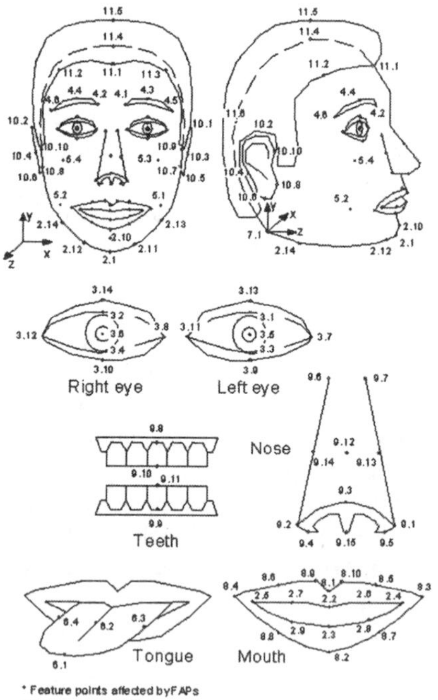

Figure1. *FDP* feature point set and feature points affected by *FAP*s.

1.2 Face Animation Parameter set

*FAP*s represent a complete set of basic facial actions, and therefore allow the representation of most natural facial expressions. The parameter set contains two high level parameters, the *viseme*, and the *expression*. The viseme parameter allows the rendering of visemes on the face without the need to express them in terms of other parameters or to enhance the result of other parameters, insuring the correct rendering of visemes. Similarly, the expression parameter allows definition of high level facial expressions.

1.3 Face Definition Parameter set

An *MPEG-4* decoder supporting the Facial Animation must have a generic facial model capable of interpreting *FAP*s. This insures that it can reproduce facial expressions and speech pronunciation. When it is desired to modify the shape and appearance of the face and make it look like a particular person/character, *FDP*s are necessary. *FDP*s are used to personalize the generic face model to a particular face. *FDP*s are normally transmitted once per session, followed by a stream of compressed *FAP*s. More detailed discussion on *FDP*s and their role in defining and creating synthetic faces can be found in[4].

2 Real-time facial animation system

This section describes a real-time interactive animation system based on *FAP*s. We use *MPEG-4* compliant faces and bodies for animation. However, to allow an inexperienced user to generate complex animations without getting into the strict specification of *MPEG-4*, we have implemented a multi-layered system that uses high-level actions to interface with the *MPEG-4 FAP* specifications. The definition of high-level actions, how they are defined and implemented will be detailed in the following sections.

2.1 From High-Level actions to FAP*s*

In order to allow an animator to work on a task level where she/he can define animation in terms of its inherent sources we use a multi-layered approach in our application [5]. Each level of the hierarchy is in the increasing degree of abstraction. It offers the advantage of providing the user a relatively low level of complexity with concepts more global than the previous layers. For instance, complex expressions, such as emotions or even speech, can be described more easily in this multi-layered system. In our whole animation system we can distinguish four levels of abstraction as shown in Figure 2. On the high-level actions layer, the animator can choose between three types of envelopes describing the evolution of the deformation of a face through time. Figure 3 displays the three available envelope shapes.

High-level actions	Description of intensity over time
↓	
Mid-level actions	Definition of movements
↓	
Low-level actions	Definition of FAPs
↓	
Deformations	Mesh deformations

Figure 2. Level hierarchy and effects

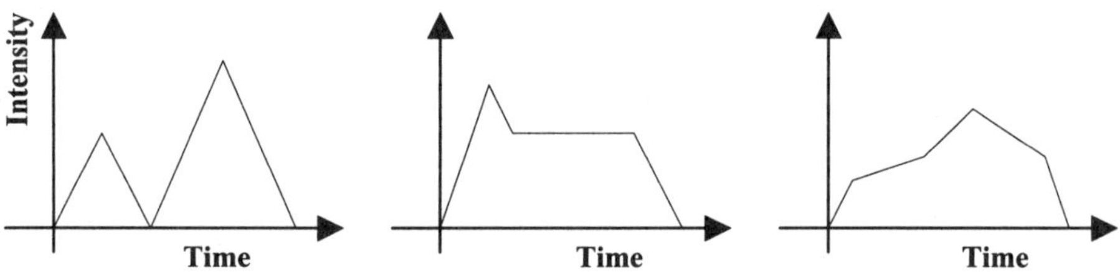

Figure 3. Three available high-level action envelope shapes

A mid-level action is a snapshot of position/expression that has been defined by the designer. Figure 4 shows six mid-level expressions. The designer has interactively set a number of values to the desired *FAP*s to obtain the desired expression. As described in subsection 2.2 these *FAP*s are generally composed/defined manually using 3D animation softwares. They can also be extracted more automatically with the help of external devices such as cameras [6,7,8], or 3D scanners [9,10].

The low-level layer is the description of the location of the *FAP* points on the face mesh in a neutral position. Among the high-level actions (the only layer visible to the user) one can distinguish three different types of actions: basic emotions, visemes and user-defined expressions. The basic emotions correspond to the 6 emotions defined in the first field of the *MPEG-4 FAP* definition: joy, sadness, anger, fear, disgust and surprise.

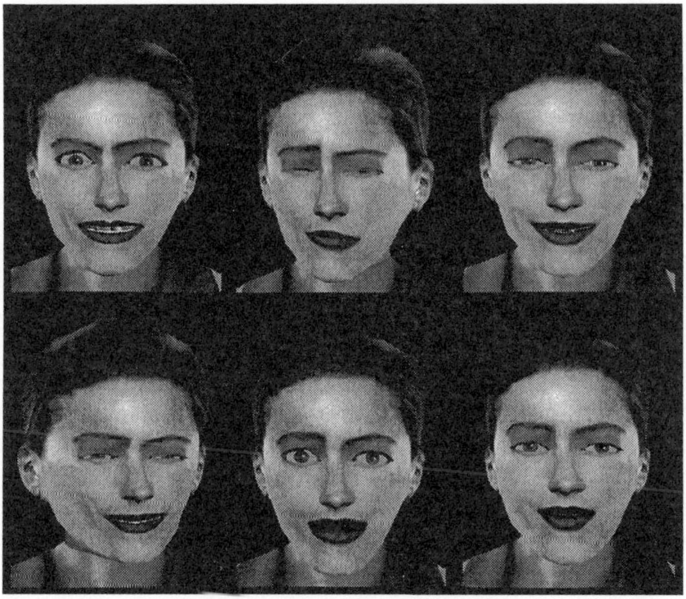

Figure 4. Mid-level face expressions

Viseme	Phoneme	Example
0	None	NA
1	p, b, m	put, bed, mill
2	f, v	far, voice
3	T, D	think, that
4	t, d	tip, doll
5	k, g	call, gas
6	tS, dZ, S	chair, join, she
7	s, z	sir, zeal
8	n, l	not, lot
9	r	red
10	A	car
11	e	bed
12	I	tip
13	Q	top
14	U	book

Table 1. *MPEG-4* viseme definition

The visemes (visual phonemes) we use are the direct correspondent to the 14 visemes defined in the second field of the *MPEG-4 FAP* standard (Table 1). A sequence of temporized visemes (with duration information included) can be saved as a high-level speech action with its corresponding audio speech stream. Finally an open set of expressions built by the user can be used to generate more original animations. Interactive real-time animation allows the animator to activate any action of any type at any time. This brings the possibility of having several high-level actions active at the same time. As long as these actions do not modify the same region of the face i.e. the same *FAP*, there is no problem. But in the other case, we have to implement a mechanism to perform their composition or blending. Good blending of several high-level actions is important to guarantee continuous animation.

The deformation of the 3D face mesh driven by *FAP* displacements is based on Rational Free-Form Deformations (RFFD) [5,11]. A surrounding control box controls each set of vertices of the face that is within the influence of a *FAP*. Setting a specific weight to a control point of the control box generates the mesh deformation.

2.2 Interactive Facial Expression Generation

Our face is the expressional support to our emotions. Through education, each person learns how to decode the different emotional states and uses them when communicating within his social group.

These states or expressions lie on the coordination of three parameters:

- The architectural shape of the face.
- The muscular tension of the shape (ranging from a relaxed position to a tense one).
- The temporal description of the expression through time.

The mixing of these three parameters shows the magnitude of the human expressions.

Before generating the expressions, we look at several pictures of a professional mime performing different expressions such as fear, joy, anger, laugh, sadness, disgust, hypocrisy, contempt, pride, greed etc and also individual phonemes. Along with the pictures, the dynamic of the expressions is also captured in short digitized films. A proprietary software is used to deform a synthetic 3D face. The software allows the designer to set individual *FAP*s, allowing the user to generate virtually every possible expression. Based on the previously taken pictures the designer composes the corresponding synthetic expressions by setting interactively the parameters of the software and ultimately generates a mid-level expression composed of several *FAP*s (Figure 5). As can be seen from the figure, the designer can set the sliders on the software panel in order to match the expression on the synthetic face with the one on the picture of a real person. This gives rise to a bank of several mid-level expressions for further use. These static mid-level expressions can be further animated permitting the designer to set the intensities of the envelope of the associated high-level action (Figure 6). Thus, the designer can compose mid-level expressions as well as static visemes, which will be used by the user of our system to generate high level actions like emotions and speech. These high-level actions are time varying, unlike mid-level static ones.

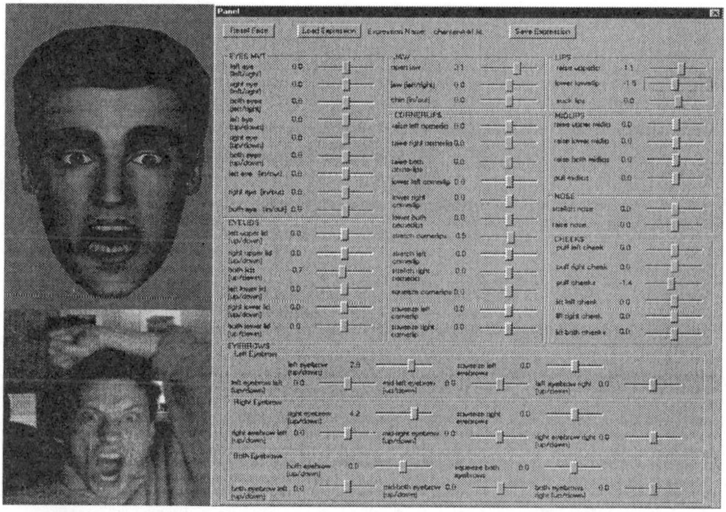

Figure 5. Generation of facial expression for a synthetic face using a real face

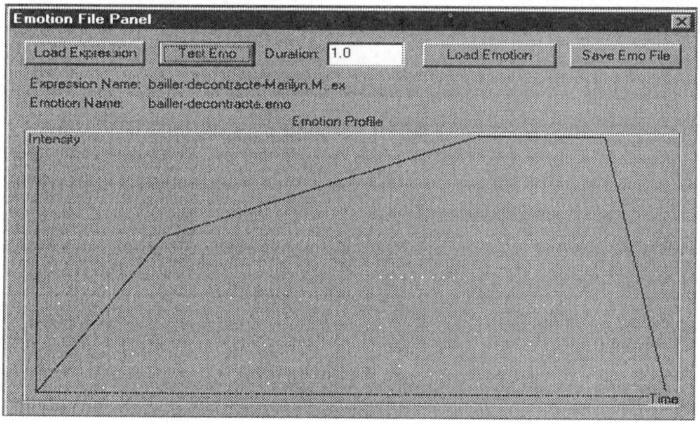

Figure 6. Defining high-level action envelope

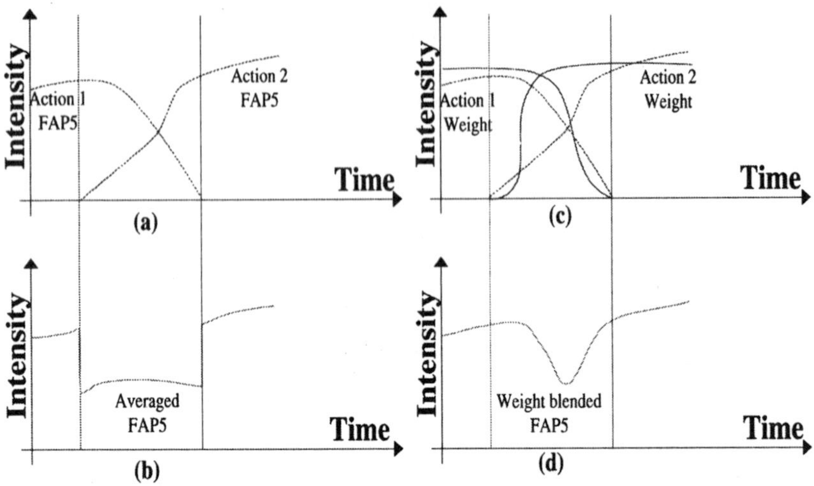

Figure 7. FAP composition problem and solution

2.3 *Action blending*

The problem of action blending increases when several high-level actions are active at the same time setting a value for the same *FAP*. If it is not handled with care it can produce discontinuities in the animation. This is particularly important if we want to get a natural facial animation. A discontinuity can happen at the activation or at the termination of each high-level action when combined with another one. For instance if we take the two *FAP* frame sequence of Figure 7(a) and compute the average of each frame, one can see that at the beginning of action two and at the end of action one we have a large discontinuity as shown in figure 7(b). This problem was treated by [12]. The solution we have chosen is to add to each high-level action a weighting curve (Fig. 7(c)), which minimizes the contribution of each high-level action at its activation and at its termination (Fig. 7(d)). The weighting curve values are generally set between 0 and 1. The composition formula used to compute the value of a *FAP* at a specific time **t** modified by **n** high-level actions is given by the following *FAP* composition equation.

$$FAP_{Final} = \frac{\sum_{i=1}^{n} Weight_{i,t} Intensity_i FAPValue_{i,t}}{\sum_{i=1}^{n} Weight_{i,t}}$$

In this equation **Intensity** is the global intensity of the high-level action **i,** and **FAPValue** is the *FAP* movement in the high-level action **i** at time **t**. This blending function is acting only at the *FAP* level and only when several high-level actions are setting values for the same action-unit. We have introduced the Intensity factor to enable the modulation of a similar high-level action in different contexts. For instance we can use the same smile (high-level action) to generate a broad smile or a small one depending on the value of the intensity. It is also used in the complex process of lip movement for speech articulation.

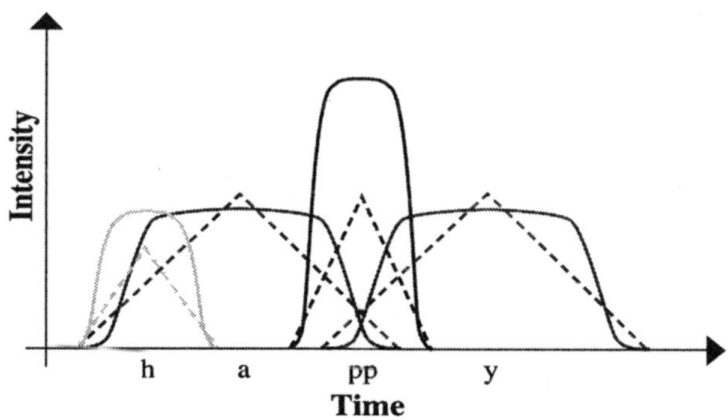

Figure 8. Viseme co-articulation for the word 'happy'

2.4 Speech co-articulation

Several pieces of work have been done in the area of speech co-articulation and visemes definition [12,13,14]. Concerning the visemes co-articulation, we have defined four types of visemes: Vowels, consonants, plosives and fricatives. Each group has its own co-articulation parameters. In the process of articulating a word or a sentence our brain and mouth do some on the fly 'pre-processing' in order to generate a fluent and continuous speech. Among these complex processings is the mixing of lip/jaw movements to compose basic sounds or phonemes of the sentence. For instance when you pronounce 'hello', even before saying the 'h' your mouth is taking the shape of the 'e' that is coming afterwards. During the pronunciation of the 'll' your mouth is also making the transition between the 'e' and the 'o'. Temporal behavior of the different vismes groups has been specified. The vowels, especially, tend to overlap the other vismes. The region of the mouth that is deformed is also specific to each viseme group. Typically the plosives act on the closure of the mouth and lip protrusion, and have little action with corner-lips. Applying the blending function that was described previously, we have associated three parameters to each viseme group: overlapping, intensity and weight. The

Overlapping describes the percentage of time that a viseme overlaps its neighbors. The intensity allows the stressing of some articulation or the simulation of shouting or whispering. Finally the weight fixes priorities to some visemes, typically plosives for which the mouth closure is mandatory. For instance if we have a high-level action of surprise (with mouth opening) and we want to articulate 'b' at the same time, we will give a low weight to the surprise action and a high one to the 'b' viseme to guarantee the closure of the mouth. Figure 8 gives an example of co-articulation for the word 'happy'.

2.5 From speech or text to mouth movements

To generate speech, various methods and softwares can be used. What we need as input is an audio file with its corresponding temporized phonemes. Two natural types of data can be used to generate phonemes: text and speech. For text to phoneme we are using Festival Speech Synthesis System from University of Edinburgh, UK, and for phoneme to speech (synthetic voice) we use MBROLA from Faculte Polytechnique de Mons, Belgium, both are public domain. To go from phonemes to visemes we have integrated a correspondence table. This table has been built by designers using a proprietary face modeling software with snapshots of real talking faces to generate the visemes actions.

The extraction of phonemes from speech signal is a more difficult task. We are using the AbbotDemo Freeware to extract the phoneme information from a speech file. To extract temporized phonemes from speech, either microphone or pre-recorded, the speech recognition software needs to be programmed as per the needs. We look at two possibilities of doing this. We can use a dictation grammar for a large vocabulary speech recognition engine, when the speech content is not known a-priori. The speech recognition software, in this case, may not output the exact speech spoken. Speaker independent continuous speech recognition softwares are far from 100% accuracy, even today. However, in this application, we are not interested in the actual words spoken, but the phonemes or even more generally, visemes content. Our experiments show that the results are quite satisfactory on phoneme level, with the use of dictation grammar on a large vocabulary speech recognition engine. If the speech content is known a-priori, then a Context Free Grammar can be used for speech recognition. Using this, speech recognition software can be programmed to recognize previously known sentences. The part of result then returned by the engine in the process of recognition, is used to extract the temporized phonemes.

It can be noted here that, the use of speech recognition is not probably the best and the most optimal way of doing phoneme extraction. Also, it has restrictions for the language, accent etc. Other methods of doing this have been tried before, some of which are explained in [15,16].

3 Virtual Human Director

In the previous sections, we described how we generate a virtual face animation based on *MPEG-4* parameters. In this section, we present a system managing the real-time animation of virtual humans based on the described animation system.

Figure 9. Real-time animated virtual humans in VHD

3.1 Real-time director

Virtual Human Director (VHD) is a real-time system developed for the creation of scenarios involving virtual humans [17]. In Figure 9 we can see different examples of virtual humans animated in VHD. A user-friendly GUI gives control of the virtual faces, bodies and cameras to a single user. The issue of the easy control of a virtual face was raised in [18]. The VHD interface provides an extension of this concept through simple and easy control of multiple actors and a camera in real-time. One key aspect is that the user can trigger the main actions in real-time, similar to a producer directing actors before a shooting. As this task is complicated, we limited the interaction to high-level actions. The speech is activated by typing/selecting simple text-based sentences and predefined facial and body animation is available in the interface. Section 3.2 highlights some of the issues related to body animation. Facial animations have been generated using proprietary facial animation software. The duration of the facial animation can be still controlled interactively from the interface. Though the actions are easy to trigger in real-time for one single virtual human, the task becomes more and more complicated with more virtual humans. In order to simplify this task, we have developed a timing control for programming the activation of actions in advance and for repeating events such as eye blinking or virtual twitch. A simple scripting language was also developed to be able to program the activation of a list of actions through time. It allows the setup of "background" virtual humans with completely predefined "behavior". The user can also use this scripting/recording tool to associate actions. For example, associating a smile, a head motion and the sentence "I am happy" into one single new action usable from the interface.

3.2 Real-time body animation

In VHD, we have two types of body motions: predefined gestures and task-oriented motion. Predefined gestures are prepared using key-frame animation and motion capture. For task oriented motions like walking, we use motion motors.

3.2.1 Motion capturing and predefined postures

A traditional way of animating virtual humans is playing key-frame sequences. We can record specific human body postures or gestures with a magnetic motion capturing system and an anatomical converter [19], or we can design human postures or gestures using the TRACK proprietary system [20]. Motion capturing can be best achieved by using a large number of sensors to register every degree of freedom of the real body. Molet et. al. [19] discuss that a minimum of 14 sensors are required to manage a bio-mechanically correct posture. The raw data coming from the trackers has to be filtered and processed to obtain *MPEG-4* Body Animation Parameters (*BAP*). Our software permits the real-time conversion of raw tracker data into *BAP*s.

The TRACK software is an interactive tool for the visualization, editing and manipulation of multiple track sequences. To record an animation sequence, we create key positions from the scene, then store the 3D parameters as 2D tracks of the skeleton joints or *BAP*s. The stored key-frames, from the TRACK system or magnetic tracker, can be used to animate the virtual human in real-time. We used predefined postures and gestures to perform realistic hand and upper body gestures for interpersonal communications. Figure 10 presents some predefined postures and a body animation part of the user interface. The users can trigger gestures and postures from a list on the main interface. Moreover the user can automate the activation of gestures and postures from the interface. Right most image on Figure 10 shows details from user interface. The upper slider "Weight" defines the weight of current active key-frame in case of a motion merge with other body animation. Under the slider there is a selectable list of available key-frames.

Figure 10. Key-frame examples with user interface

Figure 11. Walking example with interface

3.2.2 Motion motors

We used one motion motor for the body locomotion [21]. Current walking motor enables virtual humans to travel in the environment using instantaneous velocity of motion. One can compute the walking cycle length and time from which the necessary *BAP*s can be calculated for animation. This instantaneous speed oriented approach influenced VHD user interface design, where the user is directly changing the speed. On the other hand, VHD also supports another module for controlling walking, where the user can control walking with simple commands like "WALK_FASTER" or "TURN_LEFT". This simple interface allows specific user interfaces to interact with VHD easier.

A possible user interface is a touch phone to control walking. In this case setting speed and direction is impossible with our first method. The latter one solves this problem in a natural way where we can map our commands to each key on number pad. Figure 11 includes snapshots from a walking session in one picture. In many cases actors are expected to perform multiple body motions like waving while walking.

3.3 MPEG-4 *in VHD*

To create new virtual humans available in VHD, we are using heads created from two orthogonal photographs as described in [4].

3.3.1 Virtual Humans Modeling

Template bodies are created for the male and female on which we replace the generic head. The methodology used for the creation of the virtual bodies is described in paper [22]. To animate a virtual head in VHD, the only data needed is the topology and the facial-animation feature points. The heads created with our methodology using *FDP* parameters provide this information, so the heads are directly usable in VHD.

3.3.2 Animation

In order to animate the virtual humans using the *MPEG-4* parameters, we provide a set of predefined animations for each virtual human. The body is animated using key-frames based on the joint angles of a virtual skeleton, which are close to the *MPEG-4 FDP*s. A key aspect is that we can mix facial animations in real-time. For example we can "play" a smile while the virtual human is speaking and we can also mix the emotion *smile* with the emotion *surprise* to obtain a new combined expression. Figure 12 shows an example of smile combined with a speech sequence. The idea is then to provide only a simple set of facial animations as the basic emotional states of a virtual human. By the combination of these emotions we can obtain more complex animation of the virtual face. The basic set of facial emotions includes animations of the eyes and eyebrow (*eye motions, astonishment*), animation of the mouth (*smile...*), and global animation of the face (*surprise, smile, fear, happiness* and etc.). By decomposing the animation of the face into one set for the upper part, one for the lower part, and one for the global facial animation, we can obtain a great range of possible combinations. The result of such a combination can also be saved into a new *FAP* file. One can use this way to generate new facial animations, or to record a complete track of facial animations in *MPEG-4* format.

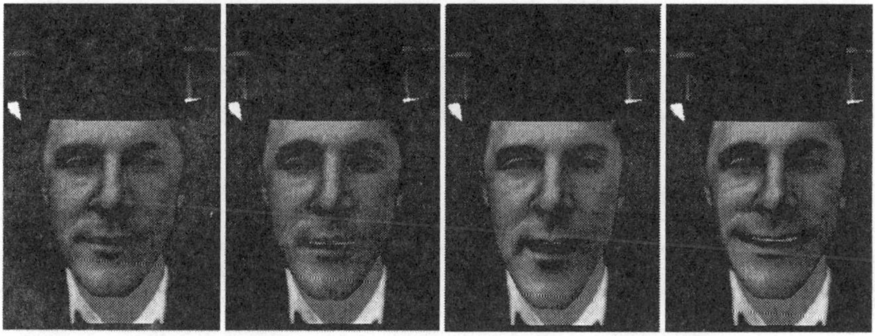

Figure 12. *MPEG-4* head animated using *FAP*

3.4 *VHD real-time performance*

We tested our software extensively within the European project VISTA together with broadcasting partners, to produce TV programs. After several tests with designers and directors, our concept of one single integrated platform for virtual humans has obtained good feedback. Our interface is a very straightforward concept and highest level of control allows designers to control virtual humans in a natural fashion. We included several traditional camera operations into our interface to allow directors to use VHD without a steep learning curve.

We tested VHD with a close-up of a virtual head made of 2313 triangles and fully textured. Figure 13 presents the results of our trials on the following computers using full screen (1280x1024) and a 400x500 pixels window:

1. O2 R5000 at 200MHz
2. Octane R10000 at 195 MHz
3. Onyx2 2x R10000 at 195MHz

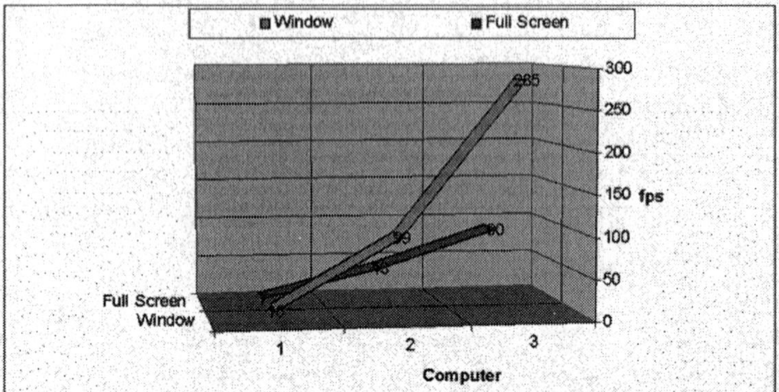

	1	2	3
Window	15	99	285
Full Screen	7	43	90

Figure 13. Number of frames per second in VHD

4 Conclusions and future work

In this paper we presented a real-time animation system. The strong points of our method are the definition of tools allowing the animation of the synthetic head at a high-level of abstraction based on the *MPEG-4* Face Animation Parameters (*FAP*), the use of speech processing tools for effective speech animation, and finally the integration of all these techniques in a real-time interactive application that allows a designer to generate a complex *MPEG-4* based animation.

5 Acknowledgments

This research was funded by the european projects VIDAS, VISTA, PAVR and the Swiss National Research Foundation. The authors would like to thank the MIRALab staff for their help and especially Dr. L.Moccozet, Dr. I.Pandzic, P. Beylot for their technical support and Dr. Zanardi, S. Hadap for their document formatting knowledge. Thanks are due to Markus Schmid, the mime artist, for generating a variety of facial expressions.

References

1. [MPEG-N1901] Text for CD 14496-1 Systems, *ISO/IEC JTC1/SC29/WG11 N1886*, MPEG97/November 1997.

2. [MPEG- N1902] Text for CD 14496-2 Video, *ISO/IEC JTC1/SC29/WG11 N1886*, MPEG97/November 1997.

3. R. Koenen, F. Pereira, and L. Chiariglione. MPEG-4: Context and Objectives, *Image Communication Journal, Special Issue on MPEG-4,* Vol. 9, No. 4, May 1997.

4. W. S. Lee, M. Escher, G. Sannier, and N. Magnenat-Thalmann, MPEG4 Compatible Faces from Orthogonal Photos, *Proc. Computer Animation'99.*

5. P. Kalra, A. Mangili, N. Magnenat-Thalmann, and D. Thalmann. Simulation of Facial Muscle Actions Based on Rational Free Form Deformations, *Proc. Eurographics'92*, pp. 59-69, NCC Blackwell,1992.

6. D. Terzopoulos, and K. Waters K. Analysis and synthesis of facial image sequences using physical and anatomical models, *IEEE Transactions on Pattern Analysis and Machine Intelligence*, 15(6):569-579, 1993.

7. A.Blake, and M. Isard. 3D position, attitude and shape input using video tracking of hands and lips, *Computer Graphics (Proc. SIGGRAPH 94)*, 28:185-192, July 1994.

8. I.S. Pandzic, P. Kalra, N. Magnenat-Thalmann, and D. Thalmann. Real time facial interaction, *Displays* 15 (3):157-163. 1994.

9. J. Kleiser. A fast, efficient, accurate way to represent the human face. In *State of the Art in Facial Animation, SIGGRAPH 89 Tutorial*, Vol. 22, pp. 37-40. 1989.

10. Y. Lee, D. Terzopoulos, and K. Waters. Realistic modeling for facial animation. *Computer Graphics (Proc. SIGGRAPH 95)*, 29(4):55-62. 1995

11. P. Kalra. An Interactive Multimodal Facial Animation System, *PhD Thesis nr. 1183*, EPFL, 1993.

12. M.M. Cohen, and D.W. Massaro. Modeling Coarticulation in Synthetic Visual Speech, *Models and Techniques in Computer Animation, N. M. Thalmann, and D. Thalmann (Eds.), Tokyo: Springer-Verlag*, pp. 139-156. 1993.

13. C. Benoit, T. Lallouache, T. Mohamadi, and C. Abry. A set of French visemes for visual speech synthesis. In *G. Bailly C. Benoit, (Eds.), Talking machines: Theories, Models, and Designs, Amsterdam: North Holland*, 485-504. 1992

14. S. E. Boyce, Coarticulatory Organization for Lip Rounding in Turkish and English. *Journal of the Acoustical Society of America* 88(6), 2584-2595. 1990

15. E. Yamamoto, S. Nakamura, K. Shikano, Lip movement synthesis from speech based on Hidden Markov Models, *Speech Communication*, (26)1-2 (1998) pp. 105-115.

16. D. V. McAllister, R. D. Rodman, D. L. Bitzer, A. S. Freeman, Lip synchronization of Speech, *Proc. AVSP 97*, Rhodes, Greece, September 1997.

17. G. Sannier, S. Balcisoy, N. Magnenat Thalmann, and D. Thalmann. An Interactive Interface for Directing Virtual Humans, *Proc. ISCIS'98*, IOS Press, 1998.

18. N. Magnenat-Thalmann, P. Kalra, and M. Escher. Face to Virtual Face, *Proc. of the IEEE.* Vol.86, No. 5, May, 1998.

19. T. Molet, R. Boulic, D. Thalmann, A Real Time Anatomical Converter for Human Motion Capture, Eurographics Workshop on Computer Animation and Simulation, R. Boulic and G. Herdon (Eds), ISBN 3-211-828-850, Springer-Verlag Wien, pp. 79-94,1996.

20. R. Boulic et. al. Goal Oriented Design and Correction of Articulated Figure Motionwith the TRACK system, Computer and Graphics, Pergamon Press, Vol. 18, No. 4., pp. 443-452, 1994.

21. R. Boulic, D. Thalmann, N. Magnenat Thalmann, A Global Human Walking Model with real-Time Kinematic Personification, the Visual Comuter, Vol. 6, No. 6, pp. 344-358, 1990.

22. J. Shen and D. Thalmann. Interactive Shape Design Using Metaballs and Splines, *Proc. Implicit Suraces, Eurographics*, Grenoble, France, 1995.

23. M. Escher, I. Pandzic, and N. Magnenat-Thalmann. Facial Animation and Deformation for MPEG-4 , *Proc. Computer Animation'98*, 1998.

MODELING METHODS FOR REUSABLE AND INTEROPERABLE VIRTUAL ENTITIES IN VIRTUAL WORLDS

MICHEL SOTO, SÉBASTIEN ALLONGUE

Laboratoire LIP6
Université Pierre et Marie Curie
75252 Paris Cedex 05, FRANCE
E-mail: Michel.Soto@lip6.fr

Virtual Worlds are facing several challenges to become a mature technology commonly used in their numerous potential applications such as games, training, education, health and collaborative work. The designing of virtual world remains an empirical process. This problem increases the cost and the needed time for designing virtual worlds. This paper proposes a methodology for decreasing these cost and needed time. The main interest of the proposed methodology is to provide virtual worlds with interoperability and reusability properties. The originality of this methodology is to rely on multiagent concepts and learning techniques.

1 Introduction

The design of virtual worlds is a difficult task because of the numerous high technologies involved: 3D image, network, distributed databases, multimedia, etc. There are also several major issues raised (e.g. latency, scaling, world consistency) due to the real-time and networked features of virtual worlds which make their design even more complex. This situation reduces the profitability of virtual worlds and slows their spread in the potential domains such as games, training, education, health and collaborative work. One way to speed up the design of virtual worlds and thus to increase their profitability is to provide them and their populating virtual entities with interoperability capabilities.

Interoperability capabilities for virtual worlds are not only needed for profitability and easier design but also needed by applications. Indeed, today's virtual worlds are closed worlds. This means, for instance, that users of one collaborative virtual world cannot collaborate with users of another different collaborative virtual world. This also means that autonomous virtual entities or users cannot travel from virtual world to virtual world in web-like manner. These limitations must be removed to make virtual worlds a basic technology used in all above-mentioned domains.

Taking into account the interoperability requirement immediately raises the problem of heterogeneity. Therefore, successful paradigms aiming at interoperability must consider it. Heterogeneity appears at any level between distinct virtual worlds: hardware, software, operating system, communication stack protocols, and input/output devices. Solutions already exist (e.g. ISO and TCP/IP protocols, ODP,

CORBA) to deal with these levels of heterogeneity and thus allowing interoperability. The point is that heterogeneity also appears at the application level that is the most important for virtual worlds. At this level, interoperability paradigms must allow to answer questions such as:

- Having users working together from their respective virtual worlds, what does their interaction capabilities become?
- What does the behavior of a virtual entity migrating from its native virtual world to a new one become?

Interoperability relies on reuse of virtual worlds and virtual entities rather than develop new ones. For example, if two groups of users in two different virtual worlds need to collaborate, interoperability allows them to do it using from their respective virtual world instead of using a new common one. In the same way, existing virtual entities developed for a specific virtual world will be reused to populate a new virtual world or to improve different existing ones. Reusability cannot be achieved with an empirical process design: modeling methods are needed.

The NOVÆ (Networked Open VirtuAl Environment) project proposes a modeling method and architectural concepts to address the issue of virtual worlds interoperability [[1]]. This paper focuses on the part of the NOVÆ project dealing with migration and reuse of virtual entities within heterogeneous virtual worlds. Section 2 presents a choice of related works and Section 3 depicts the core of the proposed modeling method and architecture to address the interoperability problem in the context of migration and reuse of virtual entities. In Section 4, we show how learning mechanisms allow going further on the way of interoperability. Section 5 presents an example of virtual entity reuse.

2 Related Works

Interoperability of virtual worlds is now accepted as a major issue in the research area of virtual worlds. This section presents a set of salient works in this domain and compares them to NOVÆ.

Distributed Interactive Simulation (DIS): DIS is the first large-scale initiative (supported by the DoD) to achieve interoperability between distributed dissimilar simulation applications [2]. However, the DIS effort only aims at interoperable simulated battlefield. The IEEE DIS standards rely on an application protocol and on communication services. The DIS standard also include guidelines for performing and managing DIS exercises. The DIS application protocol defines the format and semantic associated to each Protocol Data Unit (PDU) exchanged by participating simulations.

The simulation applications may be dissimilar in terms of technologies, purposes, vendors or OS platforms. Nevertheless, the simulation applications must be fully similar to interoperate in terms of semantic of the world they jointly simulate. Dynamical evolution of the semantic (even slightly) is not possible since it involves a revision of the DIS standard. These two last points distinguish the DIS approach from the NOVÆ approach presented in this paper. NOVÆ assumes that semantic heterogeneity between simulation applications (named virtual worlds in NOVÆ) is the rule. NOVÆ considers that semantic heterogeneity must be dynamically managed and that is not an obstacle to interoperability provided there are mechanisms to evaluate semantic (dis)similarity between virtual worlds.

High Level Architecture (HLA): HLA is part of the DoD Modeling and Simulation Master Plan and may be viewed as the natural evolution of the DIS experience. The objective of HLA is both interoperability and reuse of simulation components. The main improvement compared to DIS is that semantic heterogeneity between simulation applications is addressed. Thus, HLA provides a more generic approach of interoperability. This approach relies on two concepts: the Federation Object Model (FOM) and the Simulation Object Model (SOM). A FOM is defined as a peculiar simulation domain [3] and specifies the exchange of public information between the participants (federates i.e. an individual simulations) in a FOM. A SOM describes the capabilities of a federate provides to federations. HLA uses the SOM to calculate if an individual simulation can participate to a federation. [4]. This approach is closer of the NOVÆ's one even if NOVÆ does not organize virtual worlds within a «federation-like» concept. NOVÆ uses the theory of action called influences/reaction model detailed in section 3 to evaluate similarities and differences of virtual worlds involved in an interoperability process. The influences/reaction model is used by NOVÆ on world-to-world basis to evaluate interoperability suitability of virtual worlds. Using the HLA taxonomy, we could say that NOVÆ evaluates suitable interoperability on a SOM-to-SOM basis and, thus, NOVÆ does not need the FOM concept. At the opposite, HLA evaluates suitable interoperability on a SOM-to-FOM basis. Another difference with NOVÆ is related to the needed specification tasks. The specification of a FOM is a complex task because it must encompass all potential exchanges of data among all federates in order to be general. The specification provided by the influences/reaction model is performed for one virtual world at a time.

AVIARY allows multiple users to share multiple worlds and uses Object Oriented paradigm. In AVIARY, a world is a *world object*, which manages a set of laws and attributes. Those attributes are necessary to each entity to be in accordance with the laws of its world [5] [6]. This approach is similar to the concept of behavioral law of the world in NOVÆ.

The presented solution for interoperability and reuse mainly focuses on how an entity may be moved from its current world to another one and then behave in accordance with the laws of the new world. The proposed solution is based on a hierarchy of worlds. When an entity moved from world to world, the needed attributes of the new world are copied into the entity with default values. NOVÆ also addresses the problem of entity migration and provides two other services detailed in section 3.5 such as sharing of entities among several worlds. The AVIARY approach of entity migration is promising one but the question of the resulting behavior of the migrated entity in a new world has to be answered.

BrickNet allows multiple clients to share object's geometry and behaviors with one another, through BrickNet servers. BrickNet clients usually differ in their content from each other [7]. Like AVIARY, BrickNet uses Object Oriented paradigm for the sharing of objects between clients and the sharing of object behaviors depends on their types (simple, environment dependent, reactive and capability-based behaviors). The authors identify the interoperability and reuse problems arising when an entity is immersed in a world for which it is not designed, but don't mention any solutions.

GENOCOVE [8] presents paradigms for the design of interoperable Collaborative Virtual Environments. The approach is Object Oriented where both virtual entities and worlds are objects. Interoperability and reuse are tackled by mean of the object-object learning concept. This allows objects to acquire attributes (e.g. location, mass and temperature), to learn skills (methods) and to obtain sensors from other objects i.e. the publicly available methods by which the objects can affect another object.

Thus, an object can learn the capability, which enable it to behave in accordance with the laws of its host world. As the worlds are considered as objects, they can also learn (through object-object learning) essential capabilities that the transferred entity needs to operate in its host world.

This approach does not address conflicts that can exist between native and learned capabilities of the transferred entity. NOVÆ proposes learning mechanisms and the use of ontologies to tackle the migration entity problem. The learning mechanisms are described in section 4 while the use of ontologies is beyond the scope of this paper and but detailed in [9].

3 Modeling Paradigms

3.1 A theory of action

Users and virtual entities that behave concurrently populate virtual worlds. Most of them have a behavior ranging from purely reactive to autonomous. A reactive entity is, for example, a car, a plane or a molecule while an autonomous entity may be, for example, a virtual robot, an avatar or human user. Whatever a behavior is, i.e. reactive or autonomous, it is always the result of set of actions. Action is thus a central concept in virtual worlds and must be clearly understood and defined.

Indeed, it is a common pitfall to confuse an action and its consequences particularly when designing a virtual world.

In the real world, such a confusion will lead, for example, a car manufacturer not to design how a vehicle brakes but how it brakes on paved road, on snow, on sand, in a curve and so on. What happen now if such a car has to brake on a wet paved road and the manufacturer has not specified this? It is easy to understand that such a car design process would reduce the use of the car to very small number situations. At the opposite, only designing how a car brakes without trying to imagine all the situations it will have to brake under make the car usable in most of situations. In the real world, such a design makes no sense since the result of an action is immediately given by the laws of physics and, thus, does not have to be calculated.

Things are different in a virtual world: whatever the ruling laws are (i.e. physics or anything else), they have to be simulated and thus the result of an action must be computed. When designing a virtual world, such confusion leads to include computation of the consequences of actions within the behavior of any virtual entity.

The main point is that the result of action always depends on the state of the world where the action is performed. For example, playing guitar on the earth produces music because there is an atmosphere but playing guitar on the moon would not produce any sound because there is no atmosphere. Thus including computations of the consequences of actions within the behavior of a virtual entity makes this entity less reusable since it depends on the state of the world it has been designed for. To make a virtual entity reusable means actions of its behavior can be performed within any virtual world in conformance with the laws of such a virtual world.

For example, if the behavior of a virtual guitar is to produce sound when one touches its cords this make the virtual guitar poorly reusable since it can be only be used in virtual worlds where notion of atmosphere exists. In a virtual world where no concept of atmosphere exists the behavior of the virtual guitar is wrong since it still produces sound. The reason is confusion between the "vibrate action" of the cords and the consequence of this action when there is an atmosphere. The right design of the behavior of the virtual guitar is to make vibrate its cords when one touches them. Now the virtual guitar can be used in any virtual world since the consequence of its action is no more included in its behavior.

From this example it appears that the consequence of an action is always purely local i.e. the result is given by the world where the action performed and not by the entity performing the action. This is exactly what happens in the real world. This means that a virtual world should produce a sound when the cords of a virtual guitar vibrate if it has a virtual atmosphere and should produce no sound if it has no virtual atmosphere.

The problem illustrated by the examples above is known as the *universality problem* i.e. designing entity with a behavior that encompasses all possible situations.

Another difficulty is to represent the result of several concurrent actions when several actions are performed concurrently. When the results of actions are performed by entities themselves, concurrent actions appear to be sequential. For example, if two virtual entities push simultaneously the same object with equal strengths in opposite direction, the object will move from its initial location to left an then to the right to its initial location. The final location of this object is right but this object should have never moved. This problem is known as the *sequentiality* problem. Universality and sequentiality problems have been identified in multiagent systems and a theory of action have been defined in [10] to both address these problems. This theory proposes a model where an action is an *attempt* to change the state of the world but does not actually modify the world. Such an attempt is named *influence* and is performed by an agent. Actual modification is performed by the world itself that takes into account all the produced influences by all the agents. Such a modification is named *reaction*.

Although the influences/reactions model has been defined to solve universality and sequentiality problems within multiagent systems, we use and extend this model for improving virtual worlds interoperability and virtual entities reuse. Indeed, universality and sequentiality problems are also obstacles to virtual worlds' interoperability and virtual entities reuse. Another major benefit of using the influences/reactions model is to bring the design process of virtual worlds on the formalized way instead of the current empirical process. As shown in section 2 and in the remaining of this paper, formalization is needed to go further in design and interoperability of virtual worlds.

3.2 Influences/Reaction Model

The influences/reaction model, defines two types of laws:

- The *behavioral laws* are used to represent the behaviors of both virtual entities and virtual worlds. The behavior of a virtual entity represents for example, the way an entity responds to a collision with another entity. The behavior of the virtual world represents all mechanisms that cannot be bind to any virtual entity but the virtual world. For instance, if a designer wants to represent the wind in a virtual world, he represents it as a behavior of the world. Those two behavioral laws product influences which represent intentions to do an action.
- The *reaction laws* specify the way the virtual world is affected according to its current state and according to all the influences generated by the behaviors of the virtual entities it contains and by its own behaviors.

Therefore, when specifying the behavior of a virtual entity with this model we do not have to describe all its possible consequences on the state of the virtual world avoiding the universality and sequentiality problems. For example, if a single virtual robot pushes a virtual table, this action will modify the current state of the virtual world since the location of the moved table will change. However, the final location of the table will be different if there are, now, several robots pushing simultaneously the table in different directions. The distinction between influence and reaction allows focusing on what is the push action in the behavior of a robot without the burden of envisaging an infinity of scenarios when the action is performed. The new state of the virtual world (i.e. the final location of the table in our example) will be calculated by the virtual system using the reaction laws of the virtual world.

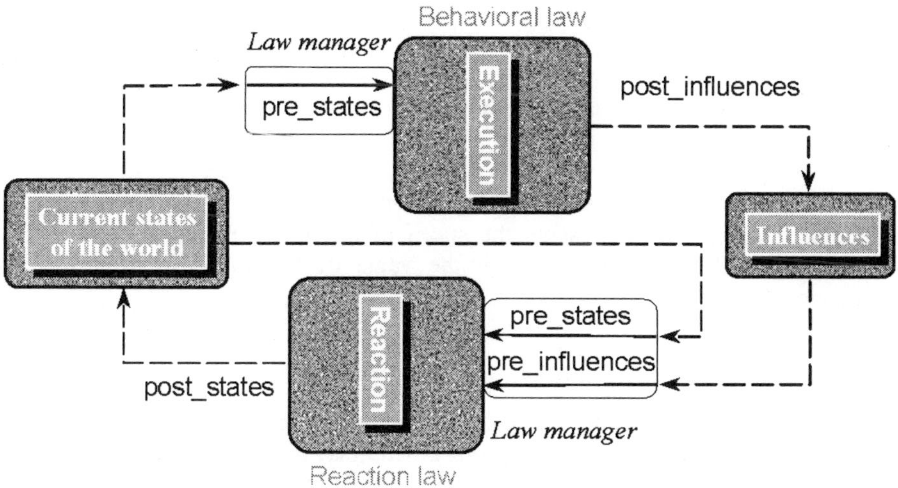

Figure 1. The influence reaction execution model.

In the influences/reaction model, the world is a set of states, built from the attributes of both the entities and the virtual world. This set represents for example, the position of an entity, its velocity, and the collision between two entities and so on. Those states are used by the *law manager* to trigger the execution of behavioral and reaction laws. They are called pre-states in the definition of a law, where they represent the preconditions for the triggering of this law.

The law manager is the architectural component in charge of the triggering of both behavioral and reaction laws. It manages the dynamics of the world, which corresponds to the influences/reaction loop. This loop is divided into the two steps described as follows and illustrated in **Figure 1**.

- Step 1: During the first step, the states of the world are analyzed in order to trigger the behavioral laws for which preconditions, i.e. pre-states and predicates, are verified. Then, the execution of those behavioral laws produces influences.

- Step 2: The dynamic state of the world is composed with the set of the world states and the set of the influences produced during the first step. This dynamic state is analyzed in order to trigger the reaction laws for which precondition i.e. pre-states, predicates and pre-influences, are verified. Then, the execution of those laws produces states, which represent the new current state of the world.

The behavioral laws (i.e. the behaviors of the entities and the behaviors of the virtual world) and the reaction laws are built using the following formalism:

Behavioral laws:	**Reaction laws:**
name (parameters)	name (parameters)
pre-states (states)	pre-states (states)
predicates (conditions)	predicates (conditions)
post-influences (influences)	pre-influences(influences)
	post-states(states)

The predicates represent conditions about the value of the pre-states. For example, if a pre-state represents the speed of an entity, a predicate can exists, representing additional conditions on the value of the speed used in the law triggering.

3.3 Compatibility evaluation

In a reuse or interoperability purpose, an entity, called *migrating entity*, can be immersed in a different world, called *host world*, for which it has not been designed. Thus, the influences/reaction model is used in order to calculate the compatibility level between the entity and its host world. This compatibility level allows the prediction of:

- the way the entity will behave in its host world, i.e. if its behaviors will be able to be triggered and if the influences generated by the entities' behaviors will be interpreted in the host world, and,
- the way the host world will interact with this new entity, i.e. if the behavioral laws of the host world are able to work with the entity, and, if all/some entities of the host world are able to interact with this entity.

This prediction is performed by an architectural component called *Interoperability Manager* (IM) in charge of all the operations related to interoperability, i.e. all operations concerning the outside of the world. The compatibility evaluation is divided into two main steps:

1. The IM analyses the way the behaviors of the entity will be interpreted in its host world. This step is split into two stages:
   - First, for each behavior law of the entity, the IM checks if its pre-states belong to the set of the host world's states. The behaviors laws for which this requirement is not verified are stamped *invalid* because they cannot be triggered in the host world. The others are temporary stamped *valid.*
   - Second, for each valid behavior law, the IM checks if the post-influences generated belong to the set of pre-influences of the host world's reaction laws. If so, these behaviors laws are stamped valid, while the others are stamped invalid.

   Thus, the IM establish the set of behaviors laws of the entity that are able to work in the host world.
2. The IM checks the ability of the behavioral laws of the host world to be applied to the migrating entity. For example, if each host world's entity is subjected to a world law called gravity, during the compatibility evaluation, the IM checks if this law can be applied to the migrating entity. In order to perform this step, the IM compares the attributes of this entity with the pre-states of the behavioral laws of the world[1]. Therefore, the IM is able to establish the set of behavioral laws of the host world operating with the migrating entity. Those laws are stamped valid.

Thus, the IM is able to predict if a migrating entity and its host world are adequate. The compatibility level, which is the ratio of the number of valid laws on the number of checked laws, reflects this adequacy:

$$\text{Compatibility level} = \frac{\text{Valid\_Behavior}_{\text{entity}} + \text{Valid\_Behavior}_{\text{Host world}}}{\text{Behavior}_{\text{entity}} + \text{Behavior}_{\text{Host world}}}$$

This compatibility level is an important information since it measures quality of interoperability of the migrating virtual entity. If this quality is poor, the IM will have to improve it using other techniques such as learning mechanisms described in the next section.

4 Learning

The influences/reaction model allows us to predict the way both an entity and its host world will interact with each other. However, if the compatibility level between an entity and a virtual world is too low to allow satisfactory interoperability, the influences/reaction model alone is not sufficient to improve it. This limitation is due

---

[1] The attributes of both entities and world are used to create the states of the world. Therefore, an attribute is equivalent to a state and to a pre-state.

to specific semantic problems, which are not taken into account by the influences/reaction model.

These problems, called *incompatibility* and *inconsistency*, concern the concepts associated with the symbols used in the formal description of both virtual entities and virtual worlds. They respectively address the fact that in different virtual worlds, different symbols can represent the same concept/meaning and the same symbol can represent different concepts/meanings. These two problems are the cause of the decrease of the compatibility level since they can invalidate some behaviors of an entity or some behavioral laws of its host world.

As an example, let us consider an entity which bouncing behavior use a world state called "elasticity", representing the density concept attached to the surface of the entities it collides with. On the other hand, in its host world, this concept is represented as an attribute called "density". Thus, the bouncing behavior of the entity does not work in the host world because of incompatibility, event though the density concept is shared between the entity and its host world.

In order to address these problems, we have enhanced the IM with learning mechanisms. These mechanisms are used to modify the description of a virtual entity in order to increase the compatibility level in when it is too low, to allow a good adequacy between the migrating entity and its host world.

4.1 Learning techniques

These learning mechanisms, called *disguise* an *imitation*, are based on the use of the Galois algorithm [11]. This algorithm is used in order to build a semantic classification of the entities of the host world; it relies on various parameters, such as attributes or behaviors, depending on the used mechanism. The classification produced by the Galois algorithm is a lattice, which represents a concept hierarchy [12].

As an illustration, let us consider three objects called O_1, O_2 and O_3 and their respective sets of characteristics {a}, {b, c} and {a, b}, where a, b and c are individual characteristics. The execution of the Galois algorithm on these objects produces the lattice shown in **Figure 2**. We can see on this figure that the objects are classified according to their characteristics, and that the base is a node containing all the characteristics of the objects and the top is a node containing all the objects. This means that none of the objects owns all the three characteristics and none of the characteristics are shared by all the objects.

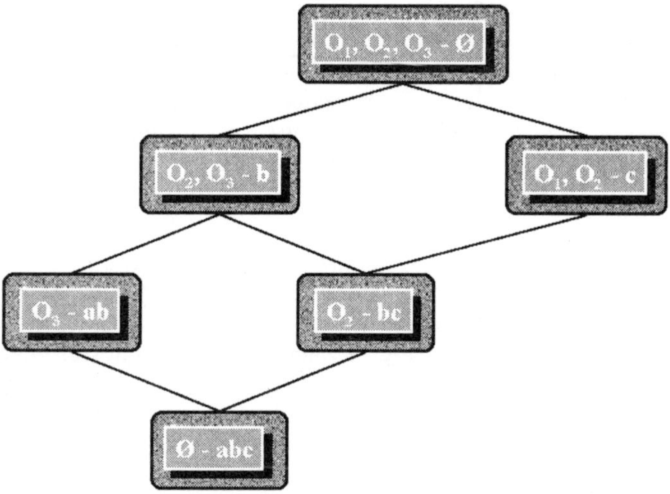

Figure 2. Galois lattice example

4.2 Disguise

During the disguise step, the migrating entity is compared with all the entities of the host world on an attribute-attribute basis. First, using the Galois Algorithm, the IM constructs a classification of the entities of the host world on their attributes. Next, using this algorithm, it adds the migrating entity to the classification. Thus, the migrating entity is identified with one or more entities, i.e. a node of the lattice, with which it shares as many attributes as possible. Finally, the IM adds to the migrating entity the additional attributes belonging to its identified entities. This stage is the quantitative stage of the disguise step. In the qualitative stage, the IM has to fix the value of those additional attributes. During this stage, it built a new lattice not only based on the attributes of the entities of the host world, but also based on the value of these attributes.

At the end of the disguise step, the migrating entity owns new attributes. On one hand, these attributes allow the entity to be reactive to the behavioral laws of the host world. On the other hand, to be able to interact with other entities in the same manner than the entities of the host world it has been identified to.

4.3 Imitation

In section 3.3, we have seen that some behaviors of the migrating entity are invalid in the host world. In the imitation step, the IM compares these invalid behaviors with the behaviors of the entities identified during the disguise step based on their pre-states and post-influences. Thus, for each invalid behavior, the IM identifies a behavior belonging to an entity of the host world with which it shares as many pre-states and pre-influences as possible. These identified behaviors are added to the migrating entity to replace the invalid behaviors. In this way, the migrating entity is able to interact in the host world in the same way than the entities with which it has been identified to.

4.4 Exploration

At the end of the disguise and imitation steps, the migrating entity gets new attributes and news behaviors, which increase its compatibility level with its host world, and obviously, which increase its interaction capabilities in the host world. As we can see, even if these two mechanisms do not provide actual answers to the two semantic problems previously mentioned in the beginning of section 4, but they answer the consequences of these problems.

A third step called *exploration* exists, to actually answer, both the incompatibility and inconsistency problems. During this step, the IM replaces the unknown pre-states and the post-influences of the invalid behaviors of the migrating entity with pre-states and the post-influences belonging to the behaviors of the entities with which the migrating entity has been identified to. Next, this behavior is performed in the host world. If the result is not satisfactory, other pre-states and other post-influences combinations are tested until a satisfactory result is reached. At the end of this step, the IM is able to establish semantic equivalence between symbols used to describe the migrating entity and symbols used to describe the host world and its entities. A lot of work is still needed to improve and to limit the execution time of this step.

5 Example

To demonstrate the benefits of these learning mechanisms, let us consider a virtual world designed for a naval military simulation purpose and an entity representing a sailing boat from a second virtual world for regatta simulation purpose. The aim of the demonstration is the reuse/migration of this entity in the military world in order to improve its realism.

In order to perform this operation, the IM of the military world first calculates the compatibility level between the sailing boat and its world. If this level is too low, it triggers the two learning steps previously described.

We do not detail the calculation of the compatibility level in this example because it requires the description of the whole world. We only discuss the way the behaviors of the sailing boat works when immersed in the military world and the way some entities of this world are able to interact with this foreign entity without performing the learning mechanisms.

5.1 Compatibility evaluation

The sailing boat and its behaviors are constructed for a virtual world that simulate the wind. Therefore, the movements of this entity are produced thanks to the wind's speed and direction. These two attributes belong to the world and are produced by a behavior law of the regatta world. The actual control of direction and speed of the sailing boat is managed by a reaction law in accordance with the wind's speed and direction. The user is only in control of the direction of the boat using a virtual helm. In addition, this boat owns an engine that is started when the boat's speed is under a given threshold.

The sailing boat is described as follows:

Attributes:

```
position, direction, speed, weight, length, width, sail_type, fuel, color.
```

Behaviors laws:

```
movement(e)
        pre-states : direction(e, d), helm (e, h)
                predicates: /* none */
        post-influences : Inf_direction(e, d + h)
```

```
rescue_engine(e)
        pre-states : direction(e, d), speed(e, s), helm (e, h), fuel(e, f)
                predicates: s < 10 /* km/h */, f>0
        post-influences : Inf_direction(e, d + h), Inf_speed(e, s × 1.1),
Inf_fuel(e, f - 0.1)
```

The reaction law calculating the actual movement of the sailing boat in accordance to the speed and direction of the wind is described as follows:

Reaction law:

```
R_movement (e)
        pre-states : position(e, e.p), speed(e, s), wind_speed(ws),
wind_direction(wd)
            predicates : /* none */
        pre-influences : Inf_direction(e, d)
        post-states : position(e, p + s*d + ws*wd)
```

In the military world, this reaction law does not exist. As the concept of wind does not exist in the military world, we may expect that the boat will move thanks to its behavior called "rescue_engine". This behavior can be triggered because all its pre-states exist in the military world. However, the speed concept, is represented in the military world with the symbol "velocity". Consequently, the influence called "Inf_speed" in the law "rescue_engine" does not correspond to any pre-influence of any reaction law of the military world. In conclusion, since the behavior law "movement" of the sailing boat is only used to change its direction, and, the behavior "rescue_engine" cannot work in the military world, the sailing boat cannot move in this world.

The military world is populated with several entities representing battleships and ornamental entities as dolphins or gulls. One of the properties of all the battleships is to be able to destroy other entities. In order to represent this characteristic, all entities contained in the military world have several attributes used when a missile collides with an entity. On one hand, these characteristics are modeled with a behavior law of the world called "collision", which detects collision between entities and generates influences called "Inf_collision". On the other hand, a reaction law which computes the result of the collision according to the kind of colliding entities. Thus, we expect this characteristic to be kept with all the new entities migrated in this world. The attribute allowing this characteristic is called "armor" and the reaction law using this attribute is described as follow:

```
R_collision_missile (e, m)
        pre-states : armor(e, a), power(m, pw)
                predicates : /* none */
        pre-influences : Inf_collision(e, m)
        post-states : armor(e, a - pw)
```

In addition, battleships are able to identify and shoot opponents thanks to an attribute called "army", used as a precondition of a behavior law called "destroy_kill_kill". This behavior allows battleships to decide if a close entity is an opponent or not. This behavior is described as follow:

```
destroy_kill_kill (e1, e2)
        pre-states : position(e1, p1), position(e2, p2), army(e1, army1),
army(e2, army2)
        predicates : |p1.x - p2.x| < 1000, |p1.x - p2.x| < 1000, army1 <> army2
        post-states : Inf_missile_creat(m, p1), Inf_vitesse(m, 200),
Inf_direction(m, |p1 - p2|)
```

Due to the absence of the attributes "armor" and "army" in set of attributes of the sailing boat, battleships are unable to attempt to destroy it. The reaction law "R_collision_missile" is also unable to compute the result a collision with a missile.

At this stage, the compatibility level of the virtual sailing boat in military virtual world is thus close to zero.

In the following, we demonstrate that the learning mechanisms allow the resolution of those two kinds of problems. First, the disguise mechanism will allow the sailing boat to acquire some of the attributes needed for the battleships to interact with it. Second, the imitation mechanism will allow the sailing boat to acquire some behaviors in order to be able to move in the military world.

5.2 Disguise Step

During the disguise step, the IM built a classification of all the entities of the military world, according to their attributes. Here, we will not detail all the entities of the military world except the battleships. These entities have several attributes in common with the sailing boat. Therefore, when the sailing boat is compared with the classification, it is identified with the battleship on the basis of the following shared attributes: "position", "direction", "speed", "weight", "length", "width", "fuel".

In addition, the battleships have three additional attributes: "army", "armor" and "power_engine". Therefore, during the disguise step these attributes are added to the sailing boat. The value of each attribute is based on the value of the shared attributes. In this case, the values of the attributes "armor" and "power_engine" are fixed depending on the values of the "length", "width" and "weight" of the battleships existing in the military world. For example, the value of the new "armor" attribute of the sailing boat is built as the average of the values of the "armor" attributes of the battleships whose values for "length", "width" and "weight" attributes are the closest to the values of those common attributes with the sailing boat. The value of the attribute "army" is determined in the same way, but in this case, this is an arbitrary choice. However, fixing the value of a string will be in most of the cases an arbitrary operation.

These additional attributes allow the battleships to attempt to destroy the sailing boat since their behavior law "destroy_kill_kill" is now able to work with the latest entity due to its new "army" attribute. Furthermore, the new attribute "armor" allows the reaction law "R_collision_missile" to calculate damages due to a collision between the sailing boat and a missile.

5.3 Imitation step

During the imitation step, the IM built a lattice, in which objects are the behaviors of the previous identified entities, in which characteristics are the pre-states, predicates, and post-influences of those behaviors. Next, it compares the invalid behaviors of the sailing boat with the nodes of the lattice. In this case, the IM compare the invalid behavior "rescue_engine" with the behaviors of the battleships. This comparison establishes that this behavior can be imitated with the behavior "engine" of the battleships, which is described as follows:

engine (e)
pre-states : direction(e, d), **velocity**(e, v), helm (e, h), fuel(e, f), power_engine(e, pwe)
predicates: /* none */
post-influences : Inf_direction(e, d + h), Inf_**velocity**(e, v × pwe), Inf_fuel(e, f - 0.1)

This equivalence is based on the following shared characteristics:

- the shared pre-states: "direction", "helm" and "fuel", and,
- the shared post-influences: "Inf_direction", and "Inf_fuel".

In addition, this behavior is able to work with the sailing boat description, since during the disguise step, the attribute "power_engine" has been added to it.

5.4 Comments

This example demonstrates that the use of the learning mechanisms can improve the reuse and the interoperability between a virtual entity and a world for which it has not been designed.

Those learning mechanisms have been developed and tested and the third step (i.e., exploration) is under construction in order to improve its feasibility in a reasonable execution time. The results of both the disguise and the imitation steps are promising although some adjustments are needed in order to fix some strange results.

6 Conclusion and Further Work

In this paper, we have presented a methodology for improving the design process of virtual worlds.

The major benefit of this methodology is to point out *action* as the main concept of virtual worlds and then to provide a definition for action. This definition states an absolute separation between an action and the consequences of such an action; it exhibits the locality property of the consequences of an action.

This locality property means that the result of an action is not always the same but depends on the state of the virtual world where the action is performed. An immediate conclusion for design methodology of virtual worlds is that the consequences of an action do not have to be calculated by the virtual entity performing the action but the virtual world where the action is performed. Furthermore, this is compliant with the security aspect since security policies are essentially local.

Thus, deconnecting actions from their consequences allow to address interoperability and reuse problems in a very effective and dynamic way. This deconnection implies an explicit and formal definition of the interface between virtual entities and the virtual worlds they populate. This interface may be then used to improve interoperability and reusability with additional mechanisms such as learning.

The use of a formalism to describe the laws allows using some formal methods to determine the consistency of critical virtual worlds. Finally, the proposed methodology is not restricted to virtual worlds but can be use in any domain where action, migration, and interoperability are salient features: mobile agents in telecommunication for example.

The proposed methodology has also drawbacks. The loop of the influences/reaction execution model, defined in section 3.2, can become a bottleneck in large-scale virtual worlds. Thus, a distributed execution model of the influences/reaction loop is needed. The need of a formalism raises the questions of its expressiveness and how is it easy to learn as a language. It would be a good thing the virtual world designer does not have to learn a new language but uses and adapted GUI for example.

Further work is to finish implementing learning mechanisms particularly the exploration step. Disguise and imitation steps already give good results but there still some aberrant imitations to be eliminated. Then, the methodology needs to be tested on larger, complex and numerous virtual worlds.

References

1. M. Soto, S. Allongue, Inter-Collaborative Virtual Environments. Collaborative Virtual Environments 1998 (CVE'98), Manchester, U.K., 1998.
2. IEEE Standard for Information Technology -Protocols for Distributed Interactive Simulation Applications, Entity Information and Interaction. Technical Report ISBN 1-55937-305-9, The Institute of Electrical and Electronics Engineers, 1993.
3. D. Miller. The DoD high level architecture and the next generation of dis. In *14th Workshop on the Standards for Interoperability of Distributed Simulation*, Orlando, Florida, USA, March 1996.
4. R. Lutz. HLA Object Model Development: A Process View Simulation Interoperability Workshop (SIW), Spring 97.
5. D. Snowdon, A. West and T. L.J. Howard. Toward the next generation of Human-Computer Interface. *Informatique'93 : Interface to Real & Virtual Worlds*, pages 399-408, March 93, Montpellier, France.

6. D. Snowdon and A. West. The aviary distributed virtual environment. In Robin Hollands, editor, *Proceedings of the 2nd UK VR-SIG Conference*, pages 39-54, 1994.
7. G. Singh, L. Serra, W. Png, A. Wong and H. Ng. Bricknet : Sharing objects behaviors on the net. In IEEE Computer Society Press, editor, *Virtual Reality Annual International Symposium'95,* March 1995.
8. M. Meehan. Interoperable Objects and Worlds for Collaborative Virtual Environments. Unpublished, June 1997.
9. M. Soto and S. Allongue. A Semantic Approach of Virtual Worlds Interoperability. *Workshop on enabling Technologies : Infrastructure for collaborative enterprises*. Cambridge Massachusetts, USA, June, 1997.
10. J Ferber and J.P. Muller. Influences and Reaction: A Model of Situated multiagent Systems. In M. Tokoro, editor, *2nd International Conference on Multiagent Systems*, Nara, Japan, 1996
11. R. Godin, R. Missaoui and H. Alaoui, Incremental Concept Formation Algorithms Based on Galois (Concept) Lattice. In *Computational IntelligenCE* ,(11)2, 1995.
12. R. Wille. Restructuring lattice theory: an approach based on hierarchies of concepts. In *Ordered sets*, pages 445-470, 1982.

Chapter 4

Information Modeling, Storage and Integration

MMM99

MODELING OBJECT CLUSTERING PERFORMANCE FOR A SPATIAL DATABASE

FANGJU WANG

Department of Computing and Information Science
University of Guelph
Guelph, Ontario, Canada N1G 2W1
E-mail: fjwang@snowhite.cis.uoguelph.ca

In the forthcoming standard of SQL/MM – SQL for multimedia applications – a large number of spatial data types have been defined for building object oriented geospatial information systems (GISs). The spatial data types may enable spatial objects of complex structures to be modeled, constructed and manipulated in a "standard" way. The new industrial standard may largely improve interoperability of GISs as well. It can be anticipated that the standard will have great impacts to the development of GIS technology. For an object oriented GIS to be accepted by its end users, it must be of high performance. Performance has been a crucial issue for successfully applying the spatial data types in SQL/MM to developing practical systems. Of the factors that may affect a system performance, physical database design is an important one. In this research, we focused on spatial object clustering of physical design and I/O cost modeling. We designed three clustering strategies for polygon objects aiming at reducing I/O costs. We conducted experiments with real data to evaluate their performance, and created mathematical models from the experimental results. The models can be used in choosing clustering strategies, predicting I/O costs in query optimization, and for many other purposes.

1 Introduction

A geographic information system (GIS) stores geospatial data of complex structures, and provides functions for retrieving, analyzing, and displaying the data stored. In recent years, there has been increasing interests in applying the object technology for developing GISs. In 1999, the standard of SQL MultiMedia (SQL/MM) will be officially published [?]. SQL/MM is based on SQL:1999 (formerly known as SQL3) that is characterized as "object-oriented SQL" and it is the foundation of several object-relational database management systems (including Oracle's ORACLE8, Informix' Universal Server, etc.) [?]. In SQL/MM, a large number of spatial user defined types (UDTs) and their structural hierarchy have been defined. A UDT is basically an object class [?]. It encapsulates a data structure and the procedures manipulating the data structure. The spatial data types defined in SQL/MM enable spatial objects of complex structures to be modeled, constructed and manipulated in a "standard" way. The new SQL/MM may largely facilitate development of object GISs. It may also significantly improve interoperability, which is becoming a major design and development consideration in GIS development.

Designers and developers of GISs have shown great interests in the model defined in the standard of SQL/MM for its good modeling power and functionality, as well as its strength in improving interoperability. However, for an object GIS to be accepted by its end users, it must have high performance. System performance has become a decisive issue that must be addressed before using the spatial UDTs in SQL/MM to develop practical object GISs. Of the factors that may affect a system's performance, physical database design is an important one.

In physical database design for a GIS, spatial object clustering is an important task, which is the grouping of spatial objects that are in some sense similar and storing them on the disk based on the grouping. Spatial object clustering largely affect the costs required for retrieving spatial objects from the disk.

In this research, we focused on spatial object clustering and I/O cost modeling. We designed three clustering strategies for polygon objects. The objective is to reduce I/O costs. We conducted experiments with real data to evaluate their performance, and created mathematical models from the experimental results. The models can be used in choosing clustering strategies, predicting I/O costs in query optimization, and for many other purposes.

2 Object clustering objectives and techniques

As described before, spatial object clustering is storing spatial objects together on the disk that are in some sense similar. The similarity between two objects depends on the probability of their being referenced together. The objective of a clustering strategy is to physically arrange the storage structure so that (1) obtaining "the next" object needed by a user query has a low probability of requesting physical access to the disk, and (2) a maximum amount of relevant data is transferred when the disk is accessed [?].

The most commonly used techniques for object clustering include the following [?].

- *class-based clustering*, in which objects of the same class are clustered;
- *value-based clustering*, in which objects having the same or similar attribute values are clustered;
- *index-based clustering*, in which objects that can be accessed from the same index node are clustered;

- *relationship clustering*, in which objects that have a certain relationship with each other are clustered;
- *aggregate object clustering*, in which component objects of an aggregate object are clustered; and
- *graph partitioning clustering*, in which a generalization graph or an aggregation graph is partitioned into subgraphs, and objects are clustered according to the partitioning.

Although research on clustering for non-spatial objects has been extensively conducted, so far clustering for spatial objects have not been paid deserved attention. Research on physical database design for spatial databases has been mainly conducted on spatial indexing [?,?,?,?]. In spatial clustering, so far the most commonly used techniques include row-order, Z-order, and the Hilbert Curve, which linearize a multidimensional space. These techniques have limitations for clustering spatial objects [?].

3 Spatial Search

Since the objective of spatial object clustering is to facilitate spatial search, before addressing spatial object clustering, we briefly describe the fundamentals of spatial search.

The data repository of a GIS is a spatial database. The database stores spatial objects and allows the objects to be searched in various ways. Search operations in a spatial database include "non-spatial search" and "spatial search". In a non-spatial search operation, the search condition can usually be specified in terms of non-spatial attributes of the objects. In a spatial search operation, the search condition involves spatial locations of objects. The former is quite similar to search operations in non-spatial databases, but the latter is special.

Range search may be one of the most important spatial search operations. Conceptually, when conducting a range search operation for spatial objects on a map, a search window (rectangle) is placed on the map at a specified location to select objects. Range search can be classified into containment search and intersection search. In a containment search, all the spatial objects that are completely contained by the window are selected as output, and in an intersection search the objects that intersect with the search window are selected. Range search is important because most of the other spatial search operations can be implemented by using containment search and intersection search.

To facilitate range search, range information is stored with each object. The information is usually represented by a *minimum bounding rectangle (MBR)*, which is the minimum rectangle binding the object. If spatial objects are indexed, range information is also included in the index. For example, if the index is structured as a tree, each tree node should include the range information of the spatial objects associated with the node.

Because of the importance of range search, we conduct range search operations in evaluating the performance of clustering strategies, and modeling I/O costs.

4 The Clustering Strategies

A clustering strategy is based on the structure of the data to be clustered. We designed our strategies based on the spatial UDTs defined in the forthcoming standard of SQL/MM and also the Open GeoData Interoperability Specification [?] For better presenting the strategies, we first describe the spatial data structure.

In SQL/MM, the spatial UDTs that can be directly used to construct spatial entities include the following: ST_Geometry, ST_Point, ST_Curve, ST_LineString, ST_Surface, ST_CurvePolygon, and ST_Polygon. ST_Geometry is a supertype of ST_Point, ST_Curve, and ST_Surface, which are the data types of the geometric primitives: points, lines, and polygons, respectively. ST_Curve and ST_Surface are abstract types that are not instantiable. ST_LineString is a subtypes of ST_Curve. ST_Polygon is a subtype of ST_CurvePolygon, and ST_CurvePolygon is a subtype of ST_Surface. ST_Point is the type of the point array of ST_LineString. ST_Curve is the type of the exterior ring and interior rings of ST_CurvePolygon.

A clustering strategy is also closely related to the index structure. We experimented our clustering strategies with two spatial indices – skd-tree [?] and R-tree [?]. The experimental results are similar. In this paper, we discuss the results with the skd-tree only.

An skd-tree is a binary tree. When an skd-tree is used as a spatial index, the root represents the space of the whole map, an internal node a subspace of the map that is partitioned, and a leaf node an unpartitioned subspace. At each internal node (including the root), a value is chosen in one of the two dimensions to partition the (sub)space into two subspaces. The two resultant subspaces usually have the same number of data objects. In this research, if all the data objects in a subspaces can be stored on a data page, a leaf node is created and the subspace is considered *unpartitioned*; otherwise, an internal node is created and the subspace is further partitioned. Using an skd-tree, a map is subdivided into a number of unpartitioned subspaces. Objects in an unpartitioned subspace is stored on a data page, and the page number is stored in the leaf node that relates to the subspace.

The following are the three strategies we designed and experimented. Differing from the existing clustering techniques mentioned above, our techniques do not linearize a multidimensional space. They are more closely related to spatial indexing, so that search with indexing can be further facilitated.

Strategy 1:

This strategy integrates the techniques of index clustering and aggregate object clustering. The data of a map are stored in one polygon data file. The file is indexed. A page in the file stores data of the polygons in an unpartitioned subspace that can be accessed from an index leaf node. For each polygon, all of its boundary curves are stored along with it in a *nested* structure. The following is the data structure of the file:

(Polygon_ID, No_of_Curves,
(Curve_ID, No_of_Points,
(Point))).

The outmost parenthesis pair represents a collection of the instances of ST_Polygon, the middle pair represents a collection of the instances of ST_Curve, and the innermost pair represents a collection of the instances of ST_Point. In this strategy, shared boundary curves are duplicated.

Strategy 2:

This strategy integrates the techniques of index clustering, aggregate object clustering, and graph partitioning clustering. Two data files are needed to store a polygon map, a polygon file and a curve file. The polygon file is indexed. A page in the polygon file stores the polygons in an unpartitioned subspace that is related to a leaf node of the index. Curve data (including XY coordinates of points) are stored separately in the curve file. The data structures of the polygon file is

(Polygon_ID, No_of_Curves,
(Curve_ID, Page_Number, Offset)).

The data structures of the curve file is

(Curve_ID, No_of_Points,
(Point)).

For a curve, the value of "Page_Number" in the polygon file data structure is the number of the page in the curve file on which it is stored. The page number can be used to directly read the page. The value of "Offset" is the starting position of the curve data page. When storing a polygon, each of its boundary curves is processed one by one. If a curve has not been stored in the curve file, it is stored along with other boundary curves of the polygon. If it has been stored, it is not duplicated. In either case, the curve's page number and offset are stored with the polygon. When storing curves in the curve file, a new page is created when the last one has no enough space for the next curve.

Strategy 3:

This strategy is similar to the second strategy: Two data files are needed to store a polygon map, a polygon file and a curve file. The files have the same structures as the ones in Strategy 2. The difference is that the curves in the curve file are not grouped based on their associations with polygons. They are stored in an arbitrary order.

Of the three strategies, Strategies 1 and 2 might be the choices for most designers when search efficiency is the major consideration, and Strategy 3 might be the choice when frequent updates to data are expected. A good knowledge of their performance can be very helpful for adopting optimal strategies for practical applications and also for estimating I/O costs in query optimization.

Although it is not difficult to have a rough prediction of the performance of the three strategies, such a prediction is far from adequate for a practical application. Accurate and quantitative information is needed. The information cannot be obtained unless careful experiments and mathematical analyses are conducted. In the rest of this paper, we describe the experiments we conducted, the experimental results, and the models created from the results.

5 Experiments

The experiments are designed to obtain information about the performance of the three strategies. Real digital polygon maps are used in the experiments. For a map, the three strategies are applied separately to cluster its spatial objects, and performance of each strategy is evaluated through conducting range search. The control parameters and performance indices are listed in the following.

Control Parameters

Control parameters are variables whose values can be changed in an experiment to affect the performance of a clustering strategy. Testing with different values of the parameters, we may understand the performance of a strategy in different circumstances; we may also obtain useful information for choosing an optimal parameter value. In this research, the control parameters include

- **page size** that is the number of bytes on a data page, and
- **size of the search window** that is given as the percentage of the area of the entire map.

Performance Indices

Performance indices are recordable experimental results that can be used to evaluate strategy performance. They are

- **number of reads** that are needed to fetch all the required data from the disk to the main memory,
- **ratio of relevant data** to all the data fetched, and
- **response time** that is the elapse time between the data request and the time when data have been fetched.

Relevant data are defined as the spatial objects whose MBRs are contained by or intersected with the search window.

Of the performance indices, the number of reads and the ratio of relevant data are primary ones. Response time is closely related with the number of reads and depends on the speeds of CPU, disk driver, data channel, and even the way in which the operating system stores a particular file. In this paper, we address the number of reads only.

For a polygon map, a strategy is used with a page size to cluster objects and create a set of database files that consists of an index (skd-tree) file and one or two data files (depending on the strategy). For each set of database files, a search procedure is applied with different search window sizes for containment search and intersection search. In a search operation, we fetch the data of all the polygons (including their boundary curves) whose MBRs are contained in or intersected by a search window. We measured the number of reads, ratio of relevant data, and response time.

The page sizes experimented are 0.5K (kilobytes), 1K, 1.5K, ..., and 8K. The search window sizes are 1%, 2%, 3%, ..., and 15% of the area of the entire map.

Consistent results have been obtained. In the next section, we present some experimental results of conducting containment search to a digital map.

Necessary analyses are given as well. In the results of containment search and intersection search, the numbers of reads and response time are the same. Only the ratios of relevant data are different. Since we do not address the ratio in this paper, we present and analyze the results of containment search only. The equipment used for the experiments is an IBM RS6000 320H machine running AIX (the IBM version of UNIX). The programs are coded in C++.

6 Experimental Results

Figure 1 and Figure 2 illustrate some of the experimental results from a geology map. The map is about 2.5MB large (when using four bytes to store a floating point number). The total number of polygons on the map is about 3461 and the average polygon size is 694 bytes. The charts in Figure 1 can be used to study the relationship between the number of reads and data page size. The four charts are generated from the results by conducting containment with window sizes of 1%, 3%, 5% and 15%.

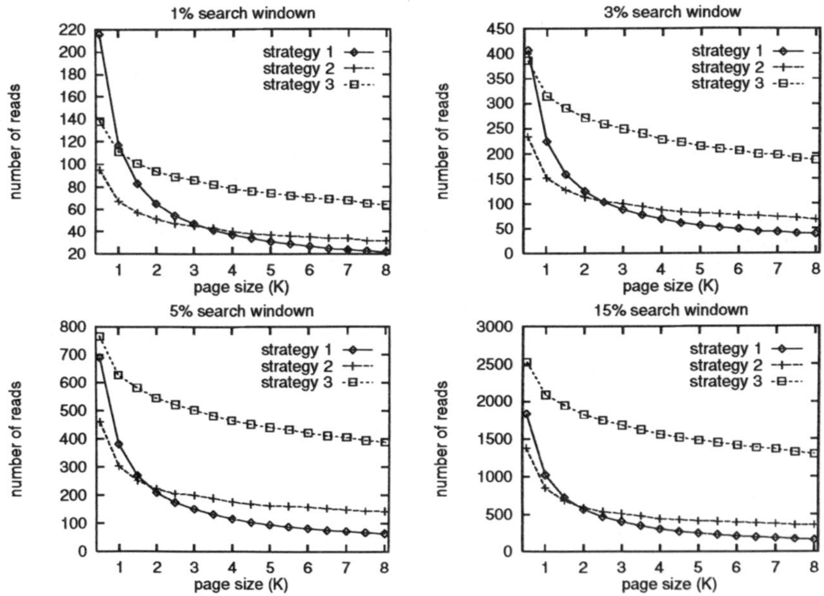

Figure 1. Actual number of reads vs data page size for the geology map.

When page size is very small (e.g. $<$ 2.5K), Strategy 1 has a larger number of reads than Strategy 2. However, when the page size is large, Strategy 1 has the smallest number. The number of reads in Strategy 3 is always greater than that in Strategies 1 and 2. When the page size is large, the number of reads in Strategy 2 is about 1.5 to 2 times of that in Strategy 1, and the number of reads in Strategy 3 is about 2.5 to 5 times of that in Strategy 1. In all the three strategies, the numbers of reads decrease with the increase of page size.

More detailed analysis reveals that in Strategies 2 and 3 a large number of reads are needed for fetching curve data pages and the numbers decrease slowly with the increase of page sizes. For example, with 3% search windows, when the page size increases from 0.5K to 8K, the number of reads for polygon pages in Strategy 1 decreases to 10%. In Strategy 2, the numbers of reads for polygon data and curve data decrease to 11% and 39% respectively, and in Strategy 3, the two numbers decrease to 11% and 59% respectively. While in Strategies 2 and 3, the number of reads for polygon data decrease as fast as that in Strategy 1, the number of reads for curve data decreases very slowly. As a result, the total numbers of reads in Strategy 2 and Strategy 3 decrease slower than that in Strategy 1 (to 30% and 48% respective) and when page size is large Strategy 1 becomes the best.

In Strategy 3, since curve objects are not clustered based on their associations with polygons, to fetch the same polygons more read operations are needed. Therefore, the number of reads for curve data is much larger than that in Strategy 2 (about 2 times). It has the largest total number of reads.

The charts in Figure 2 may provide information about the relationship between the number of reads and search window size. The three charts are generated from the results of containment search when data page sizes are 1K, 4K, and 8K.

It can be observed that in all the three strategies, the numbers of reads are proportional to the search window size. The increase rates in Strategies 1 and 2 are almost the same but the rate in Strategy 3 is much larger.

7 Mathematical Modeling

Clear and consistent patterns can be observed from the curves in Figures 1 and 2, as well as the curves for other data sets. The patterns enable us to create mathematical models for the number of reads, which is the measurement for I/O costs. We extracted a model for each strategy from the experimental results. The model is a function of the number of reads. The independent variables of the function are the data page size (in bytes), search window size (in the percentage of the entire map area), and those characterizing a map.

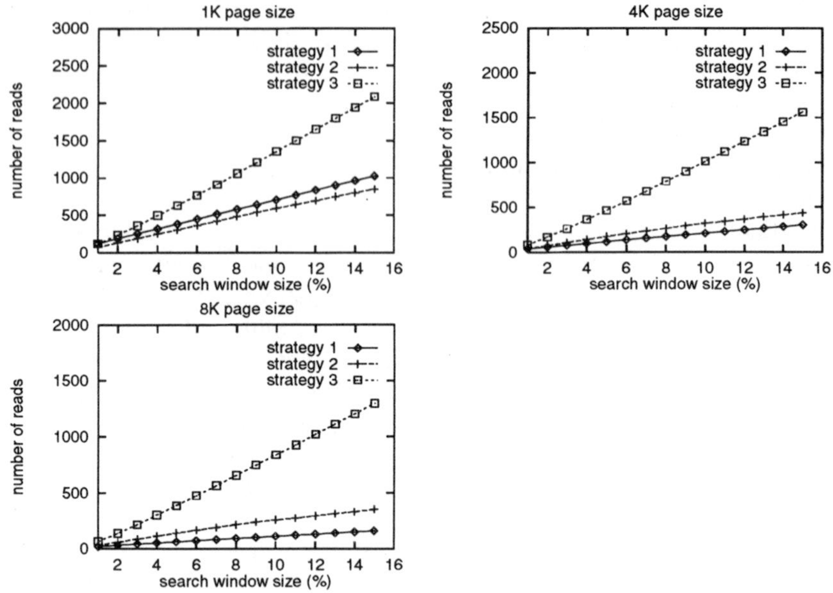

Figure 2. Actual number of reads vs search window size for the geology map.

In this research, the variables characterizing a map include the total number of polygons, and the average polygon size (in bytes). The function of the number of reads is thus

$$R = f(D, W, N, P) \tag{1}$$

where R is the predicted number of reads, D is the data page size, W is the search window size, N is the total number of polygons, and P is the average polygon size.

We use the methods of analysis, observation and non-linear regression in creating the models. In Strategy 1, polygon boundary curves are duplicated and curve data of the same polygon are stored on the same page. We can thus predict the number of reads as the quotient of dividing the amount of data to be read from the disk by the page size. We formulate the model as:

$$R_1 = C_{1,1}(WNP/100)/D + C_{1,2} \tag{2}$$

where R_1 is the predicted number of reads in Strategy 1, (WNP/100) is the predicted amount of data to be read when the search window size is W, and $C_{1,1}$ and $C_{1,2}$ are coefficients to be estimated. This model indicates that the number of reads R is proportional to search window size W and inversely proportional to data page size D. The two relationships are consistent with those illustrated in Figures 1 and 2.

To estiamte the two coefficients, we conducted non-linear regression analysis on the experimental data obtained from 10 maps of different characteristics (in terms of the number polygons, average polygon size, etc.). The estimated values of the two coefficients are 1.46 and 40. Therefore we have the model

$$R_1 = 1.46(WNP/100)/D + 40 \tag{3}$$

for the number of reads in Strategy 1.

In Strategies 2 and 3, situations are somewhat different. Polygon boundary curves are not duplicated. In Strategy 2, half of the curves are clustered based on their associations with polygons, but in Strategy 3, curves are not clustered at all. Although in the two strategies, the numbers of reads are also closely related to the amount of data to be read and the page size, it cannot be predicted by simply dividing the amount of the data to be read by the data page size.

By observing the charts in Figure 1, we can notice that in Strategy 2, approximately the number of reads is inversely proportional to $\sqrt{D}$, and in Strategy 3, the number of reads is inversely proportional to $\sqrt[n]{D}$, the nth root of the data page size ($n > 2$). The observation suggests that the models for Strategies 2 and 3 can be formulated as

$$R = C_1(WNP/100)/\sqrt[C_3]{D} + C_2. \tag{4}$$

We also use non-linear regression analysis to estimate the three coefficients. The models we create for Strategies 2 and 3 are

$$R_2 = 0.13(WNP/100)/D^{0.58} + 35 \tag{5}$$

and

$$R_3 = 0.024(WNP/100)/D^{0.18} - 100 \tag{6}$$

where R_2 and R_3 are the predicted numbers of reads for Strategies 2 and 3.

The charts in Figures 3 and 4 are generated from the predicted numbers of reads by applying the three models in Eq. (3), Eq. (5) and Eq. (6) to the same geology map. Compare the charts in Figures 1 and 3, and the charts in Figures 2 and 4. We can see that in most cases, the predicted numbers of reads fit the actual numbers very well.

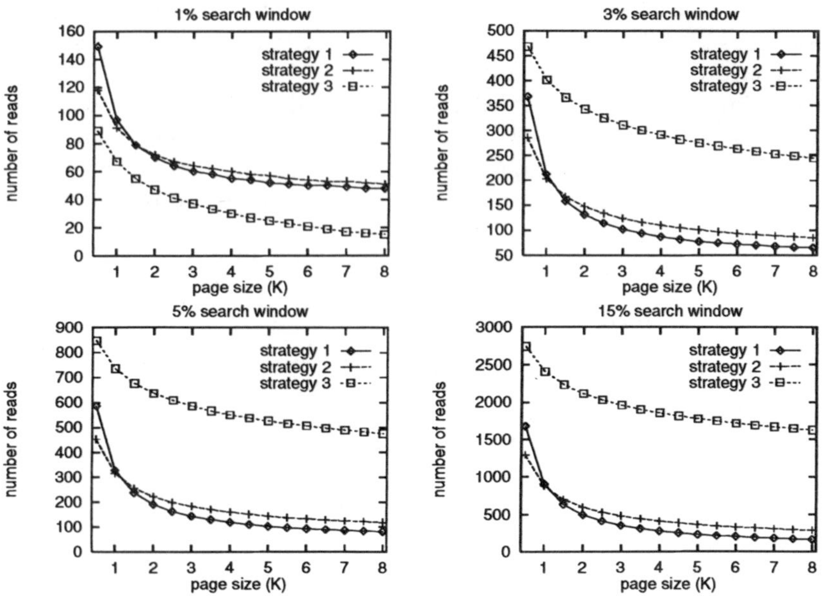

Figure 3. Predicted number of reads vs data page size for the geology map.

8 Model Validity Analysis

For a model created by using a statistical method, validity analysis is necessary before it can be used for prediction. The validity analysis usually consists of two steps: model utility analysis and model evaluation. The first step tests how well the model fits the data that are used to create the model, and the second step tests how well the model fits data which are not used to create the model. We have seen in the last section that the models fit very well the data used to create them. In this paper, we will not describe the theoretical model utility analysis. In this section we will discuss the second step – model evaluation.

The models are evaluated using several independent data sets, that is, the data which are not used for model creation. For each digital map, we conduct the experiment described above to record the actual numbers of reads, and also apply the the three models. The evaluation involves comparing the predicted numbers of reads with the actual numbers.

The charts in Figures 5 and 6 are generated from the actual and predicted

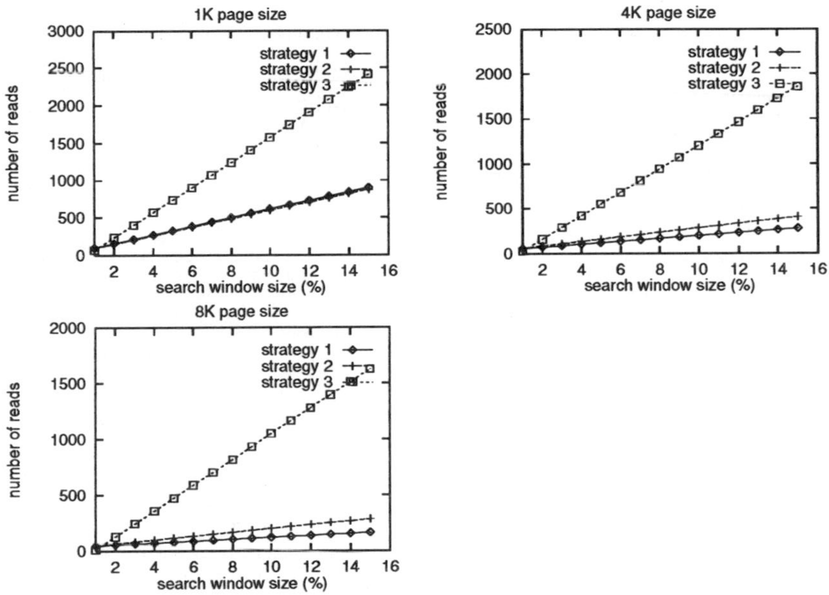

Figure 4. Number of reads vs search window size for different data page sizes.

numbers of reads for an administration map. This map is about 5.2MB large. The total number of polygons is 2037 and the average polygon size is about 2.6KB.

The following can be observed from the two groups of charts:

- For all the three strategies, the actual and predicted numbers of reads have very similar ranges.
- For all the three strategies, the changes in the actual and predicted numbers of reads are very similar. In other words, the curves for the actual and predicted reads are very similar.
- In terms of both the actual and predicted number of reads, the three strategies have the same order. That, for most page sizes, Strategy 1 has the smallest number of reads, Strategy 2 has the second, and Strategy 3 has the largest number.

The comparison indicates that the predicted values by the three models fit the actual values of this independent data set well.

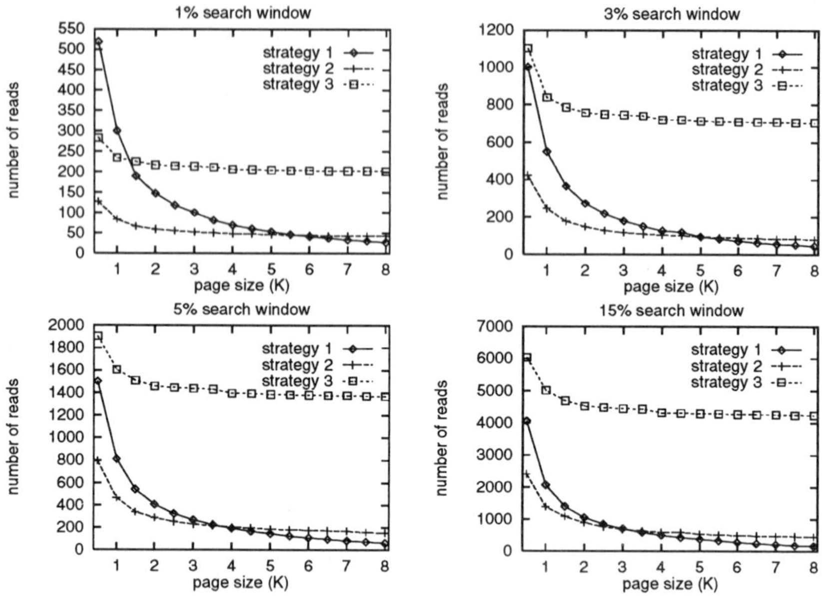

Figure 5. Actual number of reads vs data page size for the administration map.

9 Conclusion

Spatial object clustering is an important task in physical design for a spatial database. By properly clustering spatial objects, I/O costs can be considerably reduced, which are major components in the costs for performing spatial operations. In this research, we designed three clustering strategies for polygon objects and conducted experiments to evaluate their performance. The experimental results may provide relatively accurate information for studying the clustering strategies.

Based on the experimental results, we created mathematical models for the strategies. The models can be used to predict the number of reads when choosing a clustering strategy for a map, and estimate the cost for a spatial operation in query optimization. As for the independent data we tested, the models may generate very accurate prediction. The results of this research suggest that the performance of a clustering strategy can be modeled mathematically. The models created in this research can be used as a starting point to develop models for practical use, which require more experimental data

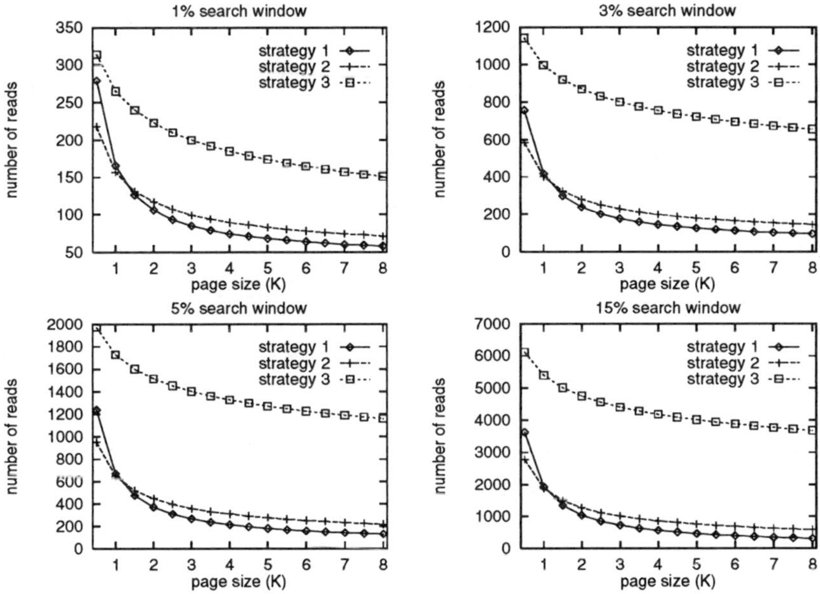

Figure 6. Predicted number of reads vs data page size for the administration map.

and closer studies.

Acknowledgements

This research is being supported by grants from the Natural Science and Engineering Research Council of Canada (NSERC).

References

1. Adam, N. R., and A. Gangopadhyay, 1997, *Database Issues in Geographic Information Systems*, Boston, Massachusetts: Kluwer academic Publishers.
2. Bertino, E., A. A. Saad, and M. A. Ismail, 1994, 'Clustering Techniques in Object Bases: A Survey', *Data and Knowledge Engineering*, Vol.12, pp 255-275.
3. Buehler, K., and L. McKee, 1996, *The OpenGIS Guide*, Wayland, Massachusetts: Open GIS Consortium, Inc..

4. Eisenberg, A. and J. Melton, 1999, 'SQL:1999, formerly known as SQL3', *ACM SIGMOD Record*, Vol.28, No. 1, pp 131-138.
5. Gaede, V. and O. Gunther, 1998, 'Multidimensional Access Methods', *ACM Computing Survey*, Vol.30, No. 2, pp 170-231.
6. Guttman, A., 1984, 'R-Trees: a Dynamic Index Structure for Spatial Searching', *ACM SIGMOD'84 Proceedings*, Vol. 14, No. 2, pp 47-57.
7. ISO/IEC, 1999, *Information Technology – Database languages – SQL Multimedia and Application Packages – Part 3: Spatial (approved version)*, The International Organization of Standardization, ftp://jerry.ece.umassd.edu/isowg3/sqlmm/YGJdocs/ygj006-sp2.ps.
8. Kulkarni, K., J. Bauer, U. Dayal, M. Kelly and J. Melton, 1994, 'ADT-based Type System for SQL', in J. C. Freytag et al eds. *Query Processing for Advanced Database Systems*, San Meteo, California: Morgan Kaufman Publishers.
9. Laurini R., and D. Thompson, 1992, *Fundamentals of Spatial Information Systems*, San Diego: Academic Press Ltd.
10. Ooi, B. C., 1990, *Efficient Query Processing in Geographic Information Systems*, Berlin: Springer-Verlag.
11. Rumbaugh, J., 1991, *Object-Oriented Modeling and Design*, Englewood Cliffs, New Jersey: Prentice Hall.
12. Shekhar, S., S. Chawla, S. Ravada, A. Fetterer, X. Liu, and C. Lu, 1999, 'Spatial Databases – Accomplishments and Research Needs', *IEEE Transactions on Knowledge and Data Engineering*, Vol. 11, No. 1, pp 45-55.
13. Stefanakis, E., Y. Theodoridis, T. Sellis, and Y. Lee, 1997, 'Point Representation of Spatial Objects and Query Window Extension: a New Technique for Spatial Access Methods', *International Journal of Geographic Information Science*, Vol. 11, No. 6, pp 529-554.

MULTI-POOL CACHING IN CONTINUOUS MEDIA SERVER

CHUTIMET SRINILTA

Department of Computer Engineering, King Mongkut's Institute of Technology Ladkrabang, Bangkok 10520, Thailand
E-mail: chutimet@ce.kmitl.ac.th

ALOK CHOUDHARY

Department of Electrical and Computer Engineering, Northwestern University, Evanston, IL 60208, USA
E-mail: choudhary@ece.nwu.edu

Efficient storage and retrieval strategies are essential to ensure a smooth and meaningful flow of information during a playback of continuous media object. Disk I/O is usually a potential bottleneck limiting capacity of a server. The number of concurrent sessions supported is usually limited by the bandwidth of a storage system. User request distribution has a direct effect on I/O load. Hence, one way to reduce number of I/O access is to reuse data that have already been fetched. Many possibilities exist for an efficient caching. A multi-pool interval cache stores data equivalent to intervals between successive playback sessions in object pools. Cache space is allocated to each object based on object's access frequency. Therefore, multi-pool caching is dynamic. Cache access efficiency is controlled by two caching parameters. These parameters can be adjusted to suit different user request distributions and object profiles.

1 Introduction

A continuous media object can be viewed as a sequence of equal size media units. One media unit may represent several physical data blocks. Each media unit is called stripe unit. A delivery of an object is called a session. One of the techniques to avoid multiple retrievals for user requests that request the same object is to group user requests and multicast data [3, 7, 9]. With this technique, some users may experience long startup delay. Another technique is to reuse the data. Sheu *et al.* [8] proposed a chaining technique where data are cached at client stations in the chaining tree. These stations help serve user requests; thus, traffic to and from server is reduced. Work done relevant to media caching was included in [1, 4, 5, 6].

It is a characteristic of continuous media object that a sequence of data is delivered in response to a playback request. Multiple playback sessions of the same object require the same sequence of data. This characteristic supports caching because it is certain that the cached data are used in the future when one or more users initiate the playback requests of that same object. The concept of interval caching proposed by Dan *et al.* [2] arose from this characteristic. Interval caching also takes into account the fact that successive playback sessions of the same object

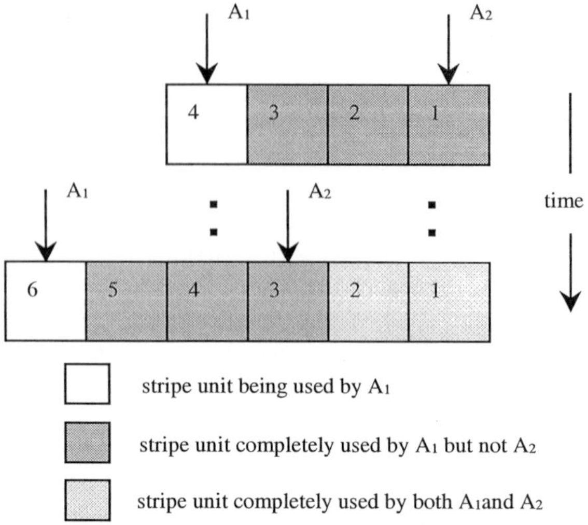

Figure 1. Fixed interval between successive playback sessions

always follow one another with fixed intervals in between. Figure 1 illustrates the situation. Suppose there are two user requests for object *A*. Let the second user request (A_2) arrive at the server when the first user request (A_1) is reading a stripe unit number 4. When A_1 is at a stripe unit number 6, A_2 is reading a stripe unit number 3. Since these two sessions are playing the same object, their paces are the same. Therefore, they are always three stripe units apart.

Interval caching keeps only the data in the interval between successive sessions in the cache. It is simple and efficient for playback operation. From Figure 1, if there are no other user requests for object *A* following A_2, stripe units are no longer needed after they are read by A_2. Hence, keeping just four stripe units in the cache is sufficient for these two sessions to share the data. By caching only the intervals, cache space is utilized more effectively. Moreover, the cache adapts itself dynamically to user request distribution as request interval is related to access frequency of object. This same concept is applied in the proposed caching scheme.

2 The Server Model

The server model is implemented on Intel Paragon parallel computer. It is composed of 16 compute nodes arranged in a pattern of 4x4 matrix. All server nodes are independent but connected. Communication between nodes is achieved by message passing.

Server nodes are categorized into three categories: manager node, dispatcher node and storage node. There are 1 manager node, 4 dispatcher nodes and 11 storage nodes in the model. Each dispatcher node has a multi-pool interval cache. Objects are striped and stored across all storage nodes. Manager node receives requests for object playbacks from users. It assigns each user request to one of the dispatcher nodes. The goal of the assignment is to maximize data sharing in the cache: user requests for the same object are assigned to the same dispatcher node. In case that the object is requested for the first time, the user request is directed to a dispatcher node handling the least number of sessions. Dispatcher node periodically sends sub-requests to groups of storage nodes to obtain object data. These data are stored in the cache and are delivered to each user according to a playback rate of the object.

The cache is implemented at dispatcher nodes in order to reduce number of sub-requests sent to storage nodes which consequently reduces both workload at storage nodes and network congestion within the server.

3 Cache Organization

A multi-pool interval cache can be viewed as a collection of equal size memory chunks. Each chunk is equivalent to one stripe unit. The cache organization is illustrated in Figure 2.

The cache is composed of a free pool, a number of object pools and a set of cache entries. The free pool contains a number of stripe units. These stripe units are available to any session. Each cache entry has a pointer to an object pool. An object pool is a circular linked list of stripe units being accessed by sessions. One object pool holds stripe units of one object. In addition to a pointer to object pool, each cache entry contains object information such as object identification number and number of stripe units contained in the object pool.

4 Cache Management

A caching window (*CW*) represents the allowable number of stripe units in the interval between any two successive sessions accessing the same object. While it is efficient when frequently accessed data are cached, it is even more efficient when those data occupy little cache space. The goal is to keep as little amount of data as possible while serving as many sessions as possible. There is a bound on the caching window. The value for caching window should be given based on frequency of access of object and total cache size. Different objects may have different caching windows. Caching window simply is the length of an object pool (in terms of stripe units).

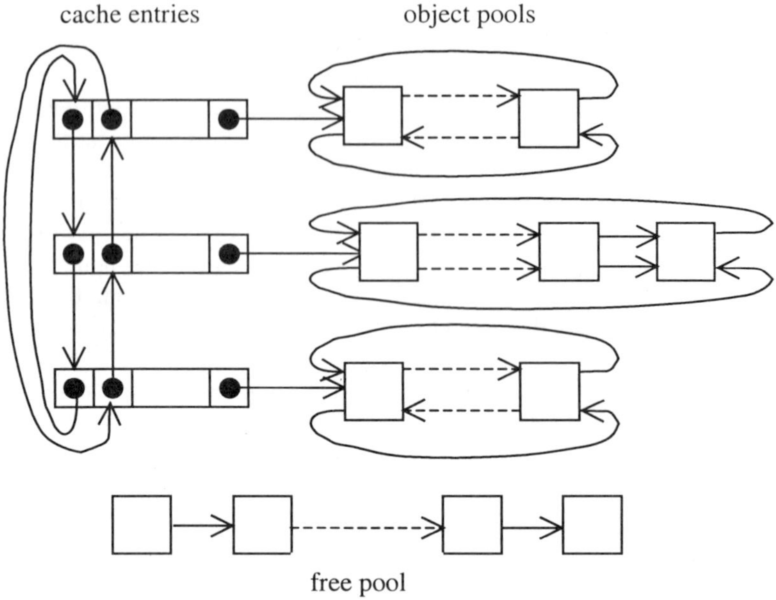

Figure 2. Multi-pool cache organization

When one object is requested by many users, these users are to share the same object pool only if their requests enter the server within an interval of the caching window assigned for the object. Each user request sharing the object pool is classified as either an initial or a duplicate request, depending upon the order in which it arrives at the server. The initial request is the first user request that requests the object, the duplicate requests are the subsequent ones. Every object pool has only one initial request, but may have more than one duplicate request. Initial request writes data to object pool and duplicate request reads data from it.

In Figure 3, let A_n be a user request for the nth playback session of an object A. User requests reach the server at times indicated by shaded boxes on a time line. Suppose object A is granted a caching window of size three stripe units. Hence, the object pool contains at most three stripe units at all times. In the figure, the numbers in object pools identify stripe units that are stored in the pools. $t_{m,n}$ represents the time when the nth stripe unit is placed in object pool M.

An object pool is created when an initial request arrives at the server. After a caching window is determined, CW stripe units are taken from the free pool to form a new object pool. In case that there is not enough stripe units left in the free pool, the new object pool is not setup.

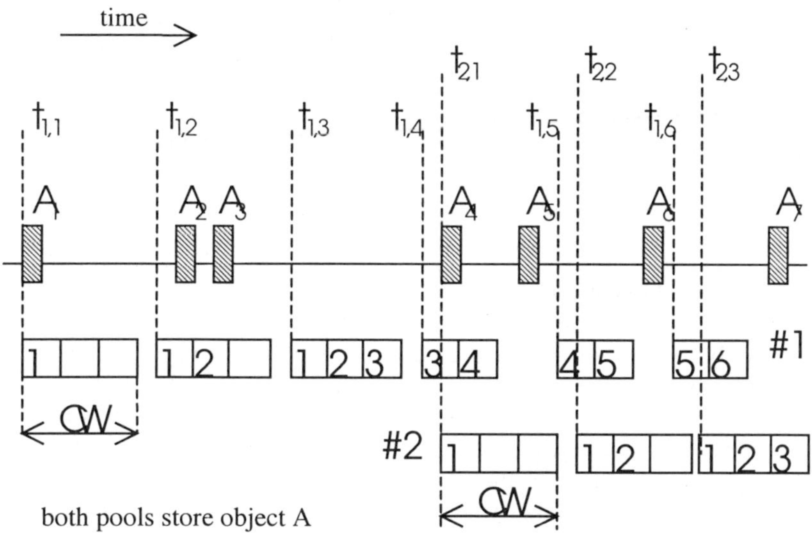

Figure 3. Logical view of the object pools (according to time)

An object pool is either open or closed at any given time. At the beginning, the object pool is open. Every stripe unit in the pool is empty. The content of these empty stripe units are filled one by one at times indicated by $t_{m,n}$'s in Figure 3. After every empty stripe unit in the object pool is filled, just before the initial request writes the content of the next stripe unit (at time $t_{1,4}$ in Figure 3), the object pool is examined to see if any stripe units can be returned to the free pool. Such stripe units are those stripe units with the most number of access. The reason for this is that those stripe units will not be accessed after the object pool is closed. In Figure 3, A_1, A_2 and A_3 are all finished with stripe units number 1 and 2 by the time $t_{1,4}$. These stripe units are no longer used by neither A_1, A_2 nor A_3 after $t_{1,4}$. Stripe unit number 1 is made available and returned to the free pool. The new stripe unit (stripe unit number 4) replaces stripe unit number 2. Object pool 1 is now closed. From then on, object pool 1 contains only two stripe units. A closed object pool holds only stripe units equivalent to the gap between the initial session and the last session reading from the object pool at the closing time. After the object pool is closed, a newly fetched stripe unit replaces the oldest one. It can be viewed as the caching window is shifting toward the end of the object one stripe unit at a time.

If another user request for that same object arrives after the object pool is closed and there is enough cache space available, a new object pool is allocated. The new object pool will capture a new set of user requests that arrive within the time when the object pool is being filled up.

In Figure 3, all user requests are for object A. A_1 is an initial request of object pool 1. A_2 and A_3 are duplicate requests of object pool 1 because stripe unit number 1 is found in object pool 1 at times when A_2 and A_3 enter the server. Object pool 1 is closed at time $t_{1,4}$. A_4 arrives the server after that. A_4 does not find stripe unit number 1 in object pool 1; therefore, it cannot retrieve data from object pool 1. A new object pool, object pool 2, is created and A_4 becomes its initial request. A_5, A_6 and A_7 are duplicate requests of object pool 2. Both object pools contain data of object A.

5 Object Pool Allocation

Consider only sessions of the same object, all sessions starting within one caching window interval from the beginning of the initial session are handled by the same object pool. Therefore, a large caching window has a tendency to serve more user requests. However, it requires more cache space. A caching window should be set to the value just long enough so that if an object has not be accessed by any other session during the first caching window interval, it is justified not to store it in the cache.

As stated earlier, a caching window should be bounded to a value based on several factors including frequency of access of an object and total cache size. Consider a database of M objects. The manager node reschedules user requests. It releases them to dispatcher nodes at rate a_r user requests per second. Let a user choose to view object i with a probability p_i, $0 \le p_i \le 1$, where $\sum_{i=1}^{M} p_i = 1$. These probabilities reflect access probability of each object. Caching window can be determined from the following equation.

$$CW_i = rounded(C \times p_i) \times \varepsilon \tag{1}$$

where,

CW_i	is caching window of an object pool containing object i,
C	is total cache size in terms of number of stripe units, and
ε	is expansion factor.

The value for a caching window is rounded to the closest integer. An expansion factor is a caching parameter used to extend object pool length. A short object pool is not very effective, especially when object's playback rate is high because object pool duration is short. The object pool is closed in a short time after it is created. As a result, it can capture only a small number of user requests. However, long object pools are not always very efficient. If a pool is long but is accessed by a small number of user requests, it may be better to obtain the data directly from the disk(s), saving cache space for more popular objects. Note that object pool replacement can be considered. However, the replacement process does add load on the server nodes. Moreover, each active object pool is currently providing some benefits. We choose objects to be stored in the cache rather than store every object and replace them later.

6 Minimum Access Probability

A multi-pool caching scheme is more effective when the difference in arrival times of user requests to the cached object is small. In other words, the scheme works well when access frequency of the cached object is high. Therefore, the cache should select to store only objects that have a tendency to be requested frequently. A threshold for the minimum access probability of a tentatively cached object is defined. Any object whose probability of access is lower than this threshold value is not cached. This threshold value depends on a number of parameters that are discussed later in the section.

6.1 *Frequency of Access*

The frequency of user requests for a particular object assigned to a particular dispatcher node (f_{dim}) depends on three factors: request arrival rate, object's access probability, and request assignment scheme. Let a_{ri} be an arrival rate at the manager node of user requests for object i, and p_{im} be a probability that the manager node directs user request for object i to dispatcher node m. f_{dim} can thus be obtained as below.

$$\begin{aligned} f_{d_{im}} &= a_{ri} \times p_{im} \\ &= a_r \times p_i \times p_{im} \end{aligned} \tag{2}$$

In our model, p_{im} is equal to 1 because user requests for the same object are always assigned to the same dispatcher node. Thus, the access frequency depends only on the request arrival rate and the probability of access of the object. Equation 2 then becomes

$$f_{d_{im}} = a_r \times p_i . \tag{3}$$

6.2 Object Pool Duration

A duration of an object pool is governed by object pool length, size of each stripe unit, and playback rate of object. Duration of object pool n containing object i (d_n) is determined from the following equation.

$$d_n = \frac{CW_i \times P_s}{R_{pl_i}} \tag{4}$$

6.3 The Bound

Content of an object pool is overwritten by newly fetched stripe units after the pool is closed. Thus, it is reasonable to cache object only when it is requested at least twice over a time interval equivalent to one pool duration. This draws a lower bound on object's access probability.

$$\begin{aligned} f_{d_{im}} \times d_n &\geq 2 \\ f_{d_{im}} &\geq \frac{2}{d_n} \end{aligned} \tag{5}$$

Equation 5 can be generalized to

$$f_{d_{im}} \geq \frac{eff}{d_n} \tag{6}$$

where,

eff is a degree of efficiency.

A degree of efficiency is another caching parameter. It indicates a minimum allowable access efficiency of each object pool. It defines object selection criterion that determines whether an object should be stored in the cache. In other words, degree of efficiency (*eff*) is a minimum number of user requests expected to access each object pool. If object's access probability does not provide that the object is to be requested more than *eff* times in one pool duration, the object is not cached. This criterion must be exercised especially when object pool replacement is not considered. In case that the value of *eff* is too high, not many objects are cached. Thus, the I/O load does not reduce much. On the other hand, if the value is too low, unpopular objects are cached leaving inadequate available cache space for popular objects that are requested later.

A minimum access probability for a tentatively cached object is obtained from equations 3 and 6. The final equation is shown below.

$$p_i \geq \frac{eff}{a_r \times d_n} \tag{7}$$

Access probability of an object must satisfy equation 7 in order for the object to be cached.

7 Experiments

A number of test cases were conducted to demonstrate server behaviors. The size of a stripe unit was set to 512KB. Cache size at each dispatcher node was 20MB. User request distribution followed the distribution in Figure 4 which conformed to Zipfian distribution. There are 400 playback sessions at a steady state.

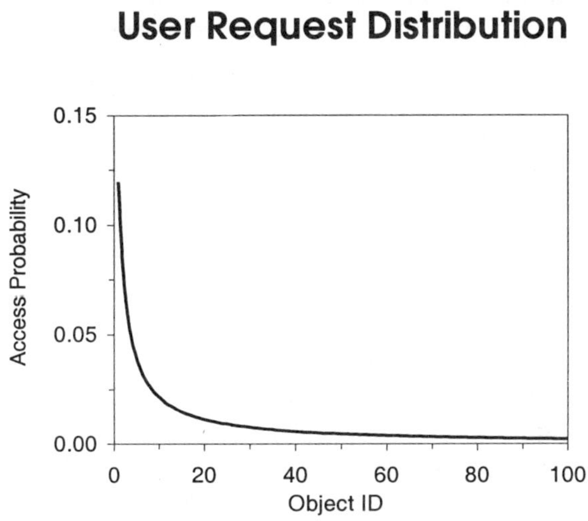

Figure 4. User request distribution

7.1 Assumptions

It was assumed that all objects belonged to a single media type: video. There were a total of 100 distinct objects in a video library. Each object had a constant playback rate of either 1.5Mbits/s (MPEG-1 standard) or 4Mbits/s (MPEG-2 standard). All objects had the same display length. They were stored at storage nodes in a compressed digital form. Compression issues were not addressed. Every object had the same storage and retrieval parameters.

Each server node was assumed to have enough disk capacity and main memory for all the playback sessions the server was serving. Disk access operations were simulated. Disk seek time and rotational latency were given using a random number generator. Disk transfer time varied according to the size of a stripe unit. Total disk service time was simulated by elapsing a system timer. Communication network between the server model and the users was assumed to be reliable and fast enough to handle the bandwidth required for object playback. Lastly, data decompression was carried out at users' sites. Communication from server to user and decompression issues were not covered in the study.

7.2 Performance Metrics

Performance metrics used in the experiment are discussed below.

- **Percentage of cache sub-requests** This metric is a ratio of the number of sub-requests satisfied from the cache to the total number of sub-requests. This metric shows the workload taken by the cache.
- **Percentage of read access** This metric is a proportion of read access in total cache access. This metric shows cache access efficiency.
- **Percentage of unused cache space** This metric represents a portion of available cache space when the server is operating at a steady state. It reflects cache space utilization.

7.3 Experimental Results and Discussion

Experiments were conducted under five object profiles: 100:0, 70:30, 50:50, 30:70 and 0:100. The name of the profile indicates the mixed ratio of playback rates of objects stored at the server. For example, a 70:30 profile means that 70% of the objects the server possesses are MPEG-1 video and 30% are MPEG-2 video.

Object pool length was varied. The value of expansion factor increased from 1 to 8. Degree of efficiency was used in test cases where *eff* was set to 2 which means that every cached object are requested at least twice in a time interval equivalent to one pool duration.

Results are presented in Figures 5-7. Percentage of cache sub-requests is shown in Figure 5. Percentage of unused cached space is shown in Figure 6. Percentage of cache read access is shown in Figure 7. The top row in each figure (labeled *a*) presents results when degree of efficiency was not used. The bottom row in each figure (labeled *b*) presents results when degree of efficiency was set to 2.

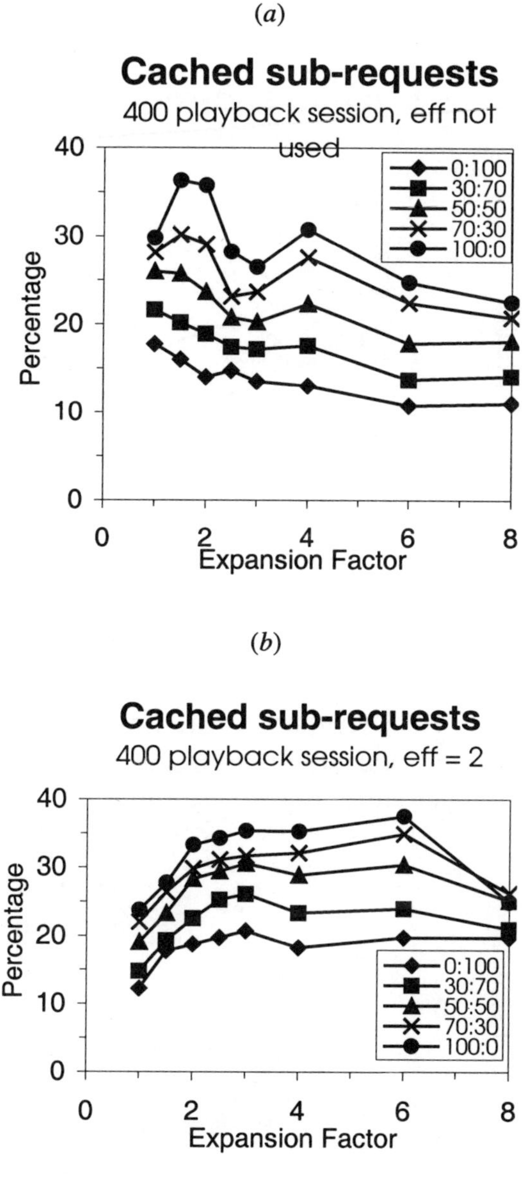

Figure 5. Cached sub-requests

(*a*)

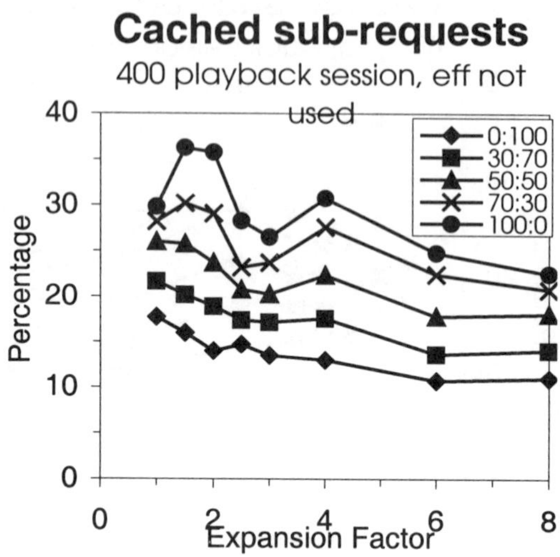

(*b*)

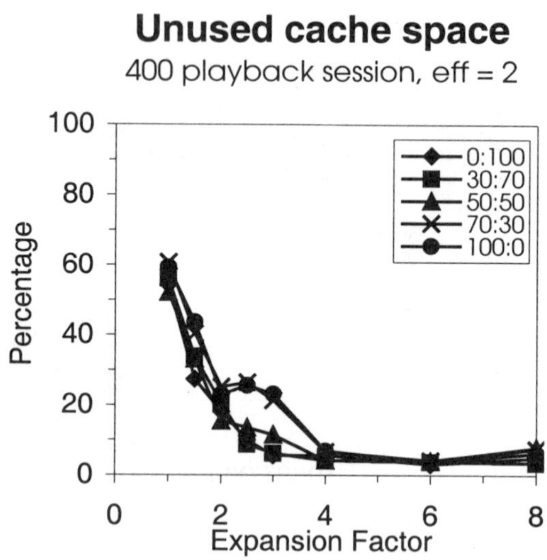

Figure 6. Unused cache space

(*a*)

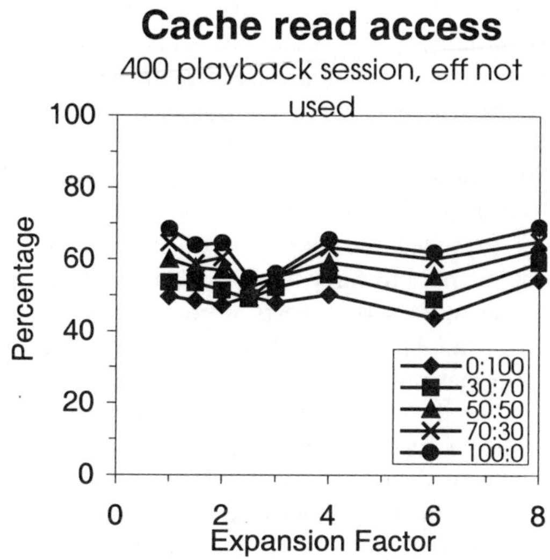

(*b*)

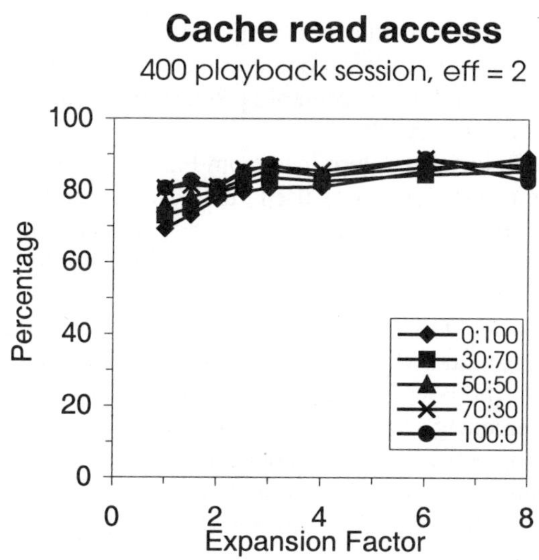

Figure 7. Cache access efficiency

In general, when degree of efficiency was not used, percentage of cache sub-requests decreased as expansion factor increased (Figure 5*a*). The percentage dropped 5-8% as expansion factor increased from 1 to 8.

When degree of efficiency was used, the trend of the graphs was different (Figure 5*b*). The graphs increased and then decreased. The peaks of the graphs were reached at a smaller expansion factor when object profile contained more of fast objects. For example, the highest percentages were reached at expansion factor of 3 in 0:100 and 30:70 profiles, where the highest percentages were reached at expansion factor of 6 in 100:0 and 70:30 profiles.

Expansion factor extended the length of object pools. Increasing expansion factor enabled each object pool to carry more stripe units. Consequently, object pool duration was longer and more sub-requests were addressed from the cache. Thus, when cache space is available (more than 20%) at a steady state, increasing expansion factor within that range increased number of sub-requests satisfied from the cache. However, when the cache was completely or nearly full at a steady state, increasing expansion factor further had a tradeoff. The unfavorable effect was that increasing expansion factor decreased the total number of object pools. The total number of cache reads might be less because fewer objects were cached although each object pool was able to address a greater number of sub-requests. This disadvantage of having fewer object pools began to override the advantage of long object pool at the value of expansion factor where the graphs started to convex down.

The percentage of cache read access reflected the effectiveness of cache access. Each object pool should serve at least one duplicate request. Since there was always one user writing to the pool, the acceptable proportion of cache read access in total cache access should be at least 50%.

Cache access efficiency is determined from Figure 7. The access efficiency was higher when degree of efficiency was used. This was because the cache selected to store only frequently requested objects. Cache read access contributed 70-90% when degree of efficiency was set to 2 (Figure 7*b*) compared to 40-70% in Figure 7*a*.

The number of cache read access was dependent on the proportion of slow objects in object profile. This again was an effect of pool duration. Percentage of cache read access was higher when object profile was dominated by slow objects.

Expansion factor did not produce a significant effect on the percentage of cache read access. The percentage varied only a little when expansion factor increased from 1 to 8. This happened because increasing expansion factor affected not only the number of cache read access, but also the total number of cache access. Therefore, the ratio of both numbers did not vary greatly upon the changes of the expansion factor.

8 Conclusion

Multi-pool caching was effective under various object profiles. In the experiment, up to almost 40% of total sub-requests were addressed from the cache. The two caching parameters, expansion factor and degree of efficiency, had an effect on workload taken by the cache as well as cache access efficiency. Expansion factor helped the cache capture more sub-requests and degree of efficiency made cache access more effective. These parameters are to be adjusted to fit the system. Since cache access efficiency was independent of the expansion factor, the expansion factor should be set to the value within the range where percentage of cached sub-requests is at the maximum. Object profile possessed by the server is another factor. It should be taken into account in selecting the value of expansion factor as well. The results showed that with a proper setting, the cache was utilized efficiently and the server had a tendency to support more concurrent sessions.

References

1. Dahlin, W., Wang, R., Anderson, T., and Patterson, D., Cooperative caching: using remote client memory to improve file system performance. *Proceedings of the first Symposium on Operating System Design and Implementation*, (1994) pp.267-280.
2. Dan, A., Dias, D., Mukherjee, R., Sitaram, D., and Tewari, R., Buffering and caching in large scale video servers. In *Proceedings of COMPCON*, (1995).
3. Dan, A., Sitaram, D., and Shahabuddin, R., Scheduling policies for an on-demand video server with batching. *IBM Research Report RC 19381*, (1994).
4. Kamath, M., Ramamritham, K., and Towsley, D., Continuous media sharing in multimedia database systems. *Proceedings of the Fourth International Conference on Database Systems for Advanced Applications*, (1995).
5. Leff, A., Yu, P., and Wolf, J., Policies for efficient memory utilization in a remote caching architecture. *Proceedings of the first International Conference on Parallel and Distributed Information System*, (1991) pp.198-207.
6. Lougher, P., Lougher, R., Shepherd, D., and Pegler, D., A scalable hierarchical video storage architecture. *SPIE Multimedia Computing and Networking*, (1996).
7. Papidimitriou, C., Ramanathan, S., and Rangan, P., Information caching for delivery of personalized video programs on home entertainment channels. In *Proceedings of the IEEE International Conference on Multimedia Systems and Computing*, (1994).
8. Sheu, S., Hua, K., and Tavanapong, W., Chaining: A generalized batching technique for VOD systems. In *Proceedings of the IEEE International Conference on Multimedia Computing and Systems*, (1997).

9. Srinilta, C., Techniques for improving performance in continuous media servers. *Ph.D. Dissertation, Department of Electrical Engineering and Computer Science, Syracuse University*, (1998).

IMMEDIATE AND ADVANCE RESOURCE RESERVATIONS ARCHITECTURE WITH QUALITY OF SERVICE ROUTING AGENTS

FARAG SALLABI, AHMED KARMOUCH

Multimedia Information and Mobile Agents Research Laboratory
School of Information Technology and Engineering, University of Ottawa
E-mail: sallabi@sol.genie.uottawa.ca
karmouch@site.uottawa.ca

We present an architecture for end-to-end resource reservations with user interactions. This architecture is based on domain agents, where in each network domain there is a domain agent. The domain agent is responsible of making immediate and advance resource reservations, and adapting the reserved resources according to user interactions. We also present an architecture for domain agents that facilitate the communications of domain agents with the receivers, the senders and the routers. It contains a QoS routing agent, to construct a QoS intra-domain path. The QoS routing agent uses a modification of Dijkstra's algorithm to find the narrowest-path with the minimum number of hops that accommodate the requested QoS. We also implemented a simulation model to monitor the rejection probability of the immediate and advance requests, and to monitor the utilization of each link in the simulated network topology.

1 Introduction

The present architecture of the Internet provides a very simple service, the best-effort service. Using this service, packets compete for the network resources, and traverse the network according to the service of the underlying routing protocol algorithm. Packets have no right to choose their paths and even ask for paths that satisfy their QoS needs. This service is not suitable for continuous real-time traffic that has stringent quality of service requirements. Therefore, new service architectures have come into existence to provide solutions to the QoS problem. The most obvious solutions are to control the number of flows injected into the network and to enable applications reserve network resources according to their QoS demands.

The first architectures for resource reservations suggest that applications could ask for reservations that start immediately and continue for indefinite periods of time [13]. These architectures also face the problem of the scarce of network resources, where most resource reservation requests are rejected. To overcome this problem, new schemes have been proposed to enable applications reserve resources in advance [6,11,12,14]. In fact, these schemes does not explicitly solve the problem of scarcity, but it enable users choose the periods of time in which resources are available. Once the resources are reserved, they will be available to users at the start of their applications. Meanwhile, advance reservations give chance to service providers in managing network resources and put cost schemes on using network resources.

Resource reservation protocols such as RSVP [13] provide a method for requesting and reserving network resources, they do not provide a mechanism for determining a network path that has adequate resources to accommodate the requested QoS. Therefore, if resource reservation protocols are used with the existing routing protocols, which use shortest-path algorithms for path computation, they will load the selected path and leave other paths unloaded. This behavior raises several problems. First, bottleneck problem where all traffic is directed into one path (shortest-path). Second, fewer flows will be admitted due to the lack of alternative paths. Third, less network links utilization, where some links are free or slightly utilized. Fourth, if the link costs are changed, to avoid the congestion problem, the traffic will change direction, use another path in which it does not have reservation, and loose the QoS.

In fact, some work has already been emerged in this area (QoS Routing) and suggested new architectures for QoS routing. Z. Wang et al [17] discuss the complexity of finding paths subject to multiple constraints, the selection of metrics for QoS routing and present three path computation algorithms for source routing and hop-by-hop routing. A. Shaikh et al [4] introduce efficient mechanisms for precomputing one or more routes to each destination, and on-demand checking of the suitability of the routes at connection arrival, based on the most recent link-state information. R. Guerin et al [8] describe extensions to the OSPF [10] protocol to support QoS routes. They present algorithm for computing QoS routes. Zhang et al [18] describe series of extensions to OSPF and MOSPF [9] that can be used to provide QoS routing in conjunction with a resource set-up protocols. Advertisements indicating the resources available and the resources used are advertised to the OSPF routing domain and paths are computed based on topology information, link resource information and the resource requirement of a particular data flow. Crawley et al [7] propose a framework for QoS-based routing in the Internet. The framework is based on extending the current Internet routing model of intra-domain and inter-domain routing to support QoS.

In this paper, we present a different approach for QoS routing. We suggest using a QoS Routing Agent (QoSRA) to carry out the QoS route calculations for immediate and advance reservations. Therefore, the underlying routing protocol (OSPF) works in its normal state, and the QoSRA is invoked only when there is need for resource reservation. We also present a QoS route calculation algorithm, which computes the narrowest-path with minimum number of hops that satisfies the desired QoS instead of using the widest-path.

The rest of the paper is structured as follows. Section 2, presents complete resource reservation architecture. This architecture includes end systems, network nodes and domain agents. Domain agents are discussed in section 3. Section 4 presents the details of QoSRA. The simulation results are presented in section 5. Then the paper is concluded in section 6.

2 Resource Reservation Architecture

The architecture, figure 1, is designed to perform three different but related phases. The first phase is the negotiation process. In this phase, the receiver negotiates the required QoS parameters and reservation periods with the sender and the network. The second phase is the reservation process, where the physical resources in the receiver, the network and the sender are reserved at the specified time. The last phase is the adaptation process. In this phase, reserved resources in the receiver, the network and the sender are adapted to reflect user interactions. For more details, refer to our paper [19].

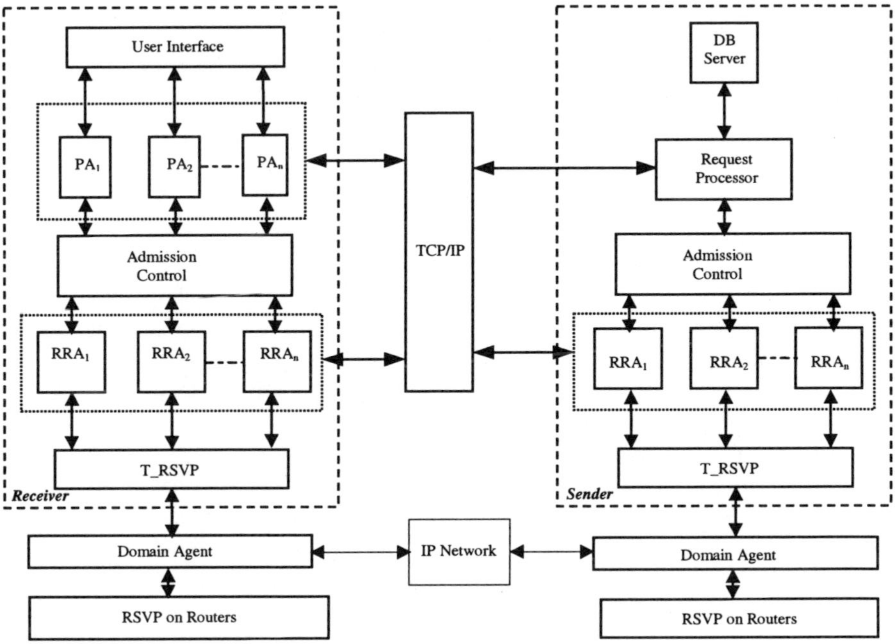

Figure 1. Resource reservation architecture

2.1 Negotiation Phase

The negotiation process is further divided into two stages. The first is between the receiver and the sender, while the second is between the receiver and the network. The reason for this division is that after the receiver and the sender agree on certain QoS and start time, the sender sends a path message to the domain agents, which start establishing the routes from the sender to the receiver(s). Then, the receiver confirms the QoS and start time with the domain agents.

2.1.1 Receiver-Sender Negotiation:

The negotiation process starts by sending a request from the receiver to the sender, as depicted in figure 2. The request contains the QoS parameters that the receiver can support and the desired starting time, in addition to other information. The sender Admission Control (AC), after receiving the scenario associated with the start time, applies the admission control algorithm, and produces three types of responses; accept, proposals or reject. If the requested QoS are accepted, a response message is sent to the receiver, otherwise proposals are generated by the AC and sent to the receiver. The idea of using proposals is first suggested by Hafid et al [12].

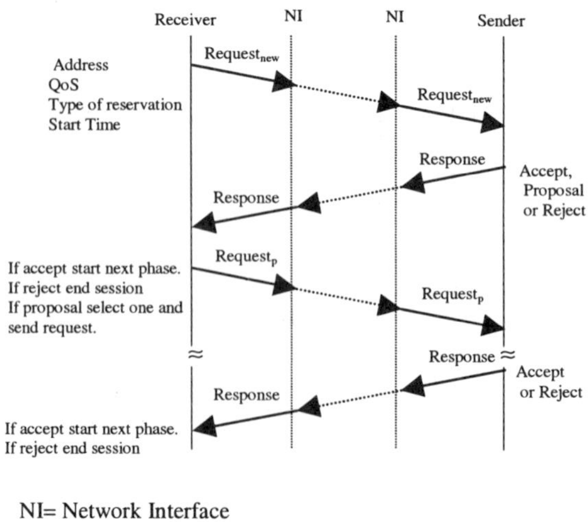

Figure 2. Receiver-Sender negotiation

2.1.2 Receiver-Network Negotiation

After finishing the receiver-sender negotiation, the sender sends a path message to the domain agent in its domain. The path message carries the session's traffic specification (Tspec), time specification (Timespec) and session addresses. The domain agent establishes a QoS route (according to the Tspec and Timespec) in the domain towards the receiver(s), and reserves resources temporarily. Then it forwards the path message to the next domain agent in the way to the receiver. This process continues until the path message reaches the receiver. At this time, the receiver sends a reserve message to the domain agent in its area. The domain agent handles the reserve message as a reserve confirmation, and makes necessary updates in the reservation state. The domain agent forwards the reserve request to the next domain agent towards the sender and sends confirmation to the previous domain agent or receiver. The process is repeated until the reserve message reaches the sender. Figure 3 shows the receiver-network negotiation.

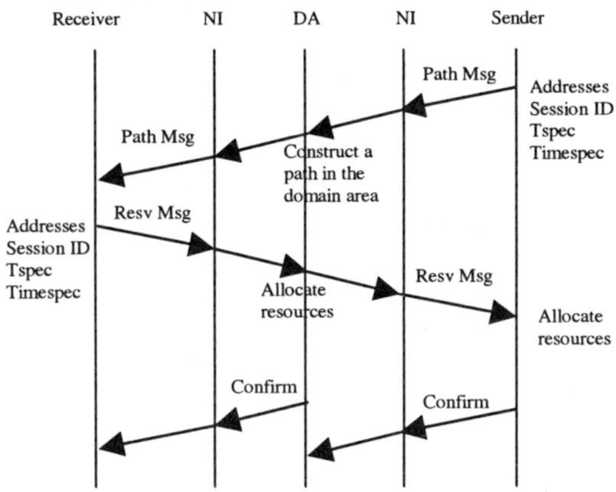

Figure 3. Receiver-Network negotiation

2.2 *Resource Reservation Phase*

This phase concerns with making the actual resource reservations in routers and end systems, and maintaining them. The T-RSVP in each domain agent and end system checks its reservation state for due sessions, if there are sessions ready to start, the T-RSVP sends messages to the routers in its domain that are involved in the session. The messages set some parameters in packet classifiers and packet schedulers to obtain the desired QoS. The domain T-RSVP is also responsible of maintaining the reserved resources by sending refresh messages at specified time intervals. The T-RSVP in the end systems sets parameters in its node to provide the due sessions its requested QoS. It also sends a refresh messages to the domain T-RSVP

2.3 *Adaptation Phase*

Adaptation is concerned with adapting reserved resources according to user interactions. The user can interactively participate in the presentation of the multimedia application. The user can use VCR like control buttons, or link to other scenarios from the current scenario, the user may also make changes to reserved resources not yet started. These interactions will certainly introduce a change in the reserved resources, either in QoS parameters or in duration.

3 Domain Agent

The idea of using static domain agents [12,14] is first suggested to solve the problem of scalability and avoid state explosion in network elements, due to resource reservations. In our architecture, we extend the functions of domain agents to include the followings:

- Make advance reservations and maintain them;
- Make immediate reservations and maintain them;
- Adapt reserved resources according to user interactions;
- Establish and maintain QoS intra-domain routes;
- Set parameters in packet classifiers and in packet schedulers to obtain the desired QoS;
- Keep history of all active domain resources;
- Send refresh messages to RSVP on routers.

To perform the above functions we propose the following domain agent architecture, figure 4. The agent could be anywhere in the domain. For reliability, there should be two agents in the same domain.

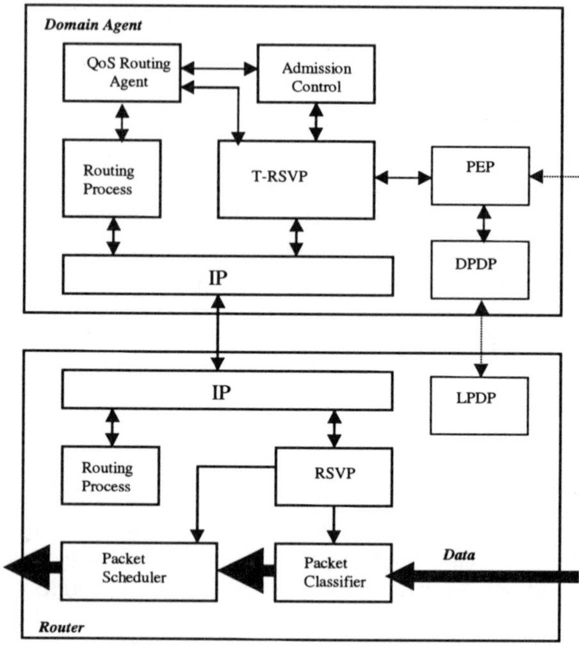

Figure 4. Domain agent architecture.

The Timed-Resource ReSerVation Protocol (T-RSVP) is the RSVP [3] augmented with session's time specification. The T-RSVP communicates with T-RSVP in other domain agents or end systems. It handles setup messages as well as user interaction messages, which are important in updating the reserved resources according to user interactions. The T-RSVP is used also to set some parameters in packet classifiers and packet schedulers in the network routers to obtain the desired QoS. For currently active sessions, the T-RSVP sends refresh messages to routers to maintain the session.

The QoS Routing Agent (QoSRA) receives the session addresses, time specification (Timespec) and the traffic specification (Tspec) from the T-RSVP, and then finds the intra-domain route that fulfils the desired QoS. The QoSRA constructs the route based on the domain topology obtained form the routing process and link states obtained from the admission control module.

The Admission Control (AC) performs two functions. First, at the session setup, where it calculates the link state at the specified time. Second, during the playback of the session, where it applies admission control on user interactions.

Furthermore, The domain agent uses policies to qualify requests against using network resources. The policy enforcement point (PEP) consults the domain policy decision point (DPDP) for policies applicable to the domain and then consults the policy decision point (PDP) for polices covering multiple areas, (service agreements).

4 Quality of Service Routing Agent (QoSRA)

The QoSRA is the essential component in the domain agent, where it decides if the new session is admitted or rejected. In fact, the QoSRA plays two roles, finding the best route and admission control. For simplicity, the QoSRA is not involved in updating routes for user interactions. User interactions are handled by the AC, which applies admission according to the existing path, if resources in this path can not accommodate the requested user interaction, the request is simply rejected.

Definition: *The best path is the narrowest route with the minimum number of hops that satisfy the requested bandwidth.*

The reasons for choosing the narrowest-path instead of the widest-path are as follows:

- To avoid resource fragmentation; resource fragmentation is a condition in which there are many scattered amounts of resources that are too small to be used productively.

- To avoid route fluctuation; by route fluctuation, we mean that, when using the widest-route the QoSRA is forced to choose different routes even if the ingress and egress of the sessions using the domain resources are the same.
- Save calculation time; using narrowest-path algorithm, we could also save calculation time by caching the most recent routes and use them for new sessions with the same source and destination addresses or ingress and egress points.

To illustrate the above points consider the following example:

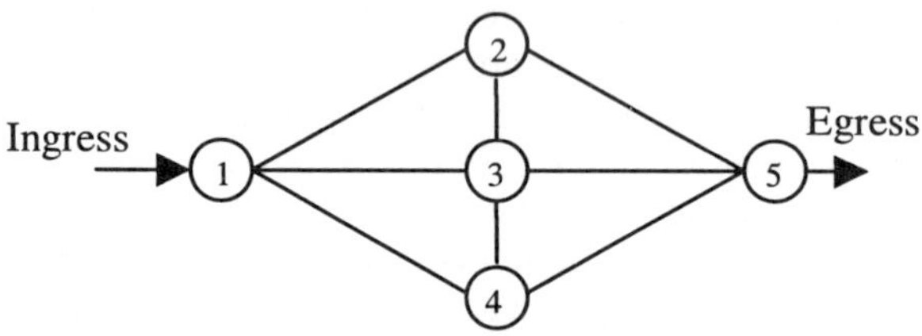

Figure 5. Widest-path problem.

In the figure above, assume each link has a capacity of 10 units, and three new flows arrive at the ingress point asking for five units each. Using the widest-path, The QoSRA will operate as follows; choose the path 1-2 for the first request, the path 1-3 for the second and 1-4 for the last. From this scenario, we conclude the following drawbacks of the widest-path algorithm:

- If another request arrives at the same ingress point asking for six units of resources, it will be definitely rejected, because there is no enough resources in the outgoing links.
- Each time a new request arrives, it will use a different path even if the ingress and egress of the previous path are the same and has enough resources. This will require unnecessary calculations and affect the performance of the algorithm

4.1 The Best-Path Calculation Algorithm

The algorithm is a modification to Dijkstra's algorithm, where we target the minimum bandwidth with the minimum number of hops that accommodate the desired bandwidth instead of the shortest path. The algorithm computes the complete path from source to destination if they are in the same domain, from the source to the egress router, from the ingress router to the egress router and from the ingress to the receiver.

The routing table includes only the transit nodes, stub nodes are checked against the destination address if it is not the destination it is discarded, otherwise the destination has been reached and the algorithm is terminated. For simplicity, the QoSRA applies only to unicast sessions, and uses a single metric calculation. Our future work is to include multicast and multi-metric calculation.

Consider a directed graph G=(V, A), where V is the number of vertices (nodes) and A is the number of arcs. Each arc (i, j) is assigned a real number b_{ij}, the available bandwidth. The algorithm proceeds in stages. By the kth stage, the best paths to the k nodes closest to the source node have been determined; these nodes are in a set M. At stage (k+1), the node not in M that has the best path and has the minimum number of hops(in case of multiple nodes with the same minimum bandwidth) from the source node is added to M. As each node is added to M, its path from the source is defined. The algorithm can be formally described as follows. Using the following notations:

b^{α} = Requested bandwidth of flow α
V= set of nodes in the network
s = Source node
M = Set of nodes so far incorporated in the algorithm
b_{ij} = Link bandwidth from node i to node j. $b_{ij} = 0$ if the two nodes are not directly connected, $b_{ij} \geq 0$ if the two nodes are directly connected.
B_n = Minimum bandwidth of the best path from node s to node n that is currently known to the algorithm

The algorithm has three steps; steps 2 and 3 are repeated until M = V. That is steps 2 and 3 are repeated until final paths have been assigned to all nodes in the network.

1. Initialize M = {s}, the set of nodes so far incorporated consists of only the source node.
   $B_n = b_{sn}$ for $n \neq s$; the initial path bandwidth to neighboring nodes are simply the link bandwidths
2. Find the neighboring node not in M that has the minimum bandwidth value from node s and equal to or greater than the requested bandwidth, incorporate that node into M; this can be expressed as:
   Find $w \notin M$ such that $B_w = \min_{j \notin M} [Bj] \geq b^{\alpha}$
   If w has more than one value, find w that has the minimum number of hops from the source. Add w to M
3. Update the best bandwidth paths:

- If $B_n < b^{\alpha}$; then
  $B_n = \min[B_w, b_{wn}]$ for all $n \notin M$
  If the new value of B_n is smaller than or equal to the previous value of B_n, restore the previous value of B_n.

- If $B_n \geq b^{\alpha}$
  $B_n = \min[B_n, \min[B_w, b_{wn}]]$ for all $n \notin M$
  if $B_n < b^{\alpha}$
  Restore the previous value of B_n.

If $\min [B_w, b_{wn}] < B_n$, and $\min [B_w, b_{wn}] \geq b^{\alpha}$ the path from s to n is now the path from s to w concatenated with the link from w to n.

One iteration of steps 2 and 3 adds one new node to M and defines the best-bandwidth path from s to that node. That path passes only through nodes that are in M. The algorithm terminates when all nodes are incorporated into M.

4.2 Example Network

The following is a network example to illustrate the operation of the narrowest-path algorithm. The result of the algorithm is shown in table 1.

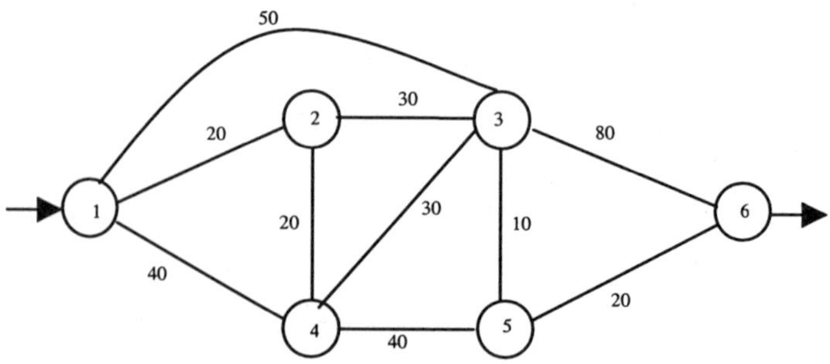

Assume $b^{\alpha} = 30$, source node = 1 and destination node = 6.

Figure 6. Network example.

Table 1: Narrowest-path with minimum hops calculation.

I	M	B2	PATH	B3	PATH	B4	PATH	B5	PATH	B6	PATH
1	{1}	20	1-2	50	1-3	40	1-4	0	-	0	-
2	{1,4}	20	1-2	30	1-4-3	40	1-4	40	1-4-5	0	-
3	{1,4,3}	30	1-4-3-2	30	1-4-3	40	1-4	40	1-4-5	30	1-4-3-6
4	{1,4,3,2}	30	1-4-3-2	30	1-4-3	40	1-4	40	1-4-5	30	1-4-3-6
5	{1,4,3,2,6}	30	1-4-3-2	30	1-4-3	40	1-4	40	1-4-5	30	1-4-3-6
6	{1,4,3,2,6,5}	30	1-4-3-2	30	1-4-3	40	1-4	40	1-4-5	30	1-4-3-6

5 Simulation

Our simulation aim to show that QoS routing is an effective way of achieving high acceptance rate of immediate and advance resource reservation requests. The simulated topology is a bottleneck link, where immediate and advance requests are directed to a QoS routing agent. The QoS routing agent applies admission control and selects the narrowest-path that satisfies the request. The network topology is pre-installed in the QoS routing agent, and is assumed constant during the simulation periods. In real implementation the QoS routing agent gets the network topology and network updates from the routing process. The network used in this paper is as follows:

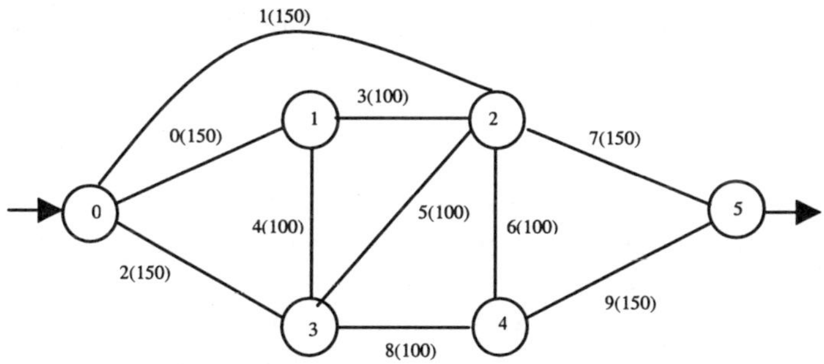

Where:
X(Y) are link Id and Link capacity, respectively.

Figure 7. Simulated network topology.

5.1 Simulation parameter choice

There are general parameters for the operation of the overall model, and there are specific parameters for each source.

- The duration of the requests is exponentially distributed with a mean of 500 simulation seconds;
- The resources requested are uniformly distributed with a mean of 3 resource units;
- The inter-arrival rate is exponentially distributed with a mean of 5.0;
- Book-ahead time is exponentially distributed with a mean of 20000;
- Minimum Booking time is equal to 1000;
- Maximum booking time is equal to 200000.

The maximum static link capacity that can be provided by the used network is 300 resource units. The simulation time is 3 x 10^5 simulation seconds. The last parameter is the Look-ahead time, which is varying during the simulation; the values used are 0, 250, 500 and 1000.

From the above parameters, we can calculate the average offered load produced by the immediate and advance sources. According to the Little's formula, which states that "for systems that reach steady state, the average number of customers in a system is equal to the product of the average arrival rate and the average time spent in the system".

$$\text{Average Offered load} = \frac{\text{Average arrival rate x Average duration x Average resources}}{\text{Total link capacity}}$$

Therefore, the total average offered load for immediate and advance sources is 200%.

5.2 *Simulation Results*

Several experiments are conducted to monitor the following performance measures:

- Rejection probability: To monitor the rejection probability of the immediate and the advance requests;
- Utilization: To check the overall utilization of each link capacity;
- Advance Duration: To check the duration of the admitted advance flows;
- Preemption probability: To monitor the preemption probability of the admitted immediate flows.

5.2.1 Rejection and Preemption Probabilities

Table 2, shows the rejection and preemption probabilities. The maximum link capacity is available to the advance requests. With 100% offered load, we get a rejection probability of zero. As time elapses, we get a steady value, which allow us to control the rejection probability by varying the offered load.

For immediate requests, the rejection probability increases as we increase the look-ahead time. At zero look-ahead time, the rejection probability is at its minimum value. The reason for this is that the admission control algorithm accounts only for currently active flows. By increasing the look-ahead time, more advance flows are included in the admission control algorithm.

The advance reservation requests have higher priority to acquire resources than immediate requests. So, at the start of every admitted advance flow, the total used resources is calculated, if it exceeds the total link capacity, one or more admitted immediate flows are preempted. The preemption probability can be changed by changing the look-ahead time. At zero look-ahead, more immediate flows are admitted, which results in high preemption probability. In fact, the look-ahead time is an essential factor for choosing the rejection and preemption probability for immediate requests. The value of look-ahead time should be chosen to get optimum values of preemption and rejection probability.

Table 2. Rejection and preemption probabilities.

	Look-ahead Time			
	0	250	500	1000
Advance Rej. Prob.	.0	.0	.0	.0
Immediate Rej. Prob.	.0	.07	.1	. 125
Preemption Prob.	.56	.08	.04	.02

5.2.2 Link Utilization

Table 3, shows the average utilization of each link in the network. All packets enter at node 0 and leave at node 5. Therefore, according to the network topology and the QoS routing algorithm, links 0,3,7 have higher utilization. When there is no enough resources in link 3, the algorithm will change the path to 0-4-5-7, which is the next best bath. After links 0 and 7 finishes their resources the algorithm will choose the path 1-5-8-9, this explains the high utilization of link 5. As we can see form the table and by following the network in figure 7, the links are utilized according to the operation of the QoS routing algorithm.

Meanwhile, the results show that as the look-ahead time increases the utilization of each link increases. At zero look-ahead time all immediate requests are admitted, but whenever a new advance flow starts using its reserved resources, one or more immediate flows are preempted. This results in a high preemption probability and low link utilization. As we increase the look-ahead time, admitted immediate flows guarantee their operation in the look-ahead period without any preemption. Using the QoSRA the rejection probability increases by small values as the look-ahead time increase, this results in a high utilization.

Table 3:.Average link utilization.

Link Id	Look-ahead Time			
	0	250	500	1000
Link 0 Ave. Util.	.959	.984	.988	.990
Link 1 Ave. Util.	.369	.767	.782	.787
Link 2 Ave. Util.	.0	.0098	.015	.0279
Link 3 Ave. Util.	.968	.993	.995	.996
Link 4 Ave. Util.	.495	.542	.543	.543
Link 5 Ave. Util.	.830	.934	.940	.947
Link 6 Ave. Util.	.129	.646	.683	.705
Link 7 Ave. Util.	.956	.982	.987	.989
Link 8 Ave. Util.	.424	.540	.538	.545
Link 9 Ave. Util.	.367	.778	.8	.817

5.2.3 Comparison with Single Path

For comparison purposes, we show in table 4 the results of earlier simulations we have done for single link admission control algorithm. The total offered load for this simulation is 170%. By comparing the results in table 2 and table 4, we can see the improvements in the immediate and advance rejection probability. The preemption probability is also slightly improved. The admitted advance duration is significantly improved, this is a very promising result where sessions with long time duration will have higher acceptance probability than sessions in single link admission control.

Table 4. Simulation results for single path.

	Look-ahead Time			
	0	250	500	1000
Advance Rej. Prob.	.07	.07	.07	.07
Immediate Rej. Prob.	.42	.75	.78	.83
Preemption Prob.	.54	.13	.06	.02

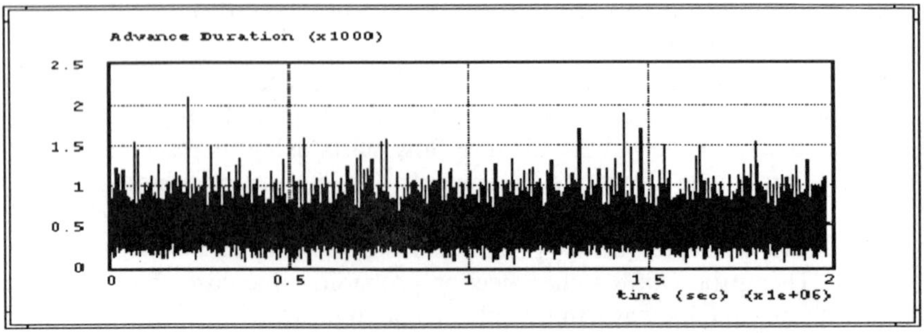

Figure 8: Admitted advance duration for single link

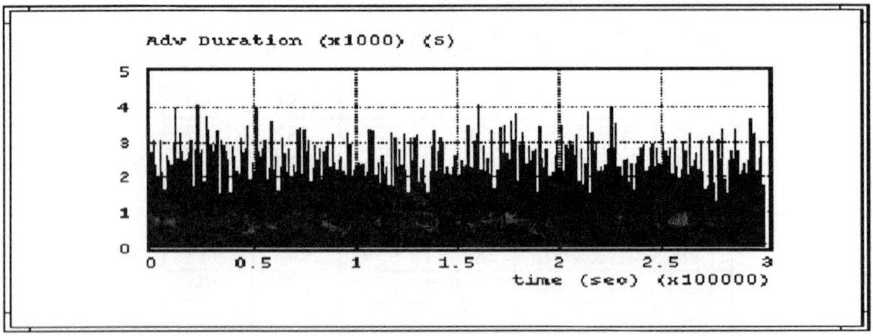

Figure 9: Admitted advance duration using QoS routing agent

6 Conclusion

Resource reservation is a very effective way of guaranteeing QoS. Multimedia applications can state their QoS demands and negotiate with the network to set aside some resources for handling their data flows. To facilitate the negotiation, we present an architecture, which make an end-to-end reservation. The architecture also handles user interactions, and update resources with any change. For scalability problem, and to isolate the receivers and senders form network problems, a domain agent is assigned to each network domain, and make it responsible for making resource reservations in its area, and establishing a route for transferring the data. The domain agent constructs a QoS intra-domain path that satisfies the reservation request.

In this paper we also presented a modification to Dijkstra's algorithm to calculate the narrowest-path with the minimum number of hops that satisfies the requested bandwidth.

References

1. A. Banerjea, D. Ferrari, B. A. Mah and M. Moran, "The Tenet Real-Time Protocol Suite: Design, Implementation, and Experiences," TR-94-059, International Computer Science Institute, Berkeley, CA, November 1994.
2. A. Campbell, G. Coulson and D. Hutchinson, "A Quality of Service Architecture," ACM Computer Communications Review, Vol.24, No.2, April 1994, pp.6-27.
3. A. Hafid, G. V. Bockmann and R. Dssouli, "A Quality of Service Negotiation Approach with Future Reservation (NAFUR): A Detailed Study," Technical Report.
4. A. Shaikh, J. Rexford, and K. Shin, "Efficient Precomputation of Quality-of-Service Routes," Proc. Workshop on Network and Operating Systems Support for Digital Audio and Video (NOSSDAV '98), July 1998, Cambridge, England, pp. 15-27.
5. D. D. Clark, S. J. Shenker, and L. Zhang, "Support Real-Time Applications in an Integrated Services Packet Network: Architecture and Mechanism," Proc. Of ACM SIGCOMM'92, Aug. 1992, pp. 14-26.
6. D. Ferrari, A. Gupta and G. Vertre, "Distributed Advance Reservation of Real-Time connections," Fifth International Workshop on Network and operating system Support for Digital Audio and Video, Durham, NH, USA, April 19-21,1995
7. E. Crawley, R. Nair, B. Rajagopolan, H. Sandick, "A Framework for QoS-Based Routing in the Internet" RFC 2386, August 1998.
8. G. Apostolopoulos, R. Guerin, S. Kamat, A. Orda, T. Przygienda, D. Williams, "QoS Routing Mechanisms and OSPF Extensions" Internet draft, December 1998.

9. J. Moy, "Multicast Extensions to OSFP " RFC 1584, March 1994
10. J. Moy, "OSFP Version 2" RFC 1583, March 1994
11. L. Wolf, L. Delgrossi, R. Steinmetz, S. Schaller, and H. Witting, “Issues of Reserving Resources in Advance,” In Proceedings of NOSSDAV, Lecture Notes in Computer Science, Pages 27-37, Durham, New Hampshire, April 1995, Springer.
12. O. Schelen and S. Pink, “Sharing Resources through Advance Reservation Agents. In Proceedings of IFIP Fifth International Workshop on Quality of Service (IWQoS’97), New York, May 1997, pp. 265-276.
13. R. Braden, L. Zhang, S. Berson, S. Herzog and S. Jamin, “Resource Reservation Protocol (RSVP)—Version1 Functional specification,” ftp://ftp.ietf.org/internet-drafts-ietf-rsvp-spec-16.ps.
14. S. Berson, R. Lindell, and R. Braden, “An Architecture for Advance Reservations in the Internet,” Technical Report, USC Information Sciences Institute, July 16, 1998.
15. W. Reinhardt, “Advance Reservation of Network Resources for Multimedia Applications,” Proceedings of the Second International Workshop on Advanced Teleservices and High Speed Communication Architectures, 26-28 September 1994, Heidelberg, Germany.
16. W3C Synchronized Multimedia Working Group. http://www.w3.org/AudioVideo/Group/.
17. Z. Whang and J. Crowcroft, "Quality of Service Routing for Supporting Multimedia Applications" IEEE Journal on Selected Areas in Communications, 14(7): 1228-1234, September 1996.
18. Z. Zhang, C. Sonchez, B. Salkewicz, and E. Crawley, "Quality of Service Extensions to OSPF or Quality of Service Path first Routing (QOSPF)" Internet draft (draft-zhang-qos-ospf-01.txt", work in progress, September 1997.
19. F. Sallabi and A. Karmouch, "New Resource Reservation Architecture with User Interactions", Accepted in IEEE PACRIM'99, August 23-25, 1999, Victoria, B.C. Canada.

DISTRIBUTED VIDEO PRODUCTION: TASKS, ARCHITECTURE AND QOS PROVISIONING[1]

NED NING REN*, RAOUF BOUTABA**, YASSER RASHEED* AND ALBERTO LEON-GARCIA*

**University of Toronto, ECE Dept., 10 King's College Rd, Toronto ONT Canada M5S 3G4*

***University of Waterloo, Computer Science Dept., Waterloo, ONT Canada N2L 3G1*

We apply a top-down approach to describe the architecture components of Distributed Video Production (DVP) systems. We first introduce the concept of a Distributed Video Production environment and describe typical DVP tasks involved. We then propose a generic layered functional model that captures the characteristics of the DVP architecture. Subsequently, we identify system and network performance parameters and discuss the network transport architecture. Finally, we propose a QoS-sensitive model for resource allocation and optimization.

1 Overview

Production equipment used in today's video production facilities is usually very expensive. Most equipment is specialized to a set of dedicated tasks and interconnected by cables, which results in expensive equipment centralized to a single physical location – the studio. However, the task of video production is distributed in nature. Production resources and live video contributions usually come from more than one physical location, e.g. daily news and weather forecasts. However editing and final touch-ups of the programs need to be done locally – where equipment belongs. Moreover, this production process requires cooperative working of personnel from each stage of the production, such as the communication between scriptwriters and the director, and between cameramen and editors, ... etc. Therefore, the operational nature of video production requires a distributed cooperative environment.

In this paper, we discuss a Distributed Video Production (DVP) approach, which replaces cable connections in traditional studios with high-speed network interconnecting equipment from remote studios, enabling users at different physical locations to work on a single task, jointly over the network. This creates a distributed working environment for the production process where production resources can be shared remotely among different users. The DVP environment therefore enables broadcasters to improve economic efficiency and time-to-market.

[1] This project is partially funded by the Canadian Institute for Telecommunication Research (CITR).

The objectives of this paper are to:

1. Identify video production tasks and their Quality of Service (QoS) requirements
2. Propose a layered architecture for Distributed Video Production systems and identify typical system and network requirements
3. Propose a QoS-sensitive model for resource allocation and optimization.

2 Distributed Video Production Tasks

In this Section, we describe typical tasks performed in a traditional production studio, then discuss how they may be carried out in a DVP environment.

2.1 Editing

The main purpose of editing is to arrange footages together and form the final presentation program. We discuss two possible situations for editing tasks in a DVP setting. In the first scenario, which we call *"local editing"*, the local studio possesses its own high quality editing system, and therefore performs editing locally. In the case the local studio does not have all the footages required, missing footages are then retrieved from a remote video server. The local studio issues commands to the DVP video server and controls the program stream that is sent back. The command signals include instructions such as play, pause and search. The program stream sent back to the local studio includes video, audio and data streams.

The second scenario is remote editing, in the case where a local studio does not possess high quality editing equipment. Therefore, the actual editing will have to be done remotely. Locally generated program streams are sent to a DVP production server, along with command signals to control the editing process. The editing process is then carried out on the production server under the control of the local studio, and the final edited program is sent back to the studio.

2.2 Keying

Keying is the process of displaying different sources of videos at various positions of the screen at the same time. An example of a key is the digital effect box over a newscaster's shoulder, where graphics or video footages related to the event can be displayed. In this case, the keying equipment cuts an "*electronic hole*" in the video signal and fills it with the graphics or video footages from another source. Studios that do not have high quality keying equipment locally may use remote keying in the DVP system. Video streams that have to be keyed together can be transported to the production server through the DVP network. The keying operation is carried out on the production server and the resultant video is delivered back to the studio.

2.3 Virtual Studio Production

Virtual studio production allows mixing of live video with synthetic or natural imagery. An example is a footage of live actors shot in the studio, mixed with computer generated graphics or outdoor scenarios that create the illusion that the performing is actually carried out on the artificially generated set. The combination of the live video and the artificial background is also called a *"virtual set."*

In the case where local studios do not have virtual studio production equipment, this task can be executed in a remote fashion within the DVP environment. A possible setup is one in which the local studio sends the foreground video stream to the DVP production server. The production server chooses a rendering server according to the type of background set that has to be rendered, and identifies the rendering server to the local studio. The local studio transmits tracking data and rendering parameters to the rendering server, which in turn processes the request and delivers rendered set to the production server where they are mixed with the live foreground video and transported back to the local studio.

2.4 Distributed Joint Production

Several geographically dispersed studios may jointly work on a program production. An example is a remote news interview program where people involved in the program are located in different studios. The DVP environment allows a distributed interview to be carried out among them.

3 Architecture of Distributed Video Production Systems

In this section, we discuss the architectural components of DVP systems and propose a preliminary functional model that can capture the system characteristics and requirements. In our model, we take into consideration the different DVP tasks, their system requirements, in addition to the computational, storage and network transport resources needed to support them. In our work, we adopt a layered model in order to highlight the separation of functions in each layer of the architecture.

Distributed Video Production (DVP) systems consist of local studios and a set of remote servers interconnected through a high-speed backbone network. Local studios connect to the backbone network through a DVP interface system. Different types of DVP servers exist, each with different functionality. Possible servers include media servers, rendering servers that provide graphics and animation, production servers that are responsible for production tasks and multi-point production servers for coordination of remote joint productions. This DVP architecture is potentially scalable by adding new servers to the network to satisfy increasing usage demand or the emergence of new task requirements.

3.1 *Local Studio and DVP Interfacing System*

In a digital environment, traditional analog routing and switching devices are replaced with a high speed Local Area Network (LAN) [1], thus enabling local studios to communicate locally and potentially utilize remote production resources.

A DVP interfacing system connects the local studio LAN to the backbone network, and provides local studios with the ability to query and request services from remote DVP servers. DVP hide the actual physical location of the remote server from control workstations on the local studio network. DVP interfaces hide the details of the DVP system from the local studio technology.

3.2 *DVP Servers*

In our architectural model, DVP servers share a common layered architecture from a functional point of view. We divide our layered functional model into three levels, namely, the application, system and transport levels. The application level consists of application software that provides clients with required services. The system level represents hardware components that support the application software. Finally, the transport level includes functions such as network and storage device interfaces. A management backplane performs system management functions, such as operation control and resource partitioning.

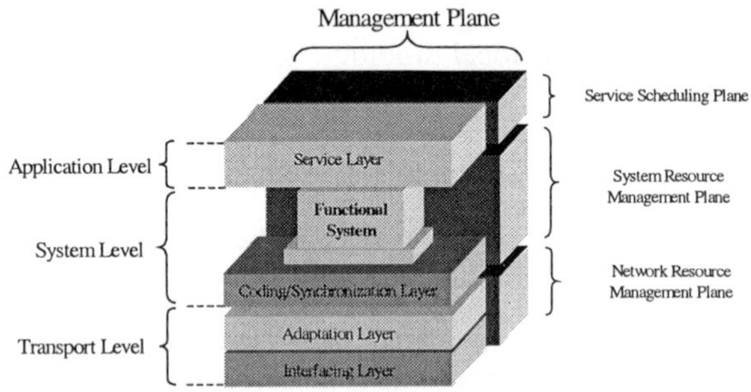

Figure 1 DVP Server Architecture

For every DVP server type, the relative levels may perform different functions. In the following sections, we first describe our layered functional for a generic DVP server, then explain the role of each type of servers in detail.

3.2.1 Generic Server Architecture

Our generic DVP server is shown in Figure 1. The application level represents the service layer, which contains software that provides each DVP server with various service capabilities, such as editing, rendering, keying, network access interfaces, ... etc. Some service layer functions supporting basic server functionality may be common to all DVP server types, such as network access and management interfaces. Meanwhile, other functions of the service layer may be unique to each individual server and specifically designed according to services the server has to provide. Examples are editing, rendering, keying and production software suites.

The system level consists of functional systems and coding/synchronization layer. The functional system is composed of the necessary hardware components that support software applications. Functional systems are in general distinct for each server, depending on the tasks the server has to perform. Examples are dedicated hardware equipment capable of providing storage, rendering and multi-point control capabilities. The coding/synchronization layer is responsible for proper coding and decoding of streams as they are passed between the system level and the transport level. This layer is also responsible for inter- and intra-media synchronization. Delay jitter introduced by the transport network, storage system and other server systems are compensated at this layer using appropriate buffering techniques. Examples of coding/synchronization layers include the MPEG coding/systems layer and Real-time Transport Protocol (RTP).

The transport level is divided into an adaptation layer and an interfacing layer. The adaptation layer performs the necessary mapping between the application and the network packet formats, in addition to adapting the QoS delivered by the network to the level of QoS requested by the application.

Management Back-Plane

The management system is divided into three planes according to the three system architecture levels we described above (application, system and transport levels). The three management planes are service-scheduling plane, system resource management plane and network resource management plane as shown in Figure 1.

The service-scheduling plane receives resource utilization information for system and network resources. Based on the resources available throughout the system and from the network, it provides a list of currently available services to local studios. This service list is communicated to the local DVP interface. Service requests originating from local studio sites are granted, modified or denied based on availability of resources. We describe the service scheduling in Section 5.

The system resource management plane manages DVP resources on a system-wide basis. It is different from conventional system management modules due to the fact that DVP deals mainly with multimedia data. The plane takes the unique high capacity, real-time and continuous characteristic of multimedia data into account while managing the system. The system management plane contains a multimedia operating system which deals with issues such as real-time CPU scheduling, memory management, I/O scheduling and multimedia file system management. The system resource information is passed to the service-scheduling plane, and is used to make admission decisions for service requests.

3.2.2 Server Functionality

We have defined four types of servers in the last section, which share similar system components with distinct functional systems as shown in Figure 2. Following is a discussion of the role of each of these servers.

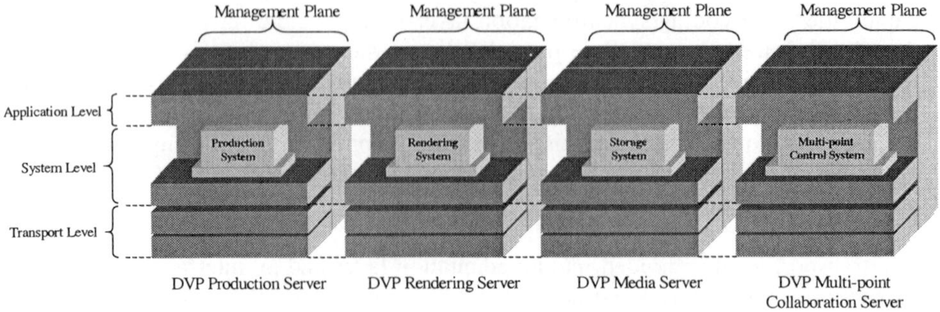

Figure 2 DVP servers layered functional model

The production server supports day-to-day production tasks required in a typical studio, such as wiping, dissolving, keying and non-linear editing. Depending on the capacity of the server, the production server may have hundreds of input and output ports in order to accommodate the needs of connected users. Each user issues production commands to the system as if it was local to them. These commands are then transmitted by the local DVP interface to the production server, along with video footages originated from the user site. Video streams and command streams enter the production system through a reserved input port for the user and are processed or mixed with video footages from other sources, such as a video server. The processed streams are finally sent back to the user through an output port.

The input and output ports, server and network resources must all be reserved prior to the beginning of a production operation. User specified QoS requirements are translated by the DVP interface at the local studio and communicated to the server. Management mechanisms in the server keep track of available server resources and decide whether user requested QoS could be accommodated.

The rendering server is responsible for providing computer-generated graphics, as requested by users. Powerful processors usually satisfy rendering needs of DVP. The rendering tasks include generating text characters, studio logos, digital effects, real-time animations and virtual sets. Some of these tasks are very complex in nature and especially if performed in production quality, they would require enormous amounts of computational power, let aside the multi-user and multitasking environment the rendering server has to support. Graphics-specialized processors are likely to be customized to support the heavy processing needs.

Media servers store large collections of footages, serving as a media database for daily production needs. Storage systems usually have large capacities in order to support high quality media. In addition, in order to satisfy the real-time characteristics of production tasks, the storage system must be able to access and serve data in real-time.

The Multi-point Collaboration Server (MCS) enables multi-site joint productions. In order to support interconnections among multiple sites, each geographical region has a MCS assigned, to which local studios in the region initiate multi-site production requests. The MCS contacts the rest of the participants to set up the session. Participants include other MCSs and servers. The MCSs decide how the multi-point connections are established and how media streams are interchanged between sites. MCSs are also responsible for managing distributed sessions by monitoring on-going sessions, performing multi-point information distribution and group cooperation control.

4 Transport Network and System Requirements for DVP applications

The DVP system can be divided into three components: system hardware, system software and network transport. In the following, we discuss the hardware and software requirements, and the communication support issues, as a baseline for DVP system implementation requirements. Other requirements may be needed in the future in order to obtain a complete set of network and system requirements.

4.1 DVP System Requirements

4.1.1 Processing Unit

Two types of processors can be found in a multimedia system [2]: dedicated multimedia processors and general-purpose processors with multimedia support. Dedicated multimedia processors are typically customized to perform specific multimedia operations, and are designed to provide large capacity and high efficiency. Complex and computationally intensive multimedia functions such as video/audio compression, 3D processing and virtual reality requires support from these dedicated processors. Advanced general-purpose processors provide support for multimedia by extending their instruction set to include multimedia instructions. These extended instructions can be executed in parallel, and provide support for generic operations in multimedia processing. An example is Intel's MMX Pentium processor, which achieves 65% to 370% performance improvements with extended multimedia support [3]. The emergence of these multimedia-extended processors allows many multimedia functions to be implemented in software, and significantly reduces cost and increases flexibility.

In order to support the high capacity demand of DVP applications, customized dedicated processors may have to be implemented in DVP servers. This will enable servers to sustain large aggregated processing loads. Furthermore, these processors can be customized to have a programmable architecture, which will enable DVP servers to be more flexible in order to accommodate future application requirements. For end-systems inside local studios, a mixture of general-purpose processors and dedicated processors can be used. The general-purpose processors will be handling less demanding tasks, with dedicated processors to back them up and support a few computationally intensive tasks. In order to lower costs and achieve higher efficiencies, dedicated processors used in local studios may not have to be programmable; flexibility can be achieved with software supported by general-purpose processors. Since computational requirements for local studios may be relatively lower, the software and general-purpose processor combination should be adequate for most tasks with supplement of a few dedicated processors.

4.1.2 System BUS

The bus is one of the traffic concentration points in a system. Bus speed is usually lower compared to processor speed, since it is limited by the maximum signal propagation delay on the wires. As more devices are attached to the bus, the total capacitance of the bus increases and further slows down signal propagation.

For DVP applications that deal with continuous streams, large amounts of data have to be exchanged between processor, memory and I/O devices. The amount of traffic involved is likely to overwhelm the system bus. A possible solution to avoid congestion on the system bus is to introduce local buses between high traffic devices, to serve as "expressways" between high traffic devices and take a portion of the traffic off the main bus. However, a local bus can only transfer data between devices attached to it. In case additional data processing has to be performed by devices that are not on local buses, media data will still have to go thorough the main bus, thus reducing flexibility in the application design.

Another possible solution is to replace the system bus with a switch architecture. Unlike in the conventional bus approach, the switch approach allows data transfers to occur between multiple pairs of devices at the same time, improving the overall system throughput. Furthermore, since a device will be connected to only one other device (a switch port), the length of the wire needed is shorter, and the total capacitive load on the wires is much smaller than a typical bus with dozen of devices attached. These factors result in faster signal propagation and further increases the communication speed of attached devices. However, the switch architecture has its disadvantages in terms of complexity, scalability and consequently cost. More details about the switch architecture mechanisms can be found in [4] and [5]. It is also possible that the switch architecture would be used to support high-speed devices in DVP servers, while slower devices may be connected by conventional bus architecture to reduce system cost.

4.1.3 Storage System

Storage devices in the DVP system must have large capacity and high throughput in order to provide access to a large amount of media data in a short time. Moreover, data blocks must be read or written in an uninterrupted fashion in order to support the continuous nature of DVP media. Special data placement, disk scheduling and admission control techniques allow continuous data access, while disk arraying techniques enable support for high capacity and throughput.

Magnetic disks are most suitable for storing media data due to their short access time, high transfer rate and random access capability. However, a single disk is not sufficient to store large multimedia files, especially in a server environment, where many files have to be stored and many users have to be served simultaneously. The solution is to group a number of disk drives together and share the load. These drives operate in parallel and thus the aggregated capacity and throughput of the disk group is proportional to the number of disks in the group. This technique is used in the Redundant Array of Inexpensive Disks (RAID) technology, where inexpensive drives are combined to increase both storage throughput and capacity. The RAID technology also uses extra disks to store redundant data information; this overcomes the unreliability associated with inexpensive drives.

Data placement techniques are used in multimedia storage management in order to support continuous data accesses. The real-time nature of media files requires data to be accessed in an uninterrupted fashion. One possible approach is contiguous placement, which places successive segments of a media stream consecutively on the disk. To retrieve a particular stream, only one seek is required to locate the beginning of the file. However, contiguous placement is likely to cause fragmentation. Constrained placement [6] [7] is a variation of this method, which avoids fragmentation by leaving constrained gaps between consecutive data blocks in a media stream, which are then used to store other media streams.

Since data transfer rate of a disk is usually higher than the playback rate of a single stream, a number of streams can be served simultaneously in a multiplexed fashion. In order to ensure efficient resource utilization, as many streams as possible should be served concurrently. However, admission control of services must be in place to prevent overload, this is especially true for DVP servers where available resources are consumed rapidly with increasing user requests. Multiplexed access and admission control alone may not be sufficient to guarantee optimal resource utilization, therefore parallel file access must also be scheduled in an orderly fashion in order to maximize the overall throughput while minimizing low seek time and latency. A number of disk scheduling algorithms exist, however traditional algorithms may not be suitable for managing storage access in DVP systems. A multimedia disk scheduling algorithm not only has to optimize disk throughput, minimize seek latency, maintaining fairness among tasks and avoiding starvation, but also has to consider the start time and deadline of real-time tasks. Details of real-time disk scheduling algorithms such can be found in [8] and [9].

4.1.4 System Software

System resources to be managed include processing power, memory space, I/O bandwidth and storage space. An OS hides the physical characteristics of these devices and provides simpler interfaces to user applications.

Traditional operating systems such as Unix, largely concerned with throughput, utilization and fairness, may be inappropriate for managing real-time multimedia tasks, which have distinct priorities, based on each task's urgency. A multimedia OS [8] [10] should be able to manage a mixture of real-time and non-real-time tasks. For real-time tasks, QoS guarantees are provided and are supported by mechanisms that perform QoS specification, admission control, resource management, scheduling and policing. QoS specifications are needed in order to indicate to the OS how many resources a new task requires. Based on QoS parameters, schedulability tests can check whether there are enough resources to accommodate the new task. If the request is accepted, the resource manager allocates the required capacity for the task and the scheduling mechanism arranges for its execution. A policing mechanism is required to prevent tasks from over-using system resources. A multimedia OS should be able to deal with both real-time and non-real-time tasks since they are both important to DVP applications. While priorities are given to real-time tasks and their QoS requirements are being satisfied, non-real-time tasks would have lower priority but they can not be neglected. Tasks should be scheduled in a proper way such that it prevents starvation of non-critical tasks while avoiding priority inversion of real-time tasks.

System resources managed by a multimedia OS can be partitioned into four categories: process, memory, I/O and file management.

Process management is responsible for scheduling the execution of each task. Continuous-media processing has a periodic nature, making the specification and scheduling of processing requirements easier. These periodic tasks perform repeated and similar operations each with their own deadlines. The goal of the process manager is to schedule as many tasks as possible, while their deadlines are all met. The problem is how to schedule the tasks effectively while maintaining a low scheduling overhead caused by operations such as schedulability test. The two most important scheduling algorithms are Earliest-Deadline-First (EDF) and rate-monotonic. Both algorithms are preemptive and assign priority to processes according to their deadline and request rate respectively. EDF is a dynamic algorithm that frequently recalculates process priorities; thus its scheduling overhead is higher. The advantage of EDF is that its processor utilization can reach 100% without failing task deadlines. The rate-monotonic algorithm is static since it fixes priority of a task at the beginning, and this causes more context switching. However since rate-monotonic algorithms have less scheduling overhead, they are more suitable for a purely periodic task environment. More details on process scheduling can be found in [8] and [11].

Memory management is responsible for assigning (and releasing) memory to processes. Virtual memory is also used to store less frequently used data, which may be swapped between physical memory and storage by paging. However, media data in multimedia systems are usually very large, a page fault would incur long swapping delay and possibly lead to missing task deadlines. Therefore, memory swapping for real-time tasks should be avoided. One possible approach is to lock the data in the memory and prevent it from being swapped to the disk, however this technique should be used with care since media data are large in size and memory space may be limited. Other approaches take advantage of the periodic nature of media tasks and pre-fetches data into the memory.

I/O management is responsible for ensuring efficient data transfers between I/O subsystems and main memory. I/O Performance is limited by many factors such as bus bandwidth and OS overhead. Traditionally, I/O devices are controlled by device drivers that exist in the kernel space of the memory. When user applications place high-level requests to an I/O device, the request is translated into a system call into the OS. The OS kernel breaks up the system call and places several low-level requests to the device driver, and the I/O device is then reached through the device driver. This hierarchy of operation requests result in overhead. Furthermore, when requested data are delivered back from the I/O device, several copying operations have to be performed in order to transfer the data thorough every level of the hierarchy. This results in inefficient operation and degrades real-time performance of the system. Each data copying between kernel space and user space would require a context switch between user and kernel processes, and these in turn incur even more operations to swap processor register to memory and vice versa.

It is clear that direct data transfers between I/O devices must be supported in a multimedia system. Data exchange could occur at the device driver level in the kernel space without going through the application space [12]. Of course, this is assuming that no application level modification has to be performed on acquired data. It is also possible to make devices "autonomous" [6], these devices would be smart enough to manage flow control and also simple operations such as checksum, then data can be exchanged between devices without going through the main memory at all. Moreover, Raghavan and Tripathi suggested granting applications direct access to I/O devices without going thorough the kernel. This would save overheads associated with system calls and context/domain switches. However, issues related to access control and run-time management must be carefully considered in such an implementation.

File management is responsible for providing users with file access and making efficient use of storage resources. The main difference of a multimedia OS file manager from a conventional one is related to the continuous, real-time nature of media data. These issues have been discussed in the storage management section.

4.2 Network Transport Requirements

This sub-section presents a preliminary quantification of network performance requirements for typical multimedia applications. Transport network performance is usually measured by three sets of parameters, namely bandwidth, delay and error/loss requirements. DVP tasks place stringent demands on the underlying transport networks due to their high quality requirements and interactive nature. It is noteworthy that, similar to multimedia applications, the actual QoS parameters depend largely on specific implementations and media contents. After consulting a number of references, we have collected a set of representative QoS parameters for typical multimedia and video distribution services. These values reflect general requirements likely to be encountered in DVP environments.

4.2.1 Bandwidth Requirements

Multimedia, and in particular video information, requires relatively large amounts of bandwidth. The requirements are even more exigent in a video production environment, where uncompressed production quality video requires transport bandwidth of 166–270 Mbps. The upcoming High definition Television (HDTV) standard further pushes these values up to 1.5 Gbps. However, with the advancements in compression algorithms such as MPEG2, standard definition TV production may be accommodated with lower bandwidth requirements.

4.2.2 Delay, Delay Variation and Inter-media Skew Requirements

Delay performance measures include constant delay, variable delay and inter-stream (skew) performance parameters. Real-time applications impose relatively more stringent requirements on network delay performance, when compared with data applications, particularly for interactive multimedia applications.

DVP applications scan a large spectrum of delay requirements. As an example, typical videoconferencing applications may withstand 200-500 ms end-to-end, while an interactive distributed joint production application may not tolerate more than 20-100 ms end-to-end [13][14]. This may in turn impose a bound on the maximum physical distance between servers involved in such an application.

Delay variation or *"jitter"* is a measure of the difference in delay experienced by different packets in the network due to variation in buffer occupancy in intermediate switching nodes. Another form of jitter is inter-stream jitter or "skew", which measures the difference in delay as seen by separate streams pertaining to the same application (such as audio and video). In order to ensure proper intra-stream synchronization, low delay variation is often required. Jitter may be compensated using buffering techniques at the receiving end. However larger the jitter, longer the buffering delay experienced, which in turn increases the overall end-to-end delay.

Accurate delay variation requirements depend on specific media types and system implementations. A general guideline is that for television quality video, jitter should be kept below 10ms [15]. Comprehensive experiments have been carried out in [16] to measure the human perception of inter-media skew, and provide a general guideline of ±80ms for inter-stream synchronization for playback application.

4.2.3 Transport Error Requirements

Error requirements for multimedia applications vary according to the application. Occasional transport errors may be more tolerable, compared with data applications. Since, multimedia information is presented to the user at a relatively rapid rate, single errors may not be perceivable by the human eye. This mostly applies to playback type of applications. DVP tasks such as remote keying may require tight error bounds for the camera tracking signals. Finally, compression algorithms add a multiplication factor to single bit errors, depending on the location of the error. This translates into a trade-off between bandwidth and error requirements.

4.3 The need for Network Adaptation Techniques

There exists a variety of DVP applications, each with different bandwidth and QoS requirements, depending on the tasks involved. In order to accommodate such a heterogeneous traffic mix with a common network transport framework, real-time adaptation functions need to be implemented, in order to perform necessary mapping between the application QoS and network performance parameters.

4.3.1 Possible Protocol Stack Realizations for DVP

In order to understand the different alternatives for a transport network to support DVP applications, we start by classifying the different types of video information sources, then work our way down in the protocol stack, identifying at each level the different protocol combinations and functionality.

At the media encoder level, the encoder type may range from a Constant Bit Rate (CBR) encoder to a Variable Bit Rate (VBR) encoder. The encoder may also be of a layered-type, generating several media layers, each of which falling into one of the previous categories. Note that for a layered-type encoder, different layers may be passed to the level below as individual streams, or alternatively, layers may be multiplexed to form a combined stream.

The next protocol level in the stack is the application-level framing layer. This is the first layer to prepare the video information for transmission over the network. Typical functions at this level include adding time stamps, sequence numbers, multiplexing identifiers and any other information needed for proper recovery at the receiver. Examples of application-level framing layers are the MPEG Systems layer and the Real-time Transport Protocol (RTP). While essentially RTP and the MPEG Systems have many features in common, there is still a possibility to use RTP to transport MPEG systems packets in order to provide full-compatibility with systems using RTP as their default application level-framing protocol. It should be noted that the encoder level and the application-level framing layer correspond to the coding/synchronization layer in the DVP system architecture.

Application packets are then passed to the network adaptation layer. We use the term *"network adaptation layer"* to include ATM Adaptation Layers (AAL) and IP transport protocols. Network adaptation protocols are intended to provide a level of adaptation of the QoS delivered by the underlying network to the QoS requested by the application. In the case where RTP is used for application framing, a network adaptation protocol is needed for encapsulation of RTP packets. This would typically be either User Datagram Protocol (UDP) for IP or AAL type 5 for ATM networks. For the MPEG Systems layer case without RTP, any underlying network adaptation protocol may be used, although it would typically be an ATM network in the transport, hence an ATM adaptation layer.

There are several alternatives for the transport network service class. For IP networks, Integrated Services IP models classes may be used to provide the necessary QoS requirements, in which case the ReSerVation Protocol (RSVP) would serve as a signaling protocol. Alternatively, Differential-Services IP classes may be used to provide higher priority for the video traffic over other less-demanding traffic types. For ISIP and Differential-services IP models, the combination of RTP/RTCP over UDP is expected to form the basis for real-time network adaptation. On the other hand, for ATM networks, it is more likely that either a Constant Bit Rate or a real-time Variable Bit Rate connection would be appropriate as defined in the User-Network Interface Version 4.0.

4.3.2 Network Adaptation Functions

We use the term *"network adaptation"* to include application-level framing protocols such as RTP/RTCP and MPEG Systems, in addition to IP transport and ATM adaptation layer protocols. Network adaptation functions (at both application and network levels) are needed for two complementary purposes: 1) mapping application traffic and QoS parameters to network-level performance parameters, and 2) adapting the QoS delivered by the network to the QoS level requested by the application. The adaptation functions are classified under the following categories:

Timing recovery and synchronization functions attempt to restore the temporal relationship between the packets constituting a real-time information stream. This is achieved by means of time stamps or adaptive clock recovery techniques at the receiver. Additionally, a playout buffer is used in order to absorb the jitter introduced in the network. Another level of synchronization is inter-stream synchronization, which deals with synchronization between several streams pertaining to a single application, such as audio and video or multi-layered video.

Error control techniques are usually based on Automatic Repeat reQuest (ARQ), Forward Error Correction (FEC) techniques, or a combination of both. For real-time applications with tight delay constraints, FEC techniques are usually favored over their ARQ counterparts. Moreover, FEC schemes are usually coupled with byte or packet interleaving in order to add robustness to the scheme, provided that the interleaving/de-interleaving delay is kept within the tolerable amounts.

Stream Multiplexing is usually used in order to avoid inter-stream synchronization problems by aggregating the different streams belonging to one or more application and transmitting them over the network as one unit. This results in a reduction in the inter-stream jitter to a relatively small and controllable amount. Multiplexing is also used to achieve better network utilization by means of statistical multiplexing.

Shaping is used to reduce the burstiness of the traffic, and hence decrease the probability of packet loss due to buffer overflows inside the network. However, shaping usually incurs delays, depending on the shaping parameters, which in return impose constraints on the amount of shaping that can be applied.

Flow control provides means to adapt the application's rate to the network congestion level as it occurs. This feature relies on the applications being adaptive in order to function properly. Shaping and flow control functions are not widely implemented in practical real-time adaptation protocols.

5 DVP Service Provision: Service Scheduling with QoS

5.1 Service Access Model

Access to DVP servers is based on a client/server model where the end user at the local studio executes DVP tasks such as retrieving multimedia objects from a multimedia server. In such a distributed environment, a number of end users from several local studios may need to access a number of DVP servers through communication networks. This scenario reveals the requirement for an access model, servicing users according to their QoS requirements, while optimizing DVP server resource utilization. For that purpose, we define a DVP service access platform that involves two basic components. The first one, at the user host, acts as the user access interface. It controls user access to the requested DVP server, and checks if the required QoS parameters are satisfied. The second component, at the server end, interfaces with the DVP server. It manages access requests to the server functionality and keeps track of the server load information. Hereafter the first component will be referred to as the "*user agent*" and the second as the "*DVP server agent.*" Depending on the system topology, the access model can involve a number of additional management components acting as traders between user agents and DVP server agents. Traders, referred to as "*managers*" in the following, direct user requests to the most appropriate servers in a transparent and dynamic manner, taking into account the QoS requirements and DVP servers' availability.

Two types of managers are defined, the *Virtual Studio Access Manager* (VSAM), and the *Domain Manager* (DM). The latter is responsible for a domain, grouping a set of DVP servers according to different criteria such as geographical constraints, DVP server functionality, or others. VSAM is responsible for a set of domains grouped according to organizational policies. It acts as a smart directory service gathering both functional and management information on the DVP domains and makes this information available to domain managers and local studios. Functional information concerns mainly the DVP tasks and multimedia content supported within the DVP domains. Management information is primarily used for managing user access to DVP servers by directing user requests to the appropriate domains based on: load information, QoS requirements and cost constraints. The Domain Manager monitors the DVP servers within its domain through the server agents associated with these DVP servers. It collects state as well as load information, and performs the appropriate allocation of user requests. It also detects multimedia server failures whenever they occur. As a result, VSAM, and Domain Managers support the appropriate exchange of messages between user agents and server agents. In addition, they maintain state information that allows the determination of the most suitable DVP server in response to a specific end user request.

The introduced agents and managers can be configured (their number, location, dependencies) to suit a given physical topology or a given DVP service provision policy. They intervene between local studios (user hosts) and DVP servers (server machines), to increase service availability and optimize resource utilization.

Figure 3, shows an example configuration of Virtual Studio Access architecture, illustrating the distributed feature of the access model. The example configuration consists of a two-level hierarchy where the Virtual Studio Access Manager is the root, Domain Managers constitute the first level, and DVP Server Agents the leaves. The Virtual Studio architecture may contain as many domain levels as necessary according to the size and feature of the overall system, e.g., the number of DVP servers, their distribution, the network topology, etc. The performance of the overall system is an important design choice to determine the number of domain levels in the access platform. The following subsections present in detail, the functions provided by the virtual studio architectural components.

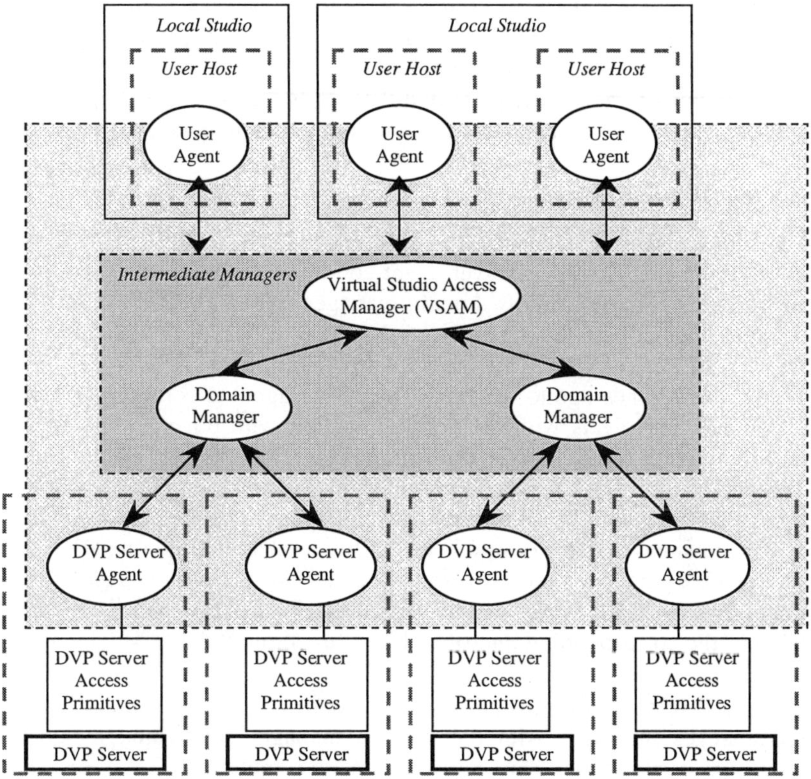

Figure 3 Virtual Studio Access Architecture

5.1.1 The User Agent

The user agent consists of three components: *user interface*, *QoS manager*, and a *client controller*. The user interface consists of two main parts. The first one provides the various DVP tasks such as a way to search and select a video object from a video server. The second one allows the specification of the desired QoS such as the quality for the presentation. It also allows to set the access cost constraints and to renegotiate the QoS parameters during the DVP service provision, e.g., during a video object display. If the specified QoS parameters conform to the capabilities of the user's host, the QoS manager invokes the client controller together with its user requirements, i.e., QoS, and user workstation capabilities like the available decoder or operating system. The client controller builds a request message before sending it to the domain manager. When the request is processed, the client controller invokes the appropriate DVP client to display the result. This is done via a message interpreter responsible for mapping Virtual Studio Access protocol data units to a specific primitive that starts the corresponding DVP client. The latter can be any of the available DVP tools such as audio/video players.

5.1.2 The DVP Server Agent

A DVP server agent is delegated to represent a DVP server within the Virtual Studio environment. The DVP server agent continuously waits at a specific service port for requests coming from its domain manager. When a request is received, the server agent checks first the capacity of the DVP server to deliver the requested service with the desired QoS. This leads to either starting the delivery by the server, or sending a reject message to the user. The server agent is composed of two main parts. The first part deals with the communication with other components of the Virtual Studio architecture like the domain manager, and the user agent. The second part is related to the DVP server represented by the corresponding server agent in our access architecture. Its implementation is specific to the encapsulated DVP server. The advantage of this design is the ability to change from one DVP server to another by changing only the corresponding part in the server agent. Similarly, introducing a new DVP server in the Virtual Studio Environment necessitates the provision of the corresponding interoperability functions at the server agent.

In the context of the Virtual Studio service requests management, a DVP server agent exchanges messages with the domain manager concerning its operational state, and its availability. This allows detecting faulty DVP servers. For this purpose, the DVP server agent periodically notifies the domain manager of its availability to handle service requests. Notification frequencies need not to be equal for all DVP server agents in the system. The notification frequency depends on a number of factors, such as the reliability of the server, and how much importance we place on these factors. Such factors can be computed according to collected statistics on the past behavior of the server. The load information of a DVP server referred to as the DVP server availability is computed as the number of service requests the server can handle with a given QoS at a given time. This highly depends on the internal implementation of the DVP server such as the processing architecture, storage capacity, access performance, etc. The DVP server agent computes the load of the DVP server it encapsulates based on the load model.

5.1.3 The Virtual Studio Access Manager

The role of the Virtual Studio Access Manager (VSAM) is to redirect user requests to the appropriate DVP domain, i.e. the domain containing the most appropriate DVP server to handle the request. For this purpose, VSAM maintains two state information tables, namely `VSAM_DVPtask_Table` and `VSAM_Load_Table`.

The first table contains two attributes: DVPtask_Id and List_of_Domains. It gives, for each DVP task identified by DVPtask_Id, the list of domains containing at least one DVP server that supports this task. Each domain in the List_of_Domains is identified by its Domain_Id. VSAM_Load_Table gives for each domain, identified by a Domain_Id, the load of this domain. The load information for each domain maintained by VSAM is received from the corresponding Domain Manager. The latter computes the domain load as the weighted average sum of the load levels of DVP servers within the domain.

5.1.4 The Domain Manager

Domains are logical structures used as flexible means for clustering DVP servers in order to control resources utilization. Each domain contains a Domain Manager, which maintains the global view of the encapsulated DVP servers. Based on global and timely knowledge of servers state, a Domain Manager can offer end users better quality and fault tolerant access to the DVP services supported by these servers. The state information on a DVP server concerns mainly its operational state, e.g., out of service, and its availability, e.g., load, response-time, etc. As described previously, domains can be defined according to geographical, organizational, service type, service performance, and other criteria. The various domains are organized into a hierarchy of domains to provide a system-wide access to DVP services. The domain structuring allows reducing the management complexity of the overall Virtual Studio environment and allows for a higher scalability. A Domain Manager performs its management task autonomously, but may cooperate with other Domain Managers in the context of global access management and service scheduling. The number and size of the domains is determined based on several factors such as investment versus revenue for the DVP service provider, and/or quality versus price of the offered services to local studios.

Similar to VSAM, but within a single domain, the Domain Manager redirects user requests to the appropriate DVP server. It maintains two state information tables, namely D_DVPtask_Table and D_Load_Table. Emphasis is given on the load distribution capability. Therefore the state information is limited to DVP servers' load information. D_DVPtask_Table contains two attribute types: DVPtask_Id and List_of_DVPserver_ DVPtask. It gives, for each DVP task identified by DVPtask_Id, the list of servers supporting the requested DVP task together with the QoS characteristics. Each item in the List_of_DVPserver_DVPtask is composed of the DVPserver_Id supporting DVPtask_Id and a list of QoS charachteristics. D_Load_Table gives for each DVP server, identified by a SVPserver_Id, the load of this server. The load information for each DVP server that is maintained by the Domain Manager is received from the corresponding DVP Server Agent. The latter computes the load of the DVP server, based on the multidimensional load model.

5.2 *Multidimensional Load Model*

5.2.1 QoS-sensitive Load Model of DVP Servers

One of the main criteria used to find the most appropriate DVP server to which to redirect users service requests, is the load of DVP servers. Load is computed as the number of processes currently executed divided by the server's speed, or equivalently the number of service requests currently handled divided by the server's speed (a function of the CPU and disk access speeds). In a multi-service environment supporting different QoS, the load information, as defined above, does not reflect the real load, and may lead to wrong placement decisions. Indeed, the "least loaded server", handling the smallest number of service requests, may not correspond to the server which has the smallest load volume. For example, a server performing a task that requires a large amount of resources, e.g., decoding and displaying a high resolution video, is effectively more loaded than a server performing tens of light tasks, e.g., text processing. To alleviate these limitations we propose a scheme, which provides an accurate information about the capacity of a server to support a given request by performing extensive measurements prior to service operation. This scheme allows determining the server, which is lightly loaded; and is able to support the user request with the desired QoS.

In the proposed scheme, QoS requirements are grouped into QoS classes. Each class represents a range of QoS parameters' values. A service request is associated with a QoS class and thus requires a certain amount of network and system resources from the DVP server. At a given time, the state of a given DVP server can be defined as the set of service instances currently supported by the server. Based on this classification, we can determine, through experiments, the set of *non-blocking*, *semi-blocking* and *blocking* states for a given DVP server. A DVP server is in a non-blocking (respectively blocking) state if it can(not) support new service request(s) without affecting the service instances currently supported. When the DVP server is in a semi-blocking state, certain new service requests can be supported while others cannot. To illustrate this QoS classification and server states determination, let us consider a simple example of a DVP server supporting only two classes of QoS $\mathtt{cl}^1$ and $\mathtt{cl}^2$. The DVP server is said to be in state (n, m) when it is currently providing n service instances of class $\mathtt{cl}^1$ and m service instances of class $\mathtt{cl}^2$. In this example, assuming that the DVP server become loaded when servicing 5 requests, states (3,2), (4,1), (2,3) and (1,4) are blocking states, which means that all new requests received by the DVP server, while in one of these states, are simply rejected. State (4,0) is a semi-blocking state, that means that the DVP server will reject all new requests belonging to QoS class $\mathtt{cl}^1$, but can provide only one new service instance of QoS class $\mathtt{cl}^2$. Similarly, states (3,1), (1,3) and (2,2) are semi-blocking states. The remaining DVP server's states are non-blocking, which means the DVP server can handle new service requests from both QoS classes. For instance, if the DVP server is in state (1,2) and receives a service request of class cl^1, it accepts it and transits to a new state, (2,2).

5.2.2 Domain Load

The Virtual Studio Access architecture introduces the domain concept as a means for grouping multimedia servers to obtain aggregated views of the DVP network and system resources, and hence a more easily manageable distribution of the overall load in the Virtual Studio as well as a higher scalability. Typically, domains are used to redirect users' requests to the appropriate DVP servers based on the global state information maintained therein. In addition to the load of each DVP server in the domain, we compute the load of the domain as a whole, which is then used for directing service requests to the most appropriate domain.

The load information of a domain is a function of the load of the DVP servers contained in it. In the next subsection, a simple approach is used to compute a domain load as the weighted average sum of the load levels of the DVP servers in this domain. The selection of the weights associated to the various DVP servers depends on several factors, such as the reliability and availability of the DVP servers. These factors can be statistically determined based on the past behavior of the DVP servers. In practice, the designer of the Virtual Studio assigns weights to the DVP servers involved in the Virtual Studio. Weights are first statically assigned based on either the designer servers' exploitation policy or the characteristics of the servers or both. The characteristics of the DVP servers are obtained from the server's vendor specifications such as the performance of the server in terms of processing power, storage capacity, access speed and so on. The weights are then dynamically adjusted according to statistics on servers operation and behavior, for example, on a day of the week or on a time of the day basis. The weights can also be adjusted to reflect a new policy of the Virtual Studio service provider.

5.2.3 Information Exchange Policy

There are a number of approaches to exchange state information between the DVP servers involved in the load distribution process. These mainly implement a polling procedure, which may be initiated by the client host or by the server. In the context of our domain-based structuring of the Virtual Studio environment, load information exchange is based on a server-initiated polling mechanism implemented for each individual domain. In order to minimize the number of messages exchanged in the system DVP server sends notifications only when significant load levels are reached. According to the defined load model, a DVP server doesn't need to send a load update notification each time it transits to a new state except if this one is a blocking or a semi-blocking state. Therefore, only the DVP servers capable of supporting user requests with the desired QoS will be considered during task placement decisions. The exchanged load information, referred to hereafter as Load_Level (LL), is expressed as:

$$LL = \Sigma w_i * b_i, \text{ where}$$

b_i is a boolean that represents the server state with respect to service requests belonging to cl^i. b_i=0 if the DVP server cannot support any new service request of class cl^i; otherwise b_i=1; initially t_i=1 for $i=\{1,..,n\}$.
w_i indicates the weight associated with cl^i ($w_i < w_j$ means that $cl^i < cl^j$ which in turn means that service requests from cl^j require more server resources than those from cl^i). Hence, the values of w_i, for $1<=i<=n$, depend on the classification of cl^i, $1<=i<=n$, in terms of grade of service.

5.2.4 Service Access Policy

Given a user request to perform a DVP task with given QoS requirements, the role of the access architecture is to locate the appropriate DVP server for this request. A service access policy is defined to guide the access architecture in the process of dynamically locating the DVP server capable of delivering the requested DVP service while satisfying user QoS requirements. Several factors are taken into account by the service access policy: 1) load of the DVP servers, 2) QoS characteristics of the DVP task; and 3) user QoS requirements and cost constraints. The ultimate goal of our access model is to minimize the blocking probability of user requests, therefore we define the service access policy such as to avoid rejecting a local studio request while there are DVP servers in the Virtual Studio, which might satisfy it. The following steps summarize the service access policy:

1) Identify the DVP servers capable to perform the requested DVP task; this gives a list of candidate DVP servers.
2) From the list in (1), select the server which can perform the requested task while satisfying most user QoS requirements, and which has the lightest load.
3) Start the DVP service delivery (e.g., displaying a video object or executing a DVP task); go to step (2) in case the selected DVP server experiences rapid load fluctuation leading to a violation of the service agreement.

6 Summary and Conclusion

Distributed Video Production systems are seen as a solution for most economical and technical challenges that a current studio faces. In this paper, we presented a comprehensive framework for DVP architectures. We described in detail typical DVP tasks and their related system and network performance requirements. We proposed a layered architecture model that captures the system and network characteristics of DVP environments. We finally proposed a QoS-sensitive model for resource allocation and optimization for distributed Video Production systems. Our architecture addresses several key issues in the design and implementation of

DVP systems. We believe that with the advancements in computational and networking technologies, DVP systems will soon become a reality.

References

1. B. Bhatt, D. Birks and D. Hermreck, ***"Digital Television: Making it Work,"*** IEEE Spectrum, October '97.
2. B. Furht, ***"Processor Architectures for Multimedia,"*** Multimedia technologies and applications for the 21st century: visions of world experts, Kluwer academic publishers, Norwell, Massachusetts, '98.
3. A. Peleg, S. Wilkie and U. Weiser, ***"Intel MMX for Multimedia PCs",*** Communications of the ACM, vol.40, No.1, Jan. '97.
4. M. Hayter and D. Mcanley, ***"The Desk Area Network,"*** ACM operating systems review, vol.25, No.4, Oct. '91.
5. T. Pfeifer, ***"Micronet machines – New Architecture Approaches for Multimedia End-systems,"*** Proceedings of 4th International workshop of network and operating system support for digital audio and video, Lancaster House, Lancaster, U.K., pp29-40, Nov. '93.
6. H. Vin and P. Rangan, ***"Designing a multi-user HDTV storage server,"*** IEEE JSAC, vol. 11, Jan. '93.
7. P. Rangan, H. Vin and S. Ramagathan, ***"Designing an On-Demand Multimedia service,"*** IEEE Communications Magazine, vol. 30, July '92.
8. R. Steinmetz and K. Nahrstedt, ***"Multimedia: Computing, Communications, and Applications,"*** PH Inc., '95.
9. A. Reddy and J. Wyllie, ***"I/O issues in a Multimedia System,"*** IEEE Computer, March '94.
10. G. Lu, ***"Communication and Computing for Distributed Multimedia Systems,"*** Artech House Inc., Norwooed, MA, '96.
11. R. Steinmetz, ***"Analyzing the Multimedia Operating System,"*** IEEE Multimedia, Spring '95.
12. D. Kandlur, D. Saha and M. Willebeek-LeMair, ***"Protocol architecture for Multimedia Applications over ATM networks,"*** IEEE Journal on Selected Areas in Communications, vol.14, No.7, Sept. '96.
13. M. Schwartz and D. Beaumont, "Quality of Service Requirements for Audio-Visual Multimedia Services," ATM Forum, July '94, ATM94-0640
14. Task Force for Harmonized Standards for the Exchange of Program Material as Bit Streams, ***"First Report: User Requirements,"*** EBU/SMPTE, April '97
15. D. Hehmann, M. Salmony and H. Stuttgen, ***"Transport Services for Multimedia Applications on Broadband Networks,"*** Computer Communications, vol.13 no.4, May '90.
16. R. Steinmetz, ***"Human Perception of Jitter and Media Synchronization,"*** IEEE Journal on Selected Areas in Communications, vol. 14, no.1, January '96.

CHAPTER 5

TOPOLOGICAL AND GEOMETRIC MODELING

MMM99

MOTION EDITING USING MULTIRESOLUTION FILTERING

Z. HUANG
Department of Computer Science, School of Computing, National University of Singapore, Singapore 119260
E-mail: huangzy@comp.nus.edu.sg

R. BOULIC AND D. THALMANN
EPFL-DI-LIG, CH-1015, Lausanne, Switzerland
E-mail: boulic, thalmann@lig.di.epfl.ch

Key frame animation is usually edited by adding, deleting and modifying key frames. We present novel motion editing techniques for animating articulated figures. The techniques are based on the *lowpass* and *bandpass pyramids* constructed from key frame sequences. We propose a motion blending method using multiresolution filtering. Then, we describe editing on frequency band. Finally, we describe motion data filtering from the pyramids. The experiment results show that the editing techniques work well.

1 Introduction

Sequences are used to represent motion of an articulated figure with multiple degrees of freedom (*DOFs*). A sequence is a set of trajectories that represents values for each *DOF* within a limited time. This paper treats sequences as signals from which *lowpass* and *bandpass pyramids* are constructed [3]. Then, the pyramids can be manipulated automatically or edited interactively. Finally, a new motion results from the signal reconstruction.

In section 1, we first describe the relevant work in motion editing and then the techniques of multiresolution filtering applied in our work. In section 2, we describe the construction of the *lowpass* and *bandpass pyramids* for key frame sequence.

We introduce our methods from section 3. First, we propose a sequence blending method based on multiresolution filtering. In this method, we construct *lowpass (Gaussian)* and *bandpass (Laplacian) pyramids* for two sequences to be blended, then we blend each layer of two *Laplacian pyramids* related to the same *DOF* at the transition period of the two sequences. This process continues for all *DOFs* and finally results in a new *Laplacian pyramid.* It is finally used to reconstruct a new sequence with a smooth transition between two sequences. We compare its results with the straightforward *weighted sum method.* In section 4, we describe a motion editing method on the coefficients of the frequency bands of a sequence. In section 5, we describe a data filtering method from *Laplacian pyramid.* The experiment results are shown for each method. Finally, we give a conclusion.

1.1 Related Work

As motion capturing is more popular in computer animation, motion editing has become more attractive too [6, 2, 9, and 8]. Bruderlin and Williams assemble a simple library of signal processing techniques applicable to animated motion. They introduce multiresolution filtering, multi-target motion interpolation with dynamic time warping, waveshaping and motion displacement mapping. They also illustrate an interactive editing technique on the coefficients of the frequency bands. Witkin and Popovic describe a simple technique for editing captured key frames based on warping of the motion parameter curves. They show that a whole family of realistic motions can be derived from a single captured motion sequence using only a few key frames to specify the motion warp. Unuma et al. apply Fourier transformations to data on human walking for animation purposes. Based on frequency analysis of the joint angles, a basic 'walking' factor and a 'qualitative' factor like "brisk" or "fast" are extracted. These factors are used to generate new movements by interpolation and extrapolation in the frequency domain, such that a walk can be changed continuously from normal to brisk walking. Recently, Guskov et al. generalize basic signal processing tools such as downsampling, upsampling, and filters to irregular connectivity 3D triangular meshes [5].

The work of Bruderlin and Williams is most relevant to ours. The major difference is that we use splines in construction of pyramids and reconstruction of signals. Splines are taking a central role in key frame animation. They interpolate key values, e.g., values of each angle or torque of each motor, to result a smooth movement. We extend the use of splines to represent signals of all layers of pyramids in the whole motion editing process. We focus on the motion blending, editing, and data filtering. For motion blending, we propose a general weighted sum method. For frequency band editing, we allow animator to change weights of the reconstruction formula instead of editing on coefficients of signals. Bruderlin and Williams did not discuss data filtering but we think it is important for a complicated model like human figure. Finally, we have implemented all these three functions and integrated them in a human animation system. The use of spline interpolation is also a major difference between motion and other signals like image.

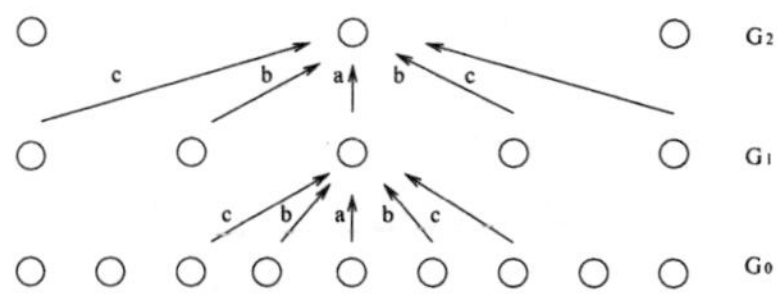

Figure 1. One dimensional graphic representation of iterative REDUCE operation used in pyramid construction.

1.2 *Multiresolution Filtering*

Multiresolution filtering is a fundamental technique of signal processing. It contains a range of digital filtering bank techniques which pass a signal through a cascade of lowpass filters to produce a set of short-time bandpass or lowpass signal components. Figure 1 is a graphical representation of the iterative filtering procedure in one dimension [3]. Each row of dots represents the samples of one of the filtered signals. The lowest row, G_0, is the original signal. The value of each node in the next row, G_1, is computed as a weighted average of a 5×5 sub-array of G_0 nodes as shown. Nodes of array G_2 are then computed from G_1 using the same pattern of weights. The process is iterated to obtain G_2 from G_1, G_3 from G_2 and so on. If we imagine these arrays stacked one above the other, the result is the tapering data structure known as a pyramid [7].

2 Pyramid Construction for Key Frames

The pyramid construction method of Burt and Adelson is adopted for key frames [3]. It is a multiresolution analysis in terms of a cubic B-spline scaling function in the currently popular wavelet parlance [4]. This method obtains the *lowpass pyramid* by successively convolving the signal with a B-spline filter kernel while the signal sampling is subsampled by a factor of 2 at each iteration as shown in Figure 1. The local averaging process is called $REDUCE$ and generates each pyramid level from its predecessor:

$$\begin{aligned} G_l &= REDUCE(G_{l-1}) \\ G_l(i) &= w(m)G_{l-1}(2i+m), \end{aligned} \tag{1}$$

where $i = 0, \cdots, n-5$ and n is the number of samples in layer $l-1$. If the original signal, i.e., G_0, contains 2^{N+1} samples, there are N layers for the pyramid ($N = 3$ in Figure 1).

The weights $w(m)$, called the *generating kernel*, can be derived in the following way: First, the weights must be symmetric, $w(0) = a, w(-1) = w(1) = b$, and $w(-2) = w(2) = c$. Second, they must be normalized, $a + 2b + 2c = 1$. Third, they must contribute the same total weight to each level $l+1$ node from each level l node, thus, $a + 2c = 2b$. If a is considered as a free variable, we have $b = 1/4$ and $c = 1/4 - a/2$.

For the example in Figure 2, the curves G_0, G_1, and G_2 are lowpass data constructed by setting $a = 0.4$. G_0, G_1, and G_2 contain $9, 5$ and 3 samples respectively. The first and final samples are copied to the next layer. Burt and Adelson refer this sequence $G_0, G_1, G_2, \cdots, G_{N-1}$ as the *Gaussian pyramid* because the equivalent weighting functions resemble the Gaussian probability density function when $a = 0.4$.

The next step is to construct the *bandpass pyramid.* It can be subtracted at each level of the low-pass *Gaussian pyramid* from the next lower level. Because arrays representing data of each layer differ in sample density, it is necessary to interpolate new samples between those of a given array before it is subtracted from the next lower array. This is done by the $EXPAND$ operation:

$$\begin{aligned} G_{l,k} &= EXPAND(G_{l,k-1}) \\ G_{l,0} &= G_l, \\ G_{l,k} &= 4\textstyle\sum_{m=-2}^{2} G_{l,k-1}\left(\dfrac{2i+m}{2}\right), k > 0, \end{aligned} \tag{2}$$

where $i = 0, \cdots, n-5$ and n is the number of samples in layer $l-1$. Now layers of the *bandpass pyramid* $L_0, L_1, \cdots, L_{N-1}$ can be derived:

$$L_l = G_l - EXPAND(G_{l+1}) = G_l - G_{l+1,l}, \tag{3}$$

where $l = 0, \cdots, N-1$.

Thus each node of L_l can be obtained directly by convolving the weighting function with the signal. The difference of the Gaussian-like functions resembles the Laplacian operators commonly used in signal processing, the sequence $L_0, L_1, \cdots, L_{N-1}$ is referred as the *Laplacian pyramid.* Each L_l represents a signal component with the same frequency. The higher the value of l, the higher the frequency. The frequency of L_l is twice as high as the frequency of its next layer L_{l-1}.

The steps used to construct the *Laplacian pyramid* may be reversed to recover the original signal G_0. The top pyramid level, G_N, is first expanded and added to L_{N-1} to recover G_{N-1}; this array is then expanded and added to L_{N-1} to recover G_{N-2}, and so on. We get:

$$G_0 = G_N + \sum_{l=0}^{N-1} L_l. \tag{4}$$

Equation 4 describes the re-constructing process. From another point of view, it represents the original signal in terms of its frequency.

We use the cubic Cardinal spines for interpolation in the $EXPAND$ process to get more samples on each layer. Suppose t_0 is time step of samples in G_0 (it is also the same in L_0), then the step t_i in layer i for both G_i and L_i is calculated from the $REDUCE$ process:

$$t_i = 2^i t_0. \tag{5}$$

Now we can list the reconstructing process:

1. Set $i = N$.
2. If i equals N, set $L'_i = G_N$.
3. Get $m-1$ more samples of L'_i at $\frac{1}{2}t_i, \frac{3}{2}t_i, \cdots$ interpolated by cubic Cardinal splines, so the number of samples in L'_i is the same as in L_{i-1}, where m is the former number of samples in L'_i; thus $m = 2^{N-i} + 1$.
4. Add the sample values of L'_i to the sample values of L_{i-1} at each time step, and use the new samples to construct L'_{i-1}.
5. If $i - 1$ equals 0, finish the process by setting $G_0 = L'_{i-1}$. G_0 represents the reconstructed motion. Otherwise set $i = i - 1$, go and repeat from step 3.

Figures 2 and 3 illustrate the construction of *Gaussian* and *Laplacian pyramids* for one DOF (wrist flexion) and trajectory reconstructed from the pyramids. From experiments, the decomposition-reconstruction introduces a small error in the reconstructed sequence. The error is acceptable with respect to the benefits presented in the following sections.

3 Motion Blending

In this section, we present a method of blending two key frame sequences into a new sequence. The method is based on multiresolution filtering. The goal is to achieve a smooth transition between two original motions represented by two sequences. The most common method is to use a straightforward weighted

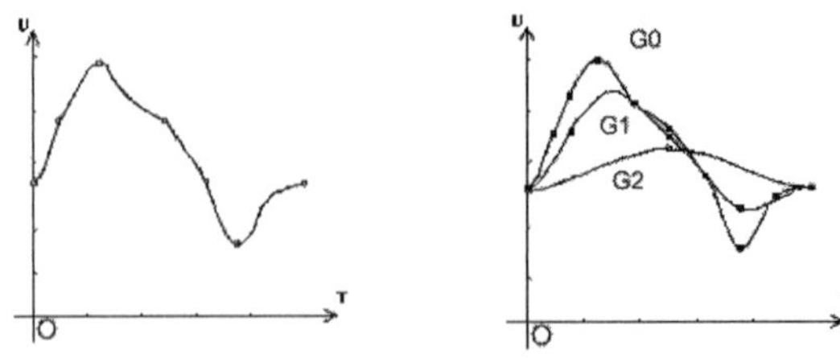

Figure 2. Left: original trajectory. Right: construction of layers of the *Gaussian pyramid*, G_0, G_1, and G_2.

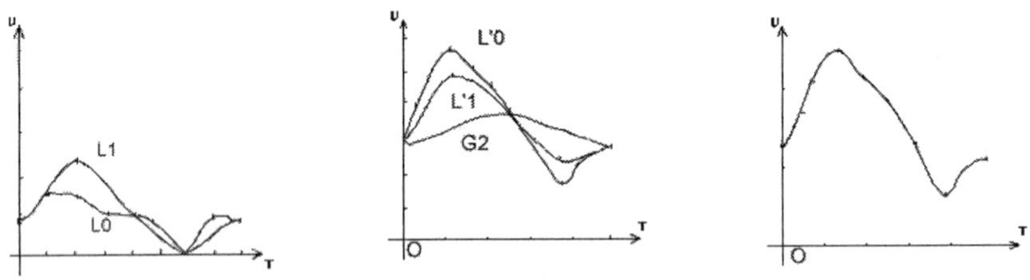

Figure 3. Left: construction of layers of the *Laplacian pyramid*, L_0 and L_1. Middle: reconstruction process, $L'_2 = G_2, L'_1 = L'_2 + L_1$, and $L'_0 = L'_1 + L_0$. Right: the reconstructed trajectory.

sum of the two motions in the transition period. Given two sequences $\theta_1(t)$ and $\theta_2(t)$ representing the motion of one DOF, the blending result $\theta_3(t)$ can be derived by

$$\theta_3(t) = w(t)\theta_1(t) + (1 - w(t))\theta_2(t), \tag{6}$$

where time t defines the transition period and $t_1 \leq t \leq t_2$. $w(t)$ is a normalized ease-in/ease-out weight function.

The *weighted sum method* is simple and its results are acceptable. Our method is to improve on the *weighted sum method* by using the multiresolution filter. This first application is similar to Burt and Adelson's approach to produce seamless image mosaic [3].

The novel blending method contains two steps more than the *weighted sum method*: pyramid construction and signal reconstruction. Suppose we have two sequences S_1 and S_2, with S_1 in period $[t1, t2]$ and S_2 in $[t3, t4]$, where $t3 > t1$ and $t4 > t2$. We carry out the following steps to blend S_1 and S_2:

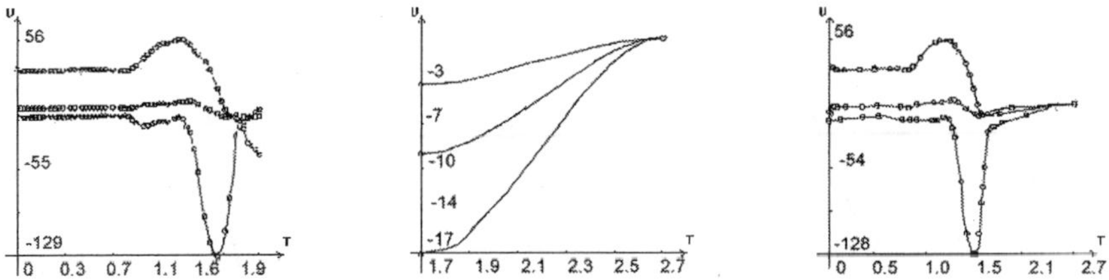

Figure 4. Left: the first sequence S_1. Middle: the second sequence S_2. Right: the resulting sequence S_3. The transition period is between 1.70 sec and 1.94 sec.

1. Construct layers of *Laplacian pyramid* L_1 and L_2 for S_1 and S_2 respectively.

2. Construct a third *Laplacian pyramid* L_3 as follows:

   (a) Copy nodes from the layers of L_1 for $[t1, t3)$.

   (b) Copy nodes from the layers of L_2 for $(t2, t4]$.

   (c) Use the *weighted sum method* for $[t_2, t_3]$: $L_{3,l} = w(t)L_{1,l} + (1 - w(t))L_{2,l}$ for each layer l.

3. Reconstruct a new sequence S from L_3.

The method works on the transition period of the two incorporated sequences. It is $[t3, t2]$ with $t3 < t2$. More interpolation samples should be in $[t3, t2]$ which is decided by the depth of pyramid layers input by the animator. Another interesting case is when $t3 > t1$ and $t4 < t2$, i.e., when the second sequence S_2 takes place inside the first sequence S_1. In this case step 2 and 3 are used in $[t3, t4]$ but with the weighting function reaching 0 at middle point $(t3 + t4)/2$ and 1 at $t3$ and $t4$. So the method is general by defining a general weighting function. From the point of view of signal processing, the component signals within a transition zone are joined using a weighting average which is proportional in size to the wave lengths represented in the band. So the result can be seamless.

We show one example in Figure 4 to 6. Two more examples are shown in video with better illustration of a smooth transition. See *http : //www.comp.nus.edu.sg/ ~ huangzy/MMM99/blend1.mps.gz* and *blend2.mps.gz*.

Figure 5. Left: a posture of S_1. Middle: another posture of S_1. Right: a posture of transition.

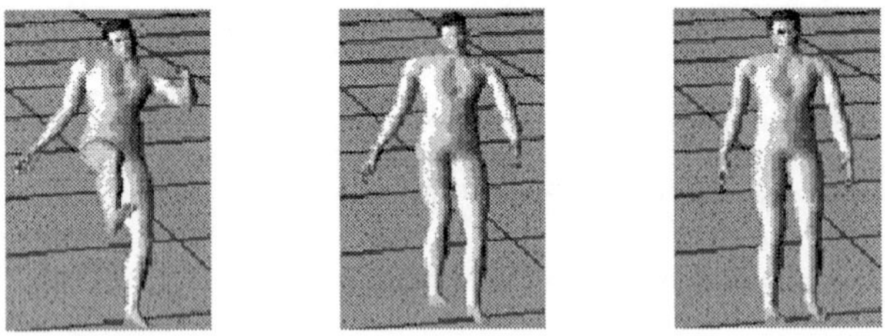

Figure 6. Left: another posture of transition. Middle: a posture of S_2. Right: another posture of S_2.

4 Interactive Editing

In this section, we describe the implementation of interactive editing of the frequency band coefficients. We start from Equation 4. It can be generalized by defining weights on each term:

$$G_0 = w_N G_N + \sum_{l=0}^{N-1} w_l L_l, \tag{7}$$

where $w_0, w_1, \cdots, w_N$ are weights. If each one is a unity, the resulting key frames are approximately same as the original ones. However, by interactively setting different values, we obtain a new sequence.

In Figure 7, there are three original key frames. We construct a pyramid with four layers and set weights $2, 1.5, 0$, and 1 for each layer respectively. Then from reconstruction, we get a new motion. Three key frames of the new motion are shown in Figure 8.

Figure 7. Three snapshots from the original motion.

Figure 8. Three snapshots from the new motion after editing. It is done by setting different weights on layers in key frame re-construction.

5 Data Filtering

Next we present the application of multiresolution filtering on a sequence. We illustrate it with an example: to filter the key frame data captured using VR device: *Flock of Birds* of Virtual Technologies. The sampling rate is 100 Hz. First, the *Gaussian* and *Laplacian pyramids* are constructed with only four layers so that G_0 and L_0 contain $17(2^4+1)$ samples. Next, a sequence from the four layered pyramids is reconstructed so the final sequence contains only 17 samples. By this manipulation, the higher frequency components are filtered out. They often represent noise or over detailed movement of the sequence. The result is shown in Figure 9 to 11. Another example is shown in video with comparison of motions before and after filtering. See *http://www.comp.nus.edu.sg/~huangzy/MMM99/filtering.mps.gz*.

This method can filter data significantly while retaining the major features of the original motion signal. The greater the number of layers used to construct the pyramid, the better the approximation with less filtering.

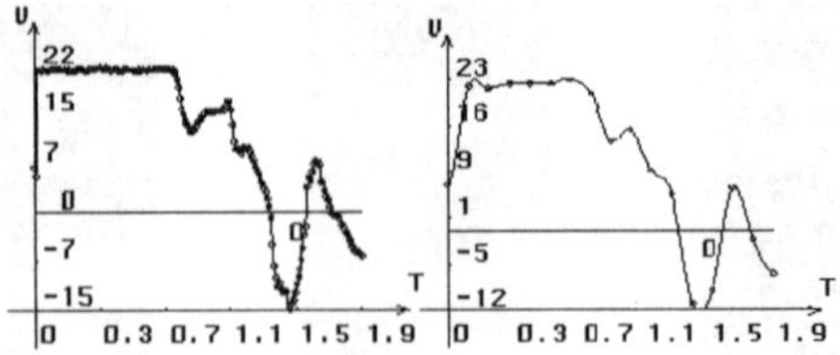

Figure 9. Left: trajectories of *DOF r_hip_twisting*. Right: trajectories of the *DOF* after filtering.

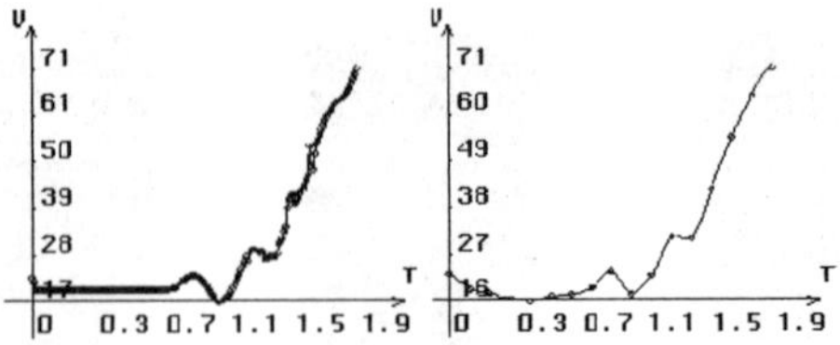

Figure 10. Left: trajectories of *DOF r_elbow_flexion*. Right: trajectories of the *DOF* after filtering.

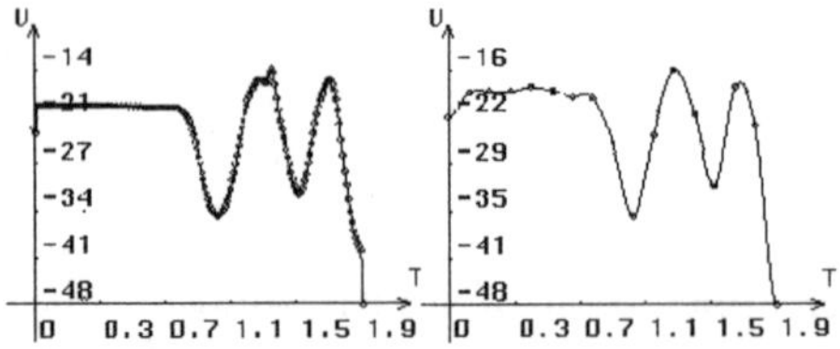

Figure 11. Left: trajectories of *DOF l_knee_flexion*. Right: trajectories of the *DOF* after filtering.

6 Conclusion and Future Work

In this paper, we proposed a motion-blending method by using the multiresolution pyramid representation. We described two sequence manipulation methods: frequency band editing and data filtering from pyramids. These techniques are important for reusing and post-processing the key frame sequence.

We have implemented and integrated them in an articulated motion control system called *Track* [1].

Work can be continued in the reuse of sequences. One of the interesting problems is how to adapt a sequence to new spatial and temporal constraints, or how to customize a sequence. A more general subject is motion recognition that is interesting for virtual reality applications.

7 Acknowledgments

This work was mainly done when the first author was studying in EPFL-DI-LIG. The work was supported by the Swiss National Research Foundation.

References

1. Boulic, R., Huang, Z., Magnenat-Thalmann, N., and Thalmann, D., *Goal-Oriented Design and Correction of Articulated Figure Motion with the Track System.* Journal of Comput. & Graphics, 18 (4), pp. 443-452, 1994.
2. Bruderlin, A. and Williams, L., *Motion Signal Processing.* Proc. SIGGRAPH'95, pp. 97-104.
3. Burt, J. P. and Adelson, E. H., *A Multiresolution Spline With Application to Image Mosaic.* ACM Transaction on Graphics, 2 (4), pp. 217-236. Oct. 1983.
4. Chui, C. K., *An Introduction to Wavelets, Series: Wavelet Analysis and its Applications.* Academic Press, Inc., 1992.
5. Guskov, I., Sweldens, W., and Schroder, P., *Multiresolution Signal Processing for Meshes*, Proc. SIGGRAPH'99.
6. Rose, C., Guenter, B., Bodenheimer, B., and Cohen, M. F., *Efficient Generation of Motion Transitions using Spacetime Constraints* Proc. SIGGRAPH'97, pp. 147-154.
7. Tanimoto, S. L. and Pavlidis, T., *A hierarchical data structure for picture processing.* Comput. Gr. Image Process. pp. 104-119, 4, 1975.
8. Unuma, M., Anjyo, K., and Takeuchi, R., *Fourier Principle of Emotion-Based Human Figure Animation.* Proc. SIGGRAPH'95, pp. 91-96.
9. Witkin, A. and Popovic, Z., *Motion Warping.* Proc. SIGGRAPH'95, pp. 105-108.

SIMULATION OF POSTOPERATIVE 3D FACIAL MORPHOLOGY USING PHYSICS-BASED HEAD MODEL

YOSHIMITSU AOKI AND SHUJI HASHIMOTO

Department of Applied Physics, School of Science and Engineering, Waseda University
3-4-1 Okubo, Shinjuku-ku, Tokyo 169-8555
JAPAN
E-mail: {aoki, shuji}@shalab.phys.waseda.ac.jp

MASAHIKO TERASHIMA AND AKIHIKO NAKASHIMA

Department of Orthodontics, School of Dentistry, Kyusyu University
3-1-1 Maidashi, Higashi-ku, Fukuoka 812-8582
JAPAN
E-mail: nakashima@dent.kyushu-u.ac.jp

We propose a prototype of the facial surgery simulation system for surgical planning and prediction of facial deformation using physics-based human head model.
Our head model has three-dimension hierarchical structure that consists of soft tissue and the skull, constructed from exact 3D-CT data of a patient. The fitting method to a specific patient's head is realized by the use of CT data and anatomic measurement points on X-ray images from both of frontal and side views.
The purposes of this research are to analyze the relationship between changes of mandibular position and that of facial morphology after orthognathic surgery, and to simulate the exact postoperative 3D facial shape. In the experiment, we predicted the facial shape after surgery for patients with mandibular prognathism using our model. By comparing the simulation results and the actual facial images after the surgery, the proposed method can be proved to be practically useful for the orthognathic treatment.

1 Introduction

1.1 Background and Previous Work

In recent years, facial image synthesis using computer graphics technique is focused in several fields and applications, such as tele-conferencing, man-machine interface, and various facial simulations.

Present methods for synthesizing facial images mostly use 3D facial models which are created by hundreds of triangular meshes. Many methods have been proposed in order to deform a facial model to create flexible facial expressions. One of them introduces action units of the FACS [1] to describe facial expressions, which defines the pure geometric deformation of points that correspond to each facial expression. These kinds of modeling methods can effectively create facial images in a short amount of computational time, and therefore can be used for applications which require the real-time performance instead of the accurate facial modeling[2]. Another facial modeling method is the physics-based one. Some studies have used physics-based facial models based on the fact that actual facial expressions are generated by the dynamics of facial muscles underlying facial surface [3][4][7][8]. These models regard the facial skin and muscles as physical springs, and can generate facial expressions by the contraction of springs.

The advantage of the physical method is that they can predict facial expressions followed by changes of facial muscles and jaw action. From this advantage, some anatomical facial models have been developed for medical applications such as the facial surgery simulation.

Since a human face plays an important role in interpersonal relationships, prediction of postoperative facial morphology for patients is a crucial problem on the occasion of facial surgery. Therefore, it is necessary for the esthetic correction of disharmony of the facial morphology as well as the functional correction. For instance, in the case of orthognathic surgery, many surgical procedures, e.g. cutting of a bone, and bringing them to a normal position, lead to changes in facial morphology. So it is important to examine the facial soft tissue changes following surgery in detail and to give an account of the obtained information for a surgery planning and prediction of facial deformation.

Regarding the prediction, surgeons draw the predicted contours of facial profiles using X-ray images of a patient. However, this kind of prediction method depends heavily on his experiences and techniques, so obtaining objective and accurate simulation is difficult. So it is clearly and strongly demanded by both of surgeons and patients to realize the simulation of the future face as accurate as possible, before the actual surgery will be carried out. In such situations, some facial model introducing actual patient data, e.g. CT scans or MRI, have been proposed for the facial surgery simulation.

Studies such as [8] describe a prototype system for surgical planning and prediction of facial shape after craniofacial and maxillofacial surgery for patients with facial deformities using finite element models. H.Mita et al. proposes a very elaborate model including underlying facial tissue from CT scanned data for a facial paralysis simulator [7]. These works show the postoperative facial morphology by the computed 3D facial image, however, the result evaluation is still not satisfactorily done because of the insufficiency of patients' data.

1.2 Motivation

In this paper, we propose an orthognathic surgery simulation system that introduces the anatomic 3D head model and the fitting method to each patient. The main features of our work are as follows:

- Because both of a face and a skull are reconstructed from exact 3D-CT data, and the fitting method to a specific patient's head from X-ray images, a highly anatomic based head model of a patient can be constructed.

- Facial modification is computed from the forces applied to the springs to simulate the elasticity of the skin and dynamics of facial muscles.
- This method can represent the process of three-dimensional facial modification naturally and smoothly with high accuracy. Especially, we simulate jaw action and some surgical procedures such as cut and resection of the jaw for orthognathic surgery.

Our goal is to analyze the relationship between changes of mandibular position and that of facial morphology after the orthognathic surgery, and to simulate the exact postoperative 3D facial deformations by the use of physics-based head model. We finally aim at the facial surgery simulator that assists surgeons in surgery planning and actual surgical procedures, by the display of realistic and accurate predicted results.

The outlines of this paper are as follows: In Section 2, we summarize orthognathic surgery and its treatment procedures to make the role of our work clear. In Section 3, we describe available data sets of a patient acquired for the modeling and fitting process, and explain the integrated head model. Section 4 presents how to compute the facial deformation caused by the action of muscles and a jaw. Next, we view our simulation system in section 5, and show some simulation results after orthognathic surgery using patients' data in section 6. In section 7, we evaluate experimental results compared with the actual surgical cases. Finally, we conclude this paper.

2 Overview of Orthognathic Surgery

This section explains the mandibular prognathism which is a typical case of jaw deformities. Next, we view the actual treatment process for those kinds of cases in order to define how our system can be available.

2.1 Mandibular Prognathism

Mandibular prognathism is one of the jaw deformities which causes functional and aesthetic disorders. In serious cases, it has bad influences in chewing and pronouncing, so orthognathic treatment and surgery are required to improve such symptoms. Fig.1(a) illustrates an example of a patient with mandibular prognathism by his facial image and X-ray image in profile, respectively. In this case, posterior transposition of the mandible was carried out with the result that the functional and aesthetic correction of disharmony of the facial morthorogy were reformed as shown in Fig.1(b).

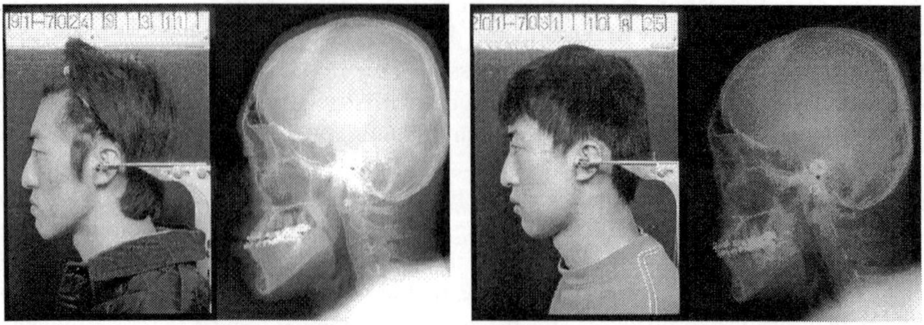

(a) Before treatment (b) After treatment

Figure1. Example of a patient with mandibular prognathism

2.2 Treatment Process

Fig.2 shows the flow diagram of a standard treatment process for orthognathic surgery, which consists of three treatment steps. We describe each step roughly in the following part of this paragraph.

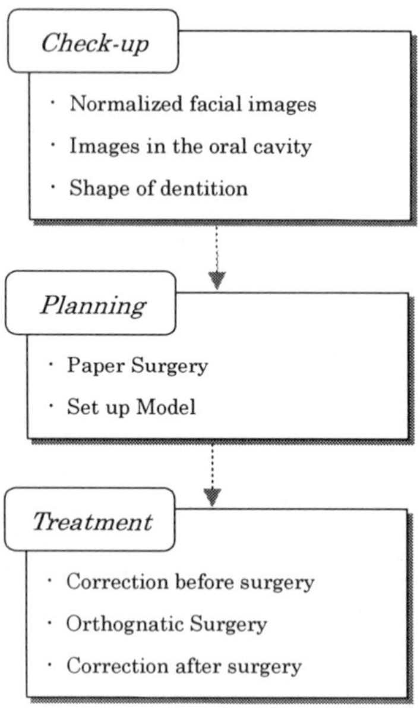

Figure2. Flow diagram of the orthognathic treatment

2.2.1 Check-up before treatment

Previous to the treatment, a dental doctor checks the condition of a patient and obtains some kinds of data for the treatment, such as facial images and X-ray images from both of frontal and side views. In addition, we acquire shape data of the dentition for the plaster cast model called "Set up model" in the field of orthodontics.

2.2.2 Treatment Planning

Using obtained data at previous step, the dental doctor determines the actual treatment way and surgical planning. Typically, the surgeon overwrites the facial contour of patient's predicted 2D profile on X-ray images. This prediction way is called "Paper surgery". Besides, Set-up-model is often used for the orthodontic planning.

2.2.3 Actual Treatment

Orthodontic treatment and surgery are carried out at the basis of surgical plan.

As stated above, the paper surgery method, which is the typical prediction way at present, only has two-dimensional information (facial contour) about facial morphology after surgery. So we attempt to simulate three dimensional changes of facial soft-tissue following orthognathic surgery using our physics-based head modeling method.

3 Modeling Method

This section describes how to generate a head model for an individual patient from anatomical data, and explains the features of a generated head model.

3.1 Data Acquisition

To construct a facial surface and a skull, we can use 3D-CT data and X-ray images from frontal and side views. Processing steps are as follows.

In the first step, CT slices of a patient's head are acquired at required intervals. Fig.3(a) shows the one of CT slices. Facial soft-tissue and hard-tissue can be separated by threshold-based segmentation, which makes use of the differences of permeability for X-rays. Next, 3D volume data of skin and skull are constructed by integrating data of CT slices as shown in Fig.3(b), and the feature points on the surface of the skin and skull are extracted at regular intervals. We selected feature points that effectively approximate the shape of the face and the skull by taking the complexity of the surface into account (Adaptive meshing algorithm). Next, we created skin and skull models using triangular wire meshes. Finally, the layer of muscles which connects the skin and the skull models was placed using feature points on both ends of the muscles.

This modeling method always requires 3D-CT, however, it costs lots of processing time, and the process includes the problem of bad effect of radiation to a human body. Therefore, we proposed the new method that fits the standard head model for an individual patient using anatomic measurement points extracted from X-ray images.

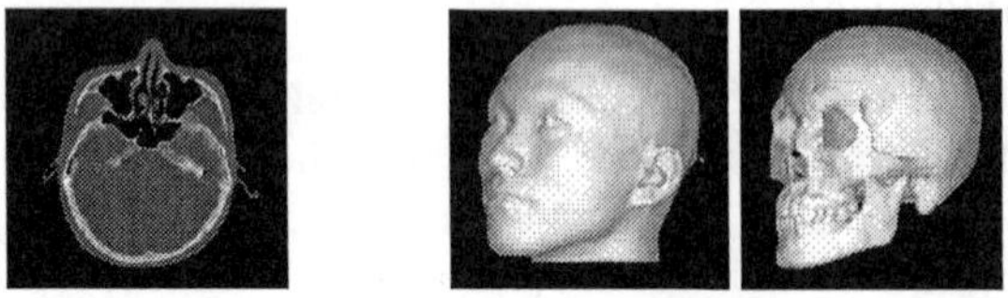

(a)CT slice (b) Segmented 3D face and skull data

Figure3. Face and Skull surface extraction from 3D-CT data model.

3.2 Standard Head Model

The generated head model including face and skull is illustrated in Fig.4(a). Facial muscles underlying skin are set between facial surface and the skull, according to the actual muscle system. The frames constructing facial surface and muscles are regarded as physical non-linear springs called "spring frames", which simulate the elasticity of actual ones. All springs have the elastic parameters that represent the stiffness of facial skin and muscles. We specially set lots of springs around the jaw in order to realize smooth and exact modification following orthognathic surgery (Fig.4(c)). The skull is modeled as a rigid body whose jaw part can realize some actions, such as rotations and parallel translations. More detailed explanation of this head model were appeared in [6].

We use this individual model as the initial model for a patient. Hereafter, we describe how to fit this initial head model for an individual patient.

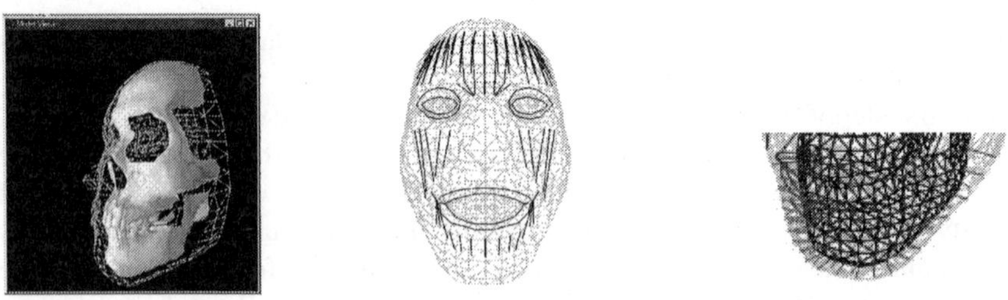

(a) Face and skull model (b) Facial muscle modeling (c) Fat modeling around the jaw

Figure4. Standard head model from CT data.

3.3 Fitting Method

In this section, we explain the fitting process to generate a patient model using X-ray images. This method is mainly divided into two steps; in the first step, the anatomic measurement points manually extracted from X-ray images are used for a rough fitting that resizes a facial width and height, translates the facial parts, i.e. eyes, mouth, and a nose, etc. In the next step, the feature points around the anatomic measurement points are locally fitted to the patient's head shape using smooth transformational function. Anatomic measurement points plotted by the doctor are shown in Fig.5. The number of the measurement points is 12 on the facial contour, 16 on the skull contour, respectively. From the 2D coordinates of points measured on two images, 3D coordinates are calculated for the fitting process.

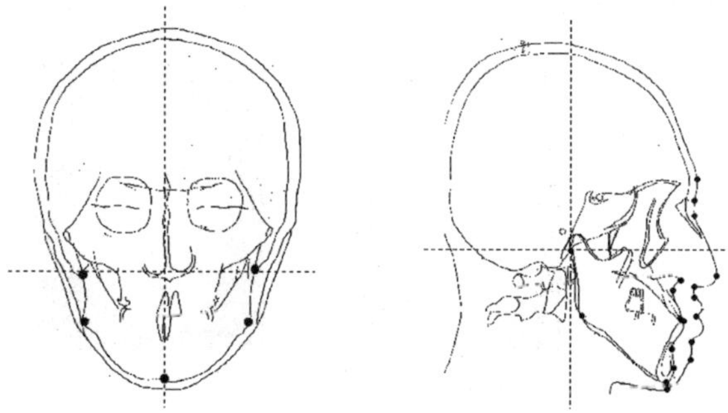

(a) Frontal view (b) Side view

Figure5. Anatomic measurement points on the sketch of X-ray images

3.3.1 Rough Fitting

First, we fit the size of the face and the skull using the 3D coordinates of measurement points. In order to fit the shape of model roughly, we divide both a face and a skull into three parts; the upper jaw, the lower jaw and the other part. At each part, its width, height, and depth information is calculated from the 3D coordinates of measurement points, so the size of each part can be fit to the actual one.

3.3.2 Detailed Fitting

After rough fitting, more detailed fitting process is necessary to reconstruct accurate head models for patients. The feature points around the anatomic measurement points are fitted to the patient's head shape using the following smooth transformation function [10].

$$f(\Delta x, \Delta y, \Delta z) = S\left\{\frac{\cos(\frac{\Delta x}{rx} + \frac{\Delta y}{ry} + \frac{\Delta z}{rz}) + 1}{2}\right\}^n \tag{1}$$

Where (Δx, Δy, Δz) is the distance between the measurement point and feature points of the model. (r_x, r_y, r_z) and S represent the deformation range along each axis and the movement of the measurement point, respectively. n indicates the acutance parameter of the modification, and this parameter for each measurement point is determined empirically.

Through these steps, the individual patient head model can be constructed with sufficient accuracy. Fig.6 shows the examples of the fitting result for two actual patients.

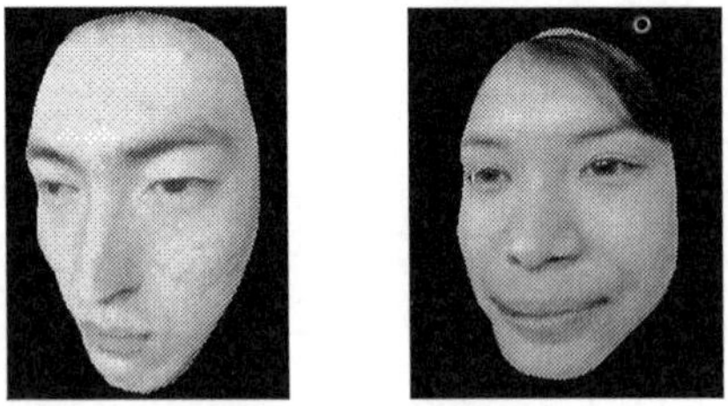

Figure6. Examples of the fitting results

4 Dynamical Facial Mechanism

4.1 The contraction of facial muscles

When we modify the face model, some movable points on the skin model are moved in order to obtain the expected modified face. The energy of the spring system can be changed by the expansion or contraction of muscles simulated by springs, and the new position of each point is obtained by calculating the energy equilibrium state. The equilibrium point is calculated by minimizing the potential energy of the entire spring system. Fig.7 shows the 3D structure of the head model. The kinetic equation for feature point i on the facial surface is given as follows:

$$m_i \frac{d^2 \boldsymbol{r}_i}{dt^2} = \boldsymbol{k}_i + m_i \boldsymbol{g} - R\frac{d\boldsymbol{r}_i}{dt} \tag{2}$$

where r_i represents the 3D coordinates of the feature point i. The first and second terms represent the total elastic force affected to the point i and the attraction of gravity, respectively. The third term is the viscous term of the facial model.

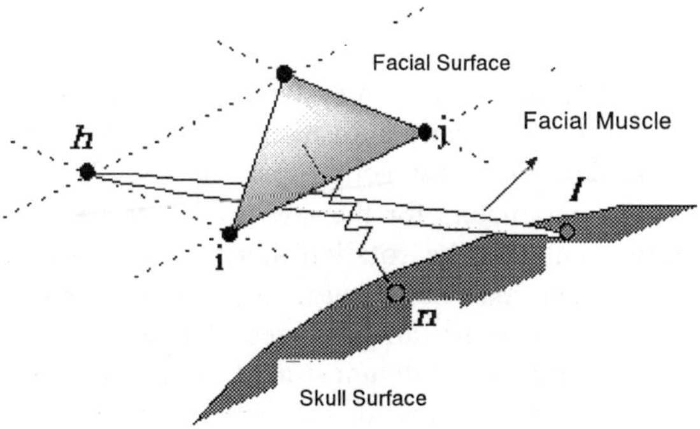

Figure7. Hierarchical structure of the head model

4.2 Motion of the jaw

The motion of the jaw can be realized by a coordinate transformation as the following equation:

$$\begin{pmatrix} x_i' \\ y_i' \\ z_i' \end{pmatrix} = \begin{pmatrix} \cos\theta_y & -\sin\theta_x\sin\theta_y & -\cos\theta_x\sin\theta_y \\ 0 & \cos\theta_x & -\sin\theta_x \\ \sin\theta_y & \sin\theta_x\cos\theta_y & \cos\theta_x\cos\theta_y \end{pmatrix}\begin{pmatrix} x_i \\ y_i \\ z_i \end{pmatrix} + \begin{pmatrix} 0 \\ 0 \\ l_z \end{pmatrix} \tag{3}$$

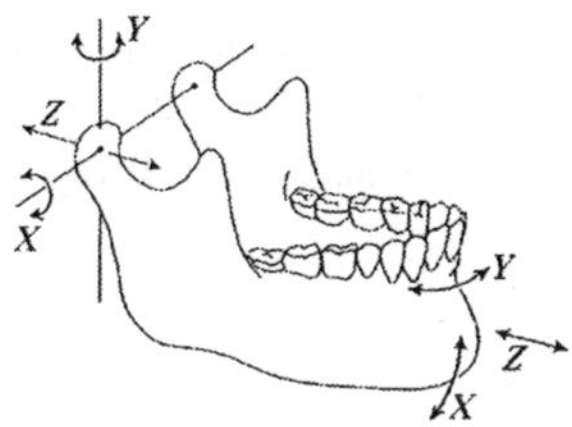

Figure8. Jaw action

θ_x and θ_y represent the degrees of rotation around the X and Y axes, respectively. lz is the parameter of the parallel motion along the Z axis. The origins of the transformation are both sides of the joint points of the jaw and the upper skull.

From this equation, the coordinates of the feature points on the jaw can be calculated. Next, the feature points on the skin model and the muscles that allocated to the jaw of the skull model move with the motion of the skull model. The energy of the entire system is generated by the transformation, and a new equilibrium point can be computed. As a result, a new position for each feature point on the skin model can be determined following jaw action.

5 System Overview

Fig.9 shows the overview of our simulation system. Using the GUI panel like (b), we can set the values of parameters easily and interactively. These parameters are the stiffness of facial muscles, and jaw action parameters. For the simulation of orthognathic surgery, the parameters for the jaw treatment are especially essential, i.e. the backward movement and the rotation angle of the jaw to bring it into a desired position. This system takes some surgical procedures into account, such as cutting and shifting of the jaw bone, and changes of facial morphology caused by them are automatically computed and demonstrated in the model view window. Our system enables surgeons to make plans for the surgery in advance, and to indicate the postoperative 3D facial images clearly. The proposed model also generates facial expressions caused by muscles' contractions dynamically, so we can demonstrate the predicted "smiling face" to a patient, for instance.

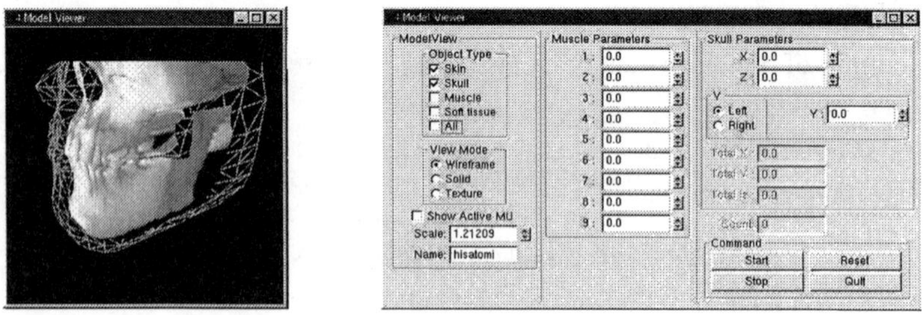

(a) Model Overview (b) Graphical User Interface for setting parameters

Figure9. Facial Surgery Simulation System

6 Computational Simulation

In this section, we simulated the predicted facial shape after orthognathic surgery for actual three patients with mandibular prognathism using the proposed head model.

6.1 Surgery Method

In the experiment, sagittal splitting ramus osteotomy (Obwegeser-Dal Pont method), which is the most popular surgical method of mandibular prognathism, was selected for actual treatment for patients. This method can be summarized as follows (Fig.10). First, the jaw is cut along some lines and divided into three parts. Then the projecting part of the jaw is set in the backward direction in order to normalize its position. Our surgery system realizes these surgical procedures for surgeons.

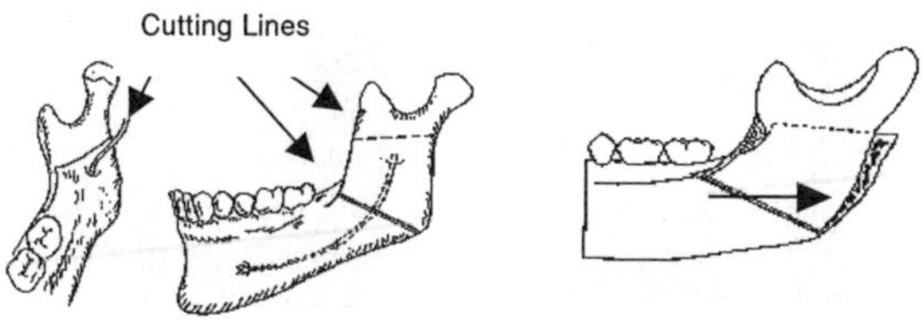

Figure10. Obwegeser-Dal Pont method

6.2 Simulation Results

The changes of facial morphology following orthognathic surgery were simulated for three patients with mandibular prognathism. In each case, backward distance of the lower jaw is determined by the medical specialist of orthodontics. Fig.11 shows the result of the jaw treatment by the Obwegeser-Dal Pont method, (a), (b) are the simulation results using the skull model and (c), (d) indicate the actual results (X-ray images) before and after surgery. It is clear that the projecting part could be set back to the desired position using our simulation system. Fig.12 illustrates the profiles of actual facial images (a), (b) and predicted results (c), (d) before and after surgery.

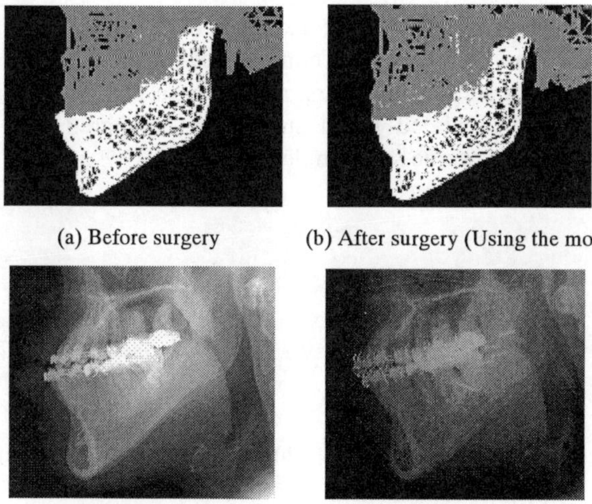

(a) Before surgery (b) After surgery (Using the model)

(c) Before surgery (d) After surgery (X-ray image)

Figure11. Surgical result following the Obwebegeser-Dal Pont method

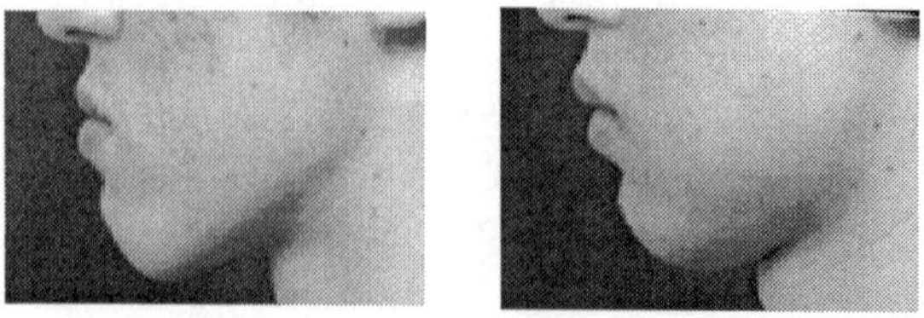

(a) Before surgery (b) After surgery (actual result)

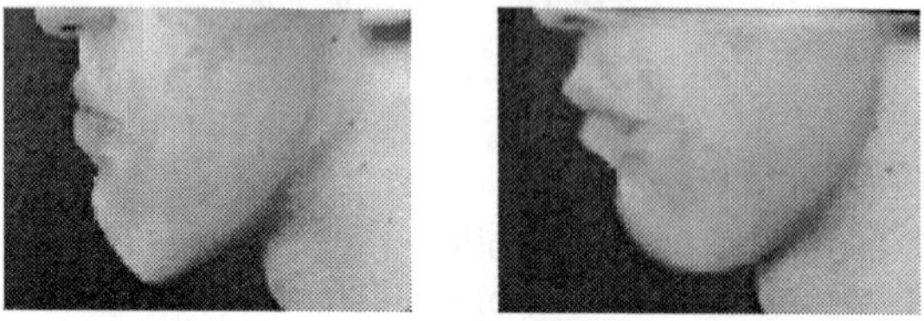

(c) Before surgery (d) After surgery (predicted result)

Figure12. Simulation result of the facial morphology

7 Evaluation and Discussion

In order to evaluate the accuracy of experimental result more obviously, the predicted profiles of three patients' are compared with the actual profiles extracted from X-ray images after surgery in layers, as shown in Fig.13. Fig.14 illustrates the points to evaluate the simulated facial surface in compared with the actual the tracing of X-ray images by some surgeon dentists.

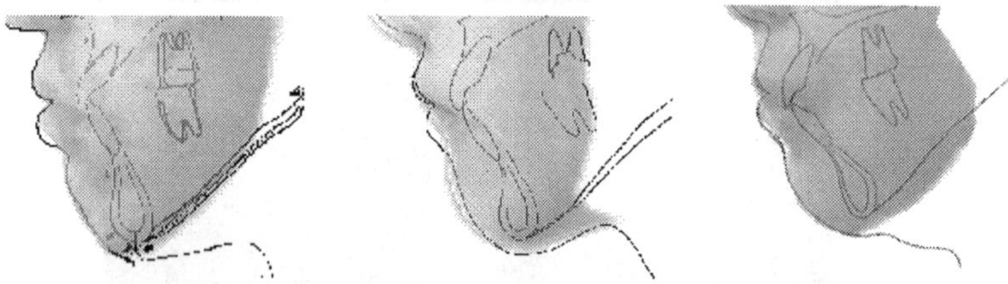

(a) Patient A (b) Patient B (c) Patient C

Figure13. Evaluation of simulation results for three patients

(Compared with the tracing of X-ray images from side view)

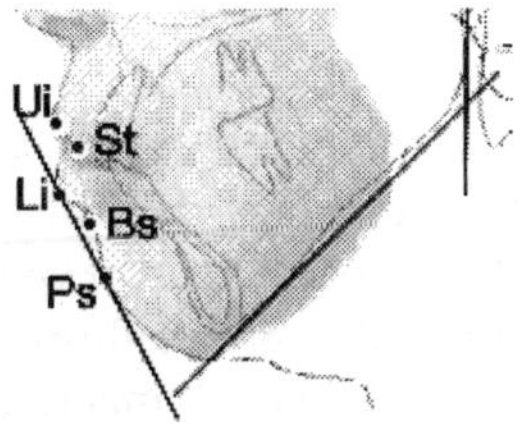

Figure14. Evaluation points on the facial surface

As shown in Fig.12, 13, the predicted facial profiles of patients are very close to actual ones after surgery. Considering the evaluation results by the surgeons, simulated position of the points around the lower jaw (Bs, Ps) is approximately close to the right position, although points around a lower lip (Li) include some error. The main reason of this error is supposed that quality of a mouth of our standard facial model is not enough for this simulation. However, these experimental results were qualitatively evaluated to be available for surgical simulation and planning by experienced surgeon dentists.

Fig.15 shows the 3D view of the predicted result for the patient C. The surgeon can observe the simulated results from desired direction at 3D space by rotating it. In addition to the prediction of facial morphology, the simulation of facial expression is strongly desired by both of doctors and patients. Our system has the ability of generating facial expressions with the dynamical motion, so it can simulate a "smiling" face after surgery as shown in Fig.16, for instance. Fig.16 indicates her smiling face generated by contraction of muscles around cheeks.

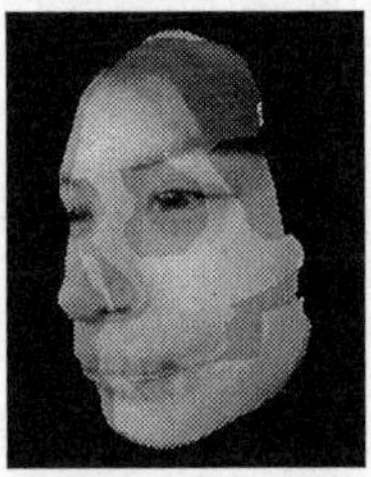

Figure15. 3D view of the result "Patient C" (superimpose)

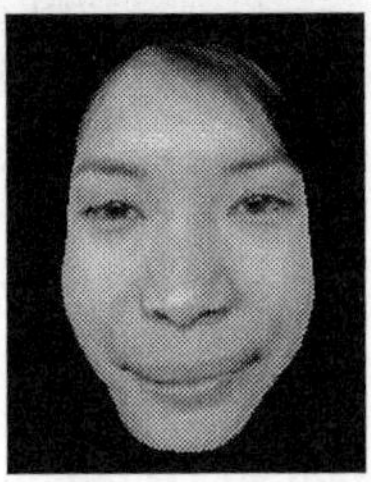

Figure16. "Smiling" face after surgery

8 Conclusion and Future Work

In this paper we proposed a prototype of the facial surgery simulation system for surgical planning and prediction of facial deformation using physics-based human head model. In the experiment, we predicted the 3D facial shape after orthognathic surgery for patients with mandibular prognathism. By comparing the simulation results and the actual postoperative facial images, the proposed method can be proved to be practically useful.

Now we are constructing a more detailed human head model and its application to obtain more accurate and realistic results of surgical simulation. Fig.17 is the prototype of the system that integrates the CT viewer and the surgical simulator. By introducing this system, an effective surgery planning and prediction can be realized for surgeons.

For future works, we should investigate how to fit the parameters of skin and muscles' stiffness for each patient in detail to improve the accuracy of the modeling. In the near future, we attempt to evaluate the difference between predicted results and actual facial shapes quantitatively using 3D-CT or MRI data of patients' head, in order to make the system more practical.

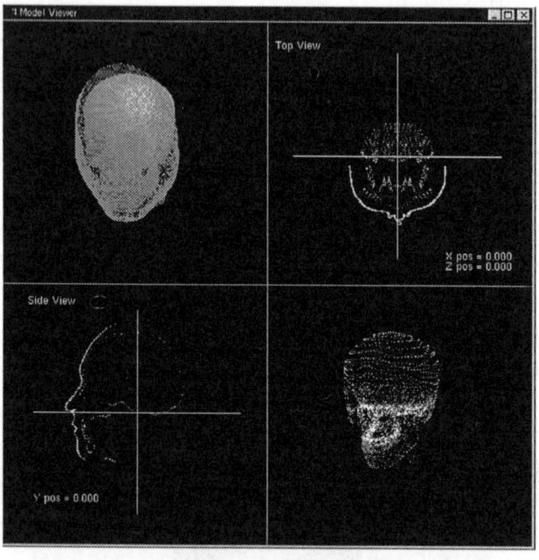

Figure17. The new head model and the simulator

9 Acknowledgement

The authors would like to thank medical Dr. Nagumo for providing the CT scanned data and his effective advice about anatomical issues.

References

1. P.Ekman, W.V.Friesen, "Facial Action Coding System", Consulting Psychologist PressInc, San Francisco, CA 1978.
2. K.Aizawa, H.Harashima, and T.Saito, "Model-based analysis synthesis image coding system for a person's face", Signal Processing: Image Commun., Vol.1, No.2, pp.139-152, 1989.
3. D.Terzopoulos and K.Waters, "Analysis And Synthesis of Facial Image Sequences Using Physical and Anatomical Models", IEEE Trans. on PAMI, Vol.15, No.6, pp.569-579, June 1993.
4. S.Hashimoto, Y.Sato and H.Oda, "Modeification of Facial Expression Using Spring Frame Model", Proceedings of IASTED, pp.9-15, 1989.
5. Y.Aoki, S.Hashimoto, "Physical Modeling of Face Using Spring Frame based on Anatomical data", Proceeding of the 4th International Conference on Multi-Media Modeling, pp.339-354, 1997.
6. Y.Aoki, S.Hashimoto, "Physical Facial Model based on 3D-CT Data for Facial Image Analysis and Synthesis", Third IEEE International Conference on Automatic Face and Gesture Recognition, pp.448-453, 1998.
7. H.Mita, T.Konno, "A Facial Paralysis Simulator for Surgery Planning", Journal of Japan society for Computer Aided Surgery, Vol.4, No.1, pp.1-5, June 1996.
8. R.M.Koch et al, "Simulating Facial Surgery Using Finite Element Models", SIGGRAPH 96 Proceedings, ACM SIGGRAPH, 1996.
9. Y.Lee and D.Terzopoulos et al, "Realistic Modeling for Facial Animation", SIGGRAPH 95 Proceedings, ACM SIGGRAPH, 1995.
10. T.Tobita et al, "A Study on the Generation of Facial Expressions using Time Generation Functions", ITE Vol.52, No.5, pp.757-763, 1998.
11. S.Morishima, T.Ishikawa, and D.Terzopoulos, "Facial Muscle Parameter Decision from 2D Frontal Image", Proceeding of 14th International Conference on Pattern Recognition (ICPR'98), Vol.I, pp.160-162, 1998.
12. K.Waters, "A Physical Model of Facial Tissue and Muscle Articulation Derived from Computer Tomography Data", Proceeding of the Second Conference Visualization in Biomedical Computing, Chapel Hill, N.Carolina, SPIE, Vol.1808, pp.574-583, 1992.
13. W.Lee, P.Kalra, N.M.Thalmann, "Model Based Face Reconstruction for Animation", Proceeding of the 4th International Conference on Multi-Media Modeling, pp.323-338, 1997.
14. V.Blanz, V and T. Vetter, "A Morphable Model for the Synthesis of 3D Faces", ACM SIGGRAPH'99, Computer Graphics, In Press, 1999.

References

1. [illegible] "[illegible]," [illegible] Computer Graphics [illegible]
2. [illegible]
4. [illegible]
5. [illegible]
6. [illegible]
7. [illegible]
10. [illegible] Computer Graphics, Vol. 32, No. [illegible]
11. [illegible]
12. [illegible]
13. [illegible]

MODELING FACIAL EXPRESSIONS BY INTERACTIVE EVOLUTION

H.-F. HEIMBRECHT, G. TROGEMANN
Academy of Media Arts
Department of Computer Science / AV-Media
Peter-Welter-Platz 2
D-50676 Cologne, Germany

E-mail: fh@khm.de, trogemann@khm.de

Artists rarely have a specific goal in mind when they begin modeling 3D shapes and motions. Especially in facial animation for 3D-characters the process of modeling is actually the search for a goal rather than the attainment of one. This type of conceptualizing process is hardly supported by conventional 3D modeling techniques. We present a new way of creating facial expressions for 3D-character animation based on the concept of interactive evolution. Instead of deforming the facial topology directly, the creation process is controlled by mutating and mating computer generated facial motions. The genetic representation is based on Active Lines corresponding to special facial structures. Basic Motions are calculated from the Active Line with the help of a fast non-physical material-function. Facial expressions are animated in realtime by merging Basic Motions.

1 Introduction

In recent years facial animation has become relevant in many different areas, for example in telecommunications, man-machine-interaction and games. But film production and advertising are still the main application areas of facial animation. In these fields two different types of figures have to be distinguished: Virtual Humans and 3D-Characters. The objective in the first case is the realistic modeling and animation of a human actor [12] whereas 3D-characters try to continue the tradition of cartoon animation [11]. In this paper we focus on the problem of facial animation for 3D-characters.

Although character animation does not require realistic behaviour it is nevertheless a difficult task to model convincing expressions for character faces. The reason can be found in special qualities of cartoon faces:

- The faces lack a uniform anatomy. Size, position and shape of typical facial structures vary heavily and often only a small subset of human facial structures is used. In contrast unusual parts of the face (e.g. ears) are often active parts of facial expressions.
- In many cases the face is very flexible and performs unusual motions compared to human faces (e.g. squash and stretch, anticipation, follow

through and exaggeration [11]). Some figures are even morphing between different facial appearances.

- The facial expressions can not be developed isolated from each other, they are closely related forming the personality of the character. Often even the shape of the face is subsequently changed if some expressions did not suit the imagined personality.

Characters do not look and behave like humans but nevertheless show convincing and believable facial expressions. They come to life through animation not through anatomic details and human-like motion. This needs an experienced animator who can control the strong interdependencies of character personality, expressions and facial shape.

Several different facial animation techniques have been developed since the first computer-generated facial model was introduced by Parke in the early 1970s [14]. As stated by Reeves [15] often simple facial models work better for character animation than complex physics-based models (e.g. [13]). Most of the anatomical complexity (bones, muscles, skin, etc.) supported by complex models is not needed in character animation. On the other hand basic cartoon animation rules are often not provided by these techniques because they are counterproductive in animating realistic faces. An example for an sophisticated animation technique supporting dynamic deformation methods for character animation can be found in [4].

Facial motions in simple facial models are often realized as composition of several isolated mesh deformations. These techniques provide total control over every aspect of motion but have a main drawback: The animator has to model the single deformations in full detail. This article deals with a new modeling paradigm trying to overcome this problem. The resulting technique allows a more creative and experimental type of modeling facial expressions. The corresponding prototype complements mesh deformation tools by a more creative sketching-like process.

2 Animation Technique

We use a simple kind of parametrization technique for character animation. In the first step several isolated motions called *Basic Motions* of the face (e.g. raising the left eyebrow) are modelled individually by mesh deformation. Basic Motions can be interpreted as generalized FACS Action Units [7] only describing the isolated deformation without making presuppositions about the anatomy and physiology of the face. Then the facial animation is constructed by defining the extent of each Basic Motion at any point of time and merging all resulting motions. Because our research is concentrated on interactive figures (e.g. co-presenters in TV-shows, Fig. 1) we developed numerical optimiziations of this method which allow a performance-based realtime animation[8] of the character.

The main advantages of this technique are the precise control over any detail of the motion, the integrative description of mimic and gesture and the realtime capabilities. The main drawback is that specifying many isolated facial deformations in full detail is a tedious and time-comsuming task and therefore hinders the creative process. The frog-character in Fig. 1 needs about 50 Basic Motions to perform facial expressions and lip-synchronization in the quality required for TV-shows. Keeping track of all the Basic Expressions interdependently forming the personality of the character therefore turned out to be another problem of this method.

Figure 1: Virtual Character "Frog" co-presenting the weather report in german TV. The character is animated in realtime using the described animation technique (ca. 80 Basic Motions) on a SGI Onyx. The motions are controlled by two actors using tracking devices for the body and data gloves for the face.

3 Modeling revisited

The basic process of our animation method is modeling Basic Motions by creating complex deformations of the facial mesh. Several advanced mesh deformation techniques like free form deformation[17], hierarchical b-splines[9], and constrained optimization modeling [22] have been developed. But in spite of these techniques modeling facial motions turned out to be a very difficult task mainly because of 4 reasons:

- The number of degrees of freedom in interacting with a complex 3D shape moving in 3D space is overwhelming. Especially the 2D projection of the shape and the commonly used devices mouse and keyboard turned out to be crude interfaces for 3D modeling.
- Apart from this problem most modeling tools require special training and knowledge about the used deformation techniques. Often the animator is not concentrated on the actual task of modeling facial expressions but on controlling the modeling technique.
- The most serious problem concerning the modeling process is basically a problem of imagination: The animator has an abstract but ambigous idea of the expression he would like to create. The difficulties in putting this idea into practice are very similar to trying to draw the face of a well-known person. It is easy to imagine the face, it is easy to recognize it, but it is quite difficult to transform the imagination to a real picture by using pencil and paper. It is not even possible to imagine details of the face exactely.
- The problem of developing isolated Basic Motions remains. As mentioned before the interplay of Basic Motions is essential for the personality of the character. A more sketching-like and experimental process is needed in which Basic Motions can be created and refined in parallel.

These problems can not be solved by a single mesh deformation technique but require a new type of modeling process. An interesting approach in this direction is the SKETCH-System [23], which allows to sketch 3D-Scenes in 2D by using a set of predefined gestures. This approach creates an environment for the needed conceptualizing modeling process but is much to imprecise for creating subtle facial motions.

4 Modeling by Evolution

Our aim was the development of a process which allows a more creative and experimental type of modeling facial expressions. It is interesting that artists achieve good results by using a trial and error process. First a rough sketch is generated which is compared to the imagination and then enhanced in several passes of correcting or restoring. The same trial and error process is used by animators when defining Basic Motions. But they have to deal with complex 3D-surfaces moving and deforming in 3D-space. Therefore the modeling interaction is complicated and hinders the creative process.

Artistic work is a highly interactive evolutionary process moving forward and backwards in the attempt to match an ambigous idea. The basic idea of our approach is to make explicit use of the evolutionary aspects of the process. The possibility of generating complex 2D- and 3D-forms by interactive artificial evolution has been demonstrated in several approaches (e.g. [5, 19, 21, 1]). The question is wether it is possible to use an evolutionary process to match a preexisting ambigous idea and wether the achievable quality is sufficient for modeling subtle facial motions.

The evolutionary modeling process performed by the user could be organized as follows:

1. The system generates a couple of random generated facial motions of a given figure and presents them to the user.

2. The user evaluates the generated expressions in 3D by rotating, zooming in details and sliding through time.

3. The user selects the best motions from his point of view and stores them into a population.

4. The user generates new random generated motion, or he decides to let the system mutate a member of the population or to mate two or more members of the population. Afterwards he continues with step 2.

The difference between the manual and the evolutionary modeling process is visualized in Fig. 2. Under the assumption that the process ensures the needed quality and very short response times it should provide the following qualities:

- No knowledge about the underlying mesh or the mesh deformation technique is needed to perform the modeling process. Only evaluation knowledge is required which can easily be provided because humans are specialists in judging facial motions.

- The process can be performed on the level of conceptualizing and ambigous ideas because a wide variety of variations can be generated fast and several ways to realize the idea can be followed simultaneously.

- Because of random factors in the operators there is even a possibility of surprising creative results not imagined by the user before.

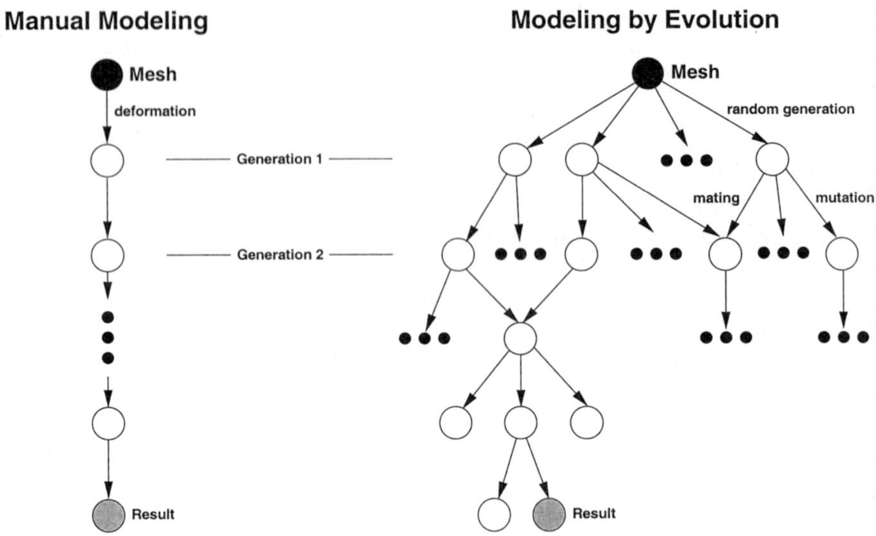

Figure 2: Comparison between the two modeling concepts.

- The system provides a simple interface. Only selecting expressions and choosing between the operators random, mutation and mating is required.

The main technical problem of this approach is the fact that the system has to generate "useful" motions. If the operators mainly produce motions which disrupt facial structures it will be almost impossible to find something good enough to proceed with.

5 Active Lines: Constructing the Search Space

The described paradigm can be interpreted as a type of search process: the user searches for a realization of his idea in the space of program-generated facial motions. The search space and the possibilities of searching are controlled by the definition of the genetic code and the evolutionary operators. In the first step it is therefore essential to identify a suitable search space of the problem. In the following we assume a facial representation of the form

$$G = (V, E), \;\; V \subset \mathbb{R}^3, \;\; E \subset V \times V \tag{1}$$

where G is a connected triangular mesh with a set of surface-points V and a set of edges E. V and E are the results of editing the raw scanning data. Any point of this mesh can move on a *path* defined by a spacecurve of the form

$$p : [0,1] \to \mathbb{R}^3 \;\text{ with }\; p(0) = 0. \tag{2}$$

Therefore a path describes the relative movement of the corresponding point. Let P be the set of all possible paths. A *deformation* of the face is a function assigning a path to every point of the facial representation:

$$d : V \to P \tag{3}$$

Let D_G be the set of all deformations of a given facial representation G. This set also contains a very small subset BAM_G of all reasonable Basic Motions. D_G is therefore a search space of the problem. But D_G is much too great to perform an interactive search and the elements of BAM_G are wide-spread and not analytically extractable. The aim is to find a production system which constructs a subset of D_G as small as possible and containing BAM_G.

To find a suitable production system some knowledge about facial motions is needed. Because of the very convincing results of 2D-character animation we first analysed the mechanisms which are used there. It is obvious that it is possible to sketch convincing facial expressions with only a few special lines. Typical lines are eyebrows, eyelids, lips and cheeks [2]. Other hints for the importance of facial lines can be found in psychology. For example line drawings are often used by psychologists to describe facial expressions (e.g. [6]). An examination of manually constructed Basic Motions shows that animators are using the principle of moving main lines even when modeling exaggerated character-specific 3D-facial motions.

This concept can be formalized by defining the *Active Line* of a facial representation $G = (V, E)$ as the vector $al = (\{v_1, \ldots, v_n\}, \delta)$, where:

[i] $v_i \in V$, $i = 1, \ldots, n$

[ii] $(v_i, v_{i+1}) \in E$, $i = 1, \ldots, n-1$

[iii] $\delta : \{v_1, \ldots, v_n\} \to P$ is the *path distribution function* of the Active Line.

If $v_1 = v_n$ the Active Line is called *closed* otherwise it is called *open*. Some examples of Active Lines are shown in Fig. 3.

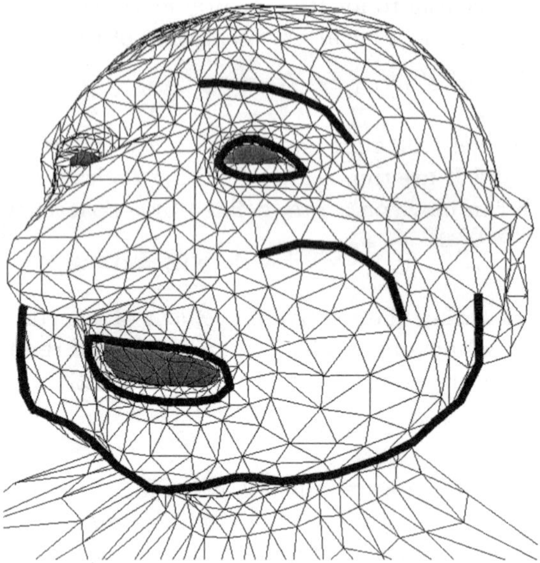

Figure 3: Examples for Active Lines.

6 Mimesys

To demonstrate the usability of the described evolutionary process and the concept of the Active Line we implemented a proof-of-concept prototype called *Mimesys* (Fig. 4) which provides easy user-interaction and a fast visualisation of the created motions.

To realize the prototype three problems had to be solved:

1. The concept of the Active Line has to be coded into a genomic structure.

2. The evolutionary operators of random generation, mutation and mating have to be defined on basis of the genome.

3. A material function has to be defined which is capable of transforming the genotype to the phenotype, i.e. is able to calculate the mesh deformation from the genomic structure.

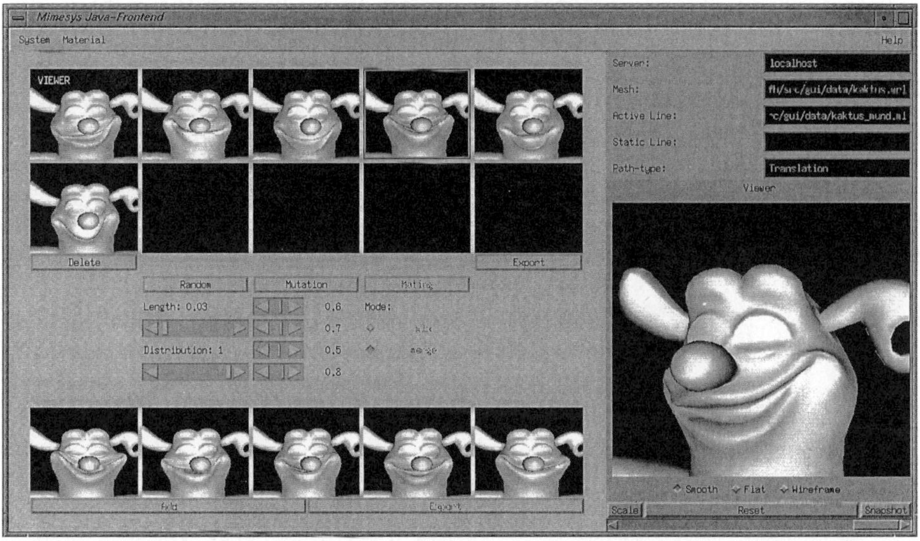

Figure 4: Mimesys-Interface. On the right there is a full 3D-representation of the character to evaluate the quality of a Basic Motion. On the top the current population is visualized, on the bottom descendants after the last operation. The modeling process is performed only by selecting individuals and using the evolutionary operators in the middle.

6.1 Genome

There are several possibilities of coding an Active Line into a genome. A naive approach would take the paths in all points of the Active Line. Because there is no relation between adjacent points this genome would spread out a search space mostly consisting of motions which destruct the facial structure. Therefore it is necessary to define constraints for the motion of adjacent points.

A more detailed examination of Active Lines shows the following properties:

- The line is unfractured and mostly waveless.
- The end parts and the middle part of the line determine the motion.

An ad hoc genome can therefore be constructed by only using the endpoints and the middle point of the line. These points are used afterwards to interpolate the motion of the other points of the line. In the case of open lines the genome therefore consists of the pathes of 3 main points, in the case of closed lines the pathes of 4 main points are used (Fig. 5).

The described structure of the genome has to be filled with suitable representations of the paths. In general any type of spacecurve (e.g. splines) can be used. It turned out that for Basic Motions path-types based on a combination of translations and rotations are sufficient because the motion complexity is achieved by merging several Basic Motions. These types are simple to code in vectors and besides can be efficiently used by the rendering pipeline. A genome for translation paths can for example simply be coded by using the 3 or 4 translation vectors of the main points of the Active Line.

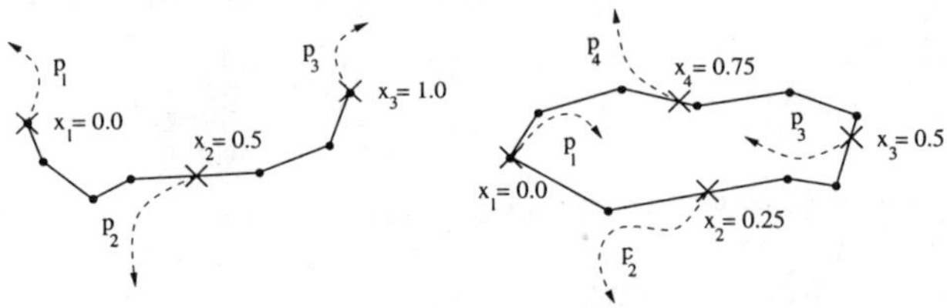

x_1	x_2	x_3
P_1	P_2	P_3

x_1	x_2	x_3	x_4
P_1	P_2	P_3	P_4

Figure 5: Genome for open and closed Active Lines.

6.2 *Operators*

Three important evolutionary operators exist: random generation, mutation and mating.

Random generation: Frequently random generation is implemented by random choice of the genomic values. To get good starting points for the evolutionary process we defined an random operator which produces specific shapes with defined probabilies (e.g. 20% of generated motions are horizontally symmetric - the motion of one end point of the line is mirrored). This shape information is not part of the genome.

Mutation: The mutation operator interprets the user-specified quality as measure for the extent of variation. If the quality is low there has to be a great change in the motion paths. To gain better control over the process different qualities can be specified for the main paths, so that mutation can be constrained to parts of the line.

In the case of translation paths for example the quality affects the mean value of a normal distribution. The value calculated from this normal distribution is used as radius for a sphere around the endpoint of the motion. One point on this sphere is chosen to be the new endpoint of the motion.

Mating: The recombination operator is simply implemented as randomly weighted interpolation between the main paths of the participating Active Lines.

6.3 Material

The Basic Motion of the face has to be calculated from the motion of the Active Line. The physically-based simulation of elasticity leads to differential equations [20] and is therefore too expensive in this case. Because the modeling process is driven by evaluation of motions the system has to produce about 10 Basic Motions per second to maintain an adequate interactivity. As an alternative to simulating elasticity the deformation can be interpreted as an interpolation problem. In the two-dimensional case of image-warping this approach showed good results [16]. In this case the points of the Active Line can be interpreted as isolated data points with values representing the vector of coefficients of the space curve.

$$M = \{(v_i, c_i) \mid v_i \in V,\, c_i \in \mathbb{R}^d,\, i = 1, \ldots, n\} \tag{4}$$

Scattered Data Interpolation Methods can now be used to interpolate each component of the vector of coefficients separately:

$$f_j : \mathbb{R}^3 \to \mathbb{R},\, \forall (v_i, c_i) \in M : f_j(v_i) = c_{i,j}\,,\; j = 1, \ldots, d \tag{5}$$

This is a well-known problem and several techniques have been developed in this area. Because a fast reaction on users input is needed, the Shepard approach seems to be suitable (Shepard 1968). It calculates the values as weighted average of the values at the data points and therefore does not require the solution of equations.

$$f_j(x) = \sum_{i=1}^{n} w_i(x)\lambda_i(x)c_{i,j} \tag{6}$$

The weight function $w_i : \mathbb{R}^3 \to \mathbb{R}$ uses the distances $d_i(x)$ from the given data points v_i:

$$w_i(x) = \frac{\sigma_i(x)}{\sum_{k=1}^{n} \sigma_k(x)} \quad \text{with } \sigma_i(x) = \frac{1}{d_i(x)^{\mu}} \tag{7}$$

The function $\lambda_i : \mathbb{R}^3 \to \mathbb{R}$ is an extension of the Shepard interpolation called *mollifying function*. These functions are used to attenuate the influence of the data points. To get controllable material-like properties we developed an extension of the Franke-Little weights (Franke 1982):

$$\lambda_i(x) = \begin{cases} 1 & \text{if } d_i(x) \le a_i \\ \left(1 - \frac{d_i(x) - a_i}{R - a_i}\right)^{\mu} & \text{if } a_i < d_i(x) \le R \\ 0 & \text{if } d_i(x) > R \end{cases} \quad (8)$$

R directly controls elasticity. With low R the generated visual effect is plastic-like, with higher R it becomes more and more elastic. The elasticity effect of a given R depends directly on the size of the actual figure. To provide a size-independent elasticity parameter e to the user, R is calculated relative to the length d_{max} of the figures bounding box diagonal as $R = e \cdot d_{max}, e \in [0, 1]$. The a_i define the area around the data points in which no attenuation takes place. This avoids peak-like deformations if an isolated point moves very far away from its original position. Therefore the a_i are calculated relative to the distance between the endpoint of the curve and the point v_i.

The distances $d_i(x)$ turned out to be more problematic. Using the surface-distance for $d_i(x)$ results in drawbacks if convex forms are calculated, because nearby points in the volume can be far away on the surface. In contrast space-distance turned out to be problematic with concave forms, because the material effect jumps over the cavity. A very good approximation of the effect of elasticity can be achieved by using the surface-distance in the weight-function and the space-distance in the mollifying function.

Because of the interpolation of coefficent vectors the selection of the representation of the path-type is essential for the visual quality of the material simulation. It turned out that it is sufficient to approximate the paths in the points of the Active Line by simple polylines. The resulting polylines after deformation are used to construct the pathes by interpolation. For more complex path-types other representations might be useful (e.g. using the control points describing a Bézier curve).

7 Experimental Results

Figure 6 shows an example for modeling a Basic Motion with Mimesys. First a set of starting points for the process is generated with the help of the random operator. It often creates directly useable motions. Interesting motions are saved in the population and varied by mutation and mating. Better offsprings are adopted to the population and used as starting points for following generations. Often the process converges and leads to a suitable result after a

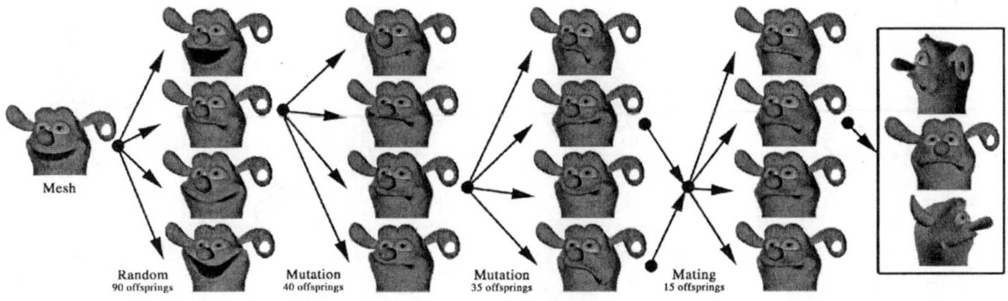

Figure 6: Modeling a Basic Motion in Mimesys. Only chosen examples of each generation are shown.

couple of generations. An extensive application is presented in figure 7. In this example we used an human-like actor to evaluate if our technique is able to produce all important human facial expressions. Fourteen Basic Motions of the eyes, eyebrows, the mouth and the chin have been generated and subsequently combined to facial expressions matching the Hjortsjo scheme[6]. Altogether approximately 500 individuals had to be created to find these Basic Motions by using the described operators.

The process itself shows the expected behaviour. It is possible to produce a wide variety of motions in a fast and easy way and to focus the process in a direction when the imagined expression substantiates. In several cases the system even produced surprising unexpected motions which can be stored and improved in parallel. The effectivity of the process depends strongly on the number of generations needed to get an acceptable result. Because the animator chooses the parent and the operator and controls the variation by constraints his experience is still an important factor in the process. But in contrast to conventional modeling the necessary experience is located at the level of evaluating, combining and varying whole facial motions.

The quality of the evolved Basic Motions is at the level of intermediate results of the modeling process which have to be enhanced manually to satisfy the quality demands of an experienced animator. These small enhancements can also be done by evolution, but the process is ineffective in this case, because a very high number of offsprings has to be generated. At this point of the process the animator knows his aim exactly but it becomes more and more difficult for him to evaluate if a small variation is an improvement. Additionally choosing parameters for constraining the variations becomes harder. These effects result in a loss of convergence and therefore in an increasing amount of time needed for small enhancements.

Figure 7: Evolved Hjortsjo scheme (angry, happy, self-satisfied, sad, sceptic, frightened, condescending, disgusted).

8 Conclusions

It is possible to enhance the process of modeling Basic Motions by using interactive evolution based on the concept of Active Lines. The approach leads to the required conzeptualizing modeling process. But the process is ineffective in doing fine adaptions or if the user exactly knows how defined points should move. The quality of the evolved motions is not fully satisfying at the moment because it is constrained by the ad hoc defined genomic structure. Several more sophisticated possibilities of coding an Active Line into the genome will be examined and evaluated. The described approach is capable of complementing mesh deformation tools by a creative sketching-like process. The integration of the process in a powerful modeling environment (e.g. as a plugin for Alias/Wavefront Maya) in which manual adaptions and conceptualizing can be performed in parallel will be the next step in development.

References

1. E. Baker and M. Seltzer, "Evolving Line Drawings", Graphics Interface '94, pp. 91-100, 1994.
2. P.Blair, "Cartoon Animation", Walter Foster Publishing, Laguna Hills, 1994.
3. O. Bunsen and G. Fleischmann, "Mesh Optimization for Animation Purposes", In: Deussen O, Lorenz P (eds) Simulation and Animation '97, Society for Computer Simulation International, 1997.
4. J. Chadwick, D. Haumann, R. Parent, "Layered Construction for Deformable Animated Characters", Proc. Siggraph'89 Conference, Boston, pp 243–252, 1989.
5. R. Dawkins, "The Blind Watchmaker", W.W. Norton, New York/London, 1987.
6. I. Eible-Eibesfeldt, "Similarities and Differences between Cultures in cx pressive Movements", In: Nonverbal Communication, Cambridge University Press, 1972.
7. P. Ekman and W. Friesen, "Facial Action Coding System", Consulting Psychologists Press, Palo Alto, 1978.
8. G. Fleischmann, R. Opalla R, A. Mähler, "Real Time Animation of 3D Characters", Proceedings of the 96 European SMPTE conference on Imaging Media, Cologne, 1996.
9. D. R. Forsey and R. H. Bartels, "Hierarchical B-Spline refinement", Computer Graphics, 22(4):205-296, 1988.
10. R. Franke, "Scattered data interpolation: Test of some methods", Mathematics of Computation, 38:181-200, 1982.
11. J. Lasseter, "Principles of Traditional Animation Applied to 3D Computer Animation", Computer Graphics, 21(4):35–44, 1987.
12. W. Lee, N. Magnenat-Thalmann, "From Real Faces To Virtual Faces: Problems and Solutions", Proc. 3IA'98, Limoges, 1998.
13. Y. Lee, D. Terzopoulos, K. Waters, "Realistic modeling for facial animation", Proc. Siggraph'95 Conference, Los Angeles, pp 55–62, 1995.
14. F. Parke, "Computer generated animation of faces", Masters thesis, University of Utah, Salt Lake City, UTEC-Csc-72-120, 1972.
15. W. T. Reeves, "Simple and complex facial animation: Case studies", SIGGRAPH 1990, Course Notes 26, 1990.
16. D. Ruprecht, H. Müller, "Free Form Deformation with Scattered Data Interpolation Methods", In: Geometric Modeling, Springer, Berlin Heidelberg New York, pp 267–281, 1993.

17. T. W. Sederberg and S. R. Parry, "Free-Form Deformation of Solid Geometric Models", Proc. SIGGRAPH 86, 20(4):151-160, 1986.
18. D. Shepard, "A two dimensional interpolation function for irregular spaced data", Proceedings 23rd. ACM National conference, pp 517–524, 1968.
19. K. Sims, "Artificial Evolution for Computer Graphics", Computer Graphics (Siggraph '91 proceedings), 25(4):319-328, 1991.
20. D. Terzopoulos, A. Platt, J. Barr, K. Fleischer, "Elastically deformable models", Computer Graphics, 21(4):205-214, 1987.
21. S. Todd and W. Latham, "Evolutionary Art and Computers", Academic Press, London, 1992.
22. W. Welch and A. Witkin, "Variational Surface Modeling", Proc. SIGGRAPH 92, 26(2):157-166, 1992.
23. R. C. Zelesnik, K. P. Herndon, J. F. Hughes, "SKETCH: An Interface for Sketching 3D Scenes", Proc. SIGGRAPH 96, pp. 163-170, 1996.

3-D HUMAN FACE RECONSTRUCTION AND ANIMATION FOR CHINESE SPEECH TRAINING IN ORAL DEAF EDUCATION

XIAODONG JIANG, QINGHUA QIANG, JIAYUE ZHU

Department of Computer Science, Nanjing University, Nanjing, Jiangsu 210093
USA
E-mail: xdjiang@public1.ptt.js.cn

In this paper, we focus on developing new techniques in model-based reconstruction of a human face which can be animated in real time using both video and audio inputs. We mainly deal with three issues in this paper: (1) a new semiautomatic method to reconstruct 3D facial model from three pictures (one front and two side views, the front and each side view are orthogonal) using our Contractive Deformation Model; (2) a new multi-directional technique for texture mapping; (3) the animation of the new constructed face using both video and audio inputs. Our system is part of the effort in developing STODE, an embodied conversational agent for Chinese speech training for children with prelingual deafness together with Nanjing Oral School under grants from National Natural Science Foundation of China. It allows integration of audio and video inputs and produces a synchronized visual and acoustic output in real time to help the deaf children overcome two major difficulties in speech learning: the confusion of different phonemes and timing within different words and syllables.

1 Introduction

The deaf people in China constitutes more than 0.5% of the entire population, i.e., more than 60 million Chinese are profoundly deaf. Statistics also show that may of them have been prelingual deaf. The overriding consequence of prelingual deafness is a dramatically lessened ability to acquire language at a rate and level that is consistent with the expectations and demands of society. It has long been agreed upon that the communication and academic learning demands placed on deaf children in school require small class size and intensive one-to-one instruction. Unfortunately, the cost of resources and energy makes it impractical, if not impossible, for such instruction to be offered to the vast majority of deaf children in China.

The recent developments in interactive technologies have offered a very promising and cost-effective way of increasing the quality of education for deaf children, particularly as it pertains to developing and refining spoken communication skills. In cooperation with teachers from Nanjing Oral School, we are developing an embodied conversational agent STODE to improve the speaking ability of prelingual deaf children. STODE assists the children in combating two major difficulties in speech learning: confusion of different phonemes and timing within different words and syllables. Consider the following scenario for a speech training process:

A hearing impaired child sits in front of a computer when a synthetic character STODE tracks the moving features of his face through a desk-mounted camera. He indicates to STODE which word he wishes to learn. STODE then displays a 3D cloning of the child's face which is animated in real time. This cloned face articulates the word with correct lip motions and timing of speech. The child imitates the facial and lip motions of the cloned face and reads out the word to STODE, who carefully collects both the video and audio of his visual speech. After analyzing the speech timing and lip motion of the child, cloned face is employed to replay the visual speech of the child according to the video and audio collected and emphasize the facial and lip motion that is wrong. The cloned face also produces a synthesized corrected visual and acoustic output to the child.

Three major technical challenges arise from the scenario: (1) how to transform a standard synthetic head to fit the geometric characteristics of a real child's head ; (2) how to map the texture picture of the real face image to the generic deformed face; (3) how to animate the new constructed face using both video and audio input in real time. To address these issues, we have presented our approach to clone a real face using pictures taken from three views (one front and two sides). We first detect predefined feature points on pictures and modify a generic 3D head model with corresponding texture mapping. We discuss both the interactive and automatic way for feature detection and propose a new semiautomatic method to combine benefits of both while avoiding their drawbacks. Then we present a way to modify the generic head smoothly using our Contractive Deformation technique. Our method of multi-directional texture-mapping using projection is also provided. In section 5, we discuss the underlying animation mechanism in our system using both video and audio input.

2 System Overview

The overall flow of our system for face model reconstruction and face animation is illustrated in Figure 1. At a high level. our system could be partitioned into three modules: the Model Reconstruction Module (MRM) , the Texture Mapping Module (TMM) and the Face Animation Module (FAM).

The Model Reconstruction Module (MRM) involves fitting the generic model to the specific model of the real face. It take as input three face pictures in neutral expression (one front and two side views) at the maximum resolution and could be partitioned into three consecutive stages: (1) the Initialization stage which makes the head magnitude of side and front views same; (2) the Feature Detection stage which performs feature points extraction with a interface for interactive correction when needed; (3) Generic Model Deformation stage which calculate displacement of non-feature points related to detected feature points in stage (2) using our Contractive Deformation technique.

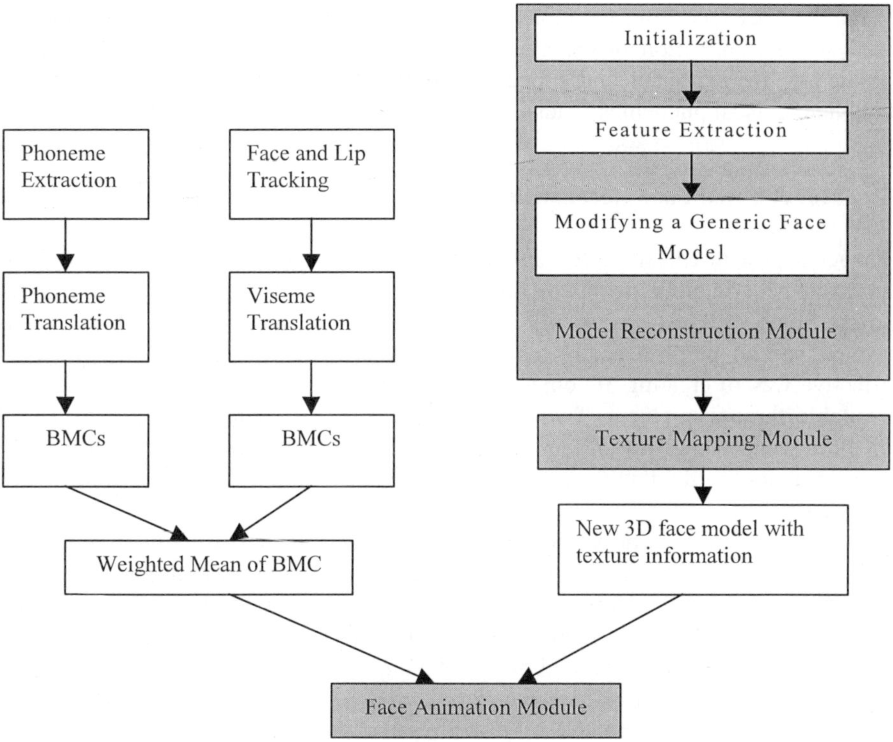

Figure 1. Overall Flow of the System

The goal of Texture Mapping Module (TMM) is to map the texture picture of the real face image to the generic deformed face. And the general idea is to have a corresponding 2D coordinates on the picture for every point of the frontal and side parts of the 3D generic model. To avoid possible texture distortion due to changes in perspective, we have developed a multi-directional texture mapping techniques which utilizes texture information in pictures from both the front and side views.

The Face Animation Module (FAM) extracts and processes information to drive the animation of the new constructed face. The video input from a desk-mounted camera provides sequence of images which are digitized to perform motion capture and generation for the face, which involves detection and tracking of moving features of the face from the images. This motion provides, after interpretation and analysis, the animation of the synthetic 3D face model. Similarly, the individual phonemes are extracted and processed from the audio input and translated into equivalent visual phonemes (facial and lip motions synchronized with speech).

3 Model-based Face Reconstruction

To get a structured shape for animation, the most typical way is to modify an available generic model with structured information such as eyes, lips, nose, hair and so on. Some methods employ 3D digitization to get a range data, but they usually require special purpose costly hardware such as laser scanners. So a more cost-effective way of creating 3D objects is reconstruction from 2D information, usually available through pictures. Two common methods are an interactive deformation method which modifies or generates a surface employing deformation, and a reconstruction method with feature points which modifies a generic model after feature detection.

The interactive deformation method utilizes an interactive editor to generate a polygon mesh for specific face modeling. As is common in most graphics software, the user creates primitives, selects objects and performs various deformation operations on them. This method is easy to understand but laborious to fulfill. Besides, it cannot guarantee to eliminate the imprecisions in the resulting model due to inadvertant mistakes made by user.

The reconstruction method is a faster method. Here, a 3D generic face model is constructed in advance, and feature points are detected automatically on several images from different views. Other points on the generic model are modified using a certain deformation technique. Then 3D points are calculated by just combining several 2D coordinates. This method is totally automatic, but the automatic feature extraction often cannot guarantee a detailed description of certain parts which are of central interest (e.g. lips and eyes). Besides, automatic feature detection is sensitive to the quality of images and is not always robust, so imprecision also arises due to the presence of noise in the images.

To combine their benefits and avoid their drawbacks, we have employed a semi-automatic approach to reconstruct a real face from three views. In the stage of feature extraction, only some most prominent feature points are extracted, they are the most characteristic points to recognize people and can be detected from front and side views. And other less prominent feature points can be interactively aligned with features in the image. The non feature points on the face mesh can be modified by using our Contractive Deformation technique. The model reconstruction take as input three face pictures in neutral expression (one front and two side views) at the maximum resolution and could be partitioned into three consecutive stages: (1) the Initialization stage; (2) the Feature Detection stage; (3) Generic Model Deformation stage, which are discussed in detail below.

3.1 Initialization Stage

The task of the Initialization Stage is aligning the scales of the three side and front views and matching with the corresponding points in the resulting framework. It performs transformation (scaling, rotation and translation) to overlay the framework on the pictures.

3.2 Feature Detection Stage

In the Feature Detection Stage, some most prominent feature points are extracted automatically with possible interactive correction if necessary. These feature points are most characteristic points to recognize people, which include hair outline, chin outline, ears, eyes, eyebrows, nose and lips. For detection of these feature points, we have used the active contour method developed by Kass etc. to fit the boundary points of maximum contrast in the images close to the predefined rough contour on the generic face model. When this technique is not robust enough and fails to give precise edge detection, we can move a few points interactively to the corresponding position to make corrections. Also, some less prominent feature points that are hard to detect can also be anchored interactively. Figure 3 shows the result for chin boundary detection after using the active contour method.

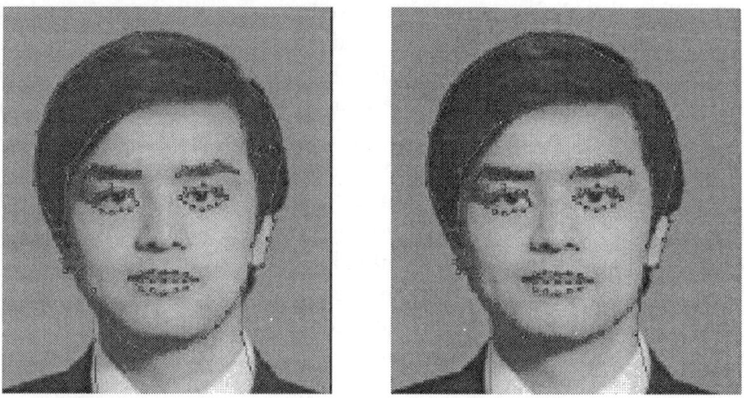

(a) (b)

Figure 2. Result for chin boundary detection using active contour method without interactive modification (a) and with interactive modification (b)

3.3 Generic Model Deformation Stage

After all feature points have been extracted and corrected, we can calculate the 3D coordinates of feature points from three 2D points on framework with predefined relations between points on the front view and two side views. Then we can modify non-feature points with certain deformation techniques. Here we use our Contractive Deformation Model to move other points according to the feature points.

3.3.1 Contractive Deformation Model

Traditional approaches to calculate displacement of non-feature points to the detected feature points have employed extensively linear interpolation which can give smooth result for the surface. The major drawback of these techniques is that local deformations in order to align specific facial features are not possible since any the movement of any single feature point will inevitably affect all other points on the face mesh by recalculating the deformation matrix. To avoid this drawback, we have proposed a new Contractive Deformation Model. The details of this Contractive Deformation Model is discussed below.

Suppose P(x,y,z) is one of the feature points on the face mesh and to be moved to a new coordinate (x', y', z'). After this movement, all other points on the face mesh can be classified into two categories: the Affected Points and the Unaffected Points. The Affected Points are those points whose positions have to be moved because of the movement of feature point P and Unaffected Points are all others on the face mesh. The determination of the Affected and Unaffected Points of a feature point P when it is moved will be based on investigations into the muscle activity of human faces. In our contractive deformation model, we have simplified this issue by taking as Affected Points all those points whose distance from P is within a certain threshold range. And this threshold is usually obtained through empirical studies.

Suppose Pa is one of the Affected Points of P and is adjacent to points P1, P2, ... , Pk. After the movement of P, Pa has to be moved because it's one of P's Affected Points. And all its adjacent points P1 ,..., Pk also have to be moved accordingly. We first assume that all points on the face mesh are connected by spring mass and are in the state of equilibrium before the movement of P. And it is intuitively justified that the face mesh should also be in the state of equilibrium after the movement. By assuming that human face is contractive in nature, i.e., all adjacent points of Pa tend to position as close to Pa as possible so long as the whole face mesh is still in the state of equilibrium, we have come to the following equation for Pa :

$$\partial \sum (\| P_i^{'} - P_a^{'} \|)^2 \Big/ \partial P_a^{'} = 0$$

Here is where the surprise comes! Previous spring-mass models generally require finding solutions for a large array of non-linear equations. It is usually computationally costly and the instability of its solution space often produces deformation effects that are undesirable. By using our contractive model, we have successfully reduced this task to finding solutions for some simple linear equations and avoided both computational inefficiency and distorted modeling caused by instability of the solution space of non-linear equations.

3.3.2 Steps in Modifying Generic Model

The process of modifying generic face model to align with feature points detected using our contractive deformation model is:

1. Apply global transformations to bring detected feature points to generic model's 3D space. These transformations involve mainly scaling and translation.
2. Apply the Contractive Deformation technique on the points of the generic face. Since the Contractive Deformation Model is suitable for performing local modification, we can also perform fine-grained alignment of some feature points without affecting other points outside their range of influence.

Figure 3 shows the result of modifying the generic model by applying Contractive Deformation Model.

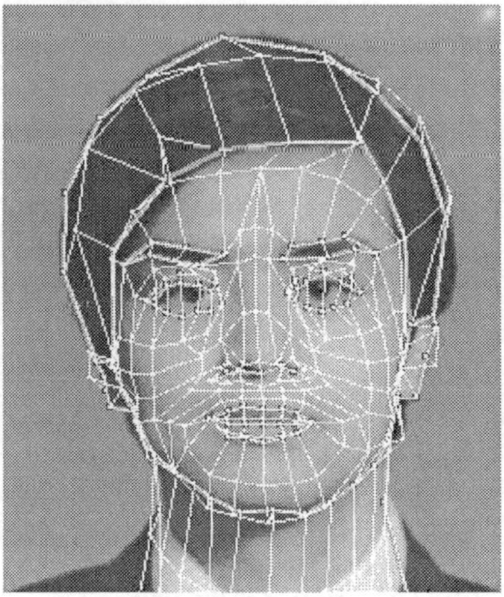

Figure 3. Result of modifying the generic model by applying Contractive Deformation

4 Multi-directional Texture Mapping

The input to the Texture Mapping Module (TMM) are pictures from both one front and two side views and the 2D coordinates of the feature points. The texture mapping process produces a face with all its points having texture coordinates. To avoid possible texture distortion when viewed from a different perspective, which often occurs with traditional texture mapping techniques, we have proposed a mulitdirectional texture technique. The whole process can be partitioned into the following consecutive steps:

1. Projection of a certain 3D point P on the face mesh onto a 2D plane.
2. Determine the angle between the normal vector on the face mesh at P and the Y-Z plane.
3. If the angle calculated above is within the range of (-45, 45), then we use the front picture to find the corresponding location of the projected point on it. If the angle is within [-90, -45), then the left side picture is used, otherwise the right side picture is used.
4. To ensure a smooth texture transition, we use interpolation to re-compute the texture information on the boundary between the three.

Figure 4 shows the result of the constructed face after applying multi-directional texture mapping.

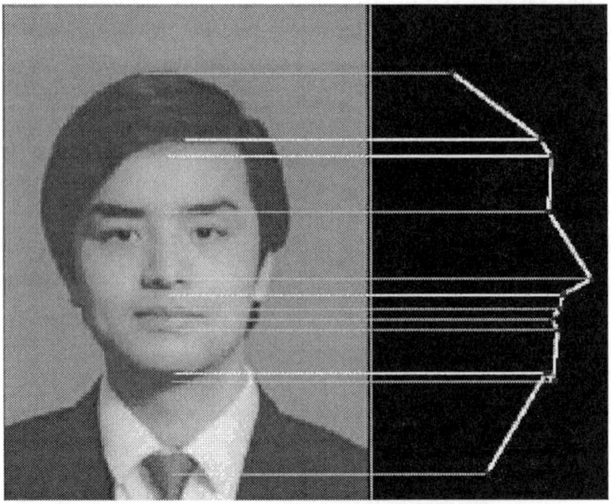

Figure 4. Result of the constructed face after texture mapping

5 Real-time Animation

The generic face model is an irregular structure defined as a polygonal mesh. We have applied Contractive Deformation and multi-directional model to the generic model to reconstruct a new model based on a specific human face. This has not changed the underlying structure, but the resulting new face is now ready to be animated. At the lowest level, facial animation is performed by employing a series of Basic Motion Components (BMCs) to simulate muscle movement.

Since our goal in reconstructing the child's face is to replay the visual speech of the child according to the video and audio collected and emphasize the facial and lip motion that is wrong, it is important to animate the synthetic face according to the facial features of the child tracked and captured. These features are tracked for use as the fundamental motion parameters in animation. The Basic Motion Components (BMCs) are driven by both audio and video input. After analyzing the input audio and video, the audio and visual phonemes are then translated into a set of BMCs in each frame for animation. It is obvious that BMCs translated from audio and visual phonemes play different roles in animating different parts of the face. As far as speech training is concerned, the animation of lip motion should consider more of the audio input, while the facial expression animation should attach more importance to visual input. So the basic conjecture here is that the final BMC should be a weighted mean of the BMC pair translated from audio and visual phonemes. However, the exact method is still under development and experiments.

6 Conclusion

In this paper, we have developed a series of new techniques in model-based reconstruction of a human face which can be animated in real time using both video and audio inputs. We have developed a new semiautomatic method to reconstruct 3D facial model from three pictures (one front and two side views, the front and each side view are orthogonal) based on our Contractive Deformation Model. We have also proposed a new multi-directional technique for texture mapping to avoid possible texture distortion when viewed from different perspectives. Finally, we give a brief overview of the animation for the new constructed face in our system using both video and audio inputs, which is still under development. Our system has been successfully used in developing STODE, an embodied conversational agent for Chinese speech training for children with prelingual deafness together with Nanjing Oral School under grants from National Natural Science Foundation of China. Initial experiments have shown that it has provided a cost-effective way to improve the quality of speech and language training for oral deaf children. We will continue to improve and refine our techniques and apply them to other contexts in the future, such as the foreign language training for normal people.

7 Acknowledgements

Support for this work has come from National Natural Science Foundation of China. We are also deeply indebted to the efforts and participation of teachers and students from Nanjing Oral School.

References

1. Parke FI (1972) Computer Generated Animation of Faces, Proc. ACM National Conference, No 1, pp. 451-457
2. Kalra (1993) An Interactive Multimodal Facial Animation System, Ph.D. Thesis Ecole Polytechnique Federale de Lausanne
3. Reinders M J T, Sankur B, van der Lubbe J C A. Facial Feature and localization and adaptation of a generic face model for model-based coding.
4. Patel M, Willis P J. (1991) Faces: facial animation, construction and editing system. In: Proc Eurographics, Vienna, Austria, 33-45
5. Loop C. (1994) Smooth spline surface over irregular mesh . In Proc Computer Graphics Annual Conference Series, Orlando. 303-310
6. Yuencheng Lee, Demetri Terzopoulos, and Keith Waters,(1996) Realistic Modeling for Facial Animation, In Computer Graphics (Proc. SIGGRAPH), 55-62
7. L. Moccozetm, N. Magnenat-Thalmann (1997) Dirichlet Free-Form Deformations and their Application to Hand Simulation, To appear in IEEE Computer Animation'97.
8. Apostolos Lerios, Chase D Garfinkle, Marc Levoy,(1995) Feature-Based Volume Metamorphosis, In Computer Graphics (Proc. SIGGRAPH), pp. 55-62
9. P.Fua and Y.G. Leclerc,(1996) Taking Advantage of Image-Based and Geometry-Based Constraints to Recover 3D Surfaces, Computer Vision and Image Understanding, 64(1):111-127

A MINIMALIST APPROACH TO FACIAL RECONSTRUCTION

M. GOTLA AND Z. HUANG
Department of Computer Science, School of Computing
National University of Singapore, Singapore 119260
E-mail: meherzad, huangzy@comp.nus.edu.sg

We propose a minimalist approach to 3D facial reconstruction. By applying cognitive and anatomical heuristics, we show that a realistic face model can be reconstructed from a generic face model using only two real facial images and minimal user interaction. There is no need for camera calibration. The method is very suitable to rapidly customize face models used as avatars in VR walk-through applications.

1 Introduction

Much work has already been done in the area of facial reconstruction [14, 17, 22, 10, 8, 11, 3, 12, 4, 6, *and* 16]. An excellent summary of the techniques used in facial reconstruction and animation can be found in [15]. However, most work emphasizes photo realistic quality that requires extensive input, a large number of sample points, and intensive user interaction.

Cognitive psychologists have demonstrated, through phenomena such as the differential inversion and the caricature advantage (Figure 2)[21], that humans appear to pay special attention to contours of facial features such as the eyes, lips, etc.(Figure 1). These are believed to form the dimensions of face space [7]. The dimensions of the face space are not formally known. "Common-looking" faces are closer to a generic face, which forms the face-space origin, while distinctive faces that are easily recognized are sparse points away from the origin. These two observed phenomena seem to corroborate this theory and provide for us a direction for our solution.

Work of cognitive psychologists inspires our solution:

1. As demonstrated by the differential inversion effect, humans process some parts of the face better than others. Obvious indicators like the eyes, mouth etc. should therefore be dealt with in greater detail.

2. The fact that humans can recognize people from just pencil sketches implies that complex texture information, while helpful, is not essential in recognizing faces. It appears that humans seem to pay special attention to the contours of facial features. Therefore, deforming the contours of a

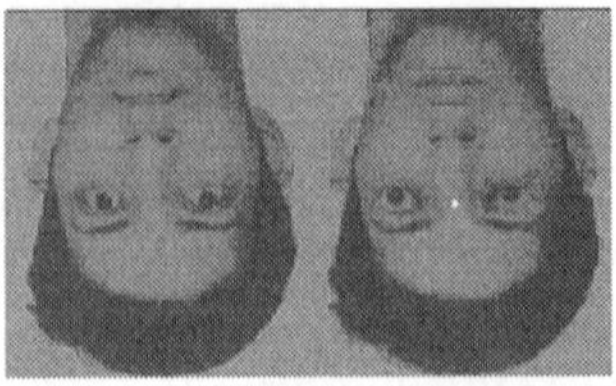

Figure 1. The eyes and mouth of the image on the right have been inverted. At a first glance, both images appear the same and everything seems normal. However, if the page is turned upside down, the grotesqueness of the image on the right becomes apparent immediately.

Figure 2. The caricatured images in the third row are more recognizable than the veridical images in the second row. Reproduced with publisher's permission.

generic face model could be a good way to reconstruct the face.

3. In addition, the caricature advantage suggests that we could potentially increase the cognitive appeal of our output by exaggerating deformations from a generic face, possibly by a low to medium degree.

We propose a minimalist approach to 3D facial reconstruction. Our goal is to minimize the quantity and quality requirement of input and human interaction while still maintaining quality of result that is good enough for human perception. The main idea is to apply cognitive and anatomical heuristics to the algorithm. We focus only on those aspects of the face, which are cognitively significant. In addition, our solution's feature extraction component takes advantage of anatomical expertise in the form of redundancies in the human face to help to trace the features of interest. This expertise is primarily in the form of rules that all human faces conform to and have been compiled in [15].

From our knowledge, all reconstruction frameworks using images need camera calibration. It is a very tedious process though significant progress has been made on techniques of self-calibration in computer vision society [18].

We can avoid the camera calibration process. We do not try to reconstruct face features precisely. Instead, we only want to get them approximately so that the resulting face is good enough for human perception. We found that we do not need the exact camera parameters. In our reconstruction solution, only two facial images from two special camera poses are used as input - a front and a profile view. Thus, we can estimate the camera position and orientation. From our experiments the reconstruction results are still acceptable, even when these two images are not taken exactly from the front and side views.

The most relevant work to ours is [12]. We follow the same trend towards automatic reconstruction. The major difference is that we introduce cognitive and anatomical heuristics into processes of feature extraction and deformation. By doing this, we can segment the extraction and deformation to multi-processes with each sub-process working on its own important feature of face model. The accuracy and efficiency of algorithm have been improved.

2 The Solution

Our solution consists of three steps - feature extraction, 3D deformation, and texture mapping (Figure 3). We apply cognitive and anatomical heuristics in feature extraction and deformation. Texture mapping is used to enhance the final results.

2.1 Feature Extraction

The function of this process is to obtain cognitively significant features represented by contours of the face space dimensions - e.g., the eyes, lips, etc. We do this by the technique of Hierarchical Deformable Templates (HDTs) which is an extension of the snake method introduced by [9]. An HDT represents hierarchically encoded anatomical expertise to help finding the cognitively significant features. Essentially, this involves taking a pre-defined face tem-

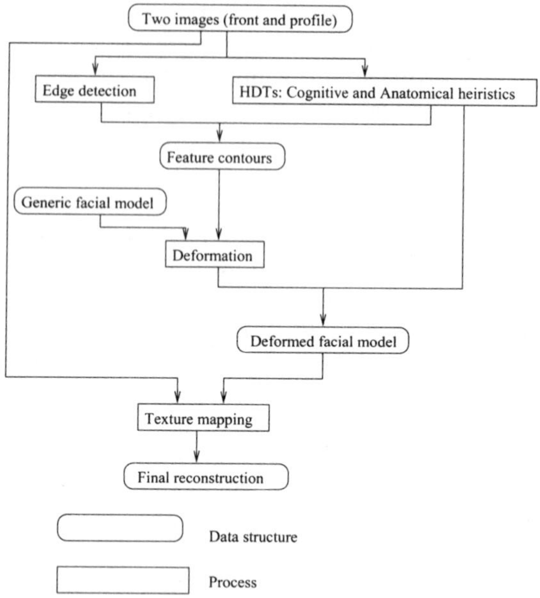

Figure 3. Function model of reconstruction process.

plate containing contours of a generic face model and allowing these contours to be deformed by facial images in a constrained fashion. These constraints are represented in a hierarchical manner and codify the anatomical expertise required to constrain the search space for individual contours.

An HDT consists of the following:

1. Child templates which are either templates or snakes (base case).

2. Approximate relative locations of these templates

3. Approximate relative size of these templates

4. Rules that its children obey.

5. References to the feature-rings of 3D generic face model.

A snake is an energy-minimizing spline guided by external constraint forces and influenced by image forces that pull it toward features such as lines and edges. The name "snake" comes from the appearance of these splines

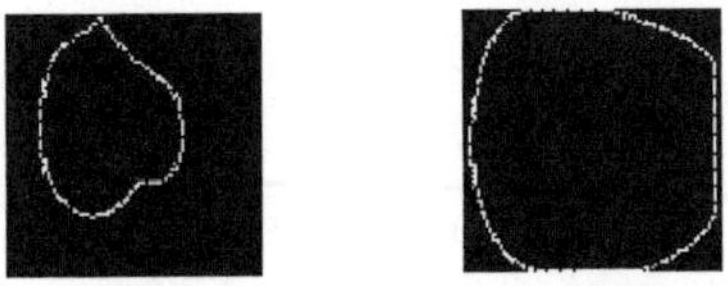

Figure 4. The illustration of snake behavior.

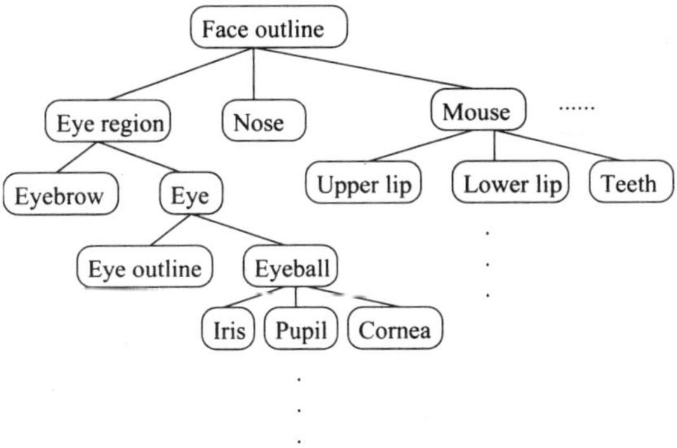

Figure 5. A top-down extraction of facial features.

to "slither" during the energy-minimization stage. The energy-minimization concept is borrowed from the classical physics. In mechanics, a ball released from a height will tend to lose energy and fall to a lower potential. In thermodynamics, a heated object will have a tendency to lose energy to its surroundings. These concepts transform readily to image processing when one views an image as a "terrain" of gradients with sharp edges acting as "cliffs". Edges can then simply be found by letting objects "fall off" these cliffs (Figure 4).

A top-down approach is used to extract the facial contours (Figure 5). First a face outline template finds the approximate location of the face. It then enforces approximate feature locations for the eyes, for instance, which are the child nodes of the face HDT. Finally the third level HDTs enforce their own set of constraints on its own children, e.g., the eye HDT enforces its set of constraints on the eye-ball (pupil, cornea, and iris) and eyelid.

For each image, we use a separate HDT to extract its contours in 2D. The results of this process are then used to deform the generic 3D model in next step.

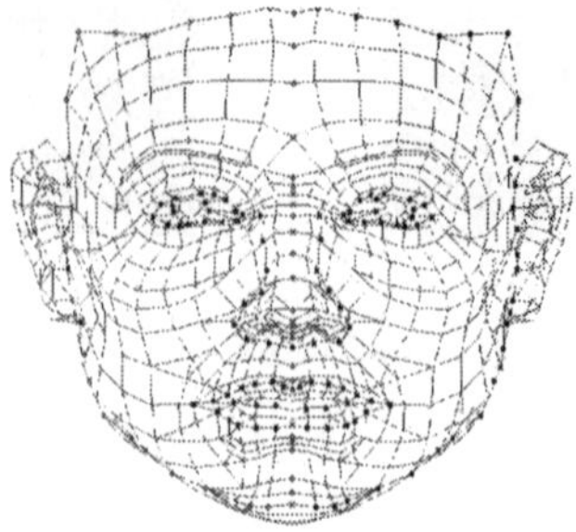

Figure 6. The front view feature-rings in a generic face model. The feature-rings are shown with highlighted points.

2.2 3D Deformation

A common technique in reconstructing the 3D structure of the face is to deform a generic 3D face instead of recreating the model from scratch (e.g. using Cyberware scanners [2]). A very general approach is Free Form Deformation (FFD) introduced by [20] that instead of deforming the object directly, the object is embedded in a space, i.e., FFD block, that is then deformed. The recent progress is the Dirichlet Free-Form Deformation (DFFD) that the FFD block is generalized by using the Voronoi diagrams [13].

Most prior work of facial reconstruction deforms the generic face using structural information derived from photogrammetric techniques. We introduce cognitive and anatomical heuristics to deformation in our approach. We pre-define a feature-ring of vertices for each facial feature on the generic face model corresponding to those extracted by HDTs in the extraction phase (see highlighted vertices in Figure 6). These features represent the most cognitively significant parts of the face. Each of these features is then deformed using the same snake-based technique to match the derived contours. The rest of the face is deformed by interpolation based on their locations relative to the feature vertices of the feature-ring.

We perform a two-stage deformation on the generic face, once for each image. We first take the front view and deform the features that reside on the XY plane with contours obtained from the front view image. After this, we deform the features that lie on the YZ plane using the contours obtained from the profile image.

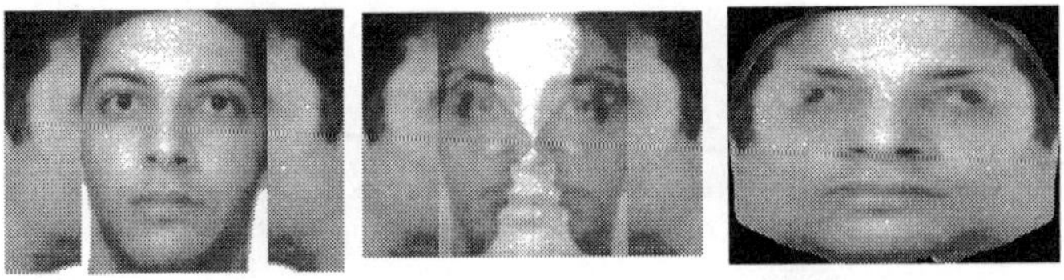

Figure 7. The process to derive a texture map from two input images.

2.3 Texture Mapping

To provide additional realism, we texture-map the two original images onto the deformed model. We blend these two images to get a texture map (Figure 7). We use a very simple inverse-distance blending function - i.e. on the final texture map, the contribution of the front image decreases in the direction away from the center while that of the profile image increases correspondingly. After creating the texture map in this manner, we project the texture map to the 3D model by using a cylinder.

3 Sample Results

A sample result is shown on the next page. Input is shown in Figure 8: two real facial images and a generic 3D face model. In Figure 9, the reconstruction results of the top row are obtained using only one image - the front view of the face. The results in bottom row are obtained using two images - front and profile. The 3D features are better reconstructed using two images. But if only the front view image is available for a face, e.g., from a web page, ID or passport photo, the 3D-reconstruction result is still very distinguishable.

However, because we use a very simple blending function for texture mapping as described in Section 2.3, sometimes the derived texture map has discontinuity (see the texture map in the top right image of Figure 10). This results in artifacts in the reconstructed 3D face.

4 Implementation

Our prototype system is implemented on PC, Windows NT 4.0 using Microsoft Visual C++ 5.0, CosmoPlayer VRML plug-in, Microsoft Vision SDK 1.0, ImageMagick DLLs, and OpenGL.

We choose the (Virtual Reality Modeling Language) VRML 2.0 standard to represent our 3D objects because it is a de-facto standard. We use Mi-

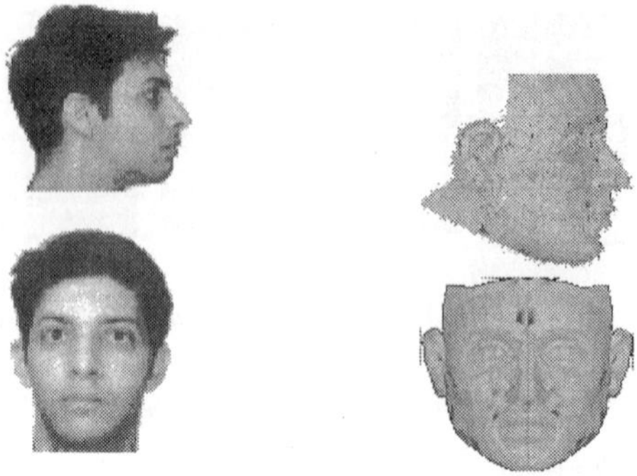

Figure 8. Two images of the first author's face (left) used as input and a generic face model (right).

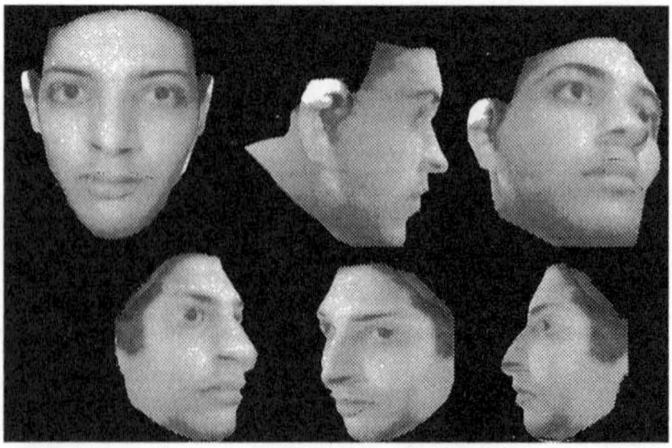

Figure 9. The reconstruction results using one image (top) and two images (bottom) after texture mapping.

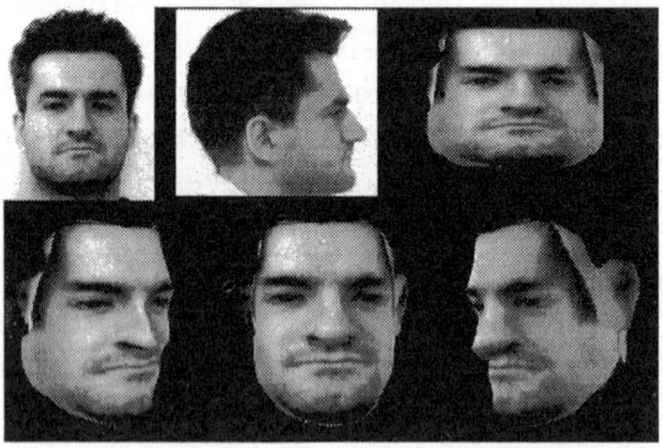

Figure 10. The reconstruction result using two images, Copyright 1995 University of Bern[5].

Figure 11. The reconstruction result using only one portrait of the second author.

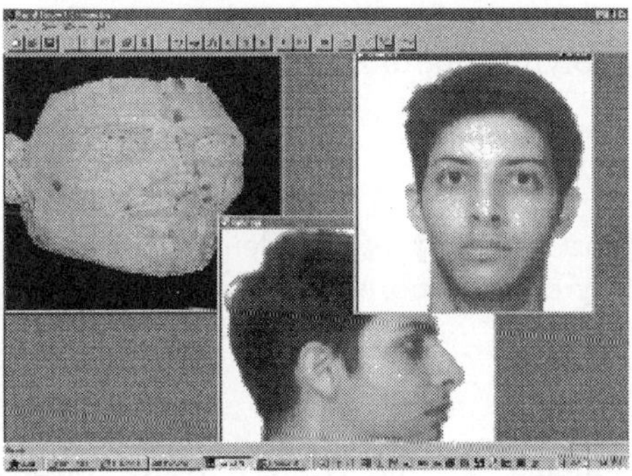

Figure 12. Some sample snapshots of the user interface.

crosoft's Vision SDK 1.0 together with image .dlls from ImageMagick. It allows us to perform low-level pixel operations in images.

The goal of our solution is to produce photo-realistic 3D face models without user interaction. The interface, in an ideal case, would therefore be a simple command line specifying details such as the generic face model and the images. However, in order to produce better results, we have an interface to allow limited manual intervention to aid the system's extraction process (Figure 12).

5 Conclusion

We have presented a minimalist approach to 3D facial reconstruction by introducing cognitive and anatomical heuristics into feature extraction and 3D deformation process. The results have shown this method can rapidly customize a generic face model using only one or two images of a real face.

6 Future Work

To achieve full automation of reconstruction is our final goal. At present, user interaction is required under some circumstances when we do not obtain optimal results from the automatic feature extraction process, e.g., noisy images. There fore, we are trying to make this process more robust. At present, we only make use of edge-gradient information and anatomical heuristics. We are exploring methods of introducing a probabilistic framework over multiple criteria. It will encode more useful target information into HDTs.

At present, our texture-blending produces artifacts because of errors in our rough estimate (front and profile) of facial poses. We are in the process of improving this by applying anatomical heuristics into the blending function.

7 Acknowledgment

This work was supported partly by Academic Research Grant (RP3982704) of National University of Singapore.

References

1. Akimoto, T., Seunaga, Y., and Wallace, R. S., *Automatic Creation of 3D Facial Models.* IEEE Computer Graphics and Applications, Vol. 13, No. 5, pp. 16-22.
2. Cyberware Laboratory, *4020/RGB 3D Scanner with Color Digitizer.* Cyberware Laboratory, Inc, Monterey, California, 1990.
3. Essa, I., Basu, S., Darrell, T., and Pentland, A., *Tracking and Interactive Animation of Faces and Heads Using Input from Video.* Computer Animation '96, 1996, pp. 68-79.
4. Fua, P. and Miccio, C., *From Regular Images to Animated Heads: A Least Squares Approach.* ECCV Conference, Freiburg, Germany, May 1998.
5. *ftp://iamftp.unibe.ch/pub/Images/FaceImages/README.*
6. Guenter, B., Grimm, C., Wood, D., Malvar, H., and Pighin, F., *Making Faces.* In the proceedings of SIGGRAPH, 1998, pp. 55-66.
7. Johnston, R.A. and Ellis, H. D., *The development of face recognition.* In Cognitive and Computational Aspects of Face Recognition : Explorations in Face Space. Routledge, 1995.
8. Kalra, P. and Magnenat Thalmann, N., *Modeling of Vascular Expressions in Facial Animation.* Computer Animation '94, pp. 50-58.
9. Kass, M., Witkin, A., and Terzopoulos, D., *Snakes: Active Contour Models.* In the proceedings of the First International Conference on Computer

Vision, 1987, pp. 259-268.

10. Kurihara, T. and Arai, K. A., *Transformation Method for Modeling and Animation of Human Face from Photographs.* Computer Animation 91, pp. 45-58.
11. Lee, Y., Terzopoulos, D., and Waters, K., *Realistic Modeling for Facial Animation.* In the proceedings of SIGGRAPH, 1995, pp. 55-62.
12. Lee, W. S., Kalra, P., and Magnenat Thalmann, N., *Model Based Face Reconstruction For Animation.* In the proceedings of MMM, 1997, pp. 323-338.
13. Moccozet, L. and Magnenat Thalmann, N., *Dirichlet Free-Form Deformation and their Application to Hand Simulation.* Computer Animation'97, pp. 60-70.
14. Parke, F. I., *A Model for Human Faces that allows Speech Synchronized Animation.* Computer and Graphics, Pergamon Press, Vol. 1, No. 1, 1975. pp. 1-4.
15. Parke, F. I. and Waters, K., *Computer Facial Animation.* AK Peters, Wellesley, Massachussetts, 1996.
16. Pighin, F., Hecker, J., Lischinski, D., Szeliski, R., and Salesin, D., *Synthesizing Facial Expressions from Photographs.* In the proceedings of SIGGRAPH, 1998, pp. 75-84.
17. Platt, S. and Badler, N., *Animating Facial Expressions.* In the proceedings of SIGGRAPH, 1991, pp. 245-252.
18. Pollefeys, M., Koch, R., and Van Gool, L., *Self-Calibration and Metric Reconstruction in spite of Varying and Unknown Internal Camera Parameters.* Proc. ICCV'98 (international Conference on Computer Vision), Bombay, 1998, pp. 90-95.
19. Prosmans, M. and Van Gool, L., *Getting Facial Features and Gestures in 3D.* In the Proceedings of the NATO Advanced Study Institute on Face Recognition : From Theory to Applications, Stirling, Scotland, UK, June 23-July 4, 1997.
20. Sederburg, T. W., *Free-Form Deformation of Solid Geometric Models.* In the proceedings of SIGGRAPH, 1986, pp. 151-160.
21. Stevenage, S. V., *Expertise and the Caricature Advantage.* In Cognitive and Computational Aspects of Face Recognition : Explorations in Face Space. Routledge, 1995, pp. 24-46.
22. Waters, K., *A Muscle Model for Animating Three-Dimensional Facial Expression.* In the proceedings of SIGGRAPH, 1987, pp. 17-24.

CHAPTER 6

INDEXING & RETRIEVAL OF MULTIMEDIA INFORMATION

VIDEO SEGMENTATION USING AN OPPORTUNISTIC APPROACH

MOHAMED AHMED AND AHMED KARMOUCH

School of Information Technology & Engineering (SITE), University of Ottawa, 161 Louis-Pasteur, Ottawa, ON, K1N 6N5, CANADA

E-mail: mahmed@sol.genie.uottawa.ca , karmouch@elg.uottawa.ca

In this paper, we present our system, MediABS, for performing key framing tasks. The main problem of video analysis is that it is a notoriously weak-structured problem. There is no fixed video style that we could use to parse directly. Moreover, there are many media formats and standards nowadays. The architecture of the system will be described. We handle three different media formats using the same process. We present a new algorithm, based on color histograms, and using Binary Penetration for achieving the key framing task taking the high performance criteria into consideration in addition to achieving effective results. The algorithm exploits the temporal characteristic of the visual information. Also, the algorithm takes into consideration solving the problems of getting false cuts and missing true cuts. A discussion, along with testing results, will be conducted to show the merits of the new algorithm relative to the old algorithm implemented within the MediABS system. This work is part of the Mobile Agents Alliance project among university of Ottawa, National Research Council (NRC) and Mitel Corporation in Canada.

1 Introduction

In the past decade, there has been significant work done in the area of image analysis and recognition so that we could partition a video source into separate segments. This process could be used to index the video within the multimedia databases and thus we could query and navigate through the database. Following are some of the algorithms used to measure the differences among consecutive frames. Pixels-Pair wise comparison [2] is a simple way to detect a quantitative change between a pair of images by comparing the corresponding pixels in the two frames to determine how many pixels have changed. The total percentage of the pixels changed is evaluated and if this percentage exceeds some preset threshold, we decide that a frame change has been detected. Many color space systems could be used for the comparison such as: RGB, HVC, HSV, YIQ or L*u*v. The advantage of this method is its simplicity. However, its disadvantages exceed the advantage. One disadvantage is that it has a large processing overhead to compare all consecutive frames. Also, it does not conclude if large objects moved within the shot before terminating the continuous shot.

The Spatial, Temporal Skips [2] (Histogram Analysis) [2,3,4,9,10] methods benefit from the redundant characteristic of the video frames either in the spatial dimension or the temporal dimension. The use of color histograms has been verified to be more robust against objects and camera movements within the same shot. Moreover, the very near video frames are similar except for the cut frames. We could compare temporally every defined number of frames, as samples, instead of all the consecutive frames and/or spatially not all the pixels within the frames. Thus, we could save great processing time and resources during the analysis. We could use the color histogram distributions of the frames to make the comparison. The histogram comparison algorithm is less sensitive to object motion than the pixels-pair wise comparison algorithm. There are many histogram difference measures that could be used to detect a shot cut.

For example:

1) Difference $= \Sigma \mid H_i(j) - H_{i+1}(j) \mid$ for $j = 1$ To N

Where, $H_i(j)$ is the histogram for color j in Frame i,
N = Number of used colors

2) Difference $= \Sigma (\mid H_i(j) - H_{i+1}(j) \mid^2 / H_{i+1}(j))$ for $j = 1$ To N

Where, $H_i(j)$ is the histogram for color j in Frame i,
N = Number of used colors

Using a preset threshold, we could discover the existence of a frame change and thus the shot cut operation is detected. Hirzalla [1] has described a new detailed design of a key frame detection algorithm using the HVC color space. First, for every two consecutive frames, the system converts the original RBG coloring space into the equivalent HVC Histogram coloring representation because the HVC space mirrors the human color perception. The system uses the Hue histogram distribution for performing the comparison instead of the intensity distribution to reduce, to some extent, the variations in intensity values due to light changes and flashes.

Pass et al. [5] proposed a histogram refinement algorithm using color coherence vectors based on local spatial coherence. Wolf [6] provides an algorithm to detect the key frames in MPEG video file format using optical flow motion analysis. Sethi et al. [7] use a similarity metric to measure the similarity through both the hue and saturation components of the HSI color space between two images. Pass et al. [8] define a notion of Joint Histograms. They use many local features in comparison including color, edge density, texture, gradient magnitude and the rank of the pixels.

We will describe the architecture and functions of the system we implemented for multi-format media browsing and processing in section 2. Then, we will focus on the media unification pre-processing function in section 3. Section 4 will represent the different video cut detection algorithms built in the system. In section 5, we will state the different possible consecutive shots cases and how the algorithm could be accommodate them. Then, in section 6, we will provide the testing results of the relative efficiency and performance of the different analysis algorithms. A conclusion statement will be described in section 7.

2 MediABS Media Browsing and Processing System

A prototype system called "*MediABS*", was implemented addressing multi video format browsing and processing. Actually, the system tries to discover the different cut changes within the video file. The system runs on Microsoft-Windows NT and Windows95 environments. In the next two sections, we will provide the system's architecture and functions description.

2.1 MediABS Architecture

Fig. 1 represents the general architecture of MediABS system. First, the input media file is provided to the M*edia Preparation module* of the system by the user, or in future it could be through an agent in a distributed computing environment.

The M*edia Preparation module* recognizes and verifies the input media file format, dimensions, resolutions, ...etc. This module is responsible also for providing a determined media unified segment to the next modules as a preparation function. We use this preparation function to unify the next processing functions irrespective of the input media format. More details regarding the media preparation pre-processing function will be explained in section 3. A third responsibility for this module is for browsing with different capabilities as will be shown in the next section.

The *Frames Management module* uses the unified media format segment for the analysis. This module is used to extract certain frames from the input segment. These frames could be requested by the *Media Analysis module.* The *Media Analysis module* specifies the region of frames, temporal skip, frames quality, color/gray condition and frames format. The *Frames Management module* does the frames extraction function. Then, it replies to the *Frames Analysis module* request with the extracted frames references (i.e. their locations on the local storage). We could make use of partitioning the file into discrete regions to be analyzed separately to compensate for the storage requirements.

The *Media Analysis module* implements two different key framing algorithms to study the relative merits of them, namely the 6 Most significant RGB bits with the use of Blocks Intensity Difference through blind search and through binary penetration as will be described. It updates the key framing index list of the required input media segment.

At the end, the *Media Analysis module* provides the result key framing index list to the *Key Frames Handling module.* The *Key Frames Handling module* either displays the key frames result report, including the total processing time, along with the used parameters configuration to the user interactively or the user could store this report into a spread sheet file on a stable storage.

The *Key Frames Handling* module could use the Frames Management module services to extract the actual frames from the media file by passing their index received in the Key Frames list from the *Media Analysis module.*

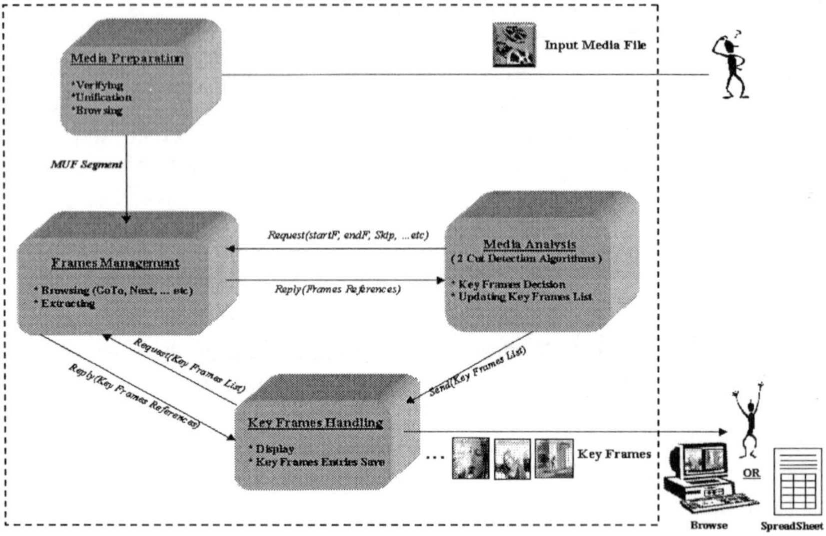

Figure 1. MediABS System Architecture

As shown, we tried to separate the different modules according to their function to facilitate the future update in any module without affecting the other ones. It is in the form of module requests services from the other modules in consistent interfaces of coordination. Thus, for example, we could adopt new media formats for processing without changing the media analysis algorithm accordingly. Another example is to change the media analysis algorithm itself for the current media formats supported.

2.2 MediABS Functions Description

The current functions and capabilities of the system are as follows:

- Media Segment:
  -Play, Pause, Resume, Stop, Repeat and Audio Volume Control
- Media Speed Adjustment
- Sound on/off
- Video Frames Random Access:
  -GoTo, Next, Previous, Begin, Middle, End, Skip and Scroll
- Verifying the Input Media Format
- Specified Frames regions Extraction and Analysis
- Temporal, Spatial skip - Defaults: 5 frames, 5 pixels respectively
- Frames save Formats: JPG, BMP : Color, Grey-scale

-Each compressed frame size is about only 4KB

- Frames Analysis:
  - * 6 Most significant RGB bits with the use of Blocks Intensity Difference
  - * The use of Binary Penetration algorithm
- Exporting Video analysis configurations and results to a Spread Sheet file

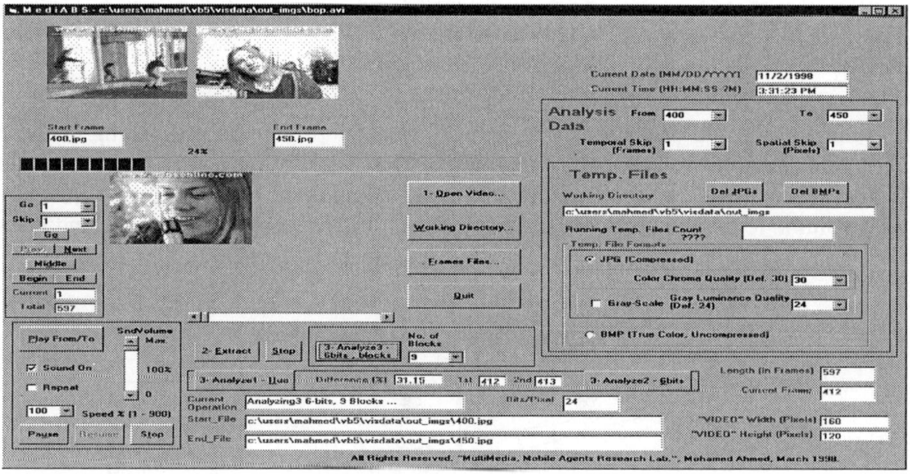

Figure 2. MediABS Main Window

The main window of the system is shown in Fig. 2. We could define a certain video segment to be analyzed. Using the temporal and spatial information redundancy within the video, we could improve the performance without sacrificing the accuracy of the algorithm results.

3 Media Unification Pre-Processing Stage

The system uses a media unification phase for different media standards before analyzing the video file. These standards are the Audio Video Interleaved (AVI), Apple Quick Time for Windows (QTW) and Motion Picture Experts Group (MPEG). The use of this process allows us to simplify the media analysis management afterwards because we don't need to worry about the different characteristics of each format for processing.

Irrespective of the information coding in these formats, we use the same processing modules for them. Thus, we could state that this simplifies managing and analyzing the video in all cases. The different components of this pre-processing stage are illustrated in Fig. 3.

The components of this stage are:

* *Media Format Handler Extension:* This component could be regarded as the media driver of each media format. It handles the special format coding of the corresponding format representation. This layer could be extended to handle other media devices (e.g. CD-ROM, CD-I, the new DVD standard, …etc). Streaming media could be processed in the same manner as well without re-doing the already implemented processing mechanisms of the next stages. We could verify the input media format and recognize the input media features such as: dimensions, resolution, …etc.

* *Media Formats Unification Module:* This module is used to unify the environment and the operations that will be used for the media processing in the next stage. For example, some of the functions of this module are controlling the speed of video display, enabling or disabling the audio component of the video, adjusting the audio volume level, the ability to specify certain video segments to analyze and browse, …etc.

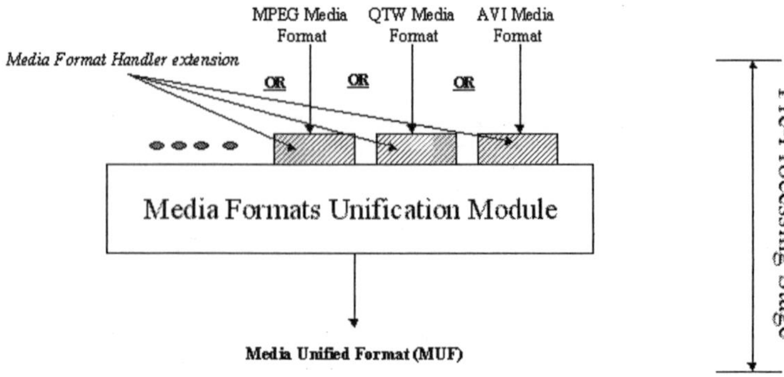

Figure 3. Media Unification Pre-Processing Stage

The output of this media pre-processing stage is seen as a *Media Unified Format (MUF)* content that will be used in further media handling operations. The use of this format will reduce the complexity of handling different input standards since we don't need the special characteristics of these formats in the current implemented media processing algorithms. Thus, for example, we don't have to worry about the format to access certain frames within the video with certain temporal skip though we know that the coding of the information is very much different between MPEG and AVI video formats for instance.

4 Video Change Cut Detection Stage

For this process, the system extracts the consecutive frames needed to detect the camera cut events. Thus, the representing frames are grabbed and stored in the computer's hard disk. The system could define various configurations for the extracted frames. They could be color or gray frames, different image qualities and different image formats (either JPG or BMP). In addition, there is a temporal skip parameter, so that we don't need to extract and analyze all the consecutive frames.

For cut detection, the system implements a spatial skip parameter as well to improve the performance without sacrificing the accuracy of the detection to benefit from the redundant information within the frames. We will describe first the original algorithm adopted within MediABS system, which is called the 6 Most significant RGB bits with the use of Blocks Intensity Difference. Then, we will present the new algorithm recommended, which we call Binary Penetration algorithm. This new approach improves the performance of the cut detection procedure taking into account the temporal heuristics of the video information.

4.1 The 6 Most Significant RGB Bits with the Use of Blocks Intensity Difference Algorithm

First, the system makes use of the 24 bits RGB color space components of each compared pixels (each component has 8 bits representation) directly. However, to speed the performance considerably, the system exploits only the 2 most Significant bits [2] of each color (using masking operation) which means actually that we define only 64 ranges of color degrees for the entire RGB color space. The system evaluates the histogram of the corresponding two frames, taking the temporal skip into account. Then, the following formula is used:

$$\text{Histogram Difference} = \tfrac{1}{2} * \Sigma \mid H_2(i) - H_1(i) \mid \;/\; \Sigma H_1(i) \qquad \text{for } i = 1 \text{ To } N$$

Where, $H_1(i)$ is the RGB Histogram distribution for frame M,
$H_2(i)$ is the RGB Histogram distribution for frame (M + Temporal Skip),
N = the possible 6 bits RGB values

Then, if this Histogram Difference exceeds some defined threshold, the 2 frames are said to represent an abrupt camera cut detected.

Initially, following the results of the initial approaches, the system gave poor results in few cases. One problem was that the previous algorithm makes use only of the global color distribution information. This results in the system not discovering cut detection even there is a cut detection in the compared frames. The two examples, shown in Fig. 4, illustrate this. The problem being that the previous algorithm ignores the locality information of the colors' distribution and especially for the cases of two frames of different shots within the same scene (i.e. the background color information is normally similar). That means that the 2 consecutive 6 MSBs color histograms are similar despite the fact that the actual spatial distributions of the colors are not the same. Thus, the algorithm was extended to suit these circumstances.

Thus, we made use of partitioning each frame into a number of disjoint blocks. This allows us to make use of the locality information of the histogram distribution, to a great extent, and in a quick decision making manner. The system evaluates every corresponding two-block histogram difference between the compared frames. Thus, the solution to the previously described problem is shown in Fig. 5.

There is another issue that was discovered while experimenting. It is the false detection problem. It occurs here mainly because of the use of the temporal skip for processing. Thus, it was realized that if this temporal skip is significantly high along with a quick change in the same continuous shot due to object movement or camera operation such as tilting, panning or zooming, the algorithm will recognize the frames as significantly different despite this not being true. Thus, an additional step is advised. After the first cut detection process, we need to analyze these specific changed frames more comprehensively [2] provided that the temporal skip is already greater than one. We do that in order to compensate for the speed of possible object and camera movements taking into consideration that the use of blocks difference magnifies the effect of any object or camera movements. Therefore, we re-analyze these region frames but with temporal skip equal to one [2]. Hence, the system first needs to extract all the frames included in the current analyzed region. The algorithm thus became more accurate in refusing false cuts obtained from the first process while maintaining true camera cut change accuracy.

Now, the modified algorithm could be described as follows for every two consecutive frames, taking the temporal skip into consideration (i.e. separated by (the temporal skip – 1) number of frames):

```
Total_Blocks_Difference = 0 ;
For BlockX = 0 To (H_Number_of_Blocks – 1)
For BlockY = 0 To (V_Number_of_Blocks – 1)
// where, H_Number_of_Blocks is the Horizontal Number of Blocks
// and V_Number_of_Blocks is the Vertical Number of Blocks

{
Histogram1(j) = 0 ;                                    for j = 0 to 63
Histogram2(j) = 0 ;                                    for j = 0 to 63

For Row = BlockX * (Frame_Height / H_Number_of_Blocks)  To (BlockX + 1) *
   (Frame_Height / H_Number_of_Blocks) Step Spatial_Skip
For Column = BlockY * (Frame_Width / V_Number_of_Blocks)  To (BlockY + 1) *
      (Frame_Width / V_Number_of_Blocks) Step Spatial_Skip
{
```

```
Frame1_Pixel_Color(Row,Column)= Six_MSB(R1(Row,Column),G1(Row,Column),
B1(Row,Column)) ;
Frame2_Pixel_Color(Row,Column)= Six_MSB(R2(Row,Column),G2(Row,Column),
B2(Row,Column)) ;
// where, Six_MSB(R, G, B) Function is used to get the 6 MSB equivalent of the R,G,B
// input parameters (i.e. return a value between 0 and 63)
   Histogram1(Pixel_Color) = Histogram1(Frame1_Pixel_Color(Row,Column)) + 1 ;
   Histogram2(Pixel_Color) = Histogram2(Frame2_Pixel_Color(Row,Column)) + 1 ;
}
```

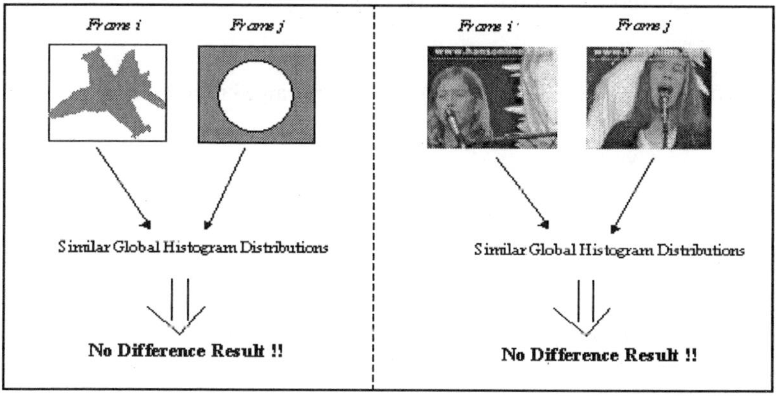

Figure 4. Wrong Frames Unchange Decision !

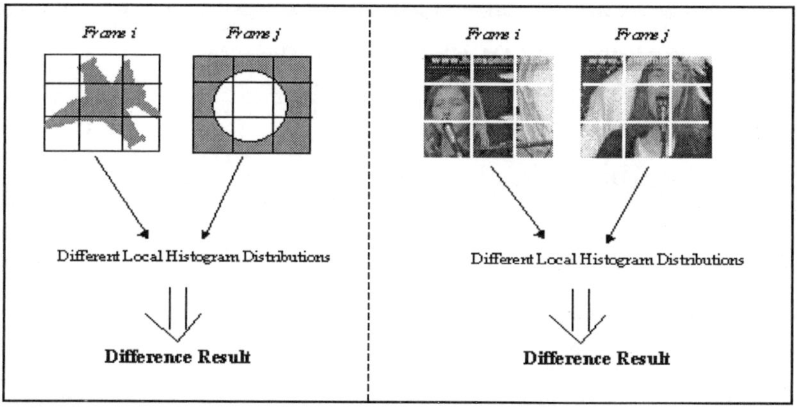

Figure 5. Correct Frames Change Decision

```
Block_Difference = ½ * Σ | Histogram2(i) – Histogram1(i) | / Σ Histogram1(i) ;
                                                              for i = 0 to 63
```

```
Total_Blocks_Difference = Total_Blocks_Difference + Block_Difference ;
}

Final_Difference_Avg = Total_Block_Difference / (H_Number_of_Blocks *
V_Number_of_Blocks) ;
IF Final_Difference_Avg > Threshold AND Temporal_Skip >1 THEN
{
Temporal_Skip = 1 ;
Extract all the current region included frames ;
Repeat the process again using Temporal_Skip =1 ;
// re-analyze again more comprehensively
}

IF Final_Difference_Avg > Threshold AND Temporal_Skip = 1 THEN
{
Decision of Cut Detection ;
Exit ;
}

Else
{
Decision of NO Cut Detection ;
Exit ;
}
```

Fig. 6 presents a snapshot of the result using this algorithm.

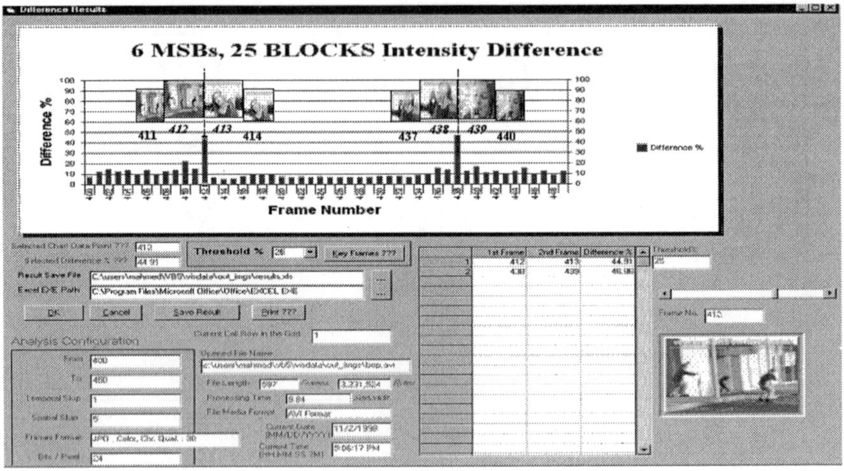

Figure 6. MediABS 6 Most significant RGB bits with the use of Blocks Intensity Difference

4.2 *Binary Penetration Algorithm*

Although the use of the 6 Most significant RGB bits with the use of Blocks Intensity Difference algorithm provided us with efficient and robust results, it lacks the high performance objective needed in these kind of systems especially in distributed architectures. Thus, we updated this given algorithm with a new approach with the use of the temporal dependencies in the visual information. Thus, we defined and implemented the Binary Penetration algorithm.

The idea behind this algorithm is to relax the step of analyzing all the consecutive frames of a certain region that is said to have a potential cut within it. The previous algorithm extracts and analyzes all the frames (i.e. equals to the temporal skip) value when the histogram difference exceeds the threshold. However, in our new algorithm, we extract and analyze the frames in a binary penetration manner as shown in Fig. 7.

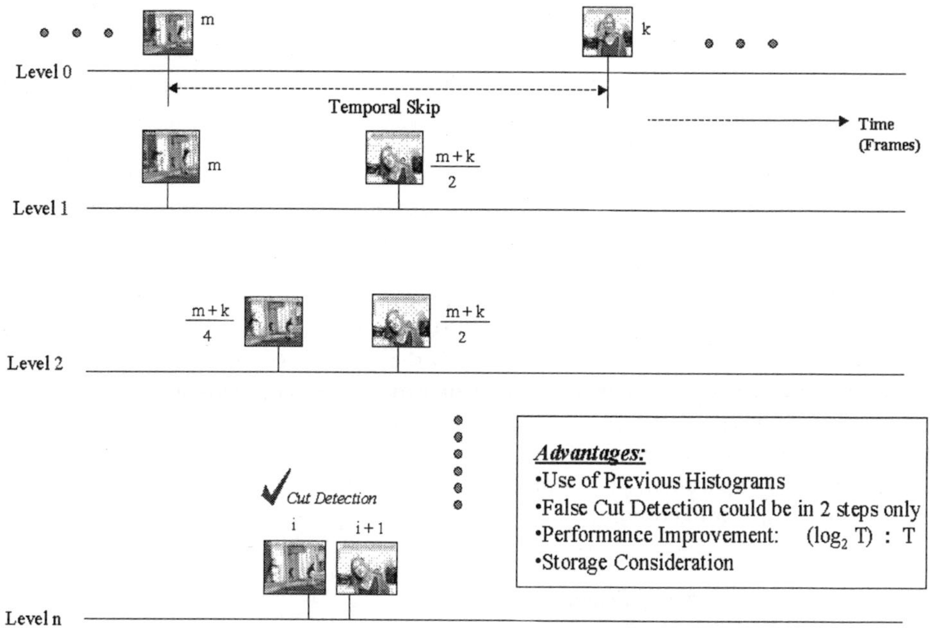

Figure 7. A Cut detected scenario using the Binary Penetration

As shown in Fig. 7, initially the algorithm compares frames m and k as discussed, using the temporal skip. Then, if the two frames difference exceeds the threshold, we extract the middle frame and compare it to both ends. If both differences are less the threshold, we declare that there is actually no cut exists in this region and continue processing for the following regions. However, if one of the two differences exceeds or even both of them exceed the threshold, we take the greater difference to represent a potential possibility to find a cut within this half region. We need to stress that the temporal skip should be a moderate value that represents a possibility of finding one camera cut operation at maximum within it. Then, we continue the same procedure with the selected half in the same manner. This continue until we get a two consecutive frames difference that exceeds the threshold which represent a camera cut operation or until both halves differences in certain region are lower than the threshold which then means that there is actually no camera cut operation in this whole region as there could be a large object moved or camera movement happened within the given region. Thus, taking into consideration the use of the temporal skip, the difference could pass this cut detection test in the first levels but this operation would be recognized in the detailed levels afterwards.

Fig. 8 describes flowchart of the whole binary penetration algorithm.

5 A Generalized Binary Penetration algorithm

The previous algorithm description is the most possible case for consecutive shots cutting. However, due to using the temporal skip parameter, there is possibility for other cases instead. They could be realized as in Fig. 9.

Studying cases number 1 and 2 of the figure, we could realize that the binary penetration algorithm described in subsection 4.2 could recognize them easily. For cases number 3 and 4, we need to make a simple generalization to the algorithm.

This generalization is simply just changing one step. It is as follows:

Instead of choosing only the higher difference of the two evaluated differences in any level and which exceed the defined threshold, we instead need to continue the penetration in each half of the level, of course if they both exceed the threshold (i.e. not necessarily only the higher of them). These modifications will leads us to discover all the cuts within the temporal skip, even if there are more than one cut included within the temporal skip frames. However, we still need to remember that these cases 3, 4 are rare if the temporal skip parameter has a moderate value, which is not large to include more than zero or one cut at maximum.

6 Testing Evaluation and Discussion

The system has been developed on a Pentium II PC-266 MHz and 64 MB RAM. Various testing experiments have been undertaken. We used different file formats (AVI, MOV and MPEG) and these files have different testing conditions such as dark shots and camera operations. We tested the two cut detection algorithms to compare their behavior with the different file formats and the different testing conditions. In addition, the testing uses some other constant testing conditions for the different algorithms such as using color, 24 bits/pixel, same quality compressed extracted frames formats, ...etc.

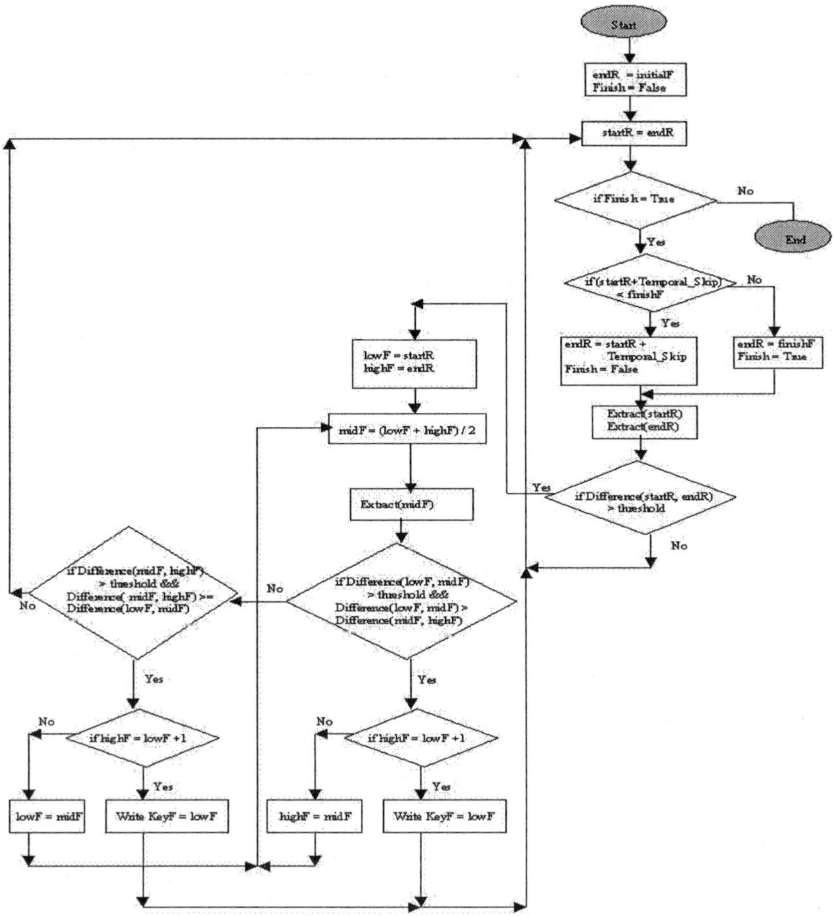

Figure 8. The Binary Penetration Algorithm

To evaluate the different algorithms, we used two well-known accuracy measures. They are the Recall and Precision measures. They are defined as:

$$\text{Recall} = \frac{\text{Correct Cuts}}{\text{Correct Cuts} + \text{Missed Cuts}} \quad , \quad \text{Precision} = \frac{\text{Correct Cuts}}{\text{Correct Cuts} + \text{False Cuts}}$$

In addition, the system evaluates the total processing time in each experiment. The testing makes use of initial spatial skip values of 5. The summary of the performance results, using the two algorithms with different values of the temporal skip parameter as an indication of the sensitivity analysis for this parameter, is shown in Fig. 10.

However, we should not forget the effectiveness comparison of the two algorithms in the presence of the performance measurements. Thus, Fig. 11 shows the recall and precision measures in each case. In both figures, we refer to the original algorithm by "Blind" and the new one by "Binary Penetration".

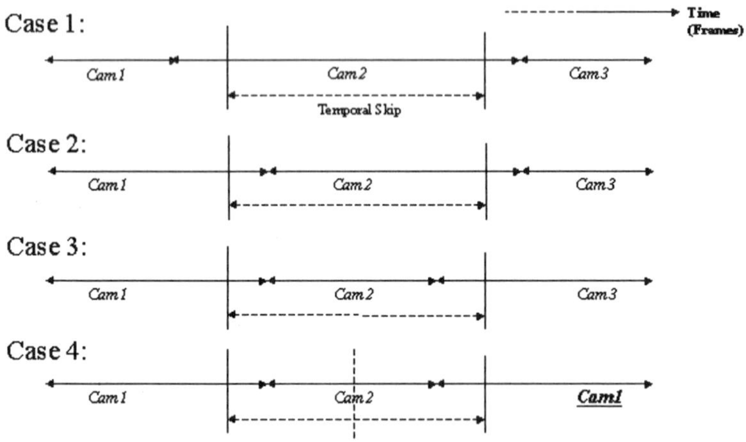

Figure 9. Consecutive shots cut possibilities

As shown from Fig. 10, the binary penetration algorithm has shown better performance in all cases. That is more realized when you use a larger temporal skip as expected. The reason for that is that the original algorithm tests all the included frames when the difference between the two ends exceeds the threshold. Thus if the temporal skip is high, there is two effects happens. Firstly, the number of frames extracted and analyzed is higher and secondly, the probability of obtaining false cut decision at the first try are larger due to any large object movement or camera operation during the same camera shot.

However, in the binary penetration algorithm, even this probability is still the same at the first level, the system could recognize this false cut operation from the second try or later without extracting and analyzing all the frames within the region two ends. Thus, this is two-fold advantage. One is the need to extract less number of frames and thus relax the memory and storage requirements. Second the speed of detecting true cut is larger by percentage ($\log_2 T / T$), where T is the temporal skip selected and could be as only two tries to detect false cut decision.

Another inherent advantage is the use of the already constructed frame histogram from upper levels. That means that we could use the histograms of the higher level (n) into the next lower level (n+1) testing. Actually, there are two histograms used from the higher level into the next lower level. For example, in Fig. 7, the histograms of frames {m and (m+k) / 2} from level 1 are used in level 2 and only histogram of frame {(m+k) / 4} is evaluated in level 2 to make the decision at this level, and so on. As we expect, this re-use of histograms saves a lot of time in computations.

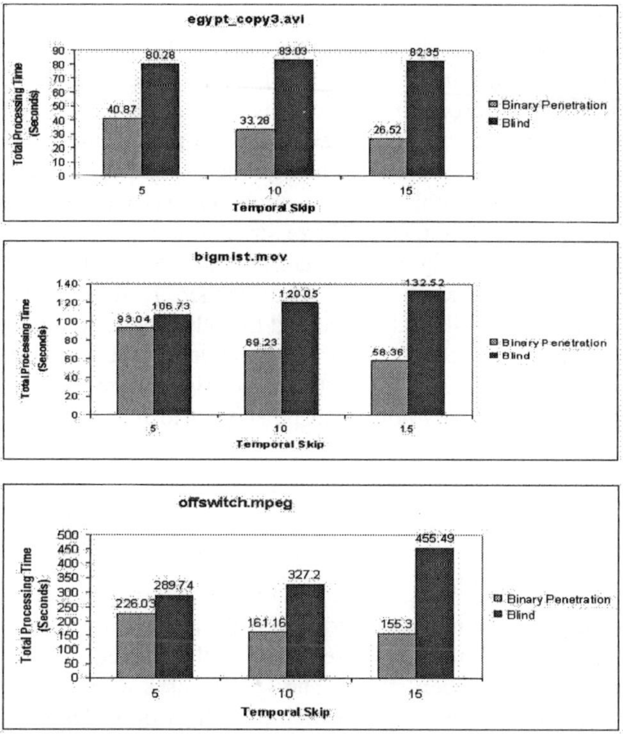

Figure 10. Performance Comparative results

egypt_copy3.avi

Blind, 5	Binary_Penetration, 5	Blind, 10	Binary_Penetration, 10	Blind, 15	Binary_Penetration, 15
RECALL = 100 % PRECISION = 100%	RECALL = 100 % PRECISION = 100%	RECALL = 100 % PRECISION = 100%	RECALL = 100 % PRECISION = 100%	RECALL = 100 % PRECISION = 100%	RECALL = 100 % PRECISION = 100%

bigmist.mov

Blind, 5	Binary_Penetration, 5	Blind, 10	Binary_Penetration, 10	Blind, 15	Binary_Penetration, 15
RECALL = 85.71 % PRECISION = 100%	RECALL = 85.71 % PRECISION = 100%	RECALL = 85.71 % PRECISION = 100%	RECALL = 85.71 % PRECISION = 100%	RECALL = 71.43% PRECISION = 100%	RECALL = 71.43% PRECISION = 100%

offswitch.mpeg

Blind, 5	Binary_Penetration, 5	Blind, 10	Binary_Penetration, 10	Blind, 15	Binary_Penetration, 15
RECALL = 75 % PRECISION = 66.7%	RECALL = 87.5 % PRECISION = 77.78%	RECALL = 87.5 % PRECISION = 77.78%	RECALL = 87.5 % PRECISION = 87.5%	RECALL = 87.5 % PRECISION = 63.64%	RECALL = 75 % PRECISION = 75%

Figure 11. Recall and Precision Comparative results

At the same time, we didn't forget the effectiveness of the algorithm while evaluating the performance of the algorithm. Thus, in Fig. 11, we evaluate the recall and precision of all the test experiments done in Fig. 10. We realize that the binary penetration algorithm shows promising effectiveness in all cases. However, from the results, we see the temporal skip of 10 frames gives best results and good performance, at the same time, in all cases. The argument behind that is that, in the binary penetration algorithm, the value of the temporal skip is sensitive. Off course, it is better to be high as possible to improve the performance. However, if this value is very high, another problem appears because in the algorithm, there is possibility to find only one camera cut within a temporal skip number of frames. Thus, if there is more than one camera cut within the temporal skip, one will be detected and the others will be missed. That means that this value should be moderate value and relative to the domain of the video information. For example, a news clips could have higher temporal skip value than musical or commercials clips. This point will be subject to more extensive research in future.

7 Conclusion

We presented our system, MediABS, developed for the purpose of media browsing and detecting camera cut operation in a media visual information. We described the architecture and its included modules used within the system. The functions and services of each module have been stated. The system uses a pre-processing stage to unify the view of the management and processing of the video files irrespective of the input file's coding format. The browsing and processing mechanisms of the different files do not change from one format to another. This eases the handling of the video files to a great extent. This architecture could be used in future to support other media formats such as streaming media.

We described the original algorithm for detecting key frames within the media segment assigned by the user for the analysis. We adopt the use of partitioning the selected frames into exclusive blocks for resolving the missed cuts problems. The system implements the use of spatial and temporal skips for improving the performance of the analysis operation. However, to compensate for the use of the temporal skip, we re-analyze all video region frames if there is a potential to find a cut within it in the first test.

Then, we explained the updated algorithm using the binary penetration mechanism. The algorithm makes use of the temporal dependence heuristics of the visual information. The new approach resulted in a good performance improvement over the original algorithm without sacrificing the accuracy results of the analysis. However, as said, further study will be realized regarding the effect of the media domain over the tuning of the adopted parameters within the system such as the temporal skip. In addition, the system will be utilized as a given service in a distributed environment system and not just a standalone application.

8 ACKNOWLEDGMENTS

This work was supported by NSERC/Strategic grant with Mitel Corp., NRC and CITO.

References

1. Hirzalla N., Media Processing and Retrieval Model for Multimedia Documents, PhD Thesis, Ottawa University, Jan. 1997.
2. Zhang H., Kankanhalli A. and Smoliar S., "Automatic Partitioning of Full-Motion Video," Multimedia Systems, Vol. 1, No. 1, pp. 10-28, Apr. 1993.
3. Swain M. and Ballard D., "Color Indexing," International Journal of Computer Vision, Vol. 7, No. 1, pp. 11-32, 1991.
4. Boreczky J. and Rowe L., "A Comparison of Video Shot Boundary Detection Techniques," Journal of Electronic Imaging, Vol. 5, No. 2, pp. 122-128, 1996.
5. Pass G. and Zabih R., "Histogram Refinement for Content-Based Image Retrieval", In IEEE Workshop on Applications of Computer Vision, pp. 96-102, Dec. 1996.
6. Wolf W., "Key Frame Selection by Motion Analysis," Proceedings of ICASSP, Atlanta, 1996.
7. Sethi I., Coman I., Day B., et al., "Color-WISE: A System for Image Similarity Retrieval Using Color," Proc. of SPIE, Storage and Retrieval for Image and Video Databases VI, Vol. 3312, pp. 140-149, Jan. 1998.
8. Pass G. and Zabih R., "Comparing Images Using Joint Histograms", ACM Journal of Multimedia Systems, 1998.
9. Ahmed M. and Karmouch A., "New Architecture for Multi-Format Video Browsing and Cut Detection", Proc. of IEEE CCECE'99 Conference, Edmonton Canada, pp. 821-826, May 9-12 1999.
10. Ahmed M., Abu-Hakima S. and Karmouch A., "Key Frame Extraction and Indexing for Multimedia Databases ", Visual Interface 99 Conference, Québec Canada, pp. 506-511, May 19-21 1999.

MOTION INSENSITIVE DETECTION OF CUTS AND GRADUAL TRANSITIONS IN DIGITAL VIDEO

SCOTT LAWRENCE, DJEMEL ZIOU AND SHENGRUI WANG
Département de Mathématiques et d'Informatique
Faculté des Sciences
Université de Sherbrooke
Sherbrooke (Qc), Canada, J1K 2R1
lawrence@dmi.usherb.ca
ziou@dmi.usherb.ca
wang@dmi.usherb.ca

Our project concerns shot boundary detection in digital video. Automatic video segmentation is a first step towards video indexing. An efficient yet robust algorithm is needed to separate video sequences into smaller segments called shots. Although many researchers have tackled the problem of finding shot boundaries, few have been able to accurately recognize gradual transition boundaries such as fades and dissolves. Because shot boundaries correspond to discontinuities in the time domain, we present an algorithm based on the video's first-order partial derivatives. By only considering areas with low apparent motion, our method is insensitive to object or camera motion. Our algorithm can accurately identify cuts as well as fades, dissolves, wipes and other gradual transitions. Experimental results show that our method outperforms other popular methods on our sample videos.

1 Introduction

In the last decade, the amount of digital video documents has grown to the point where it is now a dominating component in available multimedia data. We must now address the indexing problem emerging from the need to manage these video documents. Classical text-based indexing methods are insufficient to provide an adequate description, so a new form of indexing is needed for video sequences. Many authors [5, 6, 8, 10, 11] believe that shot boundary detection in video sequences is one of the necessary first steps in an efficient video management system. Segmentation of digital video into smaller units is also important in other domains like MPEG compression.

We define the digital video segmentation problem as the automatic detection of shot boundaries. Just as a text can be divided into sentences, a video sequence can be hierarchically divided into smaller components such as scenes and shots. A shot is defined as a sequence of images taken from a single operation of the camera and that depicts a continuous action in time and space. A scene is a group of related shots. Figure 1 shows an example of the relations between video, scenes and shots.

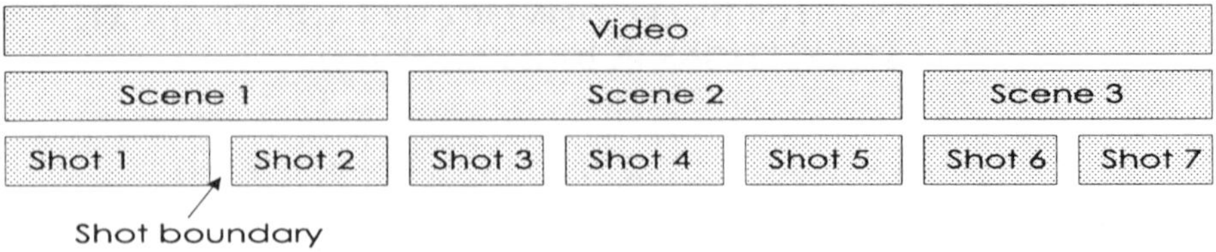

Figure 1. Digital video hierarchy model.

In the editing process, filmmakers combine shots in a variety of manners to produce the final video. Shot boundaries differ depending on the editing techniques used to combine two shots. The simplest type of shot boundary is known as a cut, and results from a simple juxtaposition of two shots. Other shot boundaries types, such as fades, dissolves and wipes, result from adding editing frames between shots to produce effects like a smoother transition or a highlight between two shots. A fade involves slowly changing the shot intensity to give the impression that a shot is appearing or disappearing. A dissolve combines a fade-out and a fade-in, as one shot vanishes, another shot appears. In a dissolve, for a shot period of time both shots are superimposed. A typical wipe involves one shot replacing the other as a line crosses the screen. As one side of the line shows the old shot, the other shows the new shot. As the line crosses the screen, the old shot disappears. In a wipe, shots are not superimposed but occupy different areas of the screen. Examples of some of the common shot boundaries are illustrated in figure 2.

Figure 2. Shot boundaries : first line shows a cut, second line shows a dissolve and third line shows a wipe.

The detection of cuts has been well established in previous work, but identifying gradual transitions still remains a challenge. This is because gradual transitions occur over many frames and the frame-to-frame differences are comparatively small. While simple cuts represent the vast majority of shot boundaries used in today's videos, we believe that detecting gradual transitions like fades, dissolves and wipes is also important. For instance, in a sample of video test data composed of television commercials, 25% of the shot boundaries were gradual transitions [4].

In this paper, we present a new method aimed at detecting all shot boundaries including gradual transitions. In the next section, we start by giving an overview of some related work. In section 3, we present our new method based on detecting temporal discontinuities caused by shot boundaries. Our method is then improved to handle motion by removing contributions from pixels in motion areas. To increase computational performance, sampling is used with little effect on results. We then give, in section 4, experimental results from two test sequences comparing our method with two other popular methods.

2 Related Work

Many methods for automatic video segmentation have been proposed in recent years. Most of these methods define a difference measure between consecutive frames and use it to identify shot boundaries. This measure has taken many forms, sometimes local, sometimes global. Here we present a short review of some related work on automatic video segmentation. Detailed surveys can be found in [4, 5].

Early research in automatic video segmentation was mainly focused on simple intensity difference measures between consecutive frames in a video sequence. In [9, 11] the authors propose a number of methods to perform video segmentation. The simplest measure is the difference in pixel intensity averages over whole frames. Another measure is the sum of pixel-to-pixel absolute intensity differences across consecutive frames.

Aigrain and Joly [1] propose a method that models the pixel intensity differences in successive frames as a combination of three factors: noise, motion and editing. The authors claim that cuts and wipes can be identified by looking for differences in the [128,255] range while fades and dissolves can be identified by looking for differences in the [7,40] range.

Another class of methods is centered on histogram differences between consecutive frames. The number of possible intensities is first reduced and a histogram is then taken for each frame. Histograms from adjacent frames are then compared and a sum of bin-to-bin differences is calculated. The differences are then thresholded. Frames corresponding to difference values greater than the threshold are labeled as shot boundaries. A number of variations of this method have been proposed. For instance, Nagasaka and Tanaka [9] determined that using a χ^2 test on color histograms results in a measure than more strongly reflects the differences between two frames. They also propose to divide the image frames into regions and use local histograms. By rejecting the regions with the highest differences, they claim to reduce motion effects. Lee and Ip [8] propose the use of local HSV histograms to provide a better measure when lighting changes occur. In [11], Zhang, Kankanhalli and Smoliar propose a twin-comparison technique to identify gradual boundaries. Instead of only one, two thresholds are used. A low threshold is used to identify possible frames at the start of a gradual transition and a high threshold is used to identify shot boundaries. If a difference value is greater than the high threshold, a shot boundary is immediately declared. If a difference value is greater than the low threshold but below the higher threshold, the corresponding frame is marked as a frame possibly starting a gradual transition. Subsequent frames are also compared to this reference frame until the difference between consecutive frames goes below the low threshold. This second comparison provides a measure of the cumulative difference between the current frame and the frame that was marked as the possible beginning of a gradual transition. If the cumulative difference reaches the higher threshold while the difference between consecutive frames steadily remains greater than the lower threshold then a gradual transition is declared.

In [6], Hampapur, Jain and Weymouth use a model driven approach to video segmentation. They separate shot boundaries into classes according to their types and formulate mathematical models for each class based on video production techniques. These models are used to design a series of feature detectors capable of identifying cuts as well as gradual transitions. Video segmentation is then formulated as a feature based classification problem.

In [10], Zabih, Miller and Mai present a feature-based method using edge detection. Their method compares edge pixel locations in successive frames. A registration technique is used to compensate for object or camera motion. The authors start by finding edges in two consecutive frames using the thresholded gradient and non-maximum suppression, resulting in two binary images E_1 and E_2. They define two values named p_{in} and p_{out} corresponding the fraction of entering edge pixels and exiting edge pixels. The first value p_{in} is the fraction of edge pixels in E_2 which are at a distance greater than a fixed value r from the closest edge pixel in E_1. Similarly, p_{out} is the fraction of edge pixels in E_1 more than r pixels from the closest edge pixel in E_2. Their measure of dissimilarity is

$$\max(p_{in}, p_{out})$$

Local maxima exceeding a threshold are marked as shot boundaries. By analyzing the spatial and temporal distributions of entering and exiting pixels, they can also classify shot boundaries according to their types (cut, fade, dissolve or wipe).

In [3], Arman, Hsu and Chiu propose a video segmentation approach for encoded video sequences. Instead of decoding frame information, their method estimates differences in successive frames by comparing a subset of DCT coefficients produced in the compression stage. Their method thereby avoids decompression overhead. No special attention was given to gradual transitions.

Ardizzone, Gioiello, La Cascia and Molinelli, [2], use a neural-network approach for shot boundary detection. Their system first resizes each frame to obtain a 16x16 pixel gray-level image. Pixel-to-pixel differences of successive frames are sent to a three-layer Multi-layer Perceptron. The authors claim satisfactory results while processing several thousand frames per second. The paper does not address detection of gradual transitions.

3 Proposed Approach

3.1 Transitions Detection

Lets us consider a video as a function of three discrete variables $V(x,y,t)$. Our approach towards the detection of shot boundaries is based on the first-order partial derivatives of $V(x,y,t)$. Our main objective is to develop a method capable of accurate detection of both cuts and gradual transition boundaries. Our initial hypothesis is that shot boundaries correspond to discontinuities in the time domain. This implies that editing induces changes in the temporal profiles of most pixels and that these changes can in turn be identified using the temporal first-order partial derivative $V_t(x,y,t)$. For a given pixel position (x_0,y_0), a pixel's temporal profile is the function $V(x_0,y_0,t)$. It shows how a given pixel's intensity varies with time (figures 3,4,5).

What we need is a measure capable of detecting all the different types of shot boundaries. Lets us first draw attention to a few facts. For a pixel position (x_0,y_0), a cut or a wipe produces a step edge in $V(x,y,t)$, it accordingly produces a maximum in $|V_t(x,y,t)|$. During a fade or a dissolve, a pixel's intensity changes slowly and it produces a blurred step edge in $V(x,y,t)$ spanning many frames. If the derivative is calculated on an interval wide enough the edge produces a maximum in $|V_t(x,y,t)|$. It is then clear that our measure should be a function of $|V_t(x,y,t)|$. It should also be global and take into consideration a large number of pixels to reduce noise and motion effects. We propose using a difference measure $d(t)$ defined as follows:

$$d(t) = \sum_{(x,y)\in I} |V_t(x,y,t)| \tag{1}$$

The sign of the derivative should not be a factor in our measure because it only indicates the relative pixel intensity values, dark to bright or bright to dark, hence the use of the absolute value. We have tried other measures such as summing the gradient magnitude or averaging $|V_t(x,y,t)|$ but experimental evidence has shown that our measure (eq. 1) is the most adapted.

The calculation of the temporal derivative $V_t(x,y,t)$ is achieved by convolution of $V(x,y,t)$ with a Gaussian mask defined by

$$G_t(x,y,t) = \frac{-t}{(2\pi)^{3/2}\sigma^5} e^{\frac{-(x^2+y^2+t^2)}{2\sigma^2}} \tag{2}$$

where σ is the Gaussian scale. Since the Gaussian filter used to calculate the temporal derivative spans more than two frames, it is better suited to identify gradual transitions taking place over many frames.

During a cut, all pixels change at the same moment in time producing a sharp peak in *d(t)*. During fades and dissolves, pixel intensities change slowly but steadily. They produce smoother peaks in *d(t)*. During a wipe, pixel intensities change rapidly but at different times also resulting in a smooth peak in *d(t)*. Figures 3, 4 and 5 show typical pixel temporal profiles and associated responses in *d(t)* responses for a few common shot boundary types.

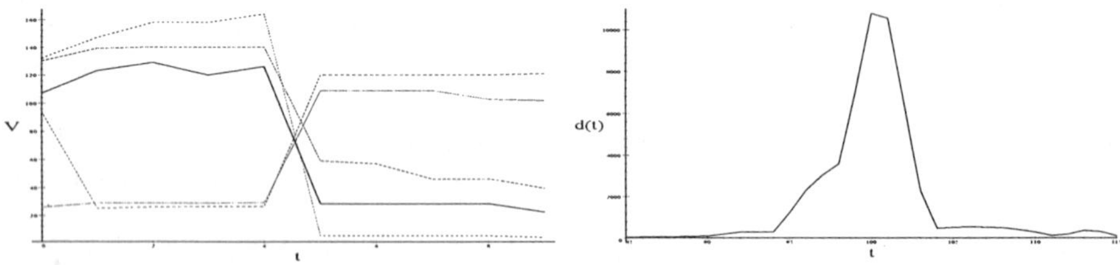

Figure 3. Typical temporal profiles for 5 pixels in a cut and associated *d(t)* response.

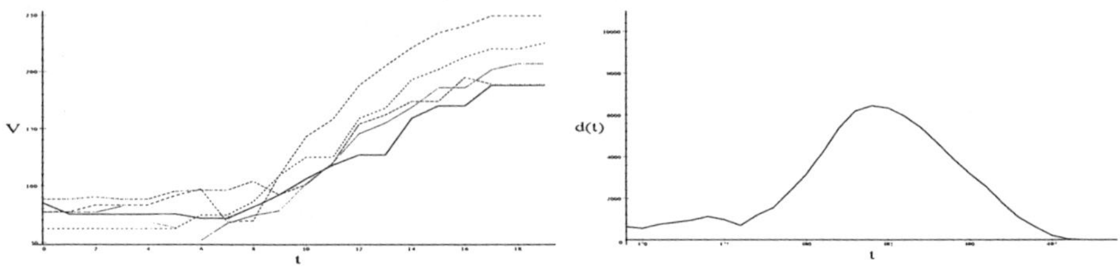

Figure 4. Typical temporal profiles for 5 pixels in a dissolve and associated *d(t)* response.

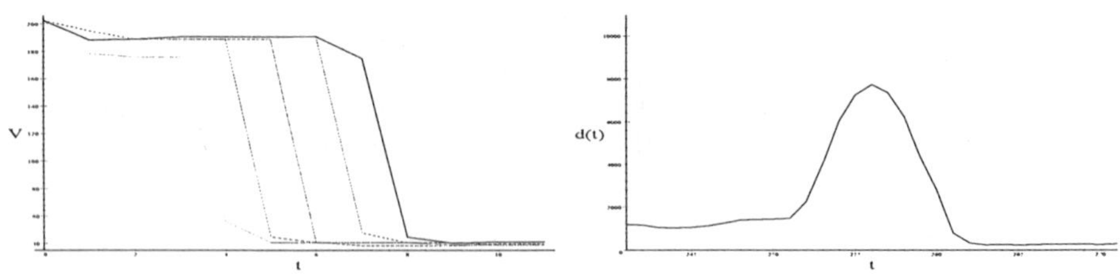

Figure 5. Typical temporal profiles for 5 pixels in a wipe and associated *d(t)* response.

We propose to locate shot boundaries in the video by identifying local maxima in our difference measure *d(t)*. From figure 6, we can see that not all local maxima in *d(t)* are due to shot boundaries, so we must remove unwanted maxima. First, to avoid multiple hits during gradual transition boundaries (labels *c*, *d* and *e*), we only label frames as shot boundaries when they correspond to local maxima over a fixed size window (only label *d* is kept). We also apply a threshold τ_1 to *d(t)* to remove small peaks caused by noise (labels *a* and *b*). The first threshold τ_1 is expressed as a percentage of the global maximum value in *d(t)*.

Experimental evidence has shown that in a number of situations, such as during gradual transitions or during high motion, many local maxima can arise. In such situations, it has become clear that a single threshold on the magnitude of *d(t)* is insufficient (maxima corresponding with labels *g* and *i* have approximately the same magnitude). We consequently use a second threshold τ_2 to eliminate local maxima corresponding to peaks of low relative amplitude (labels *f*, *g* and *h*), which are not caused by shot boundaries. The relative amplitude is defined as the average of the differences between the peak and its fore and aft minima. The second threshold τ_2 is expressed as a percentage of the value of the peak.

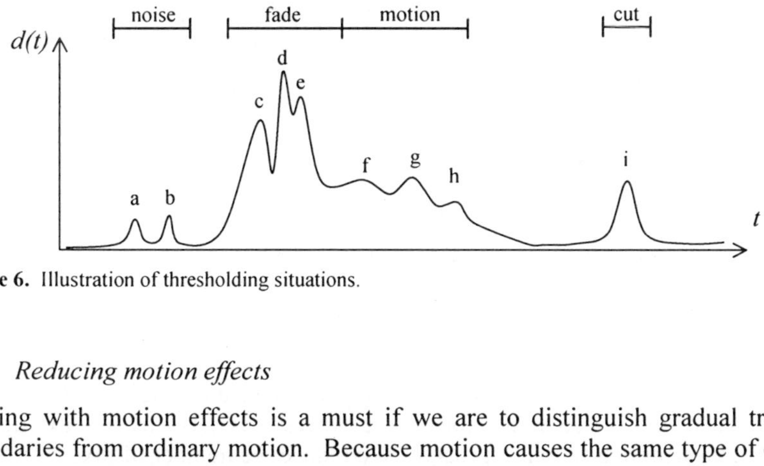

Figure 6. Illustration of thresholding situations.

3.2 *Reducing motion effects*

Dealing with motion effects is a must if we are to distinguish gradual transition boundaries from ordinary motion. Because motion causes the same type of changes as those encountered during gradual transitions, most methods for video segmentation are sensitive to motion effects. One option is to use registration techniques to compute global motion and then compensate for this motion. We have chosen not to use this approach because of the high computational cost involved. Instead, we have decided to use the first-order partial derivatives to identify areas where motion can cause problems. By identifying these motion areas, we can estimate *d(t)* only in regions that do not contain optical flow.

Motion affects shot boundary detection in areas where a pixel's intensity changes due to motion rather than editing (or both). In such areas, spatial derivatives $V_x(x,y,t)$ and $V_y(x,y,t)$ can be used to warn about possible motion effects.

To show how first-order partial derivatives can be used to reduce motion effects, we start by giving the optical flow equation [7]

$$V_x u + V_y v + V_t = 0$$

where *(u,v)* is the motion vector. From this equation, we see that if motion exists, at least one of the spatial partial derivatives must be non-zero. This brings us to propose evaluating both spatial derivatives $V_x(x,y,t)$ and $V_y(x,y,t)$ and eliminating from the sum in equation 1 pixels at which at least one of the spatial derivatives is important. This insures that high values in $|V_t(x,y,t)|$ resulting from motion are not taken into account in *d(t)*. While this also eliminates pixels lying on spatial edges, we can tolerate this because of the large number of pixels used in the estimation of *d(t)*. By eliminating contributions to *d(t)* from pixels whose spatial partial derivatives are important, we reduce motion effects on our algorithm. The influence of this algorithm designed to reduce motion effects on *d(t)* during both motion and gradual transitions is shown in figure 7. Notice how the motion areas have been reduced compared to the others. Two local maxima created in these motion areas have almost been totally removed.

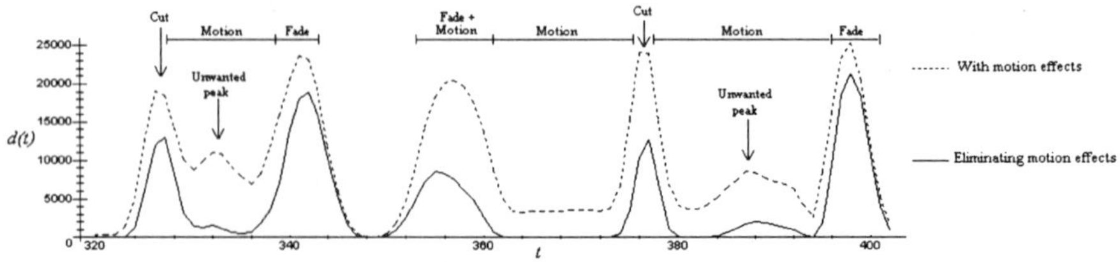

Figure 7. Reducing motion effects using spatial partial derivatives.

3.3 Sampling

While evaluating partial derivatives on every pixel in an image yields the most accurate measure, it is also a time consuming process. This is why we have decided to add spatial sampling to our approach. We reduce the number of pixels on which the derivatives are evaluated by sampling both spatial dimensions at regular intervals. Equation 1 becomes

$$d(t) = \sum_{(x,y)\in S} |V_t(x,y,t)| \tag{3}$$

where S is a sample of pixels taken from the image. Using a 1:5 ratio means that the every fifth pixel in both spatial directions in taken in S. The choice of sampling ratio is a compromise between algorithm accuracy and computational time. As the sampling ratio increases, the number of pixels in S decreases. This decrease especially impacts performance in videos with motion and gradual transitions.

With a careful choice of sampling ratio, the impact on the accuracy of the algorithm is within reasonable limits while the computational gain is considerable.

3.4 Summary of the algorithm

The algorithm is straightforward. The first step is the convolution of each frame from the video with the first order partial derivatives of the Gaussian (eq. 2) and the estimation of *d(t)* (eq. 3). The second step is the elimination of contributions from pixels exhibiting high values in at least one of the spatial derivatives. The third step is the localization of local maxima according to the algorithm presented in section 3.1.

4 Performance Evaluation

4.1 Evaluation Method

We have tested our algorithm on two separate video sequences comparing results with two other existing methods: region histograms and edge tracking. These two methods are summarized in section 2. While our choice of methods for comparison is arbitrary, both these methods have performed well when tested in survey papers [4, 5].

For the region histogram method, here are the parameters we used. We divide each frame into 16 regions in a 4x4 pattern and use 64 bin color histograms. The 8 highest difference values are dropped to compensate for motion. We use the twin-comparison algorithm to help identify gradual transitions. The thresholds varied from 1000 to 40000.

Concerning the edge tracking method, here are the parameters we used. The edge detector scale was set at $\sigma = 1.5$, the gradient threshold at 80 and the distance $r = 6$ pixels. Unfortunately the article's proposed motion registration technique is not implemented on our system. The threshold on $max(p_{in}, p_{out})$ varied from 0.1 to 0.6.

Our algorithm has many parameters influencing its performance. Here are the values we used in our tests. We use a Gaussian scale $\sigma = 1.5$ in all directions which produces good results for both sequences. To show how sampling affects accuracy, we use two different sampling ratios on both sequences. A low-resolution test uses a 1:10 ratio for the first sequence and a 1:20 ratio for the second. A high-resolution test respectively uses a 1:5 ratio and a 1:10 ratio for the first and second sequences. For the first sequence the sample set *S* has 660 pixels in the high-resolution test and 165 pixels in the low-resolution test. For the second sequence the sample set sizes are respectively 713 and 192 pixels. The local maximum window size is a compromise between reducing false positives during gradual transitions and the shortest possible shot length. Since one of the sequences contains a shot consisting of only 3 frames, we set the window size at 7. The threshold parameters are varied from 1% to 70% for the first threshold (applied to *d(t)*) and from 10% to 80% for the second threshold (applied to relative amplitude of *d(t)*).

We used two different video sequences to compare the algorithms. The first sequence is from a video trailer for the movie *Les Miserables*. The sequence was digitized at 160x120 pixels per frame and at 15 frames per second. It lasts 1715 frames and has 87 shot boundaries. The sequence contains 60 cuts and 27 gradual transitions. The second sequence is from a music video. It was digitized at 320x240 pixels per frame and at 15 frames per second. It consists of 2700 frames and contains 73 cuts and no gradual transitions. Both sequences have large amounts of both object and camera motion.

For each implemented algorithm and video sequence combination, we count the number of shot boundaries that are correctly identified, the number of missed shot boundaries and the number of false positives. If any frame in a gradual transition is marked, the boundary is considered correctly identified. But if multiple frames from the same gradual transition are marked, only one is considered correct and the others are labeled as false positives.

Comparing video segmentation methods is not easy. Depending on the application, finding an extra shot boundary at the expense of accepting many more false positives might or might not be acceptable. We have chosen a quantitative and non-contextual approach. We use recall versus precision graphs to compare the methods. Recall is defined as the number of desired items that are retrieved and precision is defined as the number of retrieved items that are desired.

$$recall = \frac{\#\,correct}{\#\,correct + \#\,missed} \qquad precision = \frac{\#\,correct}{\#\,correct + \#\,false}$$

Because the algorithms are tested using many threshold parameter combinations, many precision values are generated for a given recall value. The plots show the best precision value for a given recall value in all cases.

4.2 Experimental Results

Figure 8 shows a plot of recall versus precision values for the first video sequence. This sequence contains many gradual transitions. As can be seen from the plot, at both resolutions, our algorithm generates fewer false positives than the other methods, resulting in higher precision values for a given recall value. This is because our method is less sensitive to motion, enabling it to better locate gradual transitions. At high resolution, our algorithm does not generate any false positives at all for most recall values (recall < 86%). While the results are not quite as good in low resolution, precision is higher then with the other two methods. At high recall, our algorithm out-performs the others and does not decline as fast when recall approaches 100%.

Figure 9 shows another plot of recall versus precision values, this time for the second video sequence. This sequence only contains cuts, but it has a large amount of rapid motion. Again our algorithm outperforms the other methods. The plot lines for low and high resolution tests for superposed for most recall values, suggesting little impact from the sampling ratio. At the highest recall value of 100% (all shot boundaries found) only 2 false positives are generated in the high-resolution test and 3 false positives for the low-resolution test. At its highest recall value, the color histogram method generated 6 false positives but missed one cut. The edge-tracking algorithm did not do as good, but we did not implement the motion registration technique discussed in the article. For most recall values (recall < 98%), our algorithm does not produce any false positives.

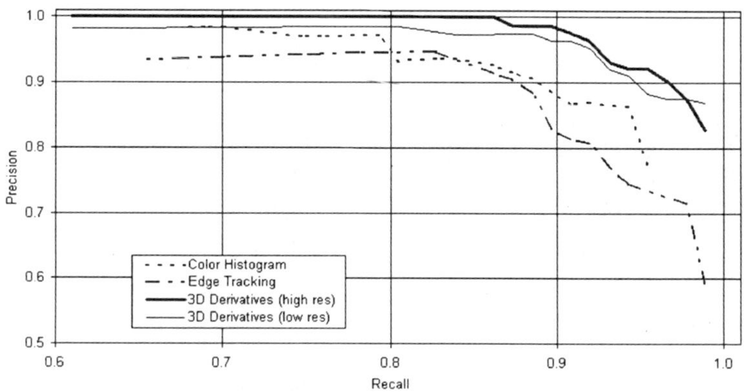

Figure 8. Recall versus precision for the first video sequence.

4.3 *Speed performance*

Both plots show that our method is accurate and robust. It has outperformed both of the others methods on both our test sequences. Table 1 gives approximate running times for the algorithms. The local color histogram method was the fastest segmenting the first sequence in 60 seconds and the second sequence in 450 seconds The edge tracking algorithm was one of the longest even without the motion compensation efforts. It took 2000 seconds to analyze the first sequence and 12000 seconds for the second. For the high-resolution test, our algorithm took a greedy 3200 seconds to segment the first sequence and 4600 seconds for the second. As expected it was faster for the low-resolution test. It took respectively 700 and 1300 seconds to segment both sequences. The respective speeds in frames per second (fps) are also given in Table 1.

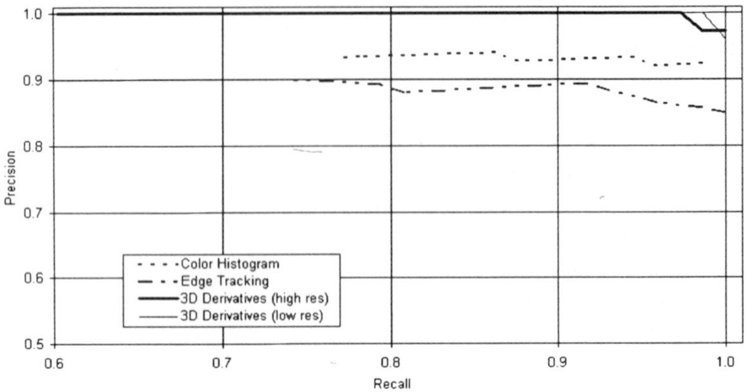

Figure 9. Recall versus precision for the second sequence (cuts only).

Table 1. Running times for the three algorithms.

	First Sequence	Second Sequence
Color Histogram	60 sec (28.6 fps)	450 sec (6 fps)
Edge Tracking	2000 sec (0.86 fps)	12000 sec (0.23 fps)
3D Derivatives (high res)	3200 sec (0.54 fps)	4600 sec (0.59 fps)
3D Derivatives (low res)	700 sec (2.45 fps)	1300 sec (2.08 fps)

5 Conclusion

For many years video indexing has been an important research area. It needs an efficient yet robust method for digital video segmentation. In this paper, we have presented a new algorithm designed to accurately identify cuts as well as gradual transitions. Using first-order partial derivatives, our algorithm recognizes shot boundaries with minimal influence from motion. Sampling considerably reduces execution time with a reasonable impact on accuracy. Experimental results confirm that our method works well with both cuts and gradual transitions. It also has shown that our method withstands large amounts of motion. Further research aims at getting a better understanding of parameter influences on the algorithm's performance. We have developed a Windows based application called Video Shot Detector (fig. 10). We plan on incorporating this video segmentation method in a future video indexing application.

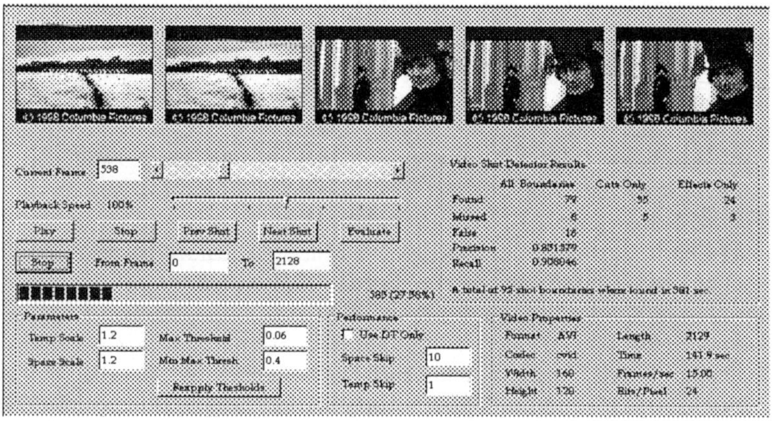

Figure 10. Example screen from our Windows based application

References

1. Philippe Aigrain and Philippe Joly, "The Automatic Real-Time Analysis of Film Editing and Transition Effects and its Applications", *Computers & Graphics* 18(1):93-103, 1994.
2. Edoardo Ardizzone, G. A. M. Gioiello, Marco La Cascia, and D. Molinelli, "A Real-time Neural Approach to Scene Cut Detection", *Proceedings of IS&T/SPIE Symposium on Electronic Imaging: Science and Technology, Conference: Storage and Retrieval for Image and Video Databases IV: Vol. 2670*, San Jose, CA, 1996.
3. Farshid Arman, Arding Hsu, and Ming-Yee Chiu, "Image Processing on Encoded Video Sequences", *ACM Multimedia Systems*, 1(5):211-219, March 1994.
4. John S. Boreczky and Lawrence A. Rowe, "Comparison of Video Shot Boundary Detection Techniques", *Proceedings of IS&T/SPIE Symposium on Electronic Imaging: Science and Technology, Conference: Storage and Retrieval for Image and Video Databases IV: Vol. 2670*, pp. 170-179, San Jose, CA, 1996.
5. Apostolos Dailianas, Robert B. Allen, and Paul England, "Comparison of automatic video segmentation algorithms", *Proceedings of SPIE Photonics East '95: Integration Issues in Large Commercial Media Delivery Systems: Vol. 2615*, pp. 2-16, Philadelphia, PA, November 1995.
6. Arun Hampapur, Ramesh Jain, and Terry Weymouth, "Digital Video Segmentation", *Proceedings of the Second ACM International Conference on Multimedia '94*, pp. 357-364, San Francisco, CA, October 1994.
7. B. K. P. Horn, *Robot Vision*, McGraw-Hill Book Company, MIT press, 1986.

8. John Chung-Mong Lee and Dixon Man-Ching Ip, "A Robust Approach for Camera Break Detection in Color Video Sequences", *Proceedings of IAPR Workshop on Machine Vision Application*, pp. 502-505, Kawasaki (Japan), December 1994.
9. Akio Nagasaka and Yuzuru Tanaka, "Automatic Video Indexing and Full Video Search for Object Appearances", In E. Knuth and L. Wegner, editors, *Proceedings of the IFIP TC2/WG 2.6 Second Working Conference on Visual Database Systems*, pp. 113-127, Budapest, 1991.
10. Ramin Zabih, Justin Miller, and Kevin Mai, "A Feature-based Algorithm for Detecting and Classifying Scene Breaks", *Proceedings of the Third ACM International Conference on Multimedia '95*, pp. 189--200, San Francisco, CA, November 1995.
11. HongJiang Zhang, Atreyi Kankanhalli, and Stephen W. Smoliar, "Automatic Partitioning of Full-motion Video", *Multimedia Systems*, 1(1):10-28, 1993.

IMAGE CLASSIFICATION TECHNIQUES FOR IMAGE RETRIEVAL ON THE WORLD WIDE WEB

N. ABBADENI*, D. ZIOU, S. WANG, N. MOURSLI AND J-C. BATISTA
Université de Sherbrooke, DMI, Sherbrooke, QC., J1K 2R1
Canada
E-mail: abbadeni@dmi.usherb.ca

N. JEMMALI
Corel Corp., Ottawa, ON.
Canada

Image retrieval is becoming an important research area with many applications in various fields, in particular in image and multimedia databases and digital libraries. In this paper, we are interested in performing image classification and retrieval on the WWW using both the image content and textual keywords. We present a prototype composed of two components. The first component corresponds to the database population part. It is composed of two tools: 1. the first tool (agent) crawls the WWW, collects images and parses HTML code in order to get some textual indices on each image; 2. the second tool performs content analyzing of each image and classifies it either as grey-level or color image, either as photo or graphic image and either as textured or non textured image. The classification into either photo or graphic is based on a multilayer perceptron neural network which uses the backpropagation algorithm. The classification into either textured or non textured image is based on an algorithm which uses the computation of image extrema. The second component corresponds to the retrieval part. Retrieval is done using both textual keywords and visual search using histogram similarity. The search can be done either in the whole database or in a specific class of images. A friendly user interface is provided to perform search and retrieval. Experimental results are very promising.
Keywords: image content, textual indices, image classification, image retrieval, neural networks, texture detection, World Wide Web.

1 Introduction

The World Wide Web is an enormous, distributed, hypermedia and non-structured information system. Tens of millions of images exist on the World Wide Web. Developing tools which would make it possible to seek specific images in this enormous image database is of an unquestionable utility and would give to the WWW all its potential. However, the search for images in the context of the WWW poses new challenges. Indeed, the incredibly large size of all these images and the extraordinary diversity of types of images

*AUTHOR OF CORRESPONDENCE

which one can find on the WWW (graphics, photos, satellite images, textured images, etc.) make this task extremely difficult.

Two fundamental issues are to be taken into account when developing such retrieval tools: effectiveness of search and effectivity of search. The effectiveness implies that one can find information in a reasonable time. With the power of the current workstations and the development of techniques such as parallel programming and multi-thread programming, the effectiveness is not a bottleneck [14]. However the effectivity (relevance) of the images retrieved compared to the request is a major problem and should be examined more closely. The majority of the retrieval tools existing on the WWW are not pertinent: many retrieved documents are not pertinent to the request (noise) and many documents pertinent to the request are not retrieved (silence).

When we are interested in images in particular, the problem becomes more crucial. Indeed, in the field of image processing and computer vision, there is no general algorithm able to process all types of images. In fact, for each type of images, one can find certain algorithms on which they work correctly and on other types they do not. For some class of images, an algorithm based on the computation of color is appropriated; for another class of images, an algorithm based on the computation of texture is more appropriated. Some algorithms work correctly on radar images but not on optical images, others work on textured images and not on non textured images and so on.

Taking into account all these facts, we believe that a preliminary and crucial step before developing an image retrieval tool on the WWW is to classify these images in many classes such as photographs, graphics, cartoons, faces, textured images, color images, etc. and then perform a search in each class. Doing so, we take at least two advantages: 1. effectivity of search is improved since search is done in a specific class and not in all the database (noise and silence are reduced); 2. we can apply appropriate algorithms on each class of images given that a general algorithm for all images does not exist.

A general architecture of our prototype is depicted in (Fig. 1). There are two major components. The first component corresponds to the collection and indexing part (database population); it collects images from the WWW and stores them in the database; HTML code is parsed and textual indices are extracted on each image; then, it performs content analyzing on each image in order to classify it either as grey-level or color image, either as photo or graphic and finally either as textured or non textured image. The second component corresponds to the retrieval part; when a query is posed, this component analyzes it and returns from the database an ordered set of images satisfying it. A user interface is provided to perform search and retrieval.

The paper is organized as follows: in section 2, a brief outline of related works is given and our work is situated among these works; in section 3, we present the image collection component; in section 4, we present the image classification component which is the most important part of this paper; in section 5, the indexing and retrieval scheme is outlined; and finally, in section 6, a brief summary of the paper is given and some important on going issues related to this project are discussed.

2 Related work

Up till now there have been many content-based image retrieval systems/prototypes developed such as QBIC [3], [8] and Photobook [19]. A lot of these systems were not developed for the WWW. Few of them were developed in order to be used in the context of the WWW. Such systems/prototypes include ImageRover [23], Webseer [10] and PictoSeek [11]. Such systems provide often keywords search combined with some content search. Color, texture and shape are the content features the most used. Some of these systems address architectural issues such as ImageRover [23] which is a distributed fleet of 32 robots running on a geographically distributed architecture in order to reduce the time of gathering images on the WWW.

The work we are presenting here fits in this global framework. In addition, we are addressing three other issues: 1. as mentioned before, a general algorithm in image processing which can be applied on each type of image does not exist. Given the extraordinary diversity of images on the WWW, it is fundamental to, first, classify these images into many classes and then apply an appropriate algorithm on each class. This will have also the benefit to reduce the search space and consequently noise and silence; 2. we are using neural networks to perform classification of images in either photos or graphics; 3. and finally, we are using an algorithm based on the computation of image extrema to classify images either as textured or non textured.

3 Image Collection

The collection of images on the WWW is a very expensive operation. On average, it takes about 80 seconds to bring back an image from the WWW [23]. Getting millions of images could take many years. In order to reduce this time, some works uses distributed architectures made up of several robots and can thus bring back up to 1 million images per month [23].

In this paper, we have not addressed such architectural issues. We have focused only on the development of a tool able to crawl the WWW and collect

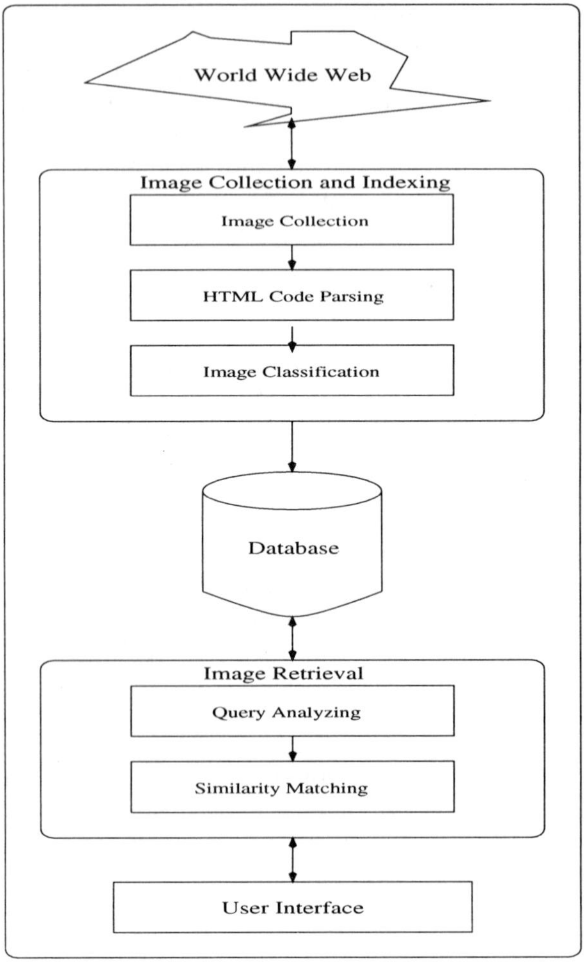

Figure 1. General architecture of our prototype.

images. The WWW crawler we have implemented works as follows:

- an HTML page is selected,
- this selected page is parsed and textual indices such as name, title, URL, caption and format of each image are extracted and stored in the

database,

- the hypertext links on this page are then selected and the corresponding pages are parsed as in the precedent step.

For experimental purposes we have collected about 1000 images from different URLs. This is sufficient for our objective. The images collected are in format GIF or JPEG (JFIF) which are the most frequent image formats on the WWW. We can easily extend to the other image formats. These images are then converted to PPM or PGM format in order to be processed in a convenient way.

4 Image Classification

Our objective here is to classify images into many categories or classes. First, each image is classified as either grey-level or color image. Second, each image is classified either as photo or graphic. Finally, each image is classified either as textured or non textured. We obtain, thus, the following classes: textured grey-level photos, textured grey-level graphics, textured color photos, textured color graphics, non textured grey-level photos, non textured grey-level graphics, non textured color photos, non textured color graphics.

To distinguish between grey-level images and color images, it is sufficient to consider the image heading. Color images have specific headings different from those of grey-level images.

To distinguish between photos and graphics, we have used techniques inspired from [10]. We compute on each image a set of content parameters. These parameters are then passed to a neural network classifier which performs classification in either photos or graphics.

To distinguish between textured images and non textured images, we have used an algorithm inspired from [16]; it is based on the detection of the granularity (coarseness) of an image and it uses the computation of image extrema.

In the following we will focus on the last two classifications. We will not discuss the first classification (grey-level or color) here since it is just a programming task in our point of view.

4.1 Photos versus graphics

General scheme

Here we want to distinguish between photos and graphics. Photos include natural scenes such as persons, faces, flowers and towns. Graphics include logos, drawings and icons. A sample of photographic images is given in (Fig. 2) and a sample of graphic images is given in (Fig. 3).

The classifier used here is a multilayer perceptron neural networks based on the backpropagation algorithm. It works as follows:

- first, the URL of an image is taken from the database, the image is read and converted to either PPM or PGM format.
- second, the content of the image is analyzed and a set of parameters is computed on the image. These parameters are based on the content of the image, especially on color or grey-levels distribution.
- finally, the computed parameters in the precedent step are passed to the neural network classifier. This neural network classifies, then, the image either as a photo or a graphic.

The classification of images in either graphics or photos is based on the following observations [10]:

- image size: graphics have, in general, a small size if compared to photos.
- number of different colors/grey-levels: graphics, in general, contain less different colors than photos.
- presence of saturated colors: saturated colors are more likely to occur in graphics than in photos.
- transitions in a pixel neighborhood: On one hand, transitions in photos from one pixel to its neighborhood are rarely null. At the opposite, in graphics, transitions from one pixel to its neighborhood are more likely to be null in one region. On the other hand, transitions in graphics between two regions are more sharper than in photos.

Based on these observations which are widely true in reality, we have derived the following parameters:

- the size of the image: this results in two parameters, one is the minimum between the two dimensions of an image, the second is the ratio between the maximum of the two dimensions and the minimum of the two dimensions. For the first parameter, graphics, in general, may score around 30; photos may score around 200. For the second parameter, graphics score, in general, more than 2; photos are likely to score between 1 and 2. These parameters are computed on both color images and grey-level images.

Figure 2. Sample of photographic images.

- the number of different colors: for photos, the number of different colors is more larger than in graphics. Photos may score between 1000 and many thousands; graphics score, in general, less than 1000 and, often, a small number between 2 and 100. This parameter is computed on both color images and grey-level images.

- the dominant color: in graphics, it is more likely to find an important number of pixels with the same color than in photos. Often, in graphics, the number of pixels with the same color is more than 10%. In photos, it is often small than 1%. This parameter is computed on both color images and grey-level images.

- the number of saturated colors: computed for four different thresholds; it results in four parameters, each related to one threshold. We have used the following thresholds: 20, 63, 100 and 180. The score of these parameters is more larger in graphics than in photos. These parameters are computed only for color images.

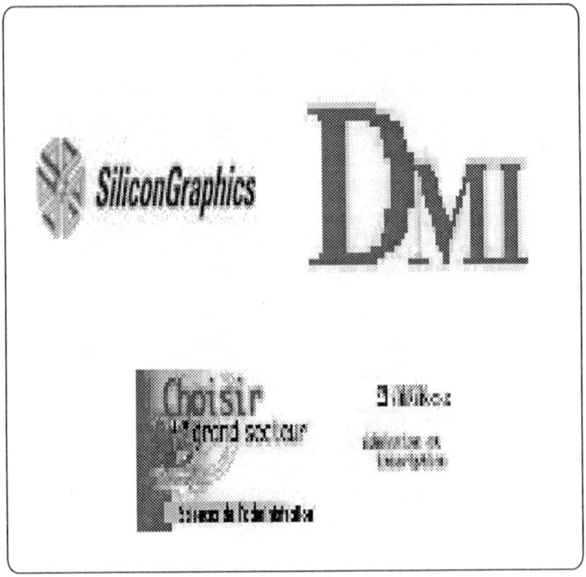

Figure 3. Sample of graphic images.

- the transitions between a pixel and its neighborhood: for color images, this results in six parameters, three of them are computed on all the RGB representation components of the image for three different thresholds, and three are computed on the intensity component of the HSI representation of the image for the same thresholds. For grey-level images, this results in three parameters computed for three different thresholds. We have used the following thresholds: 0, 1 and 20. For threshold 0, the score of these parameters in graphics is higher than in photos. For thresholds 1 and 20, the score of these parameters, in general, is higher in photos than in graphics.

So, for color images, we have computed 14 parameters: 2 parameters related to image size; 1 parameter related to the number of different colors in the image; 1 parameter related to the dominant color; 4 parameters related to saturated colors, each corresponds to a threshold; 3 parameters related to color transitions, each corresponds to a threshold; and finally, 3 parameters related to intensity transitions, each corresponds to a threshold. For grey-level images, we have computed 7 parameters: 2 parameters related to image size; 1 parameter related to the number of different grey-levels in the image; 1 parameter related to the dominant color; and finally, 3 parameters related to grey-level transitions, each corresponds to a threshold. These parameters have been normalized.

Below, two examples of such computed parameters (Tab. 1, 2, 3, 4, 5) related to two different color images (one is a photo and the other is a graphic) given in (Fig. 4).

Figure 4. a./ cma98b (photo), b./ demo (graphic).

Table 1. Number of different colors and dominant color.

Image	Number of colors	Dominant color
cma98b	0.208	0.002
demo	0.016	0.180

Table 2. Saturation computed for four different thresholds.

	Saturation			
Image	$P_1 = 20$	$P_2 = 63$	$P_3 = 100$	$P_4 = 180$
cma98b	0.997	0.609	0.458	0.217
demo	0.790	0.087	0.068	0.010

Table 3. Dimension ratio and lower dimension.

Image	Dimension	
	Dimension ratio	Lower Dimension
cma98b	1.333	0.120
demo	5.250	0.060

Table 4. Color transitions computed for three different thresholds.

Image	Color transitions		
	$P_1 = 0$	$P_2 = 1$	$P_3 = 20$
cma98b	0.000	1.000	0.870
demo	0.181	0.818	0.311

Table 5. Intensity transitions computed for three different thresholds.

Image	Intensity transitions		
	$P_1 = 0$	$P_2 = 1$	$P_3 = 20$
cma98b	0.009	0.990	0.340
demo	0.192	0.807	0.437

For image *cma98b*, these parameters have the following significance: there are $0.208 \times 256^2 = 13631$ different colors in this image; the dominant color exists in 0.2% pixels in the image; there are 99.7% pixels in the image that contain saturated colors > 20, 60.9% pixels in the image that contain saturated colors > 63, 45.8% pixels in the image that contain saturated colors > 100 and 21.7% pixels in the image that contain saturated colors > 180; the ratio between the higher dimension and the lower dimension of the image is 1.333 and the lower dimension is $0.120 \times 1000 = 120$; there are no pixels in the image with a null color transition to their neighborhood, all the color transitions between a pixel in the image and its neighborhood are $>= 1$ and 87% pixels of the image have color transition to their neighborhood $>= 20$; and finally, there are 0.9% pixels of the image with a null transition in their intensity component to their neighborhood, 99% pixels of the image have transition in their intensity component to their neighborhood $>= 1$ and 34% pixels of the image have transition in their intensity component to their neighborhood $>= 20$.

The same description can be made on the second image *demo*. If the values of the different parameters on the two images are compared, the veracity of the parameters used is verified. For example, if we take a look at the number of different colors parameter in both images, we find that in the image *cma98b* we have 13631 different colors and in the image *demo* we have 1048 different colors. This is not sufficient to distinguish between the two images since some photos may contain a number of colors similar to that in the graphic image *demo*. So, we have to examine other parameters; if we examine the dominant color parameter, we find that for the image *cma98b* the dominant color exists in 0.2% of its pixels whether in *demo* the dominant color exists in 18% of its pixels and so on.

To make a decision, we need to combine all these parameters together. Thresholding techniques cannot be used to accomplish this given the high number of parameters and the dependence between them. Neural Networks techniques seem to be more adaptable in this situation.

Classification using neural networks

Once these parameters computed, we have used them to classify images in either graphics or photos. Classification using neural networks is done in two stages. Initially, the neural network is trained on a representative sample of patterns. Once the learning process is done successfully, we can give to the trained network a set of test patterns in order to make generalization. The test patterns used were off-line training.

The multilayer perceptron used to classify color images was made up of one input layer of 14 neurons, one hidden layer of 6 neurons and one output layer of 2 neurons. The training was done on a set of 103 patterns containing as well as graphics than photos. Then, a set of test patterns was given to the network. The experimental results given below show very good results both in learning and generalization. For grey-level images, the neural network used was made up of one input layer of 7 neurons, one hidden layer of 3 neurons and one output layer of 2 neurons.

The experimental results concerning the training are given in table (Tab. 6). The experimental results concerning the test are given in table (Tab. 7). The corresponding images are shown in (Fig. 6). The images *dave2*, *daveshania*, and *deploy* are classified as photos and the images *del5*, *demo*, *dessin_accueil* and *diverse1* are classified as graphics. If we take a look at the image *dessin_accueil*, we may hesitate to classify it as a graphic or a photo. Indeed, in practice, there are some images which are neither photos nor graphics; the image *dessin_accueil* is an example.

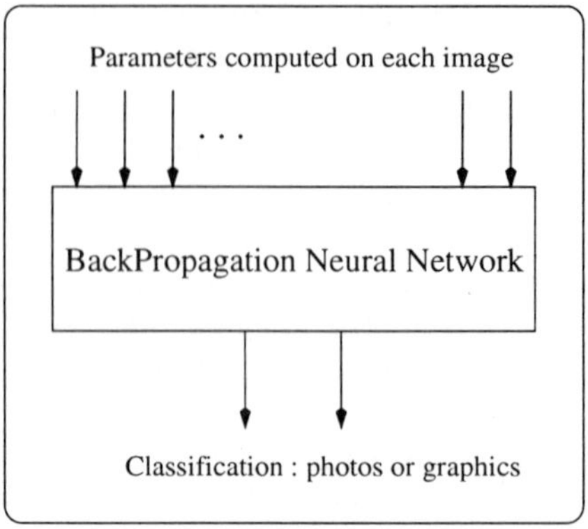

Figure 5. Backpropagation neural network.

Table 6. Experimental results of network training.

Number of iterations	Correct patterns	error/unit
400	97.09 right	0.05364
800	98.06 right	0.03981
1200	98.06 right	0.03714
1600	98.06 right	0.03585
2000	98.06 right	0.03478

Table 7. Experimental results of network testing.

Output neuron 1	Output neuron 2	Image name
1.00	0.00	dave2
0.96	0.04	daveshania
0.00	1.00	del5
0.00	1.00	demo
1.00	0.00	deploy
0.00	1.00	dessin_accueil
0.00	1.00	diverse1

4.2 Textured images versus non textured images

Texture is a fundamental feature in classification, retrieval and recognition problems. Classify images into textured and non textured ones is very useful.

Figure 6. Images corresponding to the test results of (Tab. 7).

One can search for radar images, for example, which are often textured images. In this case, it will be more efficient and more effective to restrict the search in the textured images class only. Before applying an algorithm of texture analysis on a given image, it is more suitable to ensure initially that the image in question is a textured one; elsewhere the results risk to be not significant and can induce in error [a].

Texture can be defined as the repetition of one or several primitives in a regular or a random manner. A primitive can be defined as a relatively small region in which the grey-values are steady uniform. It follows that an image is regarded as textured if it contains some primitives which are repeated in the image. So, we can think that the granularity of the primitives determine largely the presence of texture in an image: 1. if the primitives are very small (Fig. 8.(a)), the image is regarded as an image of noise; 2./ if the primitives are very large (Fig. 8.(b)), the image is regarded as containing an object shape rather than texture; 3./ if the primitives are neither very small neither very large and they are repeated either in a regular manner (Fig. 8.(c)) or in a

[a] This is not specific to texture. It exists also for many other characteristics and domains. The general problem of knowing if an image has the desired characteristic before applying a corresponding algorithm on it is similar to the problem of data clustering: before applying a clustering algorithm on a set of data, it should initially be made sure that these data have tendencies which make it possible to gather them in clusters.

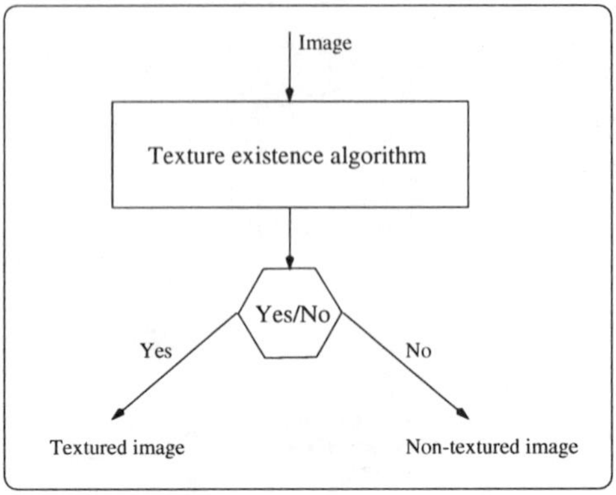

Figure 7. Texture existence algorithm.

random manner (Fig. 8.(d)), the image is regarded as textured.

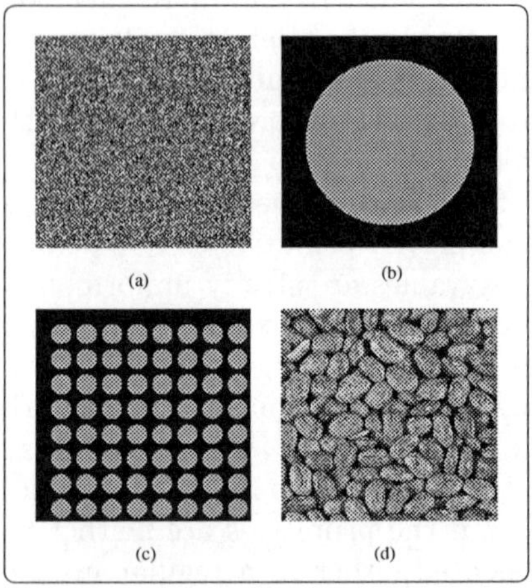

Figure 8. (a) image of noise: non textured. (b) image containing one object (disk): non textured. (c) image containing a repetition of a disk in a regular manner: textured. (d) image containing a repetition of a pattern in a random manner: textured.

The texture existence algorithm used here is based on the detection of the granularity of an image. Granularity detection is based on the computation of image extrema [16]. Let us denote the image function with $I(i,j)$ where i denotes the row coordinate and j the column coordinate. The algorithm works as follows:

- a pixel $I(i,j)$ will be considered as a local row maximum if and only if $I(i,j) > I(i,j+1)$ and $I(i,j) > I(i,j-1)$. If a set of adjacent pixels $S = \{I(i,j)/a <= j <= b\}$ has a constant grey-value such that $I(i,j) > I(i,a-1)$ and $I(i,j) > I(i,b+1)$, the local row extrema is $I(i,(a+b)/2)$.
- a pixel $I(i,j)$ will be considered as a local row minimum if and only if $I(i,j) < I(i,j+1)$ and $I(i,j) < I(i,j-1)$. If a set of adjacent pixels $S = \{I(i,j)/a <= j <= b\}$ has a constant grey-value such that $I(i,j) < I(i,a-1)$ and $I(i,j) < I(i,b+1)$, the local row extrema is $I(i,(a+b)/2)$.
- local column maximum and local column minimum are defined in a similar way.
- a pixel is considered as an image maximum (respectively minimum) if it is both a local row maximum (respectively a local row minimum) and local column maximum (respectively a local column minimum).

Granularity at a pixel is, then, computed as the density of local extrema in a small image window around the pixel.

The results computed on the images of (Fig. 8) are given in (Fig. 9): 1. in (Fig. 9.(a)), the image extrema corresponds to the image of noise (Fig. 8.(a)). Such an image contains a lot of local variations and then its granularity is extremely small. So this image does not correspond to a textured image; 2. in (Fig. 9.(b)), the image extrema corresponds to the image containing a large circle (Fig. 8.(b)). Such an image contains almost no local variations and then its granularity is very large. So this image does not correspond to a textured image; 3. in (Fig. 9.(c) and (d)), the images extrema correspond to the images of (Fig. 8.(c) and (d)). Such images contain reasonable local variations so that we can consider them as textured images.

An image is considered as textured if its density of extrema d is between a maximal threshold $MaxT$ and a minimal threshold $MinT$: if $d > MaxT$, the image is considered as non textured and is considered as an image containing object shapes; if $d < MaxT$, the image is considered as non textured and is considered as an image of noise.

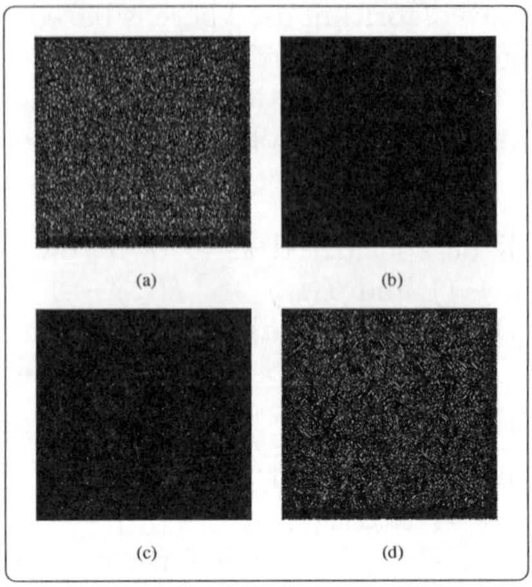

Figure 9. Image extrema computed on (a) image of noise. (b) image containing one object (disk). (c) image containing a repetition of a disk in a regular manner. (d) image containing a repetition of a pattern in a random manner.

This algorithm is now implemented for grey-level textured images only. It will be soon available for color textured images also.

5 Image Retrieval

As a first step, we have used the same algorithm for image indexing and retrieval regardless of their classes. For the moment, retrieval can be performed either with textual keywords or visual search (a QBE like interface). In both cases, the space of search can be reduced by specifying the classes of the images desired:

- textual keywords: users can provide textual indices extracted from the HTML code such as image title, image format, URL, etc. Search can be made in the whole database or a restricted portion of the database; in this case, the desired class of images is specified such as the class of color images, photos, graphics, textured photos, etc.

- visual search: given an image request, the user can select it and the system returns all the images in the database that are similar to it based on histogram similarity. The images are ordered according to their distance to the image request. The Euclidean distance is used here.

Figure 10. User interface.

A friendly user interface is provided to support search and retrieval (Fig. 10).

6 Summary and on going work

We have presented a prototype of an image classification for retrieval purposes on the WWW. We have used a neural network to classify images either as photos or graphics. We have used an algorithm based on the computation of extrema in images to classify them either as textured or non textured ones. We have insisted especially on the fact that the classification step of images in different classes such as photos, graphics, textured and non textured images is very important and may result in at least two advantages: 1. increase of effectivity (reduction of noise and silence); 2. application of appropriate algorithms on each class of images. There are many important issues related to this project under investigation. The most important are the following:

- color textured images: to classify images into either textured or non textured, we have considered only grey-level images. We are extending this classification to textured color images as well.
- more classes: we have considered grey-level *versus* color images, photos *versus* graphics, and textured *versus* non textured images. It is obvious that there are more image classes in practice. We are considering other image classes such as images of human faces, logos, etc.
- development of specific algorithms for each class of images: up till now we have used classes only to reduce the search space but we have applied the same algorithm to index and retrieve all the images in different classes. We are now developing specific algorithms for each class of images. For example, for textured images, we are using the autoregressive model to index and retrieve these textured images. For graphics, it will be sufficient to use only the dominant color(s) rather than using all the histogram like in photos; this will save space and time.

The prototype presented here is implemented in Java and C/C++. The crawler and the user interface are implemented in Java. The image content analyzing and the backpropagation algorithm are implemented in C/C++.

Acknowledgments

We thank D. Tver for providing the backpropagation algorithm implementation.

References

1. Abbadeni N., Ziou D. and Wang S., Image Classification and Retrieval on the World Wide Web, to appear in the *Proceedings of the fourth ACM Digital Libraries Conference*, Poster session, Berekely, CA, August 11-14, 1999.
2. Abbadeni N., Ziou D. and Wang S., Recherche d'images basée sur leur contenu : représentation de la texture par le modèle autorégressif, *Rapport de recherche*, N. 216, 50 p., 1998.
3. Ashley J., Barber R., Flickner M., Hafner J., Lee D., Niblack W. and Petkovic D., Automatic and Semi-Automatic Methods for Image Annotation and Retrieval in QBIC, *Proc. SPIE - Storage and Retrieval for Image and Video Databases*, Vol. 2420, pp. 24-35, 1995.
4. Athitsos V., Swain M. J. and Frankel C., Distinguishing photographs and graphics on the World Wide Web, *IEEE Workshop on Content-Based Access of Image and Video Libraries*, 8 p., June 1997.
5. Chang S-F., Smith J. R., Beigi M. and Benitez A., Visual Information Retrieval from Large Distributed Online Repositories, *Communications of the ACM*, Vol. 40, N. 12, pp. 63-71, December 1997.
6. Chang S-K. and Hsu A., Image Information Systems: Where Do We Go from Here ?, *IEEE Trans. on Knowledge and Data Engineering*, Vol. 4, N. 5, pp. 431-442, October 1992.
7. De Marsicoi M., Cinque L. and Levialdi S., Indexing Pictorial Documents by their Content: a Survey of Current Techniques, *Image and Vision Computing*, Vol. 15, N. 2, pp. 119-141, February 1997.
8. Flickner M., Sawhney H., Niblack W., Ashley J., Huang Q., Dom B. *et al.*, Query by Image and Video Content: The QBIC System, *IEEE Computer*, Vol. 28, N. 9, pp. 23-32, September 1995.
9. Furht B., Smoliar S. W. and Zhang H., Video and Image Processing in Multimedia Systems, Kluwer Academic Publishers, 1995.
10. Frankel C., Swain M. J. and Athitsos V., WebSeer: an Image Search Engine for the WWW, *Technical Report*, 96-14, Dept. of Computer Science, The University of Chicago, 23 p., August 1996.
11. Gevers T. *et al.*, Retrieving and Localizing Objects in Images on the WWW, *Vision Interface*, Trois-Rivières, May 1999.
12. Gong Y., Intelligent Image Databases: Towards Advanced Image Retrieval, *Kluwer Academic Publishers*, 1998.
13. Grosky W. I., Multimedia Information Systems, *IEEE Multimedia*, Spring 1994.
14. Gudivada V. N., Raghavan V. V., Grosky W. I. and Kasanagottu R., In-

formation Retrieval on the World Wide Web, *IEEE Internet Computing*, Vol. 1, N. 5, pp. 58-68, 1997.
15. Gudivada V. N. and Raghavan V. V., Content-Based Image Retrieval Systems, *IEEE Computer*, September 1995.
16. Karu K., Jain A. K. and Bolle R. M., Is There Any Texture In The Image ?, *Pattern Recognition*, Vol. 29, N. 9, pp. 1437-1446, 1996.
17. La Cascia M., Sethi S. and Sclaroff S., Combining Textual and Visual Cues for Content-based Image Retrieval on the WWW, *IEEE Workshop on Content-based Access of Image and Video Libraries*, 5 p., June 1998.
18. Ogle V. E. and Stonebraker M., Chabot : Retrieval from a Relational Database of Images, *Technical Report*, Department of Computer Science, the University of California at Berkeley, 1996.
19. Pentland A., Picard R. W. and Sclaroff S., Photobook: Content-Based Manipulation of Image Databases, *International Journal of Computer Vision*, 18(3), 233-254, 1996.
20. Petkovic D., Niblack W., Flickner M., Steele D., Lee D., Yin J. *et al.*, Recent Applications of IBM's Query by Image Content, *IBM Research Report*, RJ 10006 (89095), January 1996.
21. Samet H. and Soffer A., MARCO : MAp Retrieval by COntent, *IEEE Trans. on Pattern Analysis and Machine Intelligence*, Vol. 18, N. 8, pp. 783-798, August 1996.
22. Sclaroff S., World Wide Web Image Search Engines, *Position Paper for NSF Workshop on Visual Information Management*, 2 p., Cambridge, MA. 1995.
23. Sclaroff S., Taycher L. and La Cascia M., ImageRover: a Content-based Image Browser for the WWW, *IEEE Workshop on Content-based Access of Image and Video Libraries* , pp. 2-9, June 1997.
24. Wu J. K., Content-Based Indexing of Multimedia Databases, *IEEE Trans. on Knowledge and Data Engineering*, Vol. 9, N. 6, pp. 978-989, November/December 1997.
25. Zhang H., Aigrain P. and Petkovic D. Eds., Representation and Retrieval of Visual Media in Multimedia Systems, A Special Issue of *Multimedia Tools and Applications Journal*, Vol. 3, N. 3, Kluwer Academic Publishers, 1996.

CUSTOMISABLE IMAGE CATEGORISATION AND RETRIEVAL WITH INTELLIGENT INTERACTIVE USER INTERFACE

DEZHONG HONG, SUMEET SOHAN SINGH, YONG-WEI ZHU, JIAN-KANG WU

RWCP[*] Information-Base Functions KRDL Lab, Kent Ridge Digital Labs, 21 Heng Mui Keng Terrace, Singapore 119613
E-mail: dhong@krdl.org.sg, sumeet@krdl.org.sg, ywzhu@krdl.org.sg, jiankang@krdl.org.sg

Abstract: A customisable image categorisation and retrieval system is described. A method to define object models is proposed. Algorithms for image object categorisation based on the models are developed. A user friendly interface is designed to have the user in the loop for system customisation. With the interface, it is easier and more efficient for users to understand the functionalities provided by the system and to express their requirements and desire during image categorisation and retrieval. Using the concept of object category and image store, users can easily define new objects and create his/her own image indices. A novel image query and indexing method is also proposed. The refinement of image retrieval is done in a progressive way, for example, in a sequence of textural query, query by image examples, and query by image objects.

Keywords: Image retrieval, Content-based, Image categorisation, User interface, Object modelling, Supervised learning, Fuzzy C-means classifier.

1 Introduction

In the community of content-based image retrieval, most of the available techniques provide functionalities to search for images based on visual features, such as colour, texture, shape, etc.[1,2,3,5] The aim of our work is to extract and describe image contents at a level higher. At this level, queries such as "find me photos of my son at beaches" are possible. This provides means for the users to retrieve desired images in a way he/she is used to.

The implication is that techniques for image segmentation and retrieval should, therefore, be developed to "understand" image contents at a certain degree. As we already know that there exists a big gap between people and computers in understanding natural images. While looking at an image, the computer is easy to tell the contents of the image at the feature level, regarding colour, texture and shape. It can precisely measure the RGB values at every pixel. However, it is hard, in general, for a computer to say that it is a building, a tree, or a car in the image. On the other hand, people interpret contents of an image at semantic level rather

[*] This work is sponsored by the Real World Computing Partnership.

than at low feature levels. Looking at an image, we can immediately say that it consists of trees, buildings, sky, etc., even colours of sky vary from place to place. We are used to describe an image in a natural way: "This is the photo of my son playing in the beach".

Therefore, one of the kernel problems for image categorisation and retrieval is to let computers understand what users really see in an image, and to let users understand what computers describe about an image [10]. It is noticed that the difference lies at the languages and methods employed by computers and human users. A bridge should be built to fill the gap between people and computers, which is referred to as "interactive user interface" in this paper. The aim of this approach is to translate between the computer language (visual features) and the human language (semantic/textural description).

To establish the links between semantic descriptions of objects and image features, the knowledge of interested contents of images should be acquired through the user interface. The following issues are addressed in this paper:

- Image feature extraction: To extract effective features for distinguishing various objects.
- Object modelling: Three object models are briefly described: textured object model, face model and appearance model.
- A novel learning algorithm for acquiring human knowledge of visual objects on particular application domains.
- An interactive interface for on-line knowledge acquisition and query refinements.

The interactive interface is specially designed to let users customise the system in four aspects:

- Select and build object models.
- Create image stores for various collections of images.
- Training data acquisition and learning.
- Query composition and refinement with three types of query methods.

The system provides functions for object-based image retrieval. The algorithms proposed in this paper have been tested on a database with 2400 digital home photos. Preliminary experimental results are presented. In the rest of the paper, extensive discussion is given to object categories, object modelling, object clustering, image categorisation, and object-based image retrieval.

2 Semantic Object Categories

It is said that "a picture is worth ten thousands words." That means that what is contained in the image may be too difficult to put into words. On the other hand, it is true that different people may describe the same image in different ways, or different people may tell different stories about the same image. For instance, a green region with particular texture in an image can be "*trees*" in some cases, and "*forest*" in another. Similar green stuff may also be called "*meadow*", "*plants*", "*grass*", or "*mountain*". The interpretation of image content is obviously subjective and it is related to the context of the images. We also noticed that one object (e.g. sky) may have multiple appearances (e.g. clear sky, cloudy sky, sunset sky, etc.).

Therefore, the system should be designed to accommodate a large number of object categories that can be customised by the users based on their application requirements, and to support multiple appearances of object. Our goal is to build an interface and algorithms to assist the users in learning and creating customised object categories based on the personal requirements.

The diagram of object categories designed in this approach is illustrated in Figure 1. An object category is defined as a collection of the objects that possess similar properties and are described by the same object models. The semantic description associated with each object category is useful to the users to identify the included objects, such as natural category (including: sky, tree, water, field, mountain, and building), countryside category (including: plant, pond, tree, soil, cottage, and sky), vegetable category (including: cabbage, green pepper, carrot, tomato, potato, and cucumber), family category (including: John, Mary, son, and daughter), etc. The object model [1,4,9,10] assigned to each object category is employed to compute the features for each member object and separate them from each other (to be introduced in the next chapter).

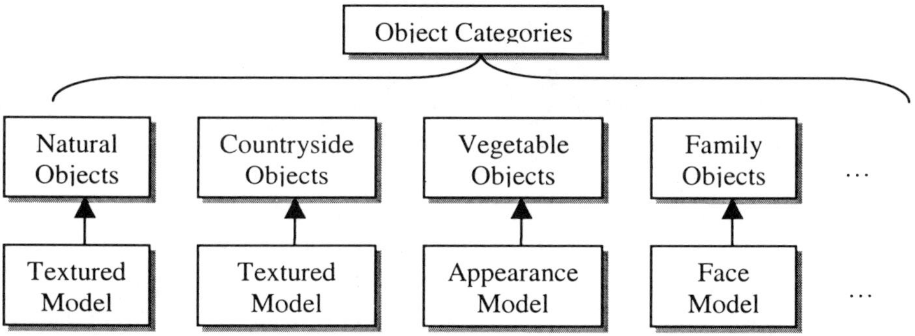

Figure 1. Object categories customised for the description of variant images.

Generally, when a user is browsing a batch of images, his interests mainly focus on a few objects presenting in the images. If we try to include all the possible objects into one object category, we may face the difficulties to distinguish them. It is impossible to create a number of universal object categories for all different purposes. An interactive interface is, therefore, presented to the user to customise the object categories based on the personal interests. From this point of view, we may conclude that one object category customised for a special case is normally effective on one or a few sets of images that may be selected by the users or pre-processing algorithms. Obviously, we cannot expect the object model for face detection and recognition to be effective on describing natural objects.

Each object in an object category is represented by a number of object clusters that are corresponding to the various appearances of the object. The object clusters are maintained by the fuzzy C-means clustering algorithm (to be detailed in the following chapter). Before applying an object category to a batch of images, the user may need to understand what kinds of objects have been defined in this category and what appearances have been included. An interactive interface is designed to let users browse the object category, which is illustrated in Figure. 2. The visual appearances presented for each object provide the users a better linkage between the semantic object descriptions and the visual features.

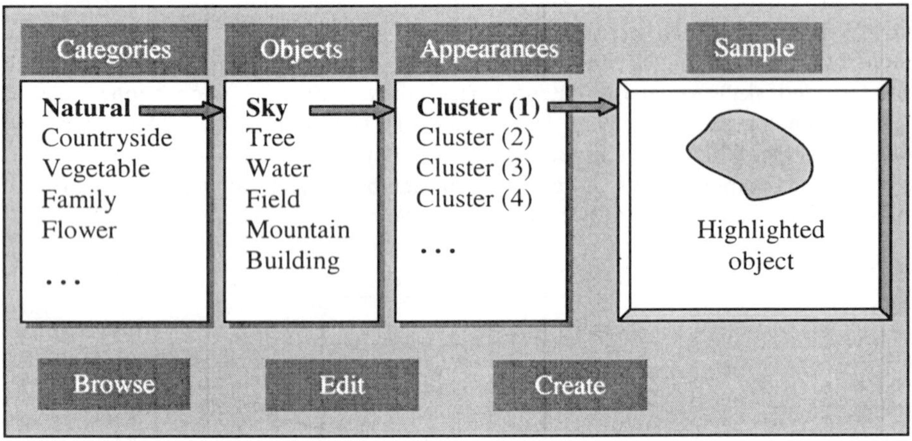

Figure 2. The interface for creating, editing, training and browsing object categories.

We do not expect users to be experienced in image processing and image retrieval. If the image retrieval model is expressed in a technical way: "Please compose the object model by 40% colour, 25% texture, 20% shape and 15% spatial relation", most of the users would be confused, and it is hard to set the percentages to satisfy different images. However, the interface shown in Figure 2 can provide the users the visual perceptual feeling of the object models defined in the system.

A number of object models may be built in the system, such as textured model, appearance model, face model, etc. They are specially designed for the definition of certain kinds of objects. For instance, we recommend that natural objects are defined by the textured model. In the system, it is unnecessary to name the object models explicitly. They are better explained by the sample object categories provided in the system. Once the users understand the object models by browsing the sample objects, they can create their own object categories for a particular batch of images. The new object categories can be derived from the sample object categories that implicitly represent the corresponding object models.

3 Object Models

The objective of the object model design is to extract effective features to distinguish and describe various objects. Due to the serious variation of different images in illumination, colour, scale, noise, geometric transformation, etc., it is not practical to design a universal filter and create a universal object model to be effective on all kinds of images.

In this approach, we have developed three types of object models:

(1) Textured model: It is for the description of natural objects, such as sky, tree, water, field, mountain, and building, which depend heavily on amount of and types of textures. It consists of three feature components [2]: LUV colour component, texture energy component, and texture direction component. The original image is initially segmented into homogeneous regions (based on the LUV colour component) by means of the MAP segmentation algorithm [11]. The homogeneous regions are treated as the *basic visual units* that are represented by a feature vector consisting of the three feature components.

(2) Face model: It is mainly for the detection and recognition of human faces presenting in images. The hypothetical face regions are firstly segmented by means of skin-colour modelling and prior shape knowledge of faces. They are further verified by a set of face templates that can be customised during training process. The PCA-based method [1] is employed to label the identity on each detected face.

(3) Appearance model: It is mainly for the description of the objects with a few strong colour components and relatively fixed spatial distributions of the colours. It may be used for representing a number of vegetables, fruits, toys, etc. Firstly, a few interested regions are segmented from the original image according to the prior knowledge of the colour distribution of objects. The colour correlograms [9] are computed on the related colour regions to confirm the labels of the objects in the image.

It may be discovered that the three types of object models take the similar procedure: 1) Initial segmentation; 2) Computation of features; and 3) Labelling objects. These are the essential steps for system training and customisation.

4 System Training

As introduced in the previous chapters, due to serious variation in the appearances of visual objects presented in images, it is impossible to employ one or a few fixed mathematical formulas to represent the visual objects [5,8]. Besides, to accommodate various requirements of different users, the human knowledge about interested objects should be incorporated into the object models defined in the system. For instance, with a semantic description (e.g. tree), a number of different visual appearances may be associated (e.g. pine, apple tree, coconut tree, etc.).

The system should, therefore, have the capability to learn from users' interactions. The purposes of the system training can be summarised as:

- Specifying an object model for object feature extraction and description.
- Establishing links between semantics and visual objects.
- Accumulating knowledge about objects on various appearances.

We have designed an interface to accumulate the training data from users' interactions for the various objects defined in the system. Speaking of the system training, many people may relate it to a word "tedious" from their previous experiences. In this design, we try to minimise the users' interactions by employing the normalised fuzzy C-means clustering algorithm (to be detailed below). The GUI for the training data acquisition is shown in Figure 3. The procedure of the training by example is just as simple as:

(1) Select the object category (e.g. Natural) that is related to a certain object model (e.g. textured model).
(2) Select a sample image. At the same time, the initial segmentation of the image is completed and the result is displayed on the interface. If some training data has been accumulated, some of the objects can be labelled in the sample image.
(3) Select a segmented region, and label it with an object title (e.g. Tree).

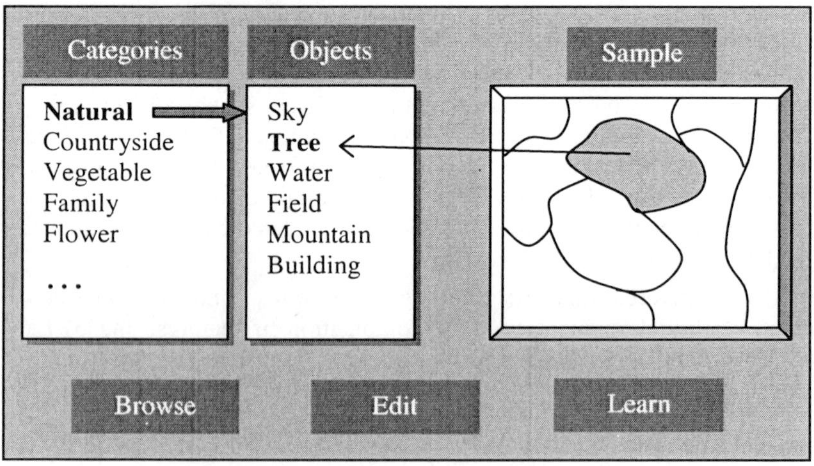

Figure 3. The interface for training data acquisition.

The system automatically compute the feature vector for the selected region based on the object model, and file it into the data set corresponding to the object title. We propose the normalised fuzzy C-means algorithm [4] to compute the object clusters from training data sets. Suppose we have the original *training data sets* $\boldsymbol{X} = \{\boldsymbol{X}_1, \boldsymbol{X}_2, \cdots, \boldsymbol{X}_O\}$ under O clusters of the object categories. Each cluster consists of a number of *data members*: $\boldsymbol{X}_i = \{x_{i1}, x_{i2}, \cdots, x_{in_i}\}$. The *feature vector* x_{ik} is used to represent a data member.

Assume the distance of two feature vectors v_a and v_b on the first feature component ***f*** is expressed as $D_f(v_a, v_b)$. The cluster computation is applied to all the training data sets and it is carried on iterately. Initially, we set the fuzzy membership $\boldsymbol{U}_i = \{u_{i1}, u_{i2}, \cdots, u_{in_i}\}$ for the data sets $\boldsymbol{X}_i$ as 1. The cluster centre for $\boldsymbol{X}_i$ can be computed by:

$$v_i = \left(\sum_{k=1}^{n_i} (u_{ik})^2 x_{ik} \right) \Big/ \left(\sum_{k=1}^{n_i} (u_{ik})^2 \right) \tag{1}$$

The fuzzy membership of the data members in the data set $\boldsymbol{X}_i$ can be computer by:

$$u_{ik} = \frac{C}{C + \sum_{j=1}^{C} \left(D_f(x_{ik}, v_i) / D_f(x_{ik}, v_j) \right)^2} \tag{2}$$

where v_i is the cluster centre of $\boldsymbol{X}_i$, and v_j represents the cluster centres of other clusters at the current iteration step. Please note that (2) is normalise by the current cluster number *C*. The new cluster centre is then updated by (1). The iteration of (1) and (2) is carried on until:

$$\max_{i,k}\{| u_{ik} - u_{ik}^{*} |\} \le \varepsilon \tag{3}$$

A threshold T_u is set to evaluate the data member in each data cluster. If:

$$u_{ik} < T_u \tag{4}$$

the data member x_{ik} will be taken out of the current object cluster to compose a new cluster under the same object category. The iteration of (1), (2), (3) and (4) is performed until converging (No new shifting of data member happens between clusters).

Now, a number of clusters may be generated for each object category, expressed as:

$$\{(S_{11}, S_{12}, \ldots), (S_{21}, S_{22}, \ldots), \ldots (S_{O1}, S_{O2}, \ldots)\} \tag{5}$$

Suppose there are C clusters totally for all the objects. To determine the intersection between the cluster $S_{ls} = (x_{ls1}, x_{ls2}, \ldots, x_{lsp} \ldots)$ under object category l and the cluster $S_{mt} = (x_{mt1}, x_{mt2}, \ldots, x_{mtq} \ldots)$ under object category m, an indicator $I_{(lt)(ms)}$ is used:

$$I_{(ls)(mt)} = \max\left(\max_{q=1}^{Q}\left\{u_{(ls)(mtq)}\right\} \max_{p=1}^{P}\left\{u_{(mt)(lsp)}\right\} \right) \tag{6}$$

where

$$u_{(lt)(msq)} = \frac{C}{C + \sum_{j=1}^{C} \left(D_f(x_{mtq}, v_{ls}) / D_f(x_{mtq}, v_j)\right)^2} \tag{7}$$

$$u_{(mt)(lsp)} = \frac{C}{C + \sum_{j=1}^{C} \left(D_f(x_{lsp}, v_{mt}) / D_f(x_{lsp}, v_j)\right)^2} \tag{8}$$

If:

$$I_{(ls)(mt)} > T_u \tag{9}$$

the clusters S_{ls} and S_{mt} are intersected.

We employ the normalised fuzzy C-means algorithm as the training engine in this system, because it has the advantages [7] over other supervised system training methods (e.g. neural networks, statistical methods), which can be summarised as follows:

- The training data can be minimised [6], if only the user can ensure that the selected training data covers all the interested appearances of the objects. One data member may be enough to be the representative of an object cluster.
- It can be used to maintain the object clusters for different object models, if only the distance functions $D_f(v_a, v_b)$ are available for the object models to measure the difference between feature vectors.
- There is no limitation for the number of the clusters maintained for each object, if only the chosen features are sufficient to distinguish variant appearances for all the objects in the category.
- The intersection indicator (9) can be given to each intersected object clusters under different object titles. That means these objects cannot be reliably labelled due to their similar appearances. By browsing the object appearances in the category, the user is able to decide whether to delete one of the intersected ones or set a higher priority to the more important one.

The system provides the interface to the users to view the training results. The users can have a direct feel of what kinds of appearances of objects have been included and how the system behaves. The system can also tell the user whether the object clusters created are effective or not in terms of the intersection indicator. The friendly interaction makes the system training no more boring. The system training can be gradually performed. Once new training data is accumulated, and new object clusters are created, the users can choose to update filed images.

5 Image Categorisation

Filing images into semantic categories can be very useful in browsing and retrieving images in the database with a large number of collections. However, it is hard to achieve fully automatic categorisation of images due to variant semantic levels. In general, he higher semantic levels we try to categorise images into, the more difficulties we may face. For instance, without prior knowledge, it is unlikely to tell an image of a farm was taken in the UK, or the USA, or Australia. Besides, every user has, normally, his own preference for filing a particular batch of images.

In this approach, an interactive interface is designed to let users create their *image stores*, as shown in Figure 4. An image store can be used to hold a batch of images with any common features, semantic contents, or higher level event descriptions. The semantic descriptions of images stores are normally assigned by users to describe their properties, such as Family Photos, Trip to US, Vegetable, etc. It is difficult to derive this kind of semantics from images due to too local information contained by individual images.

The creation of the image stores is based on the object categories that are introduced in Chapter 2. An object category is, actually, a collection of objects with certain properties that can be described by semantics. It is also related to a certain object model. One single object category can be used to create an image store with the same or different semantic title. The created image store will inherit all the objects defined in the base object category. For instance, the object store "Farm in US" is created based on "Countryside" category, as shown in Figure 4. While a batch of images are filing into this image store, the related object model (textured model) will be applied to the images and extract semantic contents in the images (named *plant*, *pond*, *tree*, *soil*, *cottage*, and *sky*).

An image store can also be created based on multiple object categories. In this case, the user should set the priorities for each associated object category (as shown in Figure 4). Normally, within one object category, the algorithm can ensure reliable object labelling in images, because the system training and object clustering are all performed within the category. However, there may be labelling conflicts (overlapped labels) across object categories, if multiple object models are applied to the same image. When labelling conflicts happen, the object with the highest priority will take over the final label.

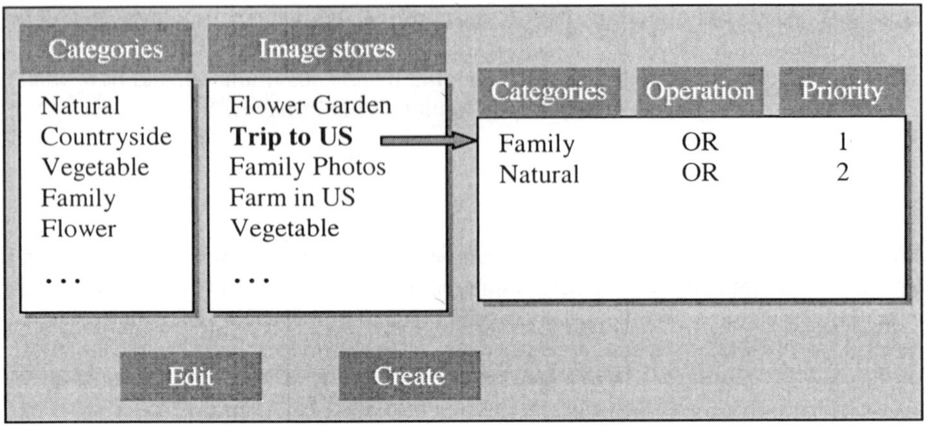

Figure 4. The interface for the creation of image stores.

While creating an image store, another option the user can set is the operation (AND, OR, NONE) related to the objects category. The operators possess the following meaning:

- AND: If all the objects under the corresponding category can be located in an image, the image can be filed into this image store.
- OR: If one of the objects under the corresponding category can be located in an image, the image can be filed into this image store.
- NONE: The labelling results under the corresponding category will not affect the image's filing direction.

When an image store is created, one or multiple object categories are associated, as shown in Figure 4. The object clusters included in the object categories may be trained for general applications or specially trained for previously created object stores. They may not be able to cover all the objects to be extracted from a particular batch of images. In this approach, we design a mechanism for the users to define a special object category attached to an image store, named *private object category*. A private object category is only effective to the attached image store. The same interface, as shown in Figure 2, is used to edit, train, and browse the private object category. The newly created private object category will be automatically added into the list of associated object categories (as shown in Figure 4), and an operator and a priority will be assigned to it by the user. When required, the user can choose to make a private object category public, such that, other image stores can share the objects defined in the private object category.

Image categorisation is automatically carried out according to the semantic objects labelled in the images. The indices for an object store can be automatically created with the same titles as the object titles included in the associated object categories, as illustrated in Figure 5. To avoid messy presentation with all the object titles in the indices table, the user is able to delete some useless indices from the list (e.g.: The user has deleted all the object titles generated from "Natural" category, shown in Figure 5). With the interface, the user is also able to create new indices based on the semantic object titles available in this image store according to the requirements. In the example shown in Figure 5, a new index is created and named as "Family Union". It is created with all the object members in "Family" and all with the same operation "AND", which means the images with all the "Family" members will be filed into this index.

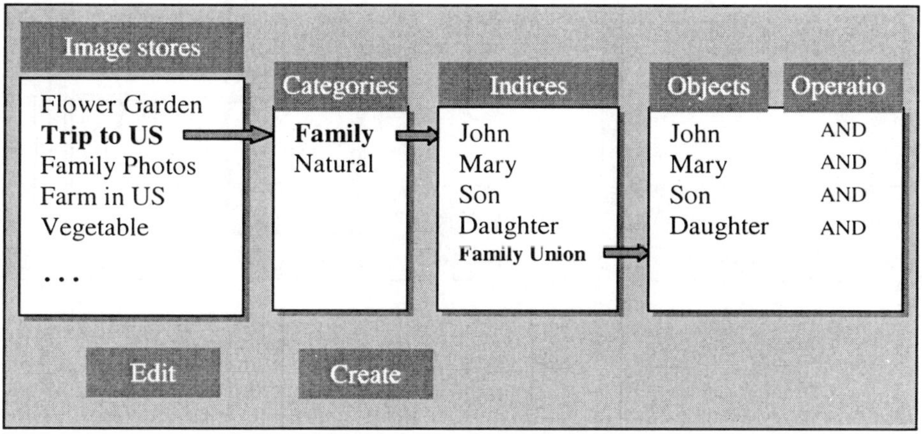

Figure 5. The interface for viewing, editing, and creating indices in image stores.

While a user is trying to file a batch of images, he may select one or a few destination image stores available in the system. The images will be directed into various indices created in the selected image stores based on the results of object labelling in images. Therefore, one image may have multiple indexed locations. This can provide the user the ability of creating highly customised indices of images with efficiency.

It may happen that some of images are wrongly filed due to mislabelled objects in these images. The reasons for mislabelling objects may include: (1) The object categories are not fully trained. (2) There are overlapped object clusters across object categories. (3) The priority settings for the object categories may be only effective to some of their member objects. It is difficult to solve the three problems completely due to the complexity of natural images. Therefore, an interface is designed for fast browsing and redirecting images within one image store, as illustrated in Figure 6.

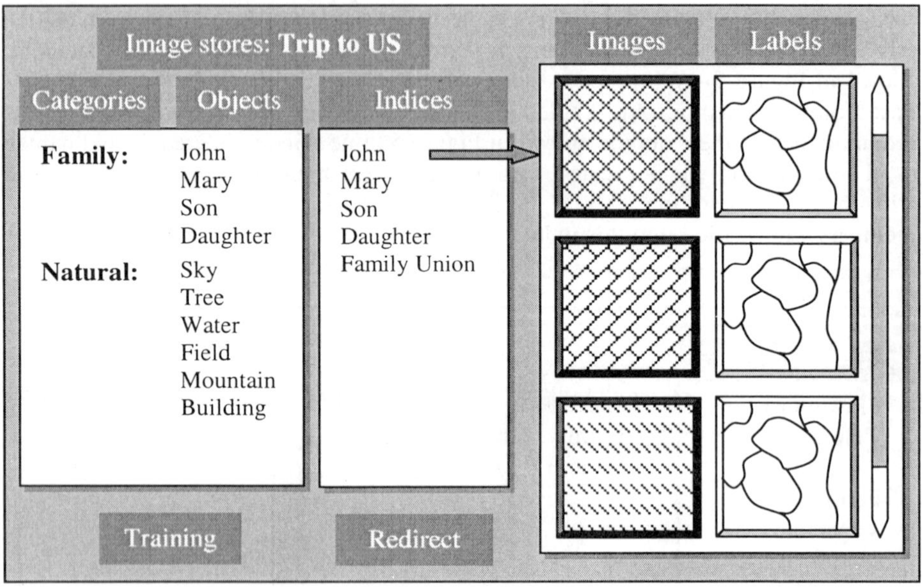

Figure 6. The interface for fast browsing and redirecting images in image stores.

With the interface, the user is able to browse the image filing results by each index title (e. g. John in Figure 6). On the left column of the display area, the original images are displayed, and on the right column, the corresponding object labelling results are displayed. In an image store, the number of effective objects is limited and relatively fixed (e.g.: there are totally 10 objects in the sample image store shown in Figure 6). By assigning a particular colour to each object label, it is easy for the user to discover mislabelled objects, especially when the user focuses on only one or a few objects that are related to one particular index title (e.g. John in the example).

The interface is designed to allow the user to re-label the mislabelled objects. In this case, the system can automatically re-file the related images into the corresponding destination indices according to the new labels. At the same time, the newly labelled objects are accepted as the training data to update the related object categories. The user can also choose to redirect the wrongly filed images into his desired indices without correcting any labels. In this case, the labelled objects in these images may not be corresponding to the index titles, and the image retrieval based on the semantic contents may not be effective on these images.

6 Image Retrieval

It is assumed that all the images have been pre-filed into the object stores in the system. By understanding the structure of the image stores with related indices, it is easy and efficient for a user to search for desired images. Obviously, the image stores and the related indices are created based on relatively fixed criteria that reflected the user's requirement at the certain time. The available indices in the system may not be effective if the user wants to submit a query beyond the existing criteria. Therefore, an interface is designed to the user to make flexible queries of images according to semantic image contents.

The system mainly supports three query methods:

- Query by semantic descriptions: The user may submit queries by one or a few semantic descriptions that describe the desired contents in images. The valid semantic descriptions are the object titles in the built-in categories. Because one semantic description may be related to multiple appearances of objects, with the vague instructions, it is unlikely to accurately estimate the actual requirements of the user.
- Query by images: The user may submit queries by one or a few images. By examining the contents in the images, the system is able to obtain the estimation of the physical objects included in the images. Because no specific object is located, the estimated contents may not accurately reflect user's actual requirements.
- Query by visual objects: The user may submit queries by pointing out one or a few visual objects presented in images, which represent more specific contents for the image retrieval.

The system records all the interactions of the user during the present retrieval period. We have made an assumption that the user always presents his most desirable retrieval interests by the latest queries. When the time goes and the new queries have been made, the significance of the past queries will be decreased gradually, which is denoted as the query state. This concept is represented by the fuzzy membership function for the query state, expressed as:

$$\mu_Q = \min(\mu_T, \mu_L) \tag{10}$$

where μ_T and μ_L are the fuzzy membership functions related to the query time and query levels respectively, which are represented by Figure 7. Therefore, each query is associated with a fuzzy membership value indicating its query state at present. It will be effective to the image retrieval until $\mu_Q = 0$.

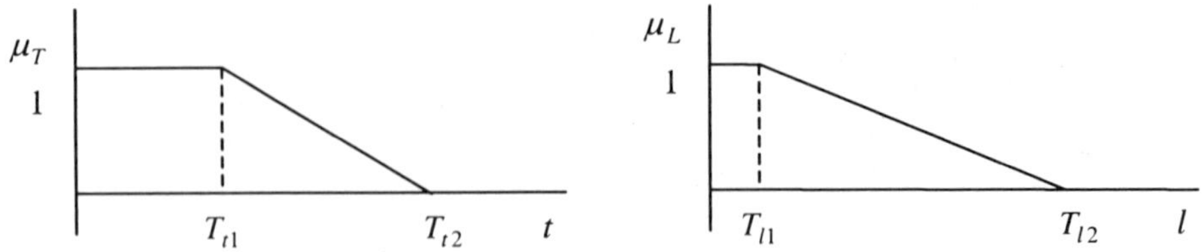

Figure 7. The fuzzy membership functions of the query time and query levels

Visually, the significance of the objects in an image can be approximately represented by their relative sizes, if there is not any object specified. We set a threshold T_S to be a certain percentage of the relative size of an object to the whole image. The fuzzy membership function μ_S of the significance of the object in the image is represented by Figure 8.

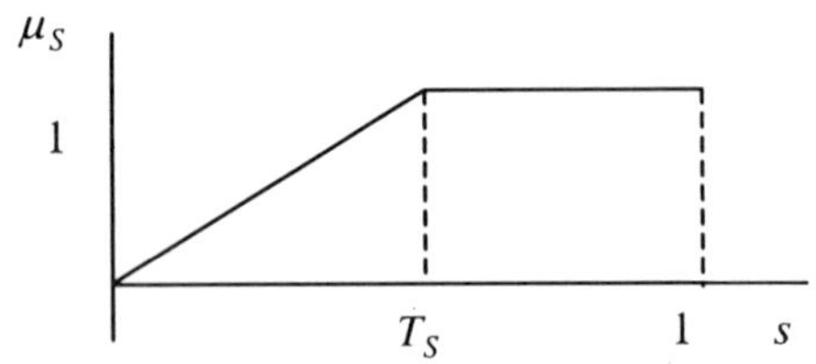

Figure 8. The fuzzy membership functions of the significance of an object

We set the ranking numbers for retrieved images at three different columns according to the query methods. The computation of the ranking numbers (related to the corresponding feature matching) varies with the types of queries. Each query is also associated with the query state μ_{Qj} (j is the order number for the current query).

- Query by visual objects: The related ranking number is set at the first column. The matching number for the column I can be obtained by:

$$\mu_{mI} = \left[\sum_{j}^{J} \mu_{Qj} \left(\sum_{k}^{K} \max_{h}^{H} \mu_{Ojkh} \right) \Big/ K \right] \Big/ \sum_{j}^{J} \mu_{Qj} \tag{11}$$

where μ_{Ojkh} represents the matchness for the object k at j query, and H indicates the total number of the query object k in the analysed image.

- Query by images: The related ranking number is set at the second column. The matching number can be computed by:

$$\mu_{mII} = \left[\sum_{j}^{J} \mu_{Qj} \left(\sum_{k}^{K} \mu_{Sjk} \max_{h}^{H} \mu_{Ojkh} \right) \Big/ \sum_{k}^{K} \mu_{Sjk} \right] \Big/ \sum_{j}^{J} \mu_{Qj} \tag{12}$$

where μ_{Sjk} represents the significance of the object in the image.

- Query by semantic descriptions: The related ranking number is set at the third column. The computation for the ranking number at this column is made by:

$$\mu_{mIII} = \left[\sum_{j}^{J} \mu_{Qj} \left(\sum_{k}^{K} \max_{h}^{H} \mu_{Sjkh} \right) \Big/ K \right] \Big/ \sum_{j}^{J} \mu_{Qj} \tag{13}$$

where μ_{Sjkh} represents the significance of the object to be analysed in the image.

By combining these three query methods, a ranking table can, therefore, be created automatically for the images according to the ranking numbers computed based on the query methods at the present query state, as shown in Table 1. The matching numbers in the first column are, of course, given the highest priority, followed by the second column and the third column. The more details the user specifies for the desired images, the more relevant the images obtained are to match user's requirements. The refinements of the image retrieval can be achieved gradually while the user is submitting his queries.

Table 1. The ranking table for image retrieval

Images	Ranking numbers		
	First column	Second column	Third column
Image 1	μ_{mI}^{1}	μ_{mII}^{1}	μ_{mIII}^{1}
Image 2	μ_{mI}^{2}	μ_{mII}^{2}	μ_{mIII}^{2}
...	...	...	...

7 Experimental Results

A prototype system of the digital home photo album has been implemented with the methods proposed in this approach. It can perform automatic categorisation of photos based on the semantic contents in photos, and it supports the three query methods introduced in the previous chapter. To simplify the presentation, we only demonstrate the principle with the textured object model.

In the experiments, six objects are defined: sky, tree, water, field, mountain, and building. Only one image store is created and it is named "Natural Scenery". There are 2400 photos in the database. To train the system, we select 160 photos. The number of the training data required for the fuzzy C-means algorithm is relatively small by comparing with other classifiers. However, during the supervised learning, it should be ensured that the selected training data should mostly cover the possible appearances of the interested objects in the images. In Table 2, we list the statistic figures and the clusters generated on each object. The number of the clusters generated under each object title mainly depends on the variation of the appearances of the object and the similarity to other categorised objects.

Table 2. The statistic figures for training semantic object clusters

Objects	Training data	Number of clusters
Tree	97	23
Sky	82	16
Water	69	31
Field	74	38
Mountain	48	19
Building	83	44

All the images in the database are semantically segmented and labelled based on the object clusters in the object category. The features extracted for the segmented regions are also stored in the database. Based on the semantic image contents, the images are categorised automatically under related object titles. They are also sorted according to the significance values of the objects contained in the images.

To determine the effectiveness of the algorithms, we randomly select 160 images in the database. The results of the precision and recall for the six objects defined in this experiments are listed in Table 3.

Table 3. The precision and recall for the semantic objects

Objects	Precision	Recall
Tree	0.74	0.84
Sky	0.69	0.91
Water	0.63	0.73
Field	0.48	0.55
Mountain	0.69	0.77
Building	0.56	0.70

The precision and recall of the semantic objects considerably depend on the coverage of the training data and the variation of the appearances of the objects. If the system can be fully trained with the data covering possible appearances of objects, both precision and recall can be largely increased.

We take an example to illustrate the process of semantic object segmentation. The original image is shown in Figure 9 (a). The result of the initial image segmentation based on colour is displayed in Figure 9 (b). After identifying individual regions with the semantic labels and merging the adjacent regions with the same labels, the complete semantic objects segmented are shown in Figure 9 (c). Obviously, the result of the semantic image segmentation is more close to human visual perception.

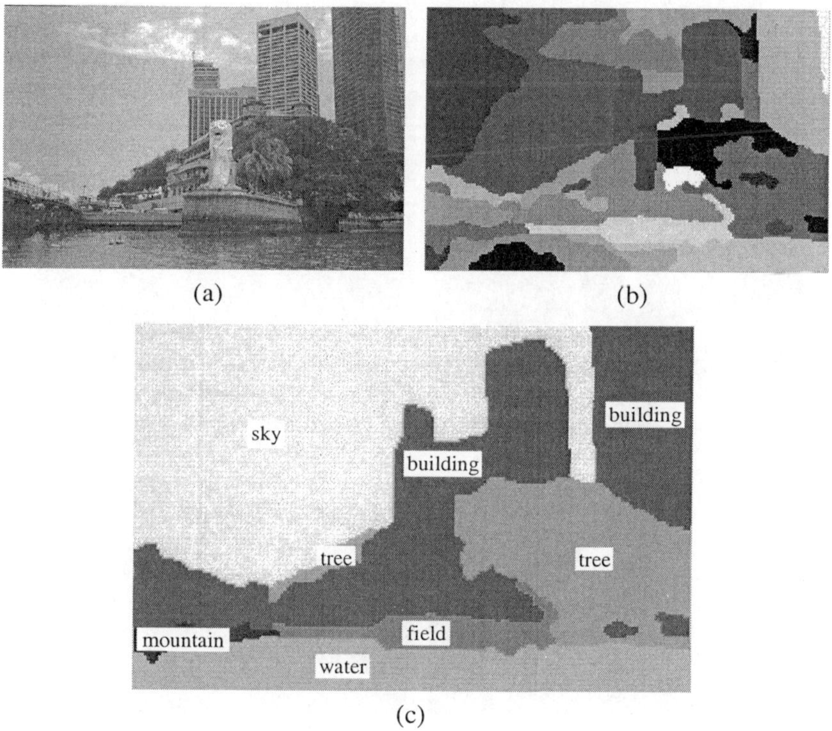

Figure 9. Semantic object segmentation with the textured object model.

Users can submit their queries in three ways as introduced in the last section. We take an example to show the process of the image retrieval and how the system refines the retrieval results when the user provide more specific requirements for particular images. When a query is made by a semantic description "building", 46 images out of the 50 first ranked images retrieved contain "buildings". We display the first 6 images in Figure 10. Then a query is made by submitting the fourth image in Figure 10, the first 6 retrieved images are presented in Figure 11. Among the first 50 retrieved images at this stage, 31 images contain *building*, *sky*, *water* and *tree*. And then another query is further made by specifying the building in the middle of the first image in Figure 11. The first 6 retrieved images are displayed in Figure 12. Among the first 50 retrieved images, 28 images contain the buildings that are visually similar to the one specified.

Figure 10. Retrieval results from a query by a semantic description "Building".

Figure 11. Retrieval results from a query by an image.

Figure 12. Retrieval results from a query by a specified visual object.

If the user wants more specific images containing some objects with particular visual features, he could just browse the currently retrieved images and point out the special objects in any images step by step. The system is able to refine the retrieval results gradually.

As introduced in the last section, the ranking priorities are different with the query methods. By making use of the three designed query methods appropriately, the user could control the retrieval results as expected. For example, a user has a large database. When he locates the specific objects, there may be thousands of images contain the same objects. To refine the retrieval results, he could simply submit one or a few images he mostly likes.

8 Conclusion

In this paper, we propose the algorithm and the methods for the semantic object definition and image categorisation. To cover the gap between the existing technology for describing image contents with the low level visual features and the human's habits in understanding images at the semantic level, the user friendly interactive interfaces are designed for various purposes, such as training data acquisition, object category creation, image categorisation browsing, etc. With the interfaces, it is easier and more efficient for users to understand the ability and functions provided by the system and to express their requirements during image categorisation and retrieval. We introduce the concept of *object category* and *image store* into the system, such that, the flexibility is provided to users to define any customised objects and to create customised image indices. With the built-in object categories and included object clusters, layman users can create personal albums. By understanding the properties of the object models with the interfaces, experienced users can build professional image libraries for various purposes. A novel image query and indexing method is also proposed in this approach. The refinements of image retrieval can be made while the users are submitting the queries telling the specific requirements.

Reference

1. A. Pentland, R. W. Picard, S. Sclaroff, "Photobook: Content-based manipulation of image databases", *International Journal of Computer Vision*, vol. 18, no. 3, pp. 233-254, 1996
2. J. R. Smith, S. F. Chang, "Tools and techniques for color image retrieval", *SPIE Proc. on Storage and Retrieval for Image and Video Database IV*, vol. 2670, 1996
3. J. K. Wu, "Content-based indexing of multimedia database", *IEEE Trans. on Knowledge and Data Engineering*, vol. 9, no. 6, pp. 978-989, 1997
4. D. Hong, J. K. Wu, S. S. Singh, "Refining Image Retrieval based on Context-Driven Methods", *Proc. of SPIE, Storage and Retrieval For Image and Video Database VII*, Vol. 3656, pp. 581-592, 1999
5. T. P. Minka, R. Picard, "Interactive learning using a 'society of models'", *Special Issue of Pattern Recognition on Image Database: Classification and Retrieval*, 1996
6. James C. Bezdek, Patrick F. Castelaz, "Prototype Classification and Feature Selection with Fuzzy Sets", *IEEE Trans. Syst., Man, Cybern.*, Vol. SMC-7, no. 2, pp.87-92, Feb. 1977.
7. Bharathi B. Devi, V. V. S. Sarma, "A Fuzzy Approximation Scheme for Sequential Learning in Patten Recognition", *IEEE Trans. Syst., Man, Sybern.*, vol. SMC-16, no. 5, pp. 668-679, Sept. 1986

8. G. Sheikholeslami, W. Chang, A. Zhong, "Semantic Clustering and Querying on Heterogeneous Features for Visual Data", *Proc. of ACM Multimedia'98*, pp. 3-12, Bristol, UK, 1998
9. J. Huang, S. R. Kumar, R. Zabih, "An Automatic Hierarchical Image Classification Scheme", *Proc. of ACM Multimedia'98*, pp. 219-224, Bristol, UK, 1998
10. A. Jaimes, S. F. Chang, "Model-Based Classification of Visual Information for Content-Based Retrieval", *Proc. of SPIE, Storage and Retrieval For Image and Video Database VII*, Vol. 3656, pp. 402-414, 1999
11. D. Langan, J. Modestino, J. Zhang, "Multiresolution Colour Image Segmentation", IEEE Trans. on PAMI, vol. 16, pp. 689-700, 1994

Chapter 7

Distributed Multimedia, Systems and Applications

MMM99

SET OF CRITERIA FOR EVALUATION AND DESIGN OF MULTIMEDIA APPLICATIONS IN INSTRUCTIONAL CONTEXT

STÉPHANE CROZAT, PHILIPPE TRIGANO, OLIVIER HU
UMR CNRS 6599 HEUDIASYC

Université de Technologie de Compiègne, BP 20529, 60206 COMPIEGNE Cedex, FRANCE
Email: Stephane.Crozat@utc.fr, Philippe.Trigano@utc.fr, Olivier.Hu@utc.fr

Making multimedia software implies knowing how to write multimedia documents. Our works is oriented toward the research of relevant literature that could help understanding what multimedia means. We specifically study multimedia software used in an educational context. We particularly focus on finding relevant criteria that describe several domains of textual, visual and sound documents, trying to underline their specificity.
This paper presents a summary of the criteria we organised, along with the description of two methods we develop to apply them: The first one is a method to assist in evaluating multimedia interactive pedagogical software and the second one is a method to help designing such applications.

Introduction

We can detect an increasing infatuation in institutions and families with the use of new technologies and multimedia, especially in an educational context. Two main problems appear: authors do not know how to write multimedia documents and users do not know how to evaluate their relevancy. People are used to dealing with paper and textual documents. Nonetheless the valid principles for those documents are mostly not transposable to numeric and multimedia documents. The experience in the field of multimedia numeric documents is not wide enough, so we do not have equivalent rules to the ones that exist in the classical domain of edition. However our research intends to help to determine the bases of such rules.
Each technical support records information on a specific way so that it determines the way it will be interpreted. An information is different depending on the support it is written on. Moreover the act of writing information on a support suppose the addition of a supplementary information, directly linked to the nature of the support [1][2]. Our purpose here is to study the supplements introduced by the use of multimedia numeric supports.

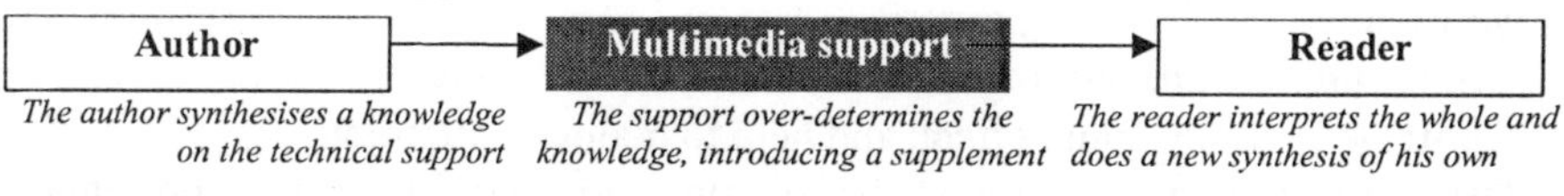

Adopting this vision on the support, we must admit that the author can not be aware of what will exactly understand the reader. Even so, understanding the specificity of

the multimedia he could better control the final interpretation and try to bring closer together the information he wants to give and the information effectively read.
We adopted the traditional separation between textual, visual and sound documents. Our approach is based on a bibliographic research in order to find **criteria** adapted to each domain. The first part of this paper present a summary of our results, with several examples of the criteria we met and selected. The second part deals with the description of the results obtained through two applications of these criteria: A method to assist in evaluating multimedia pedagogical software and a method to help designing such software. The experiences driven through these applications made it possible to validate and adapt our criteria

1 Criteria

1.1 Textual documents

1.1.1 Framework

Discovery of writing enabled to represent information in a spatial way (the surface) instead of a temporal one, like in oral tradition [3]. This new way of representing allowed building new kind of knowledge. Text is particularly adapted to deal with complex information that can be synthesised on spatial representations (lists, tables, ...) and can be re-examined several times.
Using text in instructional software is pretty bad adapted. The visual concentration imposed by reading on a vertical support, static and luminous, is especially difficult. The size and the shape of the screen also disturb the global visualisation of a set of visual elements. Nevertheless, as we can not replace textual documents by sounds or pictures, we have to deal with it, taking into account the specific conditions of **visibility** and **readability**.

1.1.2 Modern edition domain

The first field we studied was classical edition in paper industry. "A written communication depends as much on the information than on the way it is presented", translated from [4]. We think that this assertion is also totally right for texts to be visualised on screens. So we tried to adapt the principles known for typography and page design within our context. Using literature references such as [5], we gathered the following criteria:

- **Uniformity** ensures homogeneity and trust for the reader.
- **Contrast** gives dynamic effect, and help to maintain attention.
- **Density** of the page should not be too high, especially for screen presentation of the text.
- The design of the page should be discreet and **moderated.**
- The design has to represent the **logic** of the text and give repairs for reading.

- The composition of the page should present a global **harmony**.
- Elements of composition like fonts or position on the page have a proper **semantic** that should guide choices.
- Each **detail** is important.

1.1.3 Drafting

Such as reading on a screen is different from reading on the paper, a new way of drafting is to be invented. Currently too many texts are direct transposition from other supports, like scholar books. Classical rules, like quality of language (spelling and grammar), are still relevant. As in every case of communication, the language register (business, technique, academic, cultural,...) is to be adapted to the goal and the reader. But the special conditions of visibility and readability introduce new aspects to take into account, especially articulated around the simplification of the writing [6]:

- Texts should be shorts (blocs of less than 25 lines of 50 characters and sentences less than 15 words.
- Syntax should be usual (avoiding long and complex structures, sophisticated techniques, cross-references,...)
- Vocabulary should be simple and adapted to the readers (avoiding unusual words, neologisms, long words, old-fashion words, vague words,...)
- The articulation of the text should be obvious, structured and logic.
- It is important to begin with the essential part of the communication (tiredness often drives the reader not to finish the texts he begins to read)

1.2 Visual documents

1.2.1 Framework

Like oral verbal communication, visual one has a proper rhetoric. Whereas verbal one is based on a linear way of thinking (A, then B, then C,...) picture is associated to a surface way of thinking [7]. Elements of visual rhetoric are for instance heat, colour, sensuality, fascination, reject, attraction, repulsion, valorisation,... We gather these elements in two notions, central in our case: **iconicity** (measure of abstraction proposed by Abraham Moles) and **attractiveness** (subjective appreciation of the interest of the reader for the picture).

1.2.2 Picture semantic

We refer to several codes in order to give a sense to a picture. These codes can be connotative (red implies violence) or denotative (red implies Coca-Cola). Umberto Eco and Christian Metz submit relevant codes, like the chromatic code, the morphologic code the stylistic code, the topologic code, the perspective code, the support code. Referring to signification associated to codes or using stereotypes does not mean that general and non-contextual rules to follow exist. Originality remains an essential element in order to use codes discreetly [8].

1.2.3 Photography

In our society photography is associated with the real world, with a model of truth and objectivity [9]. But this idea is wrong, and like in front of any picture, the reader has to make an effort of interpretation. There is no equality between the reality and a picture of the reality. A picture is the result of selections, choices, done by the photograph [10]. Photography domain generally uses the following criteria:

- **Light** is traditionally linked with the mystic opposition between black and white [11]. The purpose of photography is not to reproduce light, but to use it to underline things [12].
- The **frame** defines organisation and equilibrium of the space and objects. He should guide the vision on important elements.
- **Colours** give global dimension to the photograph and permits to attract the eye on individual details.
- **Granularity** is a mark of quality, especially in the numeric domain where high-definition of pictures needs high use of computer resources.
- The **position** and **angle** of the camera also carries signification, especially in the case of characters.

1.2.4 Cinematography

Cinematography inherits the photography parameters adding what is specific to the movement. We generally opt for expressive movements, but without disturbing the visualisation of the pictures [13]. The rhythm, linked to plans, sequences and editing, is also an important parameter of moving pictures.

The special case of very short movies (like for advertisement) is interesting in our case, because today's possibilities of integration of long video into numeric support are quite limited. The directors in this case take care of transmitting a simple, stereotyped, strong, message [14]. They adopt three main strategies, and even if the advertising objective is quite different from pedagogic objectives, we think we can be inspired by their way of doing:

- Argumentation is mainly based on description, explanation or formalisation.
- Narration tries to catch the watcher toward a story, in order to influence him.
- Seduction uses elaborated techniques (fade for instance), attractive music, contrasts and speed to involve the watcher in the communication.

1.2.5 Didactic pictures

Realising didactic pictures consists in selecting information to submit a visual representation in order to prepare reading [7]. Examples of didactics pictures are graphs, charts, tables, maps, ... The realisation of such pictures shall follow some important principles to help understanding:

- The representation shall be simple, and go straight to the essential.
- The picture shall not be ambiguous.
- The didactic pictures shall be coherent between themselves.
- The subject of the communication shall be clear and identifiable.

Abraham Moles also proposes an iconicity degree to describe the level of abstraction of the didactic pictures. This degree, from 12 (the real object) to 0 (formal model) with intermediate values like 9 (a photography) or 5 (a technical drawing), has to be linked to the capacity of the reader to deal with an identified level of abstraction.

1.3 Sound documents

1.3.1 Framework

Oral communication is temporal so listening has to be simultaneous with speech. It is also based on a fundamentally personal and subjective relationship between human beings. Oral transmission has been modified by the analogic recording, which allows to listen several times the same speech. Numeric recording allows a better manipulation of the information, accessing a precise point of the oral information. It also permits transformation of the sound in order to upgrade it, correct it, modify it or even totally transform it. We say in the case of numeric sound that we do not listen to *what is said*, nor to *what has been said*, but to *what has been said and then transformed.* In spite of this important difference with classical sound, numeric sound conserves a **personal** and **ephemeral** character, which implies a specific way of transmitting information.

1.3.2 Audio-visual

There are three kinds of sounds in cinematography, speech, sound effects and music. Their roles are quite clearly identified in this context [12]:

- Speech drives the story.
- Sound effects reinforce objects and characters.
- Music creates an atmosphere.

To transmit information with sounds, one need, like for picture, to focalise the attention of the listener [15] :

- The localisation principle: One shall know where the sound comes from.
- The individualisation principal: The main sound shall be detached from the other ones.
- The intelligibility principle: The sound shall be audible and intelligible.

1.3.3 Musicology

We paid mostly attention to the music, often used in multimedia production. Musicology studies this domain and teaches us that music is the best way to take advantage of the empathic character of the sound [16][17]. This specificity certainly comes from repetition, regularity, and automatism that we find systematically in any kind of music [18]. It implies that music is especially capable of generating emotions to the listener, implying him in a particular ambience. It also helps in memorising.

1.4 Media and multi

1.4.1 Relations

We have just exposed proper characteristics of each kind of document, trying to find relevant criteria in order to specify them. But a fundamental aspect has been voluntarily ignored until now. A multimedia environment implies that a document is always presented along with other documents at the same time. The set of documents presented together generates a web of relations that influences the global signification. These relations are as important as each separate document's characteristics, in the process of interpretation.

Sense of information supported by multimedia documents depends on the supplements brought by each *media*, but also on the supplements brought by the *multi* aspect. Taking this into account marks the evolution from multimedia (where documents are only juxtaposed) to polymedia (where they are integrated into a coherent whole) [19].

We distinguish between two main kinds of relations, the redundancy and the complementarity. For instance when one can visualise a text and at the same time listen to the text read by somebody, we speak about redundancy. But if one can read a text on the history of a country, and at the same time visualise a geographic map of the same country, we speak about complementarity. These two kinds of relations should not be separated, but integrated in the best combination in order to generate symbiosis.

1.4.2 Element of choice

The approach we submit implies to choose between different combinations of documents in order to find the best way of transmitting the information. The choices are also fundamental not to present too many documents, risking cognitive surcharge for the reader. We distinguish three main categories of choices:

- Adequation choices: They deal with the mode of the communication (sounds help pointing, pictures help showing, texts help explaining).
- Equilibrium choices: They deal with the over or under utilisation of a kind of document.

- Semantic choices: They deal with the connotations directly linked with the kind of document.

2 Applications

This research gives us a set of principles to take into account in order to deal with multimedia documents. We used it to realise two methods, to assist in evaluating and designing multimedia instructional software.

2.1 Evaluation

2.1.1 General description

One of the problems linked to the introduction of instructional software is the difficulty of choice of a product, and more widely the problem of evaluation: How to discriminate poor contents hidden behind an attractive interface? On the other hand, how to feel in front of good pedagogical software, but which is hard to use? How to find the most adapted software for a requested situation? Does the learning software really use the potentiality of multimedia technology? To answer these questions, we need tools to characterise and evaluate the multimedia learning software. The one we submit is a helping method for the Evaluation of Multimedia, Pedagogical and Interactive software (EMPI).
We oriented our researches towards several areas: computer sciences, ergonomics and multimedia at first, and then we also look through other areas linked to cognitive sciences, social sciences, artistic sciences,... Faced with the complexity of such ambitions, we adopted an iterative approach: Firstly, we began with usability oriented studies, then worked on didactics, and ended with multimedia aspects. Each time our method was to extract criteria from the related literature, test these criteria, integrate them into a prototype, and finally evaluate them in real situation. After each evaluation we could start a new cycle, integrating new aspects we thought relevant. At each step the initial method and the previous criteria were also changed, in order to introduce new studies' constraints and ideas.
Now we hope to have reached a stable structure dividing the global evaluation into six main themes:

- The **general feeling** takes into account what image the software offers to the users.
- The computer science **quality** allows the evaluation of the technical realisation of the software.
- The **usability** corresponds to the ergonomics of the interface.
- The **multimedia documents** (text, sound, image) permit the evaluation of the contents presentation.
- The **scenario** deals with the writing techniques used in order to design information.

- The **didactic** module finally inspects the pedagogical resources mobilised in the learning context.

These themes are sub-divided in criteria, sub-criteria and questions. The whole constitutes a variable-depth questionnaire. An associated structured and contextual help describes each element of the questionnaire. The evaluation consists in answering the questions and marking the criteria. More precise description of the questionnaire contents and of the method's general principles has already been described in previous papers [20][21][22].

2.1.2 Multimedia documents theme

The multimedia documents part was realised using the research we previously described. To illustrate this application we shall give the complete organisation of criteria we submit to evaluate this theme (Figure 1), along with some examples of associated questions (Figure 2).

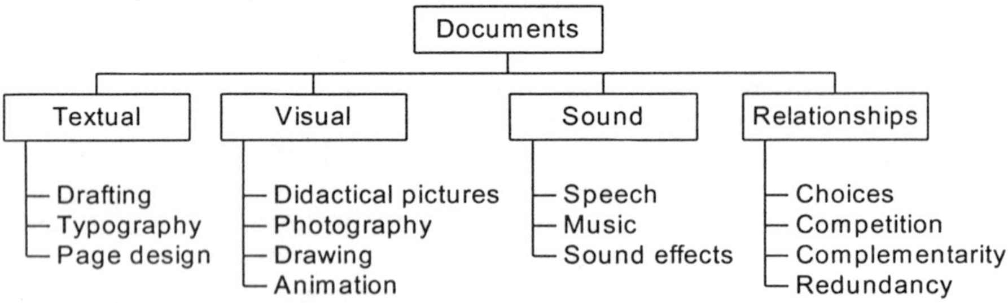

Figure 1 : Criteria of multimedia documents theme

Textual documents / Drafting
What level of language is used in the texts? *Simple / Usual / Specific / Complex*
Is drafting language reader friendly and are the texts easily understandable? *Always / Often / Sometimes / Never*
Is the vocabulary familiar to the user? *Always / Often / Sometimes / Never*
Are there any mistakes in the texts? *Never / Sometimes / Often*
Are codes or abbreviations used? *Never / Sometimes / Often*
Visual documents / Photographs
What is the quality of photographs and videos used? *High resolution / Medium resolution / Low resolution*

What part of the screen is available to visualise pictures? *Full screen / Half screen / Smaller*
Do colours, lights and contrasts underline what is important? *Always / Often / Sometimes / Never*
Sound documents / Speech
Are speeches perfectly intelligible? *Always / Often / Sometimes / Never*
Characterise speech rhythm: *Normal / Too slow / Too quick*
Are the voices pleasant to listen to (i.e. tone and key)? *Always / Often / Sometimes / Never*
Are the social and cultural characteristics (accent, sex) of voices relevant? *Always / Often / Sometimes / Never*

Figure 2 : Example of evaluating questions for multimedia documents theme

2.2 Design

2.2.1 Description

Usability domain provides sets of rules that help software designers to realise human-machine interfaces [23]. We intend to adapt this approach in order to submit design recommendations for writing of multimedia documents. Whereas the evaluation method is well developed and applied, the design method is still in a prototyping phase. Nevertheless we already have too main tools: One that provides rules to apply (example Figure 3) and one that help making choices, related to a specific context, by giving indications (example Figure 4).

Text blocs should be left aligned (best readability) or justified (best uniformity), but not right-aligned nor centred.
Titles should be well separated from the text, as short as possible, correctly positioned and give information on the text that it refers to.
Fonts should not be numerous. We advice two, one with serif and one without.
Size of characters should be proportional with importance of the message.
Styles should not be too much used. We advice bold for titles, italic for special words and avoiding the other one.
Background colour should be bright and text colour should be dark. We advice black text on green background and blue text on white background.
First information of the page should be in the upper left corner, and last one in the lower right corner. Note that left part of the screen is generally more watched

Figure 3: Example of rules for typography

Red	Yellow	Green	Blue	Black	White
Violence	Jalousy	Hope	Meditation	Sadness	Purity
Anger	Reason	Calm	Innocence	Death	Delight
Life	Happiness	Bad	Infinite	Darkness	Wedding
Power	Spirituality	Patience	Purity	Mystery	Sobriety
Action	Perception	Anxiety	Space	Evil	Innocence
Love	Stimulation	Equilibrium	Fresh	Mourning	Virtue
Murder	Magic	Rest	Wisdom	Rest	Chastity
Heat	Dynamism	Truth	Science	Depth	Cleanness

Figure 4: Example of indication for color associations

2.3 Validation program

The two methods we presented were and are still tested in situation. The evaluation method already benefits from a large set of validations. We implemented it in a software version in order to make it really effective. Local experiences concerned about ten evaluators using thirty software. Two wider experiences involved about fifty evaluators using the same piece of software. The comparison between the results permits to point out the weak and strong aspects of the questionnaire. The last experience enables us to think that multimedia criteria we used were reasonably relevant. A deeper exploitation of the results is being made in order to present precise conclusions.

The conception method is not finished yet, we are ending a piece of software that could handle the rules, recommendations and indications. Nevertheless we are testing a paper version of a set of recommendations used in a project for the realisation of a multimedia application to teach basics of algorithmic. It is still early to point out conclusions, but we can already remark that the criteria are useful as a checklist to verify that every important point has been taken into account.

Conclusion and perspectives

The experience in the multimedia domain remains quite weak. Nevertheless we intend to participate in elaborating the bases of knowledge about how to do multimedia. The criteria we proposed and organised can be useful as a starting point for deeper research, in the purpose of better understanding of the multimedia specificity. It is also a starting point for realising applications that could be of great use in the actual context of skyrocketing developments of multimedia products.

Since the evaluation method is pretty operate, we work on finalising a first version of the designing tool. We are also working on a tool that help specifying the requirements for a multimedia instructional application. Our long-term objective is to integrate all the tools we have in a unique method that could follow the process from the requirements' specification to the final evaluation of the product.

References

1. Bruno Bachimont, « Herméneutique du support et ingénierie des connaissances : de la différ*a*nce numérique », à paraître.
2. Bruno Bachimont, « L'intelligence artificielle comme écriture dynamique : de la raison graphique à la raison computationnelle », in « Au nom du sens », Actes de Cerisy la Salle, Grasset, Ed Jean Petitot, à paraître.
3. Jack Goody, « La raison graphique : La domestication de la pensée sauvage », Les Editions de Minuit, 1979.
4. Roger C . Parker, Lise Thérien, « Mise en page et conception graphique », Reynald Goulet, 1991.
5. Yves Perrousseaux, « Mise en page et impression : Notions élémentaires », Yves Perrousseaux, 1996.
6. Yveline Baticle, « Clés et codes de l'image : L'image numérisée, la vidéo, le cinéma », Magnard, Paris, 1985.
7. Joan Costa, Abraham Moles, « La imagen didáctica », Ceac, Barcelone, 1991.
8. Jean-Claude Carrière, Pascal Bonitzer, « Exercice du scénario », FEMIS, 1990.
9. Pierre Bourdieux, « Un art moyen : Essai sur les usages de la photographie », Les Editions de Minuit, 1965.
10. Jean-Marie Schoeffer, « L'image précaire », Seuil, 1987.
11. Henri Alekan, « Des lumières et des ombres », Le sycomore, 1984.
12. Pierre Sorlin, « Esthétiques de l'audiovisuel », Nathan, 1992.
13. Benoît Peeters, « Autour du scénario : Cinéma, bande dessinée, roman-photo, vidéo-clip, publicité, littérature », Editions de l'Université, 1986.
14. Francis Vanoye, Anne Goliot-Lété, « Précis d'analyse filmique », Nathan, 1992.
15. André Gaudreault, François Jost, « Le récit cinématographique », Nathan, 1990.
16. Peter Kivy, « Sound sentiment : An essay on the musical emotion », Temple University Press, Philadelphia, 1989.
17. Peter Kivy, « Music alone : Philosophical reflections on the purely musical experience », Cornell University Press, Ithaca, 1990.
18. Michel Chion, « Musiques : Médias et technologies », Flammarion, 1994.
19. Bruno Bachimont, « Du texte à l'hypotexte : Les parcours de la mémoire documentaire. », Raisons, Idéologies, Pratiques, numéro spécial sur la mémoire collective, à paraître.
20. Stéphane Crozat, Olivier Hû, Philippe Trigano, « EMPI, un guide logiciel d'aide à l'évaluation du multimédia pédagogique. », AIPU'99, Montréal, mai 1999.

21. Stéphane Crozat, Olivier Hû, Philippe Trigano, « A Method for Evaluating Multimedia Learning Software. », ICMCS'99, Florence, juin 1999.
22. Stéphane Crozat, Olivier Hû, Philippe Trigano « EMPI: A questionnaire based method for the Evaluation of Multimedia Interactive Pedagogical software. », PDPTA'99, Las Vegas, juillet 1999.
23. Jean Vanderdonckt, « Guide ergonomique des interfaces homme-machine », Presses Universitaires de Namur, 1994.
24. Jacques Aumont, « L'image », Nathan, 1990.
25. Sylvain Auroux, « La révolution technologique de la grammatisation », Mardaga, 1995.
26. Roland Barthes, « Le degré zéro de l'écriture », 1953.
27. Roland Barthes, « Le plaisir du texte », Seuil, 1973.
28. Roland Barthes, « La chambre claire : Note sur la photographie », Editions de l'Etoile, Gallimard, Le Seuil, 1980.
29. Roland Barthes, « L'aventure sémiologique », 1985.
30. André Bazin, « Ontologie de l'image photographique », Cerf, 1975.
31. Jacques Bertin, Marc Barbut, « Sémiologie graphique : Les diagrammes, les réseaux, les cartes », Gauthier-Villars, Mouton, 1967.
32. Gilbert Béville, « Images à méditer », Maloine S.A., 1977.
33. Gui Bonsiepe, « The role of design in human user interfaces », Design Recherche n°3, février 1993.
34. Jean Bottéro, « Mésopotamie : L'écriture, la raison et les dieux », Gallimard, 1987.
35. Y. Bourron, J.P. Chapuis, J.L. Ruby « pédagogie de l'audiovisuel et du multimédia », Les Editions d'Organisation, 1995.
36. Anne-Marie Christin, « L'image écrite : Ou la déraison graphique », Flammarion, 1995.
37. Bernard Cocula, Claude Peyroutet, « Sémantique de l'image : Pour une approche méthodique des messages visuels », Delagrave, 1986.
38. Geneviève Cornu, « Sémiologie de l'image dans la publicité », Les Editions d'Organisation, 1990.
39. Claude Cossette , « Les images démaquillées », Riguil Internationales, 2ème édition, Québec, 1983.
40. Stéphane Crozat, « Méthode d'évaluation de la composition multimédia des didacticiels : Proposition pour l'analyse des documents, de la scénarisation et des impressions générales. », Rapport de DEA, UTC, septembre 1998.
41. Régis Debray, « L'œil naïf », Seuil, 1994.
42. Gilles Deleuze, « L'image mouvement », Les Editions de Minuit, 1983.
43. Bernadette Donay, « Mise en page et typographie », Presses Pocket, 1991.
44. Philippe Dubois, « L'acte photographique », Edition Labor, Bruxelles, 1983.
45. Pierre Duplan, Roger Jauneau, « Maquette et mise en page », Editions du Moniteur, 1994.

46. Régis Durand, « Habiter l'image : Essais sur la photographie, 1990-1994 », Marval, 1994.
47. Umberto Eco, « Les limites de l'interprétation », Grasset, 1992.
48. Michel de Ferrières, Gérard Bouhot, « Eléments de technologie pour comprendre la photographie », editions V.M., 1991.
49. André Gardies, « 25 ans de sémiologie », CinémAction-Corlet, Télérama, 1991.
50. Laurent Gervereau, « Voir, comprendre, analyser les images », La Découverte, 1994.
51. James J. Gibson, « The ecological approach to visual perception », LEA, Londres, 1979.
52. Ernst H. Gombrich, « L'art et l'illusion », Gallimard, 1960.
53. Andre Helbo, « Sémiologie de la représentation : Théâtre, télévision, bande dessinée », PUF, 1975.
54. Antoine Hénnion, « La passion musicale : Une sociologie de la médidation », Edition Métailié, 1993.
55. Olivier Hû, « Méthodologie d'évaluation du multimédia pédagogique », Mémoire de DEA, UTC, 1997.
56. Olivier Hû, Philippe Trigano, « Proposition de critères d'aide à l'évaluation de l'interface homme-machine des logiciels multimédia pédagogiques », IHM'98, Nantes, septembre 1998.
57. Olivier Hû, Philippe Trigano, « Evaluation de l'interface homme-machine de logiciels multimédia éducatifs », Multimédia et Education, Paris, octobre 1998.
58. Olivier Hû, Philippe Trigano, Stéphane Crozat, « E.M.P.I. : une méthode pour l'Evaluation du Multimédia Pédagogique Intéractif », NTICF'98, INSA Rouen, novembre 1998.
59. Olivier Hû, Philippe Trigano, Stéphane Crozat, « Evaluation du multimédia pédagogique : La méthode E.M.P.I. », IN-TELE, Strasbourg, décembre 1998.
60. Edmund Husserl, « Idées directrices pour une phénoménologie », Galimard, 1950.
61. Ivan Illich, « Du lisible au visible : la naissance du texte : Sur l'art de lire de Hugues de Saint-Victor », Le Cerf, 1991.
62. Pierre Livet, « Image, perception et représentation », Intellectica n°5, 1998.
63. Stephen McAdams, Irène Deliège, « La musique et les sciences cognitives », Pierre Mardaga, Belgique, 1988.
64. MEDA, « Evaluer les logiciels de formation », Les Editions d'Organisation, 1990.
65. Christian Metz, « Essais sémiotiques », Klincksieck, 1977.
66. Abraham Moles, Bernard Vallancien, M. Arslan, « Phonétique et phonation », Masson, 1966.
67. Abraham Moles, « Théorie de l'information et perception esthétique », Denoel, 1972.
68. Abraham Moles, « Art et ordinateur », Blusson, 1990.
69. Abraham Moles, « L'affiche dans la société urbaine », Dunod, 1969.

70. Abraham Moles, Marie-Pierre Massé, « La lisibilité du monde comme projet du design graphique », Cours de second cycle, UTC, 1980.
71. Abraham Moles, Elisabeth Rohmer, « L'image, communication fonctionnelle », Casterman, 1981.
72. G.M. Murch, « Colour graphic – blessing or ballyhoo », Readings in human computer interaction, Morgan Kaufman Publishers, California, 1987.
73. Patick Pajon, Olivier Polloni, « Conception multimédia », cd-rom, CINTE, 1997.
74. Rémy Poinot, « Photo numérique et micro informatique », Dunod, 1991.
75. Rick Poynor, , « Typography Now : The next wave », Edward Booth-Clibborn, 1991.
76. François Rastier, « Sémantique et recherches cognitives », PUF ,1991.
77. Ruedi Rüegg, Godi Fröhlich, « Bases typographiques: Manuel pour technique et conception », Edition ABC, Zurich, 1972.
78. Fernade Saint-Martin, « Sémiologie du langage visuel », Presses de l'Université du Québec, Canada, 1987.
79. Dominique Scapin, J.M.Christian Bastien, « Ergonomic criteria for evaluating the ergonomic quality of interactive systems », Behaviour & Information Technology, n°16, 1997.
80. Dominique Scapin, J.M.Christian Bastien, « Ergonomie du multimédia et du Web : Question et résultats de recherche » , Assises du GDR-PRC I3, juin 1998.
81. Gérard De Selys, « L'école grand marché du XXIème siècle », Le Monde Diplomatique, juin 1998.
82. Jean-Claude Sperandio, « l'ergonomie dans la conception des projets informatiques », Octares, 1993.
83. Bernard Stiegler, « La technique et le temps : 1, la faute d'Epiméthée », Galilée, 1994.
84. Bernard Stiegler, « La technique et le temps : 2, la désorientation », Galilée, 1996.
85. Gary Strong, « Human centered systems research and development in the United States » , Assises du GDR-PRC I3, juin 1998.
86. J.H. Mc Type, W.D. Frommer, « Effects on character / background colour combination on CRT character lisibility », HFS'85, proceedings of human factor society, 1985.
87. Francis Vanoye, « Scénario modèles et modèles de scénario », Nathan, 1991.
88. Martial Vivet, « Evaluating educational technologies : Evaluation of teaching material versus evaluation of learning ? », CALISCE'96, San Sebastian, juillet 1996.

AN APPLICATION FRAMEWORK FOR DISTRIBUTED MULTIMEDIA DEVELOPMENT

YING-HONG WANG, CHI-MING CHUNG, HONG-ZU LIN AND SHIH-WEL LIN
Department of Computer Sciences and Information Engineering,
Tamkang University, Tamsui, Taipei Hsien, 25137 Taiwan, R.O.C.
E-mail: inhon@mail.tku.edu.tw

In this paper, a distributed multimedia application framework for is proposed. The framework is based on Model-View-Controller of Smalltalk-80. Multimedia applications are developing as a popular. However, development of highly interactive multimedia applications for today's high-powered computer is complex and time consuming. An application framework is typically composed of mixture of abstract and concrete classes along with a model of interaction and control flow among the classes. The application framework has "hooks" to allow an application programmer to plug in objects that represent the functionality unique to this application. The distributed processing of multimedia information enables advanced application areas like video conferencing, video on demand and improves the performance in other areas. Thus, it is necessary that an application framework is built for distributed multimedia.

1 1. Introduction

Multimedia applications are developing as a popular and demanding field since the potential of new multimedia technologies is challenging a variety of group user [1]. It is complex and time-consuming to develop a high interactive multimedia application for today's high-powered computers. Recently, although multimedia presentation toolkits are used to improve the developed complexity of multimedia application. However, the functionality of these toolkits is still inadequate for substantially easing the multimedia application building process. There is an apparent lack of existing tools to integrate the multimedia functionality. The existing tools can not provide mechanisms for building interactive, complex multimedia applications. Besides, there is rarely toolkits that are supporting distributed processing of multimedia information [2-7].

An object-oriented application framework is typically composed of a mixture of abstract and concrete classes along with a model of interaction and control flow among the classes. The basic idea of an application framework is to take the applications one step further and provide a skeleton for implementing an application or application subsystem. The application framework has "hooks" to allow an application programmer to plug in objects that represent the functionality unique to this application [8]. An application framework is used by deriving new concrete classes from existing classes and configuring a set of objects by providing parameters to each object and connecting them.

Multimedia application presents interaction to the combination of text, graphics, images, audio, video, and animation [17]. Recently, multimedia applications are more popular in many software systems. However, many multimedia applications have similar skeleton of design. Maybe they are using different type of media, or different operations on the media. The application programmers are coding similar applications repeatedly. Therefore, an application framework for developing multimedia system is necessary. Through a multimedia application framework, the programmers of multimedia application will build a multimedia system more efficiently and less time-consumed.

Some frameworks are proposed for multimedia presentation system [1, 9-11]. However, most of they can not provide enough high flexibility, high reusability and maintaining. To improve these drawbacks, the Model-View-Controller (MVC) strategy of Smalltalk-80 provides an appropriate idea. Thus, an application framework based on MVC for multimedia application is proposed [18-19]. The primary feature of this multimedia application framework is separating the format structure of various media and their interface operations. This feature makes for the framework keeps flexibility, reusability and maintaining. Furthermore, the proposed framework includes a networking abstract class to handle the relevant operations of distributed, heterogeneous environment.

The paper is organized as follows. In section 2 the basic concept and the advantages of MVC are introduced. Section 3 shows the related researches. The configuration of proposed application framework for distributed multimedia is presented in section 4 and section 5 concludes and gives an outlook on future works.

2. The Basic Concept of MVC

The MVC paradigm originated as a Smalltalk-80 user interface design strategy for representing information [12]. The MVC provides the framework for most Smalltalk-80 user interface [13-15]. MVC is a fundamental principle in object-oriented user interface design because it is flexible and can be applied in a variety of ways. MVC framework separates user interface applications into three components. The ***model*** class contains application-specific data, the ***view*** class displays that data on the screen, and the ***controller*** class handles user interactions that affect both models and views.

Whenever the model is changed, its representation must be updated. For this updating to be automatic, a dependency must be established between the view and the model that it represents. In addition to the dependency of the view on the model, the view and the controller must be aware of one another and aware of the model on which they are to work [16]. The relationships between a model, its view and its controller are show in the figure 2-1.

The virtues of MVC are following:

1. multiple views of the same model are possible;

2. views are built from subviews, allowing reuse of components; and
3. controllers are easily interchanged to modify application behavior.

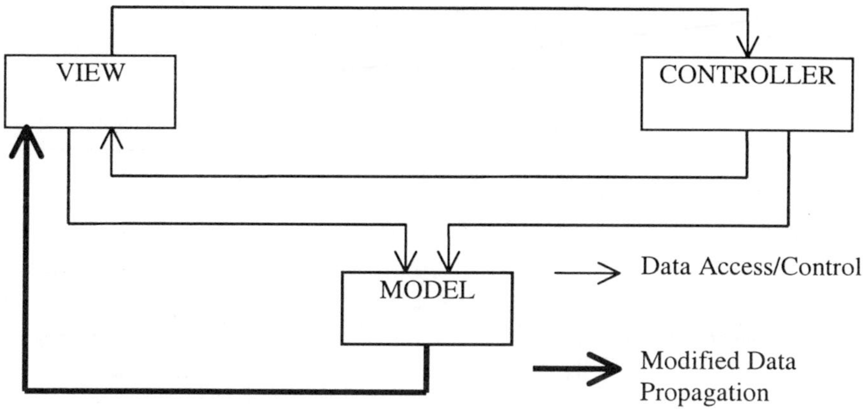

Fig. 2-1. The relationships between model, view and controller

The instances of the class *view* are windows. Two of the instance variables of this class are model and controller, which refer respectively to the *model* class and the *controller* class assigned to the view class. When several objects are to be represented in the same view, the view can be divided into several subviews. Thus, a hierarchy of views is defined, since a subview is a completely separate view. To implement this hierarchy, each view has a list of subviews and one superview. The figure 2-2 shows the relationships between models, views and controllers in the case where a view is made up of several subviews.

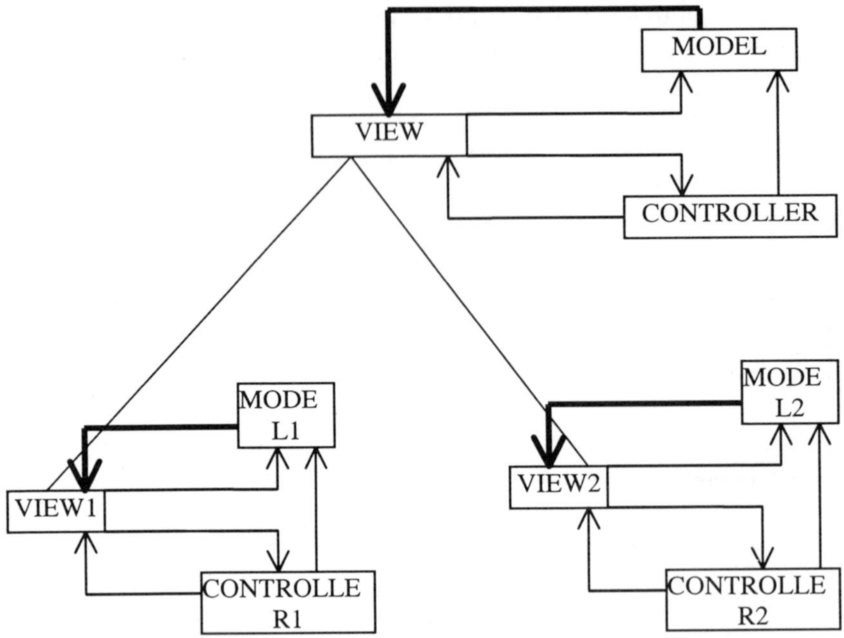

Fig. 2-2. A hierarchy of views

3. Related Researches

Before we design our framework, we have surveyed both academic researches and industrial software packages. Four previous related researches are introduced as specified below.

A multimedia presentation model is proposed by Blakowski [11]. The model is consisted of three types of object classes. They are:

1. ***Information*** classes: Instances of information classes are primary multimedia objects.
2. ***Presentation*** classes: Instances of presentation classes are objects with the ability to display themselves on a node. They exist only for the purpose of presentation and they are always generated by information objects that have to be displayed.
3. ***Transport*** classes: Instances of transport classes are objects in a state for transport, in general with data in a compressed form. If information or presentation objects have to migrate, they always convert themselves into

transport objects for the duration of the migration. Transport objects are only used for this purpose.

The main shortcoming is the information class includes all data structures and methods of the media data. Presentation class is inherited from information class and handles the presentation context information. This will restrict the flexibility and reusability. Because the methods of presentation are included in Information class.

Natarajan and Slawsky proposed framework architecture for multimedia network [9]. This architecture is applied to telecommunication system. This architecture is consisted of a logical model and an object class. The ***logical model*** defines the logical structure of information networking application. The ***object*** class define all encapsulates data and processing in the networking system. This framework is specific applied in an INA architecture for telecommunication network. Furthermore, it is same as Blakowski's model that Object class includes all data structure and presentation methods. It still restricts the flexibility and reusability.

Vazirgiannis and Mourlas proposed an object-oriented model for multimedia presentation [1]. This model is implemented as an object-oriented hierarchy. The base class of this hierarchy is called item class. The media classes are inherited from item and specific a media type -- text, audio, video, and image, respectively. The operations of presentation are implemented in the programs that use specific media objects. The main advantage of this object-oriented model is separating several operations of multimedia presentation with media classes. There are three types of presentation operation that are multimedia composition, multimedia temporal composition, and multimedia synchronization. However, the other operations of control and presentation are still included in media classes. It restricts the flexibility and reusability to develop multimedia applications. Another flaw is this model has no supporting networking functions.

A multimedia framework is presented by Gibbs and Tsichritzis [10]. This framework comprised four basic classes – media class, transform class, format class, and component class. The media class corresponds a media type; transform class represents media operations in flexible and extensible manner; format class deals with external representations of media data; and component class represents the devices and processes that modify media data. This framework provides flexible ways of extending developed multimedia applications. There are two primary drawbacks it also lacks networking functions and it has no clear definitions of the control classes and presentation classes separately. The second shortcoming will make the same media data supports to a view hierarchy as MVC model.

We also looked at the following commercial products related to multimedia authoring or presentation designs:

1. Authorware by Macromedia, Inc.;
2. Multimedia Viewer by Microsoft;

3. Multimedia Toolbook by Asymetrix Corporation;
4. Hypermedia System by ITRI (Taiwan);
5. Action! by Macromedia, Inc.;
6. Audio Visual Connection by IBM
7. Astound by Gold Disk Inc.
8. MFC class hierarchy of MS Visual C++;
9. Active-X of Microsoft;

None of the above system, however, allows the programmer create distributed multimedia applications easily and flexibly. Thus, an application framework for distributed multimedia is necessary.

4. A Distributed Multimedia Application Framework

The aim of this paper is to provide a high flexibility, high reusability, and maintaining application framework for developing multimedia applications. Furthermore, the framework supports distributed functionality. The requirements for an adequate application framework are:

- An integrated support for all kinds of media should be given.
- Separating data structure of media data with its control and presentation operations need be provided.
- Transport services have to be offered. The distribution and heterogeneity should be as transparent as possible.

In this paper, an object-oriented application framework for distributed multimedia is presented. This framework specifies interfaces, leaving open their implementation. By adding new classes through specialization the interfaces can be extended. This ability makes the framework well suited to constructing open-ended software environments for multimedia applications.

The distributed multimedia framework comprises what may first appear to be a large number of unrelated classes and methods. There is, however, an overall structure is implemented as an object-oriented hierarchy whose superclass is **Object**. Object is the root class of the class hierarchy and all other classes shown in figure 4-1 are subclasses of the abstract class, Object. There are five primary abstract classes -- ***media*** class, ***presentation*** class, ***controller*** class, ***distribution*** class and ***application*** class. The media, presentation and controller classes are similar as model, view, and controller of MVC paradigm, respectively.

Object class defines a base method, Clone(), and three abstract methods: ReadFrom(), WriteTo(), and Equal(). Clone() copies the object and its instance variables exactly and can be directly inherited by subclasses. ReadFrom() and

WriteTo() are overridden in subclasses to read and write an object to and from disk. The Equal() method is overridden in subclasses to compare objects.

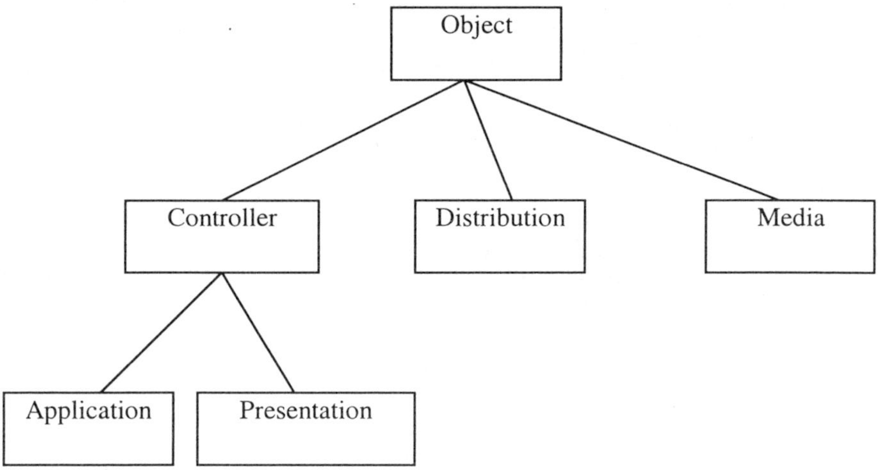

Fig. 4-1. The Primary Hierarchy of Distributed Multimedia Application Framework

The **media** class abstracts mainly administrative features (like author, format, date of creation/modification etc.) of multimedia objects. The detail class sub-hierarchy is shown as figure 4-2. It supports the MVC paradigm by maintaining a list of **presentations** dependent on its data and broadcast changes to these presentations whenever their data change. Media defines the methods: Changed() and Notify() for implementing change propagation. In this framework, the media classes such as text and video, are subclasses from the Media class. For this reason, it is usually unnecessary to subclass the Media class directly, unless you need a media of unusual data. The data structures are provided with methods to allow modification of the object's data. When these methods are invoked, they call the Changed() function which in turn calls Notify(). Notify() sends the MediaUpdated() message to each dependent presentation.

There are two types of media, static media and temporal media. The static media defines common features of time-independent media such as text, graph, and image, and so on. Temporal media defines common features of time-dependent media such as video, audio and animation.

The **presentation** class is an abstract class which is responsible for the representation of media data. Presentation defines abstract methods of multimedia operations such as Play(), Stop(), Pause(), etc. When a media sends the MediaUpdated() message to a presentation, the presentation sends a PresentUpdated() message to all sub-presentations classes that inherited from this presentation class. The design idea of presentation class inherited from controller class is the user is able to handle the specific media data when it is presenting.

The **controller** abstract class is forming a root for any classes that handle input from mouse, keyboard, or other input devices for media data. Controller defines abstract event handling methods, such as DoKeyDown() and DoMouseCommand(), for subclasses like Application class and Presentation class. All methods defined in the controller classes are expected to be overridden in subclasses.

Distribution class is responsible to migrate media data between workstation and network. The distributed environment may be homogenous or heterogeneous. The transport class defines abstract services of multimedia communication. The best suitable and available service has to selected and overridden when distributed multimedia are developed. Currently, it provides Microsoft windows socket functionality. The figure 4-3 presents the winsocket message management structure. The class hierarchy for distribution superclass is represented in figure 4-4.

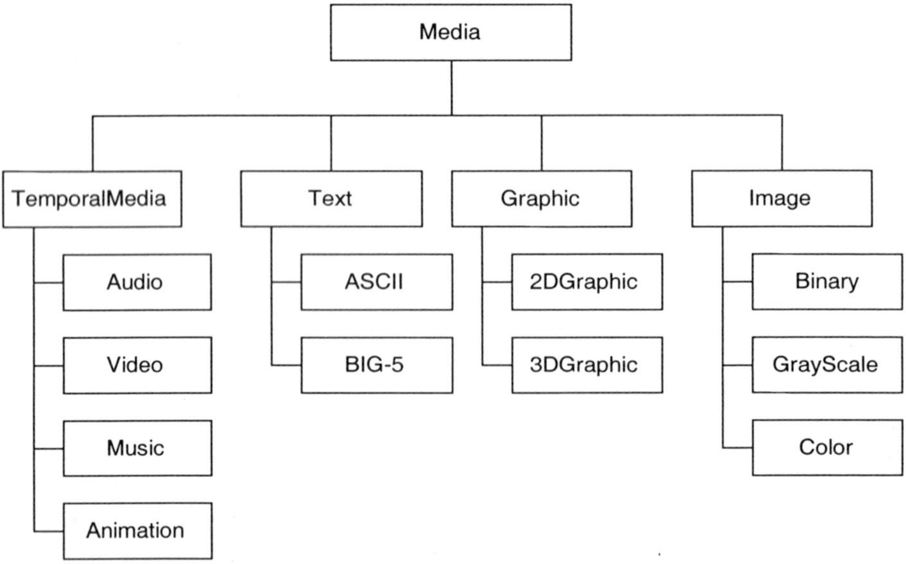

Fig. 4-2. The Media class sub-hierarchy

Fig. 4-4 The class hierarchy of Distribution Superclass

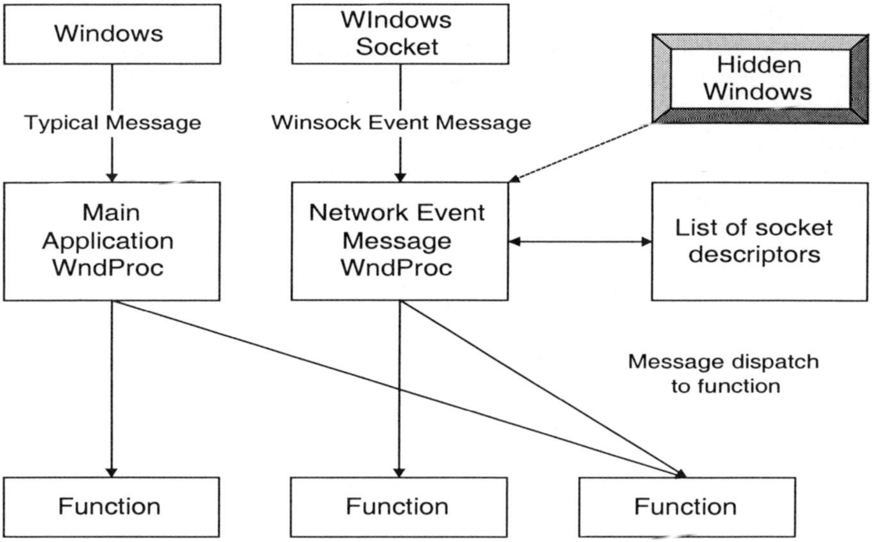

Fig. 4-3 Winsock message management structure

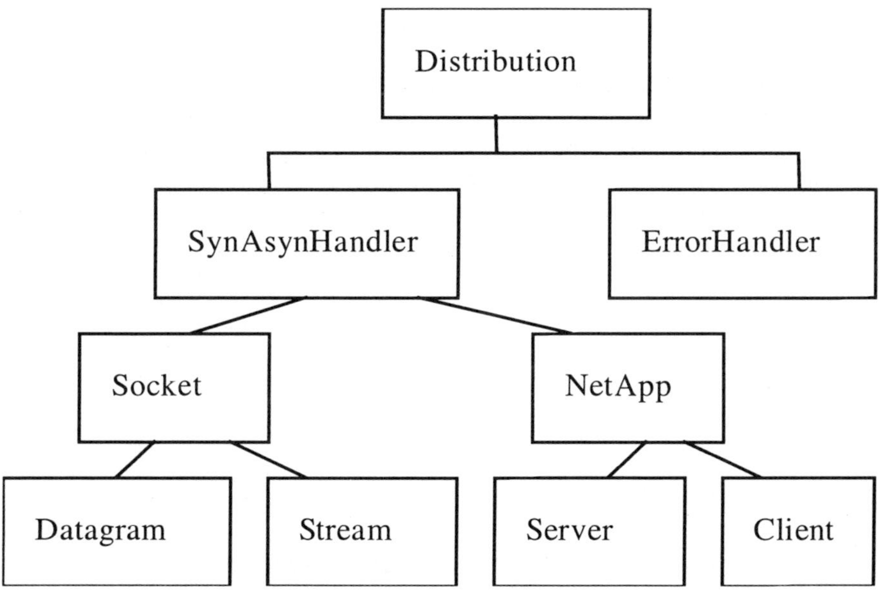

Fig. 4-4 The class hierarchy of Distribution Superclass

Application class is a hook for user main program plugging. It runs the main event loop and dispatches events to the appropriate objects to handle them. The programmer will always subclass Application and each program will have one, and only one, instance of that subclass. The abstract method Initialize() is usually overridden in the subclass of Application to perform domain-specific initialization. As the application program starts the template method Run() of the application class invokes the Initialize and CreateMenu() methods and then starts the main event loop.

5. Conclusions and Future works

Multimedia applications are more popular. The distributed processing of multimedia information enables new application areas like teleconferencing, video on demand, virtual reality, and improves the performance in other areas such as a multimedia CAI course promises as much better learning efficiency [2]. The application framework for multimedia has been heavily influenced by existing environments and research in multimedia programming. In this paper, an application framework for distributed multimedia based on MVC paradigm is proposed. The main features of the framework are (1) supporting networking capability; (2) offering a skeleton for implementing a multimedia application or application subsystem, (3) providing high flexibility, reusability, and maintaining to extend.

There are two directions in the future works. One is to concrete more common classes and builds a library. This library is able to assist programmers implement a multimedia application more efficiently and conveniently. Another is to build a browser that can aid the programmers to find proper classes. By plugging and specializing new classes to these proper classes, this ability makes the framework well suites to constructing open-ended multimedia software and can be ease to extend.

Acknowledgement: We thank the National Science Council of Taiwan to support the project. The project number is NSC 88-2213-E032-023.

Reference

1. M. Vazirgiannis and C. Mourlas, "An Object-Oriented Model for Interactive Multimedia Presentations," The Computer Journal, Vol. 36, NO. 1, 1993, pp. 78-86
2. M. Hodges, R. Sasnett, and M. Ackermann, "A Construction Set for Multimedia Applications," IEEE Software, Jan. 1989

3. Chi-Ming Chung, Timothy K. Shih, Chin-Hwa Kuo, and Ying-Hong Wang, "On the Construction of Intelligent Multimedia Presentations," Information Sciences: An International Journal, Vol.89, No.1&2, Feb., 1996, pp. 131-155
4. Ying-Hong Wang, Timothy K. Shih, C. H. Kuo, August 18-21, 1997, Baden-Baden, Germany, "MScript - A Type System and Language for the Composition of Multimedia Presentation Objects," accepted by The International Institute for Advanced Studies in Systems Research and Cybernetics,
5. Timothy K. Shih, Chin-Hwa Kuo, Chi-Ming Chung, Huan-Chao Keh, Ying-Hong Wang, Ding-Rong Jiang, and Wen C. Pai, October 12-15, 1997, Orlando, Florida, U.S.A., "A Stepwise Refinement Approach to Multimedia Presentation Designs," 1997 IEEE International Conference on System, Man, and Cybernetics,
6. H. Khalfallah and A. Karmouch, "An architecture and a data model for integrated multimedia documents and presentational applications," Multimedia Systems, Springer-Verlag, 3:238--250, 1995.
7. G. A. Schloss and M. J. Wynblatt, "Presentation Layer Primitives for the Layered Multimedia Data Model," In Proceedings of the IEEE 1995 International Conference on Multimedia Computing and Systems, May 15-18, Washington DC, pages 231--238, 1995.
8. H. Keh, W. Wittel, and T. G. Lewis, "Speedcode: A C++ framework for the Mac. Frameworks," The Journal of Macintosh Object Program Development, Aug. 1991, pp. 26-38
9. N. Natarajan and G. M. Slawsky, "A Framework Architecture for Multimedia Information Networks," IEEE Communications Magazine, Feb. 1992, pp. 97-104
10. Simon J. Gibbs, and Dionysios C. Tsichritzis, "Multimedia Programming," Addison-Wesley, 1994.
11. Gerold Blakowski, "Supporting Multimedia Information Presentation in Distributed Heterogeneous Environment," IEEE 0-8186-2088-9/90/0000/0029, 1990, pp. 29-35
12. Nancy T. Knolle, "Variations of Model-View-Controller," JOOP, September/October 1989, pp. 43-46.
13. Yen-Ping Shan, "An Event-Driven Model-View-Controller Framework for Smalltalk," OOPSLA'89 proceedings, Oct. 1989, pp. 347-352
14. S. S. Adams, "MetaMethods: The MVC Paradigm," HOOPLA! Vol. 1, No. 4, July 1988
15. G. E. Krasner and S. T. Pops, "A Cookbook for Using the Model-View-Controller User Interface Paradigm in Smalltalk-80," JOOP, Vol. 1, No. 3, August/September 1988, pp. 26-49
16. A. Goldberg and D. Robson, "Smalltalk-80: the Language and Its Implementation," Addison-Wesley, 1983.

17. P. W. Agnew and A. S. Kellerman, "Distributed Multimedia," ACM press, 1996.
18. Ying-Hong Wang, C. M. Chung, T. K. Shih, H.C. Keh, and Chyi-Jang Lee, "Distributed Framework for Multimedia Application Design," Proceedings of The Fifth International Workshop on Distributed Multimedia System, Jul. 23-25, 1998, Tamshui, Taiwan, pp. 42-47.
19. Ying-Hong Wang, Huan-Chao Keh, Chi-Ming. Chung, Hung-Zu Lin and Chy-Jang Lee, "Object-Oriented Application Framework for Distributed Multimedia Design," Proceedings of The Fourth Joint Conference On Information Sciences, Oct. 23-28, 1998, N.C., U.S.A.

MULTIMEDIA TECHNOLOGIES IN EDUCATIONAL PROCESSES: SOME EXAMPLES

NICOLETTA SALA
Academy of Architecture
University of Italian Switzerland Largo Bernasconi CH-6850 Mendrisio
Switzerland
E-mail: nsala @ arch.unisi.ch

This paper examines the role of multimedia technologies in the learning. I describe three my activities that have involved the use of multimedia technologies in educational processes in College and University. One has been developed for a first-year undergraduate course of Mathematics at the Academy of Architecture of Mendrisio, University of Italian Switzerland. It is an example of the use of multimedia technologies in support to the traditional educational tools. Second activity has been developed at the Department of Electronic - Politecnico of Torino (Italy) in the field of computer based training in electronic instrumentation and measurements using some multimedia solutions. It is a project where students have produced, for their graduation thesis, some multimedia applications to explain electronic instrumentation. Third activity has been developed for my PH-D in Science of Communication at University of Italian Switzerland. It is a constructivist model and it involves a new educational approach that I have named: "*Learning by Doing, and Creating*". Thirty students (Senior Secondary School) have searched (using the traditional media and the Internet) information on Neural Networks and they have built an hypermedia on this subject. In this way, they have built their knowledge, too.

1 Multimedia technologies in a course of Mathematics in University

The role of technology is vital in teacher education and is essential in a constructivist model of teaching [5]. Certainly, computer technology has become a fundamental part of education across the curriculum and will likely be more so in the future. Instead of simply being a source of information, computers are becoming multimedia workstations for students. Innovative use of technology combines telecommunications (e-mail, video-conferencing, online resources, Internet navigators), multimedia authoring (home page editors), user-friendly, convenient applications software and are turns students into producers as well as consumers of content [1].

At the Academy of Architecture of Mendrisio (University of Italian Switzerland, born in 1996) there is a course of Mathematics that uses also the multimedia technologies in the didactic path. This course is presented as 26 lectures, given weekly, throughout the academic year. The course intends to provide an introduction to basic facets of mathematical thought (algebra, logic, geometry, topology, analysis and stochastic). Also, it aims to introduce a host of applications. This thought is an integral part of our culture and that, frequently, it is developed in

close contact with artistic research and creations. In this course I have used some multimedia technologies (e.g., CD-ROM, computer-aided design (CAD) tools, documentaries) to raise students' attention and their knowledge, in alternative to the traditional educational tools (overhead projector or blackboard).
To explain the platonic solids, the isometry, the perspective and the axonometry, I have proposed the didactic computer-aided design Cartesio™ (it is an educational CAD produced by the Department of Architecture at University Ca' Foscari, Venice). This s/w tool, in Italian language, has an easy graphic interface and it is propaedeutic, for future architects, to learn other architectural CAD [16].
Figure 1 shows an example of an isometric orthogonal axonometry.

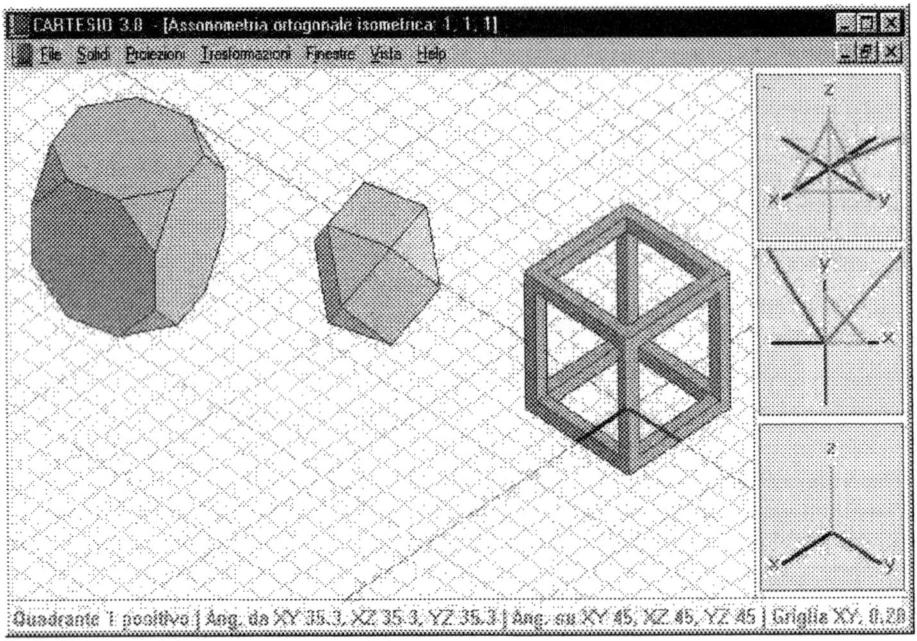

Figure 1. An example of axonometry using Cartesio™.

I have also used some scientific documentaries to expose:

- the platonic solids (produced by the Italian mathematician Michele Emmer),
- the soap bubbles (by Michele Emmer),
- the interconnections between mathematics and arts (by Michele Emmer),
- the fractal geometry and the dynamical systems (produced by Le Scienze™, and it also contains some interviews to Mandelbrot and Lorenz).

Using these scientific documentaries, I have observed a higher level of attention than a traditional explanation [16, 18]. It is a significant attribute of video that the auditory and the visual symbol systems are presented simultaneously [8]. A number of studies have compared a video program with its decomposed audio and visual presentations to determine the role of these two sources of information, individually and together [2, 3,4, 10]. In most of these studies, the combined use of visual and auditory symbol systems resulted in more recall than visual only and audio - only presentations [8].

To analyse the patterns and the groups of symmetry I have visited, with my students, the Internet site:
http: // www.geom.umn.edu/apps/kali/about.html
that contains the following applications:

- **Kali** (is an interactive editor for symmetric patterns of the plane, as seen in some of the woodcuts of M.C. Escher. It's also a fun way to learn about the 17 crystallographic symmetry groups of the plane);
- **QuasiTiler** (that generates the famous Penrose tilings, or design nonperiodic tilings of the plane; in the process, it is possible to select and visualise plane cross-sections of a lattice in anywhere from 3 up to 13 dimensions);
- **Unifweb** (that visualise families of Riemann surfaces with a specified group of symmetries. The presentation you choose for your symmetry group corresponds geometrically to a construction of the surface as a covering of a particular orbifold).
- **Lafite** (that works with any discrete symmetry group of the hyperbolic plane. Lafite can calculate the fundamental region and generators of the group you chose. The program then creates Escher-like patterns by replicating a motif through the action of that group).

To explain some fractal forms I have created:

- some algorithms, in Pascal™ and C++™ languages, to generate some iterative functions (the fern, the Mandelbrot set, the Julia set, the fractal trees) choosing the number of the iterations;
- a hypertext, to present the fractal objects and their applications in architecture, in arts and in nature.

This hypertext comprises:

- the Mandelbrot set,
- the Julia set,
- fractal forms in nature (the pineapple, the Von Koch snowflake, the dendritic structures, the fractal forms inside the human body),
- fractal worlds (created using the Computer Graphics),
- fractal architecture,

- fractal arts,
- some interesting Internet sites (with the links to other Internet sites).

The hypertext's graphic interface is "friendly" for an easy navigation, indeed it is possible to identify the existence of a similarity between navigation in the real world and navigation in a virtual world [7, 16].
Figure 2 shows a page dedicated to the pineapple.

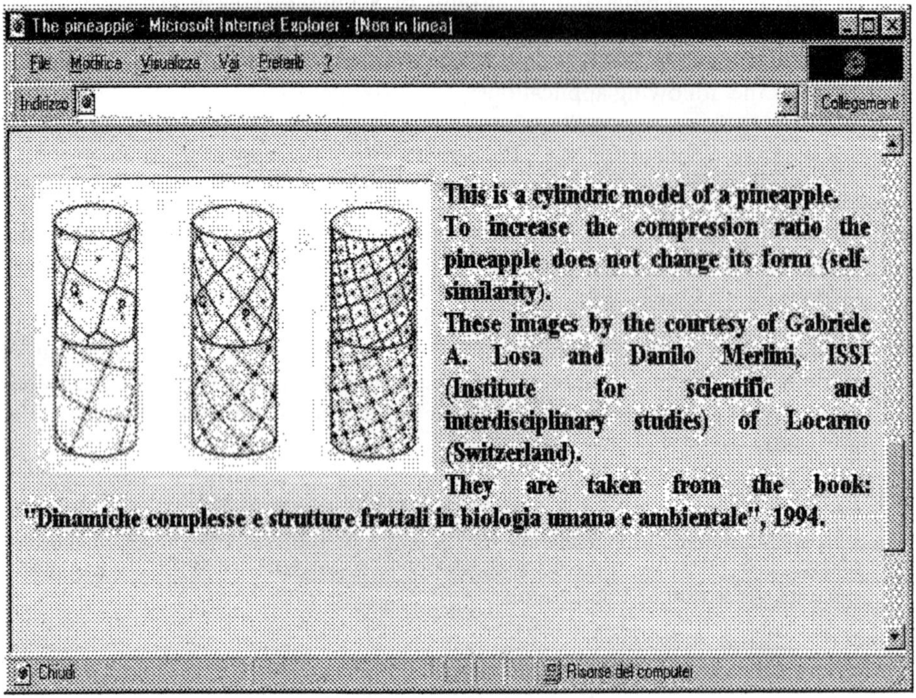

Figure 2. A page dedicated to the pineapple.

The hypertext has been carried out using the HTML (HypertexT Markup Language), and it is available at the Internet address:
http: // www. arch.unisi.ch/fractals/fract1e.htm.

In the last part of the academic year I have analysed the relationships between mathematics, architecture and arts and I have noted that is difficult to illustrate the possible interconnections using the traditional educational tools [15, 16].

For this reason I have proposed to the students the CD-ROM Escher Interactive ™ (for Windows ™) that describes the M.C. Escher's works. I have analysed the sections dedicated to:

- the tessellations,
- the morphings,
- the impossible shapes ,
- the animation (dedicated to the animation of famous Escher's spirals),
- the spheres (which describe the distortion produced when a spherical lens is placed over a two dimensional picture space),
- the convex and concave (it is a game which describes a space that could be convex or concave depending upon the perspective of the objects placed within it).

Figure 3 shows the section dedicated to the spheres (the spherical lens is placed in the top on the right of the picture) .

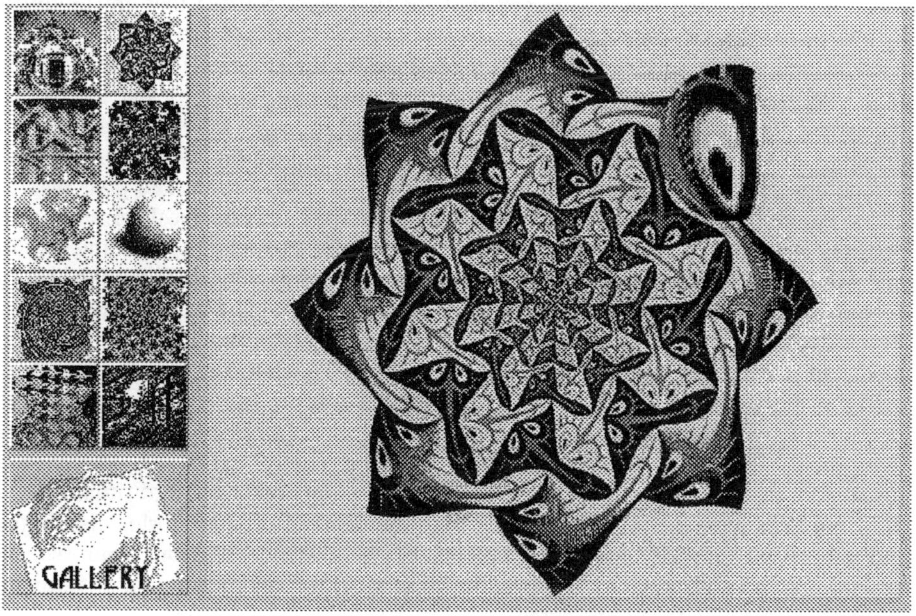

Figure 3. Escher Interactive™: the section dedicated to the spheres .

Hypertexts facilitate the application and transfer of complex knowledge to new situations. Such cognitive flexibility requires the representation of knowledge along multiple rather than single conceptual dimensions. Hypertext facilitates this cognitive flexibility because it allows a topic to be explored in multiple ways using a number of different concepts or themes [8].

For this reason I have created a hypertext (using HTML language) to introduce the interconnections between mathematics and arts.
It comprises:

- the golden section,
- the Fibonacci's sequence,
- the polyhedra,
- the fractal geometry

in arts and architecture.

3 Multimedia technologies in a course of Electronic measurements

Education in fields such as electronic measurement requires students to gain a reasonable skill in using various kinds of instrumentation [11]. The cost of basic level instruments is often low, but large classrooms means large workbench availability and a massive and qualified assistance that is not easily found [18].
Basic instrumentation teaching is required for first level courses that are followed by a large number of students.

The most of the time which the students spent in the laboratories, especially for first level courses, was devoted to learning the operating functions and the use of the same basic instruments. It was therefore decided to invest time and resources to develop an alternative solution to the laboratory replication by using the new technologies offered by computer based multimedia courseware. The goal was to allow the students to carry out a pre-training activity outside the laboratory and possibly at home; each student could thus individually adequate the learning rate to his own capabilities. After this pre-training phase, students who enter the laboratory require reduced assistance and less time to complete the training activity.
Several tutorial modules were developed that were organized like lectures, each being on a particular subject (with the support of Hewlett Packard Italy). Each module discusses theoretical and functional concepts of a basic electronic instrument and allows for a simulated instrument exercising by providing a series of instrument simulators. By means of the realistic control panel of the virtual instrument the students practice under several operating conditions and situations.
New modules were developed to tackle both the demand of laboratories distributed throughout the territory and requirements of the distance learning courses. In addition, it was decided to explore the possibility of making a real instrument laboratory available for use at home.

For this reason, the Prof. Umberto Pisani (Department of Electronic, Politecnico of Torino) has reorganized his traditional educational approach, based on lectures and successive laboratory practice, using multimedia tools which combine two different learning phases:

- a theoretical phase,
- a practice phase

in a single tutorial stage self-managed by the student. In these activities I was an expert witness for the didactic paths and the correct use of the multimedia codes in educational process.
This multimedia course is structured on a set of lessons (modules) each containing a particular topic or instrument in form of a self – contained multimedia presentation [11, 18].
These didactic modules have the following purposes:

- to expose students to a comprehensive range of electronic instruments and basic measurements techniques;
- to allow students to give practice on the particular instrument whose front panel is simulated on the monitor and the behaviour is emulated by computer.

Differently from the other multimedia applications (e.g., encyclopaedia) this case is oriented to defined objectives of knowledge and it is based on a student model with a defined knowledge background, so it was decided to guide the students through a path, based on a structured didactic methodology, to reach the proposed educational goal (we have used the Bloom's taxonomy).
Each module, developed using Multimedia Toolbook ™ (with the aid of several thesis students), is divided into subjects (pages) at the same hierarchical level; each level contains a subset of other pages, placed at a lower levels. Hyperlinks among pages have been studied to give continuity to learning trail.

In these modules different media are involved, for example:

- animation techniques (which are an efficient learning tool, when the teaching of a subject would be difficult by a written description alone),
- audio supports to emphasize some topic in a lesson (e.g., to explain an electronic circuit),
- the digital television camera images (to zoom an instrument inside).

The use of other media is calibrated to avoid the cognitive overload [14, 17].
Next figure 4 shows a page dedicated to the spectrum analyser; in this page there is the presence of a movie which explains the single instrument functions.

Each lecture includes several tests to verify the level of the acquired knowledge on the educational objectives and lesson subjects. Examinations include:

- the laboratory quizzes by multiple choices,
- some simple projects (which could require few data processing),
- some puzzles (where student must rebuild an instrument block diagram or measurement procedures).

In all exercises, the data are randomly selected to always generate new projects entry points.

The multimedia modules developed are:

- the fundamentals of the analog and digital oscilloscope,
- the fundamentals of the analog and digital voltmeters and their operating theory,
- the IEEE488 standard interface for programmable instrumentation,
- the spectrum analyser.

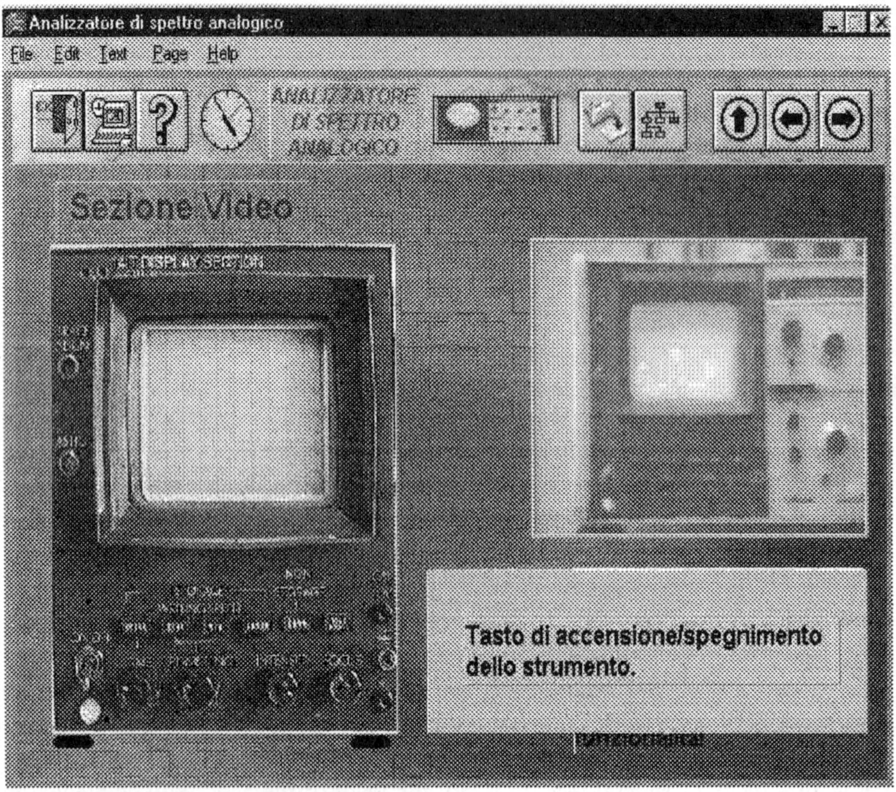

Figure 4. A page dedicated to the spectrum analyser.

After the multimedia lessons, virtual instruments are implemented in the multimedia packages (developed in the VisualBasic ™ environment with the exception of a minor part written in Microsoft C++ ™), in order to allow simple simulations of the real instruments during the self-training phase [18]. For example when learning the oscilloscope, the student has a virtual instrument panel available, where he can try to select the input signals and can evaluate the effects of the instrument setting on

the display [17, 18]. Next figure 5 shows the virtual panel of the analog oscilloscope.
Using this multimedia solution, the students can adapt the learning rate to their time availability and cultural background. They can study the theory and then self-verify their knowledge level by solving practical exercises and answering a series of questions. The student only need an inexpensive personal computer with a multimedia extension, that is available in centralized structures of the university or possibly at home.

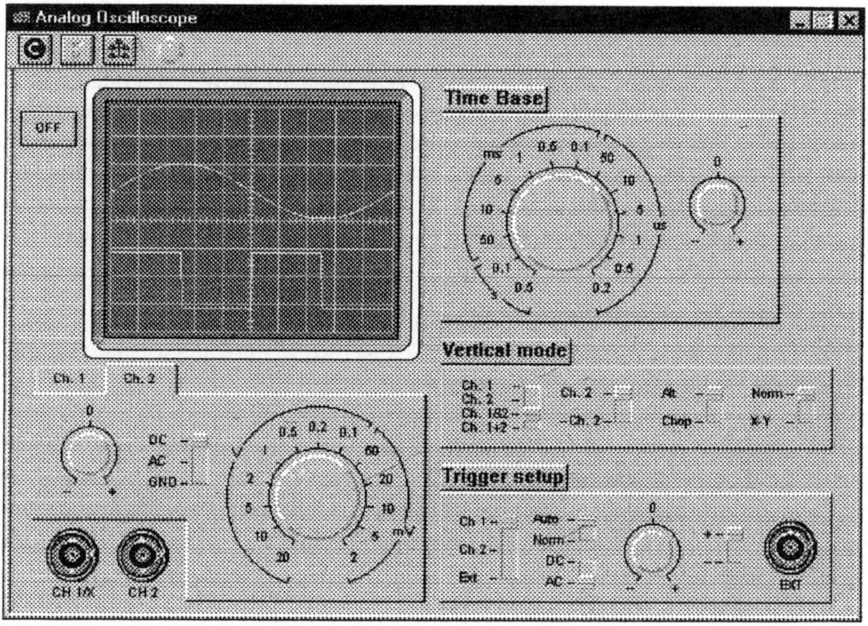

Figure 5. The virtual panel of the analog oscilloscope.

4 "Learning by Doing and Creating" in a Senior Secondary School

The reduction of overall costs and study flexibility, together with the availability of powerful telecommunications and computer systems have fostered investigation and implementation of different types of technology-supported teaching and learning system [6].

Conventional instruction has grown out of a positivist tradition, a belief system that embraces and endorses scientific methods that enable scientific inquiry to lead to understandings of problems and their remedies. Much educational research has been undertaken to find "what works" in natural classrooms so these techniques can be understood as a process-product model to be transmitted to new teachers [12]. Constructivism has emerged in opposition to conventional teaching, from the perspective of research and as well as from other education aspects. The contrasts are evident throughout education: constructivism versus instructivism, quantitative versus qualitative, standardised testing versus performance assessment, whole language versus basal reading, and fundamental epistemological conceptions. Rather than emphasizing content and presentation, the constructivist is interested more in creating authentic learning tasks, engaging the learner in realistic, thematic learning activities, and attempting to interpret the needs of learners as they become evident. These reflective teaching practices avoid interpretations of reality but direct energy into the development of individual students to accept responsibility for learning. Constructivism asserts that learners create meaning and are not passive recipients of information. There is substantial evidence to show that students do not learn effectively by passive reception of information or by memorization. Constructivist theory is based on the observation that learners construct mental models of physical phenomena. The teacher's knowledge of content, while important, is insufficient, alone, because "knowing" content does not mean that one can also teach it. Teachers must be able to make subject matter understandable to students, which requires more than a knowledge of subject matter. For knowledge to be more than information, and for students to become constructive, the curriculum must avoid piecemeal, decontextualized, teacher-transmitted learning.

The use of multimedia technologies can help the constructivist theory and they can build a "Learning by Doing" environment.

The computer plays a central role in this environment and it coordinates the use of various symbol systems [8]. In educational process the students generally build hypertext and hypermedia on topics which they know. Their teachers control and give them all information to include in hypertext. Using this approach the role of the students is passive, because they transfer, on digital documents, information furnished by the teachers.

For this reason I have thought to control some students that have researched, selected information, and produced a hybrid CD-ROM/Internet on a subject which they didn't know before. The CD-ROM's title is "Introduction to Neural Networks" .

In the details, 30 students (aged 17- 20) of a Senior Secondary School (specialization course in Information Technologies), during the school years 1997-98 and 1998-99, have researched, studied and built a hypermedia (on neural network) using the new educational technologies and they will propose this CD-ROM to other students.

This hypermedia has been developed in the Laboratory of System and Techniques of Transmission (3 hours in the week throughout the school year) in a technical institute in Italy.

I have organized my educational project in three stages.

4.1 First stage of the project

In the first stage, school year 1997 - 98, I have worked with 15 students (aged 17 - 19). I have proposed them a simple multiple choices test to control the students' knowledge on the Neural Networks. Figure 6 shows the histograms about this first test.

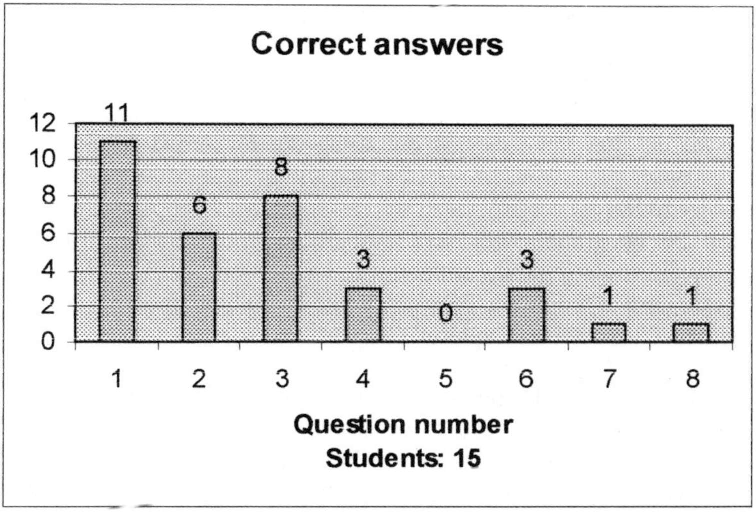

Figure 6. The histograms of the first test.

Analysing these results I have deduced that my students didn't know the subject "Neural Networks" and they were a good sample to try my "Learning by Doing and Creating" approach.
After the test, the students have researched in the Internet :

- information on hypertexts and on hypermedia; (their history and their organisation);
- how to build a hypertext (using HTML);
- how to build a hypermedia (with an introduction to Java Language and Java-Script).

I have also explained them:

- how to use some software and hardware tools to digitized the images, the movies, the sounds and so forth,
- the correct calibration of the communication codes in the educational hypermedia [16, 17, 18].

The sample of the students has:

- researched in the Internet some information on Neural Networks,
- researched the main bibliography (using the public libraries),
- selected the information,
- built the storyboard of the hypertext (they have chosen a hierarchical hypertext),
- chosen other information to insert in the hypermedia (e.g., animations or interviews to experts on information technologies),
- realized the hypermedia,
- controlled the hyperlinks.

The hypermedia has been carried out using the Hypertext Mark Up Language (HTML) because:

- it is easy to learn,
- it can be integrated with Java Applet and Java Script to introduce the multimedia codes (e.g., the animations, the movies),
- we can used a common browser without runtime module (e.g., Netscape Navigator™ or Internet Explorer™) .

During the hypermedia development, the students have put a particular care to make "friendly" the user interface, by designing:

- the icons, with shape and image which recall the linking function (e.g. a little home recalls the function which permits to go to the "home page" of the hypertext);
- the text-frames (giving brief information),
- the visual interface (which involves the choice of minimum point typeface (e.g., Arial 12), colours, background, bottom shape and so forth) [11, 13, 17].

In this hypermedia the graphic interface has been thought for an easy navigation; in fact, the navigation as a search for information still constitutes the bottleneck of most hypertext systems [11, 16, 17, 18].

The first version of this hypermedia, finished in month of June 1998, comprises:

- 20 pages of hypertext;
- 20 animations using Java language and Java Script;
- 2 movies (one is an interview to an expert on Neural Networks, the other is on the authors).

After the hypermedia production I have controlled the students' knowledge on the Neural Networks using multiple - choice tests. Figure 7 shows the histograms of this test.

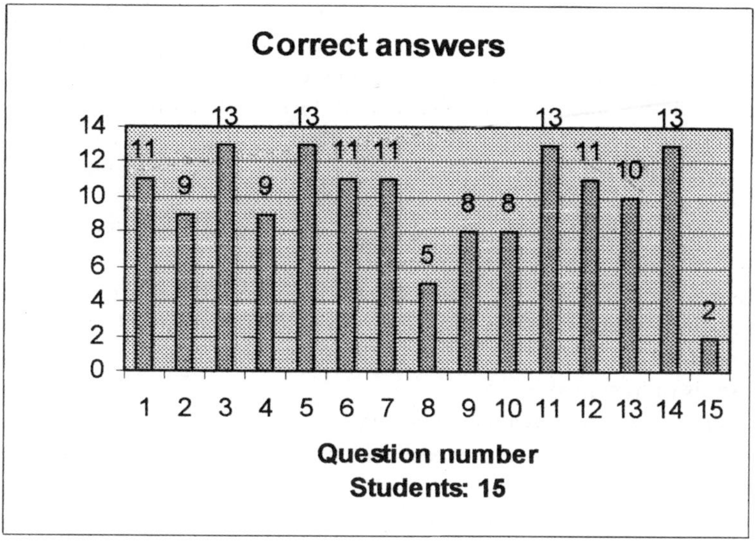

Figure 7. Histograms of the knowledge test.

The worst case of this multiple-choices test corresponds to the question 15 ("To draw some model of Neural Networks") because this subject is difficult to understand for Secondary School students.

I have also proposed to the students a test to evaluate my contribution (e.g., my interaction with the classroom, the information which I have given them, etc.) .
The results of these analysis have been encouraging, because:

- the 60% of my students have achieved the educational goals that I have established (I have used the Bloom's taxonomy),
- my contribution to the project has been well evaluated.

I have used the negative data to modify my interaction with my classroom; this feedback it has been important because all educational process was under control.

4.2 Second stage of the project

In the second stage, school year 1998 - 99, I have worked with another sample of 15 students (aged 17 - 19) of the same technical school .
This students have analysed the hypermedia produced.

They have evaluated, answering to the multiple choices test, the icons (e.g., the shape and the image should recall the linking function); the hot words, the text-frames, the visual interface, the navigation in the hypermedia.
The results of this analysis have been used to modified the first version of the hypermedia. The second sample of the students:

- have modified the contents of the hypermedia difficult to understand (e.g., some pages dedicated to the Hopfield's model);
- have added other pages (e.g., three pages dedicated to the Kohonen's model).

The new version of this hypermedia has:

- a map which performs the "here we are function". It helps the students in the navigation inside the hypermedia (to avoid the problem "lost in the hyperspace");
- 30 pages of hypertext;
- 25 animations using Java language and Java script;
- 7 movies (4 interviews to experts on Neural Networks and 3 movies on the authors);
- 30 links to other Internet sites on Neural Networks.

Figure 8 shows the home page of the second version of hypermedia.

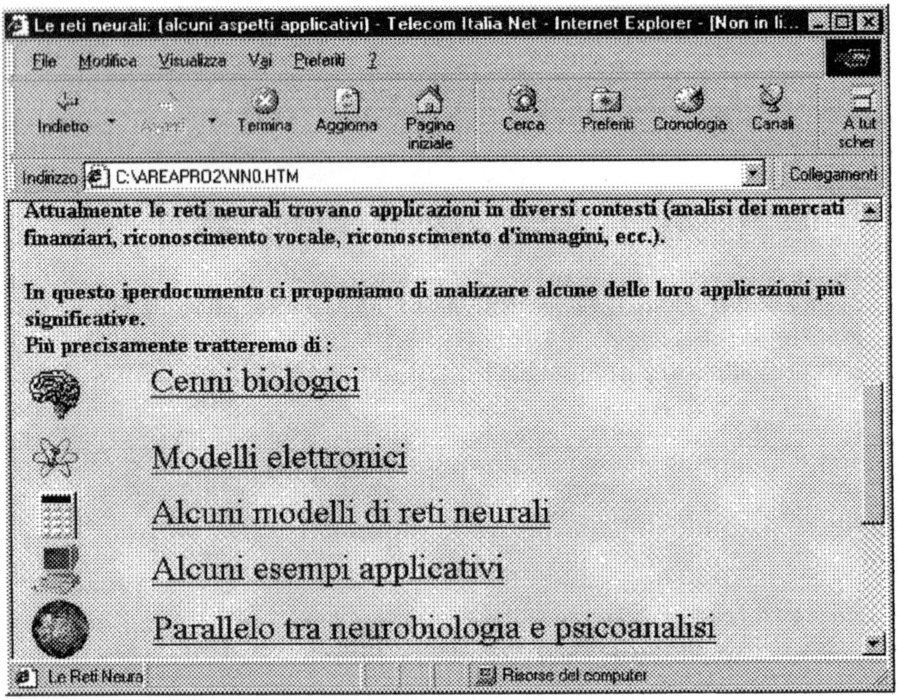

Figure 8. Home page of hypermedia.

In the last part of this second stage, I have controlled the students' knowledge on Neural Networks using the same multiple - choices test that I have proposed in the school year 1997/98. I have also made a comparison with the two samples of students using the histograms (see figure 9).

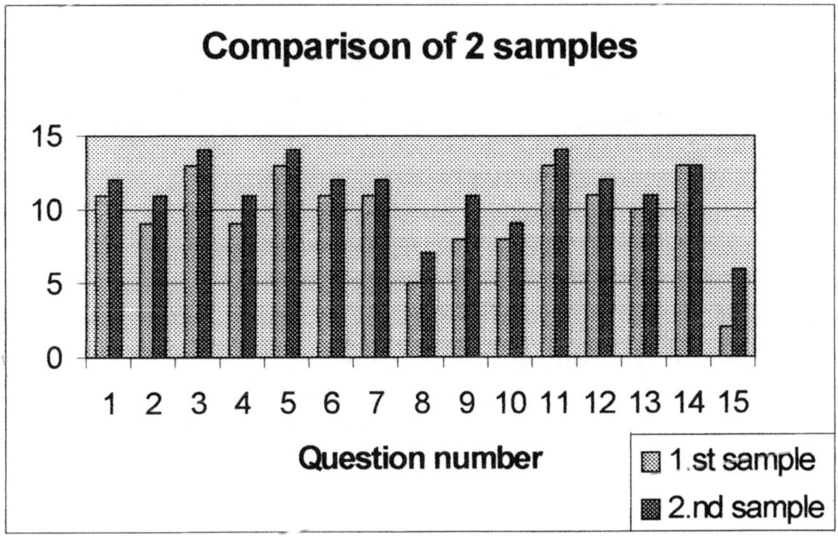

Figure 9. Comparison of two samples.

Observing the figure 9 I have deduced that the second sample of the students has achieved better results than the first sample.

The results of these tests have been encouraging, because:

- the 60% of the first sample has achieved the educational goals,
- the 75% of the second sample has achieved the educational goals,
- my contribution to the project has been well evaluated .

4.3 Third stage of the project

This educational project is a "work in progress". The next school year I will control a third sample of the students that will study the Neural Networks using the CD-ROM produced by the other two samples.

I this way, I will control the students' learning process using this multimedia solution instead of the traditional textbooks.

5 Conclusions

The term multimedia has been around for several decades [16]. Until recently, the term has meant the use for several media devices, sometimes in a coordinated fashion. The multimedia technologies can produce an innovation in the educational field, but this innovation is constituted by three domains: Topics, New Technologies, and Didactics. The intersection between these domains generates a didactic innovation (figure 10) [14].

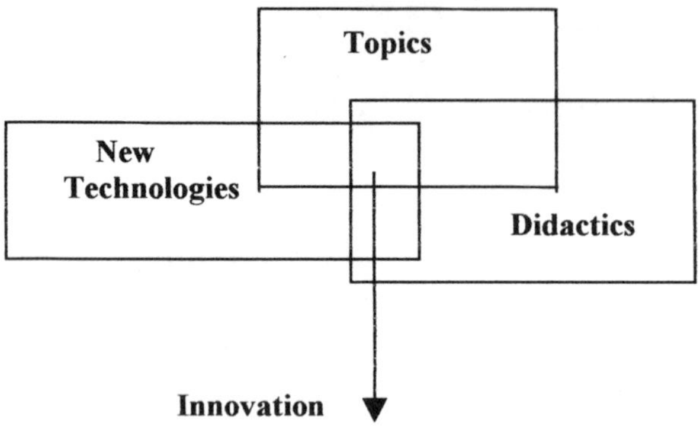

Figure 10. The didactic innovation as the intersection between three fields (New Technologies, Topics, Didactics).

Experts are ambivalent about the ways multimedia impacts a learner. One theory claims that multimedia improves motivation and thereby improves understanding . Another theory is that the varying impacts of different media influence the way we represent and process information [8]. Contrarily other theory views media merely as a vehicle which by itself does not influence student achievement The use of multimedia solutions in degree level courses has proved to be effective in several different fields. In the course of Mathematics at the Academy of Architecture of Mendrisio the use of the multimedia technologies have allowed to study in depth the platonic solids, their symmetries and perspective, to observe the tessellations; to study the fractal forms using a medium, the computer, which permits the animations in real time and which quickly elaborates the fractal algorithms [16]. The solution designed by the Politecnico of Torino, for the Electronic measurement course, is an example of an integrated solution in which the theoretical part is made available through a hypermedia and the laboratory part can be carried out by accessing real instruments through a network connection. These multimedia modules are useful for the distance education. The Department is getting involved in education experiment named "Nettuno", in which the lectures are broadcast on TV or distributed on videocassettes, but students are still required to attend laboratories to achieve practical experience under the guidance of an instructor. With these hypermedia the students can learn to use the electronic instrumentation to stay at home (it is only need a personal computer with a multimedia extension). They can study the theory and then self-verify their knowledge level by solving practical exercises and answering a series of questions. After this pre-training phase, students who enter in laboratory require reduced assistance and less time to complete the training activity [11, 17, 18]. My third research is a "work in progress". I have named this approach "Learning by Doing and Creating". It is an example of "Learning by Doing" environment where some students build an educational hypermedia and they learn while build it. I have added the term "Creating" because there is also the creativity during this hypermedia development.

Some researchers, such as Lee and Lehman [9], as well as Spiro and Jehng [19] have emphasized the active role learners must play in order to learn in hypertext-based learning environments.

Learners have to actively interact with the learning environment and contents by browsing, selecting, searching, scanning and so on.

I think that my "Learning by Doing and Creating" approach can partially refuse the Papert's accuse: "*The students consume but don't produce the knowledge*...".

References

1. Avots J. Exploring countries through telecommunications and HyperCard. *The Computing Teacher*, **22** (3) (1994) pp. 23-26.
2. Baggett P. and Ehrenfeucht A. Information in content equivalent movie and text stories. *Discourse Processes* **5** (1982) pp. 73 - 99.
3. Baggett P and Ehrenfeucht A. Encoding and retaining information in the visuals and verbals of an educational movie. *Educational Communication and Technology Journal*, **31** (1) (1983) pp. 23 - 32.
4. Beagles-Roos J. and Gat I. Specific impact of radio and television on children's story comprehension. *Journal of Educational Psychology*, **75** (1) (1983) pp. 128 - 137.
5. Brooks J. G. and Brooks M. G. *In Search of Understanding: The Case for Constructivist Classrooms.* Alexandria, VA: Association for the Supervision and Curriculum Development (1993).

6. Brofferio S. C. A University Distance Lesson System: Experiments, Services, and Future Developments. *IEEE Transactions on Education*, **41** (1) (1998) pp. 17 – 24.
7. Calvi L. Navigation and disorientation a case study. *Journal of Educational Multimedia and Hypermedia*, **6** (3/4) (1997) pp. 305 – 320.
8. Kozma R. B. Learning With Media. *Review of Educational Research*, **61** (2) (Summer 1991) pp. 179 - 211.
9. Lee Y.B. and Lehman J.D. Instructional cuing in hypermedia: A study with active and passive learners. *Journal of Educational Multimedia and Hypermedia*, **2** (1) (1993) pp. 25 - 37.
10. Nugent G. C. Pictures, audio, and print: Symbolic representation and effect on learning. *Educational Communication and Technology Journal*, **30** (3) (1982) pp. 163 - 174.
11. Pisani U., Cambiotti F., Sala N. and Sanpietro F. A Hypermedia Solution for Electronic Instrumentation and Measurements Practice. *Proceedings 3rd International Conference on Computer Aided Engineering Education, Bratislava*, (1995) pp. 175-179.
12. Rosenshine B. and Stevens R. *Teaching functions*. M.C. Wittrock, ed. *Handbook of Research on Teaching* (3rd ed.).New York: Macmillan Publishing Co (1986).
13. Sala N. A Hypermedia Solution for Electronic Instrumentation. *Proceedings IN – TELE Conference 1998*, (1998) pp. 143-144.
14. Sala N. Alcune considerazioni sull'uso della multimedialità nella didattica , in Atti del XXVII Seminario Nazionale 1998 del Gruppo di Ricerca Morin , **26** A- B n. 6 (1998) pp. 626 - 649.
15. Sala N. Matematica, Arte e Architettura, in Didattica delle Scienze e Informatica, n. 200, Casa Editrice la Scuola, Brescia (1999) p. 22- 29.
16. Sala N. How to Use Some Multimedia Technologies in a New Course of Mathematics: the Case of Architecture of the Academy of Architecture of Mendrisio . *Proceedings M-SET 99,* Editor David A. Thomas, Printed in USA, (1999) pp. 310 - 315.
17. Sala N. Multimedia Training and Remote Operating Laboratory: New Solutions for Electronic Measurements Courses. *Proceedings ED-MEDIA '99* Edited by Betty Collins & Ron Oliver Printed in the USA, (1999) pp. 792 - 797.
18. Sala N. Multimedia Technologies in University Courses: Some Examples. *Proceedings IEEE ICMCS 99*, (1999) pp. 979 - 981.
19. Spiro R. J. and Jehng J. Cognitive flexibility and hypertext theory and technology for the nonlinear and multidimensional travel of complex subject matter. In D. Nix and R. Spiro (Eds.) *Cognition, education, and multimedia: Exploring ideas in higher technology*. Hillsdale, NJ: Lawrence Erlbaum (1990) pp. 163 - 205.

MMM99

CONFERENCE ORGANIZING COMMITTEE

CONFERENCE CHAIR
Ahmed Karmouch (University of Ottawa)

TECHNICAL PROGRAM CHAIR
Ahmed Karmouch (University of Ottawa)
Tet Yeap (University of Ottawa)

TUTORIAL AUDIO VISUAL CHAIR
Roger Impey (National Research Council of Canada)

FINANCE CHAIR
Kathy Mahoney (Ottawa Center for Research & Innovation)

PUBLICITY CHAIR
Hamid Harroud (University of Ottawa)
Alex Pugh (Ottawa Center for Research & Innovation)

EXHIBITION CHAIR
Hamid Harroud (University of Ottawa)

LOCAL ARRANGEMENT CHAIR
Dianne Dinsdale (Communications and Information Technology Ontario)
Marilyn Cheek (Ottawa Center for Research & Innovation)
Alison Edgar (National Research Council)

MMM99

TECHNICAL PROGRAM COMMITTEE

Bulterman, Dick (CWI, Netherlands)
Chua, Tat-Seng (National University of Singapore)
Coulson, Geoff (University of Lancaster, UK)
Courtiat, Jean-Pierre (LAAS, France)
Diaz, Michel (LAAS, France)
Dssouli, Rachida (University of Montreal, Canada)
Fry, Michael (UT Sydney, Australia)
Earnshaw Rae, (University of Bradford, UK)
Fellner, Dieter (University of Bonn, Germany)
Gibbs, Simon (SONY Distributed Systems Labs, USA)
Glinert, Ephraim P (Renssalaer Polytechnic Institute)
Gu, Junzhong (East China Normal University, PRC)
Hafid, Abdelhakim (University of Western Ontario)
Hashimoto, Shuji (Weseda University, Japan)
Horlait, Eric (Lip6, Pierre-Marie Curie,France)
Kalra Prem (Indian Institute of Technology, India)
Karmouch, Ahmed (University of Ottawa, Canada)
Kunii, Tosiyasu (Hosei University, Tokyo, Japan)
Lee, Myeong Won (University of Suwon, Korea)
Li, Victor (University of Southern California, USA)
Magnenat-Thalmann, Nadia (University of Geneva, Switzerland)
Maurer Hermann (University of Graz, Austria)
Mueller Heinrich (University of Dortmund, Germany)
Orozco-barbosa, Luis (University of Ottawa, Canada)
Rutledge, Lloyd (CWI, Netherlands)
Sénac, Patrick (ENSICA, France)
Shimojo, Shinji (Osaka University, Japan)
Shinagawa Yoshihisa (University of Tokyo, Japan)
Suenaga, Yasuhito (Nagoya University, Japan)
Thalsmann, Danial (Swiss Federal Institute of Technology,Switzerland)
Tanimoto, Steven L (University of Washington, USA)
Whang, Kyu-Young (Institute of Science and Technology, Korea)
Wolter Franz (University of Hannover, Germany)
Wu, Jian-Kang (Kent Ridge Digital Labs, Singapore)
Zhang, Hong-Jiang (HP Research Lab., USA)

MMM99

LIST OF TECHNICAL REVIEWERS

Ahmed, Mohamed (University of Ottawa, Canada)
Bulterman, Dick (CWI, Netherlands)
Chua, Tat-Seng (National University of Singapore)
Coulson, Geoff (University of Lancaster, UK)
Courtiat, Jean-Pierre (LAAS, France)
De Saqui-Sannes, Pierre (ENSICA, France)
Diaz, Michel (LAAS, France)
Dssouli, Rachida (University of Montreal, Canada)
Earnshaw Rae, (University of Bradford, UK)
Fellner, Dieter (University of Bonn, Germany)
Fry, Michael (UT Sydney, Australia)
Gibbs, Simon (SONY Distributed Systems Labs, USA)
Glinert, Ephraim P (Renssalaer Polytechnic Institute)
Gu, Junzhong (East China Normal University, PRC)
Hafid, Abdelhakim (University of Western Ontario)
Harroud, Hamid (University of Ottawa, Canada)
Hashimoto, Shuji (Weseda University, Japan)
Horlait, Eric (Lip6, Pierre-Marie Curie,France)
Huang, Lei (University of Ottawa, Canada)
Kalra Prem (Indian Institute of Technology, India)
Karboubi, Amal (University of Ottawa, Canada)
Karmouch, Ahmed (University of Ottawa, Canada)
Kunii, Tosiyasu (Hosei University, Tokyo, Japan)
Lee, Myeong Won (University of Suwon, Korea)
Li, Victor (University of Southern California, USA)
Magnenat-Thalmann, Nadia (University of Geneva, Switzerland)
Maurer Hermann (University of Graz, Austria)
Mueller Heinrich (University of Dortmund, Germany)
Orozco-barbosa, Luis (University of Ottawa, Canada)
Owezarski, Philippe (LAAS-CNRS, France)
Rutledge, Lloyd (CWI, Netherlands)
Sénac, Patrick (ENSICA, France)

Shimojo, Shinji (Osaka University, Japan)
Shinagawa Yoshihisa (University of Tokyo, Japan)
Suenaga, Yasuhito (Nagoya University, Japan)
Tanimoto, Steven L (University of Washington, USA)
Thalsmann, Daniel (Swiss Federal Institute of Technology,Switzerland)
Tkito, Reda (University of Ottawa, Canada)
Whang, Kyu-Young (Korean Advanced Institute of Science and Technology, Korea)
Wolter Franz (University of Hannover, Germany)
Wu, Jian-Kang (Kent Ridge Digital Labs, Singapore)
Zhang, Hong-Jiang (HP Research Lab., USA)

MMM99

AUTHOR INDEX